Globe Law
and Business

Joint Operating Agreements

A Comparison Between the IOC and NOC Perspectives, Second Edition

Professor Dr Eduardo G Pereira, Anna Ovcharova and **Reg Fowler**

Authors
Professor Dr Eduardo G Pereira, Anna Ovcharova and Reg Fowler

Managing director
Sian O'Neill

Joint Operating Agreements: A Comparison Between the IOC and NOC Perspectives, Second Edition
is published by

Globe Law and Business Ltd
3 Mylor Close
Horsell
Woking
Surrey GU21 4DD
United Kingdom
Tel: +44 20 3745 4770
www.globelawandbusiness.comm

Joint Operating Agreements: A Comparison Between the IOC and NOC Perspectives, Second Edition
ISBN 9781787424388
EPUB ISBN 9781787424395
Adobe PDF ISBN 9781787424401

Table of contents

Preface

Peter Roberts
Cross Keys Energy Limited

The purpose of the first generation of the joint operating agreement ('JOA') was to effect the contractual relationship between a group of private sector oil companies which had come together to share the risks of petroleum exploration and project development. The national oil company ('NOC'), if it even existed in the petroleum sector landscape of a particular jurisdiction at that time, would almost always be absent from the JOA side of the project. It was the private sector which assumed responsibility for commercialisation of the state's mineral patrimony, and it was therefore not surprising that the terms of the JOA would have developed principally to reflect the interests of the private sector oil companies.

Over time this position would change. In the next phase of the JOA's evolution came the first appearances of the NOC as a consortium member in the JOA (although this was still a relative rarity), typically resulting from the exercise by the state of an upstream participation right. Even then, the expectation of the private sector oil companies as the incumbent JOA parties would be that the NOC would exercise a relatively passive role in the conduct of joint operations under the JOA (reflective, in part at least, of the small and often carried percentage participating interest which the NOC would have).

The present age of the JOA is witnessing the introduction of even more involvement for the NOC. One of the consequences of the emerging advent of the energy transition is the increasing trend towards private sector oil companies seeking to reduce their upstream interests in favour of more investment in renewable energy projects. This in turn could necessitate increased levels of upstream project participation by an NOC in order to maintain domestic petroleum production levels. And the next age of the JOA could see the NOC become the dominant party in the JOA, benefitting from increased provision in upstream petroleum granting instruments and mineral laws for the transition of operatorship to the NOC. Increased participation by NOCs in petroleum projects in other countries could even see the need for the JOA to reflect certain of the characteristics of a state-to-state accord.

Allied with trends towards increased localisation and a greater emphasis on capacity building as states grow in confidence, the irreversible direction of travel is that now, more than ever, the NOC will become a major participant in a JOA. As a consequence the NOC will need to know the real extent of its rights and obligations under the JOA (and, equally, the other JOA parties will need to appreciate the NOC's perspective).

As NOCs increasingly exploit the opportunities to make their presence felt in the JOA, the challenge for the persons who come together in consortium to develop a petroleum project is to ensure that the JOA represents the interests of all the parties, whether they are the private sector oil companies or the NOC. These interests will not always be aligned. The private sector oil company has its focus principally on the safe production of the greatest possible quantities of petroleum in the most cost-effective manner. This is consistent with what the NOC wants, but the NOC's ambitions could also reflect the desire to observe and to learn by doing, to train its personnel and eventually to be ready to take over the operation of the project, and at all times to be conscious of its role as the long-term steward of the state's mineral wealth, whilst at the same time also not being seen as a proxy for the role of the state. These can be difficult balancing acts to achieve within the four corners of the traditional JOA.

The purpose of this book is to shed more light on what the NOC could expect under the JOA, and on how the other JOA parties could need to approach the evolving relationship with the NOC. This book is needed more than ever, as the role and the stature of the NOC in the JOA, and the NOC's expectations as what the JOA should do, each grow to unprecedented levels.

Introduction

Historically, oil and gas upstream activities were largely open to foreign investment. However, the process of nationalisation in recent decades has concentrated the majority of natural resources with national oil companies (NOCs). Subsequently, international oil companies (IOCs) are more likely to deal with NOCs to create new and specific legal arrangements regulating their alliance.

A joint operating agreement (JOA), created by the American Association of Petroleum Landmen in the 1950s, was originally intended to be a private document to regulate the relationship between private investors. Recent changes in local laws established a requirement for NOC participation in oil and gas projects as partners in these private agreements. As a result, JOAs are now acquiring the features of public agreements, since NOCs are commonly party to such agreements and their presence is likely to dictate different rules.

This book uses the Association of International Petroleum Negotiators (AIPN) Model as its main reference, but also analyses, where applicable, a large number of JOA models from countries, including Australia, Canada, Greenland, Morocco, Norway, the United Kingdom and the United States, as follows:

- the American Association of Petroleum Landmen (American Model Form);
- the Rocky Mountain Mineral Law Foundation (Historical American Model Form);
- the Canadian Association of Petroleum Landmen (Canadian Model Form);
- the Norwegian Directorate (Norwegian Model Form);
- the Energy & Resources Law Association (Australian Model Form);
- the UK Oil and Gas Industry Associated Ltd (trading as OGUK) (British Model Form);
- the Association of International Petroleum Negotiators (International Model Form);
- the Bureau of Minerals and Petroleum (Greenland Model Form); and
- the Office National des Hydrocarbures et des Mines (Morocco Model Form).

This edition examines the key concerns and challenges that IOCs and NOCs face in this new type of joint venture and suggests alternative solutions to finding common ground between parties, which could be relevant to some standard forms.

The content is divided into three chapters: Chapter 1 deals with operation conduct (including operatorship, management committees, work programmes, local content and exclusive operations); Chapter 2 deals with financial issues related to the consortium (including budget, cash calls, cost recovery, authorisation for expenditure, default and taxes); and Chapter 3 deals with agreement boiler plate (including *force majeure*, assignment, governing law and dispute resolution).

Each chapter is analysed from the perspective of investors (ie, IOCs) and governmental entities (ie, NOCs). Explanations of the main JOA provisions and topics are provided, as well as discussions on any concerns between IOC and NOC perspectives. However, please note it is outside the scope of this book to include every detail of all JOA provisions and topics.[1]

In this second edition, the authors have updated the analysis to address emerging issues which further test the relationship of IOCs and NOCs in petroleum joint ventures. We look at the impact of economic sanctions, corporate social responsibility and the way in which conflicts of interest and conflicts of duty are dealt with in the model operating agreements. Australian, Singaporean and English law have all changed in the last five years with respect to the treatment of default clauses, and the relevant chapter has also been amended to analyse the impact of those changes.

However, NOC and IOC definitions are usually broad. A large number of entities could be combined under these definitions but they might be different in size, technical experience and financial capabilities.

This book is highly relevant for the petroleum industry. JOAs should regulate the relationship between parties and it is important to establish the modified form of the documents which aim to solve existing industry concerns regarding this new type of relationship.

The opinions expressed in this book are personal to the authors and are not representative of the opinions of, and cannot be attributed to, entities by which they are or have been employed or affiliated. The contents of this book do not represent legal advice and no attorney/client relationship is created or inferable between any of the authors and any other person.

---

1 P Roberts and R Fowler, *Joint Operating Agreements: A Practical Guide*, 4th edn, Globe Law and Business, 2020; MPG Taylor and SM Tyne, *Taylor and Winsor on Joint Operating Agreements*, 2nd edn, Longman, 1992; AB Derman, *International Oil and Gas Joint Ventures: A Discussion with Associated Form Agreements*, American Bar Association, 1992; AB Derman, *Joint Operating Agreement: Working Manual*, American Bar Association, 1986; AB Derman, *Model Form International Operating Agreement, An Analysis and Interpretation of the 1995 Form*, American Bar Association, 1997; AB Derman, *The New and Improved 1989 Joint Operating Agreement: A Working Manual*, American Bar Association, 1991; EG Pereira, *Joint Operating Agreements: Risk Control for the Non-Operator*, 2nd edn, Globe Law and Business, 2018; and EG Pereira, *Joint Operating Agreements: Mitigating Operational and Contractual Risks in Exclusive Operations*, Globe Law and Business, 2013.

1. Conduct of operations

As a general rule, any company wishing to explore for oil and gas must obtain an authorisation granted by the relevant host government,[1] since usually a state's natural resources belong to the host government.[2] This authorisation tends to be in the form of a petroleum licence, a production sharing agreement, a service agreement or a hybrid form. All these instruments provide rights and duties to the contracting parties, allowing them to explore for and produce oil and gas in a specific location.[3] Consequently, any consortium agreement must be directly linked to a granting instrument.[4]

The petroleum industry operates in a hostile environment[5] facing a range of risks, such as geological,[6] technical,[7] environmental,[8] financial and political, especially

1 JK Kaasen, *Scope of Joint Operating Agreements in Norway*, Petroleum Law Seminar, 2000, p8.

2 Most jurisdictions provide that natural resources located in the subsoil belong to the government and can only be explored if authorised by that government. However, there are exceptions to this rule, such as in US and Canadian jurisdictions. See: BG Taverne, *Petroleum, Industry and Governments: A Study of the Involvement of Industry and Government with the Production and Use of Petroleum*, 2nd edn, Kluwer Law International, 2008, p380.

3 For further information on petroleum title, see: EV Rostow, *A National Policy for the Oil Industry*, YUP, 1948, pp3–26; BGTaverne, *Petroleum, Industry and Governments: A Study of the Involvement of Industry and Government with the Production and Use of Petroleum*, 2nd edn, Kluwer Law International, 2008, p389; G Picton-Tubervill (ed), *Oil and Gas: A Practical Handbook*, Globe Law and Business, 2009, pp37–39; D Johnston, *International Petroleum Fiscal Systems and Production Sharing Contracts*, Penwell, 1994, pp87–107.

4 This book uses the term "granting instrument" to mean the agreement or instrument by which the host state in the territory where petroleum operations takes place authorises such operations by the oil companies, which in their turn might comprise the joint venture which is governed by a JOA. That granting instrument may take the form of a petroleum licence, or some form of concession agreement, service agreement, production sharing agreement or tax and royalty agreement.

5 J Wilkinson, *Introduction to Oil and Gas Joint Ventures*, OPL, 1997, p11.

6 The frontier areas are a good example of the geological risks, as little information is available on the exploration of such areas. Many jurisdictions (eg, the United Kingdom, Canada and Norway) recognise the need for a special arrangement for frontier areas. See: www.og.decc.gov.uk/upstream/licensing/lictypevar.htm;geocompendium.grid.unep.ch/reference_scheme/final_version/GEO/Geo-2-313.htm; www.pennenergy.com/index/petroleum/display/6059121972/articles/offshore/volume-70/issue-50/international-e_p/frontier-exploration.html.

7 R Fabrikant, "Oil Discovery and Technical Change in Southeast Asia – Legal Aspects of Production Sharing Contracts in the Indonesian Petroleum Industry", *OGEL* 3(1) (2005), www.ogel.org/article.asp?key=3045.

8 See also: H Douglas, "Gulf of Mexico Oil Spill: Likely Impact on UK Regulation and Contractual Arrangements", *OGEL* 8(3) (2010), www.ogel.org; J Olszewska, "Operators' Offshore Responsibilities and Liabilities Increased in Australia", *AMPLJ* 21 (2002) 104; S Tromans, "Deepwater Horizon and its Legal Ramifications", *IELR* 163 (2010); NJJ Gaskell, "The Amoco Cadiz: (I) Liability Issues", *Journal of Energy & Natural Resources Law* 3 (1985) 169.

during the exploration phase.[9] Thus, a number of factors will affect projects for the exploration and production of oil and gas in a particular region. Against this background, the oil and gas industry involves an element of gambling, as any operation will have to deal with a number of uncertainties.[10]

Financial expenditure is a critical issue for oil and gas operations. The exploration and production stages require a very large capital input, even for major companies such as Exxon, BP, Shell, Chevron and Total.[11] The Brazilian pre-salt area provides a good example of how expensive oil and gas operations can be – the reservoir could be located over 7,000 metres (m) below sea level and around 300 kilometres (km) from the shore.[12] The logistical and technical challenges make oil and gas operations extremely expensive.

Hostile environments and high levels of expenditure are the key factors that encourage companies to share and spread their costs and risks with other companies by establishing joint ventures.[13] Instead of owning 100% of a single project, the contracting parties take a share in many different projects. Consequently, if one particular project is not successful, the remaining assets might compensate these losses. The Deepwater Horizon accident in the Gulf of Mexico is a good example. If BP (the operator) and its co-venturers (the non-operators) had owned only this asset they might have gone bankrupt, as the costs and damages arising from the incident are likely to exceed US$20 billion.[14] However, they did have other assets to offset and minimise their losses.[15]

Figure 1 summarises the context in which joint operating agreements (JOAs) operate.

The goals of minimising risks and sharing costs are central to the joint venture.[16] In this sense, the joint venture provides the key instrument in achieving the investors' aims (ie, maximisation of the economic recovery of the petroleum located in the licensed area). However, this historical and traditional perspective may not be appropriate in some established regions, where the risk and cost assessments might

---

9 See also: B Manning, "Some Practical Aspects of Resources Joint Ventures" in WD Duncan, *Joint Ventures in Australia*, 2nd edn, Federation Press, 2005, p322; BG Taverne, *Petroleum, Industry and Governments: A Study of the Involvement of Industry and Government with the Production and use of Petroleum*, 2nd edn, Kluwer Law International, 2008, p380; CJ Wright and RA Gallun, *Fundamentals of Oil & Gas Accounting*, 5th edn, Penwell, 2008, p465; P Roberts and R Fowler, *Joint Operating Agreements: A Practical Guide*, 4th edn, Globe Law and Business, 2020, pp7–13; AB Derman and A Melsheimer, "Changing the Rules of the Game: Issues that Arise under the 2002 AIPN JOA when a Host Government Mandates a 'Replacement Contract'", *OGEL* 8(4) (2010) 1–7.

10 See: B Cooper and TF Gaskell, *North Sea Oil, The Great Gamble*, Heinemann, 1966.

11 For further information see: D Johnston and D Johnston, *Introduction to Oil Company Financial Analysis*, PenWell, 2006; D Johnston, *International Exploration Economics, Risk, and Contract Analysis*, PenWell, 2003; RC Nicholls, "A Review of Some Aspects of the Organization and Financing of Mineral Resource Ventures", *UNSW Law Journal* 1 (1976) 271.

12 See: www.presalt.com.

13 "Participants in the resource industry, while generally operating as competitors, will often form alliances to explore co-operatively in a particular area." J Tarrant, "Agreements to Co-Operate at Common Law", *Australian Resources and Energy Law Journal* 5(3) (2006) 281.

14 See: www.google.com/hostednews/ukpress/article/ALeqM5i60_IKLvq0xFpzU4hbNdDEcBEHBQ?docId=N0095001298375539390A.

15 See: www.google.com/hostednews/ukpress/article/ALeqM5i60_IKLvq0xFpzU4hbNdDEcBEHBQ?docId=N0095001298375539390A.

16 See: C Wilkinson, *Joint Ventures and Shareholders' Agreements*, 3rd edn, Bloomsbury Professional, 2009, pp3–5 and GMD Bean, *Fiduciary Relationships, Fiduciary Duties and Joint Ventures: The Joint Operating Agreement*, University of Cambridge, 1992, p19.

Figure 1: The background to joint operating agreements

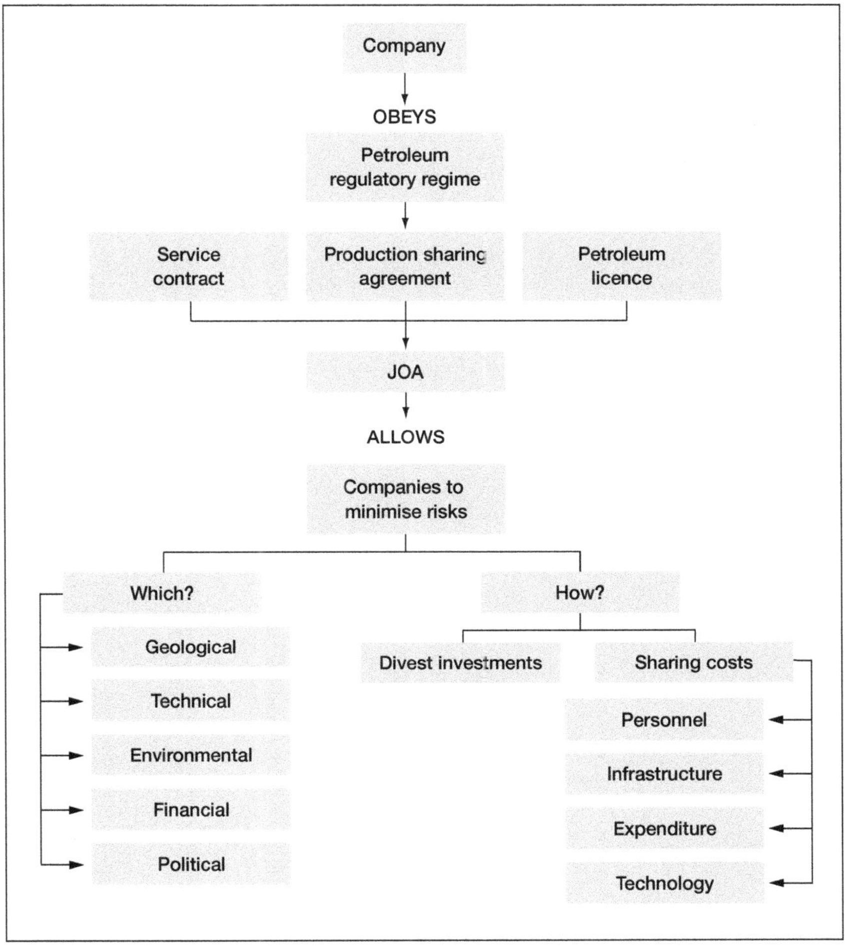

not justify the creation of a consortium. Parties may argue that the consortium could bring more problems and concerns and that the establishment of a consortium for smaller and simpler operations is not justified. Nevertheless, the majority of projects (even in established regions) will benefit from the sharing of risks, costs, technology and expertise via consortium agreements.

In the petroleum industry a joint venture[17] is commonly referred to as a joint operating agreement (JOA), as this is the document which sets out the rights and duties of the parties to the joint venture.[18] Most of the duties in any JOA are placed on the operator, which is the party responsible for administration of the day-to-day

17 For the purposes of this study JOA and joint venture will have the same meaning.

18 AT Martin, "Model Contracts: A Survey of the Global Petroleum Industry", *Journal of Energy & Natural Resources Law* 22 (2004) 291.

activities of the joint venture. Consequently, the operator is generally the party with the highest level of participation and interest in the enterprise, as usually it has the best financial and technical resources and capacity to undertake such duties. For these reasons, JOA Models and studies commonly focus on the operator's perspective. However, it is important to note that the venture is not exclusively owned by the operator. The participating non-operators also contribute to and collaborate in the success of the joint operations.

The oil and gas industry operates in different regions of the world, each of which has its own particular needs and requirements. However, these regions are not isolated from one another, as the industry operates on a global scale and most of the major companies hold assets across the globe. Thus, all regions share certain similarities and companies tend to learn from past experience in other regions so enabling them to improve their own regulations.

The same applies to JOAs. Most oil and gas regions have their own JOA Model Form to address their own particular needs. However, almost all JOAs are based on similar principles and assumptions.[19] Thus, this book will address the key provisions of a JOA based on the Association of International Petroleum Negotiators (AIPN) 2012 JOA Model Form as this is one of the most frequently updated and is a preferred standard form across most regions of the world even though it is currently under revision.[20] The US, UK, Canadian, Norwegian, Greenlandic and Australian JOA Model Forms are also considered (where applicable) in discussion of the JOA's main terms and provisions.[21]

This first chapter of the book addresses the provisions concerning conduct of operations. Anything related to the conduct of operations is central to the JOA, so these are likely to be the most disputed provisions between an international oil company and the national oil company during the negotiation and implementation of a JOA.

The sections of this chapter address in detail each of the main provisions relating to the conduct of the operations.

1. Scope

1.1 General principles

Any contract should indicate the scope and objectives it aims to achieve. This rule applies to JOAs, which commonly contain a specific provision covering the scope and objectives.[22]

---

19 CM Miles, "AIPN 2002 Model Form Joint Operating Agreement in Oil and Gas Joint Ventures", *Australian Resources & Energy Law Journal* 22 (2003) 153–160.

20 This section will not address: (i) technical (ie, geological or engineering) definitions, as they are self-explanatory in each JOA standard form; and (ii) details of each term and provision of the JOA. Rather, it will examine the essential terms and definitions to provide a solid basis for readers interested in understanding JOAs.

21 AAPL JOA Model Form 810; RMMLF JOA Model Form 1968; OGOM JOA Model Form 1985; CAPL OP Model Form 2015; OGUK JOA Model Form 2009 (amended 2020); Norwegian JOA Model Form 2020; AMPLA Joint Venture Model Form 2009; AMPLA JOA Model Form 2011; APEA JOA Model Form 1989; AIPN JOA Model Form 2012; and Greenlandic JOA Model Form 2008 & 2020.

22 For example, AIPN JOA Model Form §3.1, AMPLA JOA Model Form §3.2, APEA JOA Model Form §2.1, OGUK JOA Model Form §3.1 and Greenlandic JOA Model Form §1.1.

The JOA is the foundation document regulating the horizontal relationship between the consortium parties. Although the JOA is intended to govern joint operations, it is important to note that exclusive operations are part of the scope of the JOA, even though they are not properly defined as joint operations. Otherwise, the JOA would forbid any external operation.

The detailed scope of most JOAs is likely to focus on the upstream activities, namely exploration and production activities.[23] The main reason for this approach may be found in the granting instrument. It is important to remember that a JOA will be directly connected to the granting instrument (or several granting instruments, operated by one joint venture). A JOA can only exist if the consortium has a legal right to explore and produce oil and gas, and this is usually granted by the relevant host government.[24] Usually the granting instrument regulates the exploration and production stages rather than the downstream stages of the project.[25]

1.2 Analysis of model JOAs

The approach of focusing the JOA on upstream activities is found in the literature as well as in practice. The AIPN JOA Model Form states that:[26]

> *The purpose of this Agreement is to establish the respective rights and obligations of the Parties concerning operations and activities under the Contract, including the joint exploration, appraisal, development, production of Hydrocarbons (including treatment, storage, and handling of produced Hydrocarbons upstream of the Delivery Point), the determination of Entitlements at the Delivery Point, and Decommissioning.*
>
> *The Parties confirm that, except to the extent expressly included in the Contract, the following activities are outside of the scope of this Agreement:*
>
> > *Construction, operation, ownership, maintenance, repair, and removal of facilities downstream from the Delivery Point;*
> >
> > *Transportation of the Parties' Entitlements downstream from the Delivery Point;*
> >
> > *Marketing and sales of Hydrocarbons, except as expressly provided in Article 7.12.E, Article 8.4 and Article 9;*
> >
> > *Acquisition of rights to explore for, appraise, develop or produce Hydrocarbons outside of the Contract Area (other than through unitization with an adjoining contract area under the Contract or Laws); and*
> >
> > *Exploration, appraisal, development, or production of minerals other than Hydrocarbons, whether inside or outside the Contract Area.*[27]

---

23 S Shaw, "Joint Operating Agreements" in MR David, *Upstream Oil and Gas Agreements*, Sweet & Maxwell, 1996, p15.

24 Commonly, oil and gas belong to the government. The United States and Canada are well-known exceptions to this rule as they allow private ownership of the oil and gas located below the surface.

25 C Duval, H Le Leuch, A Pertuzio and JL Weaver, *International Petroleum and Exploration Agreements: Legal, Economic & Policy Aspects*, 2nd edn, Barrows, 2009, p287.

26 It is relevant to note that the 2012 version of the AIPN Model extended the scope of the JOA to include decommissioning, storage, treatment and handling of produced petroleum from the delivery point.

27 AIPN JOA Model Form §3.1.

The Australian Mineral Petroleum Law Association (AMPLA) JOA Model Form provides a similar approach to the AIPN in that it also focuses on the upstream activities:

> ***Objects and scope of the Joint Venture***
>
> *(a) The objects of the Joint Venture are to undertake Joint Operations associated with the Title Area and, in particular, to:*
>
> *(i) maintain the Petroleum Titles and explore and evaluate the Title Area for reserves of Petroleum;*
>
> *(ii) conduct operations for the exploration, appraisal, development, production and offtake of Petroleum from the Title Area;*
>
> *(iii) if exploration and appraisal indicates the probable existence of a commercial reservoir of Petroleum in any part of the Title Area and, if the Operating Committee approves a Development Plan, develop, produce and dispose of that Petroleum and, for such purpose, obtain all necessary further Petroleum Titles and other Authorisations;*
>
> *(iv) do all things incidental to any of the objects as resolved by the Operating Committee; and*
>
> *(v) undertake such other activities as the Participants unanimously agree from time to time, upon the terms and conditions set out in this agreement.*
>
> *(b) The following activities are outside of the scope of this agreement and are not included in Joint Operations:*
>
> *(i) construction, operation, ownership, maintenance, repair and removal of facilities downstream from the Delivery Point;*
>
> *(ii) transportation of the Entitlements of the Participants downstream from the Delivery Point;*
>
> *(iii) marketing and sales of Petroleum, except as expressly provided for in this agreement;*
>
> *(iv) acquisition of rights to explore for, appraise, develop or produce Petroleum outside of the Title Area (other than as a consequence of unitisation with an adjoining area under the terms of the Petroleum Titles); and*
>
> *(v) exploration, appraisal, development or production of minerals other than Petroleum, whether inside or outside of the Title Area.*[28]

It could be argued that the AIPN and AMPLA approach for the definition of the scope of the agreement is the standard in the industry, even though the latest version (2012) of the AIPN JOA Model Form extended the scope of the JOA to certain downstream activities. Several other model forms follow a similar standard approach, such as those of the UK's Association for Petroleum and Explosives Administration (APEA),[29] Oil & Gas UK (OGUK)[30] and Greenland.[31]

---

28 AMPLA JOA Model Form §3.2.
29 APEA JOA Model Form §2.1 and 2.3.
30 OGUK JOA Model Form §3.1.
31 Greenlandic JOA Model Form §1.1.

However, not all JOAs contain a dedicated provision on the scope of the agreement, for example the Canadian Association of Petroleum Landmen (CAPL) JOA Model Form, the Rocky Mountain Mineral Law Foundation (RMMLF) JOA Model Form and the Norwegian JOA Model Form. Nevertheless, it is possible to identify the overall scope of the JOA in different provisions of the agreement. For example, the CAPL JOA Model Form identifies the scope of the JOA within the obligations of the operator.[32] It is relevant to note that the CAPL allows downstream activities within the rights and obligations of the operator.[33]

Another example is AAPL JOA Model Form 810, which contains a provision named "Contract application" that is identical to the scope of the JOA. Interestingly, it extends the scope of the JOA to treatment and storage of hydrocarbons but clearly excludes pipelines from its scope.[34]

It is important to remember that the model forms are designed to provide guidance during the negotiation of a JOA, and may be modified in the final JOA to adjust for specific circumstances. For example, the JOA parties could decide to include midstream and downstream activities, or at least their principles, within the JOA – as is provided in some standard models such as the AIPN and CAPL JOA Model Forms. If those activities are beyond the scope of the granting instrument with the JOA parties (eg, concession agreement or production sharing agreement), further detail is necessary in drafting the JOA.[35]

Usually, the AIPN provision will be sufficient for an international oil company's need. Traditionally, the JOA parties work together until the production stage or even up to certain midstream and downstream stages. But it is unlikely that the scope of the JOA will include vertical cooperation from the field to the gas station, even though this may sometimes happen.[36]

1.3 Discussion

Commonly, once production is underway each party takes its own production as set out in the JOA or in a lifting agreement. However, not all international oil companies are the same size, or have the same balance sheets and portfolios. For this reason, a smaller international oil company may wish to extend the scope of the JOA to secure its participation in relevant midstream and downstream projects as it may not have the resources to build such facilities or processes alone.

A similar distinction happens with national oil companies. A large national oil company with international experience and an extensive portfolio might prefer the standard provision so it can decide how to deal with its own production; but a smaller national company with less capital and experience may prefer to secure

32 CAPL JOA Model Form §3.01.

33 CAPL JOA Model Form §6.01 (B).

34 AAPL JOA Model Form 810 §1.1 and 1.2.

35 KC Mildwaters, *Joint Operating Agreements, A Consideration of Legal Aspects Relevant to Joint Operating Agreements used in Great Britain and Australia by Participants thereto to Regulate the Joint Undertaking of Exploration for Petroleum in Offshore Areas with Particular Reference to their Rights and Duties*, PhD Thesis presented to the University of Dundee, 1990, p76.

36 P Roberts and R Fowler, *Joint Operating Agreements: A Practical Guide*, 4th edn, Globe Law and Business, 2020, pp100–110.

its participation in midstream and downstream projects together with the other consortium members, thus gaining further knowledge of and expertise in the different stages of the petroleum industry.

So, there is no straightforward answer. The best provision for the scope of the JOA depends on the specific circumstances of each party involved in the consortium.

2. Working interest

2.1 General principles

The rights and obligations established in the JOA are based on each consortium party's proportional share in the joint venture. This is commonly known as the working interest, participating interest or interest clause.[37]

The working interest represents the individual participation of each party in the consortium. Thus, each party's liabilities and obligations under the JOA should not exceed its working interest, unless otherwise agreed in the JOA.

However, it is important to note that commonly the JOA is a private document and this working interest is less likely to apply to liabilities to governmental authorities and third parties, as they are likely to be joint and several for all of the JOA parties.[38]

In this case if a party is sued for a share larger than its working interest (as the host government contract is likely to require joint and several liability among the consortium parties), it should seek compensation from the other JOA parties as set out in the JOA.[39] This is one of the main reasons why the consortium parties sign a JOA – it will regulate the internal relationship between the consortium parties and the external relationship with the host government contract.

In its early years the petroleum industry was controlled largely by private entities, with little or no participation by the host government. Later, host governments began to increase their involvement in and control over their natural resources. This participation may affect some JOAs as in certain jurisdictions the national oil company must be a participant in the consortium.[40]

In this sense, although the JOA was meant to be a private document between private entities, there is a possibility that a governmental entity might be party to the JOA – depending on the jurisdiction involved in the transaction – or even approve the said JOA.[41]

---

37 S Styles, "Joint Operating Agreements" in J Paterson and G Gordon (eds), *Oil and Gas Law: Current Practice and Emerging Trends*, Dundee University Press, 2007, p270.

38 The Brazilian concession contract provides a good example: The assignment in whole or in part of the area of the contract will be always an undivided share in the rights and obligations of the Concessionaire, respecting the joint responsibility between the transferor and the transferee in accordance with the applicable law. Licence Round 11 – Clause 28.5.

39 Further details about costs and liabilities will be explained elsewhere in this book.

40 For example, Morocco and Sudan.

41 C Duval, H Le Leuch, A Pertuzio and JL Weaver, *International Petroleum and Exploration Agreements: Legal, Economic & Policy Aspects*, 2nd edn, Barrows, 2009, p286.

2.2 Analysis of JOA models

The AIPN was one of the first associations to deal with this matter, and the AIPN JOA Model Form includes the possibility for participation of a government entity in the JOA:

> Optional provision, choose article 3.4, if desired. if not chosen check cross-references.
> *Government Participation*
> *If Government Oil & Gas Company elects to participate in the rights and obligations of Parties under Section ___ of the Contract. the Parties shall contribute, in proportion to their respective Participating Interests, to the interest to be acquired by Government Oil & Gas Company.*
> *ALTERNATIVE PROVISION, CHOOSE ONE*
> *ALTERNATIVE # 1*
> *The Parties shall sign such documents as may be necessary to effect such transfer of interests and the joinder of Government Oil & Gas Company as a Party to this Agreement. All payments received for the transfer of such interests shall be credited to the Parties in proportion to their Participating Interests.*
> *ALTERNATIVE # 2*
> *The Parties shall sign such documents as may be necessary to effect such transfer of interests. The rights and obligations of the Parties with respect to each other shall remain unchanged; however, they shall enter into a separate operating agreement with Government Oil & Gas Company with respect to the rights and obligations of Government Oil & Gas Company, on the one hand, and the Parties on the other. All payments received for the transfer of such interests shall be credited to the Parties in proportion to their Participating Interests.*[42]

Although participation by the national oil company has become more common over the past few decades (especially in developing countries), this is a fairly unique provision for a JOA. Traditionally, the JOA was intended to regulate the relationship between private entities.[43] Furthermore the associations developing the model JOAs, such as AIPN, AMPLA, OGUK and CAPL, have generally positioned themselves as representing privately owned oil companies even though national oil companies could be involved as well.

To put this into context, although generally the AIPN covers global operations and some regions are more likely to require government participation (such as Africa, South America and Asia), it might also be used in countries where governmental participation is not mandatory (such as France, the United Kingdom or even the United States). Therefore, the provision might not be applicable to every agreement and so it is optional.[44]

---

42 AIPN JOA Model Form §3.4.

43 The fact that the AAPL, RMMLF, OGUK, CAPL and APE JOA Model Forms do not provide for national oil company participation is a good indication of this tradition – historically the first oil and gas operations started in North America (emphasis in original).

44 CM Miles, "AIPN 2002 Model Form Joint Operating Agreement in Oil and Gas Joint Ventures", *Australian Resources & Energy Law Journal* 22 (2003) 153–160.

The inclusion of government participation is not a standard approach in the industry, at least in the Western world. The AAPL, RMMLF, OGUK, CAPL and AMPLA JOA Model Forms are issued by local associations based in the United States, the United Kingdom, Canada and Australia respectively, which do not require national oil company participation in the upstream sector, and these JOAs do not include such a provision. Drafters and negotiators should bear this carefully in mind when using the industry model forms. One purpose of this book is to indicate where the industry model forms fall short in addressing the specific JOA-related issues when national oil companies participate in the joint venture.

In considering the above reasons, an older Greenlandic JOA Model Form is used to provide a unique standard form. It is issued by the government of Greenland and expressly provides for the participation of the national oil company in the JOA.[45]

2.1.1 Percentage Interests

As of the effective date of this Agreement, the respective Percentage Interests of the Parties to the joint venture established by this Agreement are as follows:

__________________ __________________ __________________ *NUNAOIL*

____ % ____ % ____ %

____ %

Except as provided in Article VII, the Parties' Percentage Interests under this Agreement shall always be equal to the Parties' Percentage Interests under the Licence.[46]

2.4 Percentage Interest of NUNAOIL

2.4.1 The Carry

The Percentage Interest of NUNAOIL shall be subject to the provisions of Article 12 of the Licence. NUNAOIL's share of the costs, expenses, obligations and liabilities referred to in Article 2.2 (a) shall, without prejudice and subject to Article 7.7.9, be borne by the other Parties as set forth in Sections 12.02 and 12.04 of the Licence. Such bearing by the other Parties of NUNAOIL's share of costs, expenses, obligations and liabilities is referred to in this Agreement as a "carry" of NUNAOIL. Without prejudice and subject to the last sentence of Article 7.7.9, NUNAOIL shall not be entitled to any income received during the period, and in respect of the Joint Operations, with respect to which it is carried, provided always that NUNAOIL shall be entitled to its Percentage Interest share pursuant to this Agreement of any Hydrocarbons produced except for any Hydrocarbons produced and saved during the first fourteen (14) days flow period in connection with the testing of a well.

---

45 In 2020, Greenland opened discussions with oil companies on an "open door" basis in areas such as the Davis Straits and Baffin Bay, and for applications in these areas, a different form of JOA is expected. Such JOA does not anticipate the state oil company NUNAOIL participating and there is no provision for any government carry. It remains to be seen whether the state will require it to participate in licences awarded in the bid round is expected in 2021 and 2022.

46 Greenlandic JOA Model Form §2.1.

> *2.4.2 Extension of the Carry*
> *After NUNAOIL has ceased to be carried, if any wells are drilled for the purpose of evaluating or delineating the Deposit for which a request for extension referred to in Section 8.01 of the Licence has been made, NUNAOIL's payment obligation shall not extend to any obligations, costs, expenses or liabilities that arise in connection with the drilling of such wells, provided they are spudded prior to approval of a development plan for said Deposit in accordance with Section 8.08 of the Licence regardless of whether such wells are later used for production purposes.*
> *2.4.3 Payment of the Carry*
> *When and to the extent NUNAOIL is carried as referred to in this Article 2.4, all of the costs, expenses, obligations and liabilities resulting from or accrued in connection with the Joint Operations, as well as any income received as referred to in Article 2.4.1, shall be apportioned among the other Parties in proportion to the relative magnitudes of their respective Percentage Interests. If NUNAOIL participates in a sole risk operation together with one or more other Parties, then, in accordance with Article 7.7.9, such apportionment with respect to such operation shall be among the other Sole Risk Parties, consistent with the provisions of Article 7.7.9.*[47]

The Norwegian Model provides a different scenario. The Norwegian Petroleum Directorate (NPD) is an administrative body created in 1972 to provide assistance to the Ministry of Petroleum and Energy.[48] If either a single party or consortium is awarded a licence to explore for and produce oil in the Norwegian Continental Shelf, it must cooperate with the national oil company by signing an agreement in the format of a JOA,[49] but only to the extent that that government decides to take part in such an enterprise.[50] Unlike the Greenlandic JOA, the Norwegian JOA Model Form, provided by the Minister of Petroleum and Energy with the support of the NPD, does not include special provisions on national oil company participation. In Norway, the national oil company participates under the same conditions as other consortium members.

In general, the working interest of the governmental entity is likely to contain special provisions in order to secure the national oil company's participation and to avoid certain risks and liabilities.

2.3 Discussion

In any upstream project the main risk runs during the exploration phase, until the extent of any reserves is established. Therefore, commonly the national oil company has a carried interest throughout the exploration phase and an option to participate after a commercially viable discovery. The Greenlandic JOA Model is a good example for this type of national oil company carried interest. The default

47 Greenlandic JOA Model Form §2.4.
48 www.npd.no/en/About-us/.
49 www.statoil.com/annualreport2009/en/ouroperations/regulation/pages/thenorwegianlicensingsystem.aspx.
50 Section 3–4 and 3–6 of the Petroleum Activities Act 1996 (Norway).

provision is mitigated by the implementation of this carried interest as the national oil company cannot be under default until it is obliged to pay for its share in the consortium (commonly after the commercial discovery). After a commercial discovery the national oil company will be able to raise funds as some reserves are likely to be proven at that stage.

These concerns are likely to be the case for a younger national oil company without extensive experience and a solid financial base.[51] The Norwegian Model is a good example of no special provision being necessary for the participation of a national oil company (in particular, concerning the financial obligations). The national oil company could be on the same standard and qualification as any international oil company at this moment which was not the case in its earlier days. However, sometimes special provisions are demanded for strategic reasons based on the hydrocarbon law or the host government contract. For example, they might require: (i) the national oil company to exercise the role of operator;[52] (ii) the exclusion of a sole risk provision or waiver of sovereign immunity;[53] and (iii) the obligation to supply oil and/or gas to the national oil company/government until a certain stage, among others,[54] and the JOA must respect and implement such procedures.

For an international oil company, the main question is the reason for the national oil company's participation. Is it a regulatory requirement or a strategic decision? Usually, the national oil company's participation is a regulatory requirement and there is little room for negotiation. Although the key issues might be set by the relevant law or host government contract, it is less likely that these will provide detailed conditions for the national oil company's participation, so there should be some room for negotiation. Nevertheless, sometimes the international oil companies decide to join a national oil company in a consortium for strategic reasons. Brazil is a good example. Since the beginning of its licence round in 1999 several international oil companies have voluntarily joined Petrobras (the largest Brazilian national oil company) for bid proposals and later on to explore and produce oil and gas, even though there was no legal requirement to do so in the licensing regime.

Therefore, a national oil company might not participate in all petroleum transactions, but it is more likely to occur in developing countries. If the national oil company joins a consortium, the priorities of the participating international oil companies and the national oil company will not necessarily be the same. This will be analysed in the following chapters.

In conclusion, the working interest is the most relevant provision of the JOA as it determines the rights and obligations of the consortium parties (including the national oil company participation if applicable). But other provisions, such as sole risk or operator liability, might change this basic principle and they will be discussed elsewhere in the book.

---

51 This is analysed in Chapter 2.
52 Article 4 of the Production Sharing Agreement Law (Brazil).
53 For example, the Office National des Hydrocarbures et des Mines (ONHYM) JOA Model Form.
54 For example, most production sharing contracts in India.

3. Liability[55]

3.1 General principles

The allocation of liability between the state and the JOA parties is likely to be very different to the allocation of liabilities between those JOA parties. In the vertical relationship between the state and its contracting parties under the granting instrument, the state will not expect to have to recover any liability piecemeal from the JOA parties in accordance with their participating interests. It will not want to be affected by the internal arrangements of the JOA parties and will be insured against the risk of any one party becoming insolvent by having the right to enforce any liability jointly and severally against any one of them.[56] However, the JOA parties are free to agree on their internal allocation of liabilities which tend to be proportional between them as they wish to avoid the joint and several liability from the granting instrument.[57] Nevertheless, such internal agreement shall not affect third parties.[58, 59]

The operator liability provisions under a JOA are highly relevant for both an international and a national oil company. Usually, an international oil company is the operator of the consortium. But in some cases, the national oil company may be appointed to conduct the operations on behalf of the consortium, either through a requirement imposed by the state (eg, Brazilian production sharing agreement) or by the parties' voluntary decision.

A higher level of debate between the JOA parties can be expected during the negotiation period of their agreement because the oil and gas sector faces several risks. Claude Duval recognises this situation when he states that: "The question of the operator's liability is often contentious in negotiating an international JOA."[60]

---

55 It is not possible to cover all issues related to the liabilities of the parties, between themselves or with third parties, in this book. For further information see: PR Mundt, "The Assignor Giveth and the Operator Taketh Away, Oil and Gas Working Interest Owners Beware of Continuing Liability", *Tex Tech Law Review* 40 (2007–2008) 419; HL Boigon and CL Murphy, "Liabilities of Nonoperating Mineral Interest Owners", *University of Colorado Law Review* 51 (1979–1980) 153; S Harrison and C McGill, "The Liability of Directors and Officers under Mining and Petroleum Safety Legislation, What Are Their Duties, The Potential Penalties and What Can They Do to Protect Themselves?" *ARELJ* 25 (2006) 65; M Mills, "Insurance and Risk Solutions for Commercial Projects", *AMPLJ* 20 (2001) 46; M Hardy, "Better Safe than Sorry, Apologies, Liability and the Media", *AMPLJ* 19 (2000) 225; H Franklin, "Irretrievable Breakdown? A Review of Operator/Contractor Relationships in the Offshore Oil and Gas Industry", *Journal of Energy & Natural Resources Law* 23 (2005) 1; T Hewitt, "Who is to Blame? Allocating Liability in Upstream Project Contracts", *Journal of Energy & Natural Resources Law* 26 (2008) 177; JN Agrlos, "Vicarious Liability in Tort", *Alberta Law Review* 5 (1966–1967) 74; CS Kulandert and DW Lauritzen, "Flock of Trouble, Liability Under Oil and Gas Joint Operating Agreements After Seagull v Eland", *Tex Wesleyan Law Review* 14 (2007–2008) 217; S Shergold, D Beggs and S Boileau, "United Kingdom: Incidents at Offshore Facilities – Who is Responsible for Environmental Damage?" *IELR* (2010) 178.

56 C Golvala, "Upstream joint ventures – bidding and operating agreements" in G Picton-Tubervill (ed.), *Oil and Gas: A Practical Handbook*, Globe Law and Business, 2009, p45.

57 This section is based on the assumption that the operator is a member of the consortium rather than a joint operating company. If the parties decided to create a company solely to act as the operator, further consideration is required as the joint venture entity will become the operator and will be responsible against third parties as a company.

58 S Shaw, "Joint Operating Agreements" in MR David (ed.), *Upstream Oil and Gas Agreements*, Sweet & Maxwell, 1996, p16.

59 *Ibid.*

60 C Duval, H Le Leuch, A Pertuzio and JL Weaver, *International Petroleum and Exploration Agreements: Legal, Economic & Policy Aspects*, 2nd edn, Barrows, 2009, p293.

From an internal perspective (ie, the JOA parties), the basic rule governing the JOA is that the operator shall not make profit from its function within the JOA, but, on the other hand, it shall not incur any additional liability for it. Such an approach is more than consolidated within the petroleum industry, according to academics and practitioners such as Anthony Jennings,[61] Bernard Taverne,[62] Chris Thorpe,[63] Sandy Shaw,[64] Charez Golvala[65] and Hugh Dundas.[66]

Claude Duval cites an important point that the operator may recover certain costs and eventually may even charge some sort of fees in the accounting procedure,[67] but this will not affect the aforementioned basic principle:

> *The model JOAs used internationally generally favour the operator under the rationale that the operator is not authorized to profit from its operatorship. The 2002 AIPN JOA reflects the general principle underlying JOAs when it states that the operator is to "neither gain a profit not suffer a loss" from performing its duties under the JOA. The standard accounting procedures under the JOA usually reimburse the operator for its actual out-pocket expenses and an agreed-upon overhead charge, but the operatorship is not seen as a vehicle for enhancing the operating party's profit. Yet, the operator is the party most at risk of being sued by a wide variety of third parties, including subcontractors, host government agencies, landowners and other citizens of the country where it is operating.*[68]

Thus, the operator does not bear exclusive liability for loss or damage arising from the performance of joint operations, except under special circumstances. Such a limitation of liabilities is traditionally referred to as the 'exculpatory clause'.[69] The exculpatory clause determines that the operator shall not be liable as the operator of the consortium, but only in its capacity as a participant of the consortium, and to the extent of its participating interest unless the exceptional circumstances occur.[70]

---

61 A Jennings, *Oil and Gas Exploration Contracts*, 2nd edn, Sweet & Maxwell, 2008, p24.

62 BG Taverne, *An Introduction to the Regulation of the Petroleum Industry: Law, Contracts and Conventions*, Graham & Trotman, 1994, p136.

63 C Thorpe, *Fundamentals of Upstream Petroleum Agreements*, CP Thorpe, 2008, p126.

64 S Shaw, "Joint Operating Agreements"' in MR David (ed.), *Upstream Oil and Gas Agreements*, Sweet & Maxwell, 1996, p16.

65 C Golvala, "Upstream joint ventures – bidding and operating agreements" in G Picton-Tubervill (ed.), *Oil and Gas: A Practical Handbook*, Globe Law and Business, 2009, p46.

66 H Dundas, *Joint Operating Agreements: An Introduction*, 1994 Summer Programme: UK Oil and Gas Law, CPMLP 09/09, 1994, p12.

67 P Roberts and R Fowler, *Joint Operating Agreements: A Practical Guide*, 4th edn, Globe Law and Business, 2020, p160.

68 C Duval, H Le Leuch, A Pertuzio and JL Weaver, *International Petroleum and Exploration Agreements: Legal, Economic & Policy Aspects*, 2nd edn, Barrows, 2009, p294.

69 P Roberts and R Fowler, *Joint Operating Agreements: A Practical Guide*, 4th edn, Globe Law and Business, 2020, p307.

70 For further information about exculpatory clauses see: W Woods, "The Effect of Exculpatory Clauses in Joint Operating Agreements, What Protections do Operators Really Have in the Oil Patch?" *Tex Tech Law Review* 38 (2005–2006) 211, C Feasby, "Fiduciary Obligations and Exculpatory Clauses", *Alberta Law Review* 36 (1997–1998) 923 and JB McArthur, "Judging Made Too Easy, The Judicial Exaggeration of Exculpatory and Liability-Limiting Clauses in the Oilfield's Operator Fiduciary Cases", *SMU Law Review* 56 (2003) 925.

The parties will provide reciprocal indemnities in order to secure the implementation of such an exculpatory clause.[71] In this sense, the principle of no loss is clearly secured. Peter Roberts states that:

> *To reinforce this protection of the operator, the parties (including the party which is appointed as the operator, in its capacity as a party) will also undertake to indemnify the operator (in the proportion of their respective PIs) for any such loss or liability for which the operator might otherwise be responsible. Through this combination of disclaimed responsibility and indemnity coverage, the operator is effectively insulated from liability.*[72]

However, it is important to note that any indemnity provided in the JOA must be "clear and unequivocal" and/or "conspicuous", otherwise it could be struck down by the courts as an ineffective provision, especially under the jurisdiction of Texas law.[73]

Furthermore, it is important to note that commonly JOAs do not address the possibility of damage to the consortium parties' own property and personnel. If the JOA does not address this issue, the allocation of such liabilities will be in accordance with the applicable general law. Under English law, a person who causes damages to another person will be liable for those actions under tort law.[74] In this sense, if the JOA parties also wished to protect each other against the flow of tort liability on reciprocal terms, they could provide for a common procedure adopted in contracts for services, called a 'knock-for-knock' or 'mutual hold harmless' provision. In summary Peter Roberts describes this provision thus: "Under this model the parties each assume responsibility for any damage to or loss of their own property and personnel, even where such loss or damage is attributable to the act or omission of any other party."[75] Nevertheless, it is likely to be an issue as the operator should engage its own people and property, except for the joint property or in a secondment arrangement.

Although the above practices (ie, exculpatory clause) are commonly accepted, the parties may disagree on the definition of 'operator' for liability purposes. The operator is likely to request an extension of the definition to include affiliated companies and personnel so that they too can benefit from the restriction. Conversely, the non-operators will wish to keep the definition of operator used in the petroleum title in order to reduce the application of the exculpatory clause.[76]

---

71 For further information about indemnities see: G Gordon, "Risk Allocation" in G Gordon and J Paterson (eds), *Oil and Gas Law: Current Practice and Emerging Trends*, Dundee University Press, 2007), pp335–382, JS Dzienkowski, EE Smith, OL Anderson, JS Lowe, BM Kramer and JL Weaver, *Materials on International Petroleum Transactions*, 3rd edn, Rocky Mountain Mineral Law Foundation, 2010, pp546–579, DO Sabey and others, "Indemnity and Insurance Clauses in Joint Venture, Farmout and Joint Operating Agreements", *Alberta Law Review* 8 (1970) 210; JW Carter, "Contractual Indemnities, Are They Worth Having?" *ARELJ* 28 (2009) 169; P Holden, "Commentary on Contractual Indemnities in the Context of Resources Joint Venture Agreements", *ARELJ* 28 (2009) 176; and P Holden, "Contractual Indemnities in the Context of Resources Joint Venture Agreements, Some Further Thoughts", *ARELJ* 29 (2010) 171.

72 P Roberts and R Fowler, *Joint Operating Agreements: A Practical Guide*, 4th edn, Globe Law and Business, 2020, p308.

73 JS Dzienkowski, EE Smith, OL Anderson, JS Lowe, BM Kramer and JL Weaver, *Materials on International Petroleum Transactions*, 3rd edn, RMMLF, 2010, p546. See also the US, Canadian and international cases discussed by T Martin, J Gilbert and M Gusy in "A Global Review of Joint Operating Agreement Disputes" AIPN research paper 2020, Section 7.6.

74 P Roberts and R Fowler, *Joint Operating Agreements: A Practical Guide*, 4th edn, Globe Law and Business, 2020, p314.

75 *Ibid.*

76 *Ibid*, p313. See also the discussion of parent company liability in Section 1.13 (corporate social responsibility).

It is important to stress that the restrictions of the operator's liability will only apply to those actions it performs under the authority expressly provided in the JOA. If the operator performs any operation outside this authority, it will not be covered by the exculpatory clause.[77]

The exceptions in the exculpatory clause refer to the level of performance, as the operator must act diligently, prudently and in accordance with applicable laws, regulations and best oil and gas sector practice.[78] Scott Styles describes this situation as follows:

> *The nature of the duty is usually specified in the JOA as that of "a reasonable and prudent Operator" or as the duty to perform the role of operator in "a proper and workmanlike manner" in accordance with "good and prudent oil and gas field practice". The exact nature of what counts as good and prudent oil field practice will depend upon the circumstances and will also change as technology changes.*[79]

If the operator maintains the required high standard of performance in its conduct of the joint operations, it will not be exclusively liable for any event, but rather will be held liable in proportion to the percentage of its participating interest.[80] However, if the operator fails to maintain this high standard, commonly the JOAs apply the restricted liability[81] discussed above, except in two situations: gross negligence and reckless misconduct. Claude Duval recognises this situation when he states that "A common practice in the industry is to limit the operator's liability to acts and omissions which are grossly negligent."[82]

The question now is what are the definitions of these terms and the consequence of their implementation?[83] Hugh Dundas defines them as follows:

> *The position created by the BNOC 5th round proforma is that in general, the operator will only be liable for loss which results from its "wilful misconduct". This term is conventionally defined as an "intentional and conscious, or reckless disregard" of any provision of the JOA or of a programme of operations under the JOA "not justifiable by any circumstances, but shall not include any error of judgment or mistake made by any director, employee, agent or contractor of the operator in the exercise, in good faith, of any operation, authority or discussion conferred upon the operator." The BNOC proforma ensures that the operator is liable only for "wilful misconduct" or negligent failure to*

---

77 P Roberts and R Fowler, *Joint Operating Agreements: A Practical Guide*, 4th edn, Globe Law and Business, 2020, p312. See also R Fowler, "The Blank Cheque and the Cliff Edge", *Journal of World Energy Law and Business* (6) (2019).

78 "Inasmuch as the licence or contract will stipulate that the petroleum operations should be carried out according to good oil field practice, it follows that the operator is equally obliged to carry out the operations in this manner ... The operator is responsible for maintaining an adequately staffed organisation enabling him to fulfil his duties. If a party acting as operator is an affiliated company such party operator is allowed to receive and pay for technical and other assistance and services from his parent company or other affiliated companies." BG Taverne, *An Introduction to the Regulation of the Petroleum Industry: Law, Contracts and Conventions*, Graham & Trotman, 1994, p136.

79 S Styles, "Joint Operating Agreements" in J Paterson, G Gordon (eds), *Oil and Gas Law: Current Practice and Emerging Trends*, Dundee University Press, 2007, p279.

80 *Ibid.*

81 C Golvala, "Upstream joint ventures – bidding and operating agreements" in G Picton-Tubervill (ed.), *Oil and Gas: A Practical Handbook*, Globe Law and Business, 2009, p45.

82 C Duval, H Le Leuch, A Pertuzio and JL Weaver, *International Petroleum and Exploration Agreements: Legal, Economic & Policy Aspects*, 2nd edn, Barrows, 2009, p293.

83 For further information see: MPG Taylor and SM Tyne, *Taylor and Winsor on Joint Operating Agreements*, 2nd edn, Longman, 1992, pp6–7.

> *obtain insurance. However, wilful misconduct is a defined term in the agreement, thus removing much of the subjectivity from disputes.*[84]

However, the exception does not include consequential losses and, eventually, environmental liabilities since they may significantly increase the operator's liabilities, to a level which is difficult to pre-define and justify under the 'no gain no loss' principle.[85] Greg Gordon describes this situation in the following terms:

> *In addition to containing the indemnity provisions described above, a wide variety of oil and gas contracts will also include clauses which excludes, limit or put in place an indemnity regime in respect of liability for so-called "consequential or indirect" losses. Such provisions are commonplace in operator-to-contractor contracts and are seen in some (but by no means all) oil company-to-oil company contracts. Where such clauses are used, their purpose is to protect the parties from the full consequences of causing certain types of loss, typically delays in or loss of production, loss of use, loss of profits, and business interruption. The quantum of such losses is generally difficult to anticipate in advance, and may be hard to quantify even retrospectively. However, they have the potential to rise to exorbitant levels. As such, they are frequently either expensive or impossible to insure against, and the industry has by and large accepted that such losses should generally lie where they fall. Thus, we can see that economic factors very similar to those that drive the indemnity regime underpin the exclusion of consequential loss.*[86]

In other words, commonly the JOAs exclude consequential loss even when gross negligence or wilful misconduct is clearly established, in order to give more protection to the operator. However, it is advisable to define[87] 'consequential loss' (just as the terms 'wilful misconduct' and 'gross negligence' are defined in some model JOAs), because the extension and application of this term has been highly disputed under English law since the case of *Hadley v Baxendale*.[88] It is also important to note that the exclusion of consequential loss may not be recognised in certain jurisdictions (special civil law jurisdictions).[89] In addition, it is relevant to verify if such exclusions of liability would be lawful and effective under the applicable law (especially civil law jurisdictions).[90]

---

84 H Dundas, *Joint Operating Agreements: An Introduction*, 1994 Summer Programme: UK Oil and Gas Law, CPMLP 09/09, 1994, p12.

85 "It is further provided that in neither case shall the operator be liable for any consequential loss." MPG Taylor and SM Tyne, *Taylor and Winsor on Joint Operating Agreements*, 2nd edn, Longman, 1992, pp6–7.

86 G Gordon, "Risk Allocation" in G Gordon and J Paterson (eds), *Oil and Gas Law: Current Practice and Emerging Trends*, Dundee University Press, 2007, pp377–378.

87 It is important to note that there is a debate on whether it is better to define this term within an exhaustive list or use a general approach. See: G Gordon, "Risk Allocation" in G Gordon and J Paterson (eds), *Oil and Gas Law: Current Practice and Emerging Trends*, Dundee University Press, 2007, pp380–381.

88 (1854) 9 Exch 341. See: P Roberts and R Fowler, *Joint Operating Agreements: A Practical Guide*, 4th edn, Globe Law and Business, 2020, p311.

89 JS Dzienkowski, EE Smith, OL Anderson, JS Lowe, BM Kramer and JL Weaver, *Materials on International Petroleum Transactions*, 3rd edn, RMMLF, 2010, p546. For further information see: B Montembault-Héveline and A Blois, "Holding Mining Titles from Civil Law Countries on Trust, an Unpredictable and Risky Exercise", *Journal of Energy & Natural Resources Law* 18 (2000) 131.

90 See: EG Pereira and DS Olawuyi (eds), *Practical Considerations to Negotiate an Enforceable Joint Operating Agreement Under Civil Law Jurisdictions*, 2nd edn, Kluwer International Law, 2020; B Montembault-Héveline and A Blois, "Holding Mining Titles from Civil Law Countries on Trust, an Unpredictable and Risky Exercise", *Journal of Energy & Natural Resources Law* 18 (2000) 2 131–141, DOI: 10.1080/02646811.2000.11433194.

It could be suggested that gross negligence and wilful misconduct refer to a serious mistake by the operator, since anything less culpable will not result in bringing this exclusion into play.[91] Apart from consequential loss and environmental loss, the non-operators will not bear liability for any act incurred by gross negligence or wilful misconduct.[92] Anything else will be shared between the JOA parties in accordance with their participating interest.[93]

English law does not provide a single accepted definition of these terms even though the case of *Porter v Magill*[94] could give some reassurance on the use of wilful misconduct.[95] Nevertheless, it is important to define the precise extent of these terms using the relevant definition, as otherwise the parties will face difficulties when attempting to enforce them.[96] It is also relevant to note that the definition of gross negligence or wilful misconduct also involves a certain level of decision making by management.[97]

In this sense, the JOA parties can adopt a soft or harder approach, which will vary according to the definition of the terms and the level of decision making by the management involved. Charez Golvala describes the situation in the following terms:

> *The joint operating agreement will set the standard to which the operator should reference what other operators would do in similar circumstances. This industry benchmarking has variously been described as a "soft" or "high" standard depending on the exact terms used and the circumstances of the breach. However, because the operator functions on a not-for-profit basis, the joint operating agreement will maintain insurances required by the joint venture. "Wilful misconduct" is another term that is carefully negotiated and defined in the joint operating agreement; it usually includes intentional or reckless acts and the debate will focus on whether to extend the definition to include gross negligence (which is not a term that has settled meaning under English law) and what degree of foresight or seniority of management is required before wilful misconduct will have been established.*[98]

However, the major objective behind limiting the operator's exclusive liability to acts of its 'senior' management is the creation of another step before the

---

91 MPG Taylor and SM Tyne, *Taylor and Winsor on Joint Operating Agreements*, 2nd edn, Longman, 1992, pp6–7.

92 S Shaw, "Joint Operating Agreements" in MR David (ed.), *Upstream Oil and Gas Agreements*, Sweet & Maxwell, 1996, p17.

93 C Thorpe, *Fundamentals of Upstream Petroleum Agreements*, CP Thorpe, 2008, pp126–127.

94 [2001] UKHL 67.

95 P Roberts and R Fowler, *Joint Operating Agreements: A Practical Guide*, 4th edn, Globe Law and Business, 2020, pp309–310.

96 C Golvala, "Upstream joint ventures – bidding and operating agreements" in G Picton-Tubervill (ed.), *Oil and Gas: A Practical Handbook*, Globe Law and Business, 2009, p46; S Styles, "Joint Operating Agreements" in J Paterson and G Gordon (eds), *Oil and Gas Law: Current Practice and Emerging Trends*, Dundee University Press, 2007, pp279–280.

97 MPG Taylor and SM Tyne, *Taylor and Winsor on Joint Operating Agreements*, 2nd edn, Longman, 1992, pp6–7.

98 C Golvala, "Upstream joint ventures – bidding and operating agreements" in G Picton-Tubervill (ed.), *Oil and Gas: A Practical Handbook*, Globe Law and Business, 2009, p46.

operator is considered exclusively liable for its actions under the operatorship of the consortium.[99]

Additionally, if all the above protections are not enough, some JOAs go even further and provide another layer of protection for the operator by establishing a financial cap over the operator's liability to the other parties.[100] Such protection is less common than the others and it may be very difficult to agree a numerical value after the Deepwater Horizon accident in the Gulf of Mexico.[101] However, it could provide an alternative solution if the parties do not agree on implementing the relevant indemnities.[102] Even if such a financial cap is implemented, it will not affect third parties as it is an internal arrangement between the JOA parties.

The JOA can further restrict the application of wilful misconduct or gross negligence in that it may require a direct loss or evidence of physical damage or harm rather than a mere technical breach or breach having only economic impact.[103] This provision could assist operators in simple and small breaches but is unlikely to help in any serious failure of performance.

Once gross negligence or wilful misconduct has been confirmed, the JOA parties must determine the consequence. There are several alternatives available to the JOA parties. Claude Duval describes them as follows:

> *The parties to a JOA can choose to make the operator bear all damages caused by its negligence; bear only the actual cost of repairing or replacing joint property so damaged; or bear only a defined dollar amount of such damages and liabilities. If the first alternative is not selected, all parties will share proportionately in any liability in excess of the amounts in the last two alternatives. Under the 2002 AIPN JOA, the operator is never forced to bear more than its proportionate share of consequential losses or environmental losses.*[104]

For a non-operator, the first option is by far the most attractive as there is no limitation involved. For the operator, anything apart from the first option should be available, as the operator will argue that the operatorship is voluntary and so no further liability should be involved. Consequently, the parties are likely to dispute the result of this provision. However, if the operatorship is shared or delegated to a third party, it will be much easier to introduce full control of liabilities.

---

99 P Roberts and R Fowler, *Joint Operating Agreements: A Practical Guide*, 4th edn, Globe Law and Business, 2020, p310.

100 *Ibid.*

101 For further information see: H Douglas, "Gulf of Mexico Oil Spill: Likely Impact on UK Regulation and Contractual Arrangements" *OGEL* 8(3) (2010); J Olszewska, "Operators' Offshore Responsibilities and Liabilities Increased in Australia", *AMPLJ* 21 (2002) 104; S Tromans, "Deepwater Horizon and its Legal Ramifications", *IELR* (2010) 163; NJJ Gaskell, "The Amoco Cadiz: (I) Liability Issues", *Journal of Energy & Natural Resources Law* 3 (1985) 169; CB Kende, "Liability for Pollution Damage and Legal Assessment of Damage to the Marine Environment", *Journal of Energy & Natural Resources Law* 11 (1993) 105.

102 G Gordon, "Risk Allocation" in G Gordon and J Paterson (eds), *Oil and Gas Law: Current Practice and Emerging Trends*, Dundee University Press, 2007, p382.

103 P Roberts and R Fowler, *Joint Operating Agreements: A Practical Guide*, 4th edn, Globe Law and Business, 2020, p310.

104 C Duval, H Le Leuch, A Pertuzio and JL Weaver, *International Petroleum and Exploration Agreements: Legal, Economic & Policy Aspects*, 2nd edn, Barrows, 2009, p294.

Several JOAs extend the operator's exclusive liability for cases related to the operator's failure to obtain or maintain insurance.[105] Commonly, these provide a different approach for the breach in order to obtain or maintain insurance related to the joint operations.[106]

A controversial question related to the operator having breached any clause of the agreement is whether this excludes the operator's restriction of liability. Claude Duval answers this question as follows:

Perhaps surprisingly it is still not clear in many JOAs whether the limits on the operator's liability to the non-operating participants (rather than to third parties) extend to its actions which are in breach of the JOA. Some operators have argued that they may not be held liable to the non-operators for breaching the JOA's provisions unless they are grossly negligent. The United States courts have ruled inconsistently on this issue when interpreting domestic JOAs.[107, 108]

It could be suggested that the JOA parties (in particular the non-operators) should extend the application of the operator's exculpatory clause to include any breach of the terms of the agreement by the operator. Ernest Smith refers to an American case[109] where Judge E Grady Jolly addresses such danger for the non-operators as follows:

It is clear to us that the protection of the exculpatory clause extends not only to "acts unique to the operator," as the district court expressed it, but also to any acts done under the authority of the JOA "as Operator." This protection clearly extends to breaches of the JOA. It also reaches other acts including acts performed "as Operator" under the authority of the JOA that amount to tortious interference with contracts with third parties. We, therefore, hold that the exculpatory clause protects Marathon from liability for any act taken in its capacity "as Operator" under the JOA (except for gross negligence or wilful misconduct).[110]

As previously mentioned, the position with respect to liabilities of the joint venture to third parties is more complex. Generally, the JOA terms will not affect such liabilities by reason of privity of contract. The petroleum title or granting instrument will only address liability to the state for breach of its terms (typically imposing joint and several liability on the JOA parties in their capacity as concession participants). How third-party liability is allocated between the JOA parties will vary according to the arrangement of the JOA; that is, whether the operator is acting in its own name as an independent contractor or on behalf of

105 For further information see: S Styles, "Joint Operating Agreements" in J Paterson and G Gordon (eds), *Oil and Gas Law: Current Practice and Emerging Trends*, Dundee University Press, 2007, pp279–281; P Roberts and R Fowler, *Joint Operating Agreements: A Practical Guide*, 4th edn, Globe Law and Business, 2020, p312. This issue is also discussed in Chapter 2, Section 3 Insurance.

106 MPG Taylor and SM Tyne, *Taylor and Winsor on Joint Operating Agreements*, 2nd edn, Longman, 1992, pp6–7.

107 C Duval, H Le Leuch, A Pertuzio and JL Weaver, *International Petroleum and Exploration Agreements: Legal, Economic & Policy Aspects*, 2nd edn, Barrows, 2009, p294.

108 The relevant recent arbitration awards are discussed in ICC Dispute Resolution Bulletin 3, "Joint Operating Agreements in the International Oil & Gas Industry: ICC Arbitral Awards" and "A Global Review of Joint Operating Agreement Disputes" AIPN research paper 2020, Section 7.6 by T Martin, J Gilbert and M Gusy.

109 *Stine v Marathon Oil Co.* 976 F.2d 254 (5th Cir. 1992).

110 JS Dzienkowski, EE Smith, OL Anderson, JS Lowe, BM Kramer and JL Weaver, *Materials on International Petroleum Transactions*, 3rd edn, RMMLF, 2010, p572.

the consortium. In other words, it will depend whether the operator is an agent for the consortium or not.[111]

Where the operator acts as agent for the consortium, it will be the principal (as to its own participating interest) and agent at the same time for the consortium. Where the operator acts as independent contractor, it is fully liable to the third party under the relevant contract, and merely has the right under the JOA to recover costs and liabilities arising under that contract from the consortium. Where the operator acts as an agent on behalf the consortium, the operator is liable to the third party only in its capacity as a consortium member and only to the extent of its participating interest – unless the contract imposes joint and several liability on each of the consortium parties. Commonly the operator is responsible for dealing with any litigation that might arise in connection with the performance of the consortium's operations.[112]

It is also relevant to note that JOAs in which a national oil company is a party are likely to restrict its liability. Anthony Jennings describes a similar situation in the following terms:

> *Note that in some jurisdictions and often under a PSA regime the operator may be a company jointly incorporated by the participants and owned by them in equal shares, in which event it may well have no liability at all. We mentioned joint insurance and there will also be an obligation on the operator to obtain and maintain this and also a clause covering the operator's responsibilities in respect of litigation on behalf of or against the joint venture.*[113]

The governmental authorities will protect their position against any liability even in the case of a petroleum regime where no national oil company participates. Peter Roberts recognises this situation as follows:

> *The terms of the concession might also obligate the parties (in their capacity as the concession holders) to indemnify the state against any claims made by third parties against the state as the grantor of the concession, and the parties will then reallocate the indemnity liability between themselves in accordance with the terms of the JOA.*[114]

Therefore, both non-operators and operator must be very careful when agreeing the terms of the exculpatory clause as otherwise they may bear far more liabilities than desired.

3.2 Analysis of model forms

The JOA Model Forms tend to follow the principles discussed above. The British JOA Model promotes better performance of operations as it requires not only compliance with the relevant agreements and regulations, but also diligence and following good oil field practice.[115]

---

111 H Dundas, *Joint Operating Agreements: An Introduction*, 1994 Summer Programme: UK Oil and Gas Law, CPMLP 09/09, 1994, p11.

112 P Roberts and R Fowler, *Joint Operating Agreements: A Practical Guide*, 4th edn, Globe Law and Business, 2020, p317.

113 A Jennings, *Oil and Gas Exploration Contracts*, 2nd edn, Sweet & Maxwell, 2008, p24.

114 P Roberts and R Fowler, *Joint Operating Agreements: A Practical Guide*, 4th edn, Globe Law and Business, 2020, p317.

115 OGUK JOA §6.2.2.

The basic principle of no gain no loss is also recognised in this JOA, but within the accounting procedures rather than the body of the JOA.[116] The operator shall not bear personal liability for the performance of its activities (ie, exculpatory clause), except for wilful misconduct.[117] Taylor and Tyne explain the history of this provision in the UKCS as follows:

> *The JOA will invariably include a clause designed to restrict the operator's liability to the other parties in the event of its negligence or breach of the terms of the JOA. The BNOC fifth round pro forma introduced a particular form of exemption clause which, with minor variations, has become standard in modern UKCS (and onshore) JOAs.*[118]

It is important to note that the definition of 'wilful misconduct'[119] is limited to acts or omissions of the senior managerial personnel and does not refer to gross negligence at all.[120]

In addition, it is important to note that no party shall bear exclusive liability for consequential losses,[121] even in cases of wilful misconduct, which certainly benefits the operator.[122] On the other hand, the exceptions related to exclusive liability go beyond these present conditions as the provision also refers to the operator's failure to obtain or maintain insurances.[123] In other words, the exculpatory provision secures a higher level of protection for the operator.

Consequently, if the loss is not due to either wilful misconduct or failure of insurance obligations, the operator will not bear exclusive liability for the conduct of the joint operations. In addition, the operator will not bear exclusive liability for consequential losses resulting from the performance of the joint operations. As a practical application of this concept, the non-operators must indemnify the operator for any damage or costs arising out of its performance outside its participating interest.[124]

Another negative point for the non-operators is the wide scope of the exculpatory clause, which will affect all the JOA obligations as it refers to damages, claims or liabilities:

> *directly or indirectly, out of the performance, non-performance or misperformance by the Operator of any of its duties or obligations as Operator hereunder [or acting on behalf of the Participants under any Associated Agreement], irrespective of negligence and/or breach of duty (whether statutory or otherwise) on the part of the Operator.*[125]

---

116 OGUK JOA – Accounting Procedures §1.2.

117 OGUK JOA §6.2.4.

118 MPG Taylor and SM Tyne, *Taylor and Winsor on Joint Operating Agreements*, 2nd edn, Longman, 1992, p5.

119 OGUK JOA §1.1: "*'Wilful Misconduct' means an intentional or reckless disregard by Senior Managerial Personnel of Good Oilfield Practice or any of the terms of this Agreement in utter disregard of avoidable and harmful consequences but shall not include any act, omission, error of judgement or mistake made in the exercise in good faith of any function, authority or discretion vested in or exercisable by such Senior Managerial Personnel and which in the exercise of such good faith is justifiable by special circumstances, including safeguarding of life, property or the environment and other emergencies.*"

120 OGUK JOA §1.1.

121 OGUK JOA §1.1.

122 OGUK JOA §6.2.4(b).

123 OGUK JOA §6.2.4(b).

124 OGUK JOA §6.2.4(a).

125 OGUK JOA §6.2.4(a).

This provision provides security for the operator as simple mistakes or negligence will not attract exclusive liability. The non-operators will rely on the "good faith" of the operator, as the restrictions of the operator's liabilities are far too great.

It is important to stress that the British JOA is the only standard form that expressly recognises the agency relationship between the JOA parties.[126] In this situation, it includes several provisions to protect the non-operators' liabilities against third-party contractors.[127] In summary, the operator is the only body responsible for performance of the third-party contract *vis-à-vis* the contractor, and the operator has the exclusive right and responsibility to enforce any obligation of the third-party contractor on behalf of the non-operators even though it will be a disclosed agent.

The operator is responsible for controlling any claims against the joint operations up to a certain level of expenditure, as otherwise the OpCom's approval will be required, but any non-operator also has the right to participate in such a claim.[128]

In conclusion, it is clear that under the British JOA Model the operator is very well protected as its liabilities for the conduct of the joint operations will be very limited. Probably the main reasons for this approach are the higher risks involved in offshore operations and the principle of no gain no loss.

The Norwegian JOA Model requires compliance with regulations and the petroleum title; however, it does not refer to international principles such as best oilfield practices.[129] This provision is negative for the non-operators as compliance with regulations does not necessarily result in better performance of operations.

Operator liability is limited by the exculpatory clause as the basic principle of 'no gain no loss' is clearly prescribed.[130] In this situation, the operator will not bear any personal liability for the joint operations it conducts, except in cases of gross negligence or wilful misconduct. Each party will bear liabilities according to its participating interest, but the party that conducts the joint operations will be exclusively liable for cases of gross negligence or wilful misconduct.[131] Although these terms are not defined in the model, the benefits of such an exculpatory clause extend to the affiliated companies.[132]

It is important to note that the operator is not personally liable for consequential losses (including third parties), regardless of the cause (ie, gross negligence/wilful misconduct or not).

126 OGUK JOA §6.5.8.
127 OGUK JOA §6.5.7 and 6.5.8.
128 OGUK JOA §8.3.
129 Norwegian JOA §3.1.
130 Norwegian JOA §3.5.
131 Norwegian JOA §7.1.
132 Norwegian JOA §3.5.

It is very clear that the Norwegian JOA Model provides greater protection for the operator. First, there is no effective obligation to achieve and to follow a higher standard of operations. Secondly, the exculpatory clause is implemented with limited exceptions. Thirdly, no party shall be responsible for consequential loss incurred by another party. On the other hand, there is no requirement to obtain a certain level of management participation in an operator's breach to establish gross negligence or wilful misconduct.

Finally, it is also relevant to note a higher importance is given in relation to the decommissioning obligations under this model, as the parties must jointly prepare an abandonment plan.[133] It is easy to understand this emphasis for two simple reasons. First, Norway is a mature province and so is likely to face problems with decommissioning. Secondly, the host government has the right to join the consortium at any stage.

The Australian JOA's approach to the liability clause is similar to other JOAs. First, it imposes several duties on the operator, such as the establishment of 'good Australian mining practice' (ie diligence and prudence) and compliance with applicable laws, among others, to ensure that the operator performs the operations to a high standard.[134] Secondly, it establishes the exculpatory clause for the operator's performance of the joint operations. This clause excludes the operator's personal liability in any action (including actions from third parties), except in the case of wilful misconduct. The operator will bear participating party liabilities in all circumstances apart from wilful misconduct, when it will be exclusively liable.[135] This benefit applies not only to the operator, but also to any affiliated company, personnel, agent and contractors, which is a positive provision for the operator.

However, it is important to examine the JOA's particularities. It includes a definition of "wilful misconduct" which is worded to be broad enough to encapsulate what most lawyers would consider to be gross negligence. It has no separate definition of gross negligence. Regardless of this structure, it is also relevant to note that there is no requirement that a senior supervisor is responsible for the relevant act or failure, but that any of the operator's personnel can trigger such provision. However, the advantage for the non-operators is the extension of the operator's liability to include any breach of the law, the petroleum title, the JOA and the work programme and budget (except in emergencies).

It is also important to note that each party will retain liability for consequential losses it incurs, as this is not included in the scope of the reciprocal indemnities that the parties grant each other to secure the implementation of the exculpatory clause.[136] This is a positive provision for the non-operators as the consequential loss could be very large, as has been seen with the Deepwater Horizon accident.

As an exception to the principle that an operator makes no profit nor incurs any loss the AMPLA JOA includes an express provision for remuneration fees. This is as follows:

---

133 Norwegian JOA Articles 30, 31 and 32.
134 AMPLA JOA §1.1, 3.4 and 7.2.
135 AMPLA JOA §6.5, 6.6 and 6.7.
136 AMPLA JOA §3.4 and 3.5.

6.3 Remuneration of the Operator

(a) In consideration of the performance by the Operator of its obligations under this agreement, each Participant must pay the Operator its Percentage Share of the Operator Overhead payable as part of a Cash Call.

(b) The Operator Overhead may be varied by the Operating Committee by Unanimous Vote.

(c) It is intended that the Operator will neither gain nor, except where it has committed fraud or Wilful Misconduct, suffer a loss as a result of acting as Operator in the conduct of Joint Operations.[137]

This provision is contrary to the basic principle of no gain no loss, even though the parent company overhead charge provided for in many JOAs is effectively the same concept. The AMPLA accounting procedures recognise the principle in the following way:

It is the intent of this Accounting Procedure that, except as otherwise expressly provided by this agreement, no party (including the Operator) will gain or lose by reason of carrying out its duties and responsibilities pursuant to this agreement.[138]

The non-operators could argue that the exculpatory clause should be amended as the basic principle of no gain is not properly implemented. On the other hand, the operator could argue that the fee described under the body of the agreement is merely the overhead expressed differently and should not change the application of the principle.

This shows that the AMPLA JOA adopts a similar approach to liabilities provisions as most standard JOAs. However, the express reference to remuneration fees could create some problems in negotiating the exculpatory clause, as the non-operators will claim a freer hand in negotiating the operator's exculpatory clause.

The AIPN JOA Model contains several requirements which secure a higher standard in the performance of operations.[139] First, it requires diligent, safe and efficient operations in accordance with international practices. Secondly, it imposes an obligation to observe the requirements of any applicable regulations, the petroleum title and the JOA. However, unlike other JOAs, this model form makes no provision for derogation of such requirements, which is a positive provision for the non-operators.

This model form also recognises the principle of no gain no loss for the conduct of operations.[140] It contains an exculpatory clause that restricts the operator's liability in the conduct of operations. However, the construction of this clause is fairly unique in comparison with other JOAs. As previously mentioned, the AIPN aims to address

137 AMPLA JOA §6.3.
138 AMPLA JOA – Accounting Procedures §1(b).
139 AIPN JOA §4.2.
140 AIPN JOA §4.2(B)(4).

global operations so more flexibility is provided. In this situation, the JOA includes an optional[141] provision which excludes the restriction of the operator's liability for gross negligence and wilful misconduct.[142]

This optional provision requires that one of the operator's senior supervisor personnel is responsible for the relevant act or failure but the definition of senior supervisory personnel must be selected from five options in the JOA.[143] The AIPN gives alternatives from lower-level personnel to higher-level managerial personnel.[144] The former is very likely to be directly responsible for operations and the latter are less likely, as higher authority is required. The parties also determine what kind of liabilities the operator must bear exclusively arising from its gross negligence or wilful misconduct. There are three options. The first includes everything; the operator will bear all costs and liabilities related to such actions or omissions. The second option obliges the operator only to replace, repair or remove the joint property damaged. The third option makes no conceptual exclusion but a financial limit on liability to be chosen by the parties. The first option is far better for the non-operators even though it does not include consequential or environmental liabilities; the second is limited to property damage; and the third will depend on the amount defined by the parties.

If this optional provision is not chosen by the parties, the operator will have no personal liabilities to the non-operators, regardless of the cause of its poor performance.[145] In this situation, the operator will bear its liabilities as a party of the consortium and the non-operators will indemnify it for any costs or liabilities related to the performance of the joint operations to the extent of their respective participating interests.[146]

It is also relevant to note that the benefit of the exculpatory clause is fairly broad as it applies to any of the operator's personnel and any personnel in its affiliated companies; however, it does not apply to contractors.

However, no party shall be held personally responsible for consequential[147] or environmental losses.[148]

Clearly, the AIPN Model protects the operator's position in the JOA as there are several layers of protection that restrict the operator's personal liability. If the

---

141 AIPN JOA §4.6(C).

142 AIPN JOA §1.1: *"Gross Negligence/Wilful Misconduct means any act or failure to act (whether sole, joint or concurrent) by any person or entity that was intended to cause, or was in reckless disregard of or wanton indifference to, harmful consequences such person or entity knew, or should have known, such act or failure would have on the safety or property of another person or entity."*

143 AIPN JOA §4.6(C).

144 AIPN JOA §1.1.

145 AIPN JOA §4.6(A).

146 AIPN JOA §4.6(B), (D).

147 AIPN JOA §1.1: *"Consequential Loss means any losses, damages, costs, or liabilities caused (directly or indirectly) by any of the following arising out of, relating to, or connected with this Agreement or the operations and/or activities carried out under this Agreement: (i) reservoir or formation damage; (ii) inability to produce, use or dispose of Hydrocarbons; (iii) loss or deferment of income; (iv) punitive damages; or (v) indirect damages or losses whether or not similar to the foregoing."*

148 AIPN JOA §1.1: *"Environmental Loss means any losses, damages, costs, or liabilities (other than Consequential Loss) caused by a discharge of Hydrocarbons, pollutants, or other contaminants into or onto any medium (including land, surface water, ground water and/or air) relating to this Agreement or the operations carried out under this Agreement, including: (i) injury or damage to, or destruction of, natural resources or real or personal property; (ii) cost of pollution control, cleanup and removal; (iii) cost of restoration of natural resources; and (iv) fines, penalties, or other assessments."*

optional provision is not chosen by the JOA parties, the non-operators will be liable for all damages caused by the operator, regardless of the cause, in accordance with their participating interest. If the non-operators manage to get the clause included, they must ensure that the definition of a senior supervisor is included as well, as this could determine whether the criteria of the gross negligence or wilful misconduct exclusion are met. Ensuring that the JOA uses clearly defined terms is essential to achieving a watertight allocation of liability.

3.3 Discussion

In conclusion, it is clear that the purpose of the liability provision in these JOAs is focused

> *typically on a consideration of the prospective liability which the operator might have to the parties for any loss or liability which the operator causes in the exercise of its responsibilities, and how that liability might be limited in the operator's favour.*[149]

It could be said that the liability clause is no more than a mirror of the principle no gain no loss, either expressly (eg, AIPN, Norway, AMPLA, OGUK) or implicitly (eg, American models). It is very unlikely that an operator could meet the criteria to attract sole liability under the JOA.[150]

The Deepwater Horizon accident in the Gulf of Mexico demonstrated the reality of the risks of offshore operations and the very large liabilities involved.[151] The question is: are the JOA parties willing to maintain the principle of no gain no loss?[152] Are they willing to share the bill whatever the outcome of the operations (eg, consequential loss)? The answer is not as straightforward as it seems because the operator will not accept bearing further risks without receiving something in return.[153] However, it is impossible to deny that the risks involved with the exculpatory clause represent a very large burden for the non-operators.[154] From a non-operator's perspective, there are two solutions. First, the use of a third-party operator could resolve the issue as a service agreement on arm's length terms will not adopt the principle of no gain no loss. Secondly, the non-operators must bargain for the party operator to retain its functions but with the less restrictive conditions on liability they require.

It could be suggested that the non-operators face a critical problem in relation to their position in the JOA. It is very clear that the exculpatory clause will protect the operator against almost any failure of performance, so the non-operators' main protections will be their control of operations through the OpCom, the threat of

149 P Roberts and R Fowler, *Joint Operating Agreements: A Practical Guide*, 4th edn, Globe Law and Business, 2020, p307.

150 P Roberts and R Fowler, *Joint Operating Agreements: A Practical Guide*, 4th edn, Globe Law and Business, 2020, p313.

151 See: H Douglas, "Gulf of Mexico Oil Spill: Likely Impact on UK Regulation and Contractual Arrangements", *OGEL* 8 (2010) 3.

152 See: DB Shilliday and others, "Contractual Risk-Shifting in Offshore Energy Operations", *Tulane Law Review* 81 (2006–2007) 1579; WG Holt, "Problems Relating to Arctic Farmout and Joint Operating Agreements", *Alberta Law Review* 10 (1972) 450.

153 JS Dzienkowski, EE Smith, OL Anderson, JS Lowe, BM Kramer and JL Weaver, *Materials on International Petroleum Transactions*, 3rd edn, RMMLF, 2010, p545.

154 P Roberts and R Fowler, *Joint Operating Agreements: A Practical Guide*, 4th edn, Globe Law and Business, 2020, p312.

removal of the operator and the possibility of holding the operator in default.[155] However, none of the JOAs analysed here will provide the non-operators with strong control in the operations, nor will they be provided with the wider discretion to remove the operator, nor is it a simple matter to hold an operator in default. Terence Daintith describes this situation as follows:

If a JOA contains all these restrictions on the liability of the operator for wilful misconduct it would be very difficult, first, to prove wilful misconduct and then to recover any significant damages ... This leaves the non-operators with only one real remedy if the operator fails to perform its duties adequately, namely to remove the operator. This is, however, clumsy and rarely, if ever, used.[156]

In other words, in most cases the non-operators can only hope for the best as their JOA arrangements will not fully protect them against failure of the performance of the joint operations. It should not be forgotten that the operator will always bear its percentage interest share of any liability, regardless of its level of fault, in its capacity as JOA party; the greater that party's exposure to its own failings, the greater should be the care it takes with its performance. However, they are likely to rely on the fiduciary duties that may arise under their relationship with the operator so that a higher standard of performance is somehow secured.[157]

Furthermore, it is important to re-state two points addressed elsewhere in this book. First, an exclusive operation affects only the consenting parties; the non-participating parties do not bear the liabilities involved in such operations. However, it is important to remember the critical issue related to the conduct of exclusive operations; if the operator is not a party to the exclusive operations, it will be difficult to convince it to perform the operations without further assurances for the liabilities involved. Secondly, a defaulting party that has lost its participating interest through a total forfeiture or buy-out will remain liable for the activities that occurred during its participation as a member of the consortium, in particular the decommissioning issues and in accordance with the applicable law.[158] In other words, the parties must be aware of liability issues with regards to leaving the consortium, such as assignment, withdrawal, relinquishment and default, otherwise they may end up bearing more liabilities than expected.[159]

The majority of the JOAs do not directly address the issues related to third-party liabilities, but they aim to maintain the general principle that each party shall bear the liabilities related to each participating interest overall. The British JOA is the only model to address agency liabilities as it is the only model that recognises the agency relationship.

---

155 *Ibid*, 313. See also Sections 4 and 6 in this Chapter and Section 5 in Chapter 2.

156 T Daintith and G Willoughby (eds), *Adrian Hill, United Kingdom Oil & Gas Law*, 3rd edn, Sweet & Maxwell, 2009, p1141.

157 Some courts have recognised that an operator owes fiduciary duties to non-operators because of its unique authority to dispose of the non-operators' interests. See for example the decision of the Canadian first instance court in *Erehwon Exploration Limited v Northstar Energy Corporation* 1993 CanLII 7238 (AB QB). Fiduciary duties are considered further in Chapter 1, Section 4.

158 M Saunders, "Some Legal Aspects of Abandonment Agreements", *OGLTR* 11(11/12) (1993) 365–372.

159 See: B Manning, "Some Practical Aspects of Resources Joint Ventures" in WD Duncan, *Joint Ventures Law in Australia*, 2nd edn, The Federation Press, 2005, pp323–324.

Finally, the JOAs do not commonly provide financial limits on liability, but rather distinguishes between the types of damage or degree of fault that will be shared by all parties and those that are dealt with as a liability to be borne exclusively by the operator. However, such a liability provision is drafted to protect the operator's functionality in the JOA rather than anything else.

In conclusion, there is no straightforward solution for the liability provision. The outcome may depend on the party that is designated operator, a position which might be occupied either by an international oil company or national oil company and it is likely to be a highly debated topic in any JOA negotiation. Ideally it should be balanced as the operator takes the operatorship role with the main principle of no gain no loss. On the other hand, it may be better to modify the exculpatory clause by reducing the high threshold for operator liability to encourage the operator to be more cautious and implement a higher standard of performance in its operations.

4. Operatorship, removal and replacement

4.1 Introduction

All JOAs have two types of party: the operator and the non-operators. The operator acts as the leader of the joint venture, and is responsible for the day-to-day operation of the consortium.[160] Commonly, the operator will be the party with the largest interest in the joint venture, as it will need robust financial and technical resources to run the operation. Therefore, the current agreements secure a dominant position for one party, as extensive rights and duties are placed on it (the operator).

The other parties to the joint venture, the non-operators, are not involved in the running of the operations; mainly their participation is mostly restricted to financial support for the operations and lifting their share of the production.[161] However, beyond such financial contributions the role of non-operators is far less certain. Some JOA Models strengthen their position by increasing their participation and control of the joint operations,[162] while others arguably position the non-operators as mere observers of or investors in the same joint operations.[163]

The imbalance between the strength of the parties also affects the role of the parties in the JOA, as power is located on only one side of the consortium, namely the sole operatorship of the operator.

---

160 See: C Golvala, "Upstream joint ventures – bidding and operating agreements" in G Picton-Turbervill (ed.), *Oil and Gas: A Practical Handbook*, Globe Law and Business, 2009, p46; C Duval, H Le Leuch, A Pertuzio and JL Weaver, *International Petroleum and Exploration Agreements: Legal, Economic & Policy Aspects*, 2nd edn, Barrows, 2009, pp289–291; A Jennings, *Oil and Gas Exploration Contracts*, 2nd edn, Sweet & Maxwell, 2008, p24; MPG Taylor, SM Tyne, *Taylor and Winsor on Joint Operating Agreements*, 2nd edn, Longman, 1992, pp1–5; BG Taverne, *An Introduction to the Regulation of the Petroleum Industry: Law, Contracts and Conventions*, Graham & Trotman, 1994, pp135–136.

161 See: T Daintith and G Willoughby (eds), *Adrian Hill, United Kingdom Oil and Gas Law*, 3rd edn, Sweet & Maxwell, 2009; P Roberts and R Fowler, *Joint Operating Agreements: A Practical Guide*, 4th edn, Globe Law and Business, 2020, pp143–159; S Styles, "Joint Operating Agreements" in J Paterson and G Gordon (eds), *Oil and Gas Law: Current Practice and Emerging Trends*, Dundee University Press, 2007, p288.

162 S Styles, "Joint Operating Agreements" in J Paterson and G Gordon (eds), *Oil and Gas Law: Current Practice and Emerging Trends*, Dundee University Press, 2007, p286.

163 *Ibid.*

Therefore, it is easy to understand the reasons for the different views and perspectives held by these parties, as each one has a different role in the joint venture. The operator, as the manager of the joint venture,[164] seeks more power to conduct the joint operations. On the other hand, the non-operators, as participants in the joint venture, seek more control over the joint operations.[165]

Consequently, the creation of such disproportionate roles not only affects the balance of participation of the parties, but also separates their position in the JOA, which ultimately increases tension and provides grounds for dispute. This is particularly the case when national oil companies are involved as they are unlikely to accept the lack of participation in and control of the operations.

The stronger position of the operator originates with the approach of the first JOA in 1956 (ie, AAPL JOA form 1956), but it still exists in current operations. It is considered to be the traditional approach. This fact is clearly recognised by the majority of academics and professionals in the oil and gas operations sector.[166] Traditionally, the oil and gas industry has always assumed there was a need for a strong and dominant operator, which was supposed to steer the consortium and determine the pace of the operations.[167] As a consequence, the unbalanced relationship did not favour a high degree of participation by the non-operators, but rather resulted in an operator-biased document. So, the question is, why was it necessary to give one party so much authority over the others?

Commentators give three reasons for such a stronger party, which can be summarised as:

- burden;
- formation; and
- commitment.

The first theory is based on the fact that the operator has several duties to perform and comply with, so it should obtain certain benefits in order to compensate it for such a 'burden'. The second theory is based on the formation of the consortium. The theory is that a leader needs a higher level of benefit to encourage it to create and take the lead in a joint venture. The third theory, which is the most accepted by commentators in this field, is related to the level of commitment of the operator.

---

164 GMD Bean, *Fiduciary Obligations and Joint Ventures: The Collaborative Fiduciary Relationship*, Oxford University Press, 1995, pp161–175.

165 S Shaw, "Joint Operating Agreements" in MR David, *Upstream Oil and Gas Agreements*, Sweet & Maxwell, 1996, pp21–22.

166 See: T Daintith and G Willoughby (eds), *Adrian Hill, United Kingdom Oil and Gas Law*, 3rd edn, Sweet & Maxwell, 2009, p1140; GMD Bean, *Fiduciary Obligations and Joint Ventures: The Collaborative Fiduciary Relationship*, Oxford University Press, 1995, pp14–15; KC Mildwaters, *Joint Operating Agreements, A Consideration of Legal Aspects Relevant to Joint Operating Agreements used in Great Britain and Australia by Participants thereto to Regulate the Joint Undertaking of Exploration for Petroleum in Offshore Areas with Particular Reference to their Rights and Duties*, PhD Thesis presented to the University of Dundee, 1990, p427; J Wilkinson, *Introduction to Oil and Gas Joint Ventures: Volume one, United Kingdom Continental Shelf*, OPL, 1997, p40; JS Dzienkowski, EE Smith, OL Anderson, JS Lowe, BM Kramer and JL Weaver, *Materials on International Petroleum Transactions*, 3rd edn, RMMLF, 2010, p542; S Shaw, "Joint Operating Agreements" in MR David, *Upstream Oil and Gas Agreements*, Sweet & Maxwell, 1996, pp19–21; A Jennings, *Oil and Gas Exploration Contracts*, 2nd edn, Sweet & Maxwell, 2008, pp17–27; H Dundas, *Joint Operating Agreements: An Introduction*, 1994 Summer Programme: UK Oil and Gas Law, CPMLP 09/09, 1994, pp5–11.

167 H Dundas, *Joint Operating Agreements: An Introduction*, 1994 Summer Programme: UK Oil and Gas Law, CPMLP 09/09, 1994, pp5–11.

Oil and gas operations involve several risks and costs; therefore, it is very important to maintain a high level of commitment from the operator towards the success of the joint venture.

In addition, circumstances often require the operator to pay, in advance, the costs of the operation, which are later reimbursed by the non-operators according to their shares.[168] A financially stronger operator is able to deal more easily with any required advance costs.

The first and second theories are likely to be raised by the operator during the negotiation period to support its arguments in favour of a higher percentage of interest from the joint venture.[169]

However, the strongest reason for the significant interest retained by the operator is certainly the third theory, for economic reasons.[170]

A similar approach is likely to be taken in negotiations between an international oil company and a national oil company. The main reasons why national oil companies prefer to let the international oil company take the role of operator in the consortium, at least until a certain stage, are the international company's financial strength and its technical expertise. But this is no longer necessarily the case. Some of the largest oil and gas companies in the world (eg, Petrobras, Sinopec, Equinor, Rosneft) are national oil companies and they are fully able to take the operatorship role; in some cases, it may be compulsory for the national oil company to act as operator (eg, the pre-salt area in Brazil).

Additionally, a government might also exercise an important role in determining the operator's higher interest. In some jurisdictions the legal regime for the petroleum sector requires the operator to hold a specified minimum percentage interest throughout the JOA, subject to its removal if this obligation is not complied with.[171]

Both non-operators and host governments may be concerned that an operator with a smaller interest might not dedicate the necessary effort and commitment to the operations, so the operator is likely to be the party with the greatest interest and with the strongest position in the joint venture.

It could also be argued that it is the nature of business that the party that is in the better negotiating position gets more benefits.[172] In general terms this might be true, but for oil and gas operations such a scenario will be slightly different. First, the operator will not want to bear all the risks and costs of the operation by itself, as these could be very high. Consequently, the operator needs to have "partners" to share the risks and cost involved. Secondly, the non-operators are not only part of the joint venture, but also jointly liable for the operations conducted by the operator, regarding any third party and the host government. Thirdly, in general oil and gas companies spread their assets across a range of investments, so it is likely that no one party will be able to conduct all operations on its own.

---

168 C Duval, H Le Leuch, A Pertuzio and JL Weaver, *International Petroleum and Exploration Agreements: Legal, Economic & Policy Aspects*, 2nd edn, Barrows, 2009, p298.

169 T Daintith and G Willoughby (eds), *Adrian Hill, United Kingdom Oil and Gas Law*, 3rd edn, Sweet & Maxwell, 2009, p1140.

170 JS Dzienkowski, EE Smith, OL Anderson, JS Lowe, BM Kramer and JL Weaver, *Materials on International Petroleum Transactions*, 3rd edn, RMMLF, 2010, p542.

171 For example, the Brazilian petroleum regime.

172 Professor RW Bentham, "The Negotiation of Agreements", 5 (1987) *Journal of Energy & Natural Resources Law* 134.

Sometimes the parties may share responsibility for running the operations by creating another vehicle to manage the joint operations (ie, an incorporated operator), which will include all parties to the consortium.[173] In simple terms, this approach would create a joint operating company to undertake the day-to-day activities of the consortium (in a similar approach to many joint development zones using a special purpose vehicle). It might require a higher level of engagement from the non-operators, but the operator is likely to secure the control of such an entity if the size of participating interest is the determining factor for control of the vehicle.

An alternative method to avoid most of the conflicts in the conduct of the joint operations is to delegate the day-to-day operations to a third-party contractor.[174]

This approach may be problematic in those jurisdictions which require government approval. However, the host government may approve such delegation of powers if the contractor is reputable and acts without any prejudice toward the joint and several liabilities of the JOA parties.[175]

In this way the JOA parties could avoid many potential conflicts as a neutral third party would perform the work in the way decided by their OpCom,[176] and it would be easy for any JOA party to request higher levels of control and performance in such a service agreement. However, the JOA Model Forms are not designed in such way and several adjustments should be implemented in order to proceed with such approach.

Deploying a third-party operator acting as an independent contractor is an interesting alternative to balance the position between the JOA parties, as an independent party will perform the operations jointly decided by them. However, it might change the format of the JOA. First, the third party is not a member of the JOA and so the JOA will have to be adjusted accordingly. Secondly, the JOA parties will sign a separate contract with the third party. In this case, the limitations on operator liability could be relaxed as the third-party operator will make a profit for its services for which the JOA parties will expect to hold it accountable. Thirdly, the third-party operator is likely to require government approval. Consequently, the third-party operator might be an interesting solution to balance the position of the JOA parties, but the practicality of this approach is very complex. The major obstacles are the complexity of implementing two agreements simultaneously and the transfer of the operator's powers to a third party. For these reasons, the approach is not well accepted in the industry for exploration and production activities, but it is more commonly accepted for lifting agreements, where a third party will be appointed to manage the parties' lifting entitlement and accounting.

There are other ways to achieve a more balanced participation for the JOA parties in addition to using an incorporated company operator or a third-party operator are not the only solutions, such as splitting the operatorship.

However, splitting the operatorship or using a special vehicle operator are far more common in the exploration and production industry. The practicality of these

173 C Duval, H Le Leuch, A Pertuzio and JL Weaver, *International Petroleum and Exploration Agreements: Legal, Economic & Policy Aspects*, 2nd edn, Barrows, 2009, p289.

174 S Styles, "Joint Operating Agreements" in J Paterson and G Gordon (eds), *Oil and Gas Law: Current Practice and Emerging Trends*, Dundee University Press, 2007, p278.

175 P Roberts and R Fowler, *Joint Operating Agreements: A Practical Guide*, 4th edn, Globe Law and Business, 2020, pp126–127.

176 S Shaw, "Joint Operating Agreements" in MR David, *Upstream Oil and Gas Agreements*, Sweet & Maxwell, 1996, p14.

alternatives is seen not only in agreements between countries (eg, those creating joint development zones),[177] but also between private parties such as the unit operating agreement,[178] which establishes the same concept as the joint development zone inside the same jurisdiction (ie, unitisation). If the joint development zone, unit operating agreement and lifting agreement address the same situation, or a situation that is fairly similar to a JOA,[179] why is it not possible to use these alternatives in a JOA? Some practical examples from the joint development zone have shown whether they might work, but it remains a valid alternative to balance the different views and aims of operator and non-operator. The most reasonable answer is that these alternatives require a management structure which is more complex than a single party operator, and dilute the authority and control which the operator could otherwise wield.

The final question is whether the non-operators are willing to accept the imbalance imposed by the operator while continuing proportionally to share all the risks and costs involved? The conflict over liability between the JOA parties (ie, BP, Anadarko and Mitsui) involved in the Deepwater Horizon (Macondo) accident in 2010 has shown the likelihood that the non-operators will use any possible right they find under the applicable law in order to avoid their share of liability for any performance failure and its (occasionally catastrophic) consequences.[180] However, the difficulty of proving such allegations is illustrated by the decision of Anadarko (contrary to their earlier statements)[181] to drop its case and reach a settlement agreement to pay US$4 billion to BP.[182]

It is advisable for the operator to obtain the non-operators' participation or at least acquiescence in the conduct of operations, to avoid giving non-operators the opportunity to argue in legal proceedings that they had limited or no input into the conduct of the operations and should be relieved of liability on that basis. This is particularly the case if a national oil company is a non-operator as it will be unlikely to allow the operator to play a dominant role.

In conclusion, all JOAs should provide balanced and equitable provisions in order to minimise uncertainty[183] and maximise efficiency.[184] Both an international

---

177 DF Asmus, E Bastida, A Okoye, JL Weaver, S Mahmud, J Ross and TW Wälde (†), "International Unitisation of Oil and Gas Fields: The Legal Framework of International Law, National Laws, and Private Contracts", *OGEL* 2 (2007), www.ogel.org.

178 KE Barnhill Jr, "Taxation of Oil and Gas Operating Agreements, The Scope and Application of I. T 3930", *Rocky Mountain Law Review* 26 (1953–1954) 133.

179 For further information see: DE Pierce, "Coordinated Reservoir Development, An Alternative to the Rule of Capture for the Ownership and Development of Oil and Gas", *Journal of Energy Law & Policy* 4 (1983) 129; DM Ong, "The 1979 and 1990 Malaysia-Thailand Joint Development Agreements: A Model for International Legal Co-operations in Common Offshore Petroleum Deposits?" *International Journal of Marine and Coastal Law* 14 (1999) 207.

180 "As the liabilities associated with Deepwater Horizon mount, Anadarko and BP will surely square off in court to determine whether or not Anadarko has to kick in 25%. Anadarko will litigate how culpable BP was for the spill, an effort that directly aligns its interest with the plaintiffs in all the other pending litigation. Indeed, BP is currently considering initiating that war." For further information see: www.dailyfinance.com/ 2010/06/21/bp-oil-spill-update-anadarko-turns-on-bp-is-20-billion-enough.

181 *Ibid.*

182 www.spglobal.com/platts/en/market-insights/latest-news/oil/101711-anadarko-to-pay-bp-4-billion-in-macondo-settlement.

183 J Lacey, "Partnering and Alliancing, Back to the Future?" *ARELJ* 26 (2007) 82.

184 TC Marvin, "Above the Law? Dealing with the abuse of Joint Operating Agreements under the Newspaper Preservation Act", *Wayne Law Review* 42 (1995–1996) 1719; M Moy, "Beware! The Unfair Contracts Jurisdiction", *ARELJ* 24 (2005) 227; J Tarrant, "Agreements to Co-Operate at Common Law", *ARELJ* 25 (2006) 281; JD Dinnage, "Joint Activities among Gas Producers, the Competition Man Cometh", *Journal of Energy & Natural Resources Law* 16 (1998) 249.

and a national oil company could take the role of the operator in an international transaction, but the national oil company is more likely to be the non-operator and to require further control over the operations.

It is very important for all parties (including the operator) to maintain an equilibrium between the roles of each consortium party. Ultimately this will benefit all parties and both the international and the national oil companies may hold the position at some stage during the life of the JOA.

4.2 Removal and replacement of the operator

(a) *General principles*

Ideally, the operator should perform the joint operations in accordance with several rules established in the petroleum regulations and the JOA. But the operator has to comply with more than just the contractual obligations, as several other principles must also be followed, such as the requirement to follow best practices in the industry, with diligence and efficiency.

As previously mentioned, the provision on control of operations is a vital mechanism to verify the high-level performance and compliance of the joint operations. However, the long duration of most petroleum licences increases the chance of performance failure at some stage in its course, so it is necessary to secure not only the non-operators' interests but also the overall survival of the consortium, as any failure could jeopardise the whole enterprise and risk termination of the granting instrument. Consequently, JOAs should regulate the circumstances under which the operator may be removed from its function in the JOA and the election of its successor.[185] Provided the operator does not resign[186] and is not removed, it will remain the operator of the consortium until the JOA terminates.[187]

The procedure for removing the operator is another highly debated issue during the negotiation of a JOA. On the one hand, the operator will be keen to reduce the scope of circumstances in which it could lose its position in the JOA. But if circumstances potentially justifying the operator's removal do occur, the operator is likely to prefer a requirement for unanimous agreement on the removal decision. On the other hand, the non-operators will be keen to increase the number of possible reasons for removing the operator and they are likely to seek the right to do so without justification and without any control by the operator.[188]

There are several reasons why the non-operators may wish to remove the operator.[189] However, the concept behind such a provision is to protect the

---

185 S Styles, "Joint Operating Agreements" in J Paterson and G Gordon (eds), *Oil and Gas Law: Current Practice and Emerging Trends* (Dundee University Press, 2007, p278.

186 Resignation will not be fully analysed as this is a primordial right of the operator, although it may be a protection for certain non-operators to require a time limitation for such resignation.

187 P Roberts and R Fowler, *Joint Operating Agreements: A Practical Guide*, 4th edn, Globe Law and Business, 2020, p122.

188 See the discussion of US, Canadian and UK cases on the removal of operator in T Martin, J Gilbert and M Gusy, "A Global Review of Joint Operating Agreement Disputes" AIPN research paper 2020, Section 7.6. The cases illustrate the importance of properly following the procedure for removal of the operator and the significance of including a provision for the removal of operator "without cause". The US cases also discuss situations where the operator was subject to insolvency proceedings, which in some cases prevented the non-operators from removing the operator.

189 KC Mildwaters, *Joint Operating Agreements, A Consideration of Legal Aspects Relevant to Joint Operating Agreements used in Great Britain and Australia by Participants thereto to Regulate the Joint Undertaking of Exploration for Petroleum in Offshore Areas with Particular Reference to their Rights and Duties*, PhD Thesis presented to the University of Dundee, 1990, pp501–507.

consortium against performance failure. In this sense, the financial strength of the operator is a key element to secure the performance of the minimum work obligation and any other activity to explore and produce oil and gas from the licensed area.[190] As a consequence, bankruptcy is the most commonly stated grounds in a JOA for removing the operator from its function – a bankrupt operator is facing significant financial problems.

However, there may be problems with fully executing such a provision, as it may conflict with creditors' rights under bankruptcy and insolvency regulations.[191]

Bankruptcy is the most obvious reason to remove the operator from its function in the consortium,[192] but there are several other reasons, such as material breach of the JOA terms or, substantial reduction of operator's participating interest.[193]

If the national oil company is a non-operator party, it is likely to be very concerned with establishing how the operator may be removed for non-performance. But the more complex situation is the opposite, when the national oil company is the operator and it fails to perform the operations. Although the international oil companies may have the right to remove the national oil company, it may be much more complicated to implement a contractual right of this nature. Although the JOA parties have the right to remove the operator and appoint another one, the new operator will be subject to governmental approval.[194]

From a non-operator's perspective, it is highly important to exclude the operator from the decision about its removal; otherwise it will be difficult to implement such a provision.[195]

Conversely, if the operator's status with the governmental authorities is affected, the loss of status would normally make it impossible for the operator to continue in that role in the JOA, but the industry model forms do not make this automatic grounds for the operator's removal.[196]

The operator may also resign its functions as the operator of the consortium. For the non-operators, the possibility of resignation is not as important as the power to remove the operator,[197] but in certain cases specific capabilities of the operator might be crucial to complete the minimum work obligation, so the non-operators would be keen to restrict the resignation up to a certain time in the life of the JOA.[198] Nevertheless, in some cases the qualification of the Operator might be essential (eg, depending on the level of experience the Operator might obtain the status as Operator A, B or C as defined by the petroleum regulations in Brazil).

---

190 MPG Taylor and SM Tyne, *Taylor and Winsor on Joint Operating Agreements*, 2nd edn, Longman, 1992, pp20–21.

191 JS Dzienkowski, EE Smith, OL Anderson, JS Lowe, BM Kramer and JL Weaver, *Materials on International Petroleum Transactions*, 3rd edn, RMMLF, 2010, p621.

192 For further information about bankruptcy and insolvency involving a JOA see: JD Weidman, "Oil and Gas, Operator's Liens in Bankruptcy, The Model Form Operating Agreement Versus the Trustee in Bankruptcy's Avoiding Powers", *Oklahama Law Review* 37 (1984) 141.

193 C Duval, H Le Leuch, A Pertuzio and JL Weaver, *International Petroleum and Exploration Agreements: Legal, Economic & Policy Aspects*, 2nd edn, Barrows, 2009, p289.

194 P Roberts and R Fowler, *Joint Operating Agreements: A Practical Guide*, 4th edn, Globe Law and Business, 2020, p125.

195 *Ibid.*

196 *Ibid*, 113.

197 S Shaw, "Joint Operating Agreements" in MR David (ed.), *Upstream Oil and Gas Agreements*, Sweet & Maxwell, 1996, p14.

198 MPG Taylor and SM Tyne, *Taylor and Winsor on Joint Operating Agreements*, 2nd edn, Longman, 1992, p19.

The appointment of the replacement operator is another issue of debate,[199] particularly the voting ratio required to carry the decision,[200] even though some scholars argue the opposite.[201] However, the replacement must also be approved by the host government, as the change will affect the performance of the operations, which ultimately affects the maximisation of the economic recovery of the reservoir.[202] On the other hand, the host government should not unreasonably withhold its approval, which should be based on economic and technical qualification to perform the operations.[203] The terms on which the replacement operator is approved by the state is likely to reside in the granting instrument.

The appointment of the new operator will become effective when it obtains government approval; however, there should be contractual obligations on how the existing operator must perform during the interim period (between the removal and the election of the successor).[204]

If the petroleum regulations allow, an interesting alternative would be to give the operatorship to the party with the largest participating interest, or the second largest if the operator has the largest.[205] But as Peter Roberts points out, it might "result in the operatorship passing to an unwilling party (which may resign anyway)". There are possible solutions to this. "It might be preferable, therefore, to have any party eligible considered as the new operator. The JOA should provide that a party cannot become the new operator against its will."[206]

If the operator cannot vote on its removal, is it possible to argue that the operator cannot vote on the election of the new operator?[207] In theory, the removal and the election of the successor operator are two different things. So the operator would have the right to vote in the election of its successor. On the other hand, if the operator has a substantial participating interest, it would be able to block the election of a new operator and remain as the provisional operator for as long as it wished (if it wanted).

Ernest Smith describes such complexity in a case relating to a unit operating agreement, which is the same concept as a JOA but between more parties and covers a larger area (ie, a unit operating agreement results from the merging of two or more JOAs). The case of *Fasken Land and Minerals, Ltd v Occidental Permian Ltd*[208] reminds us that the removal of the operator does not secure, by itself, the position of the non-operators, they must also ensure that the election of the new operator is secured

---

199 C Thorpe, *Fundamentals of Upstream Petroleum Agreements*, CP Thorpe, 2008, pp124–125.

200 S Styles, "Joint Operating Agreements" in J Paterson and G Gordon (eds), *Oil and Gas Law: Current Practice and Emerging Trends*, Dundee University Press, 2007, p287.

201 MPG Taylor and SM Tyne, *Taylor and Winsor on Joint Operating Agreements*, 2nd edn, Longman, 1992, p21.

202 S Styles, "Joint Operating Agreements" in J Paterson and G Gordon (eds), *Oil and Gas Law: Current Practice and Emerging Trends*, Dundee University Press, 2007, p277.

203 C Duval, H Le Leuch, A Pertuzio and JL Weaver, *International Petroleum and Exploration Agreements: Legal, Economic & Policy Aspects*, 2nd edn, Barrows, 2009, p289.

204 MPG Taylor and SM Tyne, *Taylor and Winsor on Joint Operating Agreements*, 2nd edn, Longman, 1992, p20.

205 KC Mildwaters, *Joint Operating Agreements, A Consideration of Legal Aspects Relevant to Joint Operating Agreements used in Great Britain and Australia by Participants thereto to Regulate the Joint Undertaking of Exploration for Petroleum in Offshore Areas with Particular Reference to their Rights and Duties*, PhD Thesis presented to the University of Dundee, 1990, p510.

206 P Roberts and R Fowler, *Joint Operating Agreements: A Practical Guide*, 4th edn, Globe Law and Business, 2020, p126.

207 KC Mildwaters, *Joint Operating Agreements, A Consideration of Legal Aspects Relevant to Joint Operating Agreements used in Great Britain and Australia by Participants thereto to Regulate the Joint Undertaking of Exploration for Petroleum in Offshore Areas with Particular Reference to their Rights and Duties*, PhD Thesis presented to the University of Dundee, 1990, p510.

208 225 SW 3d 577 (Tex App – El Paso 2005).

(ie, they must ensure that the operator cannot block the election of a successor operator even though it has been removed from the operatorship).[209]

Consequently, it is necessary to control the operator's rights to block the election of a new operator; otherwise the removal of the operator will not be possible in practice. If the parties cannot elect another operator, the ultimate solution will be the surrender of the petroleum title.

Therefore, the removal of the operator is a key provision for the non-operators, but it will only be effective if there is clear regulation for the transition period until the appointment of the successor operator.[210]

In addition, it is important to note that the resignation or removal of the operator shall not exclude it from liabilities incurred during its performance as the operator of the consortium, and also shall not exclude the operator's right to recover the costs and expenses allowed by the accounting procedures.[211]

Therefore, a national or international oil company as a non-operator should look for a provision with the following characteristics:

- several alternatives to remove the operator (ie, with and without a good reason);
- exclusion of the operator from the vote on the removal; and
- a transition period from the removal of the operator until the election of its successor where operations shall be conducted by the non-operators (if permitted by the governmental authorities), or if the operator has to maintain the operatorship until the handing over to the new operator, the operator shall not have the right to block such election.

(b) Analysis of model JOAs

It is important to analyse how the industry JOA models deal with this topic. AAPL Model Form 810 provides two ways of removing the operator – removal upon assignment and removal for cause by vote.[212]

Removal upon assignment seeks to discourage the operator from losing its dominant position in the consortium, because if the operator dilutes its participating interest to a percentage lower than any non-operator, it may be removed by the non-operators.[213] However, it does not exclude the operator from voting on such a matter. In this situation, if a lower voting threshold is not established, then this provision might not be effective. The removal for cause by vote describes several circumstances that might lead to the removal of the operator.[214]

It is possible to suggest that the extensive list the AAPL JOA includes does not completely secure the non-operators' position, as the operator has to breach some provision or be declared insolvent before any action can be taken. In this sense, it does not secure the non-operators against weak or poor performance that complies with regulations but could be improved. However, the main difference between this and the first provision is the fact that the operator is excluded from voting on such

---

209 JS Dzienkowski, EE Smith, OL Anderson, JS Lowe, BM Kramer and JL Weaver, *Materials on International Petroleum Transactions*, 3rd edn, RMMLF, 2010, pp615–617.

210 P Roberts and R Fowler, *Joint Operating Agreements: A Practical Guide*, 4th edn, Globe Law and Business, 2020, p126.

211 *Ibid*, 125.

212 AAPL JOA Model Form 810 §4.4.

213 AAPL JOA Model Form 810 §4.4.1.

214 AAPL JOA Model Form 810 §4.4.2.

a decision, so it increases the non-operators' control. Such voting must occur within 90 days from the acknowledgement of the applicable cause.[215]

The election of the successor operator is slightly complex in regard to the voting procedure. The operator is not clearly excluded from participating in the appointment of its successor, but the provision refers to the procedure for the removal of the operator. In other words, this provision indicates that the voting procedures to elect a new operator will be the same as to remove the operator, that is, the operator will be excluded from such voting. Nevertheless, such an exclusion is not transferable, so the assignee will not suffer such restrictions. If there are only two parties, the non-operator has the automatic right to become the operator. If the non-operator does not wish to become the operator, the consortium will terminate.[216]

The removal of the operator comes into effect once approved by the governmental authority. The outgoing operator must transfer the rights and obligations related to the petroleum title to the successor operator.[217] Nevertheless, the election of the successor operator shall not exclude any right or liability incurred by the outgoing operator during its function as the operator of the consortium.[218]

In conclusion, the AAPL JOA 810 Model Form provides a reasonable degree of control over the operatorship. However, it fails to provide wide powers to remove the operator. The model allows removal related to the effectiveness of the performance of the operations.

There is no provision for the removal of the operator in the RMMLF JOA Model Form, except for on the assignment of all of its interest.[219] In other words, if the operator does not resign or sell its participating interest, the non-operators have no alternatives or mechanisms by which to remove the operator.

If the operator resigns or sells its participating interest, the non-operators must elect, by a simple majority, the successor operator. The outgoing operator shall remain as the interim operator until the new operator has been elected. But the outgoing operator shall not be required to perform as the interim operator for more than 60 days. In the case of sale, if the non-operators cannot elect a successor operator, the assignee shall become the operator. However, if no party is willing to take on the role of the operator, the consortium shall terminate.[220]

Therefore, it is clear there is a weakness in the RMMLF JOA Model Form, in that there is no mechanism for the non-operators to control the operatorship of the consortium. As a consequence, the operator has *de facto* (existing) total control of the operations, as the operatorship can only be modified at the operator's own discretion. In this sense, the lack of remedies might be a serious concern for the non-operators in securing a higher level of performance of operations.

The CAPL OP Model Form contains two provisions to remove the operator. The first allows for immediate removal and the second allows for delayed removal. The key difference between them is the urgency in removing the operator.[221]

The first provision deals with the financial strength of the operator. It is important for the consortium as this agreement is structured such that the operator

---

215 AAPL JOA Model Form 810 §4.4.3.
216 AAPL JOA Model Form 810 §4.4.5.
217 AAPL JOA Model Form 810 §4.4.7.
218 AAPL JOA Model Form 810 §4.4.6.
219 RMMLF JOA §4.2.
220 RMMLF JOA §4.3.
221 CAPL OP §2.02.

must perform the operations. If the operator cannot perform the operations, it might jeopardise the entire enterprise. Consequently, several actions that might affect the financial strength of the operator are a cause for its removal:

a) if the operator becomes bankrupt or insolvent;
b) if security against the operator's participating interest is enforced;
c) if the operator suffers dissolution, liquidation or winding up;
d) if a court order is made against the operator's participating interest;
e) if the operator is in default under the petroleum regulations;
f) if the operator attempts to assign its powers under the petroleum title.[222]

However, the non-operators must issue a notice stating the reason for the removal. In the case of removal, the party with the largest participating interest will act as an interim operator until the successor operator is appointed.[223]

The second provision deals with issues affecting the performance of the operations. This provision provides two alternatives:

a) the operator shall be removed if two or more parties holding at least 60% of participating interest decide to remove the operatorship – however, it does not mention whether the operator can vote on such a decision;
b) the operator shall be removed if its performance breaches its obligations under the petroleum title, but only if it does not remedy any breach within 30 days from the notice which must be issued by the non-operators – in this case, the operator can be replaced by an interim operator in order to protect life, property and the environment.[224]

The CAPL OP Model Form provides a unique mechanism to remove the operator, called a "challenge of the operator".[225] The idea is quite remarkable from the non-operators' perspective. First, the operator must have been performing the operations continuously for at least two years.[226] Secondly, if the former condition is met, any non-operator can challenge the operator by issuing a notice, which must state both that the non-operator can conduct the operations on more favourable terms and what these terms and conditions are. Such a notice must include sufficient detail to enable the other parties to evaluate the proposal. Within 60 days from such a challenge, the operator must state whether it can perform under the same terms. If it can perform under the same terms, the agreement will apply *mutatis mutandis* (any necessary changes having been made) but if it cannot, the operator must resign from its functions within 45 days.[227] After another two years, similar procedures are applicable for the continuation of the operations.[228] It is important to note that the proposing party shall become the operator if no other party can match its proposed terms and conditions. Any costs in excess of its proposal will be at its sole risk and expense for two years after the replacement. However, the new operator cannot

222 CAPL OP §2.02(A).
223 CAPL OP §2.02(A).
224 CAPL OP §2.02(B).
225 CAPL OP §2.03.
226 CAPL OP §2.03(A).
227 CAPL OP §2.03(A).
228 CAPL OP §2.05.

resign before the end of two years after its election.[229] No party can issue a challenge notice if it is a defaulting party or if it can be immediately removed.[230, 231]

Therefore, the challenge procedure is a valuable provision for all the parties. For the consortium, it increases the efficiency and effectiveness of the joint operations. It is also balanced as the operator cannot be removed without good reason and the challenging party must be able to match the challenge. Nevertheless, it is relevant to note that the Canadian Model does not require governmental approval to replace the operatorship of the consortium. In this sense, it is much easier to provide creative alternatives for removal of the operator. However, it is important to note that the challenging of operatorship encourages efficiency of performance, which is the most relevant issue for the host government as it will rely on the performance of the operator, for generating state income through oil and gas receipts. Consequently, such provision is likely to obtain positive support from the host government. Nevertheless, the precise extent of efficiency might be also fairly complex to determine. Ultimately it will provide a higher level of protection for all parties as the higher the efficiency, the higher the return will be for all parties.

The election of the successor operator is highly regulated. First, the parties must appoint a new operator as soon as is practicable.[232] Secondly, the outgoing operator and a defaulting party may not be appointed as the successor operator.[233] Thirdly, to obtain approval, the appointment must receive the support of at least two parties and have a participating interest greater than 50%; the outgoing Operator is entitled to vote if it is still a party to the JOA.[234] Fourthly, no party will become the operator unless it wishes to do so. Fifthly, the party with the largest participating interest (excluding the outgoing operator) shall act as the interim operator until the successor operator is appointed.[235] Sixthly, the effective date of the removal will vary according to the nature of the removal.[236]

It is important to note that the outgoing operator cannot claim recourse against the remaining parties.[237] However, it is not clear whether the outgoing operator can claim expenses incurred before the resignation or removal. The CAPL OP Model Form also regulates the transfer of property to the successor operator,[238] audit of the accounts[239] and assignment of the operatorship.[240] As with many other model JOAs, it fails to address how third-party contracts which the Operator uses to perform joint operations will be transferred contractually to the successor operator.

In conclusion, it may be suggested that the CAPL OP Model Form is by far the most favourable agreement for the non-operators. It not only guarantees extensive

---

229 CAPL OP §2.03(B).

230 CAPL OP §2.03(C).

231 The need for the relevant challenge notice to provide sufficient information for the incumbent operator to make a decision was in issue in the case of *Diaz Resources Ltd v Penn West Petroleum Ltd*, 2010 ABQB 153 (CanLII), a case which is discussed in Section 7.6 of T Martin, J Gilbert and M Gusy, "A Global Review of Joint Operating Agreement Disputes" AIPN research paper 2020.

232 CAPL OP §2.06(A).

233 CAPL OP §2.06(B).

234 CAPL OP §2.06(C).

235 CAPL OP §2.06(D).

236 CAPL OP §2.06(E).

237 CAPL OP §2.06(f).

238 CAPL OP §2.07.

239 CAPL OP §2.08.

240 CAPL OP §2.09.

grounds to remove the operator either immediately or at a later date, but also deals with the issue of efficiency. It is fairly common to provide for removal for breach or failure of performance of the material obligations of the petroleum title, but it is uncommon to allow removal for lack of efficiency, as the operator might comply with the regulations, but this does not usually guarantee a high level of performance in the operations.[241] However, this model form does not clearly address the governmental approval that shall be required to elect either the interim operator or the successor operator.

The UK JOA Model separates the reasons for removal of the operator into two categories, but both categories are subject to the determination of the OpCom. The first deals with certain issues that require a prior notice of no less than 60 days and then the operator is removed at the end of the month. The second category does not provide for such a requirement as it is used where there is a greater degree of urgency to resolve the situation.[242]

The first category addresses either a material breach of the operator which is not resolved within 28 days or the situation where the operator retains less than a certain percentage of interest. Surprisingly, although the UK Model considers these situations to be non-urgent, this is certainly not the case. A material breach is any breach that is not related to the default (ie, a cashcall or failure to obtain or maintain insurance), so it might refer to the performance of the minimum work obligation or compliance with the health and safety executive, or several other issues which might lead to the termination of the granting instrument if not remedied properly. The participating interest of the operator party, like any other JOA party, is also regulated by the granting instrument, so any breach of such instrument may also cause its termination. Consequently, the procedure to remove the operator may create problems for the non-operators if there is a failure of performance under the granting instrument as well.

The second category addresses (extensively) insolvency issues, but also refers to occasions where the operator loses its entire participating interest, where the host government withdraws its approval of the operator of the consortium and where the operator commits an act of wilful misconduct or fails to carry out decommissioning obligations (but the last could be allocated to either the first or second category).

Considering both categories which allow the removal of the operator, it is possible to suggest that the construction of such provisions is operator-friendly as the non-operators cannot remove the operator without a specific reason. It is not possible to remove the operator to improve efficiency because its performance is lower than expected. Additionally, the removal of the operator shall not affect its rights and liabilities during the time it performed the operations of the consortium.[243]

The election of the successor operator is quite well regulated. First, the model sets out the key procedures:

- the election should occur as soon as practicable;
- the new operator shall be selected by the OpCom;
- the successor party must accept the selection; and
- the host government must approve the selection.

241 A Hudec and J Paulus, "Current Oil and Gas Issues in Canada and the 1990 CAPL Operating Agreement", *Journal of Energy & Natural Resources Law* 10 (1992) 194.

242 OGUK JOA §5.3.

243 OGUK JOA §5.4.

Secondly, the model deals with the failure of an election, stating that the "the non-operator having the largest Percentage Interest and willing to assume the position of operator" shall be elected as the operator of the consortium provided that the host government consents to the nomination. But if more than one party has the same participating interest, the "Non-operator having held such Percentage Interest for the longest time shall be appointed and assume the position of operator, subject to any necessary approval of the Secretary". Thirdly, if no party wishes to undertake the role, the parties "shall be deemed to have decided to abandon the Joint Operations and to surrender the Licence in so far as it relates to the Licence Area". Thus, the election of the successor provides a high level of participation to the non-operators, as they are not compelled to accept such a role but they are given the right to perform the operations until the succession of a new operator (provided that the host government authorises it).[244]

Finally, the non-operators have a high level of control over the exclusion of the operator from participation in the decision on its removal and the election of a new operator, except when that removal is due to the dilution of participating interest.[245] In this case, the same problem as faced by the Fasken case[246] is unlikely to occur because the operator cannot block the decisions or even maintain the role of transitional operator. Additionally, the handing over to the successor operator is reasonably well regulated.[247, 248]

In conclusion, the UK JOA Model provides the non-operators a high level of control in the removal of the operator. However, the model only allows removal of the operator for specific reasons, as defined in the agreement, so it reduces the potential discretion of the non-operators.

The Norwegian JOA Model provides two different procedures for removal of the operator.[249] The first involves issues which are not urgent and the second involves issues which do require an urgent response.

In the first procedure, the OpCom must issue a notice no less than six months in advance to the operator, stating the reasons for the removal. In turn, the operator is allowed to express its views about the notice; however, the operator is excluded from voting on the decision for its removal. Nevertheless, the quorum is high, as the model requires the unanimous consent of all non-operators.[250]

In the second procedure, subject to the host government's approval, the OpCom may remove the operator immediately under the following circumstances:

a) The Operator's management or supervisory personnel has caused an economic loss to the Parties as the result of wilful misconduct or gross negligence;
b) The Operator or any of his Affiliated companies is declared bankrupt, applies for a composition with its creditors or becomes insolvent;

---

244 OGUK JOA §5.5 and 5.6.
245 OGUK JOA §5.8.
246 See footnote 208.
247 OGUK JOA §5.7.
248 The English case of to *TAQA Bratani Ltd and Others v RockRose* [2020] EWHC 58 (Comm) considered whether non-operators owed any fiduciary duty in exercising their powers to remove and appoint the operator and also considered whether, under English law, a JOA could be treated as a "relational contract" bringing obligations of mutual trust, confidence and loyalty between the parties into play. The court rejected the first argument and considered that the express terms of the JOA excluded the second.
249 Norwegian JOA §4.2.
250 Norwegian JOA §4.2.

c) Any of the Operator's Affiliated companies, as referred to in sub-section 14 litra a) of the definitions herein, is dissolved;
d) The Operator transfers his Participating interest or a substantial part thereof, to another entity.[251]

The OpCom must appoint a new operator, subject to the host government's approval, within 60 days. If it fails to appoint or if the host government rejects the appointment, the host government shall decide the new operator.[252]

It is important to note that there is no provision dealing with the interim period between the removal of the operator and the election of a new operator. Nevertheless, there is a provision requiring cooperation between the old and new operators "with regard to the transfer of the operatorship". In other words, the model indicates that the removed operator shall conduct the operations until a new operator is effectively nominated.[253]

In conclusion, the Norwegian JOA Model provides a high level of control over the operatorship as the non-operators can remove the operator for no reason or for specific reasons defined in the agreement. It is relevant to note that the operator may not participate in the decision concerning its removal. However, the model does not clearly exclude the removed operator from participation in the succession election, even though it indicates that the removed operator must hand over to the new operator several items of information and documentation.[254] It is interesting to note that the removed operator shall be liable for the expenses required to remove itself from the operatorship of the consortium.[255]

The AIPN JOA Model is once again unique as it contains standard and optional provisions for removal of the operator. The standard provisions apply in two sets of circumstances and the optional provisions in three.[256]

The first standard provision is related to insolvency and bankruptcy, enabling the consortium to continue to function notwithstanding the operator's perform its obligations and activities.[257] The second is related to material breach, but it is far more complex.[258] First, the non-operators must obtain a certain percentage of the participating interest and/or parties to issue a notice requesting that the material breach be remedied. Secondly, the operator has 30 days to remedy the material breach. If it does so, and the breach recurs, the non-operators will have to apply the same process in respect of the new breach. Thirdly, if the operator does not agree with the content of the notice of material breach, it shall remain as the operator until the final proceedings of the dispute. It is clear there are limitations on the non-operators' power to remove the operator for material breach, mostly because of the dispute process, which favours the operator.[259]

251 Norwegian JOA §4.2.
252 Norwegian JOA §4.4.
253 Norwegian JOA §4.3.
254 Norwegian JOA §4.3.
255 Norwegian JOA §4.3.
256 AIPN JOA §4.10.
257 AIPN JOA §4.10(A).
258 AIPN JOA §4.10(B).
259 One key issue which JOAs do not routinely address is whether the non-operators must obtain a final non-appealable judgment declaring the operator to be in material breach before it can be removed.

The optional provisions apply in three sets of circumstances.[260] The first provision allows the non-operators to remove the operator if the operator's participating interest is smaller than a certain percentage.[261] The second allows the non-operators to remove the operator if the operator changes its control.[262] However, the first and second provisions are not automatic as the OpCom must decide whether a successor should be elected (but the provision does not exclude the participation of the operator). The third alternative allows the non-operators to remove the operator without reason, but only if the vote exceeds a defined passmark.[263] Certainly, the last provision gives the most valuable discretion to the non-operators, as many circumstances could motivate them to remove the operator. This provision is intended to motivate the operator to improve its performance.

The election of the successor operator is highly regulated.[264] First, the model determines that the OpCom "shall meet as soon as possible to appoint a successor operator".[265] Secondly, it is clear that no party can be compelled to accept the election.[266] Thirdly, the operator cannot be a candidate for the election, except in the optional cases of dilution of the participating interest and change in control.[267] Fourthly, the removed operator shall be compensated (if applicable) for its reasonable expenses, except in the case of material breach.[268] Fifthly, the removed and the successor operators shall arrange the handing over procedures.[269] Sixthly, the removal of the operator and the election of its replacement shall not be effective until the host government's approval.[270] Seventhly, the removed operator shall be liable until the effective date of the removal.[271]

Therefore, it is possible to suggest that the AIPN JOA Model Form provides a high level of control to the non-operators, as they have several alternative methods to remove the operator, including the option of removing it without a reason.[272] However, such a high degree of control is only secured if the third optional provision is used – the first and second alternatives are not effective because they do not exclude the operator from participating in the OpCom's decision on its replacement. Additionally, there is no provision for an interim operator, so there might be a gap between the removal of the operator and the host government's approval.

The Greenlandic JOA Model starts with a provision relating to the host government's approval of any action to remove the operator.[273] It is important to remember that this model assumes that a national oil company is a member of the JOA, so it is natural to expect a higher level of concern over governmental approval.

---

260 AIPN JOA §4.10(C), (D) and (E).
261 AIPN JOA §4.10(C).
262 AIPN JOA §4.10(D).
263 AIPN JOA §4.10(E).
264 AIPN JOA §4.11.
265 AIPN JOA §4.11(A).
266 AIPN JOA §4.11(A).
267 AIPN JOA §4.11(B).
268 AIPN JOA §4.11(C).
269 AIPN JOA §4.11(D).
270 AIPN JOA §4.11(E).
271 AIPN JOA §4.11(F).
272 JS Dzienkowski, EE Smith, OL Anderson, JS Lowe, BM Kramer and JL Weaver, *Materials on International Petroleum Transactions*, 3rd edn, RMMLF, 2010, p621.
273 Greenlandic JOA §3.17.2.

There are three different grounds that the non-operators can use to remove the operator:

> a) *The Operator may be removed for cause at the end of any Month by the Operating Committee giving not less than ninety (90) days' notice to it stating such cause.*
> b) *In addition, the Operator may be removed by notice given by the Operating Committee which notice shall have immediate effect if the Operator materially defaults in the performance of its obligation under this Agreement and, where such default is capable of remedy, fails to remedy or commence actions which lead to such remedy within a reasonable period specified by the Operating Committee.*
> c) *Furthermore, the operator may be removed immediately if the circumstances described in Section 24.01 d of the Licence apply to the Operator or if circumstances occur which may in the reasonable opinion of the Operating Committee materially adversely affect the ability of the operator to continue to carry out its obligations hereunder.*[274]

It is important to note that there is a mandatory requirement that the operator shall have the right to express its views about the notice requesting its removal. Although it may be difficult to enforce such a right in cases of immediate removal, it appears to be possible under option a) above. Nevertheless, it is fair and balanced to provide such a right for the operator.[275]

It is also important to note that the operator may not vote on the decision concerning its removal. Such a decision shall be made by a certain percentage of interest of the non-operating parties.[276]

In the case of immediate removal, the non-operator that retains the largest participating interest shall act as the interim operator, unless the OpCom decides otherwise.

The election of the new operator is clearly regulated.[277] First, the parties shall elect the successor operator as soon as practicable. Secondly, a non-operator shall be appointed as the new operator. Thirdly, the nomination is subject to the nominee's acceptance and the host government's approval. Fourthly, the removed operator may not vote in the election (otherwise the election will be invalid). Fifthly, the parties shall determine the level of support from the non-operators to appoint a new operator.

Additionally, the handover process from the outgoing operator to the new operator regarding the transfer of rights, responsibilities, materials and documents is also highly regulated.[278] However, the outgoing operator shall be liable for all the actions performed during its time as the operator of the consortium.[279]

In summary, the Greenlandic JOA Model demonstrates clearly the wish of the governmental authorities to control the operatorship of the consortium. It also provides a high degree of control to the non-operators so that the host government

274 Greenlandic JOA §3.17.2.
275 Greenlandic JOA §3.17.2.
276 Greenlandic JOA §3.17.2.
277 Greenlandic JOA §3.17.3.
278 Greenlandic JOA §3.17.4.
279 Greenlandic JOA §3.17.4(b).

can achieve its expectation of high standards from the operator's performance. However, the precise definition of a material breach might be contested. Nevertheless, the non-operators could allocate such breach under the generic alternatives a) or c) since alternative b) applies as a default.

(c) Discussion

In conclusion, it is clear that each JOA takes a different approach for the removal of the operator.[280] Some provide few or no grounds for removal, such as the RMMLF Model. Others provide extensive grounds for the removal of the operator, such as the AIPN and OGUK Models. However, the Canadian Model is unique in that it allows a periodic review of the operator's performance. In this sense, any non-operator may challenge the operator, which should encourage it to improve its performance so that it is not replaced by a non-operator.

It is also important to note that the majority of the JOAs provide for the removal of the operator in the case of material breach of the agreement, or even for failure to comply with the petroleum regulations. Such an approach is reasonable as it is necessary to secure compliance with the contractual obligations and also any applicable regulations. However, the major problem that any JOA faces is the possibility of repeat occurrences of material breach. If the operator remedies the material breach within a certain period of time, it will not face any consequences. In this sense, the operator could breach the JOA as many times as it liked and still remain operator of the consortium, as long as it remedied the breaches within the allowed time.

Another important issue is the right of the outgoing operator to take part in the removal decision. As previously described the JOAs will vary on this issue, but commonly they will exclude the outgoing operator from taking part in such a decision. In turn, the operator could argue that excluding it from the removal decision-making process is not a balanced and fair approach. However, it is important to remember that commonly the quorum for such a removal is all the non-operators. Also, it is important to note that any change of operator will require governmental approval. In this sense, the operator's position will be secure, as the host government will not authorise any removal of the operatorship which could harm the good standing of the petroleum title or the commitment to perform all activities and obligations. Additionally, it is important to note that the defaulting party shall not have any right to vote or even to attend meetings, so it is logical to provide for the exclusion of the departing operator in the decision about its removal.

The operator may object to procedures which allow immediate removal of the operator. It could argue that it would be arbitrary to impose such a provision without allowing the operator to raise its defences. On the other hand, some issues do require further diligence (eg, a letter from the host government describing the lack of performance), especially for emergency issues that are not dealt with properly by the operator. Nevertheless, it is also important to recognise the need for balanced provisions, so the JOA should provide time for the operator to express its views on any notice related to the removal of its functions, as far as practicable, as in the approach taken by the Norwegian and Greenlandic JOA Model Forms.

---

280 AT Martin, "Model Contracts: A Survey of the Global Petroleum Industry", *Journal of Energy & Natural Resources Law* 22 (2004) 293.

The JOAs deal reasonably well with the transitional period between removal of the operator and the election of the successor operator. However, it is important to note that the host government must also authorise the activities of the interim operator otherwise these elaborate systems will not be effective.

The removal of the operator is a key provision for the non-operators as this is a provision which secures compliance with both the contractual obligations and the petroleum regulations. However, this alone is not sufficient, so it is essential to provide room to improve in order to achieve a higher level of performance and excellence. In this sense, the CAPL OP Model Form is the only one which clearly allows a comfort zone for the non-operators through the operator challenge process. The remaining models secure compliance with the contractual obligations, except if a broad removal clause is allowed, such as the last alternative of the AIPN or Greenlandic Models or the first alternative from the Norwegian Model (ie, removal without reason). On the other hand, removal without cause might not be balanced as the operator should have some certainty to perform its activities. So, again the Canadian Model provides a secure and balanced approach for all the parties involved. On the one hand, any non-operator can challenge the efficiency of the operator's performance, while, on the other, the operator may only be replaced if the challenging party can match its proposal and deliver on its proposal for next two years, and any extra costs will be incurred at its sole expense. In this sense, no party will be able to abuse its rights without suffering severe consequences. Finally, the non-operators must always be very careful when drafting this provision as the power to remove is the power to influence.

In addition, the minority shareholders in an incorporated operator entity have a better provision to remove the director of the board since no reason is required, only a determination by ordinary resolution.[281] However, there are no specific procedures detailing the process involved, or the voting procedure, or the interim provision. Nevertheless, it does provide the director with a right to protest against such removal.[282] The qualification and registration of the appointed director are highly regulated, but are not as important as the removal for the minority shareholder.[283] As a consequence, such an open and vague provision is positive for the minority shareholders to the extent they can exert control over the decision-making process in the board or shareholders' meeting, otherwise there will be no ground for the removal of the director. However, their position as 'minority' clearly indicates that such removal is unlikely to happen and no further security is provided for the minority shareholders to maintain the best performance by the company. Therefore, it is possible to suggest that the non-operators often are in a better position than the minority shareholders.

As previously mentioned, in the majority of cases the non-operators may only remove the operator on limited grounds. However, the most critical problem is the lack of provision to deal with repetitive material breach, which leaves the non-operators in a weaker position. On the other hand, defining the extension of such a clause is not straightforward. For example, how many times will the operator be allowed to breach without major consequences? Will it be the period between each breach (eg, two months or two years)? Will it vary according to the nature of the

281 Section 168 of the UK Companies Act 2006.
282 Section 169 of the UK Companies Act 2006.
283 Sections 157 to 167 of the UK Companies Act 2006.

breach and, if so, how would a breach of disclosure of information be distinguished from a breach concerning the award of contracts? The short answer is that this is not an easy task, but it would represent a valuable provision for the non-operators as it would encourage the operator to be more careful before breaching any provision in the JOA. Nevertheless, it will be necessary to decide reasonable terms in order to avoid any excessive demands from either side.[284]

Another alternative to deal with limited grounds to remove the operator and the lack of repetitive infractions would be the implementation of penalties or higher levels of liability for any breach of the agreement. This scenario is commonly adopted in arm's length service agreements, but it would be far more complicated to adapt to a JOA, Nevertheless, such provision would certainly inhibit any lowering of standards in the performance of the joint operations.

This section has discussed the challenges that any national or international oil company will face with the operatorship provision. However, the reality is that removal of the operator cannot protect, completely, the non-operators from a weak performance by the operator, so it is necessary to provide further protections for the non-operators. For this reason, JOAs also contain two fundamental provisions: liabilities and default. These two provisions are analysed in Chapter 1, Section 3 and Chapter 2, Section 5.

5. Information

5.1 General principles

Commonly, the operator is a member of the consortium.[285] This party is elected to represent the consortium and conduct the operations on behalf of the joint venture. One of its basic obligations is to provide information to the non-operators in a reasonable and efficient manner.

If the operator does not provide information to the non-operators, the non-operators face a serious and critical situation.[286] Without access to information, they cannot control the conduct of the operations or exercise their rights, even though their liabilities are unlikely to be reduced or waived because of this lack of information.

That is why a JOA should include an obligation on the operator to provide information to the non-operators as soon as it is available, as well as full access to any and all information as an additional right of the non-operators. This is the most protective provision for a non-operator as the operator has the primordial obligation

---

284 The proposed provision was not agreed for inclusion in the AIPN JOA but it was broadly expressed as follows: "*Consider provision for removal of Operator for repeated infractions: (a) being the three of such performance failures of material or potential material impact, then if corrective measures are not properly adopted after three of such notices of failure to perform had been sent to Operator under the conditions stated under this Article [ ], can ...; (b) A notice of failure to perform shall not be sent to the Operator: (i) before 30 (thirty) Days after the delivery of the last notice of failure to perform; (ii) if the alleged performance failure is a mere reiteration of the same kind of performance failure already detailed in a prior notice of failure to perform; (iii) or in order to complain for lack of due implementation of corrective measures of a performance failure already detailed in a prior notice of failure to perform. [Note: consider providing for the appointment of an interim substitute Operator as an alternative to this subsection (d)].*"

285 See Section 4 of this chapter.

286 "Indeed, the operator has a great advantage over the non-operators in that it controls the daily decision making, disclosure of information and has greater familiarity with the operations as a whole." Z Gounari, "Duties and Liabilities of the Operator under UK Oil and Gas Joint Operating Agreements: Is the Operator a Fiduciary?" *OGEL* Archive issue, www.ogel.org/article.asp?key=805.

to provide information and the non-operator an additional right to ask for any information related to the consortium.

5.2 Analysis of model JOAs

The AIPN JOA Model adopts this protective approach for the non-operator:

Information Supplied by Operator
4.4A Subject to Article 15.3, Operator shall provide Non-Operators in a timely manner with copies of the following information, data and reports relating to Joint Operations (to the extent to be charged to the Joint Account) in digitized format and if not available then in hard-copy as they are currently produced or compiled from Joint Operations:
4.4.A.1 All logs, and surveys;
4.4.A.2 Proposed well design and any revisions for each well;
4.4.A.3 Daily drilling reports;
4.4.A.4 All Tests and core data and analysis reports;
4.4.A.5 Final well recap report;
4.4.A.6 Plugging reports;
4.4.A.7 Seismic sections and if applicable shot point location maps;
4.4.A.8 Final, and if requested by any Non-Operator intermediate, geological and geophysical maps, interpretations and reports;
4.4.A.9 Engineering studies, and
ALTERNATIVE PROVISION, CHOOSE ONE
ALTERNATIVE #1
monthly
ALTERNATIVE #2
quarterly
and annual progress reports on Development Operations, which progress reports shall at least set out the then current development schedule, the status of each such Development Operation from inception to date, its cumulative costs to date and the cumulative commitments undertaken;
4.4.A.10 Weekly production summary and production activity reports, and monthly reports on well, reservoir, field and infrastructure performance;
4.4.A.11 Reservoir studies, annual reserve estimates, and annual forecasts of production capability, infrastructure capacity, and scheduled outages, provided that Operator makes no representations about the accuracy of its identification of reserves and that each Non-Operator retains full responsibility for making its own assessment of reserves for internal and reporting purposes;
4.4.A.12 Before filing with the Government, copies of all material reports relating to Joint Operations or the Contract required, or anticipated, to be furnished by Operator to the Government, and copies of such reports as filed;
4.4.A.13 As reasonably requested by a Non-Operator, other material studies and reports relating to Joint Operations;
4.4.A.14 Data, reports, forecasts and schedules under agreements provided in Article 9;
4.4.A.15 Copies of accounting information and reports to be furnished under Article 6.8 and the Accounting Procedure;

4.4.A.16 Monthly and annual HSE key performance data and reports;
4.4.A.17 Such additional information as a Non-Operator may reasonably request, provided that the preparation of such information will not unduly burden Operator's administrative and technical personnel, that the requesting Party or Parties pay the costs of preparation of such information, and that only Non-Operators who pay such costs will receive such additional information; and
4.4.A.18 Other reports as directed by the Operating Committee.
4.4.B Operator shall give Non-Operators access at all reasonable times during normal business hours to all data and reports (other than data and reports provided to Non-Operators under Article 4.4.A) acquired in the conduct of Joint Operations and for which a Non-Operator may reasonably request. Any Non-Operator may make copies of such other data at its sole expense.[287]

Several other JOA Models follow a similar approach,[288] such as the Norwegian JOA Model, which states that:

Reports and other information concerning the activities shall be prepared and submitted to the management committee as soon as such information is available, or as often as the management committee or one of the Parties reasonably makes a request for it. Such information shall, inter alia, include:

a) Copies of logs;
b) Copies of records on drilling operations;
c) Copies of reports on testing analysis etc.;
d) Copies of the "final well report" with the "composite log";
e) Copies of all geological and geophysical reports, maps in connection with work carried out by the Operator or by contractors engaged by the Operator, with the exception of magnetic tapes. Such magnetic tapes shall be stored by the Operator in Norway and made available to all Parties upon request;
f) Field and well data, including reservoir studies and evaluations of reserves;
g) Cores and samples of stones and liquids from the drilling wells. Samples and cores left after distribution to the Parties and Norwegian authorities shall be stored in Norway;
h) Copies of detailed final reports for each completed well and reports of subsequent alterations and reparations, including the result from completed functional tests and the "flow test";
i) Copies of daily and periodic reports on exploration, development, maintenance, production and other activities. The reports shall, inter alia, contain information on problems or accidents, with a statement of the cause and a description of repair work. The reports for the development phase shall, inter alia, provide a summary of the progress. The production reports shall, inter alia, contain information concerning the quantity and quality of the Petroleum produced;

287 AIPN JOA Model Form §4.4.
288 See: OGUK JOA Model Form §6.8 and Greenlandic JOA Model Form §6.8.

> *j) Copies of contingency plans, safety manuals, safety and accident reports;*
> *k) A chart of the Operator's organization and of how the Operator, the contractors and the subcontractors at any time man their organization with regard to activities under this Agreement;*
> *l) Copies of evaluations and reports on technical, economical as well as other issues in connection with the activities;*
> *m) Copies of reports submitted to the Norwegian authorities by the Operator, and copies of minutes and correspondence between the Operator and the Norwegian authorities regarding the activities under this Agreement;*
> *n) Periodic development reports and status reports. The reports shall give account for any substantial deviations from the approved budget and work program.*
>
> *The Operator may also be required to prepare amendments or supplements to the available information.*[289]

However, some operators might consider the obligation to share information a burden and may try to limit or restrict the scope of this obligation. That is why some JOA Model Forms try to reduce the burden on the operator to share information.[290] For example, the RMMLF JOA Model Form gives extensive flexibility to the operator to decide when and how it should share information and leaves the non-operators to request further information at their own costs:

> ***Consultation with Parties.*** *Consult freely with the other Parties concerning operations hereunder and keep them advised of all matters arising in operations hereunder which Operator deems important in the exercise of its best judgment.*[291]
>
> ...
>
> ***Access to Subject Lands and Related Records.*** *Each Party at all reasonable times, but at its sole risk, shall have access to the surface overlying the Subject Lands to inspect or observe operations, and each Party shall have access to all available information pertaining to operations hereunder, including Operator's books and records relating thereto. In addition, and with respect to each well drilled upon Subject Lands, Operator shall, upon request and as soon as available, furnish to each of the Parties the following:*
>
> *(1) Samples of cores or cuttings to be delivered at the well in containers furnished by the Party requesting same.*
> *(2) A copy of all drilling logs and well surveys, except velocity surveys.*
> *(3) A copy of all core analysis reports.*
> *(4) A copy of all reports of well tests.*
> *(5) A copy of all daily drilling reports.*[292]

289 Norwegian JOA Model Form §3.4.
290 AAPL JOA Model Form 610 Article V(D)(5).
291 RMMLF JOA Model Form §5.1(B).
292 RMMLF JOA Model Form § Article 5.1(F).

5.3 Discussion

Similar tension might occur between an international oil company and a national oil company. Commonly, the international company is elected to be the operator of the consortium, or at least for a certain length of time (eg, the development stage). Up to that stage, the national oil company is likely to put pressure on the operator to release information as soon as it is available, and assert its right to request access to any information. On the other hand, the international oil company is more likely to negotiate less frequently to share information or even to limit the information the operator should send to the non-operators, leaving the burden on the non-operator to ask and pay for the delivery of any additional information.

This clause becomes less relevant if the JOA parties decide to create a joint operating company. In this case, all parties should have access to the information at the same time in their capacity as shareholders. This is one of the main reasons why some national oil companies might not trust international oil companies to act as a single operator – they fear a lack of information and transparency in the conduct of the operations.

Finally, it is important to note that other provisions in the JOA will deal with or affect the right/obligation to request/send information.[293] Exclusive operations provide a good example as the non-participating parties are less likely to have the right to receive the exclusive operation data free of charge. Another example is default. Whenever a party fails to pay its cash call, its rights are suspended (including the right to receive information) until the settlement of the payment. These exceptions will be dealt with in the relevant sections of the book.

6. Operating committee (OpCom)

6.1 General principles

Since the operator is responsible for the day-to-day operations of the joint venture,[294] from a non-operator's perspective it is highly recommended that provision is made in the JOA for a body to control the operator's activities.[295] The operator is likely to be an international oil company (at least until a certain stage), so this provision is very relevant for any national oil company, to allow it to participate in the consortium's key decisions and to oversee the operations closely. Sometimes the national oil company acts as operator and then it will be concerned to secure its position and interests – it may have different priorities from those of an international oil company for the assets.

It is important to note that such a body can only exercise its control if the operator provides it with the relevant information and data.[296] Consequently, the duty of an operator to provide information to the non-operators is a basic right of any non-operator and will allow efficient control by the supervising body.

---

293 For example, work programme and budget, default, exclusive operation.

294 PN Swan, *Ocean Oil and Gas Drilling & The Law*, Oceana, 1979, pp65–69; C Thorpe, *Fundamentals of Upstream Petroleum Agreements*, CP Thorpe, 2008, p127; J Wilkinson, *Introduction to Oil and Gas Joint Ventures: Volume one, United Kingdom Continental Shelf*, OPL, 1997, pp38–41.

295 See also: T Daintith and G Willoughby (eds), *Adrian Hill, United Kingdom Oil and Gas Law*, 3rd edn, Sweet & Maxwell, 2009, pp1143–1145; S Shaw, "Joint Operating Agreements" in MR David, *Upstream Oil and Gas Agreements*, Sweet & Maxwell, 1996, pp18–19; A Jennings, *Oil and Gas Exploration Contracts*, 2nd edn, Sweet & Maxwell, 2008, pp24–25; S Styles, "Joint Operating Agreements" in J Paterson and G Gordon (eds), *Oil and Gas Law: Current Practice and Emerging Trends*, Dundee University Press, 2007, p278.

296 MPG Taylor and SM Tyne, *Taylor and Winsor on Joint Operating Agreements*, 2nd edn, Longman, 1992, p36.

This body is commonly referred to as the management committee or operating committee (OpCom).[297] The OpCom is the highest authority of the JOA as it is responsible for controlling and supervising the overall operations of the joint venture.[298]

As the highest authority and policy maker of the JOA, the OpCom will have the final decision on matters concerning control of joint operations.[299] Therefore, each party will wish to strengthen its position in this decision-making body. The operator will want the non-operators to have less control, to give it more freedom to act on its own judgement; the non-operators will want more control, to ensure that their views on the conduct of the joint operations are clearly addressed. It has been noted that tensions will arise between the different views of the parties in the OpCom.[300]

There could be more tension with a national oil company (especially as a non-operator) because it is likely to expect certain governmental interests to be included in the discussions, and these may be different from those of the international oil companies. In addition, an international oil company is less likely to want to upset a national oil company than another international oil company. This creates a more complex process for negotiation and implementation of the JOA. The potential for matters external to joint operations to create conflicts of interest affecting OpCom voting decisions and outcomes and the approach of the industry model JOAs are discussed in Section 8 of this chapter.

As previously described, the OpCom is very relevant for all the contracting parties.[301] However, for the non-operators, it might represent even more than mere negative control of the joint operations, as it may be their only channel of positive input and influence to (ie, participate in) the conduct of the joint operations.[302]

---

297 Arguably the role of the OpCom could be compared with the role of a shareholding meeting or a meeting of partners. See: GMD Bean, *Fiduciary Relationships, Fiduciary Duties and Joint Ventures: The Joint Operating Agreement*, University of Cambridge, 1992, pp176–177.

298 See: C Duval, H Le Leuch, A Pertuzio and JL Weaver, *International Petroleum and Exploration Agreements: Legal, Economic & Policy Aspects*, 2nd edn, Barrows, 2009, pp291–293; JS Dzienkowski, EE Smith, OL Anderson, JS Lowe, BM Kramer and JL Weaver, *Materials on International Petroleum Transactions*, 3rd edn, RMMLF, 2010, p539; T Daintith, "Right to Explore For and Exploit Petroleum: The Licence" in T Daintith and G Willoughby (eds), *Adrian Hill, United Kingdom Oil and Gas Law*, 3rd edn, Sweet & Maxwell, 2009, pp1145–1147.

299 See also: PN Swan, *Ocean Oil and Gas Drilling & The Law*, Oceana, 1979, pp66–68, KC Mildwaters, *Joint Operating Agreements, A Consideration of Legal Aspects Relevant to Joint Operating Agreements used in Great Britain and Australia by Participants thereto to Regulate the Joint Undertaking of Exploration for Petroleum in Offshore Areas with Particular Reference to their Rights and Duties*, PhD Thesis presented to the University of Dundee, 1990, p405; T Daintith and G Willoughby (eds), *Adrian Hill, United Kingdom Oil and Gas Law*, 3rd edn, Sweet & Maxwell, 2009, pp1143–1145; S Shaw, "Joint Operating Agreements" in MR David, *Upstream Oil and Gas Agreements*, Sweet & Maxwell, 1996, pp18–19; A Jennings, *Oil and Gas Exploration Contracts*, 2nd edn, Sweet & Maxwell, 2008, pp24–25; S Styles, "Joint Operating Agreements" in J Paterson and G Gordon (eds), *Oil and Gas Law: Current Practice and Emerging Trends*, Dundee University Press, 2007, p278.

300 P Roberts and R Fowler, *Joint Operating Agreements: A Practical Guide*, 4th edn, Globe Law and Business, 2020, p15.

301 See also: T Daintith and G Willoughby (eds), *Adrian Hill, United Kingdom Oil and Gas Law*, 3rd edn, Sweet & Maxwell, 2009, pp1143–1145; S Shaw, "Joint Operating Agreements" in MR David, *Upstream Oil and Gas Agreements*, Sweet & Maxwell, 1996, pp18–19; A Jennings, *Oil and Gas Exploration Contracts*, 2nd edn, Sweet & Maxwell, 2008, pp24–25; S Styles, "Joint Operating Agreements" in J Paterson and G Gordon (eds), *Oil and Gas Law: Current Practice and Emerging Trends*, Dundee University Press, 2007, p278.

302 C Duval, H Le Leuch, A Pertuzio and JL Weaver, *International Petroleum and Exploration Agreements: Legal, Economic & Policy Aspects*, 2nd edn, Barrows, 2009, p291.

Consequently, provision for an OpCom is crucial to protect and also increase the non-operator's position and participation in the JOA,[303] as all the main activities must be approved by the OpCom before the operator executes them.[304]

The use of subcommittees of the OpCom is a very effective way to increase the non-operators' participation.[305] The role of any subcommittee is to assist the OpCom with technical advice about specific issues. These specialised committees are a very effective means for the non-operators to contribute their own views and experience.[306] However, some operators may be reluctant to accept non-operators serving on such subcommittees, being concerned that their interests could deflect from the original purpose[307] and seek another layer of control of the joint operations instead of providing a vehicle for collaboration and giving input.[308]

As a consequence, the subcommittees are subject to the OpCom's supervision, to allow proper control by all parties.[309] Nevertheless, it can happen in practice that the subcommittees carry out the majority of work.[310] Thus, in such cases, the OpCom's approval may be a mere formality.[311]

A similar mechanism to obtain input from the non-operators is the project team – a body within the consortium to create another route to gather the non-operators' input on matters such as the work programme and budget and the award of contracts. However, it faces the same problem as subcommittees in that the operator will not wish to allow extensive rights for the non-operators, so commonly the project team is controlled by the operator.

The JOA needs to address several issues related to the OpCom (eg, minutes, notice of meetings, location of meetings), but certainly the voting procedure is by far the most critical concern for any party (especially non-operators)[312] as it will determine to what extent the non-operators will be able to control the conduct of the joint operations.[313] For this reason, the voting procedures are examined in detail here.

The OpCom represents all the contracting parties of the JOA,[314] because each one of them can nominate one representative to take a seat and vote on the

---

303 P Roberts and R Fowler, *Joint Operating Agreements: A Practical Guide*, 4th edn, Globe Law and Business, 2020, p143.

304 BG Taverne, *An Introduction to the Regulation of the Petroleum Industry: Law, Contracts and Conventions*, Graham & Trotman, 1994, p137.

305 P Roberts and R Fowler, *Joint Operating Agreements: A Practical Guide*, 4th edn, Globe Law and Business, 2020, p149.

306 C Duval, H Le Leuch, A Pertuzio and JL Weaver, *International Petroleum and Exploration Agreements: Legal, Economic & Policy Aspects*, 2nd edn, Barrows, 2009, p293.

307 *Ibid.*

308 P Roberts and R Fowler, *Joint Operating Agreements: A Practical Guide*, 4th edn, Globe Law and Business, 2020, p149.

309 KC Mildwaters, *Joint Operating Agreements, A Consideration of Legal Aspects Relevant to Joint Operating Agreements used in Great Britain and Australia by Participants thereto to Regulate the Joint Undertaking of Exploration for Petroleum in Offshore Areas with Particular Reference to their Rights and Duties*, PhD Thesis presented to the University of Dundee, 1990, p413.

310 C Golvala, "Upstream joint ventures – bidding and operating agreements" in G Picton-Tubervill (ed.), *Oil and Gas: A Practical Handbook*, Globe Law and Business, 2009, p47.

311 S Styles, "Joint Operating Agreements" in J Paterson and G Gordon (eds), *Oil and Gas Law: Current Practice and Emerging Trends*, Dundee University Press, 2007, p287 and S Shaw, "Joint Operating Agreements" in MR David, *Upstream Oil and Gas Agreements*, Sweet & Maxwell, 1996, p18.

312 T Daintith and G Willoughby (eds), *Adrian Hill, United Kingdom Oil and Gas* Law, 3rd edn, Sweet & Maxwell, London, 2009, p1143.

313 P Roberts and R Fowler, *Joint Operating Agreements: A Practical Guide*, 4th edn, Globe Law and Business, 2020, pp149–154.

314 BG Taverne, *Co-operative Agreements in the Extractive Petroleum Industry*, Kluwer Law International, 1996, pp68–69.

committee.[315] As a general rule, each party will have a representative regardless of the size of its interest in the joint venture, which is a valuable protection for non-operators.[316]

Each representative will have a percentage of the vote on the OpCom equivalent to their party's interest in the joint venture,[317] that is, a higher or lower input to managing the consortium depending on their party's stake in the consortium.[318] This approach may lead to tension. There is a conceptual conflict, as it could be suggested that each party can vote according to its own particular interests, which could differ from those of the joint venture.[319] On the other hand,[320] it is possible to argue that there are fiduciary duties on every party towards the joint venture whenever they exercise their voting rights on the OpCom – the parties cannot vote for their own benefit against the consortium.[321] There is no straightforward answer,[322] but it is reasonable to suggest that both arguments are pertinent and should coexist as far as it is possible. In other words, each party must seek to benefit both itself and the consortium. However, the reality is that the former is more likely to happen than the latter because, as Scott Styles argues, the JOA is not a democracy but simply a private contract.[323] This issue is more important when a national oil company participates since a government entity may have other priorities than those of an international oil company, such as local content, domestic market, and energy security which will impact its voting strategy in the OpCom.

The JOA establishes which issues must be approved by the OpCom, but usually the range will be as broad as possible.[324] Commonly, OpCom decisions will require a certain percentage of affirmative votes (a passmark) to approve a submitted

---

315 See also: C Duval, H Le Leuch, A Pertuzio and JL Weaver, *International Petroleum and Exploration Agreements: Legal, Economic & Policy Aspects*, 2nd edn, Barrows, 2009, pp291–293; JS Dzienkowski, EE Smith, OL Anderson, JS Lowe, BM Kramer and JL Weaver, *Materials on International Petroleum Transactions*, 3rd edn, RMMLF, 2010, p539; T Daintith, "Right to Explore For and Exploit Petroleum: The Licence" in T Daintith and G Willoughby (eds), *Adrian Hill, United Kingdom Oil and Gas Law*, 3rd edn, Sweet & Maxwell, 2009, pp1143–1147.

316 KC Mildwaters, *Joint Operating Agreements, A Consideration of Legal Aspects Relevant to Joint Operating Agreements used in Great Britain and Australia by Participants thereto to Regulate the Joint Undertaking of Exploration for Petroleum in Offshore Areas with Particular Reference to their Rights and Duties*, PhD Thesis presented to the University of Dundee, 1990, p407.

317 C Duval, H Le Leuch, A Pertuzio and JL Weaver, *International Petroleum and Exploration Agreements: Legal, Economic & Policy Aspects*, 2nd edn, Barrows, 2009, p291.

318 See: J Wilkinson, *Introduction to Oil and Gas Joint Ventures: Volume one, United Kingdom Continental Shelf*, OPL, 1997, p41; S Shaw, "Joint Operating Agreements" in MR David, *Upstream Oil and Gas Agreements*, Sweet & Maxwell, 1996, pp18–19; T Daintith and G Willoughby (eds), *Adrian Hill, United Kingdom Oil and Gas Law*, 3rd edn, Sweet & Maxwell, 2009, pp1143–1145.

319 P Roberts and R Fowler, *Joint Operating Agreements: A Practical Guide*, 4th edn, Global Law and Business, 2020, p147.

320 For further information see: GMD Bean, *Fiduciary Relationships, Fiduciary Duties and Joint Ventures: The Joint Operating Agreement*, University of Cambridge, 1992, pp176–208.

321 PD Finn, "Fiduciary Obligations of Operators and Co-Venturers in Natural Resources Joint Ventures" *AMPLA Yearbook* (1984) 160, 170.

322 See also: S Fisher, "Formation and Structure" in WD Duncan, *Joint Ventures Law in Australia*, 2nd edn, Federation Press, 2005, pp165–171. See also *TAQA Bratani Ltd and Others v RockRose* [2020] EWHC 58 (Comm) Para 38 as discussed in Section 8.2 of this chapter.

323 See: S Styles, "Joint Operating Agreements" in J Paterson and G Gordon (eds), *Oil and Gas Law: Current Practice and Emerging Trends*, Dundee University Press, 2007, p287 and P Roberts and R Fowler, *Joint Operating Agreements: A Practical Guide*, 4th edn, Globe Law and Business, 2020, pp147–148. See also *TAQA Bratani Ltd and Others v RockRose* [2020] EWHC 58 (Comm) discussed in footnote 248 above.

324 S Shaw, "Joint Operating Agreements" in MR David, *Upstream Oil and Gas Agreements*, Sweet & Maxwell, 1996, p18.

proposal, but certain issues will require unanimous approval.[325] The default provision for approval at the Opcom level is the passmark; the requirement for unanimous approval is an exception.[326] It is important to note that any decision taken by the OpCom will bind all contracting parties.[327]

The determination of the passmark and the definition of the issues that require unanimous approval are important topics during JOA negotiations,[328] as these definitions can determine the amount of control exerted by non-operators in the joint venture.[329] The presence of a national oil company in the consortium could raise further tensions as it may claim special rights and protections in the decision-making process. Nevertheless, it is important to recognise that the existence of non-consent and sole risk clauses may reduce the tension caused by those issues (if the national oil company accepts the concept of an exclusive operation with them).[330]

In other words, if a higher passmark is set, it is probable that the operator will depend on securing the agreement of one or more of the non-operators in order to achieve the passmark, as illustrated in Example 1.

Example 1

	Company A	Company B	Company C
Role	Operator	Non-operator	Non-operator
Interest	60%	20%	20%
Passmark	70%		

Example 1 shows a case where the operator cannot achieve the passmark on its own. It needs the cooperation of at least one non-operator to achieve the passmark. However, in the same example, if the issue requires unanimous consent, it would be even harder since any non-operator could block the approval.

On the other hand, if the passmark is low, the operator can achieve the passmark by itself and so approve the overall operations with little difficulty,[331] as illustrated in Example 2.

325 For further information see: BG Taverne, *An Introduction to the Regulation of the Petroleum Industry: Law, Contracts and Conventions*, Graham & Trotman, 1994, p137; MPG Taylor and SM Tyne, *Taylor and Winsor on Joint Operating Agreements*, 2nd edn, Longman, 1992, pp21–24; C Golvala, "Upstream joint ventures – bidding and operating agreements" in G Picton-Tubervill (ed.), *Oil and Gas: A Practical Handbook*, Globe Law and Business, 2009, p47; P Roberts and R Fowler, *Joint Operating Agreements: A Practical Guide*, 4th edn, Globe Law and Business, 2020, p151; C Duval, H Le Leuch, A Pertuzio and JL Weaver, *International Petroleum and Exploration Agreements: Legal, Economic & Policy Aspects*, 2nd edn, Barrows, 2009, p293.

326 C Thorpe, *Fundamentals of Upstream Petroleum Agreements*, CP Thorpe, 2008, pp127–131.

327 KC Mildwaters, *Joint Operating Agreements, A Consideration of Legal Aspects Relevant to Joint Operating Agreements used in Great Britain and Australia by Participants thereto to Regulate the Joint Undertaking of Exploration for Petroleum in Offshore Areas with Particular Reference to their Rights and Duties*, PhD Thesis presented to the University of Dundee, 1990, p416; BG Taverne, *Co-operative Agreements in the Extractive Petroleum Industry*, Kluwer Law International, 1996, pp68–69.

328 C Golvala, "Upstream joint ventures – bidding and operating agreements" in G Picton-Tubervill (ed.), *Oil and Gas: A Practical Handbook*, Globe Law and Business, 2009, p47.

329 S Styles, "Joint Operating Agreements" in J Paterson and G Gordon (eds), *Oil and Gas Law: Current Practice and Emerging Trends*, Dundee University Press, 2007, p287.

330 These clauses will be further analysed in Chapter 1, Section 9.

331 P Roberts and R Fowler, *Joint Operating Agreements: A Practical Guide*, 4th edn, Globe Law and Business, 2020, p150.

Example 2

	Company A	Company B	Company C
Role	Operator	Non-operator	Non-operator
Interest	60%	20%	20%
Passmark	50%		

It is important to note that some JOAs provide a secondary criterion for decision approval at the Opcom level: even if a proposal has achieved the passmark (using the percentage of participants' interests), it must also have the support of a certain minimum number of parties. This provision prevents a decision being carried by one party with a large participating interest.[332] This is a very positive provision for non-operators as, commonly, the operator retains the largest interest in the joint venture and the non-operators have smaller interests (at least individually).[333]

If this secondary level of protection is adopted by the JOA parties, it would be possible for parties to block the OpCom's decisions simply by not attending the meeting, so that the minimum number requirement would not be reached. However, it is possible to avoid this situation by providing that any absence shall be considered as an affirmative or negative vote or to allow a secondary meeting with a lower requirement.[334]

It is also possible to provide different levels of passmark according to the nature of the proposal and its significance for the parties,[335] that is, more contentious issues shall require a higher passmark (eg, a declaration of commerciality or decision to stop production) and less contentious issues shall require a lower passmark (eg, acquisition of data or the award of low value contracts).[336]

The key elements to determine the system of voting procedure are the connection between the number of parties, the participating interest and the relevance of the proposals.[337]

332 C Duval, H Le Leuch, A Pertuzio and JL Weaver, *International Petroleum and Exploration Agreements: Legal, Economic & Policy Aspects*, 2nd edn, Barrows, 2009, p292.

333 P Roberts and R Fowler, *Joint Operating Agreements: A Practical Guide*, 4th edn, Globe Law and Business, 2020, p152.

334 KC Mildwaters, *Joint Operating Agreements, A Consideration of Legal Aspects Relevant to Joint Operating Agreements used in Great Britain and Australia by Participants thereto to Regulate the Joint Undertaking of Exploration for Petroleum in Offshore Areas with Particular Reference to their Rights and Duties*, PhD Thesis presented to the University of Dundee, 1990, p413; Ch Golvala, "Upstream joint ventures – bidding and operating agreements" in G Picton-Tubervill (ed.), *Oil and Gas: A Practical Handbook*, Globe Law and Business, 2009, p47; P Roberts and R Fowler, *Joint Operating Agreements: A Practical Guide*, 4th edn, Globe Law and Business, 2020, p154.

335 C Thorpe, *Fundamentals of Upstream Petroleum Agreements*, CP Thorpe, 2008, p129.

336 See also: S Styles, "Joint Operating Agreements" in J Paterson and G Gordon (eds), *Oil and Gas Law: Current Practice and Emerging Trends*, Dundee University Press, 2007, p287; C Golvala, "Upstream joint ventures – bidding and operating agreements" in G Picton-Tubervill (ed.), *Oil and Gas: A Practical Handbook*, Globe Law and Business, 2009, p47; P Roberts and R Fowler, *Joint Operating Agreements: A Practical Guide*, 4th edn, Globe Law and Business, 2020, p154; C Duval, H Le Leuch, A Pertuzio and JL Weaver, *International Petroleum and Exploration Agreements: Legal, Economic & Policy Aspects*, 2nd edn, Barrows, 2009, pp292–293.

337 BG Taverne, *An Introduction to the Regulation of the Petroleum Industry: Law, Contracts and Conventions*, Graham & Trotman, 1994, p137.

Unanimous voting is another complex issue in the voting procedure.[338] As mentioned above, some matters will require the approval of all parties, such as voluntary surrender, modification of the JOA's scope and unitisation.[339] In this case, the position of the non-operators is considerably stronger as any non-operator (regardless of the size of its participation interest) can block the approval of the proposal; however, this could also lead to a deadlock[340] if no consensus is established. Some national oil companies may push for unanimous consent on all decisions in order to obtain full control of the decision-making power from the consortium.

Consequently, the unanimous approval requirement is very beneficial for non-operators, but it may also jeopardise the existence of the joint venture if the parties cannot reach agreement.[341] It is important to provide alternative approaches in order to avoid deadlocks, such as through alternative dispute resolution (eg, mediation, mini-trial, expert determination) or simply by lowering the passmark if a particular proposal is "repeatedly brought back to a committee".[342] However, the most common approach in JOAs is to resolve deadlocks via exclusive operations, as will be discussed in Section 9 of this chapter.

Therefore, in a traditional JOA negotiation, the operator will seek a lower passmark and the minimum number of issues requiring unanimous approval. On the other hand, the non-operators will seek opposite: a higher passmark and more issues requiring unanimous approval.[343]

It is very unlikely that the non-operators will obtain overall control of the joint operations, but it is important for them to secure preventative control over critical issues so that the operator is forced to obtain their consent.

Scott Styles argues that the passmark should reflect the strength of the parties during negotiations as against some form of contractual democracy.[344] Although the JOA is a private agreement, it is important to maintain a certain level of equilibrium, as, if the passmark is set very low, the role of the OpCom is redundant, but if it is very high it will create bureaucracy that will harm the effectiveness of the joint venture.[345] In other words, the parties should negotiate the exact percentage for this particular clause, but they must also bear in mind the importance of reasonable terms for all parties in the interest of an efficient, clear and balanced consortium.

Thus, it can be seen that the OpCom is a crucial instrument to protect the non-operators' position, as it allows proactive participation by non-operators in the

---

338 KC Mildwaters, *Joint Operating Agreements, A Consideration of Legal Aspects Relevant to Joint Operating Agreements used in Great Britain and Australia by Participants thereto to Regulate the Joint Undertaking of Exploration for Petroleum in Offshore Areas with Particular Reference to their Rights and Duties*, PhD Thesis presented to the University of Dundee, 1990, p415.

339 C Golvala, "Upstream joint ventures – bidding and operating agreements" in G Picton-Tubervill (ed.), *Oil and Gas: A Practical Handbook*, Globe Law and Business, 2009, p47.

340 "where two parties, each of whom is to hold one-half of the shares and neither of whom is willing to surrender control to the other." C Wilkinson (ed.), *Joint Ventures and Shareholders' Agreements*, 3rd edn, Bloomsbury Professional, 2009, p171.

341 P Roberts and R Fowler, *Joint Operating Agreements: A Practical Guide*, 4th edn, Globe Law and Business, 2020, pp153–154.

342 C Golvala, "Upstream joint ventures – bidding and operating agreements" in G Picton-Tubervill (ed.), *Oil and Gas: A Practical Handbook*, Globe Law and Business, 2009, p47.

343 S Shaw, "Joint Operating Agreements" in MR David, *Upstream Oil and Gas Agreements*, Sweet & Maxwell, 1996, p18; P Roberts and R Fowler, *Joint Operating Agreements: A Practical Guide*, 4th edn, Globe Law and Business, 2020, pp150–151.

344 S Styles, "Joint Operating Agreements" in J Paterson and G Gordon (eds), *Oil and Gas Law: Current Practice and Emerging Trends*, Dundee University Press, 2007, p287.

345 C Thorpe, *Fundamentals of Upstream Petroleum Agreements*, CP Thorpe, 2008, p129.

joint venture and ultimately allows any non-operator to control the conduct of the joint operations.[346]

However, the mere existence of an OpCom is not enough to secure the non-operators' position since it could be another vehicle dominated by the operator.[347] Thus, in order to make an effective difference, the OpCom must follow balanced provisions to secure the non-operators' control over and participation in the joint operations.

Consequently, a non-operator party negotiating a JOA should be seeking an OpCom with the following provisions:

- representation of all parties regardless of the size of their interest in participating in the joint venture;
- establishment of subcommittees allowing effective participation of non-operators and/or project teams;
- establishment of a voting procedure based on participating interest and number of parties;
- establishment of a voting system, including:
  (i) a number of issues subject to unanimous approval; and
  (ii) other issues subject to different passmarks according to their importance; and
- establishment of deadlock resolutions that are not significantly detrimental to the non-operators' position.

6.2 Analysis of model JOAs

The following paragraphs examine how various JOA Model Forms regulate their OpCom provisions. However, it is important to note that not every JOA will provide for the existence of an OpCom, and why this happens and who controls the joint operations instead are also discussed.[348]

AAPL Form 810 does not provide for the existence of an OpCom. It could be argued that such a model allows the operator to act without any major interference (to act freely) by the remaining parties. In such a model form, the majority of protection available for non-operators would be the non-consent clause,[349] which, in brief, allows a party not to participate in a joint operation.[350]

346 KC Mildwaters, *Joint Operating Agreements, A Consideration of Legal Aspects Relevant to Joint Operating Agreements used in Great Britain and Australia by Participants thereto to Regulate the Joint Undertaking of Exploration for Petroleum in Offshore Areas with Particular Reference to their Rights and Duties*, PhD Thesis presented to the University of Dundee, 1990, p414.

347 C Duval, H Le Leuch, A Pertuzio and JL Weaver, *International Petroleum and Exploration Agreements: Legal, Economic & Policy Aspects*, 2nd edn, Barrows, 2009, p291.

348 See: P Roberts and R Fowler, *Joint Operating Agreements: A Practical Guide*, 4th edn, Globe Law and Business, 2020, pp144–145; S Styles, "Joint Operating Agreements" in J Paterson and G Gordon (eds), *Oil and Gas Law: Current Practice and Emerging Trends*, Dundee University Press, 2007, p286; MPG Taylor and SM Tyne, *Taylor and Winsor on Joint Operating Agreements*, 2nd edn, Longman, 1992, pp21–24.

349 For further information about the non-consent clause see: BG Taverne, *Petroleum, Industry and Governments: A Study of the Involvement of Industry and Government with the Production and Use of Petroleum*, 2nd edn, Kluwer Law International, 2008, pp387–388; A Jennings, *Oil and Gas Exploration Contracts*, 2nd edn, Sweet & Maxwell, 2008, pp92–93, T Daintith, "Right to Explore For and Exploit Petroleum: The Licence" in T Daintith, G Willoughby, and A Hill (eds), *United Kingdom Oil and Gas Law*, 3rd edn, vol 1, Sweet & Maxwell, 2009, pp1152–1153; S Shaw, "Joint Operating Agreements" in MR David, *Upstream Oil and Gas Agreements*, Sweet & Maxwell, 1996, pp22–23; MPG Taylor and SM Tyne, *Taylor and Winsor on Joint Operating Agreements*, 2nd edn, Longman, 1992, p47; S Styles, "Joint Operating Agreements" in J Paterson and G Gordon (eds), *Oil and Gas Law: Current Practice and Emerging Trends*, Dundee University Press, 2007, p288.

350 MPG Taylor and SM Tyne, *Taylor and Winsor on Joint Operating* Agreements, 2nd edn, Longman, 1992, pp21–23; P Roberts and R Fowler, *Joint Operating Agreements: A Practical Guide*, 4th edn, Globe Law and Business, 2020, pp144–145; T Daintith and G Willoughby (eds), *Adrian Hill, United Kingdom Oil and Gas Law*, 3rd edn, Sweet & Maxwell, 2009, p1143.

However, it is not entirely correct to say that under such a JOA Model Form the non-operators have no control over the conduct of the joint operations. There are provisions for approval of operations by the non-operators.[351] AAPL Form 810 provides four general classes of activities or operations: (a) those requiring approval by vote; (b) those requiring approval by election; (c) those requiring approval by unanimous agreement; and (d) those within the discretion of the operator.[352]

This system is a mixture of voting procedures commonly regulated in the OpCom. The parties should decide the percentage of interest required to approve a specific proposal, which could range from a simple passmark to unanimous consent.[353] It also makes a distinction between the percentage of the participating interest and the number of parties involved. In other words, AAPL Model Form 810 adopts, for the first time, a similar flexibility to the AIPN Model. This is probably the upper limit of control and influence for the non-operators under this model form (if a high percentage passmark is implemented).

However, the model form does not provide a specific mechanism for the resolution of deadlocks, which might benefit the non-operators, but, on the other hand, might jeopardise the whole consortium if the deadlock is not resolved quickly. The natural answer is the possibility to proceed as an exclusive operation. Another issue which is not available in this model form is the effective participation of non-operators in the joint operations, as there is no OpCom or subcommittee available to obtain input from the non-operators and the non-operators cannot participate in the determination of the overall policies of the consortium. However, the model form does provide for the existence of project teams, which have a fairly similar scope to a subcommittee,[354] although they will be under the direction of the operator.[355] This provides a route for the non-operators to give their input; however, it is for the operator to decide whether to take their comments into consideration. Nevertheless, it is important to recognise that AAPL JOA Model Form 810 allows the non-operators to retain some control of the joint operations.

Consequently, under the AAPL 810 Model Form the non-operators' position is not strong as they cannot determine the overall policy and supervision of the consortium. Also, there is no effective provision to obtain input from non-operators. In addition, the model requires unanimous consent or participation in certain operations but it does not provide for deadlock resolution.[356] For this reason, arguably the AAPL JOA Model treat the non-operators as mere investors.[357]

Like all other North American Model JOAs, the RMMLF Model does not provide for the existence of a management committee. The operator has the maximum possible power and authority, since this model states that the: "Operator shall direct and have control of all operations conducted hereunder and shall have exclusive custody of all materials, equipment and other property owned by the parties."[358]

---

351 P Roberts and R Fowler, *Joint Operating Agreements: A Practical Guide*, 4th edn, Globe Law and Business, 2020, p219.

352 AAPL Form 810 §8.1.

353 AAPL Form 810 §§10.1, 11.1, 11.2.2, 12.2.1, 12.3.2, 12.7.6, 12.8, 13.1.1. 13.1.2.

354 AAPL Form 810 §§6.2.2.2, 12.3, 12.8.

355 AAPL Form 810 §2.58.

356 AAPL Form 810 §8.1.

357 S Styles, "Joint Operating Agreements" in J Paterson and G Gordon (eds), *Oil and Gas Law: Current Practice and Emerging Trends*, Dundee University Press, 2007, pp286–287.

358 RMMLF JOA §4.1.

It is important to remember that such a model provides that the operator should consult the non-operators about matters considered relevant in the sole and "best" judgement of the operator.[359] This is not a very positive provision from a non-operator's perspective as it allows extensive discretion to the operator.

As with the Canadian Model, this model only allows the non-operators to opt out of or to join a particular operation,[360] that is, the party can only decide whether to share the costs and join the operation or whether to exercise its right of non-consent. Consequently, a non-operator cannot block a proposal or even effectively participate in the ongoing activities via subcommittees or project teams.

Therefore, a non-operator in North America is likely to be in a weaker position than a non-operator in other regions (eg, the United Kingdom, Greenland, Norway) or under an international model, as the existence of an OpCom is a clear and effective way to ensure that the non-operators can control and participate in decisions that determine the conduct of the joint operations, but effective control and participation will only occur if the non-operators have *de facto* positive or negative control of such a decision-making body. As a consequence, it is unlikely that these model forms should be used outside North America – any national or international oil company will wish to retain more control of the activities if they are a non-operator.

The CAPL Model adopts a similar approach to AAPL Form 810 as it does not provide for an OpCom, nor does it adopt an elaborate voting procedure.[361] However, it does expressly state that: "The Operator will consult with the Parties periodically about the exploration, development and operation of the Joint Lands ... and management of the Joint Property."[362] The mere obligation to consult does not represent a high degree of control, as the operator may consult with the non-operators but reject their views and continue with its own plans.

Some later provisions in this model explain the process of consultation by the "Forecast of Operations", which means that after consultation the operator should "create a written forecast outlining all anticipated Joint Operations during the next 12 months period and their estimated cost".[363] However, the model clearly states that such a procedure is solely for information purposes.

Considering the above comments, it may rightly be suggested that the non-operators have no real control of the joint operations, but the only alternative available to non-operators is the right of non-consent, that is, the parties can decide either to join or to refuse to join an operation.[364]

Thus, the CAPL Model does not provide a high degree of participation and control of the joint operations. It clearly mentions the duty on the operator to consult the non-operators but without further explanation, so it offers "soft" influence instead of a truly effective clause which, ideally, would aim to obtain the input and views of the non-operators towards an efficient and effective joint venture.

---

359 RMMLF JOA §5.1 (B).
360 RMMLF JOA §§5.5, 9.2.
361 MPG Taylor and SM Tyne, *Taylor and Winsor on Joint Operating Agreements*, 2nd edn, Longman, 1992, p22.
362 CAPL OP §3.01.
363 CAPL OP §5.04.
364 CAPL OP §7.01.

The British JOA[365] Model does provide for the existence of an OpCom to control and supervise the overall activities of the joint venture.[366] The provisions adopted in this model are fairly similar to those provided by the AIPN, but they are not exactly the same.

Each party can nominate a representative to the OpCom, regardless of the size of its participating interest, as in the AIPN JOA Model.[367] Such a provision is useful as it will secure a wider participation of all the contracting parties.

This model also allows the creation of subcommittees for advisory purposes, just as the AIPN JOA Model does. However, a clear difference between the models with regard to representation of the parties is that, in contrast to the AIPN JOA Model, the British Model does not expressly determine the right of each party to nominate a representative to the subcommittees.[368] In this case, the operator is unlikely to accept any reduction in its dominant position by allowing a higher degree of participation in subcommittees by the non-operators, which could use this opportunity to increase their degree of control over the joint operations. It is unhelpful for non-operators and the consortium that this provision does not allow the non-operators to provide input via subcommittees.

The voting procedure is also quite similar to that provided by the AIPN JOA Model as the parties must negotiate the applicable passmark.[369] As mentioned above, this system may weaken the non-operators' position if they cannot secure a high passmark during the negotiations. On the other hand, the British JOA Model secures the application of unanimous consent on certain issues, which clearly raises the degree of control and participation of the non-operators over the joint operations; this is not guaranteed in the AIPN JOA Model.[370]

It is important to note that decisions shall be based on a certain percentage of interest (passmark), which must be defined by the parties.[371] However, this model does not state the number of parties required to approve any proposal without establishing a minimum, so again it is possible that the operator could move from its dominant position to one where a single party is sufficient to approve a proposal and this provision is likely to benefit the operator. In order to avoid such a situation, the model should determine at least a minimum number of parties (any number equal to or higher than two). On the other hand, this may raise difficulties if there are only two parties in the consortium, when any passmark would need unanimous agreement. This would be a very positive outcome for the non-operator, but not for the operator.

Additionally, this model does not determine how parties should proceed in the case of a deadlock. Instead, the model only "provides that the agreement, approval or consent of the Joint Operating Committee is not to be unreasonably withheld or

---

365 Historically the British Model did not have an OpCom as it was based on the AAPL JOA Form 610, but in the mid-1970s the United Kingdom established the OpCom provision for the first time within the British National Oil Company pro-forma model. In the current OGUK JOA Model, the OpCom is provided in clause 9. See: T Daintith and G Willoughby (eds), *Adrian Hill, United Kingdom Oil and Gas Law*, 3rd edn, Sweet & Maxwell, 2009, p1143; MPG Taylor and SM Tyne, *Taylor and Winsor on Joint Operating Agreements*, 2nd edn, Longman, 1992, pp21–23.

366 OGUK JOA §9.

367 OGUK JOA §9.2.

368 OGUK JOA §9.7.

369 OGUK JOA §9.8.

370 OGUK JOA §9.8.3.

371 OGUK JOA §9.8.2.

delayed in respect of any matter".[372] So what would happen if a party unreasonably withheld its vote? Or even, if any party had reasonable grounds for withholding its approval, what would happen if unanimous consent is required? The model seeks to provide a solution for the minimum work obligations, but only if the OpCom does not object within 28 days. In this case, there will be some measure of resolution for the minimum work obligations. In general terms, it seems that the dispute resolution process should apply and, in this case, the dispute resolution provision would deal with such an issue. However, this might be time-consuming, expensive and could put the very existence of the consortium at risk.[373] The most reasonable interpretation is that deadlock resolution for the OpCom's decisions is the route via exclusive operations, which will be analysed further in Section 9 below.

As a general rule, possibly the main difference between the AIPN and British JOA Models is the flexibility available in the AIPN Model with its options and alternatives. At first glance, this flexibility is not beneficial to a non-operator, as it may have to negotiate all the issues that should have a higher passmark, and those that require unanimity. On the other hand, eventually this flexibility could increase the non-operators' power, if they can retain a strong position in the negotiation, which might not be the case unless if the non-operator is a major international company or national oil company.

The British Model left the passmark provision empty, just as the AIPN did, so that the parties can agree on a case-by-case basis. In addition, the British JOA Model has a weaker provision regarding subcommittees, as it does not provide a high degree of participation for non-operators on subcommittees. On the other hand, it secures a high degree of non-operator control by establishing issues which require the unanimous approval of all parties.

Therefore, like the AIPN JOA Model, the British Model adopts a relatively high degree of control of the joint operations by the non-operators. However, its provisions to obtain the non-operators' input are limited and it does not deal with possible deadlocks, which benefits a non-operator from a short-term perspective as it strengthens its position in the joint venture, but it could jeopardise the joint venture if a resolution is not agreed within a short time.

The Norwegian JOA Model Form establishes a management committee (ie, an OpCom) to control and supervise the conduct of the joint operations.[374] The principles that govern the OpCom are highly balanced, as follows:

> *The management committee is the supreme body of the joint venture. Each Party shall contribute to the management and control of the joint venture activities. The management committee shall have a key role in the joint venture's strategy process focusing on goals, the choice of direction and the monitoring of the activities. The Management Committee shall ensure the balance between strategic organization, monitoring and control. The management committee shall establish guidelines for and exercise control over the Operator's activities. The management committee may issue general and specific directions for the Operator's performance of its duties.*

372 OGUK JOA §9.8.5.
373 OGUK JOA §29.
374 Norwegian JOA §1.1.

> *The management committee may demand that all matters concerning the joint venture activities be presented to it, and may make decisions concerning such matters.*[375]

The management committee will be composed of one representative from each party of the consortium.[376] However, the operator's representative will chair the committee.[377] The composition is fairly balanced – all parties can participate in the decision-making process, although the operator will have stronger control via its chairmanship.

There is clear provision allowing the existence of subcommittees. Each party has the right to have a representative on each subcommittee, even though the model suggests that the parties might decide otherwise. All subcommittees are restricted to an advisory role unless otherwise decided by the OpCom.[378] Consequently, this is a balanced approach to the extent that equal representation is secured.

The OpCom may address a large variety of issues, as follows:

> *The management committee itself shall deal with and decide matters pertaining to:*
> *a) Appointment of an auditor for the joint venture and for the Operator's activities;*
> *b) Such circumstances as referred to in Article 3.3 [3.4] of the Special Provisions;*
> *c) All matters pertaining to co-operation with licensees of other licence areas;*
> *d) Claims for damages which are of importance as a matter of principle or which are of considerable economic importance;*
> *e) Any other matter being submitted for consideration by any of the Parties;*
> *f) Any other matter as specified in this Agreement; and*
> *g) Procurement and contract strategy, unless otherwise provided by this Agreement.*[379]

It is important to note that the voting procedures are not addressed inside the body of the JOA, but outside it in the "Introduction" part of the agreement, entitled "Agreement concerning Petroleum Activities pursuant to Production Licence No. [ ]". In fact, the JOA structured as an attachment to the Introduction.

The voting procedures are based on the participating interest of each party.[380] Decisions are taken by a combination of the number and the participating interest of the parties. In other words, this agreement secures the negative control of the joint operations for the non-operators.[381]

However, some issues will require unanimous consent, such as "relinquishment of acreage within the licence area or surrender of the Production Licence".[382] In fact,

375 Norwegian JOA §1.3.
376 Norwegian JOA §1.1.
377 Norwegian JOA §1.2.
378 Norwegian JOA §1.3.
379 Norwegian JOA §1.4.
380 Norwegian Agreement Concerning Petroleum Activities §3.1.
381 Norwegian Agreement Concerning Petroleum Activities §3.2.
382 Norwegian Agreement Concerning Petroleum Activities §3.4.

the voting procedures are not a private issue between the parties but also are relevant for the governmental authorities. This is made clear in the provision that if any change occurs within the voting rules the parties must obtain the governmental authority's approval.[383]

Another advantage is the provision that: "The management committee shall make no decision which could render an unreasonable advantage to certain Parties or others to the detriment of other Parties or the joint venture."[384] This favours the consortium and not a specific party as it applies to both sides (ie, the operator and the non-operators).

Under this model the OpCom must not make a decision that is contrary to the petroleum regulations, and authorises the state or the manager (ie, the state direct financial interest entity) to reject such a decision, as follows:

> *3.3 [The State or the Manager may oppose a decision by the management committee which would not respect the conditions and requirements, specified in this Production Licence, regarding the State's depletion policies or the State's financial interests. If the Manager's Member in the management committee declares that an adopted decision is of a nature as described in paragraph one, such decision cannot be executed. If the matter is not brought before the Ministry of Petroleum and Energy ("the Ministry") within 4 weeks after the day of adoption, the decision may nevertheless be executed.]*[385]

Such a provision regarding state control is standard and reasonable to expect in a licence, but not in a JOA. This again shows that a JOA issued by a host government may have particular provisions.

In conclusion, the Norwegian JOA Model Form is more beneficial for the non-operators as it requires their participation in any decision regarding the joint operations. On the other hand, it secures a balance, as no decision in the OpCom can benefit one party exclusively so it also favours the operator. The most interesting fact is that the voting procedure is provided outside the scope of the JOA but inside a short introduction to the consortium agreement. Arguably, the main flaw in this model form is the lack of regulation regarding deadlock resolution, which may create a problem for the parties (even though there are provisions for sole risk operations), especially regarding minimum work obligations and decisions which require unanimous consent, but also the greater power that the manager has to override the decisions made in the OpCom.

The AIPN JOA form secures the existence of an OpCom as the highest authority of the JOA. This provision is clear as it states that: "To provide for the overall supervision and direction of Joint Operations, there is established an Operating Committee."[386]

The representation in the OpCom is well balanced as each party can nominate a representative regardless of the size of its participation interest.[387] However, some

383 Norwegian Agreement Concerning Petroleum Activities §3.5.
384 Norwegian Agreement Concerning Petroleum Activities §3.2.
385 Norwegian Agreement Concerning Petroleum Activities §3.2.
386 AIPN JOA §5.1.
387 AIPN JOA §5.1.

parties might raise concerns about the extent of the representatives' authority.[388] As mentioned above, such an approach is very positive for non-operators because it will allow all parties to participate in the main decision-making body of the JOA. In particular, such a democratic provision will benefit participants with smaller participating interests.

The OpCom determines the creation of subcommittees, which in principle should be for advisory purposes, but the parties may change the purposes by unanimous agreement. The most important part of the provision is that: "Each Party shall have the right to appoint a representative to each subcommittee."[389] This is a valuable procedure to gather non-operators' input and their experience and expertise on each applicable subcommittee, as all parties will be able to nominate a member on these subcommittees.

The comments above refer to provisions from the standard part of the model, as they must be included in any JOA draft. However, it is important to remember that the AIPN Model is unique in providing flexible terms. Alternatives are provided in several provisions of the model draft so the parties can choose the one which best suits their requirements, such as for voting procedures, where the AIPN JOA gives two main options.[390] The first is quite simple as it adopts one passmark for all proposals. The second is more complex as it provides three different scenarios (A, B and C) with different percentages for each scenario.[391] In this case, the parties can choose which areas will require a higher passmark and which a lower one. Commonly, scenario A represents a simple majority, scenario B requires a higher passmark (usually 70%) and scenario C requires unanimous approval.

Certainly, the second option provides a greater degree of balance between protection to the non-operators and the need for prompt decision making, as they can exercise more control on complex and sensitive issues and less on issues that are not important to them. However, the flexibility of such a model might affect the non-operators negatively, as the operator may successfully negotiate lower passmarks. It is suggested that such flexibility suits a mature province stage, where parties are in more equal negotiating positions, but not traditional operations where the non-operators are likely to accept unbalanced terms. As a consequence, for current operations, a defined percentage or at least a defined range between the minimum and maximum percentages, could be more beneficial for non-operators and also would re-establish the balance between the parties. It is also relevant to note that if a deadlock occurs, there is no clear provision on how to proceed and resolve the issue, save in cases where protracted deadlock might endanger the concession agreement or licence, by delaying performance of licence obligations such as minimum work obligations.[392] In this case, it is likely that it would be dealt with as a dispute, which could take a long time to resolve, except for a minimum work obligation, as the model provides that the ultimate decision on a minimum work obligation lies with the operator.[393] But the idea of the AIPN is to allow the sole risk operation as a resolution process,

---

388 DF Asmus, "The 1995 Model Form International Operating Agreement", *Journal of Energy & Natural Resources Law* 14(1) (1996) 14–36.

389 AIPN JOA §5.4.

390 AIPN JOA §5.9.

391 See DF Asmus, "The 1995 Model Form International Operating Agreement", *Journal of Energy & Natural Resources Law* 14 (1996) 10.

392 AIPN JOA §6.1.G, 6.4.D, 6.5.D.

393 AIPN JOA §6.1 (D).

which may be an alternative to resolve some problems, but not all of them, as will be examined in Section 9 of this chapter, "Exclusive operations".

Furthermore, it is important to recognise that both alternatives regarding the voting procedures are based on both the percentage interest and the number of participants.[394] However, there is no determination on the minimum number of parties required to approve any proposal, so it is possible that one party may be sufficient to approve a proposal. Clearly the operator will benefit if the parties do not adopt the requirement of more than one party to approve any decision, as its larger percentage interest will allow it supreme authority over the joint venture, and it will be able to make, by itself, the decisions of the OpCom, even though it might be a minority in terms of the number of parties.

It is important to note the possibility of voting by notice, which aims to improve flexibility and speed when voting for a particular proposal. In theory, this could benefit the whole consortium, as certain decisions might require urgent determinations; however, the problem with the provision is the discretion of the operator to determine whether such urgency is applicable.[395]

Thus, the AIPN JOA Model secures a relatively strong position for non-operators, but only if they are able to negotiate a higher passmark. If they cannot, the concept of the OpCom could be a mere formality as the operator would be able to conduct the joint operations in accordance with its own views, regardless of the opposition of the non-operators. Nevertheless, it is important to note that if the representation with regards to the governmental authorities involves some kind of committee for operations,[396] the non-operators shall also have a seat and vote on this committee, or at least have the right to observe the meetings.

The Australian JOA Model does provide for the existence of an OpCom (referred as a management committee), to supervise the overall operations of the joint venture and also determine its major policies.[397] The representation is very similar to the British and AIPN JOA MODELs, as each member of the joint venture can nominate a representative to the committee regardless of the size of its participating interest.[398]

The voting procedure is unique compared with the other JOA Models. First, the operator is expressly not allowed to vote on the OpCom as an operator, but only as a party; this is common practice in JOAs but is rarely addressed properly in model JOA terms.[399] Secondly, it does not consider the number of parties voting in favour of a particular decision. Instead, it only considers the percentage of the participating interest, which ultimately could be only one party.[400] Thirdly, as a rule the passmark is a simple majority but certain subjects require a unanimous vote, even though these are cited as examples rather than standard terms (eg, surrender, decommissioning and management fees).[401] However, the model does not provide resolution for deadlock situations. All these procedures are different from the approach taken by the British and AIPN Models, except for the lack of clear regulation of deadlock resolution.

394 AIPN JOA §5.9.

395 PR Weems and M Bolton, "Highlights of Key Revisions – 2002 AIPN Model Form International Operating Agreement", *OGEL* 1 (2003) 5.

396 DF Asmus, "The 1995 Model Form International Operating Agreement", *Journal of Energy & Natural Resources Law* 14 (1996) 21.

397 AMPLA JOA §5.1.

398 AMPLA JOA §5.1(a).

399 AMPLA JOA §5.5(b).

400 AMPLA JOA §5.5(a).

401 AMPLA JOA §5.5(c) and Schedule 1.

This model also ensures the possibility of creating subcommittees if the OpCom decides to do so.[402] The subcommittees should provide advisory guidance for the OpCom. However, it is important to note that the composition of these subcommittees shall be determined by the OpCom, which does not guarantee the participation of all parties.

In its current form, this JOA fails to provide a high level of participation by the non-operators as there is no minimum requirement for the number of parties involved in the decisions, so the strong position retained by the operator (ie, from its larger participating interest) is likely to determine any proposal without the support of any other party (ie, the non-operators) in the joint venture.

Thus, the non-operator faces the same problem as it does in any JOA with regards to the OpCom provision, whereas an effective control only exists if the non-operator obtains a higher passmark to enable it to block decisions.

The Greenlandic Model establishes the existence of the OpCom just as the AIPN, British, Norwegian and Australian Models do.[403] It is important to note that, for better participation of the non-operators, each party can nominate a representative regardless of the size of its participating interest in the OpCom. The same procedure applies for any subcommittee which is subject to the OpCom regulations.[404]

The passmark percentage is open to negotiation, as it is left blank, as is the number of parties required to approve any proposal.[405] This model also faces the same problem as the previous models regarding negotiation of passmark percentage and the number of parties required. However, it does establish the requirement to obtain unanimous consent for certain issues just as the British JOA Model does.[406] This is a valuable guarantee that certain issues will not be passed without the non-operators' consent.

This model does address deadlock situations, adopting the following approach:

> *If the Operating Committee cannot decide on the manner of carrying out any Work Obligations or surrender of acreage required under the Licence in sufficient time to fulfil those obligations within the Licence terms and in accordance with the Licence conditions, then such Work Obligations will be carried out or satisfied or surrender of acreage effected in such manner as shall be favoured by the Party or Parties holding individually or in aggregate the greatest Percentage Interest, and all Parties shall be bound by any such decision and such manner of carrying out the Work Obligations or surrender of acreage shall be deemed adopted as part of the Programme and Budget for the year in question.*[407]

The result of this provision is likely to favour the operator rather than the non-operators, as the operator will have the largest percentage interest in the joint venture, so will decide such matters. It is possible to argue that the unanimous

402 AMPLA JOA §5.7.
403 Greenlandic JOA §4.1.
404 Greenlandic JOA §4.2.
405 Greenlandic JOA §4.7.2.
406 Greenlandic JOA §4.7.2.
407 Greenlandic JOA §4.7.4.

consent provided in this JOA Model Form is a mere formality because ultimately the party holding the greatest percentage of interest will make the decision. On the other hand, it could be argued that the interest of the consortium and the licence is greater than a particular party's views, so it will be necessary to adopt special measures to protect the licence if there is a real danger of losing the whole investment.[408] Both arguments are valid, so a balanced provision between the protection of the consortium and the parties' interest would be the way forward.

It could be suggested that this model adopts a similar provision to the AIPN model regarding representation of the parties on subcommittees and a similar approach to the British Model regarding the voting procedure.[409] But the main difference is the deadlock resolution process, which is particular to this model. On the one hand, the result is not positive for non-operators, as the dominant position of the operator shall prevail, but, on the other, it might secure the existence of the whole consortium or even the licence. Although the AIPN provides a similar provision for deadlocks regarding a minimum work obligation, the Greenlandic Model does not give the final decision to the operator, so it provides slightly more balanced terms.

6.3 Discussion

In conclusion, the OpCom is a valuable provision for the protection of non-operators, allowing them some degree of control of the conduct of the joint operations,[410] and, in addition, it is a great opportunity to gather input from the non-operators on maximising the efficiency of the joint venture. This is often the case for the national oil company: the operator is likely to be an international oil company so the national oil company will be concerned to be involved in key decisions and control of the operations. However, not all JOAs have provisions for such management committees.

In North America, the operator has far more discretion in the conduct of operations, as the non-operators cannot exercise adequate control over the joint operations.[411] They cannot collaborate or give their input to the operations.[412] It is very unlikely that any national oil company would accept to use the North American models unless it was the operator since otherwise it would have very little control over the operations.

It could be argued that this situation in North American operations has arisen because they may not be as expensive and risky as elsewhere in the world (ie, they have extensive onshore operations), so there is no need to provide a greater amount of participation and control for the non-operators. Furthermore, there are no companies operating in North America which are owned and controlled by the US or Canadian governments.

Considering the fact that the CAPL, AAPL Form 610 and the RMMLF JOA Models aimed to address onshore operations, which are far less expensive and risky than offshore operations, the cost and risk explanation might stand, but it certainly does

408 S Shaw, "Joint Operating Agreements" in MR David, *Upstream Oil and Gas Agreements*, Sweet & Maxwell, 1996, p19.

409 AIPN JOA §5.4, OGUK JOA §9.7.

410 S Styles, "Joint Operating Agreements" in J Paterson and G Gordon (eds), *Oil and Gas Law: Current Practice and Emerging Trends*, Dundee University Press, 2007, pp269–270.

411 JS Dzienkowski, EE Smith, OL Anderson, JS Lowe, BM Kramer and JL Weaver, *Materials on International Petroleum Transactions*, 3rd edn, RMMLF, 2010, p542.

412 H Dundas, *Joint Operating Agreements: An Introduction*, 1994 Summer Programme: UK Oil and Gas Law, CPMLP 09/09, 1994, pp4–5.

not apply to AAPL Form 810, which aims to address offshore operations. The Deep Horizon operation in the Gulf of Mexico was regulated by AAPL Form 810 and this practical example clearly illustrates how expensive and risky such offshore operations can be. Nevertheless, even Form 810 does not allow the non-operators fully to control and participate in the conduct of the joint operations. If costs and risks are not the reason why AAPL Form 810 allows little participation for non-operators, what is the reason? There is no straightforward answer; however, it is likely to be the lesser US experience in deep water operations. AAPL Form 810 was a large improvement on the previous Form 610, but it still follows historical tradition, where the operator conducts the joint operations "freely", that is, without any major control by the non-operators unless the non-operators obtain unanimous consent on most of the decisions. It is likely that there will be further modifications to the model in order to increase the non-operators' participation. Nevertheless, it is important to note that North American jurisdictions do not require any national oil company participation and these models are intended to be used by private entities or, eventually, a national oil company operating internationally (ie, a national oil company such as Equinor or Sinopec, which does not expect any special rights in the host jurisdiction).

On the other hand, the remaining models[413] provide better control of the joint operations through the existence of an OpCom, as this body will be the highest authority to determine the overall policies and supervision of the JOA. This is more likely to be the case when a national oil company participates as it should require more involvement and participation in the consortium.

The existence of an OpCom can provide security for the non-operator's position in the joint venture as it can effectively participate in the conduct and supervision of the joint operations, but this can only happen if the provisions inside the OpCom also secure the effective participation of the non-operators; otherwise it will be a powerless body which will increase the administrative load without any real benefit to the non-operators.

When the JOA provides for the existence of an OpCom, commonly it is provided that each party shall nominate a representative for the committee regardless of the size of its participation interest.[414] This is a very positive provision from a non-operator's perspective, as it will secure a higher degree of participation by the non-operators.

The provision allowing the creation of a subcommittee offers a very effective means of gathering input from the non-operators, but only the AIPN Model secures the representation of all parties on such a subcommittee.[415] The other models refer to the OpCom decision to determine such procedures, which can be positive or negative.[416] If the non-operators have a strong position in the OpCom, it is likely to determine a higher degree of their participation on each subcommittee created, but the opposite is more likely to occur in current operations, as the operator retains a dominant position. However, the creation of subcommittees is not the only way to gather the non-operators' input, as project teams can be a valuable route to allow their participation. Nevertheless, it is unlikely there will be a high degree of

413 T Daintith and G Willoughby (eds), *Adrian Hill, United Kingdom Oil and Gas Law*, 3rd edn, Sweet & Maxwell, 2009, p1143.

414 AIPN JOA §5.1, OGUK JOA §9, Greenlandic JOA §4.2, AMPLA JOA §5.1(a).

415 AIPN JOA §5.4.

416 OGUK JOA §9.7, AMPLA JOA §5.7, Greenlandic JOA §4.2.

participation by the non-operators in subcommittees or project teams as the operator will control such bodies. However, it is still a way for non-operators to give their input. This is another critical issue for a national oil company, as it could gain a lot of knowledge through subcommittee discussions.

The voting procedure is the most critical issue involving the OpCom as it can determine the extent to which the non-operators will be able to control and participate in the conduct of the joint operations.[417] The AIPN and AAPL Form 610 expect the parties to negotiate the detailed definition of the voting passmark.[418] The British, Norwegian and Greenlandic Models also leave the parties to negotiate this provision,[419] but these models suggest the topics that require unanimous consent.[420] As mentioned above, the question remains whether the operator will be able to negotiate a passmark that allows it to control OpCom outcomes by leveraging the strength of its position in the consortium.

However, the Australian Model is the only model that clearly determines the voting procedure by simple majority as a rule and provides exceptions which are decided by unanimous consent.[421] It could be argued that a simple majority might not be beneficial to a non-operator, as the operator is likely to be able to override the other parties' interests.[422] As a consequence, there is no practical difference from such a restriction. However, it could be a very useful provision to correct the imbalance of power between the operator and the non-operators if such a restriction also applied to the operator as a party, except in matters requiring unanimous consent. In this case, the operator would participate in the preparation of the proposals and approval of very important issues and the non-operators would participate in the decision on the proposals made by the operator.[423] In other words, this would be an interesting solution to minimise the operator's significant powers over the conduct of operations.

On the other hand, it is important to note that the CAPL, the RMMLF and AAPL Form 610 do not provide for a passmark or unanimous approval, as there is the right to join or to refuse participation in any proposal.[424] Nevertheless, the participation of all parties is mandatory for some operations.[425] This is expected to be a highly contested topic between any international oil company and a national oil company during JOA negotiations and special rights for the national oil company to veto certain projects or issues to secure the governmental interest can be expected.

In addition, it is important to note that most JOAs do not provide a resolution for deadlocks, which might be useful for a non-operator at first glance,[426] but it might jeopardise the consortium if the parties have to go to litigation or arbitration every time a consensus is required.[427] Ideally, JOAs should include a dispute resolution

417 T Daintith and G Willoughby (eds), *Adrian Hill, United Kingdom Oil and Gas Law*, 3rd edn, Sweet & Maxwell, 2009, p1143.

418 P Roberts and R Fowler, *Joint Operating Agreements: A Practical Guide*, 4th edn, Globe Law and Business, 2020, pp149–151.

419 OGUK JOA §9.8, Greenlandic JOA §4.7.2, Norwegian ACPA §3.2.

420 OGUK JOA §9.8.3, Greenlandic JOA §4.7.2, Norwegian ACPA §3.4.

421 AMPLA JOA §5.5(c).

422 AMPLA JOA §5.5(b).

423 AMPLA JOA §7.2(b).

424 MPG Taylor and SM Tyne, *Taylor and Winsor on Joint Operating Agreements*, 2nd edn, Longman, 1992, p22.

425 AAPL JOA Form 610 Article VI(A).

426 P Roberts and R Fowler, *Joint Operating Agreements: A Practical Guide*, 4th edn, Globe Law and Business, 2020, p154.

427 S Christensen and B Duncan, "Default, Deadlock and Remedies" in WD Duncan, *Joint Ventures Law in Australia*, 2nd edn, The Federation Press, 2005, p295.

mechanism,[428] but with a high degree of flexibility whenever there is a real danger to the whole consortium so that the dispute can be resolved more quickly. But other, lower priority matters could be resolved via alternative dispute resolution procedures, which will guarantee the position of the non-operators.[429] In other words, provisions relating to urgent matters, which might affect the existence of the joint venture, should aim to protect the consortium and allow flexibility, just as the Greenlandic JOA Model provides for minimum work obligation even though this might not be the most balanced provision.[430] But other matters which are not as urgent (eg, voluntary surrender) should have a more elaborate system to resolve the conflict without weakening the non-operators' position, by adopting different levels of dispute resolution.[431]

It is important to note that all JOA Models fail to secure a wider participation in the OpCom, as it is not standard practice to obtain the approval of more than one party. Instead, most JOAs leave this issue blank so the parties can negotiate it.[432] In this case, it is suggested that it is dangerous not to set the number of parties required to approve any proposal, because it is possible to have a situation where a single party alone could determine the result of a proposal, even though the majority of the other parties do not agree, if its participating interest is too great. Thus, the JOA should determine a minimum number so the parties avoid the risk of missing such a provision in the negotiation process.

As Gerry Bean states, it is possible to establish a comparison between the role of the OpCom and shareholders' meetings.[433] However, others draw a comparison with another decision-making body of the company, namely the board of directors.[434]

Certainly there are more similarities between the OpCom and the shareholders' meetings than with the board of directors, as the former is the higher authority of its vehicle just as the OpCom is for the JOA.[435] Additionally, the shareholders' meeting secures the participation of each shareholder, whereas this is not guaranteed with the board of directors.[436] For the shareholders' meeting, British law provides a large discretion for the dominant shareholder.[437] This situation is very clear as, ordinarily, decisions will require a simple majority and, exceptionally, will require a 75%

---

428 *Ibid*, p294.

429 P Roberts and R Fowler, *Joint Operating Agreements: A Practical Guide*, 4th edn, Globe Law and Business, 2020, pp355–356.

430 Greenlandic JOA §4.7.4.

431 For further information on alternative resolutions for deadlocks see: M Coyle, "Panel Discussion on Deadlock Breaking Mechanisms in Mining and Petroleum Joint Ventures", *AMPLA* 2 (1979–1980) 334; C Wilkinson, *Joint Ventures and Shareholders' Agreements*, 3rd edn, Bloomsbury Professional, 2009, pp171–176; S Christensen and B Duncan, "Default, Deadlock and Remedies" in WD Duncan, *Joint Ventures Law in Australia*, 2nd edn, Federation Press, 2005, pp294–302.

432 AIPN JOA§5.9, OGUK JOA §9.8, AMPLA JOA §5.5(a).

433 See: GMD Bean, *Fiduciary Relationships, Fiduciary Duties and Joint Ventures: The Joint Operating Agreement*, University of Cambridge, 1992, pp176–177.

434 S Fisher, "Formation and Structure" in WD Duncan, *Joint Ventures Law in Australia*, 2nd edn, Federation Press, 2005, pp165–167. See also the discussion in Section 8 of this chapter.

435 See also: P Roberts and R Fowler, *Joint Operating Agreements: A Practical Guide*, 4th edn, Globe Law and Business, 2020, p19; C Golvala, "Upstream joint ventures – bidding and operating agreements" in G Picton-Tubervill (ed.), *Oil and Gas: A Practical Handbook*, Globe Law and Business, 2009, p46.

436 C Wilkinson (ed.), *Joint Ventures and Shareholders' Agreements*, 3rd edn, Bloomsbury Professional, 2009, pp181–182. Furthermore, it may be the case that a shareholder should retain a certain percentage to nominate a director. Consequently, this potential right may be limited according to the shareholders' agreement.

437 UK Companies Act 2006 Sections 282 and 283.

passmark.[438] There are few provisions demanding unanimous approval under the UK Companies Act 2006,[439] but shareholders can be provided with extensive veto[440] rights under the shareholders' agreement, which would allow a similar effect.[441] Thus, the parties' relative bargaining power might result in more or fewer cases for unanimous voting.[442]

In addition, representation on the board of directors will be regulated by the shareholders' agreement and articles of incorporation, as the UK Companies Act 2006 only requires one director for a private company.[443] In this case, a high degree of control over the board of directors by the largest shareholder can be expected.[444] Consequently, it could be suggested that the non-operators will enjoy better control of the joint operations via the OpCom and subcommittees than the minority shareholders in the shareholders' meetings and board of directors.[445] Thus, it could follow that a minority shareholder in the United Kingdom is in a similar position to a non-operator in North America, but curiously is in a weaker position than a non-operator in United Kingdom.

In conclusion, a non-operator in North America will have less control of the joint operations than a non-operator in any other region examined in this book.[446] Different JOA Models provide better provisions for non-operators regarding participation on subcommittees or voting procedures, but most of them fail to secure the effective participation of more than one party and an adequate resolution of deadlocks, even though there are provisions for exclusive operations.[447] In other words, the current JOAs do not establish effective participation for the non-operators in the joint operations, as the operator can conduct the joint operations without major interference by the non-operators. Nevertheless, it is important to recognise that some JOAs will secure the non-operators' participation in critical issues by requiring unanimous consent, but they do not allow full collaboration of the non-operators in the JOA.

Alternatively, the current JOA could adjust the participation of non-operators by adopting an amendment based on the Greenlandic JOA Model, which provides for "cooperation" from another party that is regulated in a specific agreement.[448]

438 C Wilkinson (ed.), *Joint Ventures and Shareholders' Agreements*, 3rd edn, Bloomsbury Professional, 2009, p177.

439 UK Companies Act 2006, eg, Sections 188, 190 and 223.

440 C Wilkinson (ed.), *Joint Ventures and Shareholders' Agreements*, 3rd edn, Bloomsbury Professional, 2009, p185.

441 *Ibid*, p202.

442 *Ibid*, p195.

443 UK Companies Act 2006 Section 154.

444 C Wilkinson (ed.), *Joint Ventures and Shareholders' Agreements*, 3rd edn, Bloomsbury Professional, 2009, pp181–182.

445 *Ibid*, p177.

446 See also: T Daintith and G Willoughby (eds), *Adrian Hill, United Kingdom Oil and Gas Law*, 3rd edn, Sweet & Maxwell, 2009, p1143; H Dundas, *Joint Operating Agreements: An Introduction*, 1994 Summer Programme: UK Oil and Gas Law, CPMLP 09/09, 1994, pp4–5; S Styles, "Joint Operating Agreements" in J Paterson and G Gordon (eds), *Oil and Gas Law*, pp269–270; JS Dzienkowski, EE Smith, OL Anderson, JS Lowe, BM Kramer and JL Weaver, *Materials on International Petroleum Transactions*, 3rd edn, RMMLF, 2010, p539.

447 The Greenlandic Model is an exception as it provides a resolution for deadlocks, but it is still not the best procedure from a non-operator's perspective. See: Greenlandic JOA §4.7.4.

448 Greenlandic JOA §3.1.2: "As from the development phase NUNAOIL will act as a Co-Operator. The rights and obligations of NUNAOIL as Co-Operator shall be specified in the Co-Operation Agreement to be entered into prior to submittal of a request for extension for the purpose of development and production. The Co-Operation Agreement shall be in accordance with the principles of the model form attached hereto as Appendix B."

This is an interesting approach for a national oil company's participation but it is important to remember that in the Greenlandic Model the national oil company's participation is determined by the legislation, so as there is little space to negotiate. If a party wishes to become an operator in such a region, it must accept and deal with those terms. Nevertheless, it is a good practice, demonstrating the importance of sharing decisions and participation between the international and the national oil companies.

Another option would be to provide the OpCom with wider powers in representing the consortium; that is, it would represent the consortium in day-to-day operations and also in the overall supervision of the operations.[449]

This is a very positive solution to achieve equitable management, but it is far from the reality, and it might prove difficult to manage daily operations on such a level of cooperation. Thus, it is important to recognise that in current operations, private parties are unlikely to accept an agreement on these terms, but in a mature operation it might be possible. Nevertheless, what cannot be denied is the right of the non-operator to participate with regard to the conduct of the joint operations.

In short, a national oil company is more likely to have the concerns of a non-operator as commonly the operator of the consortium will be an international oil company. But eventually the national oil company might be or become the operator and the international oil company would then face the concerns of the non-operators and be very keen to control the pace and conduct of the operations. In addition, many oil and gas companies might end up taking projects with operator and non-operator positions. This is why balanced terms are important for the entire duration and smooth execution of the JOA.

7. Award of contracts

7.1 General principles

As discussed in Section 4 of this chapter, the operator acts on behalf of the joint venture in order to perform joint operations. Where the Operator acts as agent, the operator has powers to award contracts on behalf of the consortium. However, on certain occasions, it might be agreed that the operator will award contracts in its own name rather than on behalf of the consortium.[450]

For the purposes of this book, the primary focus is the agency status of the operator as it is the common route for awarding contracts. However, where relevant, the award of contracts outside the scope of an agency duty will be examined. Additionally, this section will discuss the relationship between the JOA parties rather than the relationship between the JOA parties and third parties (ie, contractors).[451]

The complexity of oil and gas operations and the long duration of the petroleum title usually require expert services, all of which are unlikely to be provided by the

449 S Fisher, "Formation and Structure" in WD Duncan, *Joint Ventures Law in Australia*, 2nd edn, The Federation Press, 2005, p165.

450 KC Mildwaters, *Joint Operating Agreements, A Consideration of Legal Aspects Relevant to Joint Operating Agreements used in Great Britain and Australia by Participants thereto to Regulate the Joint Undertaking of Exploration for Petroleum in Offshore Areas with Particular Reference to their Rights and Duties*, PhD Thesis presented to the University of Dundee, 1990, p539.

451 For further information about the relationship with third parties see: H Franklin, "Irretrievable Breakdown? A Review of Operator/Contractor Relationships in the Offshore Oil and Gas Industry", *Journal of Energy & Natural Resources Law* 23 (2005) 1.

operator itself.[452] The operator will perform the joint operations through the award of contracts to several third parties during the life-span of the consortium.

Therefore, control of the procedures by which the operator may award contracts (which commonly are referred as procurement) is a very important mechanism for controlling expenditure.[453] The importance of this mechanism for control of expenditure is supported by several experts in the field, such as Taylor and Tyne,[454] Charez Golvala,[455] and Anthony Jennings,[456] among others.[457] It is a very important tool by which both national oil companies and international oil companies control the direction, pace and cost of the consortium's operations as most of the activities are likely to be outsourced.

Usually, the award of contracts clause will determine what rules the operator must follow before hiring or acquiring any services or goods related to the joint venture. However, the difficult part is deciding the details of such a process, as it is up to the parties to determine the procedures and processes in the award of contracts without violating the local laws and regulations.[458]

The extent of the parties' control over the award of contracts is a potential cause for tension and controversy between the operator and the non-operators. In the same way this tension arises between an international and a national oil company as one of them will act as the operator and the other as the non-operator within the consortium.

The operator will seek to retain as much discretion as possible, so that it will be able to act freely without any major control or interference from the other parties. On the other hand, the non-operators will seek to impose as many restrictions as possible in order to implement a transparent and efficient procedure for the control of cost and scope of work. This tension is clearly noted by several scholars in the field, such as Taylor and Tyne,[459] Sandy Shaw[460] and Charez Golvala.[461]

Since oil and gas operations require expert and highly technical services, the award of contracts to third parties is the most common route to acquire services. However, on certain occasions, the award of contracts to the operator's affiliates may be important for non-operators, as a major operator might be able to deliver several services through its affiliated companies, possibly at a competitive price. In addition, some national oil companies may have affiliated companies in the service sector and may wish to give preference to their own entities.

There is no doubt about the necessity of awarding contracts and the non-operators should have no objection to the operator doing this.[462] However, there are

452 S Shaw, "Joint Operating Agreements" in MR David, *Upstream Oil and Gas Agreements*, Sweet & Maxwell, 1996, p20.

453 P Roberts and R Fowler, *Joint Operating Agreements: A Practical Guide*, 4th edn, Globe Law and Business, 2020, p195.

454 MPG Taylor and SM Tyne, *Taylor and Winsor on Joint Operating Agreements*, 2nd edn, Longman, 1992, p45.

455 C Golvala, "Upstream joint ventures – bidding and operating agreements" in G Picton-Tubervill (ed.), *Oil and Gas: A Practical Handbook*, Globe Law and Business, 2009, pp47–48.

456 A Jennings, *Oil and Gas Exploration Contracts*, 2nd edn, Sweet & Maxwell, 2008, p29.

457 P Roberts and R Fowler, *Joint Operating Agreements: A Practical Guide*, 4th edn, Globe Law and Business, 2020, p195.

458 C Duval, H Le Leuch, A Pertuzio and JL Weaver, *International Petroleum and Exploration Agreements: Legal, Economic & Policy Aspects*, 2nd edn, Barrows, 2009, p293.

459 MPG Taylor and SM Tyne, *Taylor and Winsor on Joint Operating Agreements*, 2nd edn, Longman, 1992, p45.

460 S Shaw, "Joint Operating Agreements" in MR David, *Upstream Oil and Gas Agreements*, Sweet & Maxwell, 1996, p20.

461 C Golvala, "Upstream joint ventures – bidding and operating agreements" in G Picton-Tubervill (ed.), *Oil and Gas: A Practical Handbook*, Globe Law and Business, 2009, pp47–48.

462 P Roberts and R Fowler, *Joint Operating Agreements: A Practical Guide*, 4th edn, Globe Law and Business, 2020, p188.

several concerns for the non-operators regarding the mechanism for determining the award of contracts.[463]

A practical solution to minimise conflict between the parties is to apply a monetary limit, whereby the operator must apply a process of competitive tender if this a limit is exceeded. Below such a financial restriction, the operator will have more discretion over less important contracts and the non-operators will have more control over substantial contracts. A financial cap is used by an operator to reduce the use of the contracting mechanism by non-operators to control expenditure, according to academics and experts in the field such as Taylor and Tyne,[464] Scott Styles[465] and Bernard Taverne.[466, 467]

As previously mentioned, the most common route for procurement is the award of contracts by the operator (on behalf of the joint venture) to third parties. However, if it is not expressly restricted in the JOA, it is also possible for the operator to provide services or goods from its own resources,[468] or via the affiliate route.[469] This is a common practice, but it may create a conflict of interest.[470]

From an operator's perspective, it may be preferable to award contracts to its affiliated companies as this will allow it even more control of the operations and also may increase its profit from the project.[471] The operator will desire more flexibility for such contract procurement procedures, which may not be the same as for the usual award of contracts.[472]

On the other hand, the non-operators will have a different attitude to such affiliate awards.[473] Peter Roberts describes the two main concerns for the non-operators, namely the cost and the quality of the services.[474]

It was reasonable for Peter Roberts to suggest that an element of profit could be allowed for the provision of such services. However, this clearly contradicts the principle governing the JOA that the operator should not make any profit or loss from the conduct of the joint operations. It would create an exception to the principle, which could encourage the operator to change the focus of the joint operations to that of providing as many contracts as possible to its affiliate companies in order to maximise its profits in the joint operations. Nevertheless, it is important to remember that the operator may suffer losses from its operations and it may try to restrict its liabilities for possible failure of performance. In this case, if the profit is acceptable, should the operator lose the benefit of restricted liabilities? It seems reasonable to

463 S Shaw, "Joint Operating Agreements" in MR David, *Upstream Oil and Gas Agreements*, Sweet & Maxwell, 1996, p20.

464 MPG Taylor and SM Tyne, *Taylor and Winsor on Joint Operating Agreements*, 2nd edn, Longman, 1992, p45.

465 S Styles, "Joint Operating Agreements" in J Paterson and G Gordon (eds), *Oil and Gas Law: Current Practice and Emerging Trends*, Dundee University Press, 2007, p280.

466 BG Taverne, *An Introduction to the Regulation of the Petroleum Industry: Law, Contracts and Conventions*, Graham & Trotman, 1994, p136.

467 MPG Taylor and SM Tyne, *Taylor and Winsor on Joint Operating Agreements*, 2nd edn, Longman, 1992, p46.

468 P Roberts and R Fowler, *Joint Operating Agreements: A Practical Guide*, 4th edn, Globe Law and Business, 2020, p190.

469 BG Taverne, *An Introduction to the Regulation of the Petroleum Industry: Law, Contracts and Conventions*, Graham & Trotman, 1994, p136.

470 MPG Taylor and SM Tyne, *Taylor and Winsor on Joint Operating Agreements*, 2nd edn, Longman, 1992, pp45–46.

471 P Roberts and R Fowler, *Joint Operating Agreements: A Practical Guide*, 4th edn, Globe Law and Business, 2020, p190.

472 *Ibid.*

473 P Roberts and R Fowler, *Joint Operating Agreements: A Practical Guide*, 4th edn, Globe Law and Business, 2020, p191.

474 *Ibid.*

accept market price for such services, but at the same time it is reasonable to require full standards of performance backed up with liability provisions consistent with arm's length market practice, as any third party must perform or it will be liable for the loss it causes, albeit subject to a financial cap on liability.[475]

In practice, it is more common for contracts to be awarded to third parties than to affiliates. Therefore, usually the non-operators are keen to forbid or carefully control such awards. However, this more restrictive approach may not be in the best interests of the consortium.[476] The same situation may occur when a national oil company is a non-operator but has large entities within its group that could deliver some services to the consortium. The main issue here is the potential conflict between an international oil company and the national oil company and typically the international company will wish to avoid any conflict with the national oil company. Thus, it would be difficult for an international oil company operator to reject a recommendation from the national oil company or even a ministry of petroleum to use more services from national oil companies.[477]

Achieving balance in the contracting procedure is very important if all parties' interests are to be protected without damaging the consortium's efficiency. That balance should apply to the use of affiliates of an international oil company as it would to state-owned companies which are affiliates of a national oil company. One of them will be the operator and the other the non-operator. The non-operators may take some comfort if the operator owes them fiduciary duties or a duty of good faith, but whether either actually apply will depend on the express wording of the JOA and its applicable law.[478]

The non-operators may not object to the affiliate service route since this may bring benefits for the consortium, but they must check carefully whether this route will achieve a high standard of services at no more than the fair market price. In order to secure such high standards, the non-operators should have the right to participate during the awarding process so that they can verify compliance with the regulations and also assist the operator in achieving a better performance. The non-operators will also be keen to verify that the operator is complying with all the relevant regulations related to the procurement, such as the EU Procurement Directive for European countries, any local content regulations which may be established in the petroleum title and any other regulation.[479]

Therefore, both international and national oil companies should seek a JOA with balanced and highly efficient awards of contract procedures in order to achieve higher standards of operations at a fair market price. On the other hand, these companies should also allow some flexibility in the conduct of the joint operations – a financial cap should suit this purpose as it will provide some flexibility to the operator while giving control of important services to the non-operators. Both international and national oil companies should not rule out the affiliate service route as it may bring benefits to the consortium, especially when time is critical. However, this route must be carefully controlled in order to avoid abuse by the operator. Probably the most

475 *Ibid.*

476 *Ibid.*

477 This conflict may also arise in the context of "local content" discussions in which the national oil company and/or state are keen to ensure that the greatest proportion possible of the operator's contracts are let to businesses operating in that state; see Section 11 of this chapter.

478 P Roberts and R Fowler, *Joint Operating Agreements: A Practical Guide*, 4th edn, Globe Law and Business, 2020, p192.

479 *Ibid*, p188.

common solution chosen by the model JOAs is to require the operator to provide a certificate issued by its external auditors confirming the relevant service was provided without any element of profit or mark-up. Prudently this should be backed up by the non-operators' right of audit of the operator's financial records, which is routinely provided for in the Accounting Procedure. Finally, the participation of the non-operators in important roles may increase the efficiency of the joint venture.

7.2 Analysis of model JOAs

As a general rule, AAPL Form 810 gives extensive discretion to the operator, which has almost absolute control of the operations, as follows: "Except as otherwise provided, the Operator has the exclusive right and duty to conduct (or cause to be conducted) all activities or operations under this Agreement."[480]

This approach puts the operator in a very strong position to conduct the joint operations. There is no doubt about the operator's control over the award of contracts in the following paragraph:

> *With the exception of any Feasibility Team or Project Team formed under this Agreement, the Operator shall select and determine the number of employees, Affiliates, contractors, and/or consultants used in conducting activities or operations under this Agreement and the hours of labour and the compensation for those employees, Affiliates, contractors, and/or consultants.*[481]

The non-operators face another difficult problem under this JOA Model Form, as there is little regulation of the award of contracts to affiliated companies, but only to third entities:

> *The Operator may have drilling operations conducted by qualified and responsible independent contractors who are not an Affiliate of the Operator and are employed under competitive contracts.*[482]

However, there is a provision which could reassure the non-operators as regards drilling operations:

> *If the Operator's or its Affiliate's equipment, personnel, drilling rig, Workover rig, or snubbing unit is employed in conducting operations under this Agreement, the terms, conditions, and rates for that employment shall be consistent with those currently prevailing in competitive contracts for the deepwater OCS.*[483]

---

480 AAPL Form 810 §5.1.
481 AAPL Form 810 §5.1.
482 AAPL Form 810 §5.3.
483 AAPL Form 810 §5.3.

Consequently, if the operator employs an affiliate, this provision should reassure the non-operators and secure the high standards they require. The main hope of the non-operators will be that the word 'competitive' refers to the level of fees rather than just a higher standard of performance. However, the flaw in such a provision is the lack of enforcement, as it only allows an operator to hire qualified and responsible independent contractors, but does not allow the non-operators a mechanism to enforce the obligation without the operator's consent and participation. In other words, if the operator abuses its power (ie, by using the affiliate route) it will be very difficult for a non-operator to exert control over it or make objections against it.

It is important to note that the operator awards contracts as an independent contractor, not as an agent of the non-operators. A third party may initiate a lawsuit to recognise the liabilities of the non-operators, even if expressly excluded from the contract, but the trend of US court decisions suggests this will not be successful.[484]

Thus, the non-operators have little or no say in the award of contracts. Even if the project team has some participation in the process of awarding contracts, this will be only in an informative role as the operator has the ultimate decision about such matters. In this case, the non-operators must rely on the duty put on the operator to "timely commence and conduct all activities or operations in a good and workmanlike manner, as would a prudent operator under the same or similar circumstances".[485]

The AAPL form puts the operator in a comfortable position since it can determine for itself the award of contracts without any significant interference from the non-operators.[486] Such findings are quite surprising as the higher costs and risks involved in offshore operations for which Form 810 is used usually would mean that a higher degree of control and participation was given to the non-operators. The AAPL Form 810 does not allow effective participation by the non-operators. In fact, it fails to provide a clear and transparent procedure for tendering and for the operator to disclose this information to the non-operators.[487]

Finally, there is no doubt that the AAPL JOA Model avoids overly elaborate procurement procedures,[488] as these could create a greater administrative burden for the conduct of operations. The AAPL JOA Model provides almost total control of the operations to the operator so it is very difficult for a non-operator to exert any effective measure for control of expenditure via the mechanism of awarding of contracts.[489] This model form is unlikely to be used by either international or national oil companies because of its lack of balance between the parties.

The RMMLF JOA Model Form offers by far the best position for the operator, as there is no control whatsoever of the conduct of the joint operations. This JOA Model Form states very clearly that the "Operator shall direct and have control of all operations conducted hereunder and shall have exclusively custody of all materials, equipment and other property owned by the Parties."[490]

---

484 See *US Trucks v Texaco Inc.* 337 S.W.2d 497 (Tex. App. – Eastland 1960, writ ref'd) which is discussed in T Martin, J Gilbert and M Gusy, "A Global Review of Joint Operating Agreement Disputes" AIPN research paper 2020, Section. 7.4.2.

485 AAPL Form 810 §5.2.

486 AAPL Form 810 §5.2.

487 The Canadian Model has a similar approach (§3.3(B)), as there is no clear and effective way to control this process and it does not allow for the effective participation of the non-operators.

488 MPG Taylor, SM Tyne, *Taylor and Winsor on Joint Operating Agreements*, 2nd edn, Longman, 1992, p45.

489 See: C Thorpe, *Fundamentals of Upstream Petroleum Agreements*, CP Thorpe, 2008, p126.

490 RMMLF JOA §4.1.

In turn, the non-operators can only hope to be consulted by the operator during the "process of awarding a contract" as follows:

> *Consultation of the Parties. Consult freely with the other Parties concerning operations hereunder and keep them advised of all matters arising in operations hereunder which Operator deems important in the exercise of its best judgement.*

However, the reality is that such a provision is a mere permission rather than an obligation and also is subject to the operator's discretion.[491] In other words, there is no provision to enforce any control of the conduct of the operations, nor the process of awarding any contract, or any guidelines about the rules or principles that the operator must follow.

Additionally, the model does not include any provision recognising or denying the existence of the operator's agency status, although there is no doubt that the operator will act on the behalf of the remaining parties of the consortium.

Therefore, the RMMLF is the least attractive JOA from a non-operator's perspective, as there is no provision to enforce any control over the operator's operations and the model does not provide any guidance on the operator's procedures before awarding a contract. In this case, the non-operator is comparable to an investor. Again, this type of imbalance is unlikely to be appreciated by an international oil company and a national oil company during negotiation.

The Canadian Operating Procedure Model Form secures a greater amount of power for the operator so that it can award contracts at its own discretion.[492] The operator has very strong control of the joint operations.[493]

However, there are restrictions which establish the principles that must be followed before awarding any contract, so the operator must follow the "good contracting practices in the oil and gas industry" and also base its decision in accordance with several criteria, such as "reliability, safety, environmental protection, technology, cost, quality of service, delivery time and other factors relevant to the contract".[494] This is a valuable provision for the non-operators as they have clear grounds for comparison and are able to verify whether the operator is complying with the principles imposed in the JOA.

Additionally, the operator must proceed with the award of contracts on a competitive basis. As mentioned above, such a competitive procedure is beneficial for the non-operators as higher standards can be secured at fair market prices. However, there are exceptions to such requirements in four different situations:

- where the operator deploys its own resources or uses affiliate resources;
- there is an agreement between the operator and a supplier applicable to the operator's wider activities in the relevant basin;
- it is a requirement of applicable local content regulations; and
- the contract's value is less than C$ 50,000.[495]

491 RMMLF JOA §5.1(B).
492 CAPL OP §3.03.
493 CAPL OP §3.03(A).
494 CAPL OP §3.03(B).
495 CAPL OP §3.03(B).

On the one hand, the last exclusion is fairly reasonable as less expensive services do not need the same attention as major operations. On the other hand, the first two exclusions require more caution on the non-operators' part as these may weaken their position in the joint venture, especially the provision related to services provided by the operator from its own resources or by affiliated companies.

It is important to note that the operator is considered to be an independent contractor, so there are no agency issues are raised even though this could be challenged by the relevant parties or third parties.[496]

The Canadian Operating Procedure Model Form provides extensive discretion to the operator to determine the award of contracts. On the other hand, it also provides reasonable guidelines that the operator must follow before awarding any contract, in order to secure higher standards for the operations. However, the exclusion of some operations from the obligation to award competitively could be a problem for the non-operators, as this may grant the operator too many rights and provide few control mechanisms for the non-operators to verify the operator's standards. Finally, the troublesome feature of this approach is its lack of provision for non-operator participation, as the operator can, unilaterally, make all decisions on the award of contracts. If the operator does this, the only right available to non-operators is the general obligation on the operator periodically to consult the non-operators on the joint operations.[497] A similar situation is faced by all North American JOA Model Forms, where the imbalance between operator and non-operator is significant. This discourages both international and national oil companies from using these model forms outside those jurisdictions.

The British JOA Model authorises the operator to award contracts for services and goods, if such expenditure is approved by the work programme and budget and the authorisation for expenditure provisions.[498] Such a connection between the award of contracts and both mechanisms for controlling expenditure is beneficial for the non-operators, but only if the mechanisms effectively allow the non-operators control over and participation in the joint operations. It is also worth noting that this model form clearly establishes the agency relationship between the parties, as the model states that the operator acts on the behalf of the whole consortium.[499] The model also provides a mechanism intended to shield the non-operators from liability to any third-party contractor, which is further discussed in the "Liability" section of this book (Chapter 1, Section 3).

The key mechanism to restrict the operator's discretion to award contracts is one based on financial caps. The parties must determine three different processes and three different financial caps for awarding contracts.

The first process deals with services and goods provided by the operator or its affiliated company.[500] The parties must decide the financial limit above which the OpCom's approval of the contract will be required. As mentioned previously, it is important to achieve a balance between the interests of operator and non-operators, so using a financial cap is a good solution; however, the limit should be agreed with care. A lower financial cap could inhibit the conduct of the joint operations, and a higher financial cap could give too much discretion to the operator.

496 CAPL OP §3.03(A) (B).
497 CAPL OP §3.01(A).
498 OGUK §6.2.1.
499 OGUK §6.5.8.
500 OGUK §6.5.2(b).

The second mechanism provides another financial cap for contracts which support the operator's multi-field operations.[501] In this case, the operator must also obtain the OpCom's approval before awarding the contracts, but the level of information (such as sensitive and confidential issues) that must be provided to the OpCom is reduced at the operator's discretion.

The third mechanism provides a financial cap only for third-party contracts, and these contracts must meet certain criteria before they can be awarded. This mechanism is divided into two categories. The first requires a higher level of participation by the non-operators, competitive tender and the OpCom's approval.[502] The second requires a lower level of participation by the non-operators and requires OpCom approval only if the operator awards the contract to an entity which is not the best qualified in the competitive tender.[503]

The main difference between the two categories is the financial cap. The first secures a higher level of control by the non-operators for higher expenditure and the second reduces the non-operators' control over moderate expenditure (ie, contracts for amounts above the minimum requirement to tender but below the first category's limit). It seems an intelligent system that provides flexibility to the operator while also protecting the non-operators' position. The main flaw with this elaborate system is its lack of guidance on services and goods provided by the operator from its own resources or by its affiliated companies. The non-operators could argue that Clause 6.5.6 requires the operator to put any contract outside the scope of the previous clauses up for tender.[504] However, this is a weak provision, as it also provides that the operator is not obliged to put a contract out to tender if it considers, at its own discretion, that it is impractical or inefficient to do so.

Clearly, the British Model allows more participation for the non-operators, especially for higher expenditures. In addition, there is a general duty on the operator to consult the non-operators on the joint operations, but this is not a clear obligation as it uses the words "freely consult".[505] Also, the provision makes reference to a "project team" but gives no further detail.[506] A project team would be a valuable body to gather the non-operators' views on and input to the joint operations. The model also provides an intelligent and effective system of awarding contracts based on the financial level of each contract. However, its major flaw is the weak control over services provided by the operator from its own resources or affiliated companies. The British and other non-North American JOA Model Forms are more likely to be used between international oil companies and national oil companies, as they provide a more balanced agreement between the operator and non-operator.

On initial inspection, the Norwegian Model appears to favour the operator's position as it is the party responsible for "carrying out and administer[ing] the day-to-day management of the joint venture activities".[507] However, the operator is not the highest authority of the JOA – it is subject to the OpCom's decisions (or "management committee" using the terminology of the Norwegian JOA). Thus, as a

501 OGUK §6.5.3.
502 OGUK §6.5.4.
503 OGUK §6.5.5.
504 OGUK §6.5.6.
505 OGUK §6.5.1.
506 OGUK §6.11.1(a).
507 Norwegian JOA §3.1.

general rule, the operator must prepare the proposals, but then submit them to the OpCom for approval.[508]

This is exactly the case for the award of contracts, as the operator must prepare the procurement strategy for significant expenditure, which must be approved by the OpCom.[509] Such a provision secures a high degree of control for the non-operators over relevant contracts, but at the same time allows more flexibility for the operator, as smaller contracts will be subject to fewer requirements. The operator must provide detailed information to the OpCom, as follows:

> *When presenting a budget proposal for activities in the coming Year, the Operator shall include an overview showing what significant purchases the Operator is planning for the budget year. Among others, this overview shall state the expected contract value for each individual purchase, contain a market evaluation and describe suitable framework agreements. When considering the budget proposal, the management committee shall decide which purchases are to be included in the plan for significant decisions for the coming Year. For purchases, the duration of which exceed the budget for the Year, the Parties shall organize themselves such that the joint venture may commit itself according to the duration of the purchase.*[510]

It could be argued that the combination of the work programme and budget system and such detailed procurement provisions is very positive for the non-operators, as they can take significant decisions at the OpCom level.

This is a very effective provision for balancing the position of the parties. On the one hand, more control of the operations is given to the operator, so it can prepare and plan the procurement strategy. Consequently, the parties must cooperate and make reasonable decisions in order to achieve progress and efficiency. There is also a provision to ensure the non-operators do not abuse their right, as they must take reasonable decisions in the OpCom and not disadvantage the operator:

> *The management committee shall make no decision which could render an unreasonable advantage to certain Parties or others to the detriment of other Parties or the joint venture.*[511]

The question of efficiency is also important; there can be a conflict between the governance of programmes and budgets and the approval of key third-party contracts. If the OpCom has already approved the programme and budget, should it have the right to refuse to approve a third-party contract which is intrinsically necessary for the operator to perform that approved programme and budget? Likewise, should the OpCom approve a multi-year third-party contract which commits the consortium to

508 Norwegian JOA §3.3.
509 Norwegian JOA §13.1.
510 Norwegian JOA §13.1.
511 Norwegian ACPA §3.2.

making expenditure in future years for which no approved programme and budget is yet in place? There is some guidance on this point from the English case; *Spirit Energy Resources v Marathon*[512] can be argued as authority for the proposition that the OpCom must approve expenditure necessitated by activities the OpCom has previously approved.

This is a valuable provision for the non-operators, as they can effectively participate in decisions on important contracts. At the same time the provision gives some relief to the operator as abuse of power by the non-operators is not allowed. Also, as previously mentioned, some flexibility is provided to the operator as it is not obliged to send all contracts to the OpCom, only high-value ones. In other words, financial caps are established, which determine the procurement system, as follows:[513]

> *In respect of purchases which the Operator expects will have a contract price of more than NOK 50 million, or NOK 25 million without competitive bidding, a proposal shall be made to the management committee for a decision concerning specific purchase strategies including a bidding list and approval of the supplier. A decision shall be made within 5 working days after the Operator has submitted his proposal to the management committee.*
> *By a unanimous resolution, the Parties may change the amount of the thresholds.*
> *The Operator shall upon request send a copy of the bid invitation to the Parties.*
> *Procurements with an agreed contract value exceeding NOK 10 million shall be subsequently reported to the management committee.*

This model form recognises the potential conflict of interest regarding the award of contracts to affiliated companies, as it requires a report to the OpCom before such an award:

> *If a Party has an ownership interest in a company which is a bidder for a purchase, or has a self-interest in the purchase or in any other way is in a possible conflict of interest, the management committee shall be made aware of this fact before the contract is entered into.*[514]

It should be noted that the provision does not categorically require the OpCom's approval for such a contract because it is only an informative procedure. In this case, the level of control the non-operators have will depend on the financial threshold: if the limit is exceeded, the operator cannot participate in the voting procedure under the contract. Nevertheless, it is clearly provided that the operator "shall in its capacity as such neither have profit nor loss through the execution of its duties".[515]

---

512 *Spirit Energy Resources Ltd v Marathon Oil UK LLC* [2019] EWCA Civ 11.
513 Norwegian JOA §13.1, 13.2, 13.3.
514 Norwegian JOA §13.4.
515 Norwegian JOA §3.1.

Additionally, the operator must carry out the operations in accordance with not only the rules established in the JOA, but also any applicable regulation in the mineral law or any other legislation.[516] There is no doubt about the agent status of the operator, as it must conduct the joint operations on behalf of all the parties of the joint venture.[517]

The operator is responsible for the preparation and planning of the procurement strategy, but is not required to obtain the non-operators' input at this stage. The only obligation is to "keep the management committee informed of events and circumstances which may be of importance to the joint venture".[518] In other words, the effective participation of the non-operators will only occur if the financial threshold is exceeded, when they must approve such contracts. On the other hand, the non-operators do not participate in procurement related to contracts below the financial threshold, which is relatively high. The Norwegian JOA Model creates a very useful body to gather the parties' views during execution of the joint operations, referred to as the "partner forum":[519]

> *The Operator shall establish a partner forum (Partner Forum) for joint ventures having the same operator. Each participant in the joint ventures shall appoint one member and one alternate member, and may at any time make new appointments. In the Partner Forum, matters shall be subject to common discussions. The Partner Forum has no authority to make decisions.*
>
> *The Partner Forum shall deal with matters that are common to all the joint ventures of the Operator concerning the Operator's charging of costs and other matters of common interest within the scope of the provisions of Attachment A – Joint Operation Agreement, Attachment B – Accounting Agreement and applicable legislation. Such matters comprise, among others:*
>
> *a) The Operator's allocation methods for the charging of costs;*
> *b) Criteria for charging of the Operator's costs to the Joint Account and the Operator's own costs;*
> *c) The Operator's hourly rates, efficiency measures and stretch targets;*
> *d) Benchmarking of the Operator's costs;*
> *e) Reorganization or restructuring costs that the Operator proposes to charge to all joint ventures according to rules set forth in Attachment B – Accounting Agreement; and*
> *f) Unsettled audit claims from a multi-venture audit of the Operator according to procedures set forth in Attachment B – Accounting Agreement.*

However, as clearly stated, the partner forum shall only exist "for joint venturers having the same operator", that is, it requires more than one joint venture, and will only then be a useful provision for the non-operators.

In conclusion, the Norwegian JOA Model provides a reasonable degree of participation by the non-operators, and it is curious that its own national oil company

516 Norwegian JOA §3.1.
517 Norwegian JOA §3.2.
518 Norwegian JOA §3.3.
519 Norwegian JOA §5.1, 5.4, 5.5.

(ie, SDFI) is excluded from the procurement decision process. Nevertheless, however, the problem for the non-operators is the high level of the financial threshold for contract approvals and the high threshold for competitive biddings. So, this model provides an interesting approach to balance the role of the operator and non-operators in the joint venture, but it still provides a high degree of discretion to the operator in its performance of the procurement procedures. Interestingly, in Norway several international oil companies have signed this JOA with Equinor, which gives a clear indication that this format should work from both an international and a national oil company's point of view.

In the AIPN JOA Model, the operator is responsible for conducting the joint operations on behalf of all parties. As usual, the model contains provisions on the operator's power to conduct the joint operations, including the awarding of contracts:

> *Subject to the terms and conditions of this Agreement, Operator shall have all of the rights, functions and duties of Operator under the Contract and shall have exclusive charge of and shall conduct all Joint Operations. Operator may employ independent contractors and agents (which independent contractors and agents may include an Affiliate of Operator, a Non-Operator, or an Affiliate of a Non-Operator) in such Joint Operations.*[520]

However, the award of contracts is not entirely within the discretion of the operator, as there are specific rules for such procedures. There is some flexibility in the model that allows the parties to choose between two optional procedures for the awarding of contracts. The first alternative allows greater discretion for the operator, as there is no obligation for it to put the contract out to tender or to inform the OpCom for contracts up to a certain amount. But if the amount is exceeded, the OpCom's approval will be required.

> *ALTERNATIVE NO. 1*
> *Subject to the Contract, Operator shall award the contract to the best qualified contractor as determined by cost and ability to perform the contract without the obligation to tender and without informing or seeking the approval of the Operating Committee, except that before entering into contracts with Affiliates of Operator exceeding [_________ U.S. dollars], Operator shall obtain the approval of the Operating Committee.*[521]

The operator only has the obligation to award the contract to the best-qualified contractor based on cost and ability to perform the contract. In practice, it is quite difficult to find the best-qualified contractor if there is no tender, so there is not as much discretion as the operator would expect from this provision, but the decision still remains within the operator's discretion.

520 AIPN JOA §42(A).
521 AIPN JOA §6.6.

The second alternative is a system of thresholds on a sliding scale, which allows greater participation to the non-operators as the expenditure involved increases at different stages of the joint venture:[522]

ALTERNATIVE NO. 2 (From Paragraph (A) to (C))

Subject to the Contract, Operator shall award each contract for Joint Operations on the following basis (the amounts stated are in thousands of U.S. dollars):

	Procedure A	**Procedure B**	**Procedure C**
Exploration and appraisal operations	0 to ______	___ to ______	>
Development operations	0 to ______	___ to ______	>
Production operations	0 to ______	___ to ______	>

As previously described, if the parties decide on the second alternative, they will implement a system with three different procedures. Procedure A is exactly the same as the first alternative, where the operator does not have to tender or to inform the OpCom up to a certain amount of expenditure, but has to award the contract to the best-qualified contractor. Procedure B imposes more duties on the operator, including the obligation to put the contract out to tender. In addition, such a procedure will allow the non-operators to participate in the tender process, which is a valuable provision for them, and their approval of awards of contracts to the operator's affiliates is required if a certain threshold is exceeded. Procedure C is similar to Procedure B, but goes beyond Procedure B and secures more control for the non-operators by requiring the OpCom's approval of a 'recommended bid'. The last procedure is the most beneficial for the non-operators as it allows them the highest degree of participation and control.

There is little regulation of the power of the operator to award contracts to affiliated companies, except the obligation to obtain the OpCom's approval if the contract exceeds a defined value.[523] The non-operators could argue that in awarding a contract to an affiliated company, the operator must also comply with all the procedures described in the second alternative (if applicable), but the model does not expressly address this. On the other hand, the operator could argue that the second alternative contains an express provision requiring it to obtain the OpCom's approval before awarding a contract to one of its affiliates, with no further requirements. Beyond the OpCom approval requirement, the precise regulations on awarding contracts to affiliated companies if the expenditure threshold is exceeded are not clear.

It is important to note that the non-operators can control the operator's performance not only through the procurement procedures, but also by ensuring

522 AIPN JOA §6.6.

523 AIPN JOA §6.6(A), (B)(4).

that the operator complies with all the general duties placed on its performance of the joint operations, especially the duties to:

> *(1) perform Joint Operations in accordance with the provisions of the Contract, the Laws/Regulations, this Agreement, and the decisions of the Operating Committee not in conflict with this Agreement;*
> *(2) conduct all Joint Operations in a diligent, safe and efficient manner in accordance with such good and prudent petroleum industry practices and field conservation principles as are generally followed by the international petroleum industry under similar circumstances;*
> *(3) exercise due care with respect to the receipt, payment and accounting of funds in accordance with good and prudent practices as are generally followed by the international petroleum industry under similar circumstances;*
> *(4) subject to Article 4.6 and the Accounting Procedure, neither gain a profit nor suffer a loss as a result of being the Operator in its conduct of Joint Operations, provided that Operator may rely upon Operating Committee approval of specific accounting practices not in conflict with the Accounting Procedure*[524]

Therefore, it could be said that under the AIPN JOA Model Form, the non-operators will have a higher degree of control over and participation in the award of contracts if they can ensure the following:

- a low financial threshold is set, so that the non-operators can control the majority of the contracts;
- the second alternative in the model is used, rather than the first; and
- the non-operators' control over the OpCom, putting them in a position to block certain proposals.

A major concern for non-operators in this model form is that the alternatives have to be negotiated by the parties, and the non-operators are usually in a weaker bargaining position than the operator. Another concern for non-operators is the loose control over the award of contracts to the operator's affiliated companies. Nevertheless, the non-operators can secure higher standards of operations by enforcing the general duties imposed on the operator's performance of the joint operations. In short, this JOA Model Form provides good guidance to balance the interests of the international and the national oil company.

In the Greenlandic JOA Model, the operator must act on behalf of all parties to the joint venture. It is responsible for conducting the joint operations "by itself, or through its Affiliates, its agents or its contractors, under the overall supervision and control of the Operating Committee".[525] In addition, the operator has to perform several duties during the execution of the joint operations, especially:

> *(f) The planning for and obtaining of all requisite services and Material;*
> *(g) The direction and control of accounting services;*
> *(h) The provision of all technical and advisory services required for the efficient performance of the Joint Operations.*[526]

524 AIPN JOA §4.2(B).
525 Greenlandic JOA §3.2.
526 Greenlandic JOA §3.2.

The operator must not act as agent for the joint venture; the JOA mandates that the JOA parties shall not have direct liability under procurement contracts unless the OpCom otherwise decides.[527] Equally important is the operator's authority to perform the joint operations, including acquiring services and goods. One example of the operator's powers mentioned in this model is its discretion in the use of its own personnel: "The number of employees of the Operator employed in connection with its activities hereunder shall be determined by the Operator."[528]

However, there are provisions dealing with the procedures for the award of contracts. First, the operator is subject to the national oil company's decisions (if there are any). Secondly, the operator must work within the limits of approved work programme and budget. However, the provisions on the award of contracts do not refer to the authorisation for expenditure provisions contained in this JOA Model Form. If the first and second conditions are fully complied with, the operator shall have the right to determine the award of contracts as follows:

> *Subject to the rules and regulations laid down by BMP, subject to the provisions of any approved Programme and Budget and subject to Article 3.6.2, the Operator shall have the right to determine the contractors, vendors and others to provide goods and services in connection with the Joint Operations.*[529]

However, the operator is not completely free to determine the procurement system as there are procedures which it must follow:[530]

> *the Operator shall utilize its reasonable efforts to*
> *(a) Assign contracts, sub-contracts, purchases of supplies and services in accordance with Section 21.02 of the Licence, and in accordance with rules and regulations issued by BMP; and*
> *(b) Ensure that each contract is entered into under the best commercial practice and provides the most beneficial terms and rates for the goods and services based on various criteria depending on the contract in question such as, eg, price, quality, availability and reputation. Thus, under normal circumstances bids from several non-affiliated suppliers should be obtained. The Operator shall at the request of any Party inform the Operating Committee fully about the administration of the provisions of this Article 3.6.*

The model also provides more duties related to the procurement procedures, as follows:[531]

527 Greenlandic JOA §3.6.3.
528 Greenlandic JOA §3.5.
529 Greenlandic JOA §3.5.
530 Greenlandic JOA §3.6.1.
531 Greenlandic JOA §3.6.2.

Generally, for proposed contracts for the Joint Operations, the operator shall:

(a) Obtain competitive bid tenders;

(b) Consult with the Parties regarding the contractors to be invited to tender on a timely enough basis to allow the Non-Operators to make recommendations, by forwarding to the Non-Operators the proposed list of such contractors (including any known subcontractors) provided that if any Non-Operator has not responded within five (5) Working Days of such consultation it shall be deemed to have approved the contractors to be invited to tender;

(c) Forward copies of the tender documents to the Non-Operators if requested to do so;

(d) After the expiry of the period allowed for tender and the opening of the bids, promptly submit to the Non-Operators evaluations and recommendations and, upon request, report details of all bids received, and any rebids, amendment to bids, and subsequent negotiations to the Non-Operators;

(e) Use its reasonable endeavours to ensure that any such contract can be fully assigned to any of the Non-Operators in the event of any change of the Operator;

(f) Promptly notify the Non-Operators when a commitment is entered into and upon request promptly supply the Non-Operators with confirmed copies of each such contract and any subsequent revisions thereto;

(g) When an agreement for the delivery of goods or services with an anticipated contract value of seven million Kroner (DKK 7,000,000) or more is to be concluded, furnish to the contract committee established according to Article 4.6 the material referred to in Articles 3.6.2(b), (c) and (d); and refrain from entering into such agreement until the contract committee has submitted to the Operator a recommendation on which of the bids received should be accepted, or in case no contract committee has been established furnish to the Operating Committee the material referred to in Articles 3.6.2(b), (c) and (d) and refrain from entering into such agreement until the Operating Committee's approval has been obtained;

(h) When an agreement for the delivery of goods or services with an anticipated contract value of twenty million Kroner (DKK 20,000,000) or more is to be concluded, and the recommendation of the contract committee established according to Article 4.6 (if any) has been received, obtain the Operating Committee's approval of the bid and the applicable terms and conditions prior to the conclusion of the agreement.

It is very clear that the non-operators have a high degree of control over the operator's discretion in the procurement system, and in addition there are opportunities for non-operators to give their input to the mechanism of procurement. However, there is no regulation on services provided by the operator from its own resources or by the operator's affiliated companies. This approach is negative for the non-operators, as, lacking regulation, the operator could abuse its position. On the other hand, the non-operators may rely on the general terms to secure a higher standard of control by the operator in the joint operations and ensure that it pays the fair market price for the services/goods acquired.

The obligation on the operator to pay the fair market price for goods and services is secured by the general provision which states that the "Operator shall neither gain a profit nor incur a loss as a result of the Joint Operations or the discharge of the Operator's responsibilities, obligations or liabilities under this Agreement."[532]

In addition, the operator may, from time to time, request to amend the expenditure limits previously described, but only if the OpCom agrees by unanimous decision.[533] This is a reasonable provision, as all parties must agree to such an important modification.

The Greenlandic JOA Model provides non-operators with a high degree of control over and participation in the procurement procedures. This is to be expected if a national oil company will be a party in the JOA (especially if it is a non-operator party). However, there is no regulation regarding the award of contracts to the operator itself or its affiliated companies, which could create difficulties for the non-operators to control such awards.

7.3 Discussion

It is clear that control over the procurement process is important to non-operators if they are to be able to control the operator's spending. However, the JOAs vary considerably regarding such mechanisms of expenditure control as some provide the non-operators with little or no control while others give non-operators a high degree of control.[534]

Again, note that extensive discretion is provided to operators in the North American JOAs, where the operator can award contracts at its own discretion with little or no control or participation by the non-operators. This is another indication that the North American JOAs treat non-operators as investors because, in a business sense, investors do not have any operational control, only financial control.

On the other hand, the remaining JOA Models (Norwegian, British, international and Greenlandic) provide not only a high degree of control and participation to the non-operators, but also secure a higher standard of performance by the imposition of competitive tenders.[535] Nevertheless, it is important to note that the existence of a tender is not enough, as the non-operators must have access to the details of the tender and must be allowed to participate in the tender procedure in order to verify that high standards of operations are achieved.[536]

A common feature of these models is that the non-operators have more rights and increased participation as the expenditure rises, and the approval of the OpCom is necessary if the expenditure level exceeds the agreed limit.[537]

---

532 Greenlandic JOA §3.3.1.

533 Greenlandic JOA §3.6.5.

534 KC Mildwaters, *Joint Operating Agreements, A Consideration of Legal Aspects Relevant to Joint Operating Agreements used in Great Britain and Australia by Participants thereto to Regulate the Joint Undertaking of Exploration for Petroleum in Offshore Areas with Particular Reference to their Rights and Duties*, PhD Thesis presented to the University of Dundee, 1990, p538.

535 Kenneth Charles Mildwaters, *Joint Operating Agreements, A Consideration of Legal Aspects Relevant to Joint Operating Agreements used in Great Britain and Australia by Participants thereto to Regulate the Joint Undertaking of Exploration for Petroleum in Offshore Areas with Particular Reference to their Rights and Duties*, PhD Thesis presented to the University of Dundee, 1990, 538.

536 KC Mildwaters, *Joint Operating Agreements, A Consideration of Legal Aspects Relevant to Joint Operating Agreements used in Great Britain and Australia by Participants thereto to Regulate the Joint Undertaking of Exploration for Petroleum in Offshore Areas with Particular Reference to their Rights and Duties*, PhD Thesis presented to the University of Dundee, 1990, 538.

537 OGUK JOA §6.5.

There are some differences between the models. The AIPN Model provides a higher degree of control for non-operators in sliding scale systems, but only if this alternative is chosen. The British have adopted a simplified scale system but with no alternative, which avoids uncertainties for the non-operators. The Greenlandic Model does not use a scale system but secures a good level of control and participation by the non-operators over the procurement systems. Of these model JOAs, the best model for non-operators is the Norwegian one, as it balances the roles of the operator and the non-operators by requiring the operator to prepare the procurement strategy. In summary, it is clear that the British, international, Greenlandic and Norwegian JOA Models recognise the important role of the non-operators, as under these models they have more effective control of the process of contract awards.

On the other hand, from a non-operator's perspective, a common flaw in all the JOAs is the lack of clear regulation of the award of contracts to its affiliated companies, or performance of a contract by the operator itself, which could make it difficult for the non-operators to secure a high standard of performance at a fair market price. Another common problem with the JOAs that contain OpCom provisions is the lack of effective control by the non-operators over such a decision-making body. If the non-operators have no control over the OpCom, it will be only a bureaucratic body, securing little or no benefit for the non-operators. But the most difficult task for any non-operator is to negotiate the amount of expenditure which will require a more rigid control of the process of awarding contracts (if applicable) as lower amounts will increase the non-operators' control over the operator's discretion and higher thresholds will reduce this control.[538]

Furthermore, as previously described, the JOAs provide a high degree of discretion to the operator regarding the acquisition of goods and personnel.[539] One source of comfort for the non-operators is that the operator must always secure a high standard of operations in accordance with the best practices of the industry, and act diligently and prudently in the operations. The very large scale of many oil and gas operations and the complexity involved often demands highly specialised services, which commonly are provided by third parties. Control over the award of contracts to third parties is usually of more importance to non-operators than control over the personnel the operator allocates to the operation, but in some cases the latter issue may also be a concern.

Finally, the non-operators will wish to establish that the operator is complying not only with the JOA procurement rules, but also with other related regulation, such as Procurement Directive 2004/18/EC (for EU members),[540] restrictions imposed by the host nation's petroleum legal regime (eg, local content regulations) and any other regulation which is applicable to such operations. The obligation to provide information is very important for the non-operators as it will help them

538 KC Mildwaters, *Joint Operating Agreements, A Consideration of Legal Aspects Relevant to Joint Operating Agreements used in Great Britain and Australia by Participants thereto to Regulate the Joint Undertaking of Exploration for Petroleum in Offshore Areas with Particular Reference to their Rights and Duties*, PhD Thesis presented to the University of Dundee, 1990, p538.

539 KC Mildwaters, *Joint Operating Agreements, A Consideration of Legal Aspects Relevant to Joint Operating Agreements used in Great Britain and Australia by Participants thereto to Regulate the Joint Undertaking of Exploration for Petroleum in Offshore Areas with Particular Reference to their Rights and Duties*, PhD Thesis presented to the University of Dundee, 1990, pp538–539.

540 See: www.ogc.gov.uk/procurement_policy_and_application_of_eu_rules_european_procurement_directives.asp.

to exert the necessary control to ensure that the operator is complying with the applicable regulations.[541]

All of those issues should be considered from both an international and a national oil company's perspective as they will be acting as either an operator or a non-operator. The award of contracts is a key process to control the pace, quality and cost of the operations, so all parties should be interested in maintaining an efficient, transparent and professional conduct of operations.

8. Conflicts of interest

8.1 General principles

The purpose of this section is to address conflicts of interest in the management of any joint venture governed by a JOA in which international oil companies and national oil companies participate. The concept of 'conflict of interest' is confused and controversial, not least because there is a lack of consensus as to what a conflict of interest is. It includes, but is not limited to, personal conflicts of interest which arise when an individual has a duty, the performance of which is affected by, or may be perceived to be affected by, a different interest, duty or role which may influence him or her in the exercise of that duty. The latter interest, duty or role might arise because of family connections or loyalties, past employment, or, in an extreme case, bribery. Following the passing of the UK Bribery Act in 2010, many international oil companies have adopted procedures and established corporate compliance departments with the intention of availing themselves of the statutory defence in Section 7(2) of the Act, which excuses commercial organisations from vicarious liability for acts of bribery if the relevant corporation can show that it had the appropriate anti-bribery procedures and safeguards in place, notwithstanding that the procedures and safeguards failed to prevent a specific act of bribery or corruption. National oil companies have adopted similar anti-bribery procedures,[542] and follow international oil companies in requiring employees to avoid situations where their loyalty to their employer is compromised by another relationship, or at least to report any such conflict, and recuse themselves from acting on behalf of their employer if appropriate.

To some extent, this focus on this particular form of personal conflict of interest has detracted attention from other forms of conflict of interest, particularly those conflicts affecting strategic decision making and the use of information. It is a characteristic of upstream oil and gas operations that many joint ventures are formed around a contractual framework and not a corporate one. With some exceptions, operations are not conducted by a special corporate vehicle deploying its own dedicated management, employees, property and resources. Instead, the

541 "The Operator is under a duty to give to the Participants a detailed procedure of how it intends to implement its undertaking in respect to the employment of personnel and the entering into of contracts. The procedure will usually require the Operator to give notice to the Participants of its requirements in this regard and to give them sufficient time to consider and respond to the proposals of the Operator in respect of such requirements." KC Mildwaters, *Joint Operating Agreements, A Consideration of Legal Aspects Relevant to Joint Operating Agreements used in Great Britain and Australia by Participants thereto to Regulate the Joint Undertaking of Exploration for Petroleum in Offshore Areas with Particular Reference to their Rights and Duties*, PhD Thesis presented to the University of Dundee, 1990, p538.

542 For example the Qatar Petroleum Code of Conduct available at https://qp.com.qa/en/SupplyManagement/Pages/BusinessEthics.aspx.

operator deploys its own in-house managers, employees, property and resources in performing operations for any and all of the joint ventures for which it acts as operator. This is counterintuitive for corporate lawyers from an English law tradition, expecting company directors or persons performing a similar managerial role to act exclusively for, and to owe a fiduciary duty of loyalty to the companies they manage, as now partly codified by the UK Companies Act 2006.[543] Similarly, partners owe a duty of good faith to fellow partners under the Partnership Act, at least in the conduct of partnership business.[544] Lastly, English case law has recently established that representatives acting on behalf of a member of a limited liability partnership owe fiduciary duties to that LLP, even if the LLP members themselves do not owe such duties to each other.[545]

By contrast, the joint-venture operator will deploy its own managers and staff to conduct joint operations as well as other operations for other joint ventures simultaneously, often with the full knowledge of, and tacit consent of, the non-operators in each joint venture. Similarly, operator and non-operator representatives on the OpCom are likely to act in such capacity on other OpComs for other joint ventures. Whilst such representatives and managers are likely to receive training on the confidentiality and antitrust obligations relevant to their multiple roles, no common perspective exists between international oil companies on how such representatives or managers may address conflicts of interest arising because of their multiple roles, even if they accept that such conflicts of interest arise.

There is an argument that OpCom representatives act only for the JOA party that appoints them and that the scope for conflicts of interest in their role is reduced. After all, they act in a capacity similar to a corporate shareholder representative, upon whom no fiduciary duty is imposed by law,[546] and rarely by shareholder agreement. But in the interests of cost saving, it is often the case that non-operators will use the same representatives in several OpComs for joint ventures working in the same region, with the result that conflicts of interest may arise for them just as often as they may arise for operator OpCom representatives.

The non-operators may also second their employees into the operator organisation, for the purpose of participating in a joint project team; this will blur the distinction between loyalties owed to their employer and to the operator, and between information that they can share with their employer and information they cannot share.

It might be more appropriate to expect higher degrees of trust and loyalty from a joint-venture manager employed by the operator, who acts at a similar level of responsibility and authority to a company director. In such cases, conflicts of interest can routinely arise – an operator joint-venture manager may be incentivised to maximise returns for the operator, encouraging him or her to focus on the joint venture(s) which is most profitable to the operator, or the manager may have access to information relevant to all the joint ventures for which he or she is responsible, but he or she may wish only to disclose that information selectively to those joint ventures best able to monetise that information, to the ultimate benefit of the operator.

---

543 Companies Act 2006 Sections 170–177.

544 *Helmore v Smith* (1886) 35 ChD 436.

545 *F&C Alternative Investments (Holdings) Limited v Barthelemy & Anor.* [2011] EWHC 1731 (Ch).

546 *Ellard v Andrews* [2002] All ER (D) 133; *McKillen v Barclay* [2012] EWHC 521 (Ch).

The issue is also bound up with the law applicable to fiduciary duties. Where a fiduciary duty applies, the duty holder must "act in good faith; he must not make a profit out of his trust; he must not place himself in a position where his duty and his interest may conflict; he may not act for his own benefit or for the benefit of a third person without the informed consent of his principal".[547] In other words, where a fiduciary duty exists, the duty holder must prefer the interest of his or her principal over any other conflicting interest. However, it is wrong to assume that conflicts of interest only arise in the context of a fiduciary duty or that the nature and scope of such fiduciary duties are the same in whatever context or role they arise.

Whilst some industry sectors, such as financial services, are making progress towards establishing codes of practice and guidance on the management of conflicts of interest based on the expectations of market practitioners rather than legal principles,[548] the oil and gas sector has not reached consensus on the recognition of, and management of, such conflicts of interest. Such personal conflicts of interest are not addressed in model JOAs, nor indeed in any negotiated JOAs of which the authors are aware. This feature of upstream project governance can be problematic for operators which are responsible for running unincorporated and incorporated joint ventures by deploying the same team of managers, because those managers acting as directors in the incorporated joint ventures will owe fiduciary duties, and those managers acting as senior supervisors of unincorporated joint ventures will not. This is also surprising given that the OpCom plays a role which is closer in nature to a company board in terms of its level of engagement in operational detail, compared to the general meeting of company shareholders. Again, these are issues that are not routinely addressed by JOAs, but routinely give rise to allegations of bad faith and dispute between the joint-venture participants.

This *laissez faire* approach to conflicts of interest affecting individuals responsible for joint operations opens up more opportunities for dispute where the non-operators include a national oil company, and especially where the joint venture is acting under a granting instrument with the State controlling such national oil company. This section now looks at conflicts of interest between JOA parties, which may manifest themselves as conflicts between individuals acting as OpCom representatives or between operator managers and the non-operator representatives they deal with, but they arise from underlying differences of strategy and objective between the companies they represent.

8.2 Analysis of model JOAs

In many ways, it can be argued that a standard JOA recognises and manages the conflicts of interest inherent in the operator role. Many standard JOA provisions set the expectations for the operator specifically, defining the boundaries of its responsibilities, and the restrictions imposed on it within those boundaries. For example:

- the operator is likely to be selected with the approval of the OpCom, may be dismissed on certain grounds and a replacement operator approved by the OpCom; Operatorship is not a transferable asset belonging to the operator (see Section 4 of this chapter);

547 *Bristol and West Building Society v Mothew* [1998] Ch 1 16 per Millet LJ.

548 See for example the OICV-IOSCO report to the Board of the International Organization of Securities Commissions "Conflicts of interest and associated conduct risks during the debt capital raising process" FR08/2020 September 2020 Available at www.iosco.org/library/pubdocs/pdf/IOSCOPD612.pdf.

- the scope of the operatorship function is limited by subject matter (routinely defined by approved work programmes and budgets and/or authorisations for expenditure), in time (the duration of the JOA) and in scope (most JOAs list the responsibilities of the operator in some detail) (see Chapter 2, Sections 1 and 2);
- strategic investment decisions are made by, or at least approved by, the OpCom, and not the operator acting alone (see Section 6 of this chapter);
- high-value procurement decisions are also approved by the OpCom (see Section 7 of this chapter);
- the operator is required to charge its expenditures to the joint account at cost, making no profit and incurring no loss;
- related party transactions are controlled by the terms of the accounting procedure, which may require the costs incurred under such transactions to be certified by an independent audit body (see Section 7 of this chapter);
- the costs of parent company support provided to the operator by its affiliates are routinely capped at a percentage of annual approved expenditure (see Chapter 2, Section 8);
- the operator is obliged to provide information in a regular and structured fashion to the non-operators with respect to joint operations (see Section 5 of this chapter).

Thus, in piecemeal fashion, the JOA addresses specifically the issues which give rise to conflict between the operator and non-operators. However, the same JOAs routinely and expressly exclude any fiduciary duty owed by the operator to the non-operators in respect of the joint operations. In other words, the JOA codifies the non-operators' expectations of the operator and seeks to limit any recourse against the operator for non-performance purely to breach of those contractual terms, without opening up the field of remedies which can be deployed against the operator to include implied duties arising out of theories of law such as equity, trust and duties of good faith or loyalty. English law respects the right of legally advised parties to exclude such non-contractual sources of legal duty and remedies by the express terms of the relevant contract,[549] but other jurisdictions do not.[550]

JOAs do not usually address the question as to whether the non-operators owe any duty of good faith or loyalty to the joint venture. In one sense, the non-operators' duties to the joint venture are also codified; the non-operators must pay cash calls issued in accordance with the JOA and Accounting Procedure on time (see Chapter 2, Section 6); they must appoint OpCom representatives (see Section 6 of this chapter); they must lift their participating interest shares of produced petroleum in accordance with the relevant lifting or balancing agreements (see Section 14 of this chapter). The question arises whether a non-operator (or indeed the operator voting its own participating interest) is free to vote in the OpCom in accordance with its own wishes, irrespective of the general interest of the joint venture. Take for example the non-operator which has an interest in another joint venture on the point of approving development of a hydrocarbon field which will produce hydrocarbons for delivery into an over-subscribed downstream transportation system; if it votes in favour of a similar development ready for approval by

549 *Ross River Ltd v Waverley Commercial Ltd* [2013] EWCA Civ 910.

550 See, for example, the discussion in *Hewitt on Joint Ventures*, 6th edn, Sweet & Maxwell, 2016, Section 11-09.

the OpCom, then it may find that one or both of the joint ventures will have to find alternative and potentially costly alternatives for the evacuation of their hydrocarbons, significantly impacting the economic viability of those projects. Can it vote against one project in order to maximise its profit in another, thereby maximising its return on investment?

The model JOAs are not consistent on this point. The AIPN JOA requires the operator to avoid conflicts of interest,[551] but does not address the position of non-operators. It does expressly state that the JOA parties do not owe each other fiduciary duties,[552] but that might not exclude lesser duties of good faith and loyalty which are imposed upon parties to a long-term agreement which relies upon such cooperation for its success.[553] The CAPL JOA is perhaps the only model form which addresses this point squarely by stating:

> *Each Party acknowledges that the Parties are engaged in the oil and gas business. Each party is free to conduct its business in such manner as it, in its sole discretion, sees fit, even if it is (or may be) in competition with potential Joint Operations. Nothing in the Agreement restricts a Party from making elections or decisions in what it perceives to be its own interests, economic or otherwise, subject to: (i) any trust, trust duty or fiduciary relationship imposed at law or in equity; (ii) any duty of good faith (or similar duty) contemplated in Subclause 1.05 a; and (iii) the other provisions of the Agreement, including any specific obligations not to exercise discretion unreasonably.*[554]

As discussed in Section 6 of this chapter, the Norwegian form JOA tries to square this circle by imposing upon the management committee an obligation to avoid decisions which have unfair advantages or disadvantages for a subset of the parties. However, such provision is extremely difficult to apply in practice and to enforce.[555]

The English courts have recently interpreted one JOA as allowing the parties to vote for their interests in accordance with their individual commercial priorities, and not in the interests of the joint venture as a whole. In *TAQA v Batani*, the court said:

> *The relationship was one that ultimately depended on the interests of the parties to it being aligned. Where that ceased to be so the parties were free to act what they perceived to be in their respective individual best interests.*[556]

This statement is an important one for the understanding of JOAs – the courts generally will not intervene to impose a decision upon the OpCom if there is no

---

551 AIPN JOA §20.2.

552 AIPN JOA §14.1.

553 See P Roberts and R Fowler, *Joint Operating Agreements: A Practical Guide*, 4th edn, Globe Law and Business, 2020, pp137–138; *Hewitt on Joint Ventures*, 6th Edition, Sweet & Maxwell, 2016. See also *TAQA Bratani Ltd and Others v RockRose* [2020] EWHC 58 (Comm), referring to *Braganza v BP Shipping Limited and another* [2015] UKSC 17.

554 CAPL JOA §1.05B.

555 Norwegian Agreement Concerning Petroleum Activities §3.2.

556 *TAQA Bratani Ltd and Others v RockRose* [2020] EWHC 58 (Comm) Para 38.

consensus. Nor will it choose between different strategies using the yardsticks of good faith or fiduciary duty to make that choice. This makes it doubly important that JOA negotiators understand how deadlocks will be resolved.[557]

8.3 Discussion

The terms of standard JOAs used by the industry do not expressly impose any fiduciary duty or duty of good faith and loyalty on non-operators, and routinely expressly exclude such duties. As a result, it is difficult for international oil companies to complain if national oil companies exercise their rights under such JOAs consistently with the interests of the state that controls that national oil company. After all, when deciding how to vote in the OpCom, it is legitimate for a national oil company to follow a business strategy set by the state just as it is legitimate and expected for an international oil company to follow the corporate strategy set for it by head office. However, if the joint venture acts as the state's counterparty under a granting instrument, the participation of national oil company is more likely to give rise to significant conflicts of interest that will give rise to certain disputes and complicate others. Given that petroleum licence terms often allow the state to step into joint ventures at the development and production stage, or for their share of costs and liabilities to be carried by the international oil companies up to that point, the JOA negotiators should consider how standard industry JOAs should be adapted to take into account these additional conflict of interest exposures. Just because there is no national oil company participation at the outset of the JOA does not mean that the JOA should not address later national oil company participation if such participation is a likely consequence of the joint venture's success.

In theory, the state will exercise its control over the joint venture's performance of the relevant granting instrument through the governance committees appointed by the agreement (typically a management committee), as well as supervision by the regulatory authorities to inspections, audits and statutory reporting. Arguably, there is no need for the state to "double down" on that control by influencing national oil company in its OpCom decision making and voting. Conflicts may arise because the national oil company has a dominant position in the downstream market for oil or gas, possibly exacerbated by state control of pricing. Likewise, the national oil company may have preferential access to downstream transportation or processing capacity because of its overall larger footprint on state territory. The national oil company may find itself misaligned with the joint venture when the joint venture is called upon to sell hydrocarbons at fixed price to the state to address a local supply emergency. In a sense, these are just different forms of the same kind of commercial conflict that a joint venture has to address if a participating international oil company has a dominant and conflicting position.

However, it is inevitable that the national oil company will wish to align itself with state policy in its engagements with the joint venture. In many developing countries, where the oil and gas sector represents a very significant source of state

557 In the case of *Spirit Energy Resources Ltd v Marathon Oil UK LLC* [2019] EWCA Civ 11, the English court reached the conclusion that JOA parties are not free to vote their interests unconditionally. In that case, the OpCom was required to approve expenditure which was necessitated by projects previously approved by it, and the OpCom could not use its voting discretion to avoid approving and paying for expenditure which would otherwise have to be incurred by the operator in any event. But the court did not have to make any finding that a fiduciary duty of loyalty and good faith existed to reach this conclusion.

budgetary income, the state may have different drivers with respect to the cost and revenue profile of the project compared to the international oil companies, wishing to defer investment and increase cash flow to replenish state coffers, when the international oil companies wish to invest based on stand-alone economic criteria.[558] Another key area of potential conflict is legislative reform. The national oil company will have interests in most of the oil and gas projects in state territory and will comply with the latest regulatory and taxation requirements applicable to the sector. Indeed, it may be a key advocate of legislative reform. By contrast, the granting instrument is likely to guarantee the joint venture with legal and tax stability, fixing the legislation applicable to the joint-venture operations to laws in force at the time the agreement was signed. The state and national oil company may be aligned in preferring the joint venture to apply current law to all the national oil companies' operations, including joint operations conducted by the joint venture.

Another key area for conflict relates to local content, and the efforts by the state to enhance wealth generation by ensuring that the joint venture spends as much of its budget as it reasonably can within state territory on state goods and services (see Section 11 of this chapter). The national oil company may already be familiar with local sources of such goods and services and may even have its own federal contracts which it will wish the operator to use – as will the state (see Section 7 of this chapter). Likewise, the national oil company may align itself with the state at times of oil price stress when the international oil companies will pursue a strategy of cash preservation and may significantly retrench discretionary expenditure such as drilling when the national oil company and the state may be prepared to continue with such spending in the interests of the regional economy, even at an economic loss.

Given that JOAs do not impose duties of good faith and loyalty upon non-operators as a general rule, and permit international oil companies to use their voting powers in the OpCom to pursue their separate corporate objectives, is it not legitimate for a national oil company to pursue objectives aligned with the state in this way? The better answer is that standard JOAs do nothing to prevent this, but other industry sectors are encouraging a more transparent form of relationship in public and private partnerships and, arguably, the oil and gas sector should be no different. In 2015, OECD published the Guidelines on Corporate Governance for State-owned Enterprises,[559] arguing that state participation in industry should follow a corporate approach to state ownership. This would include establishing and publishing an ownership plan, describing the state's objective for its participation, providing its stakeholders and joint-venture partners with some predictability as to the priorities against which its state shareholder assesses its performance.

In conclusion, standard JOAs are not fit for the purpose of managing the conflicts of interest that come into play when a national oil company participates in a joint venture which itself is performing a concession agreement with the state which is that national oil company's controlling shareholder. Those JOAs take a *laissez faire* approach in relation to international oil companies' participation in other joint ventures and the conflicts that may then arise, so that they are ill-equipped to address national oil companies' conflicts which may cause deadlock in the OpCom more frequently. Perhaps that can be avoided if the national oil company is

---

558 See D Johnson, "Upstream Concessions and Contracts" in P Roberts (ed.) *Oil and Gas Contracts – Principles and Practice*, 2nd edn, Reuters, 2019.

559 Available at www.oecd.org/corporate/guidelines-corporate-governance-SOEs.htm.

prepared to adopt policies similar to the OECD Guidelines, to share and pursue its business objectives transparently, whilst resisting pressures from the state to pursue unrelated priorities.

9. Exclusive operations

9.1 General principles

The basic principle underlying any JOA is encapsulated by the word 'joint', as the parties combine forces to share the higher costs and risks of oil and gas operations.[560] This principle provides both the concept and the definition of a JOA.

The starting position is that the operations will be performed jointly. Consequently, the initial desire of all JOA parties is to exclude or forbid any operation that goes against the basic principle of "jointly and shared costs and risks".[561] However, the shortest and the easiest route may not be the best option for the parties, as the standard model should provide the essential provisions in adequate depth to provide reassurance and stability for the consortium.

As with any kind of consortium, the JOA parties do not always share the same opinion on how to proceed in order to maximise the efficiency of the joint enterprise.

In fact, the JOA is not a simple consortium, but an agreement which is established to regulate the relationship between parties that desire to engage in highly risky and costly operations so the potential for different views is even greater than for a regular consortium.[562]

The nature of oil and gas operations demands a certain measure of flexibility as it is not possible to predict all possible scenarios at the drafting stage.[563]

This is exactly the scope of the sole risk and non-consent provisions, as they allow operations in which not all of the consortium parties take part (ie, exclusive operations).[564] A sole risk clause is used when a proposal of work does not achieve the required passmark in the OpCom. In this case, a party that fails to obtain the passmark but wishes to proceed independently will have the right to carry out the proposed work at its sole risk and cost.[565] The non-consent clause is used in the opposite situation, where the passmark vote is achieved but a party does not wish to proceed in the activity approved by the majority of the consortium. In this case, if unanimous approval is required, the non-consent will be "superfluous, because a passive participant can protect its economic interest simply by voting against the proposed operation/investment to which it is opposed".[566]

The main difference between sole risk and non-consent clauses is where the power lies in the OpCom. The sole risk clause is used when the proposal does not reach the passmark required by the OpCom but nevertheless the party decides

---

560 J Wilkinson, *Introduction to Oil and Gas Joint Ventures*, OPL, 1997, p42.

561 *Ibid.*

562 MPG Taylor, SM Tyne, *Taylor and Winsor on Joint Operating Agreements*, 2nd edn, Longman, 1992, p47.

563 See also: *Const v Harris* (1824) Turn & R 496; 37 ER 1191, *Blisset v Daniel* (1853) 10 Hare 493; 68 ER 1022.

564 C Duval, H Le Leuch, A Pertuzio and JL Weaver, *International Petroleum and Exploration Agreements: Legal, Economic & Policy Aspects*, 2nd edn, Barrows, 2009, p295.

565 The non-sole risk or non-consent party could refer to one or more parties.

566 BG Taverne, *Co-operative Agreements in the Extractive Petroleum Industry*, Kluwer Law International, 1996, p70.

to move on with the proposed work.[567] The non-consent clause is used when the proposed work is approved by the OpCom but the party decides not to engage in it.[568] However, both clauses have a common feature in that they both modify the principle of 'majority rule' as in both situations the sole risk and non-consent parties were out-voted, either positively or negatively.[569]

Even though the JOA requires flexibility, the existence of exclusive operations conflicts with the JOA and its main principles such as joint operations, shared costs and risks, and rule by OpCom. The possibility of performing exclusive operations is probably the most distinctive difference between JOAs and any other similar arrangements (eg, corporate joint ventures, partnerships).

The question here is how far can you change the concept of the agreement to secure its own existence? The answer lies in the goals that the exclusive operation aims to achieve, which cannot be straightforwardly stated; any provision allowing for exclusive operations to a greater or lesser degree changes the concept and philosophy behind the JOA, so it will involve highly complex provisions. As a consequence, sole risk and non-consent clauses are by far the most complex clauses to be drafted in a JOA, as clearly recognised by the majority of academics and practitioners in the field, such as Viviane Gayrner,[570] Terence Daintith[571] and Claude Duval,[572] among others.

On the other hand, it is possible to argue that the concept of exclusive operations is fairly simple,[573] but drafting the terms to regulate and implement the concept is a more difficult task. The complexity involved in implementing such clauses cannot be questioned.

In practice, the complexity surrounding such clauses reduces their use.[574] They may be included in the JOA, but the parties prefer not to exercise such rights.[575] Another reason for the complexity of sole risk provisions is that they are intended to create a mechanism which can be applied without the need for negotiation and further approvals by any of the JOA parties; they are intended to be stand-alone so that the proposing party cannot be held back by the non-consenting parties in prosecuting its purpose.

567 See: MPG Taylor and SM Tyne, *Taylor and Winsor on Joint Operating Agreements*, 2nd edn, Longman, 1992, p48; S Shaw, "Joint Operating Agreements" in MR David, *Upstream Oil and Gas Agreements*, Sweet & Maxwell, 1996, p23; A Jennings, *Oil and Gas Exploration Contracts*, 2nd edn, Sweet & Maxwell, 2008, pp288–289; H Dundas, *Joint Operating Agreements: An Introduction*, 1994 Summer Programme: UK Oil and Gas Law, CPMLP 09/09, 1994, p10.

568 See: MPG Taylor and SM Tyne, *Taylor and Winsor on Joint Operating Agreements*, 2nd edn, Longman, 1992, p48; S Shaw, "Joint Operating Agreements" in MR David, *Upstream Oil and Gas Agreements*, Sweet & Maxwell, 1996, p23; A Jennings, *Oil and Gas Exploration Contracts*, 2nd edn, Sweet & Maxwell, 2008, pp288–289; H Dundas, *Joint Operating Agreements: An Introduction*, 1994 Summer Programme: UK Oil and Gas Law, CPMLP 09/09, 1994, p10.

569 C Duval, H Le Leuch, A Pertuzio and JL Weaver, *International Petroleum and Exploration Agreements: Legal, Economic & Policy Aspects*, 2nd edn, Barrows, 2009, p295.

570 V Gayrner, "Sole Risk and Non-Consent under UK Joint Operating Agreements", 1994 Summer Programme: UK Oil and Gas Law, CPMLP 09/09, 1994, p1.

571 T Daintith and G Willoughby (eds), *Adrian Hill, United Kingdom Oil and Gas Law*, 3rd edn, Sweet & Maxwell, 2009, p1153.

572 C Duval, H Le Leuch, A Pertuzio and JL Weaver, *International Petroleum and Exploration Agreements: Legal, Economic & Policy Aspects*, 2nd edn, Barrows, 2009, p297.

573 C Thorpe, *Fundamentals of Upstream Petroleum Agreements*, CP Thorpe, 2008, p133.

574 T Daintith and G Willoughby (eds), *Adrian Hill, United Kingdom Oil and Gas Law*, 3rd edn, Sweet & Maxwell, 2009, p1152.

575 A Jennings, *Oil and Gas Exploration Contracts*, 2nd edn, Sweet & Maxwell, 2008, p25.

Most of the time, such clauses are used as a deterrent to the parties, to avoid an exclusive operation, as the consequences could be quite negative.[576] In other words, their complexity and the harsh effect of their implementation could be an effective way to encourage parties to keep to joint operations wherever possible.[577]

The same principle applies for non-consent operations since if a party decides to opt out of an operation, it may be much more expensive for it to buy-back later on than it would have been to pay its share in the first place. Thus, in this sense, both clauses support the main principle of the JOA, which is the performance of joint operations instead of exclusive operations.[578]

However, the main idea behind a sole risk operation is the incentive to perform as much work as possible, regardless of the number of parties involved.[579] Thus, it could be suggested that sole risk clauses are more important and useful than non-consent clauses. If there is a strong and dominant party in the JOA, which can control the OpCom, and several small parties with little influence, it could be argued that the acceptance of a sole risk operation is the middle way between the parties' interests (ie, joint operations and non-consent).[580]

On the other hand, it is also possible to argue that the execution of a sole risk operation may create even more discord between the parties as it can result in some of the parties operating under their own segregated JOA.[581] In order fully to understand and to answer the fundamental question about the extension where sole risk and non-consent clauses effect the existence of their own JOA, it is necessary to analyse the application and distinctions between them.[582]

First, it is important to stress that sole risk or non-consent operations should be truly balanced provisions, as all parties could use such provisions (both international and national oil companies). However, the traditional dominant position of the operator suggests that these clauses must have rigid terms so as not to encourage the non-operators to avoid the joint operations. In other words, in a general sense, the operator would encourage the existence of sole risk operations, but not non-consent clauses.

A sole risk operation is more likely to occur than a non-consent operation.[583] There are several reasons for this. First, the sole risk operation aims to provide

---

576 C Golvala, "Upstream joint ventures – bidding and operating agreements" in G Picton-Tubervill (ed.), *Oil and Gas: A Practical Handbook*, Globe Law and Business, 2009, p49.

577 T Daintith and G Willoughby (eds), *Adrian Hill, United Kingdom Oil and Gas Law*, 3rd edn, Sweet & Maxwell, 2009, pp1151–1153.

578 "Thankfully, in practice, sole risk is used more as a threat to bring other parties along in support of a proposal, than it is a means of alternative operations." S Shaw, "Joint Operating Agreements" in MR David, *Upstream Oil and Gas Agreements*, Sweet & Maxwell, 1996, p24.

579 *Ibid*, p23.

580 MPG Taylor and SM Tyne, *Taylor and Winsor on Joint Operating Agreements*, 2nd edn, Longman, 1992, pp48–49.

581 T Daintith and G Willoughby (eds), *Adrian Hill, United Kingdom Oil and Gas Law*, 3rd edn, Sweet & Maxwell, 2009, p1152.

582 "As mirror images of each other, these provisions can be complex and, because they run contrary to the basic premise of the joint operating agreement, the consequences of non-consent or sole risk need to be set out in detail." C Golvala, "Upstream joint ventures – bidding and operating agreements" in G Picton-Tubervill (ed.), *Oil and Gas: A Practical Handbook*, Globe Law and Business, 2009, p48.

583 See: J Wilkinson, *Introduction to Oil and Gas Joint Ventures*, OPL, 1997, pp42–43; S Styles, "Joint Operating Agreements" in G Gordon and J Paterson (eds), *Oil and Gas Law: Current Practice and Emerging Trends*, Dundee University Press, 2007, pp288–289; H Dundas, *Joint Operating Agreements: An Introduction*, 1994 Summer Programme: UK Oil and Gas Law, CPMLP 09/09, 1994, p10; B Manning, "Some Practical Aspects of Resources Joint Ventures" in WD Duncan, *Joint Ventures Law in Australia*, 2nd edn, The Federation Press, 2005, pp323–324.

additional work, which could benefit all parties if the late-joining rights are fully exercised.[584] A non-consent clause can be seen as creating additional risk for the JOA parties, in so far as it allows a party to opt out of an operation with the result that the remaining parties bear an increased share of the cost, risk and liability in it.[585] Drafters should consider disapplying the right of non-consent to key decisions such as project development so that a non-consent decision does not cause the other parties to reconsider their position.[586] By contrast, the sole risk provision enables one or more parties to pursue options which the joint venture has decided not to pursue,[587] and therefore allows for additional work to be done notwithstanding the lack of consensus on the OpCom.[588] As we discussed below, the disadvantage with the sole risk provision is that it enables operations to proceed that may ultimately conflict with current or future joint operations.[589]

The more common use of sole risk clauses has led to some standard terms and provisions,[590] but there are few standard terms for the less frequently used non-consent clauses and, on some occasions, the draftsmen may have no model clauses to guide them.[591] Thus,[592] the non-consent clause is more likely to vary according to the specific agreement.[593]

All the above reasons explain why the non-consent operation is not well-developed in the oil and gas industry, but probably the most important reason is the benefit such a provision provides in protecting the minority and most likely the financially weaker party.[594]

However, current JOAs are based on the operator retaining a dominant position, so it is very unlikely that such provisions will become the rule. Sole risk operations deal with greater risks, but also greater rewards which clearly is a situation that a stronger party can accept more easily than smaller parties.[595] Nevertheless, if the consortium includes several strong parties, they may negotiate changes to the main provisions of the model agreement and adopt their own version, as the current standard JOA forms are not balanced.

On the other hand, sole risk clauses tend to benefit the strongest party of the consortium as they aim to enable parties to perform as much work as possible.[596]

---

584 C Penman, "Sole Risk Operations in Petroleum Joint Ventures" [1986] *AMPLA Yearbook*.

585 B Manning, "Some Practical Aspects of Resources Joint Ventures" in WD Duncan, *Joint Ventures Law in Australia*, 2nd edn, Federation Press, 2005, pp323–324.

586 J Wilkinson, *Introduction to Oil and Gas Joint Ventures*, OPL, 1997, p42.

587 S Shaw, "Joint Operating Agreements" in MR David, *Upstream Oil and Gas Agreements*, Sweet & Maxwell, 1996, p23.

588 T Daintith, "Right to Explore for and Exploit Petroleum: The Licence" in T Daintith and G Willoughby (eds), *Adrian Hill, United Kingdom Oil and Gas Law*, 3rd edn, Sweet & Maxwell, 2009, p1152.

589 P Roberts and R Fowler, *Joint Operating Agreements: A Practical Guide*, 4th edn, Globe Law and Business, 2020, p233.

590 S Shaw, "Joint Operating Agreements" in MR David, *Upstream Oil and Gas Agreements*, Sweet & Maxwell, 1996, pp22–23.

591 MPG Taylor and SM Tyne, *Taylor and Winsor on Joint Operating Agreements*, 2nd edn, London, 1992, pp49–50.

592 GMD Bean, *Fiduciary Obligations and Joint Ventures: The Collaborative Fiduciary Relationship*, Oxford University Press, 1995, p18.

593 *Ibid.*

594 V Gayrner, "Sole Risk and Non-Consent under UK Joint Operating Agreements", 1994 Summer Programme: UK Oil and Gas Law, CPMLP 09/09, 1994, pp7–8.

595 KR Saville, "Comment on Sole Risk in Mining and Petroleum Ventures" [1986] *AMPLA Yearbook*.

596 *Ibid.*

Thus, it is clear that the scope of sole risk is to allow not only different interests to coexist within the same enterprise,[597] but also, and most of all, to produce as much work as possible in the licensed area and to encourage parties to stay together as a group.[598]

However, it could be argued that a strong party may resist not only a non-consent clause, but also a sole risk provision as it would itself be the *de facto* majority of the consortium.[599]

If a party has total control of the OpCom, it will not need a sole risk clause as it will be able to achieve approval any operation by its own vote. However, this is unusual and more often the dominant party will need the support of some of the other parties. In this case, the sole risk clause is a useful provision for the dominant party as it may persuade the remaining parties to join an exclusive operation that has not been approved as a joint operation. The sole risk provision may also benefit a smaller participant that has been unable to get its proposal approved in the OpCom.

Although common practice is to allow the inclusion of sole risk provisions but not of non-consent provisions, for various reasons (as previously described) it is not correct to say that only non-consent provisions are an exception to passmark approval as this is exactly the same situation with sole risk provisions. Both clauses contradict the concept of passmark voting as one allows operations to progress where the parties do not achieve the minimum requirement and the other allows a party to opt out of the passmark determination.[600]

Additionally, it is important to note that a sole risk provision could favour a party that has an under-used drilling rig on long-term contract which the joint venture does not wish to use, or if the project was not approved on technical grounds.[601]

However, the non-consenting parties could decide to reject such an operation based on the high cost of the drilling. In this case, a non-consenting party has to face a difficult sole risk dilemma, if such a project is proposed under a sole risk notice, given the significant cost of re-entering the project if it proves to be successful. It could equally turn out to be an expensive and unsuccessful venture.[602]

There is no doubt about the complexity of this situation, as the views of the consenting and non-consenting parties will often diverge. It seems unfair to forbid such a sole risk operation even if it sounds too expensive, as the sole risk parties will bear all the costs involved. The control of expenditure is vital in a consortium, but only for the participants in the operation. In a situation like this, a stronger party might even overestimate the costs deliberately to discourage the remaining parties from participating – but it will also suffer the consequences.

One drawback of the voting procedure in the OpCom is that most of the time no provision is made for deadlock resolution. However, the explanation for this approach is that the JOA is structured such that the sole risk and non-consent clauses act as a means of deadlock resolution.[603] Thus, if a party cannot control the OpCom

---

597 J Wilkinson, *Introduction to Oil and Gas Joint Ventures*, OPL, 1997, p42.

598 GMD Bean, *Fiduciary Obligations and Joint Ventures: The Collaborative Fiduciary Relationship*, Oxford University Press, 1995, p18.

599 KR Saville, "Comment on Sole Risk in Mining and Petroleum Ventures" [1986] *AMPLA Yearbook*.

600 MPG Taylor and SM Tyne, *Taylor and Winsor on Joint Operating Agreements*, 2nd edn, Longman, 1992, pp48–49.

601 *Ibid*, p58.

602 *Ibid*.

603 H Dundas, *Joint Operating Agreements: An Introduction*, 1994 Summer Programme: UK Oil and Gas Law, CPMLP 09/09, 1994, p10.

decisions, it can still manage to proceed with an exclusive operation or opt out of a joint operation.[604]

Some of the problems related to deadlocks in the OpCom may be avoided if both clauses are drafted into the JOA.[605] However, not all authors recognise this function of exclusive operations, especially with the non-consent clause as here the majority will have already approved a decision and so there is no deadlock to be resolved.[606] It is true that in many cases there is no deadlock, only a conflict with the wishes of a party. Nevertheless, it is impossible to deny the deadlock resolution function of sole risk operations if the passmark is not obtained (ie, if they are unable to agree with a specific activity) but they might be still allowed to proceed with such a particular operation.[607] However, it will not resolve the issue if such clauses do not apply to the particular decision or project at hand.

The exclusive operation clause could be very important for an international oil company if the consortium includes a national oil company. If for some reason it does not agree with a particular decision, it could continue the work as an exclusive project. In this case, the national company may limit the scope of the exclusive operations in the JOA negotiations to protect national interests. The existence of a carried interest could mitigate the use of an exclusive operation as the costs will be covered by the international company and sometimes the national oil company is not required to repay to the international oil company the costs previously carried when the carry period comes to an end, for example in Morocco.[608] The non-consent provision is less likely to be a concern as both the international and the national oil companies should have some control of the decision-making process in the consortium.

A very controversial issue for any JOA negotiation is the definition of the type of operations that may be undertaken as sole risk and non-consent operations. A simple clause may allow any operation to be conducted as a sole risk or to be opted out of by non-consent unless it interferes with the joint operations.[609, 610]

JOAs often prohibit the use of these clauses before the completion of the minimum work obligations (even though some exceptions could be implemented),[611] decommissioning obligations[612] (ie, it is forbidden to use such provisions before the completion of any mandatory licence obligation[613]), and during emergency situations, since failure in any of these cases could jeopardise the existence of the whole consortium.[614] In emergency situations, work programmes and budgets and authorisations for expenditure are not required as the situation must be addressed urgently.

---

604 S Shaw, "Joint Operating Agreements" in MR David, *Upstream Oil and Gas Agreements*, Sweet & Maxwell, 1996, p22.

605 T Daintith and G Willoughby (eds), *Adrian Hill, United Kingdom Oil and Gas Law*, 3rd edn, Sweet & Maxwell, 2009, p1150.

606 C Penman, "Sole Risk Operations in Petroleum Joint Ventures" [1986] *AMPLA Yearbook*.

607 JH Waite, "Sole Risk in Mining and Petroleum Ventures: The Australian Position" [1986] *AMPLA Yearbook*.

608 See: www.onhym.com/en/conventional-petroleum/partnership-and-cooperation-2.html.

609 P Roberts and R Fowler, *Joint Operating Agreements: A Practical Guide*, 4th edn, Globe Law and Business, 2020, pp233–235.

610 BG Taverne, *An Introduction to the Regulation of the Petroleum Industry: Law, Contracts and Conventions*, Graham & Trotman, 1994, p137.

611 C Duval, H Le Leuch, A Pertuzio and JL Weaver, *International Petroleum and Exploration Agreements: Legal, Economic & Policy Aspects*, 2nd edn, Barrows, 2009, p295.

612 BG Taverne, *Co-operative Agreements in the Extractive Petroleum Industry*, Kluwer Law International, 1996, p70.

613 C Golvala, "Upstream joint ventures – bidding and operating agreements" in G Picton-Tubervill (ed.), *Oil and Gas: A Practical Handbook*, Globe Law and Business, 2009, p49.

614 V Gayrner, "Sole Risk and Non-Consent under UK Joint Operating Agreements", 1994 Summer Programme: UK Oil and Gas Law, CPMLP 09/09, 1994, p1.

However, some authors believe that non-consent options should be allowed at any time, including for compulsory obligations imposed by the licence or regulations, such as work obligations and decommissioning. Their main argument is based on the free will of the parties whether to participate in the operations.[615]

It is possible to accept the argument in favour of sole risk operations regarding minimum work obligations as which party carries out the operations is irrelevant,[616] but the argument should not apply to the non-consent provision:[617] every party knew the precise terms and conditions of the licence when the consortium was established, so it would not be reasonable to allow a party to avoid any commitment necessary to maintain the existence of the petroleum title.[618]

The exclusive operations terms will commonly state that joint operations will take priority over exclusive operations.[619] This priority often extends to the first sole risk operations, so later sole risk operations will not interfere with previous sole risk operations.[620]

However, the definition of what constitutes interference with the joint operations is quite controversial.[621] In addition, the extension of such an application is controversial.[622] The controversy is understandable: as on the one hand, the participating parties will wish to use the joint property as much as possible (ie, to minimise their costs) and the non-participating parties will wish to avoid the use of the joint property as much as possible (ie, to reduce their risks).[623]

The use of the joint property for the exploration of a well should be less controversial,[624] but other stages may be more difficult, as they will depend not only on the goodwill of the non-consenting parties but also on the capacity of the current infrastructure being used for existing operations. Nevertheless, restrictions will be imposed on any sole risk operation in order to preserve the joint operations. A practical example of such a restriction is the obligation not to drill any well within a specified distance from a well drilled in a joint operation; this is commonly accepted by the parties,[625] but there may also be further relevant regulations under applicable law.[626]

Conversely, Bill Manning raises the interesting question of whether, when the non-participating parties take some benefit from the exclusive operation, should they pay something back to the participating parties?[627]

---

615 KR Saville, "Comment on Sole Risk in Mining and Petroleum Ventures" [1986] *AMPLA Yearbook*.

616 JH Waite, "Sole Risk in Mining and Petroleum Ventures: The Australian Position" [1986] *AMPLA Yearbook*.

617 *Ibid*.

618 P Roberts and R Fowler, *Joint Operating Agreements: A Practical Guide*, 4th edn, Globe Law and Business, 2020, p221.

619 C Golvala, "Upstream joint ventures – bidding and operating agreements" in G Picton-Tubervill (ed.), *Oil and Gas: A Practical Handbook*, Globe Law and Business, 2009, p49.

620 B Manning, "Some Practical Aspects of Resources Joint Ventures" in WD Duncan, *Joint Ventures Law in Australia*, 2nd edn, Federation Press, 2005, pp323–324.

621 T Daintith and G Willoughby (eds), *Adrian Hill, United Kingdom Oil and Gas Law*, 3rd edn, Sweet & Maxwell, 2009, p1152.

622 P Roberts and R Fowler, *Joint Operating Agreements: A Practical Guide*, 4th edn, Globe Law and Business, 2020, p228.

623 KC Mildwaters, *Joint Operating Agreements, A Consideration of Legal Aspects Relevant to Joint Operating Agreements used in Great Britain and Australia by Participants thereto to Regulate the Joint Undertaking of Exploration for Petroleum in Offshore Areas with Particular Reference to their Rights and Duties*, PhD Thesis presented to the University of Dundee, 1990, pp211–212.

624 MPG Taylor and SM Tyne, *Taylor and Winsor on Joint Operating Agreements*, 2nd edn, Longman, 1992, p58.

625 C Penman, "Sole Risk Operations in Petroleum Joint Ventures" [1986] *AMPLA Yearbook*.

626 UK Model clauses 19 and 20 of the Petroleum Licensing (Production) (Seaward Areas) Regulations 2008.

627 B Manning, "Some Practical Aspects of Resources Joint Ventures" in WD Duncan, *Joint Ventures Law in Australia*, 2nd edn, Federation Press, 2005, pp323–324.

Although it would be fair to evaluate such benefits in order to compensate the sole riskers, the process of evaluation and compensation seems complex.

It is important to provide that the approval of the OpCom should not be unreasonably withheld,[628] and that any applicable fees should be fair and balanced.[629]

However, the determination of such fees may create more conflicts. The consenting parties will wish to charge market prices, while the non-consenting parties will wish to pay only for the applicable costs. The consenting or non-consenting parties might wish to charge or pay for the market price or costs as the case might be convenient for them.[630]

It is commonly accepted that any party may exercise the non-consent or sole risk clauses regardless of their participating interest.[631] For example, a party could retain a 1% participating interest and still have the right to use such clauses.[632] In practice, the licence regime, rather than the JOA, may introduce restrictions regarding minimum percentages, as some jurisdictions do not allow parties with less than a certain percentage. On the other hand, the dominant parties may not welcome such provisions as the likelihood of a party initiating a sole risk operation would become very high with more minority stakeholders.[633]

Provided the security of the joint operations and the consortium is not affected,[634] at any stage of the project the parties may exercise the right of non-consent or undertake a sole risk operation. However, in practice there are other situations that may encourage additional restrictions on the use of sole risk and non-consent clauses, so the clauses may be extremely complex if they are fully structured in a balanced form.[635]

As a general rule,[636] there is little doubt about the possibility of allowing sole risk or non-consent clauses for exploratory wells or even appraisal work,[637] but the possibility of using the clauses for development work is more contentious.[638] In fact, a sole risk operation is more likely to occur in the exploration phase and a non-consent operation in the development phase,[639] but this could change in specific circumstances.[640]

---

628 KC Mildwaters, *Joint Operating Agreements, A Consideration of Legal Aspects Relevant to Joint Operating Agreements used in Great Britain and Australia by Participants thereto to Regulate the Joint Undertaking of Exploration for Petroleum in Offshore Areas with Particular Reference to their Rights and Duties*, PhD Thesis presented to the University of Dundee, 1990, pp211–212.

629 MPG Taylor and SM Tyne, *Taylor and Winsor on Joint Operating Agreements*, 2nd edn, Longman, 1992, p58.

630 *Ibid.*

631 *Ibid.*

632 V Gayrner, "Sole Risk and Non-Consent under UK Joint Operating Agreements", 1994 Summer Programme: UK Oil and Gas Law, CPMLP 09/09, 1994, p1.

633 MPG Taylor and SM Tyne, *Taylor and Winsor on Joint Operating Agreements*, 2nd edn, Longman, 1992, p58.

634 JS Dzienkowski, EE Smith, OL Anderson, JS Lowe, BM Kramer and JL Weaver, *Materials on International Petroleum Transactions*, 3rd edn, RMMLF, 2010, p605.

635 T Daintith and G Willoughby (eds), *Adrian Hill, United Kingdom Oil and Gas Law*, 3rd edn, Sweet & Maxwell, 2009, p1152.

636 P Roberts and R Fowler, *Joint Operating Agreements: A Practical Guide*, 4th edn, Globe Law and Business, 2020, p221.

637 J Wilkinson, *Introduction to Oil and Gas Joint Ventures*, OPL, 1997, p43.

638 C Golvala, "Upstream joint ventures – bidding and operating agreements" in G Picton-Tubervill (ed.), *Oil and Gas: A Practical Handbook*, Globe Law and Business, 2009, p49.

639 KC Mildwaters, *Joint Operating Agreements, A Consideration of Legal Aspects Relevant to Joint Operating Agreements used in Great Britain and Australia by Participants thereto to Regulate the Joint Undertaking of Exploration for Petroleum in Offshore Areas with Particular Reference to their Rights and Duties*, PhD Thesis presented to the University of Dundee, 1990, p174.

640 KR Saville, "Comment on Sole Risk in Mining and Petroleum Ventures" [1986] *AMPLA Yearbook*.

A sole risk seismic operation could be important at any stage of the project, but especially at an early stage.[641] Sole risk seismic may be very useful if the licence involves a large acreage as it would increase the overall understanding of the licensed area, and this may increase the amount of work to be performed.[642]

If sole risk seismic is permitted, this may raise questions about whether there should be a premium involved for purchase of the results by non-participants[643] and controversial issues about the right of access to such data.[644] The easiest solution is to forbid sole risk operations involving seismic work.[645] However, this may not be the best solution as results from the seismic operation could be important in encouraging the parties' decision whether to proceed with further exclusive operations.[646]

In practice, the JOA must find a balance between the participating and non-participating parties, especially on access to data.[647] The non-participating parties will want access to any information from seismic data obtained as part of a sole risk operation.[648] They may need further information before making a decision on whether to join subsequent sole risk operations in the same acreage.[649] Of course, these parties will wish to obtain such information on the sole risk seismic free of charge.

The non-participating parties will argue that it is in the interest of the participating parties to share the information from the sole risk operations so the remaining parties can take a view on, and potentially join, subsequent operations, which will benefit all participating parties. The non-participating parties will share the costs and risks again and the participating parties will receive some compensation for their sole risks.[650]

By the same token, the non-consenting parties will wish to apply equitable terms to the sole riskers' right to use information derived from joint operations.[651] By contrast, the non-consenting parties will insist that the JOA principle is applied, whereby the operator provides them with current operational reports, including data information. However, in the case of exclusive operations, the situation is quite different: it is not a joint operation as the parties are not following the basic principle of sharing the costs and risks.

Alternatively, the non-consenting parties may take another, less radical approach such that the participating parties would retain the property in the sole

---

641 T Daintith, "Right to Explore for and Exploit Petroleum: The Licence" in T Daintith and G Willoughby (eds), *Adrian Hill, United Kingdom Oil and Gas Law*, 3rd edn, Sweet & Maxwell, 2009, p1152.

642 JH Waite, "Sole Risk in Mining and Petroleum Ventures: The Australian Position" [1986] *AMPLA Yearbook*.

643 KR Saville, "Comment on Sole Risk in Mining and Petroleum Ventures" [1986] *AMPLA Yearbook*.

644 B Manning, "Some Practical Aspects of Resources Joint Ventures" in WD Duncan, *Joint Ventures Law in Australia*, 2nd edn, Federation Press, 2005, pp323–324.

645 BG Taverne, *Co-operative Agreements in the Extractive Petroleum Industry*, Kluwer Law International, 1996, p70.

646 V Gayrner, "Sole Risk and Non-Consent under UK Joint Operating Agreements", 1994 Summer Programme: UK Oil and Gas Law, CPMLP 09/09, 1994, p1.

647 KR Saville, "Comment on Sole Risk in Mining and Petroleum Ventures" [1986] *AMPLA Yearbook*.

648 P Roberts and R Fowler, *Joint Operating Agreements: A Practical Guide*, 4th edn, Globe Law and Business, 2020, p225.

649 KC Mildwaters, *Joint Operating Agreements, A Consideration of Legal Aspects Relevant to Joint Operating Agreements used in Great Britain and Australia by Participants thereto to Regulate the Joint Undertaking of Exploration for Petroleum in Offshore Areas with Particular Reference to their Rights and Duties*, PhD Thesis presented to the University of Dundee, 1990, pp174–175.

650 P Roberts and R Fowler, *Joint Operating Agreements: A Practical Guide*, 4th edn, Globe Law and Business, 2020, pp225–226.

651 MPG Taylor and SM Tyne, *Taylor and Winsor on Joint Operating Agreements*, 2nd edn, Longman, London, 1992, p58.

risk information but non-consenting parties would retain a right of access to that information – that is, they would expect to be permitted to consult such information at the sole risker's office even if they are not allowed to take copies of it.[652] The argument for this approach is grounded in the same basic principle that obliges the operator to provide information to the non-operators and how such an operation might affect the joint operations or even to decide if they wish to rejoin such an exclusive operation.[653]

Regardless of the approach taken by the non-consenting parties (ie, conservative or moderate), the key element is the right of access to information, free of costs and charges.[654] In the worst case scenario, the non-participating parties would be willing to pay the costs involved, but no premium until they decide to join the exclusive operation.[655] However, the acknowledgement of the participating parties' proprietary rights would lead to an acceptance that the participating parties could trade the sole risk data, without sharing such benefits, as the ownership of the data rests with the consenting parties.[656] There are no major concerns if the non-consenting parties do not exercise their right to buy-back, but if they do so, the question of their share from such trade, if they join the exclusive operations later on, will be raised.[657] It is unreasonable to claim benefits from a time when the party was not a member of the operation, nor the owner of the data.

It is possible to argue that it is not reasonable to grant free access to any data obtained from a sole risk operation, as this would not recognise one principle of the sole risk clause, which is to secure benefits for the risk taker.[658]

In many cases, the sole risk data will be the determining factor in the decision whether to continue as a sole risk operation, so it will be valuable information that could save a very large amount of expenditure.[659] Clearly, the right of the non-consenting parties to have access to sole risk information is very important.[660]

However, the question is not about the right of access, but only how to exercise this right, as it must involve some compensation. It is not reasonable to allow the non-sole risk party to access such valuable information free of costs. On the other hand, the agreement must not impose high penalties as access to information is crucial to enabling the party to make a final decision on whether to join the sole risk operation. Thus, it is reasonable to charge the costs involved and a fee of, say, the same amount as the costs, which would recognise the importance of the work

652 *Ibid*, p67.

653 KC Mildwaters, *Joint Operating Agreements, A Consideration of Legal Aspects Relevant to Joint Operating Agreements used in Great Britain and Australia by Participants thereto to Regulate the Joint Undertaking of Exploration for Petroleum in Offshore Areas with Particular Reference to their Rights and Duties*, PhD Thesis presented to the University of Dundee, 1990, pp211–212.

654 KR Saville, "Comment on Sole Risk in Mining and Petroleum Ventures" [1986] *AMPLA Yearbook*.

655 P Roberts and R Fowler, *Joint Operating Agreements: A Practical Guide*, 4th edn, Globe Law and Business, 2020, pp225–226.

656 MPG Taylor and SM Tyne, *Taylor and Winsor on Joint Operating Agreements*, 2nd edn, Longman, 1992, pp63–64.

657 *Ibid*, p67.

658 *Ibid*.

659 KC Mildwaters, *Joint Operating Agreements, A Consideration of Legal Aspects Relevant to Joint Operating Agreements used in Great Britain and Australia by Participants thereto to Regulate the Joint Undertaking of Exploration for Petroleum in Offshore Areas with Particular Reference to their Rights and Duties*, PhD Thesis presented to the University of Dundee, 1990, pp211–212.

660 MPG Taylor and SM Tyne, *Taylor and Winsor on Joint Operating Agreements*, 2nd edn, Longman, 1992.

without creating prohibitive conditions to allow a non-consenting party to take an informed decision about the sole risk operation. Nevertheless, if such a sole risk operation reaches development, the premium should be slightly higher.

On the other hand, the sole risk parties could argue that since they took all the risks and costs involved in the seismic work, they should also own the data,[661] and that the non-participating parties should not enjoy the benefits of the sole risk operation, which would include the access to any data obtained.[662] A fair balance would be to allow restricted[663] access to the data and secure a reasonable benefit to the sole risk parties if the seismic work results in a successful operation.[664] But if the operation is not successful, or even if the non-participating parties decide not to join the sole risk parties after analysing the seismic data, is it fair for them to have free access? This contradicts the basic principle of the existence of the sole risk operation as the risk takers are gaining no extra benefit from the results of the operation. In this sense, it is reasonable to determine some compensation for their costs. The sole risk parties are saving the non-consenting parties a lot of expense as they would have to pay a premium and also share the costs if they continued such an exclusive operation, so it is reasonable to recognise the fact by some measure of compensation.

In practice, the proposing party or parties must issue a notice to the other parties so they can decide whether to join the operations. The financial implications will be considered further, but clearly the key issue at this point relates to the information provided about the sole risk project proposed. Should the proposing parties provide all the information attached to the sole risk operations (if available)? If so, should the proposing parties also provide a cost estimate? Or should the matter of costs be raised only if any non-consenting parties decide to join later on? As previously mentioned, a balance must be struck between the proposing parties' freedom to proceed and the right of the remaining parties to receive adequate information on which to make a good judgement about the exclusive operation.

Therefore, the sole risk notice should provide detailed information. Needless to say, such a notice is very important and the non-participating parties will analyse it carefully as it may have major financial consequences for them.[665]

Possibly there should be some restrictions on sole risk operations at the development stage as it is a later stage of the project.[666] The limited grounds where a sole risk or non-consent operation can take place at the development stage leads some authors to consider that sole risk clauses concerning such a phase should be simple rather than complex.[667] In practice, this will be unlikely because some sole risk developments are likely to lead to the need to subdivide the contract area applicable to the concession, and to establish separate OpComs, if not separate JOAs, to govern the relations of the sole risk parties responsible for those sub-areas. On the other hand, some JOAs may provide that no party can be forced to take part in the development stage.[668] The main reason for such flexibility is the requirement for firm

---

661 C Penman, "Sole Risk Operations in Petroleum Joint Ventures" [1986] *AMPLA Yearbook*.

662 V Gayrner, "Sole Risk and Non-Consent under UK Joint Operating Agreements" (1994 Summer Programme: UK Oil and Gas Law, CPMLP 09/09, 1994) 4.

663 *Ibid.*

664 C Penman, "Sole Risk Operations in Petroleum Joint Ventures" [1986] *AMPLA Yearbook*.

665 C Penman, "Sole Risk Operations in Petroleum Joint Ventures" [1986] *AMPLA Yearbook*.

666 *Ibid.*

667 *Ibid.*

668 *Ibid.*

commitments to cover the costs related to the development instead of waiting for the unwilling party to trigger a default later in the operation.[669] In other words, the higher costs mean a party is allowed to decide whether it still wishes to take part in the operation.[670]

The high costs may not be the only reason for allowing such a right. The host government must approve the development plan. Since the plan involves maximising production from the reservoir, it will be very important from a governmental perspective as production is a major source of income for the government. So it could be argued that the government will be keen to confirm that all parties are committed to developing the field; it may have some concerns if one party is not.[671]

On the other hand, the opposite could be argued. The development stage is very costly, so all parties must contribute otherwise it may be impossible to perform such an operation; the reason why the parties decided to form a consortium was to minimise the risks and costs involved in the industry.[672]

According to this line of argument, no non-consent right should apply to the project's development stage, as it could require a major financial investment.[673]

Thus, there is no straightforward answer to the application of non-consent provisions during the development stage, as it will vary according to the nature, philosophy and financial resources of the parties involved in the consortium. However, it is reasonable to accept non-consent provisions at this stage because it is not logical to force a party to participate in something with which it does not agree as, ultimately, this may lead to default.

Another complex issue involving the development stages is whether the sole risk parties are obliged to proceed with their sole risk operations having proposed it. Can the non-consenting parties compel the sole risk parties to proceed with their exclusive operations, even when, for whatever reason, they do not wish to continue?[674]

This would be a draconian measure as no one could enforce such a provision, unless it is decided by the governmental petroleum regime. If the parties establish that development is not economically viable, it may even be possible to change the work obligations with the consent of the governmental authorities. In this sense, it would be unreasonable to provide the non-consenting parties with a right to compel the development of the exclusive operation, as they are not party to the operations.

However, it is not reasonable to accept that the sole risk parties could stop a development operation and remain with exclusive rights over the area. It would be more reasonable to establish a time limit during which, if the operations stop for any reason, the sub-area created by the exclusive operation would fall back to the general area owned by all parties.[675]

Another critical question is the time at which parties are allowed to exercise a sole risk or non-consent right.[676] A more practical question would be, when can a non-consent or sole risk operation be proposed? Is it at the work programme and budget

---

669 *Ibid.*
670 MPG Taylor and SM Tyne, *Taylor and Winsor on Joint Operating Agreements*, 2nd edn, Longman, 1992, p72.
671 *Ibid.*
672 JH Waite, "Sole Risk in Mining and Petroleum Ventures: The Australian Position" [1986] *AMPLA Yearbook.*
673 *Ibid.*
674 MPG Taylor and SM Tyne, *Taylor and Winsor on Joint Operating Agreements*, 2nd edn, Longman, 1992, p72.
675 *Ibid.*
676 *Ibid*, pp49–50.

stage, or later on during the authorisation for expenditure procedures? In order to answer such questions, it is important to remember the debate about the levels of information provided in the work programme and budget and the authorisation for expenditure.[677] As previously mentioned, if the work programme and budget does not provide enough information, it will be very difficult for the non-operators to formulate a sole risk proposal or reach a satisfactory decision.

A lack of information in the work programme and budget could lead a financially weaker party to exercise its non-consent right too early as it may prefer to opt out rather than take unforeseeable risks.[678]

Another problem involving the work programme and budget is the right to amend it. Should the parties have a right of non-consent to an amended work programme and budget?[679]

One solution could be to modify the timing to move the application of a non-consent or sole risk operation from the work programme and budget to the authorisation for expenditure procedure; authorisations for expenditure are routinely presented to the OpCom when the relevant project and expenditure is better understood and more specifically described.[680]

The authorisation for expenditure link may be a complicating factor, as the consenting parties could exercise the right of non-consent or sole risk when the operator seeks approval to amend an approved authorisation for expenditure to allow the approved expenditure to be exceeded.[681] In other words, if the operator overspends the authorisation for expenditure, could the parties exercise the right to non-consent to such an operation or could the operator continue as a sole risker? There is no one reasonable approach as it will vary according to the situation; for example, the difference may be minor or substantial. However, the most complex situation may occur with a JOA that provides for work programme and budgets and authorisation for expenditures. If all the parties approved the work programme and budget, a later rejection of the authorisation for expenditure may create an obstacle for the parties that were expecting the performance of such activities.[682]

On the other hand, the remaining parties could argue that they should not be forced into an operation which they are not keen to develop, or to continue an increasingly expensive operation, as it may eventually lead to a default.[683] An intermediate solution would be to limit the exercise of the non-consent or sole risk to within a certain time after the approval of the work programme and budget.[684]

However, this would not solve the problem since commonly a work programme and budget does not provide enough detail, so the efficacy of such a provision will depend on the level of the information regardless of the timing.[685] Peter Roberts recognises this when he states that since usually the work programme and budget is a rough prediction, the authorisation for expenditure is more suitable for such a proposal.[686]

---

677 *Ibid*, pp55–56.
678 *Ibid*.
679 *Ibid*, pp56–57.
680 *Ibid*, pp55–56.
681 *Ibid*.
682 *Ibid*.
683 *Ibid*.
684 *Ibid*.
685 *Ibid*.
686 P Roberts and R Fowler, *Joint Operating Agreements: A Practical Guide*, 4th edn, Globe Law and Business, 2020, p217.

As previously mentioned, the party proposing a sole risk operation must notify the remaining parties so that they can decide whether to participate in the operation.[687] The sole riskers must provide enough detail on the proposed operation to allow the other parties to take an informed decision.[688]

The notice must be carefully drafted in order to avoid later problems with the validity of the exclusive operations – that is, it is important to comply with formal obligations in order to secure the validity of the operation.[689]

In principle, only the participating parties will benefit from such operations.[690] However, the non-participating parties are not completely excluded as they can decide to join the operations at a later stage, provided that a premium is paid.[691] The conditions under which non-participating (either from a sole risk or even a non-consent operation[692]) parties may buy-back their rights into the exclusive operations is another highly debated issue.

First, the non-participating parties must pay all the costs that they would have had to contribute if they had joined the exclusive operation in the first place.[693] Secondly, they must pay a premium, commonly referred as a 'penalty',[694] to the risk takers for bearing all the costs and risks by themselves.[695] However, 'penalty' is not the best term for such a provision as this payment is not related to a breach of a contract[696] but rather is a premium to the other parties, as will be discussed below. The controversial issue involves the second payment as commonly it is set at a high rate to discourage parties from opting out of the operations.[697]

The level of such premium can vary from 100% to 2,000% of the original costs of the operations.[698] The amount is negotiable but should be set out in the final JOAs so that it is not a matter for dispute when the first sole risk project is considered under the JOA.

Sole risk clauses are more common than non-consent clauses and there is a sense that the latter may be more sensitive for the consortium as a whole. Some authors suggest that a non-consent buy-back premium should be higher than a sole risk

687 S Shaw, "Joint Operating Agreements" in MR David, *Upstream Oil and Gas Agreements*, Sweet & Maxwell, 1996, pp22–23.

688 DF Moroney, "Sole Risk in Mining and Petroleum Ventures: An International Perspective" in AJ Beal, "Comment on Sole Risk in Mining and Petroleum Ventures: An International Perspective" [1986] *AMPLA Yearbook*.

689 T Daintith, "Right to Explore for and Exploit Petroleum: The Licence" in T Daintith and G Willoughby (eds), *Adrian Hill, United Kingdom Oil and Gas Law*, 3rd edn, Sweet & Maxwell, 2009, p1153.

690 H Dundas, *Joint Operating Agreements: An Introduction*, 1994 Summer Programme: UK Oil and Gas Law, CPMLP 09/09, 1994, p10.

691 C Golvala, "Upstream joint ventures – bidding and operating agreements" in G Picton-Tubervill (ed.), *Oil and Gas: A Practical Handbook*, Globe Law and Business, 2009, p49.

692 *Ibid.*

693 J Wilkinson, *Introduction to Oil and Gas Joint Ventures*, OPL, 1997, p43.

694 MPG Taylor and SM Tyne, *Taylor and Winsor on Joint Operating Agreements*, 2nd edn, Longman, 1992, p48.

695 S Styles, "Joint Operating Agreements" in G Gordon and J Paterson (eds), *Oil and Gas Law: Current Practice and Emerging Trends*, Dundee University Press, 2007, p289.

696 P Roberts and R Fowler, *Joint Operating Agreements: A Practical Guide*, 4th edn, Globe Law and Business, 2020, p232. See also *Bonn Operating Co v Devon Energy Production Co*, a US Court of Appeals decision 613 F.3d 532 (2010), which is discussed in T Martin, J Gilbert and M Gusy, "A Global Review of Joint Operating Agreement Disputes" AIPN research paper 2020, Section 7.4.2.

697 A Jennings, *Oil and Gas Exploration Contracts*, 2nd edn, Sweet & Maxwell, 2008, p25.

698 See: C Thorpe, *Fundamentals of Upstream Petroleum Agreements*, CP Thorpe, 2008, pp134–135; S Shaw, "Joint Operating Agreements" in MR David, *Upstream Oil and Gas Agreements*, Sweet & Maxwell, 1996, pp22–23.

premium.[699] However, this may not be a good idea. Passmark voting is disregarded by both provisions and the effect of both is to disrupt joint operations to the same extent, so it is better to have fair and balanced terms for both provisions.[700] Thus, the premium for a sole risk clause should be the same as for a non-consent clause,[701] and any difference in the "penalties" in each should be based on the level of risks and costs involved instead of the level of support in the OpCom.

It could be argued that as the risks involved get greater, so the costs to a party to buy-back their rights in the operation should be higher,[702] but the costs could also vary according to the stage of the project.[703] If the non-participating parties do not exercise their buy-back right, they will not enjoy any benefit from the exclusive operations.[704] On the other hand, they will not bear any of the costs associated with the exclusive operation.[705] In this case, the participating parties must rearrange their participating interest in the exclusive operation in accordance with their participation and bear an increased proportionate share of the risk and cost.[706]

However, it is impossible to determine fully the rearrangement of costs until all parties have decided whether they will join the sole risk operation.[707] Thus, the sole riskers cannot determine the participating interests in the operation in the sole risk notice since they cannot know which other parties may elect to participate.[708]

The complexity of determining the participating interests may increase over the course of the exclusive operations as some sole risk parties may leave and some may join later.[709]

It is difficult to determine the premium for a seismic operation. However, there is no question that if an exclusive operation is successful, the sole risk parties that carried out the seismic work should receive some measure of compensation.[710]

Thus, it is very difficult to implement a provision that is both balanced and fair. On the one hand, the sole risk and non-consent provisions aim to achieve more work regardless of the number of parties by providing higher rewards for the participating parties, but, on the other, the provisions aim to allow the non-participating parties a contingent right to re-enter. This is one reason why some JOAs do not set the level of the premium, but instead leave the parties to determine it. Nevertheless, there is only one certain criterion for such a 'premium', which is the direct connection between the premium and the level of risks involved.[711]

---

699 B Manning, "Some Practical Aspects of Resources Joint Ventures" in WD Duncan, *Joint Ventures Law in Australia*, 2nd edn, The Federation Press, 2005, pp323–324.

700 KR Saville, "Comment on Sole Risk in Mining and Petroleum Ventures" [1986] *AMPLA Yearbook*.

701 *Ibid.*

702 C Duval, H Le Leuch, A Pertuzio and JL Weaver, *International Petroleum and Exploration Agreements: Legal, Economic & Policy Aspects*, 2nd edn, Barrows, 2009, p296.

703 C Thorpe, *Fundamentals of Upstream Petroleum Agreements*, CP Thorpe, 2008, pp134–135.

704 S Styles, "Joint Operating Agreements" in G Gordon and J Paterson (eds), *Oil and Gas Law* , p289.

705 *Ibid.*

706 C Duval, H Le Leuch, A Pertuzio and JL Weaver, *International Petroleum and Exploration Agreements: Legal, Economic & Policy Aspects*, 2nd edn, Barrows, 2009, p295.

707 P Roberts and R Fowler, *Joint Operating Agreements: A Practical Guide*, 4th edn, Globe Law and Business, 2020, pp221–223.

708 DF Moroney, "Sole Risk in Mining and Petroleum Ventures: An International Perspective" in AJ Beal, "Comment on Sole Risk in Mining and Petroleum Ventures: An International Perspective" [1986] *AMPLA Yearbook*.

709 MPG Taylor and SM Tyne, *Taylor and Winsor on Joint Operating Agreements*, 2nd edn, Longman, 1992, p75.

710 JH Waite, "Sole Risk in Mining and Petroleum Ventures: The Australian Position" [1986] *AMPLA Yearbook*.

711 *Ibid.*

Payment of the buy-back premium is commonly by cash or in kind,[712] although there are other possibilities, such as dilution, or swap of assets.[713] The choice of option will depend on the financial strength of the parties, regulations, allowances and tax considerations.[714] A cash payment of a premium is likely to be treated as a capital gain by the sole risk parties for capital tax purposes. Indeed, it is essential that the parties agree in the JOA whether the premium is pre- or post-tax. The preferred option may be a combination of forms of premium payment. [715] Commonly, payment out of production is preferred as it reduces the requirement for upfront costs.[716] Some authors argue that the production payment approach is the only viable alternative available for the non-participating parties,[717] due to the difficulty in enforcing an acreage transfer without governmental approval and the high costs of upfront cash.[718] The parties should avoid changing their legal status or transferring legal rights in order to minimise the need for third-party consents (ie, the government); rather they should only change the purely commercial arrangement as far as possible.[719] In other words, a payment in kind is the most practical solution.[720]

Thus, it can be seen that the buy-back is not a penalty but a harsh "carried interest",[721] which increases its rates in accordance with the risk and stage of the project.[722] Conversely, if this provision were considered a penalty it might get relief in court, as intended by the non-operator in *Hamilton v Texas Oil & Gas Corp.*[723] So the main difference between such a carry of interest and a penalty is breach of the contract, which is required for the latter, but does not occur in the former as it is a commercial arrangement.

The buy-back provision is a very complex provision, but it is less complicated if the parties opt out only once and at the first stage of the operation.[724] However, it is important to remember that such a carry will become far more complicated if parties exit during the execution of an exclusive operation.[725] In this case, if a consenting party decides to opt out at a later stage, would it be fair to share, to some extent, the profits, if such an operation turns out to be profitable? As mentioned above,

---

712 T Daintith, "Right to Explore for and Exploit Petroleum: The Licence" in T Daintith and G Willoughby (eds), *Adrian Hill, United Kingdom Oil and Gas Law*, 3rd edn, Sweet & Maxwell, 2009, pp1152–1153.

713 JH Waite, "Sole Risk in Mining and Petroleum Ventures: The Australian Position" [1986] *AMPLA Yearbook*.

714 B Manning, "Some Practical Aspects of Resources Joint Ventures" in WD Duncan, *Joint Ventures Law in Australia*, 2nd edn, The Federation Press, 2005, pp323–324.

715 JH Waite, "Sole Risk in Mining and Petroleum Ventures: The Australian Position" [1986] *AMPLA Yearbook*.

716 V Gayrner, "Sole Risk and Non-Consent under UK Joint Operating Agreements", 1994 Summer Programme: UK Oil and Gas Law, CPMLP 09/09, 1994, p1.

717 KR Saville, "Comment on Sole Risk in Mining and Petroleum Ventures" [1986] *AMPLA Yearbook*.

718 C Penman, "Sole Risk Operations in Petroleum Joint Ventures" [1986] *AMPLA Yearbook*.

719 JH Waite, "Sole Risk in Mining and Petroleum Ventures: The Australian Position" [1986] *AMPLA Yearbook*.

720 *Ibid.*

721 "In essence, the buy-back right is similar to the non-participating party having a hard carried interest with an uplift, in that the non-operating parties are relieved of the costs of participation, but can later become participants upon repaying the forgone costs, with a premium." P Roberts and R Fowler, *Joint Operating Agreements: A Practical Guide*, 4th edn, Globe Law and Business, 2020, p231.

722 C Duval, H Le Leuch, A Pertuzio and JL Weaver, *International Petroleum and Exploration Agreements: Legal, Economic & Policy Aspects*, 2nd edn, Barrows, 2009, p296.

723 648 S.W.2d 316 (Tex. App. 1982). The Texas Appeals court decided that the premium was not a penalty and was an enforceable term of the JOA. B Manning, "Some Practical Aspects of Resources Joint Ventures" in WD Duncan, *Joint Ventures Law in Australia*, 2nd edn, The Federation Press, 2005, pp323–324.

724 C Duval, H Le Leuch, A Pertuzio and JL Weaver, *International Petroleum and Exploration Agreements: Legal, Economic & Policy Aspects*, 2nd edn, Barrows, 2009, p297.

725 BG Taverne, *Co-operative Agreements in the Extractive Petroleum Industry*, Kluwer Law International, 1996, p70.

this issue involves a complicated exercise in rearranging the parties' participating interests in the case of success.

On the other hand, if the buy-back provision is not exercised,[726] inevitably the implementation of an exclusive operation will lead to the segregation of the consortium by the creation of a sub-area inside the licensed area.[727] This segregation may be a very complex issue to determine as the parties will have to agree the extent of the sub-area.[728] The complexity arises because of the different interests: the non-participating parties will wish to limit the sub-area as much as possible while the participating parties' objective will be the opposite.[729]

However, the problems are not exclusively related to the definition of the sub-area,[730] as such a segregation affects the scope of the joint venture. The parties must draft this provision very carefully so that their intentions are clearly secured.[731] It is most important to determine how this sub-area will coexist and deal with the main issues of the JOA, especially regarding relinquishment, liabilities and default.[732]

It is important to stress that a non-participating party will not bear any of the costs or risks of the exclusive operations.[733] The participating parties must indemnify the non-participating parties from any liability related to the exclusive operations.[734] The non-participating parties should check that the exclusive operations provisions secure their position against any liability.[735, 736]

Conversely, it is possible to argue that the non-consenting parties should have some measure of liability regarding the exclusive operations as they may exercise their buy-back right and in any event remain party to the same granting instrument under which the exclusive operation is conducted.[737]

Another important issue that the JOA must determine is the party responsible for the conduct of the exclusive operations. In general, the same party will act as operator for both the consortium and the exclusive operations.[738]

The situation is more complicated if the operator does not participate in a particular operation.[739] On the one hand, the operator (ie, the joint-venture

726 P Roberts and R Fowler, *Joint Operating Agreements: A Practical Guide*, 4th edn, Globe Law and Business, 2020, p227.

727 C Thorpe, *Fundamentals of Upstream Petroleum Agreements*. CP Thorpe, 2008, p137.

728 A Jennings, *Oil and Gas Exploration Contracts*, 2nd edn, Sweet & Maxwell, 2008, p25.

729 V Gayrner, "Sole Risk and Non-Consent under UK Joint Operating Agreements", 1994 Summer Programme: UK Oil and Gas Law, CPMLP 09/09, 1994, p6.

730 "The sole risk area will form a separate area within the JOA/Licence area, which may cause some difficulties in dealing with the asset, both within a group and in relation to third parties." S Shaw, "Joint Operating Agreements" in MR David, *Upstream Oil and Gas Agreements*, Sweet & Maxwell, 1996, pp22–23.

731 GMD Bean, *Fiduciary Obligations and Joint Ventures: The Collaborative Fiduciary Relationship*, Oxford University Press, 1995, pp18–19.

732 B Manning, "Some Practical Aspects of Resources Joint Ventures" in WD Duncan, *Joint Ventures Law in Australia*, 2nd edn, The Federation Press, 2005, pp323–324.

733 A Jennings, *Oil and Gas Exploration Contracts*, 2nd edn, Sweet & Maxwell, 2008, p25.

734 V Gayrner, "Sole Risk and Non-Consent under UK Joint Operating Agreements", 1994 Summer Programme: UK Oil and Gas Law, CPMLP 09/09, 1994, p4.

735 DF Moroney, "Sole Risk in Mining and Petroleum Ventures: An International Perspective" in AJ Beal, "Comment on Sole Risk in Mining and Petroleum Ventures: An International Perspective" [1986] *AMPLA Yearbook*.

736 *Railroad Commission of Texas v Olin Corporation* (690 S.W.2d 628 (Tex.App. – Austin 1985, writ ref'd n.r.e.). is a case where the courts upheld a regulator's right to require a non-consenting party to plug and abandon a well, as the operator was no longer contactable.

737 C Duval, H Le Leuch, A Pertuzio and JL Weaver, *International Petroleum and Exploration Agreements: Legal, Economic & Policy Aspects*, 2nd edn, Barrows, 2009, p297.

738 A Jennings, *Oil and Gas Exploration Contracts*, 2nd edn, Sweet & Maxwell, 2008, p25.

739 V Gayrner, "Sole Risk and Non-Consent under UK Joint Operating Agreements", 1994 Summer Programme: UK Oil and Gas Law, CPMLP 09/09, 1994, p5.

operator) may have the right to decide whether it will act as the operator in a particular exclusive operation, even if the participating parties do not want it to, or the opposite as the consenting parties may force the operator of the consortium to act as the operator for a sole risk project even though it may be a non-consenting party.[740] On the other hand, this provision might be difficult to apply in practice, as the granting instrument may not consider the existence of an exclusive operation.[741]

Commonly, the granting instrument recognises the existence of only one operator,[742] so if the consenting parties decide to choose another party to conduct an exclusive operation, they must obtain governmental approval.[743] If approval is not granted, the operation cannot be performed.[744] In this case, could the participating parties force the joint-venture operator to conduct the operation against its will? If the JOA contains a precise provision allowing the participating parties to force the operator to act in these circumstances it would be possible, but in the absence of such a provision it would be difficult. The operator could argue that if a party can opt out of an operation, why should it be forced to conduct the operation? In this case, the practical solution is for the operator to conduct the operation to the extent it is possible.[745]

The operator might argue that it must refuse to conduct the exclusive operation, as doing so may interfere with and harm the conduct of the joint operations.[746] The participating parties might argue that they have grounds to compel the operator since refusal could jeopardise the operations and, in any event, the JOA requires the exclusive operation to be conducted in a manner which does not prejudice joint operations. Also requiring two different operators to act under the same JOA in the same contract area would over-complicate the operations and be wasteful of resources.[747]

Additionally, even if the granting instrument does not clearly regulate the drilling of exploratory wells (which is uncommon), it is unlikely to provide for the same flexibility for the development phase, as the host government will wish to ensure that the operator exploits the reservoir in the most effective way.[748] In other words, sooner or later the consenting parties will be required to obtain the host government's approval of the operatorship. It is not a straightforward issue, but the argument for compelling the joint-venture operator to conduct as many of the operations as possible seems more reasonable than the others.

On the other hand, in theory, control of the exclusive operations should be a less contentious issue, as the sole risk parties have the right to "make up their

740 H Dundas, *Joint Operating Agreements: An Introduction*, 1994 Summer Programme: UK Oil and Gas Law, CPMLP 09/09, 1994, p10.

741 P Roberts and R Fowler, *Joint Operating Agreements: A Practical Guide*, 4th edn, Globe Law and Business, 2020, p227.

742 See: model clause 24 (1) of the Petroleum Licensing (Production) (Seaward Areas) Regulations 2008.

743 KC Mildwaters, *Joint Operating Agreements, A Consideration of Legal Aspects Relevant to Joint Operating Agreements used in Great Britain and Australia by Participants thereto to Regulate the Joint Undertaking of Exploration for Petroleum in Offshore Areas with Particular Reference to their Rights and Duties*, PhD Thesis presented to the University of Dundee, 1990, p212.

744 C Duval, H Le Leuch, A Pertuzio and JL Weaver, *International Petroleum and Exploration Agreements: Legal, Economic & Policy Aspects*, 2nd edn, Barrows, 2009, pp295–297.

745 MPG Taylor and SM Tyne, *Taylor and Winsor on Joint Operating Agreements*, 2nd edn, Longman, 1992, pp62–63.

746 P Roberts and R Fowler, *Joint Operating Agreements: A Practical Guide*, 4th edn, Globe Law and Business, 2020, p226.

747 T Daintith and G Willoughby (eds), *Adrian Hill, United Kingdom Oil and Gas Law*, 3rd edn, Sweet & Maxwell, 2009, p1152.

748 MPG Taylor and SM Tyne, *Taylor and Winsor on Joint Operating Agreements*, 2nd edn, Longman, 1992, p58.

own Operating Committee".[749] That is, the exclusive operations will be controlled by a committee composed of the participating parties.[750] However, the extension of the sole risk operations and how this will affect the joint operations are of critical concern for the non-participating parties, so they will require some measure of control of these operations.

Thus, it could be suggested that the sole risk parties will have the main control of exclusive operations and only limited control will be allowed to the non-consenting parties, generally in relation to the effect of the sole risk operation on the joint operations; they will focus on the need for separate accounting, allocation of costs and the use of joint property. Since the participating parties will have exclusive control over the exclusive operations, including the award of contracts and approval of expenditure, the non-participating parties must accept that their rights to buy-back into that operation will require them to pay their share of the costs and uplift as an *fait accompli*.[751]

Some authors suggest that a new JOA should be created to govern only the exclusive operation. However, commonly this is not accepted in practice as it may create more problems than solutions within the joint operations.[752]

Commonly, it is provided that the remaining clauses from the JOA will apply to the exclusive operation *mutatis mutandis*.[753] However, this approach could create problems later in the joint venture, since the parties may question the extent to which some clauses are applicable to newly proposed operations.[754] Thus, it is safer to determine the extent of the provision's application during the drafting stage rather than leave such issues open for future debate.[755] However, the extension of an exclusive operation will not affect the non-participating parties' rights in general, on the basis that their participating interest must not be modified outside the scope of the exclusive operation.[756]

It is important to note that in all the JOAs discussed in this book (with the exception of the AIPN JOA), the petroleum legal regime is connected to the JOA via a licence regime. However, in some jurisdictions a production sharing agreement may be used instead of a licence, or a combination of the two, or another type of agreement.[757] In this case, special provisions will be necessary in order to adjust for the existence of a production sharing or other agreement.[758]

---

749 V Gayrner, "Sole Risk and Non-Consent under UK Joint Operating Agreements", 1994 Summer Programme: UK Oil and Gas Law, CPMLP 09/09, 1994, pp1–4.

750 S Styles, "Joint Operating Agreements" in G Gordon and J Paterson (eds), *Oil and Gas Law* , pp288–289.

751 MPG Taylor and SM Tyne, *Taylor and Winsor on Joint Operating Agreements*, 2nd edn, Longman, 1992, pp59–60.

752 P Roberts and R Fowler, *Joint Operating Agreements: A Practical Guide*, 4th edn, Globe Law and Business, 2020, p223.

753 MPG Taylor and SM Tyne, *Taylor and Winsor on Joint Operating Agreements*, 2nd edn, Longman, 1992, p62. See also R Fowler "Sole Risk, Non-Consent and Default; the curse of *mutatis mutandis*" in E Pereira and W Zahari (eds), *Joint Operating Agreement: The Applicability and Enforceability of Default Provisions*, Rocky Mountain Mineral Law Foundation, November 2018.

754 B Manning, "Some Practical Aspects of Resources Joint Ventures" in WD Duncan, *Joint Ventures Law in Australia*, 2nd edn, The Federation Press, 2005, pp323–324.

755 P Roberts and R Fowler, *Joint Operating Agreements: A Practical Guide*, 4th edn, Globe Law and Business, 2020, p223.

756 *Ibid*, p227.

757 C Duval, H Le Leuch, A Pertuzio and JL Weaver, *International Petroleum and Exploration Agreements: Legal, Economic & Policy Aspects*, 2nd edn, Barrows, 2009, p297.

758 BG Taverne, *An Introduction to the Regulation of the Petroleum Industry: Law, Contracts and Conventions*, Graham & Trotman, 1994, p140. See also the discussion of AIPN JOA Article 19 by R Fowler, P Roberts and E Pereira, *The AIPN Joint Operating Agreement: A Practical Guide*, Globe Law and Business, 2019.

In conclusion, fair and balanced provisions are required since some circumstances may change during the long life-span of the licence, such as:

- each party's:
  - participating interest;
  - financial strength;
  - viewpoint; and
  - priorities; and
- the maturity of the oil and gas region which will naturally balance the position of the parties.

Thus, a fair and balanced provision must be negotiated for the JOA and, ultimately, a new JOA will be required if an exclusive operation is fully implemented.[759]

Bearing all these comments in mind, in the following paragraphs we examine some standard model JOAs to determine whether their approach clarifies the complexity of these provisions or they fail to address various critical points, leaving the agreement open to future debate and possibly to litigation.

9.2 Analysis of model JOAs

The RMMLF JOA Model offers a fairly simple approach to dealing with sole risk and non-consent provisions. They are fairly short, and certainly do not address the majority of the issues related to these clauses.

Sole risk operations are allowed for drilling and development activities, but the right to exercise and conduct a sole risk seismic is clearly excluded.[760] There are no other restrictions on proposing or conducting a sole risk operation, such as completing the minimum work obligations or even protecting the joint operations.

Although a proposal to drill a well is not exclusively related to sole risk operations, it will provide extensive detail in the applicable notice, such as location, depth and itemised costs.[761] The RMMLF sole risk provision makes reference to such a provision, so the other parties should receive a moderate amount of information before deciding whether to join a drilling operation.

This JOA Model Form indicates that the consortium operator will act as the operator for an exclusive operation, although there is no clear obligation on this.[762] This leaves an area open to debate as it does not compel the practice even though the licence may require it. Most importantly, it does not mention the right of the consenting parties to elect one of their number to conduct the exclusive operations.

All consenting parties will bear the costs of the exclusive operation, but the non-consenting parties will be excluded from its activities.[763] Nevertheless, the right to buy-back is secured if 100% of the costs are paid, along with a premium that is agreed between the parties.[764]

In conclusion, it is clear that these provisions are vague as the majority of issues arising from such clauses are not mentioned at all or are weakly provided for.

759 S Shaw, "Joint Operating Agreements" in MR David, *Upstream Oil and Gas Agreements*, Sweet & Maxwell, 1996, pp22–23.
760 RMMLF JOA §9.2, 9.3, 9.4, 9.5, 9.6.
761 RMMLF JOA §9.2.
762 RMMLF JOA §9.2, 9.3, 9.4, 9.5, 9.6.
763 RMMLF JOA §10.1.
764 RMMLF JOA §10.2.

The model does not help the parties to resolve any disputes, but rather increases the chances of litigation because of its lack of clarity and procedures. However, the parties' lack of participation in the policy and overall decisions of the consortium creates an environment where the operator has far too much discretion to conduct the joint operations. For this reason, the RMMLF Model provides a non-consent right allowing the non-operators to opt out of any operation approved by the operator.[765]

The Norwegian JOA Model allows sole risk operations for most activities, such as seismic, drilling, testing and development operations.[766] This model provides far fewer restrictions at any of these stages than other JOAs, except for the development stage, where it requires unanimous consent.[767]

The starting point is that any development approval will require unanimous consent of all parties, but if the operator does not consent and yet the development goes ahead on a sole risk basis, the parties must elect a different operator subject to the approval of the state.[768] However, the intention of the clause is to obtain the approval of all parties for any development as it will affect the whole consortium even though a party might not be part of the operation. The development stage is the last stage during which a party may exercise its right to buy-back into the operation.[769]

However, certain general restrictions apply to any sole risk operation; such operations must not include minimum work obligations or jeopardise the integrity of joint operations.[770] In other words, the parties will not be allowed to proceed with a sole risk operation before the minimum work obligations finish or if the proposal might harm the joint operations.

The sole risk proposal must include a "detailed description of the work to be carried out, along with a corresponding budget estimate".[771] This wording indicates a higher level of information, but ultimately the proposing party determines the level. Nevertheless, the requirement to attach an estimated budget to give the parties practical information about the costs of the proposal is very positive.

It is important to note that a sole risk proposal may become a joint operation if it receives support equal to or higher than that required for a joint operation. It is not necessary to obtain 100% support to become a joint operation; the proposal will only be a sole risk project if it receives a lower level of support than the required passmark.[772]

As a general rule, the operator will conduct the sole risk operations. However, as with sole risk development, if the operator is not a participating party, "one of the other participants may be approved as operator for the project".[773] Such a simplified approach does not clarify whether the operator would still be obliged to conduct the operation if another operator is not approved by the governmental authorities.

---

765 RMMLF JOA §6.1, 6.2 and 6.3.

766 Norwegian JOA §18.1.

767 Norwegian JOA §19.4: "A proposal for a sole risk development in accordance with Articles 19.1 shall be considered to have been adopted when the proposal has obtained a 100% Participating interest."

768 Norwegian JOA §19.5: "If the Operator does not participate in the development, the participating Parties shall select an operator. Such selection is subject to approval by the Ministry."

769 Norwegian JOA §19.6.

770 Norwegian JOA §18.3.

771 Norwegian JOA §18.4.

772 Norwegian JOA §18.5.

773 Norwegian JOA §18.7.

The participating parties will have the right to use the joint property in accordance with the "reasonable conditions established by the management committee" and to the extent that it "does not unreasonably disturb the joint activities".[774] In other words, the OpCom cannot unreasonably withhold its approval, but also cannot determine high fees for its approval nor allow proposals which might harm the effectiveness of the joint operations. However, there is no clear definition of the extent of such interference, so this provision gives extensive discretion to the OpCom.

The sole risk project is "in its entirety owned by the participating Parties and is managed by a separate management committee, consisting of the participating Parties only".[775] This provision includes data and information obtained from the sole risk project. It seems extensively to protect the participating parties and gives little control to the other parties. However, this is the only JOA Model Form to establish an obligation on the participating parties, as they "must keep the non-participating Parties informed about the project".[776] The duty to keep the non-participating parties informed is the most beneficial condition in this model form as it secures for them some measure of control over the exclusive operations.

The participating parties will be responsible for the liabilities and expenses related to the sole risk project.[777] This is a fairly standard provision in the industry, but it is not completely fair as the non-participating parties can obtain some benefits from the exclusive operations. In this sense, it would be reasonable to provide that the non-consenting parties are liable to a certain extent for the exclusive operation until their right to buy-back their interest is enforced.

This JOA Model Form attempts to resolve the controversial issue of buy-back rights: it sets the level at 1,000% of the costs of the sole risk development project.

The Norwegian Model takes the approach that the sole risk operation should be governed by the terms of the JOA save to the extent that clauses 18 and 19 (the sole risk provisions) otherwise apply. In practice, it may be difficult to apply the JOA provisions to sole risk operations in circumstances of default, relinquishment or assignment.[778]

On the other hand, the model form includes a positive provision for the non-consenting parties as it sets a time limit that the exclusive operation must commence within 12 months of its approval;[779] otherwise the participating parties will "lose their right to carry out the project" and: "In such event, the relationship between the Parties shall be as if the project had never been proposed."[780] It should not be forgotten that the sole risk project will still be governed by the licence or concession agreement terms, and may need to be approved by the state. Accordingly, the sole risk project may be subject to an agreed timescale for its performance, just as may apply to joint operations.

In conclusion, the Norwegian JOA Model does not address properly all the relevant issues related to exclusive operations as it adopts a fairly simplified approach for this complex issue. The implications of this approach were clearly noted in discussion of the provisions regarding the rearrangement of the participating interest,

774 Norwegian JOA §18.8.
775 Norwegian JOA §18.10.
776 Norwegian JOA §18.11.
777 *Ibid.*
778 Norwegian JOA §18.13.
779 Norwegian JOA §18.14.
780 *Ibid.*

the buy-back right and the conduct of operations, among others. However, the main disadvantage with this model form is that it does not provide for the existence of a non-consent right, which is a significant omission from the perspective of the smaller participants.

However, it is important to note that there are some positive provisions, such as a time limit on the commencement of sole risk operations and the right to use joint property, among others. Also helpful is the provision in this model form obliging the participating parties to inform non-participating parties on the progress of the sole risk project. This is a valuable provision for the non-participating parties as it allows them to check that the sole risk project is complying with the petroleum regulations and also not interfering with joint operations.

Sole risk operations are clearly authorised by the AIPN JOA Model Form and there are almost no changes from the 2002 to 2012 model forms with regard to exclusive operations.[781] On the other hand, non-consent operations are included as an optional provision.[782] Sole risk operations are highly regulated, but there is almost no regulation of non-consent operations or clarification of their application, except for the right of further non-consent[783] (ie, a second right to opt out of an operation).[784]

There are very few restrictions on the non-consent right, except for a reference to the activities that could be allowed as exclusive operations and a second opportunity to vote on an operation.[785]

There are more restrictions on the implementation of a sole risk operation. No operation may conflict with any operation previously approved, which can be either a joint or an exclusive operation.[786] Both provisions are reasonable but, as is common in many JOAs, the AIPN Model Form lacks clarity in the detail of such 'conflict'.

Another common restriction on sole risk operations concerns the minimum work obligations. As a general rule, the AIPN JOA Model Form forbids any exclusive operation which may threaten the good standing of the granting instrument and/or constitutes a specific obligation under the granting instrument which is binding on all the JOA parties. However, it contains an optional provision to allow drilling operations to be undertaken before the minimum work obligations are met.[787] This is a very positive provision as the petroleum title will not be affected whether drilling operations are carried out as a joint or exclusive operation, and the JOA should encourage as much work as possible rather than restrict it, as this will benefit not only the sole risk parties but also the whole consortium. Nevertheless, the sole risk provision imposes certain limits on the activities that can be executed as a sole risk operation before the completion of the minimum work obligations.[788]

---

781 AIPN JOA §5.13(A).

782 AIPN JOA §5.13(B).

783 CM Miles, "AIPN 2002 Model Form Joint Operating Agreement in Oil and Gas Joint Ventures", *Australian Resources & Energy Law Journal* 22 (2003) 153–160.

784 PR Weems and M Bolton, "Highlights of Key Revisions – 2002 AIPN Model Form International Operating Agreement", *OGEL* 1 (2003) 5, 16.

785 *Ibid.*

786 AIPN JOA §7.1(A).

787 AIPN JOA §7.1(B).

788 CM Miles, "AIPN 2002 Model Form Joint Operating Agreement in Oil and Gas Joint Ventures", 22 *Australian Resources & Energy Law Journal* (2003) 153–160.

Apart from the above restrictions,[789] the parties may decide the type of works that can be proposed as a sole risk operation.[790] The first alternative allows any operation to be proposed as a sole risk, except for the development plan.[791] The second alternative provides a restrictive list of the types of work that may be proposed as a sole risk operation.[792] Although the first option is broader than the second, both allow the most important activities to be undertaken as a sole risk operation, including seismic work.[793]

If the sole risk proposal is clearly permitted by the JOA, the proposing party will issue a sole risk notice, specifying the work, location, objectives and estimated costs of the operation.[794] This is a positive approach as it secures a description of the most important information in the sole risk proposal, although the notice should not be limited to these requirements since other issues may be relevant, such as information on the need to use the joint property. Thus, there should also be a general provision to provide all relevant information on the proposal or to provide further information if so requested.

If all parties decide to participate in the proposed operation, it will become a joint operation, which is a different approach from other JOAs.[795] Some JOAs provide that if a sole risk proposal achieves the required passmark it will become a joint operation.[796] The former approach protects the minority parties as they will not be dictated to by the majority. The latter approach is based on the spirit of the agreement as the minimum percentage to start a joint operation will have been achieved.

The AIPN JOA Model Form adopts a reasonable provision on the costs and liabilities of an exclusive operation. In general, the participating parties will bear all the risks and costs.[797] The AIPN provisions with respect to responsibility for the costs of decommissioning sole projects are somewhat conflicting and contradictory. The key principle is stated in Article 7.3.B, which states that sole risk parties are only responsible for decommissioning cost to the extent that the sole risk project increased the cost of decommissioning; by contrast, Article 10.1.C (part of the decommissioning provisions) states that the sole risk parties are entirely responsible for existing joint property and facilities which they take over as part of a sole risk operation.

An issue directly related to the parties' liabilities is the allocation of participating interest, for which there are two main options. The first is a simple form proportional to each party's interest in the consortium. The second operation is more complex as it allows more flexibility for the parties to decide the percentages.[798]

Access to information is open to all parties, including the non-participating parties, except for seismic work. If a non-participating party requires access to

789 DF Asmus, "The 1995 Model Form International Operating Agreement", *Journal of Energy & Natural Resources Law* 14 (1996) 7.

790 CM Miles, "AIPN 2002 Model Form Joint Operating Agreement in Oil and Gas Joint Ventures", *Australian Resources & Energy Law Journal* 22 (2003) 153–160.

791 AIPN JOA §7.1(D).

792 AIPN JOA §7.1(D).

793 DF Asmus, "The 1995 Model Form International Operating Agreement", *Journal Energy & Natural Resources Law* 14 (1996) 7.

794 AIPN JOA §7.2(A).

795 AIPN JOA §7.2(B).

796 For example, the Norwegian and Greenlandic JOAs.

797 AIPN JOA §7.3(A).

798 AIPN JOA §7.2(E).

seismic information, it must pay a fee proportionate to the cost it would have had to contribute upon the execution of the work.[799] This indicates that any information, excluding seismic, should be available free of premium and in no circumstances should a premium be charged for access to information. The AIPN Model adopts the approach to provide the most information to the non-participating parties so that it will be easier to exercise the buy-back provision, and only requires payment for the data costs of seismic work.

It could be argued that the JOA must facilitate the exchange of information so the parties have a better chance of exercising the buy-back right, which will provide compensation for the sole risk parties and also return to the main principle of sharing costs and risks. On the other hand, it also conflicts with the main principle of the sole risk operation, which aims to recognise the risk taken by the sole risk parties and information is the key element for the sole risk operation. In this sense, one of the most valuable outputs of sole risk operations (ie, the information) may be available free of charge. It seems right to encourage the exchange of information, but some measure of compensation would be fair and reasonable.

The timing for exercising of buy-back is clearly defined in accordance with the stage of the sole risk operation.[800] However, it is interesting to note the greater level of drafting detail in this agreement regarding the governance of an exclusive development if not all parties participate in it (either directly or via the buy-back provision):

> *If after the expiry of the period in which a Non-Consenting Party may exercise its option to participate in a Development Plan the Consenting Parties desire to proceed, Operator shall give notice to the Government under the appropriate provision of the Contract requesting a meeting to advise the Government that the Consenting Parties consider the Discovery to be a Commercial Discovery. Following such meeting such Operator for such development shall apply for an Exploitation Area (if applicable in the Contract). Unless the Development Plan is materially modified or expanded prior to the commencement of operations under such plan (in which case a new notice and option shall be given to the Non-Consenting Parties under Article 7.4I), each Non-Consenting Party to such Development Plan shall:*
> *(1) if the Contract so allows, elect not to apply for an Exploitation Area covering such development and forfeit all interest in such Exploitation Area, or*
> *(2) if the Contract does not so allow, be deemed to have:*
> *(a) elected not to apply for an Exploitation Area covering such development;*
> *(b) forfeited all economic interest in such Exploitation Area; and*
> *(c) assumed a fiduciary duty to exercise its legal interest in such Exploitation Area for the benefit of the Consenting Parties.*
> *In either case such Non-Consenting Party shall be deemed to have withdrawn from this Agreement to the extent it relates to such Exploitation Area, even if the Development Plan is modified or expanded subsequent to the commencement of operations under such Development Plan and shall be further deemed to have forfeited any right to participate in the construction and ownership of facilities outside such Exploitation Area designed solely for the use of such Exploitation Area.*[801]

799 AIPN JOA §7.4(A).
800 AIPN JOA §7.4(C).
801 AIPN JOA §7.4(D).

Thus, the AIPN JOA Model Form allows for development to be carried out as a sole risk project even if the non-consenting parties and/or the petroleum regulations object to it.

The payment regarding the buy-back right is clearly defined as a premium rather than a penalty. There are several issues related to such a right. First, the non-consenting parties will have to reimburse all the costs they would have incurred if the operations had been executed as a joint operation from the start. This payment may either be a monetary payment or a commitment to meet all cash calls from the joint or exclusive operation until the applicable costs have been repaid (both options are available, but the parties must choose one of them).[802] It is important to note that the previous edition of the JOA allowed payment in kind, which is not allowed in the current model form[803] because the approach had not been accepted in practice.[804]

This provides further proof that even an international JOA aims only at wider acceptance instead of being a balanced agreement between the parties, as payment in kind is not even mentioned as an optional provision. Payment in kind may be the best mechanism for a non-consenting party to buy its right back, as it has a delayed financial impact, which is likely to benefit a smaller party. However, it makes more sense for an operator to reduce the flexibility of the sole risk provisions, so making it harder for a smaller party to opt out of a proposal for a sole risk operation. Secondly, the non-consenting parties should pay a premium to the sole risk parties as initially they did not share the risks and costs. The percentage of the premium could vary according to the type of work and its level of inherent risk, namely seismic and drilling work, but the percentage is left blank so the parties can define it.[805] The payment of such a premium follows the same procedure as for the sunk costs payments.

It is important to note that any previous exclusive operations will take priority over new proposals.[806] If more than one proposal is made, the one that receives the most support will take priority over the remaining proposals. However, the model does not specify how this priority will take place or the process to evaluate the remaining proposals.[807, 808]

The model form has one compulsory provision on the use of joint property and four additional options that may be implemented by the parties. The basic provision secures the use of most of any equipment not being used by the joint operations, free of cost, as follows:

> *The Parties participating in any Deepening, Testing, Completing, Sidetracking, Plugging Back, Recompleting or Reworking of any well drilled under this Agreement shall be permitted to use (free of cost) all casing, tubing and other equipment in the well that is not needed for operations by the owners of the wellbore, but the ownership of all such equipment shall remain unchanged.*[809]

802 AIPN JOA §7.5(A).
803 CM Miles, "AIPN 2002 Model Form Joint Operating Agreement in Oil and Gas Joint Ventures", *Australian Resources & Energy Law Journal* 22 (2003) 153–160.
804 PR Weems and M Bolton, "Highlights of Key Revisions – 2002 AIPN Model Form International Operating Agreement", *OGEL* 1 (2003) 5.
805 AIPN JOA §7.5(B).
806 AIPN JOA §7.6(A).
807 AIPN JOA §7.6(C).
808 AIPN JOA §7.6(E).
809 AIPN JOA §7.9(A).

However, a more complex formula may be required to determine the share of expenses for the decommissioning costs if different parties have used the equipment during the existence of the petroleum title.

On abandonment of a well in which operations with differing participation have been conducted, the Parties abandoning the well shall account for all equipment in the well to the Parties owning such equipment by tendering to them their respective Participating Interest shares of the value of such equipment less the cost of salvage.[810]

The first optional provision mentions the use of spare capacity of facilities for the purposes of drilling, but not for development or production, which is a right reserved for the owner of the facility. If the owners of the platform are part of the exclusive operation, no fee will be charged, but if not, they must pay a reasonable contribution to the overall costs of the platform:

Consenting Parties in the well shall pay to the owners of the platform until all wells drilled by such Parties have been plugged and abandoned a monthly fee equal to (1) that portion of the total cost of the platform (including costs of material, fabrication, transportation and installation), divided by the number of months of useful life established for the platform under the tax law of the host country, that one well slot bears to the total number of slots on the platform plus (2) that proportionate part of the monthly cost of operating, maintaining and financing the platform that the well drilled under this Article 7.9(B) bears to the total number of wells served by such platform.[811]

The second option addresses any spare capacity with equipment used in processing and transporting production. All parties will have the right to use such equipment, subject to specific procedures and requirements.[812] The parties must define whether payment for such use will be based on arm's length rates or cost basis.[813] The third option clarifies that no legal interest in property used in the previous options transfers to the user by reason of that use.[814] This seems reasonable if there is no fee applicable or only usage fees, but if the sole risk parties pay fees related to the overall costs of the infrastructure it would be reasonable to expect some sort of participation in the equipment's ownership. The final option excludes the owners of the infrastructure from any liability or expenses that may arise from the sole risk operation.[815] This is a reasonable provision as the sole risk parties must be liable for such risks. Consequently, it is possible to suggest that the AIPN Model

810 AIPN JOA §7.9(A).
811 AIPN JOA §7.9(B).
812 AIPN JOA §7.9(C).
813 AIPN JOA §7.9(C).
814 AIPN JOA §7.9(D).
815 AIPN JOA §7.9(E).

Form secures a higher level of regulation regarding the right to use joint or exclusive property, which was a problem in previous editions.[816]

The model form also addresses a critical issue for the joint operations regarding the integration of the exclusive operation with joint property. If the process of integrating the exclusive operation into a joint operation facility (ie, a tie-in process) results in any loss of production, the sole risk parties will bear the losses, so it is reasonable to charge the sole risk parties for such costs.[817]

There is also an optional provision that may be applicable to petroleum titles which require production bonuses.[818] None of the jurisdictions related to the JOAs examined in this book adopt such a requirement, but it is fairly common to find such a disposition under a production sharing agreement.[819]

Detailed provisions are established to deal with the conduct of the sole risk operation, such as the computation of liabilities, separate accounting and cash calls, among others.[820] In fact, the proper conduct of the exclusive operations is well defined. In general, the consenting parties must conduct the sole risk operations subject to the petroleum title regulations.[821] If the operator does not take part in the development of a sole risk discovery, it has the following options:

> *Check one Alternative.*
> *[ ] ALTERNATIVE NO. 1*
> *may resign, but in any event shall resign on the unanimous request of the Consenting Parties, as Operator for the Exploitation Area for such Discovery, and the Consenting Parties shall select a Consenting Party to serve as Operator for such Exclusive Operation only.*
> *[ ] ALTERNATIVE NO. 2*
> *may resign as Operator for the Exploitation Area for such Discovery. If Operator so resigns, the Consenting Parties shall select a Consenting Party to serve as Operator for such Exclusive Operation only.*
> *Any such resignation of Operator and appointment of a Consenting Party to serve as Operator for such Exclusive Operation shall be subject to the Parties having first obtained any necessary Government approvals.*[822]

However, there is no provision concerning the conduct of a sole risk operation if it is not the development of a discovery and if the governmental authorities do not permit the consenting parties to conduct the operation (eg, sole risk seismic or sole risk drilling of an exploratory well).[823]

---

816 DF Asmus, "The 1995 Model Form International Operating Agreement", *Journal of Energy & Natural Resources Law* 14 (1996) 7.
817 AIPN JOA §7.10.
818 AIPN JOA §7.11.
819 DF Asmus, "The 1995 Model Form International Operating Agreement", *Journal of Energy & Natural Resources Law* 14 (1996) 8.
820 AIPN JOA §7.12.
821 AIPN JOA §7.12(A).
822 AIPN JOA §7.12.
823 DF Asmus, "The 1995 Model Form International Operating Agreement", *Journal of Energy & Natural Resources Law* 14 (1996) 23.

In conclusion, it can be seen that the AIPN JOA Model Form is a very balanced and detailed agreement, which addresses the main issues regarding exclusive operations. There are few restrictions on proposing sole risk operations. It is the only model form that allows the possibility of proposing a sole risk operation before the completion of the minimum work obligations, which is a valuable provision for the consortium as a whole.

The model also provides the non-consenting parties with easier access to information, but at the same time reduces the importance of the sole risk operations as no real compensation is provided for the information obtained from the exclusive operations. The importance of information is clearly noted by all JOAs, as the main duty of any operator is to provide information to the non-operators and no drilling operation is executed without a reasonable amount of data. Consequently, it would be fair to provide higher, but not prohibitive, fees for access to such information. Another very positive approach taken by this model form is the inclusion of fair and balanced provisions regarding the use of joint property.

The model could be improved in other areas, such as the conduct of operations if the governmental authorities do not consent to the operatorship being modified, as well as a clear determination of the connection between the sole risk provisions and other JOA provisions, among others. It tries to address the situation where the state does not permit the concession area to be divided and to create a concession area specific for the sole risk development; it requires the non-participating parties to hold their interest in the sole risk development as a fiduciary for the sole risk parties.[824] This is a strange formulation because it is not clear exactly what fiduciary duties the non-participating parties might hold. It would be better to adopt the approach that the non-participating holding parties hold their interest on trust for the sole risk parties. This is exactly the approach that the AIPN JOA adopts for handling a parallel situation which may arise where a party forfeits its interest in the consortium by reason of its default subject to the given procedures and regulations.[825] However, the most serious problem with the AIPN Model Form is that it does not provide for full implementation of the non-consent right,[826] as this appears as an optional provision. Nevertheless, even if the non-consent provision is not chosen, the parties may exert similar control via the provision in the AIPN Model JOA which allows a party to propose an exclusive operation in respect of an authorisation for expenditures if the second option is chosen. This could be considered as another kind of non-consent.[827]

If a smaller party cannot secure the implementation of either the optional non-consent provision or a requirement that a work programme and budget approval be followed up by approved authorisations for expenditure, and if that party has no control over the OpCom, it will have to follow the strongest parties. This means no remedy is available to protect it, save for withdrawal or a tactical default. Such an approach could be positive for the integrity of the consortium, but it may lead to the smaller party defaulting because it is unwilling to participate in such an operation. A non-consent clause can be double-edged for a non-operating party – it

824 AIPN JOA §7.4.F.2.

825 AIPN JOA §8.4.I.

826 CM Miles, "AIPN 2002 Model Form Joint Operating Agreement in Oil and Gas Joint Ventures" *Australian Resources & Energy Law Journal* 22 (2003) 153–160.

827 AIPN JOA §68.

may permit other parties to opt out of an expensive development, leaving the other non-operating parties with a tough choice; either to accept a larger share of the costs and risk in the development conducted on a sole risk basis, or to non-consent itself.

The Greenlandic JOA Model allows sole risk operations for seismic, drilling, testing and development.[828] This is a positive approach, as it allows sole risk operations at almost any stage of the project. However, this is not the case for non-consent operations as there is no provision for non-consent rights. This is a negative point for the smaller parties (most likely non-operators) as they may have to accept the decisions of other parties in any joint operation.

It is possible to propose a sole risk operation at any stage of the project. However, there are a number of restrictions on sole risk projects, such as the timing of the sole risk proposal or the conditions for their proposal.[829] Usually, a sole risk proposal is made at the time of an authorisation for expenditure rather than a work programme and budget,[830] but in some cases it may be the other way round.[831] Nevertheless, as with the Norwegian Model, sole risk projects may not be carried out in relation to minimum work obligations or if they threaten the integrity of the joint operations.[832]

Provisions that ensure the protection of the joint operations are a key feature in several JOAs.[833] However, a common problem faced by JOAs is their lack of clarity on the definition and extent of such protection. The Greenlandic JOA Model addresses these concerns by clearly defining the priority and potential interference with the joint operations, as follows:

> *If in the reasonable judgement of any Party there is a substantial risk that the proposed Sole Risk Drilling would appreciably impair the present or potential future production from an existing well which is then producing or capable of producing or would unreasonably interfere with Joint Operations or would fail to conform to the principles of good and prudent industry practice, such Party shall so advise the other Parties stating the reasons substantiating its objection and the Sole Risk Drilling shall not be undertaken if the Operating Committee agrees with such advice and determines that Sole Risk Drilling should not be undertaken.*[834]

Another key issue relevant to interference with joint operations is the right to use joint property. As a general rule, the sole risk parties have the right to use joint property, unless the OpCom refuses such a right on "reasonable operational grounds".[835] The sole risk notice should provide all relevant information on any

828 Greenlandic JOA §7.1.
829 Greenlandic JOA §7.2.2.
830 Greenlandic JOA §7.3.1. One of the peculiarities of the Greenlandic JOA is that it, in theory, allows for a sole risk project to be proposed if the OpCom does not approve an authorisation for expenditure required to carry out an activity already approved in the current work programme and budget. The situation could arise where the relevant drilling programme has already been partly paid for at the expense of the joint account and all the participants, only for that expenditure to be thrown away by the non-approval of a subsequent authorisation for expenditure and the continuation of the drilling programme on a sole risk basis.
831 Greenlandic JOA §7.3.2.
832 Greenlandic JOA §7.2.1.
833 Greenlandic JOA §7.2.4(a).
834 Greenlandic JOA §7.2.4(b).
835 Greenlandic JOA §7.2.6.

operations, which must include the use of joint property in the sole risk project. In this case, the most reasonable interpretation is that a sole risk party can use joint property up to the capacity of the infrastructure. Nevertheless, if any charges for the use of such joint property are made, they should be made on a "reasonable and equitable basis".[836]

Before starting any sole risk operation, the party proposing to carry out the operation is required to issue a sole risk notice. The notice must include all relevant information about the proposal, but the model does not provide any more detail on the obligation.[837] It is a broad provision that could favour both parties. On the one hand, the non-participating parties will have the right to request access to any relevant information they need in order to make an informed decision on whether to join the sole risk proposal. On the other hand, there is no provision detailing the information that must be provided in the sole risk proposal – that is, it could be seen as providing more flexibility to the proposing party. On balance, the wording of this provision gives far more discretion to the proposing parties to define the extent of the required information.

Data is a critical issue for any exclusive operation. This model provides that the property in the sole risk data remains in the possession of the sole risk parties. However, if the non-consenting parties decide to exercise their buy-back interest in the exclusive operation, the information must be shared among all parties.[838] On the other hand, the non-consenting parties may have access to the exclusive operation before exercising their rights to buy-back their interest in the operation, although some measure of compensation may be required. In this case, it is important to note that access to the data may be treated differently depending on the stage of the operation. For a sole risk seismic, the non-consenting parties may obtain access to such information if they pay, in cash, the equivalent of 200% of their original contribution to the sole risk operation.[839] For sole risk testing, the payment is based on the basic costs without any additional charges.[840]

In summary, all parties have the right to access any information, but some measure of compensation may be involved. The idea is to allow more information to the non-participating parties so they can make an informed decision on whether to join a sole risk operation, but at the same time the model also aims to recognise the risk taken by the participating parties. However, ownership of the information will transfer only after the full exercise of the buy-back right, which means that, before then, the sole risk parties may trade the sole risk data without any involvement from the non-consenting parties.

The conduct of the exclusive operation is a critical issue and, in this case, will vary according to the type of proposal (ie, whether it is a drilling, seismic or development operation), but always subject to governmental approval:

---

836 Greenlandic JOA §7.2.6.

837 For example, Greenlandic JOA §7.3.3, 7.3.4, 7.6.2.

838 Greenlandic JOA §7.2.7.

839 Greenlandic JOA §7.6.6.

840 Greenlandic JOA §7.7.8.

7.2.8 Subject to any necessary consent of the BMP, a Sole Risk Project shall be carried out by the Operator on behalf of the Sole Risk Party under the provisions of this Agreement provided always that:

(a) if the Operator is not a Sole Risk Party in Sole Risk Drilling then the Sole Risk Party shall be responsible for providing all equipment and personnel reasonably requested by the Operator to carry out the Sole Risk Drilling and provided further that if the BMP approves the appointment of a Sole Risk Party as operator for the sole purpose of conducting the Sole Risk Drilling, the Operator may decline to carry out the Sole Risk Drilling in which case the Sole Risk Party so appointed shall carry out such Sole Risk Drilling on behalf of each Sole Risk Party mutatis mutandis *as between such Parties as if it was the Operator under the provisions of this Agreement;*

(b) if the Operator is not participating in a Sole Risk Development and such Sole Risk Development does not involve the use of Joint Property as provided under Article 7.2.6, the Operator shall not be obliged to conduct the same and shall in any event only carry out the Sole Risk Development with the consent of all the Sole Risk Parties. If such consent of all Sole Risk Parties is not given, the Sole Risk Development, subject to any necessary consent of the BMP, shall be carried out by the Sole Risk Party or such one (1) of their number appointed by them if there is more than one (1) Sole Risk Party and such Sole Risk Party shall, unless the context otherwise requires, be deemed to be the Operator in respect of the independent application of this Agreement as provided in Article 7.2.9; and

(c) Sole Risk Seismic shall be carried out by the Sole Risk Party or such one (1) of their number appointed by them if there is more than one (1) Sole Risk Party.

7.2.9 Sole Risk Development shall in respect of the area comprised therein be regarded as creating a Sub-Area subject to Article 12.10, provided that the Sole Risk Party shall have a right of access to the Sub-Area. The Parties agree that, in the event of the creation of a Sub-Area or Sub-Areas pursuant to this Article 7.2.9, the surface area above the Sub-Area or Sub-Areas shall, to the extent permitted under the Licence and subject to the surface area above any area comprised in any development carried out under the Joint Operations and authorised by the BMP prior to his authorisation of the Sole Risk Development having priority, be included in the part of the Licence Area to which the Licence is to continue to apply.[841]

The conduct of the exclusive operations will be subject to the supervision of the sole risk parties.[842] This is a fairly common procedure and also positive for the sole risk parties, but it does not resolve completely the issue of control of such operations. From a non-consenting party's perspective, this is not a reasonable provision as it will require some measure of control over the exclusive operations to the extent necessary to confirm compliance with the petroleum regulations and stop interference with the joint operations.[843] In other words, some issues related to the exclusive operations may affect the non-consenting parties, so it is reasonable to allow the exchange of any information necessary for such purposes.

841 Greenlandic JOA §7.2.8 and 7.2.9.
842 Greenlandic JOA §7.10.
843 Greenlandic JOA §7.2.10(a).

The exercise of the buy-back right may be difficult. The buy-back provision for drilling and appraisal is straightforward as the non-consenting parties have to pay 200% of all the costs that they would have contributed previously.[844] However, for a development stage the cost will be higher and involves a complex formula to determine the payment that the non-participating parties must make to the participating parties.[845]

If the non-consenting parties do not exercise their right to buy-back their interest in the operation, the task of rearranging the parties' participating interests will be complex. This model form recognises the complexity of rearranging the participating interests for the development stage. They will be easier to determine for drilling operations.[846] The development stage is far more complicated than any other stage as it may involve different layers of sole risk operations inside the same project, rather than a single sole risk operation.[847] Whilst the Greenlandic JOA recognises that a sole risk development may need to be treated as creating a sub-area, it does not answer the question whether the operation of the buy-back provision would be treated as a transfer between the parties, possibly subject to pre-emption (Article IX in the Greenlandic JOA), and necessitating Bureau of Minerals and Petroleum's approval.

Regarding costs and liabilities, this model form provides a fairly common approach, as the sole risk parties will bear all the risks and costs of the sole risk operation.[848] The sole risk parties must indemnify the non-consenting parties for any damage arising from the exclusive operation, "excepting only damage inflicted to the subsurface including any reservoir".[849]

This exclusion of reservoir damage from the sole risk indemnity is potentially controversial; the AIPN JOA[850] and Norwegian JOA[851] require the sole risk parties to indemnify the non-participants fully, and the AIPN clause expressly includes consequential loss and environmental loss in the scope of that indemnity. The OGUK JOA[852] follows the Greenlandic JOA by excluding reservoir damage from the scope of the indemnity. It could be argued that the risk of reservoir damage and potential impact on joint operations can be assessed by the parties at the time the sole risk project is proposed. However none of the JOAs enable non-participating parties to block a sole risk project at that point and for that reason, unless they can show that it will conflict with existing joint operations. It is not clear that such provisions would allow the non-participating parties to block a sole risk project that might, unintentionally, damage the reservoir from which hydrocarbons are, or are likely to be, extracted for the joint interest. Furthermore, the granting instrument might require the joint-venture parties to indemnify the state for loss or damage to the reservoir arising from the joint venture's performance of the concession agreement, a liability which falls on all the parties, irrespective of whether the damage arose from joint operations or a sole risk project. Since the non-participating parties are not represented on the OpCom that manages a sole risk project and have no other

844 Greenlandic JOA §7.6.3.
845 Greenlandic JOA §7.4.2.
846 Greenlandic JOA §7.5.6 and 7.5.7.
847 Greenlandic JOA §7.5.6 and 7.5.7.
848 Greenlandic JOA §7.2.3.
849 Greenlandic JOA §7.2.5.
850 AIPN JOA §7.3.
851 Norwegian JOA §18.11.
852 OGUK JOA §15.2.5(c).

means of preventing damage to the reservoir, it is submitted that the AIPN JOA and Norwegian JOA are more comprehensive. They in turn take a more balanced approach by requiring the sole risk parties to indemnify non-participants for damage to the reservoir caused by a sole risk project. After all, it is highly unlikely that the risk of damage to the reservoir would be insurable.

It is important to note that if the national oil company decides to take part in the sole risk operation, it will also bear liability for any incremental participation over and above the participation attributable to its participating interest in joint operations – such liability will continue to be carried by the international oil companies.[853]

Notwithstanding the other provisions of this Article VII, if NUNAOIL elects to participate in a sole risk operation during the period in which NUNAOIL is carried, the provisions in Article 12 of the Licence and in Article 2.4 of this Agreement concerning the carry of NUNAOIL shall apply to the other Sole Risk Parties, subject to this Article 7.7.9. The carried Percentage Interest of NUNAOIL in a sole risk operation shall not exceed the carried Percentage Interest of NUNAOIL in Joint Operations in the area in which the sole risk operation is carried out. Thus, NUNAOIL shall be required to bear a portion of the risks, costs, expenses and liabilities of any sole risk operation equal to the difference between its carried Percentage Interest in Joint Operations as aforesaid and any larger Percentage Interest it may acquire in a sole risk operation pursuant to this Agreement. If NUNAOIL is the only participant in a sole risk operation, it shall be responsible for all risks, costs, expenses and liabilities connected with the same, and shall be entitled to receive all such payments in respect thereof.[854]

However, it is difficult to foresee the imposition of any liability on the national oil company, especially in the case of a default. This is a difficult reality that any international oil company must face when their consortium includes a national oil company.

Commonly, the JOAs provide that if a sole risk proposal obtains the participation of all parties, it will become a joint operation. However, the Greenlandic Model Form provides that a sole risk proposal for seismic acquisition which obtains affirmative votes equal to or higher than the passmark for the joint operations will also become a joint operation.[855] In other words, it will be only an exclusive operation if the participating interest remains lower than the original passmark. Both provisions are sustainable. This effectively means that parties can be voted into a seismic project which is proposed by any party and obtains the necessary OpCom passmark.

853 For example, if NUNAOIL's participating interest in a joint venture is 25% in a proposed well costing USD 100 million, but the well is pursued as a sole risk project with the result that NUNAOIL's participating interest is 33%, the carry will apply to the USD 25 million to which the carry would have applied had the well been drilled as joint operations, but not to the incremental USD 8 million which is payable by NUNAOIL on account of its increased interest in the sole risk well. This provision protects the IOCs as carrying parties from having to pay increased carry costs by reason of NUNAOIL's decision to participate in a sole risk well which they cannot control and which would otherwise be a "free option" for NUNAOIL.

854 Greenlandic JOA §7.7.9.

855 Greenlandic JOA §7.6.3.

By contrast, a development proposal needs unanimous approval of all parties, and must be proposed to the OpCom a joint operation first.[856]

Finally, it is important to note that this JOA Model Form also adopts the common approach of stating that the remaining provisions of the JOA shall apply *mutatis mutandis* to the sole risk provision.[857] As previously mentioned, this is the easiest but not the best approach as it will postpone uncertainty instead of determining from the very start the extension of such application.

In conclusion, the Greenlandic Model provides a reasonable approach to the main issues concerning the sole risk clause, such as the possibility to propose a sole risk operation at any stage of the project, a fair regulation of access to information, a good explanation of the extent of any interference with the joint operations and a detailed procedure for the conduct of the operations. The Greenlandic JOA Model is unique in that the participation of the national oil company increases governmental control, which is clearly demonstrated by the requirement for the national oil company's approval before proceeding with a sole risk operation.[858] However, the model's biggest problems are, first, its lack of a non-consent provision, which means the smaller parties must follow the stronger parties, and, secondly, the problems which could arise from the national oil company's participation in the consortium. Another important concern is the lack of definition for extending the provisions of the main JOA into the sole risk JOA and the interaction between the sole risk provisions and the provisions of the main JOA.

The most interesting and unique approach is taken by Morocco. The Office National des Hydrocarbons et de Mines (ONHYM) is the national oil company for the Kingdom of Morocco, and has a legal power to represent the state on signing and monitoring certain oil and gas activities.

The ONHYM JOA Standard Model offers probably the shortest and simplest sole risk provision in the industry. Clause 12 focuses on two topics: (i) the types of operations and (ii) the parties involved. It is clear that sole risk operations are only allowed for drilling activities. It is also clear that the national oil company/government will not be affected by any use of the sole risk provision.

> *The provisions of this Clause 12 shall apply to all drilling operations undertaken pursuant to the Petroleum Agreement and this Contract, provided however that if the drilling operations to be conducted are not part of the Development and Exploitation Works voted by the Management Committee undertaken under Exploitation Concession(s) and are proposed by PETCO, then this Clause shall only apply to PETCO and other eventual Parties, other than ONHYM and their respective Percentage Interest(s). If drilling operations during the exploitation Period are requested by ONHYM alone, in such case ONHYM will bear the entire cost of such Sole Risk drilling.*
> *It is the intent of the Parties under this Clause that ONHYM's Percentage Interest shall not be affected by any Exploration Work sole risk operations undertaken by PETCO and in which ONHYM does not participate.*[859]

856 Greenlandic JOA §7.5.1.
857 Greenlandic JOA §7.2.10(f).
858 Greenlandic JOA §7.2.8.
859 www.onhym.com/pdf/en/Model_Association%20Contract.pdf.

Morocco's approach is to simplify the sole risk provision by limiting the types of activities that may be undertaken as a sole risk operation and by exempting the national oil company from any effects of the exclusive operation in which it is not involved.

Clearly, this is a negative provision for any investor. The complex issue is not regulated and excessively protects the national oil company, as the rules do not apply to it. The government's aim is to exert more control over exclusive operations and not lose its national oil company's participation in any upstream activity.

This is a good example of how far a national oil company may change the JOA in order to protect the government's interest.

9.3 Discussion

It could be argued that the sole risk and non-consent clauses do not promote the essential purpose of a JOA, because they do not observe the basic principle of sharing costs and risks. However, it could also be argued that usually sharing costs and risks are expressly addressed in both clauses, as these clauses permit a party that initially decides not to join a proposal/approved work (the non-sole risk or non-consent party) to join at a later time, provided that it pays a premium.[860] From that time, all the parties will share the costs and risks involved in the operation(s). However, if the buy-back right is not exercised, there will be no joint sharing of risks and costs.

The sole risk and non-consent clauses affect the basic principle of sharing costs and risks in different ways. Initially, the sole risk clause aims to share the costs and risks as the sole risk notice invites the other parties to join the proposer's efforts. However, the non-consent clause clearly contradicts the principle of sharing costs and risks from the very beginning. Nevertheless, either a sole risk or a non-consent right may lead to an exclusive operation, which does not involve the joint sharing of costs and risks. In fact, this is the most reasonable explanation for the fact that most JOAs with governmental participation prohibit sole risk operations before the completion of the minimum work obligations as the host government will be keen to ensure the parties' combined financial strength is deployed in performing the minimum work obligations. The host government agreement will normally make no distinction between joint operations and sole risk operations. Any NOC in the joint venture will be required to make the election between participating and not participating in a sole risk operation, and taking the consequences of its election like any other party, unless the NOC is able to negotiate special treatment such as the right to have some of its costs of participation carried by the participating parties.

If we accept that the principle of sharing costs and risks does not justify the existence of such clauses, why are these clauses allowed in JOAs? If the consortium includes a dominant party which retains total control of the OpCom, there is no need for such clauses, as both clauses clearly contradict the principle of passmark voting, either positively or negatively. In this sense, is it possible to suggest that sole risk and non-consent clauses favour the smaller parties, that is, the non-operators?

In theory, the sole risk operation favours a smaller participant since any party may propose a sole risk operation, regardless of its participating interest (no JOA

860 The premium could vary according to the stage at which the procedure is required. Therefore, it could be suggested that later joining (development) will be more expensive than joining in the early stage (exploration). However, the most relevant factor is not the stage of the activity but rather the risks and costs involved, so the higher the risks involved, the higher the premium.

examined in this book provided any restriction on the issue).[861] However, the reality is slightly different, as in many consortiums the dominant party does not have total control of the OpCom, only negative control (ie, the power to block a decision), so it may need to obtain the support of smaller parties to approve an operation. Thus, such a sole risk operation may be useful for almost all the parties.[862] The strongest party may use this clause to coerce the smaller parties into joining its exclusive operation, since the premium for them to join later could be too expensive. If this advantage were not enough, the sole risk operation has additional benefits, as it aims to ensure more work is performed in the licensed area, which ultimately benefits the consortium, as more information is obtained and participants earn additional production entitlement and revenues. In other words, the sole risk party is working for the benefit of the whole enterprise, which carries out activities to find and develop oil and/or gas. It is clear that the sole risk operation favours a lot of parties, and so it is understandable that JOAs usually allow a sole risk clause.

The same is not true for the non-consent clause. There is no doubt that the aim of such a provision is to protect the smaller parties, as the right to opt out is only available if a decision is approved by the majority. In this context, it seems fair to suggest that this action could harm the existence of the consortium if, for instance, the capital raised were not enough to execute the operations. Consequently, the non-consent clause is not well accepted and is not found in several JOAs, as it favours the smaller and weaker consortium parties.

However, surprising as it may be, the strongest provisions for the operator (ie, the dominant party and the one which proposes the joint operations) are offered by the JOAs which provide for the existence of non-consent clauses. This is exactly what happens in the North American JOAs, due to the lack of participation and control by the non-operators in that region. If the North American non-operators cannot control the joint operations through the OpCom and cannot approve a work programme and budget, it is reasonable to provide that they can at least reject a decision that they do not agree with, that is, this is a minimum protection given to non-operators. However, clearly it does not resolve the problem of lack of control as these models only give the non-operators two options: join in, or opt out and bear the consequences. In other words, the non-operators in North America are in the same situation as a tourist on a city tour bus service. He or she cannot decide the route to the destination. S/he can only board the bus and let someone guide him/her or, if it is not suitable, s/he can leave the bus.

Therefore, the non-consent clauses are included in JOAs where the operator has total control over the joint operations and is not subject to supervision by the OpCom, such as in the American (AAPL and RMMLF) and Canadian Models. However, models that allow the non-operators more contribution to decisions concerning the joint operations (eg, the UK and international JOA Models) may not include non-consent clause on the basis that there are several alternative mechanisms in the JOA that permit non-operators some degree of influence over joint operations, such as the approval of work programmes and budgets by the OpCom.[863] On the other hand, this participation may not be a reality in practice as the non-operators can only exert

861 V Gayrner, "Sole Risk and Non-Consent under UK Joint Operating Agreements", 1994 Summer Programme: UK Oil and Gas Law, CPMLP 09/09, 1994, p1.

862 *Ibid*, pp5–6.

863 See P Mandler, "New Oil & Gas UK Standard Joint Operating Agreement (JOA)" *IELR* 4 (2008) 111, 112.

real control or enjoy real participation if their participating interests allow them to block any decision at the OpCom; otherwise their position will be more that of an investor, similarly to non-operators in North American JOAs that do not provide for the existence of an OpCom.

It is important to remember that most consortiums will encounter disagreements at some stage of the project. Sole risk and non-consent clauses often represent useful tools for helping the JOA to survive, as they will provide flexible ways of dealing with some disagreements within the joint venture. It is essential to keep the consortium in existence for the duration of the petroleum title, which could last for a couple of decades.[864] This is more likely to happen if sole risk and non-consent clauses are contained in the agreement because they give the necessary flexibility to allow different interests to coexist in the same enterprise in order to maintain the integrity of the consortium (in the long term). Nevertheless, it is also important to stress that there are major restrictions on any exclusive operation. The exclusive operation must not harm the joint operations or the standing of the petroleum title.[865] In this sense, it is important to recognise the valuable provision of the AIPN JOA Model Form (as an option),[866] which allows sole risk operations to take place in a well drilled to meet minimum work obligations to take advantage of the opportunity to deepen or sidetrack a well while the rig is on location. However, the remaining JOA Model Forms (including JOAs with national oil company participation) maintain a conservative provision, allowing only joint operations until the completion of the minimum work obligations.

As previously mentioned, it could be argued that these operations aim to benefit a minority party, which in essence is true as the majority is clearly denied by the non-consent and sole risk clauses, either in a positive or negative way.[867] The sole risk clause may be useful for a strong party that does not have total control of the decisions, but has enough power to block any decision. On the other hand, a non-consent right only benefits a smaller party with limited financial resources.[868] It could even be argued that a sole risk operation benefits the whole consortium, since it aims to produce more work and also allows later participation,[869] but the non-consent clause aims precisely to protect the interests of a smaller party.[870] Consequently, sole risk provisions are far more common than non-consent provisions.[871]

In theory, the JOA should apply equitable terms for sole risk and non-consent provisions as they are both contrary to the basic principle of passmark voting and also lead to an exclusive operation.[872] The restriction that can be imposed on the non-consent provision could also apply to the sole risk provision as both contradict the basic principle of passmark voting.[873]

---

864 C Golvala, "Upstream joint ventures – bidding and operating agreements" in G Picton-Tubervill (ed.), *Oil and Gas: A Practical Handbook*, Globe Law and Business, 2009, pp45–46.

865 MPG Taylor and SM Tyne, *Taylor and Winsor on Joint Operating Agreements*, 2nd edn, Longman, 1992, p58.

866 AIPN JOA §7.1.B.

867 C Penman, "Sole Risk Operations in Petroleum Joint Ventures" [1986] *AMPLA Yearbook*.

868 "This non-consent right could be a particularly attractive option for a party with limited financial resources or for which investment instead into another (competing) JOA relationship might be a more attractive proposition." P Roberts and R Fowler, *Joint Operating Agreements: A Practical Guide*, 4th edn, Globe Law and Business, 2020, p217.

869 *Ibid.*

870 *Ibid.*

871 MPG Taylor and SM Tyne, *Taylor and Winsor on Joint Operating Agreements*, 2nd edn, Longman, 1992, p48.

872 C Penman, "Sole Risk Operations in Petroleum Joint Ventures" [1986] *AMPLA Yearbook*.

873 P Roberts and R Fowler, *Joint Operating Agreements: A Practical Guide*, 4th edn, Globe Law and Business, 2020, p218.

Thus, there is no reason to treat a sole risk provision differently from a non-consent provision, since if the former contradicts the spirit of a JOA, then the latter does too.[874] There is no difference in the result of the two clauses, which is an exclusive operation (provided that a buy-back is not exercised), so a balanced JOA would contain both clauses rather than only one of them.

However, the real difference between the effect of the two clauses is not the likelihood of more or less work,[875] but rather which party will benefit more from these clauses. As a result, the existence of sole risk provisions is very common but non-consent provisions are much less so.[876]

The examination of each JOA has shown just how long and complex the provisions addressing operations undertaken by any number of parties fewer than the total in the consortium can be. The complexity involved in any exclusive operation clause is a reasonable motivation for avoiding them, as Claude Duval points out:

Perhaps this complexity explains why most international operations are done jointly. Because the sole risk feature is not often used, it has been difficult to foresee some of the difficulties in its use and to draft clearer provisions in model forms.[877]

However, that complexity is necessary because a sole risk provision does not work as a deterrent if it can only be implemented with the consensus of all the parties, necessitating negotiation and compromise. There is a parallel here with complex pre-emption provisions governing the transfer of interests in joint ventures; those provisions are only fully effective if they are compulsory and comprehensive, eliminating any opportunity to undermine the process by exploiting any uncertainty or inadequacy in the drafting.

The JOA parties should think carefully before proceeding with any exclusive operation, as it may have adverse consequences for both non-participating and participating parties.[878]

The parties should draft carefully the non-consent and sole risk provisions in relation to their relationship, but also bear in mind how these operations will affect the joint operations and the JOA as a whole.[879]

A common problem in most JOAs arises with a general provision stating that the remaining provisions of the JOA will apply *mutatis mutandis* to any sole risk and non-consent projects, but there is no clear provision on the extent to which these provisions should apply. For example, if a party fails to contribute to an exclusive operation, would it be appropriate for it to forfeit its rights to the whole area or only to the area of the exclusive operation? If a party decides to relinquish its rights to a sub-area or to assign its rights, how would this interact with the JOA? Should a new JOA be issued to govern this exclusive operation? There are many doubts, so it is prudent to set out the provisions in a clear way rather than leaving these issues

---

874 *Ibid*, p233.

875 *Ibid*, p234.

876 MPG Taylor and SM Tyne, *Taylor and Winsor on Joint Operating Agreements*, 2nd edn, Longman, 1992, pp49–50.

877 C Duval, H Le Leuch, A Pertuzio and JL Weaver, *International Petroleum and Exploration Agreements: Legal, Economic & Policy Aspects*, 2nd edn, Barrows, 2009, pp295–297.

878 V Gayrner, "Sole Risk and Non-Consent under U.K. Joint Operating Agreements", 1994 Summer Programme: UK Oil and Gas Law, CPMLP 09/09, 1994, p1.

879 P Roberts and R Fowler, *Joint Operating Agreements: A Practical Guide*, 4th edn, Globe Law and Business, 2020, p227.

open for future debate. The easiest solution may not always be the best solution. The AMPLA JOA is the only model that seeks to provide a solution to this issue as follows:

> (f) *The Sole Risk Participants must promptly and in good faith negotiate and execute a new joint venture agreement in relation to the Sole Risk Operation in the Sole Risk Area (Sole Risk JOA) but unless and until they agree, the provisions of this agreement apply with necessary modification to the Sole Risk Joint Venture.*
> (g) *Upon execution of the Sole Risk JOA, the Sole Risk Area is excised from this agreement and the non-Sole Risk Participants must do all things necessary to transfer the Petroleum Title (or part thereof) over the Sole Risk Area to the Sole Risk Participants, or to facilitate the grant of a new Petroleum Title over the Sole Risk Area to the Sole Risk Participants.*[880]

Another issue which is likely to be controversial is the definition of the sole risk project itself. As with pre-emption clauses mentioned above, there is only one opportunity to define the scope of the sole risk project – in the notice provided by the providing party to the other JOA parties at the outset. That definition is likely to prove inadequate over time as the sole risk project develops, and other projects develop on its margins. Only the AIPN JOA has an optional provision which seeks to address the conflict which may arise when a sole risk well does not proceed to the original depth proposed in the applicable notice.[881] But no model JOA provides for any bespoke expert determination process to help reconcile conflicts between sole risk joint operations that will routinely arise.

There is no doubt about the complexity involved in sole risk and non-consent provisions, but this does not mean that the parties should not use them.[882] They are important for preserving the consortium since the participants' views may change during the consortium's life-span. Most importantly, they will encourage the parties to produce more work (ie, through sole risk projects). In addition, they may provide some measure of deadlock resolution (ie, through a party threatening a sole risk project). Finally, they sometimes provide more protection for smaller parties (ie, non-consent provisions), even though the spirit of the JOA could be affected by such operations and a sub-area will be created if the exclusive operation is successful.

It could be argued that if these clauses were not routinely included in JOAs, it would be very difficult for the joint enterprises to continue over an extended time, because termination would be the only solution available in the event of a major disagreement. For this reason, it is clear that both clauses succeed in keeping the parties together in a long-term relationship. Nevertheless, if the parties do not approve a joint operation or do not exercise the right to buy-back, the consortium will fragment, but at least there are still several restrictions to protect the performance of the joint operations and, most importantly, the good standing of the licence.[883]

---

880 AMPLA JOA §13.2.

881 AIPN JOA §7.6.E.

882 P Roberts and R Fowler, *Joint Operating Agreements: A Practical Guide*, 4th edn, Globe Law and Business, 2020, pp233–235.

883 BG Taverne, *Co-operative Agreements in the Extractive Petroleum Industry*, Kluwer Law International, 1996, p69.

The overall restrictions are based on the petroleum regulations, not on the type of proposed work (activity) even though some JOAs may establish some limitation in specific types of work (ie, seismic).

In the event of conflict, the parties should re-read the sole risk or non-consent clauses in a methodical and thorough way. Probably the first issue they may verify is the validity of the exclusive operation, so the provisions relating to the necessary notice are very relevant.[884] This is a complex issue as there is often no guidance on the level of detail that should be provided in the sole risk notice.

Our analysis of the JOAs shows this to be true. The provision often contains an open and vague requirement to provide enough or all the relevant details but leaves the proposing parties to determine the extent of such information. Consequently, the non-participating parties could argue that the sole risk proposal did not provide enough information, and so did not allow them fully to exercise their buy-back right or that the sole risk operation is invalid. This is the type of concern that may arise from a sole risk notice, so it is worth spending more time drafting these clauses and the applicable sole risk notices properly, rather than wasting a lot more time later in an eventual dispute.[885] However, any problem regarding the sole risk notice should be addressed as soon as possible.[886] The sooner the parties correct any problem, the more likely that it will be a simple process and will reduce the chance of a long, difficult and expensive dispute later on.[887]

The decision to join a sole risk operation or to avoid joining a non-consent operation will be based on a risk assessment, which each party must make, but sensible, flexible terms in the clauses will help the parties.[888]

However, the complexity of such exclusive operations may lead to unforeseen scenarios in which standard model forms cannot assist.[889] Thus, these provisions should offer balanced terms and flexibility, and it is important to remember that the parties' participating interests, or even their financial strengths, may change, so balanced terms will benefit all parties in the long term.[890] Balance and flexibility are key for these provisions as the parties' goals and financial positions may change over time.[891]

If the parties cannot resolve a dispute between themselves, an expert determination could be a valuable alternative if the conflict relates to technical issues, which are likely to happen with such complex provisions.[892] The majority of

884 DF Moroney, "Sole Risk in Mining and Petroleum Ventures: An International Perspective" in AJ Beal, "Comment on Sole Risk in Mining and Petroleum Ventures: An International Perspective" [1986] *AMPLA Yearbook*.

885 *Ibid.* Further examples of litigation where a sole risk notice or the obligations that triggered it were in dispute are discussed in T Martin, J Gilbert and M Gusy, "A Global Review of Joint Operating Agreement Disputes" AIPN research paper 2020, Section 7.7.

886 "It is probably reasonable that a party aggrieved in this way should bring to the sole risk party's attention as early as possible the alleged deficiencies of the sole risk notice." MPG Taylor and SM Tyne, *Taylor and Winsor on Joint Operating Agreements*, 2nd edn, Longman, 1992, p58.

887 DF Moroney, "Sole Risk in Mining and Petroleum Ventures: An International Perspective" in AJ Beal, "Comment on Sole Risk in Mining and Petroleum Ventures: An International Perspective" [1986] *AMPLA Yearbook*.

888 JH Waite, "Sole Risk in Mining and Petroleum Ventures: The Australian Position" [1986] *AMPLA Yearbook*.

889 KR Saville, "Comment on Sole Risk in Mining and Petroleum Ventures" [1986] *AMPLA Yearbook*.

890 *Ibid.*

891 C Penman, "Sole Risk Operations in Petroleum Joint Ventures" [1986] *AMPLA Yearbook*.

892 DF Moroney, "Sole Risk in Mining and Petroleum Ventures: An International Perspective" in AJ Beal, "Comment on Sole Risk in Mining and Petroleum Ventures: An International Perspective" [1986] *AMPLA Yearbook*.

academics and practitioners recommend the inclusion of sole risk and non-consent clauses, but at the same time they expect that such clauses will never be used, as they are highly complex and sometimes almost impossible to draft in a consistent manner.[893] In other words, at the same time as arguing these clauses are important to include, they warn that it is dangerous if such provisions are fully exercised.[894] Thus, it could be argued that in practice sole risk and non-consent clauses should rarely be used,[895] serving more as a psychological threat than anything else. However, one of the problems with the complexity of exclusive operations provisions is the potential attraction of cutting corners in order to speed up the conclusion of a negotiation. For example, initially the parties may be encouraged by the area's geological data to move too fast, with insufficient concern for the terms of the agreement, but later on when the situation becomes less certain, the JOA will be read in detail – so it is better to spend more time sooner rather than later.[896]

As previously mentioned, the possibility of buying back the right to participate in operations involving fewer than all parties is a highly debated issue.[897] This is a highly sensitive area since, on the one hand, the sole risk parties may consider it unfair that they have to allow late participation by a party once the success is real and tangible.[898] On the other hand, the non-participating parties may take the view that they had participated fully until the sole risk operation, which therefore would not exist without their contribution. Consequently, some restrictions on such rights are commonly provided, but mainly related to the type of activities which are allowed and the costs involved. It is natural to expect a provision that favours the sole risk parties, but the spirit of such a clause should be based on the level of risks and costs involved, instead of the type of work.[899] The majority of JOAs leave these percentages blank so the parties can negotiate them, but some pre-determine them. The most suitable approach is a mixture of both where the percentage is left blank but with an upper limit provided.

Another highly debated issue is access to the data obtained from the exclusive operations. Some JOAs, such as the AIPN Model, authorise the exchange of information almost free of charge. This is positive for the consortium as a whole and for the non-consenting parties, but it does not encourage or compensate the risk takers, as the Greenlandic Model does. However, a balance must be achieved since the right of access to information must be secured, as it is a very important factor in the decision whether to join the sole risk project, but at the same time the provision should recognise the importance of such sole risk data. The same principle applies for the use of joint property as it must be right to allow this to the extent there is spare capacity, but fees should be charged to the extent necessary to cover operating costs and possibly to make a contribution to sunk capital costs.

Control of the exclusive operations must remain with the sole risk parties, but this does not exclude the obligation to inform the non-participating parties so they

893 C Penman, "Sole Risk Operations in Petroleum Joint Ventures" [1986] *AMPLA Yearbook*.
894 JH Waite, "Sole Risk in Mining and Petroleum Ventures: The Australian Position" [1986] *AMPLA Yearbook*.
895 C Penman, "Sole Risk Operations in Petroleum Joint Ventures" [1986] *AMPLA Yearbook*.
896 P Warne and J Aidersey-Williams, "Oil and Gas Contracts in the UKCS – How to Survive Them" *Journal of Energy & Natural Resources Law* 19 (2001) 302, 16.
897 P Roberts and R Fowler, *Joint Operating Agreements: A Practical Guide*, 4th edn, Globe Law and Business, 2020, pp230–232.
898 *Ibid*, p231.
899 *Ibid*, p232.

can verify compliance with petroleum regulations and non-interference with the joint operations, as both situations clearly affect them. Only the Norwegian JOA Model secures such rights for the non-consenting parties, whereas they should be provided in any JOA.[900]

Conduct of the exclusive operations is a problem in most of the JOAs as the operator for such operations must be approved by the governmental authorities. However, there is no clear regulation if this consent cannot be obtained. Can the consenting parties force the operator to carry out these operations against its will? It seems reasonable to compel it to the extent this does not harm the joint operations. On the other hand, the non-consenting parties may wish to compel the sole risk parties to perform a sole risk operation against their will. In this case, it would be more reasonable to limit the sole risk parties' obligations to a certain time period (as the Norwegian JOA Model Form does[901]), but if any further operation is executed in the same area, they should be compensated.

In conclusion, the sole risk and non-consent clauses are important provisions to balance the interests of the parties and also to provide a solution for some cases of deadlock in the OpCom.[902] However, the real function of the sole risk provision is to force the other parties to join a proposal for joint operations and the main purpose of the non-consent clause is to protect the smaller parties from aggressive larger parties. It is also important to note that the parties' participating interests may change, as may their priorities or even their financial strength, during the life-span of the petroleum title. Thus, it is important to have a balanced provision that any party (both international and national oil companies) may use without any draconian consequences for the remaining parties.

Finally, it is important to note that these clauses demonstrate probably the most significant difference between the non-operator and the minority shareholder, as the sole risk and non-consent clauses do not exist in any company law or partnership act. It is exclusive to this kind of association. Generally, these clauses are a key element of a JOA, even though their goals and consequences may appear to be against the very concept of joint operations.

Both the national and the international oil companies may make use of an exclusive operation and that is why the clauses should balance the interests between the operator and the non-operator. However, the interests of international oil companies and national oil companies may differ in detail with respect to sole risk provisions. Sole risk and non-consent provisions which work to balance the interests of operator and non-operator, as well as majority and minority interest holders, may create, not moderate, conflicts between international oil companies and national oil companies. The state is likely to have different drivers with respect to cash expenditure and generation compared to an international oil company. Constraints on the state budget may drive it to compel the national oil company to accelerate or decelerate cash expenditure and hydrocarbon development for reasons that are not connected to oil price and rate of return. These are drivers which are more likely to align than misalign the international oil companies. The sole risk and

---

900 Norwegian JOA §18.10.

901 Norwegian JOA §18.14.

902 Waite states that: "Thus non-consent can operate as an investment brake for joint venturers and resolve deadlocks on technical and investment matters between them." JH Waite, "Sole Risk in Mining and Petroleum Ventures: The Australian Position" [1986] *AMPLA Yearbook*.

non-consent provisions may help a national oil company to influence the pace of expenditure and development in accordance with the state's wishes. It may pursue a sole risk project which generates cash or employment but has a poor rate of return, against the wishes of international oil companies; conversely, it may exercise a non-consent right to avoid capital expenditure only because the state budget is short of cash. International oil companies should consider these points very carefully before using an industry model JOA as a starting point for negotiating national oil company participation.

10. Secondment, project team and staffing

10.1 General principles

After the geological quality of the asset and the financial capability of the participants, staffing is one of the most important contributors to a project's success. It is important to ensure that the project is staffed by professional and capable people. It is very often said that people are the main asset of each project.

The national oil company and the international oil company may have different views on the secondment of staff, since usually this is one method for a non-operator to influence joint operations. Thus, where either the national or international oil company takes on the role of non-operator, it will be more interested in establishing a transparent and effective secondment structure, effectively allowing it to alter the course of operations at each stage of the project: exploration, development and production. The non-operator will want to secure for itself the key positions in the project's operational structure and to ensure that the mechanism to allow this is set out in the JOA. It is probable that the operator will be reluctant to allow the non-operator this additional lever over operations and so will oppose a specific mechanism in the JOA.

Different countries take different approaches. In Europe, the United States and Asia, it is usual for the international oil company to take the role of operator; there is no requirement that the national oil company should operate the project. However, in some South American countries, such as Brazil, eastern countries, such as Algeria, and east European countries, such as Russia, the national oil company has a significant role in the operations and often acts as the operator, although this is not necessarily the direct requirement of the local legislation.

It is the operator's responsibility under the JOA to engage, retain and involve the employees necessary for the operations under the JOA.[903] The operator may have unlimited discretion to engage and retain employees for the project – that is, it is free to engage any employees for the project at its sole discretion – or it may have limited control such that it may engage only those employees who are reasonably necessary to conduct joint operations. The Operator may also establish the organisational structure of the project. However, such discretion may be limited, if the approval and modification of the organisational structure lies within the competence of the OpCom and such decision requires all parties' involvement. This

903 If a joint venture company is set up (comprising the interests of both the national and the international oil companies), it will be the project operator and the placement of personnel in the structure will be regulated at the level of the joint venture or the shareholders' agreement and decided by the corporate bodies of the incorporated joint venture.

could be particularly the case where the JOA parties wish to achieve a certain balance of influence and control in the organisational structure of the operator by ensuring that certain key roles within that structure are filled by non-operator secondees (see Section 10 of this chapter).

The opportunities and need for secondment will depend on the manner in which the operator is structured. If the operator is an existing company of one of the participants, it will deploy its own employees to conduct operations – and indeed those employees may work for several joint ventures simultaneously. In this case it might be difficult to allocate time dedicated to the joint project as against other projects. Different allocation procedures might be established in the joint venture to properly address the issue. However, even in this case there is room for the partners to discuss whether to employ the partners' personnel in the operator's company or to use other structures for engagement of the partners' secondees in the joint operations.

However, if the partners decide to incorporate a special purpose vehicle to act as Operator uniquely for that joint venture and potentially being owned by the same partners, that vehicle will need to hire human resources for its own account. These might be employed by the operator entity directly, depending on the stage, scale and maturity of operations. In the early stage of operations, when the operator requires a small team, it is more likely that the JOA parties will provide the majority of the staff to the operator entity by way of secondment and, as a result, the staff will be employed directly by the operator or special services agreements will be concluded to complement with some specific services.

The secondment of staff into the operator organisation can be useful also where the operator's corporate group has specialist employees appropriate for deployment in the operator entity, who can be seconded into the operator.

The non-operator secondment allows the involvement of its personnel in the project and thus those trusted personnel who are temporarily assigned to the project can supervise the process. The parties to the project may pre-agree and formalise in the provisions of the JOA: (i) the key employees' organisational structure, (ii) rotation rules securing particular positions for their employees and (iii) thereby allowing different partners to have their fair representation at different stages of the project development. There might also be special procedures established as to how such employees are being appointed to ensure that the candidates cannot be unreasonably rejected by the operator. Such procedures might include transparent qualification criteria such as experience, education and so on. The subcommittee of the OpCom dedicated to human resources issues can also interview the candidates before their appointment into the project structure. There might also be some rules agreed that certain personnel, for example financial and technical staff, are appointed by the primary operator from a list of candidates provided by the particular partner. It all depends on the value of the expertise the particular partner has. For example, one of the international oil companies, being the partner in an Arctic project, might have a particular reputation for its extensive technical expertise in resolving Arctic challenges. Thus, it will be beneficial to employ such a partner's knowledge and expertise to the maximum extent possible and to allow such partner to appoint chief operational/technical/subsurface officers and to have involvement in the selection process of the other technical employees. The relevant mechanics might be formalised in the provisions of the JOA.

The parties might also decide that the operator will have discretion and decide the number of secondees and the necessary expertise. It might set the scope of the secondment, its duration and location, and the duties and responsibilities of the secondees. This scenario provides the operator with a broad discretion and does not leave significant leverage for the non-operators to influence the day-to-day activity of the operator.

If the operator is a national oil company (which commonly is the case, since many local governments require that oil and gas project operators should be a local company, which is often the national oil company), it will be keen to use the international oil company's expertise and to develop its own expertise through working with the international company's secondees.

The secondment issue is crucial for a national oil company if the international company acts as operator and it tries to limit the national oil company's involvement in operational activities. In such a case the national oil company may insist on specific provisions in the JOA securing placement of its candidates within the organisational structure of the operator.

10.2 Analysis of model JOAs

Usually, the JOA will contain special provisions for the number of secondees and specific positions at each stage of the project (exploration, development, production), and the areas of expertise (eg, technical, drilling, financial), qualifications (eg, should be a graduate of a certain institute, with specific admissions and certifications) and minimum experience (number of years' experience, including in the particular area, eg, upstream or downstream).

For example, the Greenlandic Model JOA provides that the number of employees of the Operator employed in connection with its activities hereunder shall be determined by the Operator.[904]

The 2012 AIPN Model JOA provides that the operator has discretion in relation to project staffing issues and will engage and/or retain only such employees, contractors, consultants, and agents as are reasonably necessary to conduct Joint Operations. Subject to the Contract and this Agreement, the Operator shall determine the number of such employees, contractors, consultants, and agents, the selection of such persons, their hours of work and their compensation.

The AIPN alternative below provides some specifics in relation to the partners' secondees and allows the operator to decide on the number of secondees as well, whilst the first alternative establishes only the discretion in relation to the other staffing, not touching upon the matter of secondees.

> *ALTERNATIVE #2*
> *Operator shall engage and/or retain only such employees, Secondees, contractors, consultants, and agents as are reasonably necessary to conduct Joint Operations. Subject to the Contract and this Agreement, Operator shall determine the number of such employees, Secondees, contractors, consultants, and agents, the selection of such persons, their hours of work, and (except for Secondees) their compensation.*[905]

904 Article 3.5 of the Greenlandic Model JOA.
905 Article 4.3 of the 2012 AIPN Model JOA.

The AMPLA Model JOA also provides the operator with the discretion to determine whether secondees are necessary in particular professional areas, such as technical and management, and then to set the number of these employees and their remuneration:

> *The Operator may request that Participants second to the Operator suitable management and technical personnel for particular Joint Operations, and each Participant may propose secondees for particular Joint Operations, on terms and conditions acceptable to the Operator. However neither the Operator nor a Participant is required to accept or provide any proposed secondee.*[906]

In this case the non-operator might propose for the operator's consideration candidates who have the designated expertise and meet the requirements. The JOA may provide a specific procedure for such nomination and the selection process, for example the non-operator may be required to submit the résumés of three candidates, and designate the scope of the secondment, its duration and the estimated costs for the secondee, thus meeting the JOA's requirements, and the operator has the obligation to choose between these candidates and to start the process of nominating such candidates into the operator's structure.

The 2012 AIPN Model JOA provides that:

> *Any Party may propose Secondment for a designated purpose related to Joint Operations. Any proposal for Secondment must include the:*
>
> *(a) Designated purpose and scope of Secondment, including duties, responsibilities, and deliverables;*
>
> *(b) Duration of the Secondment;*
>
> *(c) Number of Secondees and minimum expertise, qualifications, and experience required;*
>
> *(d) Work location and position within Operator's organization of each Secondee; and*
>
> *(e) Estimated costs of the Secondment.*
>
> *(2) If a proposed Secondment meets the requirements of Article 4.3.C.1, Operator shall as soon as reasonably practicable.*

The AIPN JOA also describes some further obligations of the operator to consider and either approve or reject the nominees, proposed by the non-operators.[907] The second alternative proposed by the AIPN JOA provides more detailed provisions in relation to the process of assessment and approval or rejection, including some reasons for rejections.

906 Article 7.8(b) of the AMPLA Model JOA.

907 Article 4.3.C.5 of the AIPN Model JOA.

> *ALTERNATIVE PROVISION, CHOOSE ONE*
> *ALTERNATIVE #1*
> *approve or reject any Secondment proposed by a Non-Operator, in Operator's sole discretion.*
> *ALTERNATIVE #2*
> *approve (such approval not to be unreasonably withheld) or reject any Secondment proposed by a Non-Operator. Without prejudice to Operator's right to conduct Joint Operations under this Agreement and the Contract, Operator shall consider such Secondment proposal in light of the: (i) expertise and experience required for the relevant Joint Operations; (ii) expertise and experience of Operator's personnel; and (iii) potential benefits of such Secondment to the conduct of Joint Operations.*
> *(1) Any proposal for one or more Secondment positions approved by Operator is subject to: (i) the Operating Committee's authorization of an appropriate budget for such Secondment positions; and (ii) Non-Operators continuing to make available to Operator Secondees qualified to fulfil the designated purpose and scope of such Secondment.*
> *(2) As to each approved and authorized Secondment position, Operator shall request Non-Operators to nominate, by a specified date, qualified personnel to be the Secondee for such position. Each Non-Operator may nominate for each Secondment position one or more proposed Secondees, whom such Non-Operator considers reasonably qualified to fulfil the designated purpose and scope of such position.*
> *(3) Following the deadline for submitting nominations, Operator shall consider the expertise and experience of each such nominee in light of the expertise and experience required for the approved and authorized Secondment position.*[908]

In practical terms, giving the operator discretion to choose when a secondee is deployed in operations means that the non-operator has no right to deploy a secondee in joint operations, so non-operators should avoid granting the operator such wide discretion in the JOA. The OGUK Model Form states that:

> *The Participants agree that in certain circumstances a collaborative effort between them may be beneficial to Joint Operations. Such collaborative effort may include the secondment by a Non-Operator of personnel to the Operator's organization.*[909]

Allocation of secondees can be a controversial matter from the confidentiality and conflict of interest point of view.[910] As well as providing an opportunity to influence operational decision making within the operator, a non-operator secondee may also enhance the non-operator's familiarity with operations in the flow of information. However, secondees will find themselves under a duty to conduct

908 Article 4.3. of the 2012 AIPN Model JOA.
909 Article 6.11. of the OGUK Model Form.
910 The potential for a conflict of interest in these consequences is discussed in Section 8 of this chapter.

themselves transparently and fairly, not disclosing information to their seconding company without also making the information available to the other joint-venture parties in the strict compliance with the rules established in the JOA. The national oil company might have a particular advantage in securing itself key secondee roles in the operator organisation; the granting instrument is likely to require the joint venture to meet targets for the employment and training of national employees. The national oil company can use these obligations as a lever to secure such positions for itself.

As already elaborated, the secondment may be achieved through two main schemes: direct employment by the operator or through secondment/services agreements. Below are some examples of how these issues are addressed in different JOA Models.

The OGUK Model Form provides that the secondee is placed either:

> *(a) to work on a term assignment as a member of a project team; or*
> *(b) to fill organisational positions.*[911]

However, the Greenlandic Model JOA provides only one method for personnel involvement in the project – direct employment by the operator. It is interesting to note that the Greenlandic Model JOA also provides limitations on the region from which the operator's employees may be drawn:

> *the Operator shall use its reasonable endeavours to employ manpower from Greenland or Denmark, the Operator shall also determine their selection, hours of work and remuneration. However to the extent necessary for the Joint Operations the Operator may employ staff from other countries, if manpower with similar qualifications does not exist or is not available in Greenland or Denmark.*[912]

The Norwegian JOA also provides only for the possibility of direct employment of the personnel in the operator's organisational structure. This JOA addresses many details of such employment, for example joining employees' trade unions and meeting their requirements.

10.3 Discussion

The choice of assignment scheme will be based on the tax and regulatory implications. Since in many cases some functions within the project are undertaken by foreign citizens, the tax and immigration aspects become very important. It may take a significant time to obtain a work visa or permission to work, and will require substantial commitment from the employer. Under certain circumstances (eg, short-term commitments or specific services) the secondment/services scheme may be preferable; however, for long-term managerial commitments and roles necessary for

911 Article 6.11.1 of the OGUK Model Form.
912 Article 3.5 of the Greenlandic Model JOA.

the day-to-day operational activities of the project, the direct employment scheme will offer more benefits.

The direct employment scheme may be the most tax efficient, which will reduce the project costs, and is frequently used by the parties. The cost of deploying expatriate secondees into the operator is a disincentive for the non-operators. However, such costs are likely to be invoiced by the non-operator for payment by the joint account, enabling the non-operator to "socialise" the cost of its secondees, as discussed below.

The 2012 AIPN Model JOA and some other model forms provide that the secondee shall at all times remain the employee of the non-operator, but should be assigned to the operator and introduced to the operator's structure.

The OGUK Model Form states that:

> *... such person shall remain the employee of the Participant which seconded him and such Participant shall remain responsible for all the legal obligations of an employer associated with such employment...*[913]

The JOA's requirement that the secondee shall at all times remain the non-operator's employee might at first sight jeopardise the idea of the direct employment by the operator, but in practice this will not be the case, since the employment by the operator might be the secondary employment.

It may be preferable for the non-operator (often an international oil company) providing staff for such staff to be directly employed by the operator because the non-operator is likely to have less residual liability for such staff, and the process of obtaining work permits for them may be more straightforward compared to the work permit process which applies to seconded staff.

The non-operator will assign each secondee to work either as the operator's employee at the secondment location and for the agreed secondment period. The secondee is integrated into the operator's organisational structure and so will be subject to the operator's supervision and control, its instructions and directions, and will report to the operator. However, this is not always the case: if the staff are provided through the services scheme, when the staff remain the full-time employee of the non-operator, the staff will be subject to both the operator and the non-operator's instructions, although the non-operator's instructions will be limited by the terms and conditions of the relevant services agreement.

Since usually the costs and expenses of the secondees are charged to the joint account, thus shared by all parties to the project, and shall be designated and approved in the relevant work programme and budget, it is in the parties' best interests to choose the most efficient scheme of secondment, which is most tax efficient and complies with local legislation.

Certain costs arise due to the non-operator's standard internal procedures and usually these are allocated to the non-operator, which has seconded its personnel to the project structure through the services or secondment agreement, and which will be charged to the joint account:

913 Article 6.11.2 (a) of the OGUK Model Form.

- the secondee's basic salary and all other compensation, including standard allowances, entitlements and benefits, accrued during the secondment period;
- payroll taxes, withholding taxes or any other form of cost or charge assessed by any governmental authority in respect of the secondee's employment;
- health insurance, pension plan, defined contribution plan, profit sharing or stock option plan, or any other employment-related contributions for the benefit of the secondee as an employee of the non-operator, whether statutory or otherwise;
- the non-operator's (as employer) liability insurance, including insurance against compensation claims by third parties, and all obligations arising under applicable workers' compensation laws in respect of the secondee;
- the secondee's local expenses and taxes while in the secondment location;
- any other direct costs, charges or expenses assessed against an employer under any applicable laws or regulations in relation to the employment of persons such as the secondee; and
- all administrative costs and other indirect charges that are directly attributable or fairly allocated to the secondment or secondee.

If the secondee is provided to the operator under the secondment agreement, the non-operator employer will charge the operator for the costs and expenses it incurs related to the secondment and that would be chargeable to the joint account under the accounting procedure of the JOA, on a monthly basis. If the person is seconded on the basis of services agreement, that agreement will form a direct contractual arrangement between the operator and non-operator and the costs incurred with respect to such person under such services agreement will still be charged to the joint account periodically based on the payment schedule set out in the services agreement.

In addition to the monthly charge, the employer non-operator shall, to the extent chargeable to the joint account under the JOA, charge the operator for the costs it incurs in relation to relocating the secondee between his or her home country and the secondment country and location there. These costs might potentially consist of the following elements:

- transport and travel expenses;
- initial accommodation, meals and any other arrival expenses;
- relocation agency costs; and
- air and sea freight and insurance charges.

If the staff member is directly employed within the operator's organisational structure, all the above-mentioned costs and expenses will be incurred directly by the operator and will still be charged to the joint account. It is practical for the parties to discuss the potential amount of the above-mentioned costs and to agree in advance on a specific capped amount as it will be reasonable to control the costs and make them compliant with the relocation policies which the operator might wish to adopt in relation to the project.

One important aspect of the secondment is each party's liability in relation to the secondee. There are several approaches to this matter. Under the most common approach, liability arises only if the secondee is a senior supervisor and engages in gross negligence or wilful misconduct. Also, commonly, any gross negligence on the part of a secondee caused by the non-operator's interference in his or her functioning under the JOA are considered to be senior supervisory gross negligence and the non-operator will be liable for the consequences. In all other cases the senior supervisory secondee is appointed and acts under the operator's instructions and thus any gross negligence or wilful misconduct by the secondee will be the operator's sole liability.

Frequently the operator provides the non-operator with an indemnity against any claims related to the operator's employees, other than claims brought by the operator's employees due to the wilful misconduct of the non-operator. Similarly, the non-operator provides the operator with an indemnity against any claims brought by the non-operator's employees, other than those brought by the non-operator's employees due to the operator's wilful misconduct.

These standard terms are widely accepted and in practical terms mean that in case of secondment through direct employment, the operator will always be held liable for the secondee's actions. The liability of a non-operator for services provided through a services agreement is discussed below.

The JOA might also deal with allocation of responsibility for obtaining the work and other services permits necessary for secondees. In many cases, JOAs provide that the non-operator is responsible for obtaining the necessary work permits, visas and other administrative authorisations required to allow the secondee, and, if applicable, his or her dependants, to work and reside in the secondment location, and must keep these in force for the whole secondment period. If the non-operator is responsible for obtaining this documentation, the operator's obligation is merely to assist the non-operator in its licence-obtaining processes.

However, in practice this may not be the best approach since commonly the operator will be the national oil company and thus will have a better local network and capacity in relation to permits and authorisations, if such are required, than the non-operator, which in many cases is the international oil company. In these circumstances it would be reasonable for the international oil company, as non-operator, to request the national oil company, as operator, to take the lead in the work permits and authorisation process.

As an alternative to providing a secondee who will be employed full-time and dedicated to the operator organisation and subject to the particular restrictions of the local legislation,[914] the non-operator may provide services in the form of professional expertise under the personnel services agreement. In such a scheme the non-operator, acting as service provider, supplies the necessary personnel, who will have the specialised skills and qualifications necessary for their roles, most commonly drilling management and project management services. They are provided on a full-time basis for a period agreed between the parties or may involve the performance of a particular scope of professional work to an agreed time frame. If the work is performed at the operator's work sites, the operator provides the assigned personnel with the facilities and equipment needed to perform their work, and is responsible for provision of security, safety and first aid services and facilities. Usually, the operator will train the service personnel in its policies and procedures and in certain circumstances will instruct the service personnel directly without the service provider's involvement. Commonly, the non-operator service provider will be liable for failure to perform the service agreement, though the liability may be capped at

914 For example in Russia the use of agency labour is prohibited.

a multiple of the service fee chargeable. Interestingly, such service agreements do not necessarily require the service provider to charge no profit or mark-up – but the granting instrument may require this as a condition of cost recovery.

It is important to consider the specific situation when, due to the demands of a particular stage of the project, the operator requests that a special team, known as an integrated project team, with the expertise to deal with those particular challenges, is set up.

For instance, these challenges might arise during the development stage of the project and require a separate team dedicated to the planning, design, engineering, fabrication, transportation and installation of a production system and associated facilities, such as: offshore surface structures, subsea structures and any other kind of structures to develop and produce hydrocarbons offshore, or facilities located downstream of the wellhead connections and installed either within or outside the contract area.

If such a team is required to accomplish a particular task, the operator will designate the specific scope of the work that falls within the joint operations or, in the case of exclusive operations, the scope of the work for the parties to the agreement, and document this as a specific memorandum to be approved by OpCom.

It is important to note that the scope of work might not fall outside of the scope of the JOA itself and thus will form the integral part of the JOA.

The sole purpose of setting up an integrated project team is to pool the talents and capacities of all parties in order to conclude a particularly challenging part of the project and to assist the operator in conducting operations under the JOA.

It is essential to understand that the performance of functions within the agreed scope of work will be delegated to the integrated project team, which will substitute for the operator in that work within the joint operations. OpCom will approve the integrated project team. To this effect the party, or alternatively the operator itself, wishing to set up an integrated project team must send a memorandum describing in detail the anticipated scope of the work to be undertaken by the team, the estimated type and number of staff required to complete the work, the estimated duration of the project and the costs (proposed modifications to the work programme and budget) to all parties, an agreed number of days before the work starts.

OpCom may approve or reject the setting up of such an integrated project team, after considering the existing expertise and experience of the operator's and other seconded personnel, and the potential benefits of an integrated project team to the joint operations or exclusive operations, as applicable.

Commonly, an integrated project team may be set up to prepare the development plan, to design above-ground infrastructure provided for in a development plan, to procure above-ground infrastructure provided for in a development plan or for any other issues of a particularly challenging nature.

If the use of an integrated project team is approved, the operator will set it up. Approval is contingent on the OpCom's authorisation of the proposed expenditures within the applicable work programme and budget.

It is common practice for the operator to appoint a project manager for the integrated project team, who may be removed and replaced under the procedure provided by the JOA for the appointment of senior supervisory personnel/key personnel.

The operator is likely to appoint the project manager from among the integrated project team members promptly after OpCom approves the setting up of the team.

The project manager will be responsible for directing, supervising and overseeing the work of the integrated project team. Subject to the scope of work and the decisions of OpCom, the project manager will determine the manner, means and method by which the team undertakes the work, and the locations where it is performed.

At certain points it may be advantageous for the parties to create a steering committee, a special body to decide and mediate difficult cases, which cannot be resolved for certain reasons by OpCom and might potentially lead to deadlocks. This committee will consist of representatives of high-level management of the parties and has the purpose of providing solutions for operational, managerial team and management.

The project manager is usually required promptly to prepare an organisational chart for the integrated project team and submit it to OpCom for approval. Each participant is entitled to nominate representatives as candidates to serve on the integrated project team, subject to the terms of the agreement. All integrated project team members must have the required qualifications and experience commensurate with the scope of work assigned to the team and must be either employees or contract workers of a participant or its affiliates.

11. Local content

11.1 General principles

Different forms of legal obligation are employed by the host government in order to increase domestic and foreign investments, employment, and technology and knowledge transfer from the international oil companies involved in local oil and gas projects to local companies. Most local petroleum laws provide a requirement that every oil and gas project should use a certain amount of local goods and services, usually expressed as a percentage. Commonly, such requirements are also embedded in the different forms of granting instruments, including production sharing and licence agreements where national oil companies, representing the local government's interests, are parties. However, the absence of the national oil companies among the parties in the granting instrument does not mean that the local government lacks the opportunity to impose certain obligations in relation to the involvement of the local labour force and services. The requirements on local content may also be included in public tendering rules (as in Mozambique and Angola) as well as in any granting instrument.

The legislation of developing countries, such as Angola, Equatorial Guinea, Indonesia, Kazakhstan, Nigeria and Zimbabwe, will usually contain local content requirements. Some other countries provide such rules in their tendering procedures or introduce them in the licensing procedure.[915]

The Kazakh legislation on subsoil use requires that the concessionaire buys 50% of goods and services from local contractors.[916] The same legislation in 2018 introduced a requirement that subsoil users invest 1% of the funds invested in the

915 U4 EXPERT ANSWER Local content and corruption in the oil and gas industry. www.transperancy.org, published on 16 December 2014 as the U4 Helpdesk answer.

916 Code of the Republic of Kazakhstan dated 27 December 2017 No. 125-VI "on Subsoil and Subsoil Use", Article 28. Please note that some of the experts conclude that this proportion seems to be unrealistic: "Shared Value, Shared Responsibility: A New Approach to Managing Contracting Chains in the Oil and Gas Sector", www.pubs.iied.org.

relevant subsoil operations into research and development projects provided by Kazakh companies, a further 1% into training of Kazakhstan personnel and another 1% into the socio-economic development of the relevant region.[917] In Indonesia the legislation requires a local content of not less than 35% for offshore projects (which are naturally more technically complicated and thus the government allows a less burdensome requirement for the local content) and a 90% requirement for onshore projects.[918]

In Nigeria the minimum level of local content and minimum percentage of local personnel for oil and gas companies is determined by the Oil and Gas Industry Content Development Act 2010. Under the special exhibit to this act the requirement on local content may vary from 40 to 100%.[919]

In Angola the legislation on goods and services public tendering rules provides specific requirements on the local source for certain goods and services. In some circumstances international companies can participate in the tenders only in cooperation with local Angolan companies.[920]

Often, the parties' obligation under governmental requirements on local content and hiring a specific percentage of local personnel is met in private level arrangements, for example JOAs.

11.2 Analysis of model JOAs

Thus, the Angolan operating procedure text provides the principle that the operator should attract contractors and award contracts "in accordance with the local preference requirements under the regulations or the title documents or under the Operator's normal contracting policy for use of local suppliers."[921]

Extracts from JOA Model Forms show that the principle of local content requirement can be embedded not only in the JOA but in other procedural documents. Often the procurement policies of an operator include the principle that, when awarding contracts on behalf of the consortium, the operator will primarily select local services if the price quality and other conditions offered by the local contractors are comparable with non-local contractors.

The operator might also try to include a requirement to use local content in arrangements with its third-party contractors, who in turn engage subcontractors. Such arrangement with the third-party contractor may oblige it to engage only local subcontractors for the certain type of services, as a logical extension of the operator's local content policy.

The explicit provisions in this regard might be even found in the JOA Models, thus clause 4.2 of the AIPN Model provides:

> *In the conduct of Joint Operations Operator shall to the extent practical and lawful include in its contracts with independent contractors the provisions that require such*

917 Code of the Republic of Kazakhstan dated 27 December 2017 No. 125-VI "on Subsoil and Subsoil Use", Article 129.

918 Ministry of Energy and Mineral Resources Regulation 2013 (Indonesia), www.ssek.com.

919 Nigerian Oil and Gas Industry Content Development Act 2010, www.placng.org.

920 U4 EXPERT ANSWER Local content and corruption in the oil and gas industry, www.transperancy.org, published on 16 December 2014 as the U4 Helpdesk answer.

921 https://iclg.com/practice-areas/oil-and-gas-laws-and-regulations/angola.

contractors to comply with applicable Laws, including registration to do business, immigration, import/export, local preference, national content, tax withholding and payment, and the HSE Plan.

The operator's obligations under the AIPN Model include the obligation to meet certain requirements on national content in their conduct of the joint operations, in practical terms, meaning that the operator must attract local companies or hire the local employees for the joint operations.

The definition of 'local content' is very important. In a broad sense it is understood to mean the involvement of local companies for the provision of services or hiring local citizens into the operator's structure or for the operator's activity.

In some jurisdictions local companies are considered to be those which are registered nationally. However, this is merely a formal characteristic of 'locality'. The most objective characteristic should be the percentage of local citizens employed by the local company or owned locally. In the interests of the host government and the national oil companies it represents, as well as from a practical perspective, the objective criteria should be taken into account and local companies should be understood to be only those involved in actual local manufacturing and those with significant ownership, management and employment of local citizens. Angola, for example, has recently changed its local content legislation to specify that only companies wholly owned by Angolan interests qualify for preferential treatment.[922]

There are some other considerations that need to be taken into account in deciding which goods and services might be included in the understanding of local content:

- the type of work to be provided by the local service providers: for example front-end engineering and detailed engineering design for all oil and gas projects (as well as seismic data-processing projects and reservoir management studies). Some constructions works of the heavy floating platform types and other forms of pre-fabrication are necessarily conducted at local manufacturing yards;
- the type of goods to be provided by the local manufacturers: for example, the fabrication of certain categories of equipment (eg, topsides of fixed onshore and offshore platforms, piles, deck anchors, buoys, jackets, bridges, flare booms, and storage tanks);
- equipment and materials manufactured locally that are fully utilised in the project.

Attracting local companies or employees to the project might be difficult for both the international and the national oil companies. The main concern is that in most cases the local content, including hiring the services of the local companies, is more expensive and may not meet the high standards required by the projects, especially for those projects which are technically and managerially challenging. The requirements for certain projects may be technically very challenging; this will be

922 www.plmj.com/xms/files/03_Novidades_legislativas/2020/10_outubro/NI_Colab_BCSA-PLMJ_New_local_content_rules_for_the_oil_sector.pdf.

the case with Arctic projects, any offshore projects, projects requiring multilateral and fishbone wells or any other types of horizontal drilling with the applicability of chemical fracturing and so on. The particular technologies to be applied for these types of projects are typically available from the international service providers and thus it may be difficult to perform such a project to the appropriate industry standard whilst also achieving the required level of local content.

Some jurisdictions allow oil and gas project parties some discretion, permitting them to give priority to the local content in so far as their prices, qualities, quantities, delivery terms and sales conditions are comparable to the goods and services available abroad and do not incur additional economic burden for the project.

However, in practical terms such a comparison and the provision of evidence that the non-local goods and services are cheaper and better than the local ones may be complicated, so the project participants could still find themselves obliged to hire the local companies and personnel.

This complication could be addressed fairly substantially by including in the JOA terms and provisions such that if the materials and services are not available locally or at reasonably comparable quality standards the operator is entitled to involve non-local companies. They may also involve a monitoring system through the national resource company or a specialised government agency or procurement office which has the role of ensuring that international companies make the maximum use of locally available goods and services when they are comparable in quality to internationally sourced goods and services.

11.3 Discussion

There are a number of challenges for the JOAs parties in relation to "local content" requirement. The interests of a national oil company party will not be the same as those of an international oil company as parties to the JOA, since the international oil company will be more interested in the project's commercial success while the national oil company will also pursue the ancillary political interests, such as increasing investment in local sources and decreasing local unemployment.

The most challenging aspects of hiring local companies are that:

- often the local companies do not meet the project's high health and safety standards;
- the local companies may be somewhat flexible in relation to ethics and other compliance matters and thus threaten the high standards required for the project, a critical reputation issue for the international oil companies;
- conflict of interest may come into play as national oil companies come under pressure to support local companies in order that the state meets political commitments to its population;
- potential local employees may be under-skilled and unable to meet the high professional skills required of project employees and service providers, which will vary depending on the type of project, both offshore and onshore;
- the drive to enhance local content may also work against competitiveness, simply because the local markets are unlikely to have the necessary scale to sustain several suppliers qualifying for local content preferences;
- lastly, several developing countries such as Kazakhstan have joined or aspire to join the World Trade Organization which itself requires members progressively eliminate certain local content preferences.

Certain solutions to these challenges may be available, such as specific training, exchange programmes and the involvement of the local employees in the implementation of the public and private partnerships.

It is often hard to measure the true percentage of local content involved since the measurement's criteria are not clear. Should it be measured by the actual headcount, the amount of compensation for services rendered by the local companies, and so on? In order to clarify the situation, the regulators in some jurisdictions have created an online local content calculator and made it available on their websites.[923]

When meeting the local content requirement might lead to an oil and gas project not being economically viable, the national oil company and international oil companies together might ask the local government to decrease the required percentage of local companies and employees.

The other solution is that the governmental bodies by themselves ease the requirements in relation to the local content. Thus, in anticipation of the pre-salt bid rounds in Brazil in 2013, Petrobras, as the national oil company, asked the state regulator Agência Nacional do Petróleo, Gás Natural e Biocombustíveis (ANP) to reduce the strict local content requirements.

According to the Brazilian National Agency of Petroleum, Natural Gas and Biofuels (ANP), the objective of the local content clause is to increase the share of the domestic industry of goods and services in the projects for exploration and production development of oil and natural gas, on a competitive basis. The expected result of this clause is to boost technological development, the training of human resources and the generation of jobs and income in this segment.[924] Local content requirements are set by the host government and are commonly contained in the granting instrument, so all private arrangements based on the granting instrument must follow that instrument's terms and conditions and must not breach them. However, it is often the case that neither the national industry nor the foreign investors are able to meet the minimum local content requirements. In Brazil, as a result of ongoing controversies and market reaction, in 2018 the ANP approved lower requirements for the use of locally produced goods and services in oil field development, including a concession to shipbuilders and removed local content as a factor in determining winning bids during the 14th bid round. A diversified approach was chosen. Under new rules oil and gas companies were required to use 50% local content during the exploration and production phases of onshore oil and natural gas projects. Naturally, due to complexity of operations the local content levels for offshore exploration were set at 18%, while the requirements for local content in the offshore production phase are divided into three subgroups: 25% for well construction, 40% for subsea systems and 40% for stationary production units.[925]

While deciding whether to join a hydrocarbons project and accept the terms and conditions of the granting instrument, an international oil company should first evaluate its capacity to meet the requirements of the granting instrument and

923 For example, South African National Standards, including the formula on calculation of the local content, www.thedti.gov.za.

924 www2.deloitte.com/br/en/pages/energy-and-resources/upstream-guide/articles/local-content.html.

925 www.spglobal.com/platts/en/market-insights/latest-news/oil/041218-brazils-anp-approves-revised-local-content-rules-appeases-shipbuilders.

compare the outcome of meeting the "local content" requirement with the expected standards of the operations.[926]

12. Health, safety and environment

12.1 General principles

It is a well-known fact that hydrocarbons operations are associated with health, safety and environmental (HSE) risks. It is always the JOA parties' understanding that the joint operations will be undertaken in accordance with the HSE requirements of the local legislation and also that the operator shall meet high industry standards in this regard.

The major events that could cause potential risks to human health and safety are:

- a well blow-out at a drilling or production site, or the rupture of a pipeline and subsequent release of large amounts of oil into the environment – oil spill;
- loss of well or hydrocarbon control, including the release of toxic gases such as hydrogen sulphide, marine oil spills, and ignition of explosive gases, land and marine pollution, including contamination of groundwater sources and productive marine environments.

Since safety of the environment and health is a primary issue during hydrocarbons operations, each model JOA has provisions dealing with the HSE standards for hydrocarbons operations. To develop JOA HSE standards further within the course of conduct of operations, it might be also recommended for the OpCom to approve more detailed and specific HSE internal rules and standards for the joint venture.

Commonly the local law contains extensive provisions on HSE issues for hydrocarbons operations. Since such local law provisions in most cases will have overriding force, they will be applicable to the hydrocarbons operations under a JOA, irrespective of whether the local law is chosen as the applicable law for the JOA. Any operator under any JOA will be bound by the local environmental law provisions by default, and will face the negative consequences in any case of breach. The state usually employs the range of special state services to monitor and control the consortium or the license's holder compliance with the imperative provisions of the local legislation in relation to HSE. Such state authorities operate only by local legislation and are indifferent to the provisions of the JOA, which could not even be available for them due to the confidential nature of the document. Authorities visit operational work sites and check the conduct of operations as part of routine inspections and for unplanned inspections if something goes wrong, for example explosions, oil spills, damage to the health of the team members. These authorities become the participants of the commissions that are involved in the investigation of the HSE incidents. This sphere of operator's activity is very closely regulated by such administrative procedures and requires a lot of caution by the operator, since any violations or incidents might lead to different types of penalties, including the instruction to stop operations.

926 The changing scope of local content legislation can be a matter for dispute between IOCs and the state, particularly where the relevant concession agreement includes stabilisation provisions, preventing the state to a greater or lesser degree from increasing the economic cost of the project by legislative changes. In one sense, it is reasonable to expect IOCs to absorb such costs because, ultimately, they are likely to be compensated in cash or in-kind by the state for the costs of investment under the terms of the relevant concession agreement.

12.2 Analysis of model JOAs

Almost all model petroleum JOAs contain provisions dealing with HSE, and some provide that an HSE plan should be adopted yearly at the level OpCom. The requirement to adopt HSE plan could be also be a particular requirement of the local legislation.

Since the HSE sector is very sensitive and violation of the HSE rules could result in litigation and reputational risks for the investors (international oil company) and the government (national oil company), the parties' expectations are that the JOA's rules and the requirements of the local legislation should be followed during the hydrocarbons operations.

Some JOAs take the view that OpCom involvement in the HSE plan should be minimal and that the operator will present the HSE plan to the OpCom for information purposes only, while others recognise the importance of the HSE plan and accept the OpCom's involvement in the process of adopting the plan.[927]

The AMPLA Model Petroleum JOA recognises the importance of the HSE plan and the necessity of the OpCom's involvement in the process of its adoption. It further provides that HSE plan shall be adopted yearly and shall be compliant with the Good Australian Oilfield Practice:

> (a) *Before the beginning of each Year, the Operator must prepare and submit to the Operating Committee for its approval a plan of Health, Safety, Environment and Community (HSEC) matters containing the policies which will govern the Joint Operations and the objectives and targets for that Year consistent with Good Australian Oilfield Practice.*

The AMPLA JOA Model gives some attention to the potential elements of HSE plan and contains the list of its essential components:

> (a) *The HSEC plan must:*
>   (i) *include an assessment of the health, safety and environmental impact of Joint Operations;*
>   (ii) *include an alcohol and drugs policy and enforcement procedure, which prohibits employees and agents, contractors and invitees in any area in which Joint Operations are being undertaken from using or distributing unprescribed controlled substances, including alcohol; and*
>   (iii) *take into account of any specific policies, objectives and targets adopted by the Operating Committee.*
>
> (b) *The Operator must conduct Joint Operations and any Sole Risk Operations in accordance with the HSEC plan.*
>
> (c) *The Operator must report regularly on the implementation of the HSEC plan and promptly advise the Operating Committee of any adverse matter arising out of*

927 P Roberts and R Fowler, *Joint Operating Agreements: A Practical Guide*, 4th edn, Globe Law and Business, 2020, pp370–371.

Joint Operations, such as an occurrence which negatively affects the environment or could or does cause any serious illness, injury or death.

(d) The Operator must audit, or cause to be audited, the HSEC plan regularly at the cost of the Participants. Each Participant may join in such audit upon reasonable notice given to the Operator.[928]

Under Article 12.4 of the Norwegian Agreement concerning petroleum activities (Norwegian JOA form), the annual work programme and budget model form provides a specific line item dealing with HSE activities: "activities related to HSE work as well as licence". This line item deals with the costs and expenses related to HSE activities and is the integral part of annual work programme and budget. This means that it is operator/joint venture's responsibility to take care of the HSE aspects of hydrocarbons operations and it ensures that the partners dedicate a particular amount of budget on HSE issues. The operator will be then obliged to provide the OpCom with the report on how the budget on HSE has been spent and what preventive and other activities have been conducted.

The Greenlandic Model JOA establishes a special capacity within the scope of the project subcommittees for a technical subcommittee to discuss all technical, safety and environmental matters relating to the joint operations.

The most robust provisions dealing with HSE issues are provided by the 2012 AIPN Model JOA, including the operator's obligations to provide HSE information and to prepare the HSE plan. Under this model JOA, the operator shall supply HSE key performance data and reports both monthly and annually to OpcCom and or participants. It contains detailed provisions on the HSE plan as well as the possibility to conduct audits of the plan's implementation and HSE issues:

HSE Plan

Operator shall in the conduct of Joint Operations:

Prepare and establish an HSE Plan designed to achieve safe and reliable conduct of operations and activities, to avoid significant and unintended impact on the safety and health of people, on property, and on the environment, and to comply with Laws relating to HSE;

Carry out the HSE Plan in conformance with Laws relating to HSE and in a manner consistent with standards and procedures generally followed in the international petroleum industry under similar circumstances;

Plan and conduct Joint Operations consistent with the HSE Plan; and

Design and operate Joint Property consistent with the HSE Plan.

The Operating Committee shall at least annually review and approve:

ALTERNATIVE PROVISION, CHOOSE ONE

ALTERNATIVE #1

the details of the HSE Plan, the implementation of the HSE Plan, and of the effectiveness of the HSE Plan.

---

928 Clause 7.9 of the AMPLA Model Petroleum Agreement.

ALTERNATIVE #2
an HSE report and letter of assurance from Operator in a form acceptable to the Operating Committee providing adequate evidence that the HSE Plan fulfils the requirements of Article 6.6.A and is in place, that Operator is properly carrying out the HSE Plan, that any major HSE issues have been brought to the attention of the Operating Committee and are being properly managed, and that the HSE Plan as carried out is effective.
In the conduct of Joint Operations, Operator shall:
ALTERNATIVE PROVISION, CHOOSE ONE

The following wording of the AIPN Model provides the different schemes of HSE assessment. Thus, under one of the schemes the assessment is carried out in accordance with the internally established procedures and by the operator itself. The second scheme contemplates annual assessment by the independent external auditor.

ALTERNATIVE #1
establish and carry out a program for regular HSE assessments. The purpose of such assessments is to periodically review HSE systems and procedures, including actual practice and performance, to verify that the HSE Plan is in place and fulfils the requirements of Article 6.6.A, that the HSE Plan is being properly carried out and that the HSE Plan as carried out is effective. Operator shall, at a minimum, conduct such an assessment before entering into significant new Joint Operations and before undertaking any major changes to existing Joint Operations. Upon reasonable notice given to Operator, Non-Operators shall have the right to participate in such HSE assessments.
ALTERNATIVE #2
establish an annual audit program in which independent auditors review and verify that the HSE Plan is in place and fulfils the requirements of Article 6.6.A, that the HSE Plan is being properly carried out, and that the HSE Plan as carried out is effective.[929]

As discussed, the AIPN Model is the most robust among others existent in relation to HSE provisions. It gives detailed understanding about possible elements of the internal rules and separately requires the operator to include in its agreements with contractors a stipulation that the contracts comply with the operator's HSE rules and regulations.

Operator shall require its contractors, consultants, and agents undertaking activities for the Joint Account to manage HSE risks in a manner consistent with the requirements of HSE Plan.

929 Article 6.6.C of the AIPN Model JOA.

> *Operator shall establish and enforce rules consistent with those generally followed in the international petroleum industry under similar circumstances that, at a minimum, prohibit within the Contract Area the misuse of prescribed drugs and the possession, use, distribution, or sale of any of the following:*
> *Firearms, explosives, or other weapons without the prior written approval of Operator's senior management;*
> *Alcoholic beverages without the prior written approval of Operator's senior management; and*
> *Illicit or non-prescribed controlled substances.*[930]

On top of the above, the AIPN Model also provides the possibility for a non-operators' audit in relation to HSE issues. Such provisions might be also complimented with the obligation of the operator to provide relevant documentation upon the request of the non-operators.

> *OPTIONAL PROVISION, CHOOSE IF DESIRED. IF NOT CHOSEN CHECK CROSS-REFERENCES,*
> *Without prejudice to a Party's rights under Article 4.2.B.8, with reasonable advance notice, Operator shall permit at all reasonable times during normal business hours each Non-Operator (at its own risk and cost) to conduct an audit of the HSE Plan, its implementation and effectiveness. Where there are two or more Non-Operators, the Non-Operators shall make a reasonable effort to conduct joint or simultaneous HSE audits in a manner that will result in a minimum of inconvenience to Operator.*[931]

12.3 Discussion

It appears that HSE matters are issues of mutual interest for the national oil company and the international oil company and that all participants in the JOA will wish to ensure that the hydrocarbons operations are conducted following the standard or best industry practices in this regard and at least in compliance with the local HSE rules.

The stricter the HSE obligations in the JOA are, the greater liability the operator should bear in relation to the standards in the hydrocarbons operations, subject, of course, to the general rules of operator's liability based on "no gain, no loss" concept. Thus, depending whether the national oil company or the international oil company is to be the operator, either the national or the international company will be reluctant to accept strict HSE provisions, since the operator will be responsible for preparing the HSE programme to be approved at the OpCom, and to ensure that it and other HSE requirements (eg, joint venture HSE policies) are followed during the day-to-day operational activity.

930 Article 6.6.D&E of the AIPN Model JOA.
931 Article 6.6 of the 2012 AIPN Model JOA.

Bhargava *et al* criticise JOAs for failing to contain express, detailed provisions governing operations with respect to greenhouse gases, water resources, gas flaring, community engagement and compliance with local environmental laws.

Quite often, those drafting these agreements are concerned first and foremost about minimizing their company's environmental liability rather than negotiating clauses that establish strong pro-environment standards. While understandable, this orientation has the unintended effect of limiting a non-operating partner's ability to hold the operator to strong environmental standards which could stop environmental problems before such liability clauses are needed.[932]

It is perhaps wrong to criticise JOAs agreed 20 or 30 years ago for failing to meet modern expectations. Secondly, it is also inappropriate for a JOA to add an additional level of environmental rule-making on top of the national and international standards that will apply as a matter of law and will have obligatory effect by default – and may change over the life of the JOA. What is legitimate is to expect the JOA to require the operator to present to the OpCom its procedures for meeting environmental requirements for approval, together with proposals for key performance indicators, audit and assurance provisions, and reporting of such indicators to the non-operators. In principle, local and international law will define what the operator is supposed to achieve, but the JOA can support compliance by requiring the operator to demonstrate compliance to the operational committee on a regular basis and can even establish a more robust and developed framework for HSE rules compliance. This is what is intended to be achieved in the AIPN Model. Developed provisions on HSE matters in the JOA provide the operator with the flexibility to apply its corporate procedures, and thereby to protect its brand and corporate reputation, but gives the non-operators the tools by which to hold it to the task.

Poor adherence to the HSE rules, simple negligence or just unforeseen circumstances might result in severe consequences. One of the most well-known examples is the Deepwater Horizon case.

In April 2010 the mobile operating drilling unit Deepwater Horizon was completing operations at the Macondo well in the Gulf of Mexico on the outer continental shelf of the United States. During the operations, control of the well was lost, resulting in the release of liquid and gaseous hydrocarbons, multiple explosions and the death of 11 people. This became the grounds for multiple lawsuits and BP had to pay, in total, more than 60 billion dollars in fines, clean-up costs and compensation by 2018.

The Deepwater Horizon case is not the only example of environmental cases in the sector. Another example is the Oil Spill case, Bohai Bay, China (2011). The joint venture (ConocoPhillips (49%) and CNOOC (51%)) was a special joint venture set up to run operations in the Penglai field in the Gulf of Bohai, China. As a result of litigation, CNOC, the non-operating party, was obliged to pay a large amount of compensation in favour of the Chinese fund for environmental protection. Other

932 S Bhargava, J Bamford, N Joseph and J Kwicinski, "Fixing Flawed Environmental Clauses in Joint Venture Legal Agreements: How Operators and Non-Operators Can Live Up to Their Environmental Stewardship Promises", *OGEL* 18(5) (2020), www.ogel.org/article.asp?key=3923.

cases include the explosion of the drilling platform Piper Alpha, UK (1988);[933] the oil spill in North Alaska, USA (2006);[934] the explosion on the island Varanus, Australia (2008);[935] and the oil Spill in Nigeria (2006).[936]

As international consensus grows for the need to reduce greenhouse gas emissions, achieve the target of zero carbon emission and improve environmental performance generally, international oil companies and national oil companies need to re-engage on the value of environmental performance. In the past, national oil companies may have associated high safety standards with "gold-plating" the practice of maximising project expenditure on the pretext that the state will fully compensate the contractor for that expenditure in kind or in cash under the concession agreement.[937] Alternatively, they may consider such expenditure as driven by the international oil company's desire to placate stakeholders and activist shareholders in their countries of incorporation. The recurrence of industrial accidents, with associated penalties, liability and reputation damage, as well as the increasingly global attention to climate change should help the OpCom to take an aligned position on environmental issues.

13. Corporate social responsibility

13.1 General principles

The purpose of this section is to consider the relevance of corporate social responsibility to JOAs and the governance of joint ventures. "Corporate social responsibility" refers to the evolving concept that businesses owe duties of care to wider society beyond their employees, shareholders and contractual counterparties for the impact that their global business operations may have on the environment and human rights. It is directly connected with the so-called "social license to operate" which society expects such companies to observe in their operations. Oil and gas companies are under extreme pressure to respond to this agenda because their operations regularly have significant environmental impact, either in terms of direct pollution or carbon emissions, and those operations may take place in countries with poor human rights records. The same operations generate significant revenues which are returned to shareholders and pension funds that are increasingly themselves under pressure to defend the sustainability of their sources of funds.[938]

Corporate social responsibility extends to a very wide range of potential concerns and societal issues. At the time of writing the second edition, environmental protection and climate change are probably the most significant, but oil and gas companies currently must take into account civil society initiatives on a range of issues such as child labour, modern slavery, the trade in illegal forest products, anti-bribery and corruption, disclosure of government revenues and

---

933 See: www.smd.qmul.ac.uk/risk/yearone/casestudies/piper-alpha.html.

934 Tim Bradner, "Drilling and Spilling on Alaska's North Slope State Wins $255 Million in 2006 Pipeline Leak Arbitration", *Alaska Journal of Commerce* (8 November 2012).

935 K Bills and D Agostini, "Offshore Petroleum Safety Regulation Varanus Island Incident Investigation", Commonwealth of Australia, Department of Resources, Energy, and Tourism, June 2009.

936 https://oilspillmonitor.ng/ Oil spills in the Niger Delta in Nigeria.

937 D Johnston, "Upstream Concessions and Contracts" in P Roberts and R Fowler (eds), *Oil and Gas Contracts – Principles and Practice*, 2nd edn, Sweet & Maxwell, 2019.

938 See the *Economist*, "Big Business is Beginning to accept Broader Social Responsibilities", 24 August 2019 available at www.economist.com/briefing/2019/08/22/big-business-is-beginning-to-accept-broader-social-responsibilities.

human rights generally; many of these initiatives have resulted in specific country or multistate legislation.[939]

Emerging focuses of civil society attention include racial and gender equality as well as economic inequality and access to employment opportunities.

The corporate governance applicable to joint ventures, particularly unincorporated versions, creates very specific issues with respect to managing corporate social responsibility. Since the publication of the UN Guiding Principles on Business and Human Rights in 2011, joint ventures may have taken the view that corporate social responsibility could be left to the joint-venture operator to implement and report upon, in the same way that it implemented and reported upon health and safety performance. After all, the specific technical requirements for compliant petroleum operations are dictated by local law. For several reasons, this is no longer the case.

First, the country of incorporation of each JOA party may impose duties to report on the environmental and human rights performance of its global operations, including non-operated businesses. It is increasingly likely that these duties to report will be enhanced by duties of due diligence, requiring such companies to take proactive steps to avoid or mitigate environmental and human rights impacts of such businesses.[940] As will be discussed in relation to the UN Human Rights Council deliberations on a binding instrument on transnational corporations and other business enterprises with respect to human rights[941] and the proposed EU Directive on Corporate Due Diligence and Corporate Accountability,[942] the legislation is unlikely to address directly the question whether a non-operator has responsibility for non-operated businesses, whether or not they are able to exercise control via the OpCom on the content and manner of performing joint operations.

Secondly, there is a trend in several legal systems to permit parent companies whose subsidiaries are accused of human rights or environmental violations in other jurisdictions to be held responsible for failing to detect and address those violations, to a greater or lesser extent prioritising environmental and human rights protection over the principle of corporate separateness, limited corporate liability and the corporate veil.[943] In some measure, this trend takes its lead from the United Nations "Guiding Principles on Business and Human Rights" elaborated by Professor

939 See for example the materials listed in Annex 1 "Key Resources" in the EU's "Oil and Gas Sector Guide on implementing the UN Guiding Principles on Business and Human Rights" available at https://op.europa.eu/en/publication-detail/-/publication/e05fc065-f35c-4c0d-91e9-7e500374ee0f; up-to-date descriptions of environmental risk and human rights risk are provided by Article 3 of the draft text of the EU directive on corporate due diligence and corporate accountability available at www.europarl.europa.eu/doceo/document/A-9-2021-0018_EN.html.

940 See for example France's "Loi de Vigilance LOI n° 2017-399 du 27 mars 2017 relative au devoir de vigilance des sociétés mères et des entreprises donneuses d'ordre", available at www.legifrance.gouv.fr/loda/id/JORFTEXT000034290626/.

941 Second revised draft available at www.ohchr.org/Documents/HRBodies/HRCouncil/WGTransCorp/Session6/OEIGWG_Chair-Rapporteur_second_revised_draft_LBI_on_TNCs_and_OBEs_with_respect_to_Human_Rights.pdf.

942 See footnote 939.

943 A summary of the position under French, Italian, Dutch, Swedish and UK law is provided by the EU document "Access to legal remedies for victims of corporate human rights abuses in third countries" Section 5 available at www.europarl.europa.eu/RegData/etudes/STUD/2019/603475/EXPO_STU(2019)603475_EN.pdf. For the position under US federal law, see R Mares, "Responsibility to Respect: Why the Core Company should act when Affiliates infringe Human Rights", available at www.biicl.org/files/5800_mares_15-09-11_biicl.pdf. For Canadian law see R Chartier and KL Johnston, "ESG Considerations in Oil and Gas Deals: Risks and Opportunities (Canada & Globally)" *OGEL* 5 (2020), especially discussion of *Nevsun Resources Ltd v Araya et al.*

Ruggie in his capacity as the United Nations' Special Representative on the issue of human rights and transnational corporations and other business enterprises.[944] This trend was entirely unforeseen by the drafters of the model JOAs and executed JOAs which now govern the operations most likely to be the target of such parent company liability.

This is bound to cause concern both for operator and non-operator parent companies; on the one hand, the operator's parent company will wish to ensure that operations are conducted in a manner that minimises the risk of such liability being incurred by it in its jurisdiction, with the result that it may insist upon the joint venture adopting policies of reporting and due diligence consistent with the laws of its country of incorporation.

By contrast, the parent companies of the non-operators face a dilemma: should they, through their non-operator participants, insist that the operator enhances its environment and human rights performance to be consistent with the expectations of each parent companies' home state laws by insisting the JOA contains additional audit rights and/or seek to appoint secondees to key roles in the operator organisation and/or more control over the operator conduct of operations via the Opcom?[945] Should the joint venture simply adopt a strategy of following the most onerous applicable legal regime? How acceptable might that be to the joint venture, given the implications in terms of cost and disclosure of information will depend on whether the terms of the joint-venture agreements would 'socialise' any liability incurred by any participant to the others, creating the necessary degree of alignment. This point is considered in the next section.

Reaching consensus in the joint venture on how to respond to this legislation may entail difficult conflicts and compromises with the expectations of the operator parent company which will itself be potentially subject to different laws. Or should the non-operators instead allow the operator freedom to act, adopting a *laissez faire* approach, in the hope of sustaining the argument that their non-operator subsidiaries lacked the necessary control and influence over the operator and/or legitimately relied upon the operator to meet the relevant environmental and human rights standards of performance? This is a risky strategy for reasons explained below.

These dilemmas are particularly significant for a joint venture comprising international oil companies and national oil companies seeking to perform its obligations to a host state under the applicable granting instrument. How that joint venture meets its environmental and human rights obligations will be heavily influenced by the scope of its licence to operate and the programmes and budgets for the joint venture which the state approves. If the granting instrument is a production sharing agreement or service agreement, it is likely that the state will ultimately compensate the joint venture for its costs and will have the right to review and approve the joint venture's operational programmes and budgets. It will therefore have a say in the joint venture's strategy and budget for corporate social responsibility compliance (if it is a cost recovery item to be approved). Will the state consider such expenditure as unnecessary "gold-plating"? Will the state allow the joint venture to take remedial action on human rights and environmental issues at its cost, if it does not wish to admit that such issues exist in its jurisdiction? It may be that the

---

944 Available at www.ohchr.org/documents/publications/guidingprinciplesbusinesshr_en.pdf.

945 It should be borne in mind that JOAs often limit non-operator audit rights to financial matters only; those audit rights may need to be expressly extended to include human rights and environment issues.

state and its national oil companies wish to be able to access international financial markets, may participate in other international ventures and may even aspire to partial or total privatisation of state-run enterprises in future, reasons encouraging them to adopt and implement international good practice on these issues.[946]

The importance of this issue cannot be exaggerated. The trend towards imposing legally enforceable obligations to conduct environmental and human rights due diligence, and allowing rights of action and remedies against parent companies may make it harder for the state and joint venture to reach mutually acceptable agreement on environmental and human rights performance. If the state and any national oil company in the joint venture are not aligned with the other participants in aspiring to the same broad objectives and standards, the joint venture may be faced with the choice of leaving such issues unaddressed, exposing it to litigation and liability in the participants' home jurisdictions,[947] or terminating its granting instrument and potentially disengaging from that state altogether.[948] The stated objective of the EU Directive is to create a level playing field for all European incorporated enterprises and ultimately all enterprises globally, by imposing a single uniform standard of environmental and human rights performance;[949] if such legislation does not take into account the influence which the host state has upon environmental and human rights performance of a joint venture, it may result in compliant joint ventures being forced to withdraw their business from states which are prepared to function with lower environmental or human rights performance standards. This will shrink the size of the so-called "level playing field".

There are at least three key consequences of these initiatives which are relevant to the functioning of joint ventures governed by JOAs:

- How will each joint venture be treated for the purpose of accountability – as a single business enterprise, or an association of business enterprises with interlocking accountability?

---

946 The EU's "Oil and gas sector guide on implementing the UN guiding principles on business and human rights" remarks:

> *"National O&G Companies (NOCs) are subject to the same responsibility to respect human rights as all other O&G companies, but will also need to take into account the human rights obligations of the state that owns or controls them. These obligations suggest a number of roles for the state, for example:*
> *– Ensuring policies that are consistent with human rights standards and coherent across all ministries that engage with the NOC (such as energy, health, foreign affairs, education and research);*
> *– Including human rights issues in regular 'owner dialogues' between the government and the company;*
> *– Developing guidance for all state-owned entities on human rights.*
> *NOCs may be particularly well-placed to raise with government representatives the benefits of these kinds of approaches for both the state and the company." Section III.1 E Page 24.*

947 Some joint ventures may resolve the dilemma by deciding to meet the costs of such environmental and human rights compliance with their own resources, without seeking the state's approval for such expenditure, and recovering such expenditure as cost petroleum under the terms of the relevant granting instrument. There are two dangers with this approach; a non-cooperative state may challenge the joint venture's rights to conduct due diligence and to take appropriate mitigation actions, if those actions are potentially the responsibility of the state's own competent authorities. Also, the granting instrument may actually prohibit the joint venture from taking action which is not pre-approved by the state, even if the joint venture has no intention of recovering the costs of such action from the state.

948 The United Nations General Principles make it quite clear that a business enterprise should consider terminating an operation which is causing or contributing to a human rights violation, having exhausted any leverage to remedy the situation. See J Ruggie, "Guiding Principles on Business and Human Rights", commentary on Principle 19, pp21–22.

949 Refer to Recital 8 of the proposed text for the EU Directive on corporate due diligence and corporate accountability.

- What levels of accountability and responsibility are to be imposed upon the operator's parent company, the non-operators and the non-operators' respective parent companies, and how can such responsibilities be discharged within the scope of a JOA?
- If an operator's parent company incurs a liability for infringement, can that liability be passed on to the non-operators under the JOA?

The first two questions can be addressed together.

The draft terms of the proposed legislation do not clarify the allocation of responsibility for human rights compliance between operator, non-operators and their respective corporations. The approach adopted by the UN Special Representative is captured by the following statement:

The corporate group structure does not make any difference to whether entities within the group have to respect human rights. It simply affects how they go about ensuring that rights are respected in practice, for instance through their contractual arrangements, internal management systems, governance or accountability structures. If human rights abuses occur, it will be the national law in the relevant jurisdiction that determines where liability rests.[950]

There are probably two reasons for this – first, in the context of human rights, corporate separateness has been treated as a defensive strategy used by corporations to isolate the parent company from human rights controversies and liabilities in the countries in which their subsidiaries operate.[951] Secondly, the United Nations[952] recognises that participating states are in a better position to implement the purposes of the legislation in their domestic laws, taking into account the peculiarities of business laws and corporate structures in their jurisdictions. In any event, the draft legislation is purposefully widely drafted to capture any form of for-profit business organisation with a particular focus on businesses conducting transnational activity and to allocate to it an appropriate level of responsibility to address human rights risks and infringements anywhere in its value chain.

Helpfully the United Nations Special Representative and the EU have both published interpretative guidelines in support of their stated policy positions, which the legislation is intended to implement.[953] These guidelines are broadly consistent in their approach to the allocation of responsibility and it is hoped that the legislation, as implemented into domestic laws by participating states, will follow the same

950 "The Corporate Responsibility to Respect Human Rights – an Interpretative Guide" Q.17 available at www.ohchr.org/documents/publications/hr.pub.12.2_en.pdf.

951 See Prof. J Ruggie, "Protect, Respect and Remedy: A Framework for Business and Human Rights" Report the UN Human Rights Council 7 April 2008, para 13, p5, available at https://media.business-humanrights.org/media/documents/files/reports-and-materials/Ruggie-report-7-Apr-2008.pdf. See also Section 3.5.1: "Legal barriers that can prevent legitimate cases involving business-related human rights abuse from being addressed" in "Access to legal remedies for victims of corporate human rights abuses in third countries" referenced in note 947 above.

952 See UN Guiding Principles Foundational Principle A.2: "States should set out clearly the expectation that all business enterprises domiciled in their territory and/or jurisdiction respect human rights throughout their operations."

953 "The Corporate Responsibility to Respect Human Rights – an Interpretative Guide" referenced in footnote 950 above; "Oil and gas sector guide on implementing the UN guiding principles on business and human rights" referenced in footnote 939 above.

approach and be equally clear. The EU "Oil and Gas Sector Guide on implementing the UN Guiding Principles on Business and Human Rights" sets out a scheme for attributing levels of responsibility as follows:

To identify the best ways to address potential impacts, a company first needs to understand the nature of its involvement:

Where the company is at risk of causing an impact, it should take the necessary steps to prevent the impact from occurring.

Where the company is at risk of contributing to an impact, it should first take steps to avoid this contribution.

Where it does not control those who may contribute to the impact, it should use its leverage with them to mitigate the remaining risk.

Where a negative impact may be directly linked to the company's operations, products or services through a business relationship, even without a contribution by the company itself, it should use whatever leverage it has to mitigate the risk that the impact occurs.[954]

It may be attractive for non-operators and their parents to "downplay" the level of control and influence they exercise in the joint venture with the objective of arguing that they merely have an obligation to use such leverage as they do have to mitigate any human rights infringement risk. This is unlikely to succeed because the UN Guiding Principles and their interpretive guidelines make it clear that joint-venture partners are expected to seek means of increasing their leverage in order to ensure that human rights infringements are eliminated and ultimately to consider leaving the joint venture rather than hide behind the assumed role of a passive investor. It is more likely that non-operators will be considered at least as contributing to any human rights impact caused by joint-venture operations: because they approve the strategy for the joint-venture operations through programmes and budgets and AFEs, they are kept closely informed of operational outcomes and contribute to its financing. Such concern might impact the outsourcing and procurement strategies of the joint venture as well.

On the other hand, the prospect of legal liability for human rights risks and violations being imposed upon parent companies for activities abroad by subsidiaries (including the subsidiaries of other corporations where that subsidiary acts as operator) is likely to attract corporate head office attention and resources. The UN Guiding Principles expect corporations to establish and implement corporate policy commitments to human rights compliance and to maintain the appropriate stamp of senior management approval for embedding such policy commitments into the corporation's global practice.[955]

There is the risk therefore that each of the joint venture's parties will be expected by their respective parents to implement their own corporate versions of good practice in the joint venture. The EU Guidelines sensibly suggest that this conflict can be avoided by the joint venture implementing local procedures delivering the necessary due diligence, grievance and remediation processes which the guidelines advocate,

954 EU "Oil and Gas Sector Guide on implementing the UN Guiding Principles on Business and Human Rights", Section III C p44.

955 UN Guiding Principles Foundational Principle 15(a).

whilst facilitating the reporting of human rights practice by the participating corporations at head office level. Such a "local" approach has many advantages to it – it will be adaptable to the particular local environment, will be best placed to respond to local grievances on a timely basis and will be accessible to the individuals and communities it seeks to protect.[956] The key relationships which the joint venture has with the state through which many human rights issues will be negotiated and resolved will necessarily also be local. It will be for the OpCom to deliberate upon and approve such local procedures, achieving alignment between the participating corporations' objectives. This should also be attractive to the operator which should prudently avoid a situation where it allows its parent to override the OpCom and impose its own corporate procedures without obtaining the OpCom's support.[957] However, such a joint-venture specific procedure may not meet the requirements of the non-operator and/or its parent company; this may arise if the EU and UN member states take different approaches in implementing the new legislation. It will then be down to the non-operator and its parent to decide if they can adequately mitigate any human rights risk associated with such difference or, in an extreme case, need to withdraw from the joint venture altogether.

In summary, therefore, it is impossible to predict how the participating states may implement these rules into their domestic legislation and how, in particular, responsibility for compliance will be allocated to operators, non-operators and their parents incorporated in those territories. However, if the legislation follows the guidelines, the operator, non-operators and their parents will each have an appropriate level of responsibility, and it will not be possible for non-operators to hide behind their minority participation in the joint venture.

13.2 Analysis of models JOAs

If the operator's parent company is sued in its own jurisdiction for the operator's failure to meet human rights and environmental standards, will the operator be able to recover a proportion of such liability from the non-operators pursuant to the JOA? On the one hand, the liability squarely arises from the conduct (or misconduct) of petroleum operations by the operator; on the other hand, the liability is incurred by the parent company, and not the operator entity itself, and the parent company is not a signatory party to the JOA. There is a conundrum here: by imposing a duty of care directly upon parent companies, the principles of corporate separateness and the corporate veil are circumvented for the objective of providing the victims of human rights and environmental violations with a remedy against the parent company, but the parent company may be unable to share that liability with the other joint-venture participants precisely because it cannot avail itself of the rights applicable to the operator as it is not party to the JOA.

---

956 "Oil and Gas Sector Guide on implementing the UN Guiding Principles on Business and Human Rights" referenced in footnote 939 above. See for example Section III A page 43, Section 3 V page 64, Section VI A Page 72.

957 The potential for a parent company to attract liability to itself by intervening in its subsidiary's activities "on the ground" is illustrated by the English Supreme Court cases *Vendanta Resources Plc v Lungowe* [2019] UKSC 20 and *Okpabi v Royal Dutch Shell plc* [2021] UKSC 3.

The answer to this question will turn on the wording of the operator's indemnity clause discussed in Section 3 of this chapter. The critical issue will be whether the beneficiary of the indemnity provided by the JOA parties in respect of joint operations is limited to the operator or is extended to the operator's affiliates. The AIPN JOA extends the scope of the operator indemnity to any "Operator Indemnitee" which is defined as follows:

> *Operator Indemnitee means any of the Operator, its Affiliates, or their respective directors, officers, and employees. Operator Indemnitees means all of them.*[958]

The AMPLA JOA and CAPL JOAs follow the AIPN JOA in extending the operator indemnity to include liabilities incurred by the operator's affiliates.[959]

The AAPL JOA form 810 permits the operator to recover the costs of settling "Claims" defined as:

> *Any claim (including any third party claim for contractual indemnity), demand, lawsuit, hearing (administrative or judicial) or other proceeding made against a Party or other person or entity on account of a matter involving activities or operations under this Agreement or affecting the Leases or the Contract Area.*[960]

That wording is sufficiently wide to enable the operator to recover liability incurred by its parent company, but there are other provisions in the AAPL JOA which would help the non-operators to contest that interpretation.

By contrast, the Oil & Gas UK JOA specifically limited the operator's indemnity to the operator entity only,[961] until the 2011 edition extended the scope of beneficiaries of the indemnity to include the Operator's affiliates. The Greenlandic JOA limits the scope of the operator's indemnity to the operator itself acting in such capacity, but interestingly extends that indemnity to include any party to the JOA (including NUNAOIL) which incurs a liability while performing the functions of the operator in its place; that will not assist the recovery of a liability incurred by the operator's parent company because it is neither a party to the JOA nor was the liability incurred as a result of the parent company's performance of operator tasks.[962]

The Norwegian JOA is difficult to interpret on this point; the relevant provision in favour of the operator is worded as follows:

958 AIPN JOA Article 1.1.
959 AMPLA JOA Article 6.6; CAPL JOA Article 4.02.
960 AAPL JOA Form 810 Article 2.10.
961 Oil & Gas UK JOA Article 1.1, 6.2.4.
962 Greenlandic JOA Article 3.3.

> *Unless otherwise specified in this Agreement, the Parties shall be primarily liable to each other on a pro rata basis, secondarily jointly and severally liable for all obligations arising by virtue of the joint venture's activities. This applies irrespective of a liability towards third parties.*[963]

Arguably, a liability incurred by the operator's parent company may be said to arise "by virtue of the joint venture's activities", particularly because the trigger for liability will be the breach of relevant standards by the operator, and not any particular action or inaction by the parent company, save for its failure to intervene and prevent such breach.

13.3 Discussion

Even in cases where the JOA does not extend the operator indemnity to the operator's affiliates, the operator may still be able to recover a contribution from non-operators. This will be via the joint account if it itself is liable to its parent company in its capacity as operator under the terms of the separate services agreement put in place between the parent company and the joint venture to govern the parent company's activities for the joint venture. Similar concerns might occur with a large variety of service providers and their relevant supply chain. The difficulty here may be that the scope of the services agreement may be activity specific and may not extend to the supervision of the operator in terms of human rights and environmental performance which is the trigger for the parent company's liability. Chapter 2, Section 8 discusses overheads and the additional fee which the operator may be entitled to levy from the joint account as compensation for corporate support from the operator's head office, including its parent company. The non-operators will argue that the additional fee, usually expressed as a percentage of the overall costs of joint operations, is also a limit on the joint account's liability for such head office activities, preventing the operator from recovering the parent company liability in excess of that amount.

Lastly, the operator will doubtless invoke the principle that it should not incur a gain or loss with respect to joint operations, the principle discussed in Chapter 2, Section 6. Again, the non-operators will argue that such a principle extends only to the position of the operator entity acting in accordance with the JOA, and not its parent company. Furthermore, the court is unlikely to interpret that principle to be wider in scope than the operator indemnity set out in the relevant JOA.

The operator should also consider whether the joint-venture insurance policies put in place with respect to third-party liability will respond to claims in respect of parent company liability and/or other third parties like service contractors.

14. Disposition of production

14.1 General principles

Each participant is entitled to receive its participating interest share of the oil and gas production at the point of delivery described in the JOA from the operator in accordance with the terms of the underlying granting instrument and/or JOA.

---

963 Norwegian JOA Article 7.1.

A national oil company's share in the hydrocarbons production will be proportional to its participating interest in the project, in the same way as an international oil company. However, the national oil company's right to production entitlement may be postponed if the national oil company's share of costs has been carried by the other parties on terms that the carried amount is repayable by recovering the cost of the carry from the value of the national oil company's share of production. Under these terms and conditions, the national oil company will only be entitled to its share of the production once the carrying parties have fully recovered the carry amount. Depending on the amount of carry provided, it could take several years for the carrying parties to recover the value of that carry from the national oil company's share of petroleum.

Generally, under the applicable national petroleum law or the granting instruments (eg, concession agreements, licence agreements, licences, petroleum agreements, production sharing agreements), the total amount of the petroleum produced will be transferred into the ownership of the state and the participating companies by the operator.[964] However, certain jurisdictions provide in their constitutional documents that the host government will solely own the produced hydrocarbons. Thus, the law on Subsoil of the Russian Federation provides that initially the state has ownership over all subsoil resources. Hence, the state has the primary right over what is being produced from the subsoil and the granting instrument provides the terms and conditions of how the extracted hydrocarbons will be split in between the state and license holder,[965] taking into account the fact that it is license holder who will be responsible for investments in the licensed fields.

The host government may have the right to reserve a certain amount of the hydrocarbons produced and to retain them for public purposes, such as a mandatory supply on the domestic market. The matter of allocation and disposition is a very commercial issue (though certain aspects such as metering, hydrocarbon quality and pressure are likely to be governed by local regulations) and will mainly be addressed in such instruments as the granting instrument and JOAs. The granting instrument will initially establish the allocation of hydrocarbons between the government and the license holder and JOA will establish purely commercial terms of further allocation. These two instruments will serve as the basis for further detailed hydrocarbons allocation instruments such as lifting agreements, crude oil supply agreements and gas balancing agreements.

In the case of production sharing agreements, the companies usually bid on the percentage of the production that the host government receives (this may be variable with the oil price). Generally, the lifting provisions of any JOA will deal with the allocation between the parties of hydrocarbons allocated to them by the concession agreement or other type of granting instrument; this may include cost petroleum (hydrocarbons allocated as compensation for the costs of the investment) and the JOA parties' share of profit petroleum (remaining petroleum allocated to them jointly by the concession agreement).

It should be noted that the participants have not only the right to dispose of their share of the hydrocarbons, but also the obligation to dispose of their share and an obligation to take the title over the hydrocarbons after the point of delivery.

---

964 P Roberts and R Fowler, *Joint Operating Agreements: A Practical Guide*, 4th edn, Globe Law and Business, 2020, p198.

965 Article 1.2. of the Law on Subsoil, dated 21 February 1992.

14.2 Analysis of model JOAs

Most of the current model JOAs, in dealing with the disposition of production, provide explicit obligations for the parties to offtake their portions (with the exception of the situations when the party becomes the defaulting party), for example, the Norwegian Agreement concerning petroleum activity, the AMPLA JOA, the 2012 AIPN Model JOA and the Greenlandic Model JOA. Some of the JOAs, such as the OGUK Model, deal mainly with the right of the parties to dispose of the extracted entitlements.

The Norwegian Agreement concerning petroleum activity provides explicitly for the "right" and "obligation" to take and dispose of petroleum:

> *Each Party has the right and obligation to take in kind and dispose of a share of the produced Oil, which shall be equivalent to his Participating interest.*[966]

Similarly, the AMPLA JOA deals with the "rights" and "obligations" to dispose of the petroleum and, moreover, specifically to ensure equal treatment of all parties provides that the operator shall not use the infrastructure, which could favour one party over the others:

> *the Operator must deliver a Participant's Entitlement to the Participant at the Delivery Point and, if separately delivered, by use of equipment and techniques which are specifically designed and intended not to favour any one Participant over another*[967]

Likewise, both precedent JOA Models in the 2012 AIPN JOA provide the right and obligation to dispose of the hydrocarbons:

> *each Party shall have the right and obligation to own, take in kind and separately dispose of its Entitlement.*[968]

Unlike both precedent model JOAs, the OGUK JOA mainly deals with the rights of the parties to dispose of the hydrocarbons and makes a clear exclusion for circumstances when the operator needs the petroleum for the joint operations:

> *each of the Participants shall have the right to take in kind and separately dispose of its Percentage Interest share in the total quantities of Petroleum available under this Agreement, provided always that the Operator shall have the right to use in any Joint Operations as much of such Petroleum as may be needed by it for that purpose*

966 Article 20.1 of the Norwegian Agreement concerning petroleum activity.

967 Article 4.3 of the AMPLA JOA.

968 Article 9.1 of 2012 AIPN Model JOA.

and the quantities to be so used shall be excluded from the estimates to be provided by the Operator.[969]

The Greenlandic Model JOA takes a very similar approach to the OGUK JOA and provides the right to dispose and equal treatment principles:

Each of the Parties participating in a development shall have the right to take in kind and separately dispose of its Percentage Interest share of the total quantities of Hydrocarbons available under this Agreement, provided always that the Operator shall have the right to use in any operations relating thereto as much of such Hydrocarbons as may be needed by it therefore. Each of such Parties shall have the obligation to lift and separately dispose of its Percentage Interest share of all Hydrocarbons produced and/or stored at such point or points of delivery, at such times, in such quantities and in accordance with such offtake procedures as may be agreed.[970]

It should be noted that the "obligation" to dispose has the same importance as the "right" to dispose as this is essential that during hydrocarbons operations the hydrocarbons are lifted properly from the disposition point and there is no need to arrange storage of the extra non-lifted oil. Given the incremental capital expense, it is rarely justifiable to build crude oil storage facilities for the storage of produced crude oil, beyond what is necessary to store two to three days of crude oil production for operational reasons. Since the parties are likely to market and sell their crude oil shares separately, there will be potential misalignment between them as to when to store crude oil and when to release it, and the question of how such incremental crude oil storage is controlled will be controversial. Furthermore, the granting instrument may require the parties to maximise production and the option to store crude oil may conflict with that requirement.

Before the start of production, the operator leading the process, together with the participants, ought to agree on and ensure that the production plan for the relevant year and the lifting programme are approved by the management committee. In many cases, under local regulation the parties will have obligation to provide the production plan to the hydrocarbon regulator. The management committee will also designate the point of delivery for the hydrocarbons. This is important since the title over the hydrocarbons is supposed to be transferred to the project participants at the point of delivery and thus the parties will acquire the right of ownership over the hydrocarbons after this point and will have burden and responsibility for any loss of hydrocarbons.

Most of the model JOAs specifically deal with this matter and provide that the parties shall decide in advance on the point of delivery, lifting programme and so on. The Norwegian Agreement concerning petroleum activity makes detailed provision in relation to the point of transfer of ownership, responsibility of the operator to prepare and submit the production plan and a detailed lifting programme. The

969 Article 18 of the OGUK JOA.
970 Article 8.1 of the Greenlandic Model JOA.

production plan and lifting programme shall be approved by the Management Committee, which means that all parties will be involved in discussions and decision-making processes in relation to the said documents:

> *The property right, and the liability and risk pertaining to the produced Oil, is transferred to the individual Party at a point of delivery which shall be determined by the management committee prior to the commencement of production.*
> *The Operator shall, at the point of time decided by the management committee, submit to the management committee a production program covering the Year in which production is to commence. If production is expected to commence after 1 June, the program shall also cover the subsequent Year. Thereafter, and before 1 June of each Year, the Operator shall submit to the management committee and to the Ministry a production program which comprises the three (3) subsequent Years and a production estimate for the rest of the field's life. The program shall be specified for each Quarter and shall describe the quality of the Oil which is expected to be produced.*
> *At the same time as the production program is submitted, the Operator shall submit to the management committee a draft Petroleum lifting program for the Program period in question.*
> *The draft lifting program shall be adapted to the production program and to information collected in advance concerning the Parties' plans for lifting and shipment of Oil. The draft shall contain a schedule for the lifting as well as detailed terms and conditions concerning lifting, delivery and transportation of Oil, and shall specify the requisite steps in a lifting and shipment procedure.*
> *The management committee shall establish the lifting program within thirty (30) days following receipt of the draft.*[971]

The OGUK JOA provides a very general approach to the matter. Rather than stipulating that allocation and lifting procedures shall be agreed in advance, it leaves this detail to the parties, which is generally included in their internal rules, to be approved by the management committee:

> *the Participants which have or may have Percentage Interests in respect of such development shall prior to the commencement of production agree allocation, attribution and lifting procedures.*[972]

The Greenlandic Model JOA states:

> *The Parties participating in a development shall meet as soon as practicable following the approval of a development plan ... and shall, prior to the proposed commencement of production, agree on necessary supplemental provisions to this Agreement covering lifting and operating procedures in respect of such development.*[973]

---

971 Article 20 of Norwegian Agreement concerning petroleum activity.
972 OGUK Model JOA §18(C).
973 Greenlandic Model JOA §8.2.

Some JOAs provide a special regulation for situations when one of the parties is underlifting or overlifting the oil. In practice, if one of the parties is underlifting (eg, for reasons beyond its control), the other parties (or some of them) will inevitably be overlifting. Usually, the operator takes the lead in situations of underlifting and monitors the amounts that have been underlifted. The underlifted amounts are offered to the other parties and, if taken, the underlifting party will be entitled to compensation in kind from those which are overlifting. This raises the question of the necessity of storage for underlifted hydrocarbons. The matter has been discussed in more detail above in this section.

The Norwegian Agreement concerning petroleum activity addresses "overlifting" and "underlifting" in some important details, specifying the Operator's rights and obligations when the situations of "underlifting" and "overlifting" occur, providing with the definitions of the terms "Overlift" and "Underlift" etc:

> *Each Party shall, during the Program period, seek to lift its share of the produced Oil at an even pace and in conformity with the lifting program. When calculating the quantity which a Party has lifted during a one (1) Year Program period, the Party may demand that the lifted quantity during the first or the last sixty (60) days of such a Program period shall be considered as having been made in the previous or the succeeding Program period respectively.*
> *If a Party, for reasons beyond its control and wholly related to the completion of the lifting program, has lifted a lesser quantity of Oil during the Program period than it is entitled to, it shall be considered as an "Under-lifter" and the quantity which it has not lifted will be considered as an "Under-lift".*
> *If one or more Parties are Under-lifters, the Operator shall promptly notify the Parties and specify the quantity of each Party's Under-lift. Each Party which is not an Under-lifter shall have the right to lift the Under-lift, in addition to its own share. If two or more Parties want to take the Under-lift, it shall be apportioned between them in proportion to their Participating interest.*
> *A Party lifting an Under-lift or a part thereof pursuant to this provision shall be considered an "Over-lifter" and the quantity which thereby has been lifted shall be considered as an "Over-lift".*
> *When Over-lift has taken place, the Under-lifter is entitled to compensation for its Underlift, to the extent it is covered by the Over-lift.*
> *Unless the management committee has established another compensation arrangement, 10% of each Overlifter's share shall be placed at the Underlifters' disposal as compensation until the Over-lift is balanced, commencing as of the first Quarter in a succeeding Year. If there are more than one Underlifter, the quantity placed at their disposal shall be apportioned amongst them in proportion to their Under-lift.*
> *If an Under-lifter during a Quarter fails to lift a quantity which has been placed at its disposal as compensation, it shall nevertheless be considered to have received that quantity.*
> *In such event, the quantity which is not lifted by the Under-lifter shall be placed at the disposal of those Over-lifters who have offered the compensation with an acceptance time limit of 48 hours.*

The AMPLA JOA deals with underlifting in the way that the operator may sell the underlifting party's interest in hydrocarbons on its behalf:

> *if a Participant fails to take its Entitlement within 14 days after receiving notice from the Operator requiring the Participant to take delivery, the licence of the Participant to take in kind and separately sell and dispose of its Percentage Share of Petroleum products in the ordinary course of business is terminated, and the Operator may sell all or part of that Entitlement as agent for the Participant at not less than the available arm's length market value (as determined by the Operator acting reasonably) for that Petroleum. The Operator must account to the Participant for the proceeds of any such sale after first deducting its reasonable expenses and additional storage costs incurred in the sale.*[974]

At the same time the AMPLA JOA states that:

> *The failure of a Participant to take and dispose of its Entitlement must neither prevent the production of Petroleum from the Title Area nor prevent the other Participants from taking and disposing of their respective Entitlements.*[975]

It specifically emphasises that underlifting shall in any case not hinder the production process or the lifting procedures of the other participants. However, it leaves unanswered the question of what happens if the other parties do not have the desire to take the underlifted share or if the operator fails to sell the underlifted amount. Providing crude oil storage is an expensive and controversial option as noted above; natural gas storage is not technically feasible save for moderate amounts of linepack (pressure management).

In the same way as the AMPLA JOA, the Greenlandic JOA provides that if a participant fails to take the produced amount in kind, the operator has a right to sell this amount on behalf of the underlifting party:

> *In the event that any of the Parties for any reason fails to lift such quantities of liquid Hydrocarbons as are to be lifted by it in accordance with agreed offtake procedures or consistently nominates less than its full entitlement of liquid Hydrocarbons and thereby in the reasonable opinion of the Operator prejudices the efficiency of the production operation, the Operator shall arrange to lift, or have lifted, the relevant underlifted quantity of liquid Hydrocarbons of said Party or Parties on behalf of said Party or Parties and at said Party or Parties sole risk, and shall dispose of the same at such prices as it can reasonably obtain in all the circumstances and shall credit to said Party or Parties the price obtained therefore net of the costs and expense of such sale and after deduction of a reasonable handling fee.*[976]

974 Article 4.3 of the AMPLA JOA.
975 Article 4.3 of the AMPLA JOA.
976 Article 4.3 of the AMPLA JOA.

The parties' rights to the entitlement could be restricted or suspended in certain circumstances, such as a default position of one of the parties, exclusive operations or a recoverable carry.

In the event of default, the party that has not fulfilled its obligations under the JOA (a defaulting party) will not be able to exercise its rights under the JOA, including the right to entitlement in the extracted hydrocarbons. The situation will be remedied once the defaulting party rectifies its default in compliance with the provisions of JOA.

In the event of exclusive operations, the non-consenting party will not be entitled to receive its share of hydrocarbons extracted from exclusive operations. In order to join the production operations and thus obtain rights over its share, the non-consenting party must pay a (fairly substantial) premium which might be many times higher than the actual costs and expenses in relation to the exclusive operations.[977]

The other situation where a particular participant's entitlement to hydrocarbons is suspended arises in relation to the repayment of a recoverable carry. As discussed above, a recoverable carry refers to a commercial arrangement whereby some parties have financed another party's share of the cost of operations in its place. Such party (the carried party) will not have a right over entitlement until the whole amount of carry (possibly with interest) is fully reimbursed.

Delivery of hydrocarbons production to which any participant is entitled takes place within the framework of an offtake agreement. The offtake agreement is an important commercial and legal framework for when, how, in which amount and on the basis of which conditions the hydrocarbons will be lifted and disposed. Commonly a party's entitlement or share of production is equal to that party's participation interest. However, the deviations are also possible within a particular timeframe and are connected mainly with "carry" situations or exclusive production situations.

A proper system of measurement must be established in order to assess the exact amounts of hydrocarbons extracted. The emphasis here should be on better precision and accuracy of the system. The measurement system should follow local government and international measurement standards and requirements to ensure proper design, installation and calibration which is also important for the state, as the state is interested in the correct calculation of royalties on the basis of the production sharing agreement.

A good measurement system will ensure better accountability for all parties as well as necessary transparency of production operations. It has the utmost importance for all parties.

JOAs usually address this issue under the heading of so-called 'custody measurement', related to the transfer of deliverable hydrocarbons at the point where title over the hydrocarbons changes (the delivery point), providing quantity and quality information to be used for the physical and fiscal documentation regarding the change in ownership and/or risk in the hydrocarbons between transferor (usually the state in which title of produced hydrocarbons initially vests) and the transferees (the JOA parties) under binding terms of contractual agreements, that is, offtake agreements and JOA.

977 See discussion in Section 9 of this chapter, "Exclusive operations".

Examination of the different model JOAs shows that the essential provisions relating to hydrocarbon lifting common to each of the model JOAs, and which will be repeated in the oil lifting and gas balancing agreements, are: a) identification of the delivery point; b) recognition of the possibilities of overlifting and underlifting as well as stipulation of certain procedures related to the said circumstances; c) reservation of the operator's right to retain a portion of the oil, which will be used for the purposes of conducting the joint operations; and d) reservation of the operator's rights and responsibility to deal with the situations of 'overlifting' and 'underlifting'.

Commonly, due to the specifics of gas production and the relatively greater complexity of gas disposition in comparison with crude oil disposition, the terms and conditions of natural gas disposition are different from the terms and conditions of oil dispositions and thus there are usually separate sections in JOAs dealing with natural gas disposition. Oil lifting agreements tend to follow a recognised industry format whereas gas balancing agreements need to be adapted to the relevant venture and gas market.

Usually, natural gas production will be disposed of on a joint and integrated basis and sold to a single buyer in accordance with the terms of a single long-term gas sales agreement (or a number of identical gas sales agreements, each covering the share of an individual participant).

The basic principles of natural gas disposition are the same as for crude oil disposition, namely, each JOA participant will be entitled to dispose of its share in the gas produced, and this share will be proportionate to its participating interest in the project. The agreement will define the point of delivery and address overlifting and underlifting situations. However, there will be certain specifics, such as: a) the provisions concerning allocation, which will be expressed mathematically and will deal with the specific allocation within the specified periods (monthly, quarterly, etc); b) attribution – that is, when an underlift of the natural gas (measured against the allocated amounts of gas) by a party at the delivery point is made good through a substitution from the natural gas entitlement of another party. In other words, these provisions deal with the borrowing and lending of the gas between the parties.[978] The allocation provisions are not always contained in the same agreement as the attribution provisions.

The most important model JOAs deal with natural gas disposition as follows.

The Norwegian Agreement concerning petroleum activity provides that:

> *Each Party has the right and obligation to take in kind and dispose of a share of produced Natural Gas which shall be equivalent to its Participating interest.*[979]

As with the principle relating to crude oil change of ownership, the principle relating to change of ownership in gas provides:

978 P Roberts and R Fowler, *Joint Operating Agreements: A Practical Guide*, 4th edn, Globe Law and Business, 2020, pp205–207.

979 Article 20.1 of Norwegian Agreement concerning petroleum activity.

the property right, and the liability and risk pertaining to the Natural Gas are transferred to the individual Party upon lifting at a delivery point which shall be determined by the management committee prior to commencement of production.[980]

The Norwegian Agreement further provides that a single gas lifting agreement shall be concluded by the parties and submitted to the governmental oil and gas authority for approval. The terms and conditions of the agreement must be unanimously approved by the management committee. It is typical for all JOA Model Forms that such type of agreements will be in the list of the reserved matters, being agreements that must be approved by each JOA party acting autonomously and are not subject to an OpCom passmark vote. As a specific point for the model Norwegian Agreement, such agreement must be approved by the Norwegian Ministry:

The Parties shall enter into a gas lifting and balancing agreement which is subject to approval by the Ministry prior to the commencement of production. For adoption of the gas lifting and balancing agreement, a unanimous vote by the management committee is required.
No later than 8 (eight) working days after the first day of each month the Operator shall submit to the management committee an overview of produced and lifted Natural Gas for the previous month and for accumulated volume since commencement of production.[981]

The disposition of gas is undertaken on the basis of the sole agreement concluded by the parties to the JOA with the offtaker, or with a marketing company. If the natural gas were disposed of by the individual parties, imbalances might occur. The AIPN Model provisions on disposition of natural gas deal with the specific events of imbalances:

Natural Gas to be produced from an Exploitation Area shall be taken and disposed of in accordance with the rules and procedures set out [this Article 9.3]. ...
The Parties recognize that, in the event of individual disposition of Natural Gas, imbalances may arise with the result being that a Party will temporarily have disposed of more than its Participating Interest share of production of Natural Gas. Accordingly, if Natural Gas is to be produced from an Exploitation Area, the Parties shall, in good faith and no later than the date on which the Development Plan for a Natural Gas project is approved by the Operating Committee, negotiate and conclude the terms of a balancing agreement to cover the disposition of Natural Gas produced under the Contract, regardless of whether all of the Parties have entered into a sales arrangement or sales contract for their respective Entitlement of Natural Gas. The

980 Article 20.1 of the Norwegian Agreement concerning petroleum activity.
981 Article 22 of the Norwegian Agreement concerning petroleum activity.

Natural Gas balancing agreement shall, subject to the terms of the Contract, make provision for:
9.3.A.1 the right of a Party not in default to take delivery of Natural Gas (and to thereby use all relevant facilities) more than its Participating Interest share of production, subject to the right of an undertaking Party to take later delivery of make-up Natural Gas; provided that, such make-up Natural Gas shall in no month exceed _______ percent of total Natural Gas production produced monthly from the Exploitation Area, and further provided the such undertaking Party shall lose its right to such make-up Natural Gas if it has not taken delivery of the make-up Natural Gas within _________ [months/years] after the excess Natural Gas was originally taken; ...
9.3.A.6 each Party's provision to Operator of such information regarding such Party's arrangements for the disposition of its Entitlement of Natural Gas production as Operator may reasonably require in order to conduct Joint Operations;
9.3.A.7 each Party's regular periodic nominations to Operator of the amount of such Party's Entitlement of Total Available Production of Natural Gas which it wishes to accept during a defined future period, along with Operator's regular periodic advice to the Parties of estimates of total Natural Gas production (as reasonably in advance as practicable in order to assist the Parties to plan Natural Gas disposition arrangements); provided, however, that the Parties recognize that Operator's estimates may vary from the actual Natural Gas volumes produced and that the Parties may rely upon any such information at their own risk; and
9.3.A.8 the allocation of Cost Hydrocarbons and Profit Hydrocarbons regarding such individual Natural Gas disposition.[982]

If the parties are willing to agree a multiparty arrangement for disposition of the natural gas and this arrangement is not prohibited by law, the parties may enter into a multiparty natural gas disposition agreement and agree to dispose of the natural gas produced under the contract on a multiparty basis to a common purchaser or purchasers. The possibility of multipartite arrangement is recognised by some of the model JOAs. Thus, under the 2012 AIPN JOA Model, the multiparty natural gas disposition agreement shall make provision for:

9.3.B.1 The terms of sale or disposition of Natural Gas on a multiparty basis.
9.3.B.2 The Parties' rights and obligations regarding the disposition of Natural Gas on a multiparty basis, including the extent to which Operator is designated as the Parties' authorized representative to conduct marketing studies, designing and constructing necessary facilities, investigating financing opportunities, and negotiating sales agreements.
9.3.B.3 The managerial structure for making decisions governing the multiparty disposal venture.
9.3.B.4 The scope and duration of the multiparty disposal venture.

982 AIPN JOA §9.3.

9.3.B.5 The extent, if any, to which the costs of the multiparty disposal venture are chargeable to the Joint Account.
9.3.B.6 The obligation of the Parties to participate in all Natural Gas infrastructure necessary for such multiparty Natural Gas disposal, and the multiparty disposition venture governing only such Natural Gas infrastructure as is necessary to deliver Natural Gas to the point where fiscal calculations are made for the purposes of the Contract.
9.3.B.7 The extent to which a Party shall have, or shall be permitted to hold itself out as having, the authority to create any obligation for the multiparty disposal venture.
9.3.B.8 Confirmation that the relationship among the Parties shall be contractual only and shall not be construed as creating a partnership or other recognized association.
9.3.B.9 Confirmation that formation of the multiparty disposal venture shall not create any rights in any persons not a party thereto.
9.3.B.10 The allocation of Cost Hydrocarbons and Profit Hydrocarbons concerning the multiparty Natural Gas disposal.

The AMPLA JOA deals with the disposition of gas in a very general manner, recognising that some specific detail may be required for natural gas disposition:

If there is a discovery of Natural Gas, each party recognises that there may need to be special arrangements for the offtake and disposal of the Natural Gas. In such event the parties agree to negotiate to amend this agreement and/or make a separate agreement to make provision for such arrangements.[983]

Similar to the AMPLA JOA, the Greenlandic Model JOA provides that the disposition of gas may have some specific requirements and thus the parties should additionally discuss and agree such terms and conditions:

The Parties recognize that, in the event of the production of natural gas, it may or will be or become desirable for them to enter into special arrangements for the disposal of the same and they agree that, in such event and upon the request of any of them, their respective representatives shall meet together as necessary to consider their entry into such arrangements and that, if and to the extent that any such arrangements are agreed, they will adopt and undertake the same.[984]

As the disposition of natural gas has some specific requirements, it is often the case that the gas lifting or offtake agreements will include gas balancing agreement

983 Article 4.5 of the AMPLA JOA.
984 Article 8.4 of Greenlandic Model JOA.

provisions. It might be practical for the national oil company (if not a party to the JOA) to join as a party to the gas balancing agreement or become a shareholder in the gas marketing company together with the other participants of the project, on the basis that the local government may be interested in buying any gas surpluses. In this situation, the parties to the JOA may add further provisions to the gas balancing agreement, requiring the national oil company to meet certain specific obligations, for example ensuring access to gas transportation infrastructure, gas market and export routes. However, in this case the parties should be very cautious in formulating the particular provisions to make sure they meet compliance requirements and will not be considered as breaching antitrust laws.

The 2012 AIPN Model JOA provides that:

> *9.4 The Government Oil & Gas Company may, if necessary and practicable, also be party to the balancing agreement ... and/or the multiparty disposition venture ... If the Government Oil & Gas Company is party to the balancing agreement, then the Parties shall endeavour to obtain its agreement to the JOA. Furthermore, if the Government Oil & Gas Company is party to the multiparty disposition venture, then the Parties shall endeavour to obtain its agreement to the JOA principles.*
> *9.4.B In addition, the Parties shall endeavour to include in the Contract, and in any other agreement with the Government Oil & Gas Company concerning the disposition of Natural Gas, the following principles:*
> *9.4.B.1 Assured access to a fair share of the available Natural Gas market, including suitable assurances for Government controlled sales.*
> *9.4.B.2 The right to market and to export all Natural Gas, including the Government's share, to the highest value outlets (domestic or export).*
> *9.4.B.3 A minimum contractual term that provides a reasonable period to develop a Natural Gas market and enables Natural Gas reserves to be produced for their full economic life.*
> *9.4.B.4 Assured access to infrastructure for the purposes of processing and/or transporting Natural Gas at a competitive tariff.*[985]

14.3 Discussion

The JOA provisions with respect to oil and gas lifting may seem prosaic and operational, but in practice they can provide fertile ground for misalignment between international oil companies and national oil companies in the joint venture. One issue this section has touched on is the parties' obligation to lift; given that the joint venture does not extend to joint oil marketing, and not always to joint gas marketing, the participants make independent marketing and sale decisions. This may mean that they are not aligned when called upon to agree production strategies in the OpCom, and agreeing the annual production plan may be complicated by the different agendas of their separate downstream marketing arrangements. More significantly, the national oil company may be in a very different position; it is more likely to have other interests in the relevant oil province, may have access on

985 Article 9.4 of the 2012 AIPN Model JOA.

preferential terms to existing downstream transportation systems and may, directly or indirectly through the state's authority, be able to influence downstream gas prices. The national oil company may be charged by the government with achieving the state's objectives of delivering inexpensive gas to local industry, a task which may conflict with the objective of maximising the cash value of produced hydrocarbons, in order to minimise the amount of production allocated to cost hydrocarbons and maximising profit hydrocarbons for the joint venture and the state.

Finally, it should not be ignored that the granting instrument will also require the parties to agree production targets with the state, the performance of which may be jeopardised if one or more parties fail to lift their hydrocarbon entitlements. Such underperformance may affect all the parties' entitlement to cost and profit hydrocarbons, for which reason JOAs and lifting agreements should allow the operator or other parties to step in to lift an underlifter's share, so as to avoid production being curtailed overall.

It is also advisable for the parties to review the *force majeure* and default clauses under the JOA; often the *force majeure* clauses are treated as applying only to the operator's obligations, whereas in fact it will also apply to the parties' obligations to lift their hydrocarbon entitlements. The drafting may be inappropriate for this purpose. The default clauses might address the situations of not fulfilling the obligations to lift the hydrocarbons and may provide certain procedures incentivising the defaulting parties to meet their obligations to lift.

15. Relinquishment, surrender and withdrawal

15.1 General principles

Almost all JOA Models address the situation with withdrawals, surrender and relinquishment. Withdrawals may be either based on particular events, designated in the JOAs or without any events or causes, and will be at the JOA participants' discretion. If withdrawal is based on the participants' discretion, no specific requirements need be met to make the withdrawal effective – withdrawal becomes effective a specific time (as designated in the JOA) after prior written notice has been given. However, as will be discussed further in this section, some liabilities in relation to the hydrocarbons operations will still remain with the withdrawing party even after such party ceases to be party to the JOA.

National and international oil companies are likely to have different views with respect to withdrawals. The national oil company, representing the host state interest, by its nature is unlikely to withdraw from the project and probably will retain its interest in the project under any circumstances. It is likely to prefer to keep the other partners within the agreement with the aim of continuing sharing geological and other risks. The national oil company may have a particular interest in maintaining the financial support of the international oil company in the project, especially if the national oil company's interest is being carried.[986]

As a general principle, no participant is entitled to withdraw until the minimum exploration programme has been completed and thus the minimum exploration financial commitments have been met. In practice, the JOAs define the following

986 It is often the case that an international oil company joining a local market project is required to run the operations from a specified point, such as the commencement of production.

points in time, after which the participants may withdraw: drilling of the first exploration well; inability to reach the agreement in relation to the development plan after drilling of the first of a particular series of exploration wells; drilling the appraisal well; commercial discovery. Sometimes the withdrawing point is defined more generally, for example upon completion of all the exploration commitments as defined under the relevant granting instrument, including a production sharing contract or the licence. The national oil company will probably prefer the withdrawing event to occur as late as possible, so that the participants stay in the project longer and thus share the commitments and liabilities for a longer time.

The international oil company's interest will be to provide itself with more flexibility to have a right to withdraw, even during the earlier stages of the project; for example at any point in the exploration period, such as following unsatisfactory results from the seismic tests. However, many JOAs contain a restriction on withdrawals until at least some of the exploration works under the licence have been completed.[987] Such restrictions are typically based on the imperative provisions of the granting instruments and are directly related to the commitments made to the host government. Usually, while negotiating the JOA, the other parties may be willing to accept early withdrawal (before the end of the exploration period), but subject to the withdrawing party making an advance payment of its share of the exploration costs or guaranteeing that it will continue funding the exploration operations costs even after withdrawal.

A withdrawing party will remain liable for future costs resulting from the commitment jointly made by all parties prior to the notice of withdrawal. The most common and expensive are the decommissioning and abandonment costs, the other costs might be related to pre-existing commitments to complete the construction of certain infrastructure. A withdrawing participant may be required to provide adequate financial security for these future liabilities, including in the form of the bank guarantee for these future liabilities. The share of the costs to be contributed in advance (or guaranteed) might be identified based on the length of time the withdrawing participant has benefitted from production from the asset.

Older JOAs which are not based on current industry model formats may not address ongoing liability for decommissioning or environmental liabilities in respect of activities carried out or facilities installed before withdrawal. The remaining parties may struggle in such circumstances to force the withdrawing party to acknowledge its ongoing exposure in the novation deed recording its departure from the JOA. However, the remaining parties may invoke the recent case of *Spirit Energy Resources v Marathon* where it was successfully argued by the operator that the non-operators had to approve expenditure necessitated by activities and projects they had previously approved. This is an important but arguable connection; it could arguably be extended to the decommissioning costs of facilities installed prior to a party's withdrawal, provided that the JOA expressly imposes liability on the withdrawing party for expenditure necessitated by activities the withdrawing party approved or

987 For example, the provisions restricting withdrawal until the minimum exploration work obligations are completed in the OGUK Model JOA. Article 10.1.3 of the Greenlandic Model JOA provides that a party participating in the development programme cannot withdraw until the works under the programme are completed: "*Withdrawal from a Development Programme. No Party participating in a development Programme may withdraw from the Licence and this Agreement prior to the completion of all the works comprised in such development Programme.*"

was voted into while party to the JOA.[988] But should such decommissioning liability be imposed with respect to a particular development plan which was not approved by the withdrawing party? Would it be a balanced position? This question remains open in some JOAs and should be addressed with the outcome largely depending on negotiation leverage of the parties.

The participating interest of the withdrawing party will be distributed among the remaining participants *pro rata* to their respective participating interests, if otherwise not provided for in the JOA.

As a general rule, the withdrawing party will not be entitled to any compensation for the investments it has made in the project. The position may be more complicated where the withdrawing party is carrying the costs of non-withdrawing parties and/or shares the burden of that carry with other parties. Whether that is a soft carry, on terms that the carry is later repaid in cash or in kind, or a hard carry (where no such conversation is payable), it is highly unlikely that the carried parties or the other carrying parties would agree to compensate the withdrawing party for its investment. This is because the withdrawal increases their participating interest share to ongoing costs and to the cost of the carry, even though they may escape repaying the carry to the withdrawing party at a later date. However, even this complication might be resolved if the parties might have some common interests in the future and willing to settle amicably in order to be able to cooperate well in the other projects. One of the solutions might be that the withdrawing party will be compensated for the amount of carry provided out of further hydrocarbons proceeds.

As a general rule, any assignment of the participating interest requires approval by the host governmental body, and the validity of this approval is subject to receipt of the governmental body's consent. The 2012 AIPN Model JOA addresses this issue and the withdrawing party to cooperate by providing the information and the documents needed for the application for consent to the assignment in favour of the remaining parties as follows:

> *A withdrawing Party shall promptly join in such actions as may be necessary or desirable to obtain any Government approvals required in connection with the withdrawal and assignments. The non-withdrawing Parties shall use reasonable endeavors to assist the withdrawing Party in obtaining such approvals. If the Government does not approve a Party's withdrawal and assignment to the other Parties, then the withdrawing Party shall at its option either (1) retract its notice of withdrawal by notice to the other Parties and remain a Party as if such notice of withdrawal had never been sent, or (2) to the extent allowed under the Contract and Laws hold its Participating Interest in trust for the exclusive benefit of the non-withdrawing Parties with the right to be reimbursed by the non-withdrawing Parties for any subsequent costs and liabilities incurred by it for which it would not have been liable, had it successfully withdrawn. Any penalties or costs incurred by the Parties in connection with such withdrawal shall be borne by the withdrawing Party.*[989]

988 *Spirit Energy Resources Ltd v Marathon Oil UK LLC* [2019] EWCA Civ 11. That case addresses the position of existing non-operators – not a party that had previously withdrawn from the JOA. However, it would be hard to apply that principle to existing non-operators, but not a party which had previously withdrawn, if the JOA expressly provides that a withdrawing party should remain so liable.

989 Article 13.7 of the 2012 AIPN Model JOA.

There is also a specific situation of 'deemed withdrawal', which has now been recognised by the case law. The judgment in the Supreme Court of Western Australia involving Empire Oil (Empire) found that there had been a valid and legally effective deemed withdrawal from a JOA following the failure of a party to the JOA to pay cash calls.[990]

In this case, the claimants, Empire, and ERM Gas Pty Ltd (ERM),[991] and the defendant, Wharf Resources PLC (Wharf), were the registered owners of a petroleum permit granted under the Petroleum and Geothermal Energy Resources Act 1967 (WA), known as Exploration Permit 389 (EP 389). Activities in relation to EP 389 are governed by a JOA dated 30 November 2007. Empire, ERM and Wharf were parties to the JOA. Empire was the operator. Under the JOA, the operator was authorised to issue cash calls to the joint venture and the participants' default in meeting those cash calls could lead to the defaulting party being deemed to have given a notice of withdrawal from the joint venture. In that event, the JOA provided for the appointment of the operator as the lawful attorney of the defaulting party for the purposes of executing any documents necessary to give effect to the withdrawal.

It was found that the process of approval of the authority for expenditures, the process of service of cash calls and the mechanism which led to a deemed withdrawal from the joint venture were all undertaken in accordance with the JOA. Since Wharf's assertions that Empire lacked authority to issue cash calls and alleged breaches by Empire of the JOA were not accepted by the court, Wharf was deemed to have withdrawn from the joint venture on 8 April 2013. The court also declared that Empire had validly executed transfers of EP 389 and PL 96 as attorney for Wharf pursuant to the JOA.

Joint-venture participants are sometimes concerned that a forced withdrawal of a party for failure to pay cash calls (or another default under the JOA) will not be effective. Each case will turn on its own facts, but provided that procedures in the JOA are followed, a forced withdrawal of a defaulting party can be valid and effective.[992]

15.2 Analysis of model JOAs

The model JOAs address withdrawal issues in different ways.

The OGUK Model provides that, as a general rule, withdrawal is not allowed:

> *No Participant may withdraw from the Licence (in so far as it relates to the Licence Area) or this Agreement otherwise than in accordance with the following provisions of this clause.*[993]

However, the same model document provides a right to withdraw under certain circumstances:

990 www.gadens.com/publications/Pages/Court-declares-effective-withdrawal-following-default.aspx.
991 *Empire Oil Company (WA) Limited v Wharf Resources PLC* [2014] WASC 179 (23 May 2014).
992 See Chapter 2, Section 5, "Default".
993 Article 24.1 of the OGUK Model Agreement.

Any Participant may, subject to clauses 9.9, 24.2.3 and 24.3 and always provided that all Work Obligations set out in schedule 4 to the Licence have been completed, at any time up to and including the date of the meeting to be held pursuant to clause 9.9.3 to decide whether to continue the Licence beyond the Initial Term, give notice to the other Participants that it wishes to withdraw from the Licence (in so far as it relates to the Licence Area) and this Agreement. Within thirty (30) days of receipt of such notice (but in any event no later than the date of such meeting), any of the other Participants may similarly give notice that it wishes to withdraw from the Licence (in so far as it relates to the Licence Area) and this Agreement. If all the other Participants give such notice no assignment shall take place, the Participants shall be deemed to have decided to abandon the Joint Operations and the Licence (in so far as it relates to the Licence Area) shall be surrendered on the earliest possible date. If less than all the other Participants give such notice the withdrawing Participants shall withdraw from the Licence (in so far as it relates to the Licence Area) and this Agreement on the earliest possible date and shall assign their respective interests in the Licence and in and under this Agreement to the non-withdrawing Participants in accordance with clause 24.3 without any compensation whatsoever.[994]

The Norwegian Agreement concerning petroleum activity provides that:

A Party may withdraw from this Agreement when the obligatory work obligation described in the Production Licence has been carried out. If a Party has acceded to a development plan, it may only withdraw when the Ministry has determined that the plan is completed.
A notice of withdrawal must be submitted to the management committee at least four (4) months in advance. The other Parties shall within 30 days notify the management committee of whether they want to take over the Participating interest. A Party failing to give such notice within the expiry of the time limit, will lose his right to take over the Participating interest unless otherwise agreed by the other Parties.
After a notice of withdrawal has been submitted, the withdrawing Party ceases to be liable for decisions taken by the joint venture which involve expenses not comprised by the agreed budget. A withdrawal from the Agreement shall be effective as of the first day of the month following the expiry of the four-month time limit which started when the notice of withdrawal was submitted to the management committee. Notwithstanding the above the withdrawing Party is liable for expenses comprised by the agreed budget, resulting from a decision taken within the first day of the month subsequent to the expiry of the four-month time limit, unless the Party taking over has accepted to cover such expenses.

The important point is that the Norwegian Model agreement establishes the principle of continuing liability in relation to the obligations, already incurred and

994 Article 24.1 of the OGUK Model Agreement.

not met at the time of the withdrawal. A specific reference is made in relation to the decommissioning liability and the requirement to provide security to ensure that the liability will be met. It should be noted that not all of the jurisdictions have detailed and direct requirements in relation to decommissioning costs as well as specific security instruments in this regard.[995]

> *The withdrawing Party shall continue to be liable for obligations which are not met at the time of withdrawal, and which have been established by damage, resolution by the authorities or in any other way independently of any decision made by the joint venture.*
> *The other Parties may require that a satisfactory guarantee be provided concerning a proportionate share of the joint venture's liability for decommissioning of facilities belonging to the joint venture at the time of withdrawal.*
> *If the other Parties as well as third parties do not want to take over the Participating interest pursuant to Article 23, the other Parties are entitled to take over their proportionate share of the Participating interest without compensation. An amendment to this Agreement following the withdrawal of a Party shall be submitted to the Ministry, cf. Article 8 of the Special Provisions.*
> *If nobody wants to take over the Participating interest pursuant to Article 24.4, the joint venture shall be dissolved pursuant to the provisions of Articles 25.2 and 25.3. In such case, the effects of a notice of withdrawal will lapse.*[996]

The 2012 AIPN Model JOA addresses the issue very simply as follows:

> *any Party not in default may at its option withdraw from this Agreement and the Contract by giving notice to all other Parties stating its decision to withdraw. Such notice shall be unconditional and irrevocable when given ...*
> *The effective date of withdrawal for a withdrawing Party shall be the end of the Calendar Month after the Calendar Month in which the notice of withdrawal is given, provided that if all Parties elect to withdraw, the effective date of withdrawal for each Party shall be the date determined by Article 13.9.*[997]

The fact that one party is withdrawing from the JOA and consequently from the relevant petroleum concession and other types of granting instruments could trigger the rights of the remaining participants to withdraw as well because remaining parties will find that their financial and other burdens of participation increase to a point which they had not considered as a possible scenario when

995 For example in the Russian Federation the legislation does not address the issue of necessity to provide the security measures in relation to the decommissioning costs. Based on this, the parties to the JOAs or other types of joint-venture agreements have tended not to address the decommissioning issues in the joint venture agreements. The situation is changing now as the Russian legislator has started establishing the rules in relation to the decommissioning.

996 Article 24 of the Norwegian Agreement concerning petroleum activities.

997 Article 13.1 of the 2012 AIPN Model JOA.

the particular party entered into the agreement. Thus the 2012 AIPN Model JOA addresses such a situation:

> *Within thirty (30) Days of receipt of each withdrawing Party's notification, each of the other Parties may also give notice that it desires to withdraw from this Agreement and the Contract. If all Parties give notice of withdrawal, the Parties shall proceed to abandon the Contract Area and terminate the Contract and this Agreement. If fewer than all of the Parties give such notice of withdrawal, then the withdrawing Parties shall take all steps to withdraw from the Contract and this Agreement on the earliest possible date and sign and deliver all necessary instruments and documents to assign their Participating Interest to the Parties that are not withdrawing, without any compensation whatsoever, under Article 13.6.*[998]

The 2012 AIPN Model JOA also addresses the withdrawing party's rights and obligations, including under the circumstances when the production has been already started:

> *A withdrawing Party shall have the right to receive its Entitlement produced through the effective date of its withdrawal. The withdrawing Party shall be entitled to receive all information to which such Party is otherwise entitled under this Agreement until the effective date of its withdrawal. After giving its notification of withdrawal, a Party shall not be entitled to vote on any matters coming before the Operating Committee, other than matters for which such Party has financial responsibility.*

It is most important to address the obligations and liabilities of a withdrawing party and provide specific rules in this regard. It is logical for the JOA to anticipate that liability for the appropriate share of costs of expenses already committed and approved or incurred but not paid, any breaches, emergency cases as well as any other obligations accrued before the withdrawal shall remain with the withdrawing party.

> *A withdrawing Party shall, after its notification of withdrawal, remain liable only for its share of the following:*
> *Costs of Joint Operations, and costs of Exclusive Operations in which such withdrawing Party has agreed to participate, that were approved by the Operating Committee or Consenting Parties as part of a Work Program and Budget (including a multi-year Work Program and Budget under Article 6.1.E) or AFE before such Party's notification of withdrawal, regardless of when they are incurred;*
> *Any Minimum Work Obligations for the current period or phase of the Contract, and for any subsequent period or phase that has been approved under Article 11.2 and with respect to which such Party has failed to timely withdraw under Article 13.4.B;*

998 Article 13.1 of the 2012 AIPN Model JOA.

> *Expenditures described in Articles 4.2.B.14 and 13.5 related to an emergency occurring before the effective date of a Party's withdrawal, regardless of when such expenditures are incurred;*
> *All other obligations and liabilities of the Parties or Consenting Parties, as applicable, concerning acts or omissions under this Agreement before the effective date of such Party's withdrawal for which such Party would have been liable, had it not withdrawn from this Agreement; and*
> *In the case of a partially withdrawing Party, any costs and liabilities concerning Exploitation Areas, Commercial Discoveries and Discoveries from which it has not withdrawn.*
> *The obligations and liabilities for which a withdrawing Party remains liable shall specifically include its share of any costs of plugging and abandoning wells or portions of wells in which it participated (or was required to bear a share of the costs under Article 13.4.A.1) to the extent such costs of plugging and abandoning are payable by the Parties under the Contract. Any Encumbrances that were placed on the withdrawing Party's Participating Interest before such Party's withdrawal shall be fully satisfied or released, at the withdrawing Party's expense, before its withdrawal. A Party's withdrawal shall not relieve it from liability to the non-withdrawing Parties concerning any obligations or liabilities attributable to the withdrawing Party under this Article 13 merely because they are not identified or identifiable at the time of withdrawal.*
> *Despite the foregoing, a Party shall not be liable for any operations or expenditures it voted against (other than operations and expenditures described in Article 13.4.A.2 or Article 13.4.A.3) if it sends notification of its withdrawal within five (5) Days (or within twenty-four (24) hours for Urgent Operational Matters) of the Operating Committee vote approving such operation or expenditure. Likewise, a Party voting against voluntarily entering into, or extending, an Exploration Period or Exploitation Period or any phase of the Contract, or voting against voluntarily extending the Contract shall not be liable for the Minimum Work Obligations associated therewith provided that it sends notification of its withdrawal within thirty (30) Days of such vote under Article 11.2.*[999]

A significant challenge arises if a party purports to exercise its rights to withdraw from the JOA when it does not have the right to, or fails to obtain the necessary approval for, its withdrawal from the granting instrument. This may result in the withdrawing party remaining formally party to or bound by the granting instrument but not a participant in and entitled to exercise rights under the JOA. This situation might be considered as analogous to the position of a non-participating party in a sole risk development or indeed a case where a party is deprived of its participating interest upon its default, but is not released from the granting instrument by the state. However, the withdrawing party, like the defaulting party, does not have the option to rejoin the sole risk development joint venture by paying the appropriate premium under the granting instrument on trust for the continuing parties[1000]

---

999 Article 13.3 and 13.4 of the 2012 AIPN Model JOA.
1000 AIPN JOA §13.7.

and the OGUK JOA simply provides that the withdrawal is suspended until the state's consent is obtained.[1001] Practical problems might remain because not all the jurisdictions recognise the concept of trust instruments whereby the withdrawing party holds its interest on trust for the other parties. If the withdrawal is suspended, then how would the rights to vote and take the entitlement to hydrocarbons under the agreement be exercised? The OGUK JOA prudently provides a template trust instrument which addresses these concerns its impact on the OpCom passmarks. Many JOAs seek to protect the interests of non-operators by requiring a vote to be passed not only by reference to a minimum score of percentage interest voting in favour but also a minimum number of parties voting in favour. This protects non-operators in cases where the operator has a significant participating interest. If a non-operator withdraws, the number of voting parties naturally reduces, changing the dynamic of how passmarks may be achieved. If the JOA was drafted for a joint venture of the three parties and one withdraws, a provision requiring every passmark to be achieved by the positive vote of at least two parties becomes automatically the JOA requiring unanimous support for every proposal. Such situation requires further negotiations. It is not a rare case that JOAs contain provisions, proposing the remaining parties conduct good faith negotiations to address the new reality, including in relation to the corporate governance, when one of the parties withdraws.

Commonly, the concession agreements, production sharing agreements, licence and other granting instruments will include conditions that at certain intervals, for instance after the lapse of the initial exploration period, part or some parts of the licence may be relinquished if the results of the exploration activity within the area are not satisfactory and a decision on commercial development is unable to be taken.

Generally, similar provisions (duplicated in the granting instruments) are provided in the JOAs. If no commercial discovery has been made by the end of the exploration period and the parties are not able to agree on the approval of the development plan and take an investment decision in relation to the project and thus the project has not moved on to the development stage, usually there are two possibilities:

- to extend the exploration stage (if sufficiently reasonable grounds can be provided to the competent authority for an extension); or
- to surrender or relinquish the exploration area to the host government and possibility terminate the project.

There are no negative consequences (such as the imposition of fines) for the participants if the licence area or its portion is surrendered at the end of the exploration period without commercial discovery, provided, however, that minimum license obligations at the exploration stage have been properly met. Once the relinquishment is approved by the regulator, the parties to the JOA and granting instruments will have no further liability for completing the hydrocarbons activity in relation to the surrendered portion of the exploration area.

The decision to surrender, and the size, shape and coordinates of the area to be surrendered, must be agreed in good time by the JOA parties; otherwise, the state may impose its own surrender terms. Since surrender of the area is the obligation of the participants, towards the government, it is important to ensure that the decision is not

1001 OGUK JOA §24.3(b).

blocked by the other participants, including the minority participants. Thus, the AIPN JOA provides that if the decision is not taken unanimously (and where the minority participant might have wished to block the decision), it will be decided by the majority of votes at the subsequent meeting of OpCom. If no decision can be reached at that meeting, the operator is entitled to take the decision on surrender. Since commonly the obligation to surrender is imposed by the applicable law, there must be a mechanism to allow the operator to comply with the requirements of the law. This is one specific example of how JOAs may address deadlocks.

The model JOAs have fairly different approaches to surrender issues.

The AMPLA Model provides that:

> *If the Contract requires the Parties to surrender any portion of the Contract Area, Operator shall advise the Operating Committee of such requirement at least one hundred and twenty (120) Days in advance of the earlier of the date for filing irrevocable notice of such surrender or the date of such surrender. Before the end of such period, the Operating Committee shall determine under Article 5 the size and shape of the surrendered area, consistent with the requirements of the Contract. If a sufficient vote of the Operating Committee cannot be attained, then the proposal supported by a simple majority of the Participating Interests shall be adopted. If no proposal attains the support of a simple majority of the Participating Interests, then the proposal receiving the largest aggregate Participating Interest vote shall be adopted. In the event of a tie, Operator shall choose among the proposals receiving the largest aggregate Participating Interest vote. The Parties shall sign any documents and take such other actions as may be necessary to effect the surrender. Each Party renounces all claims and causes of action against Operator and any other Parties on account of any area surrendered in accordance with the foregoing but against its recommendation if Hydrocarbons are later discovered under the surrendered area.*[1002]

The Greenlandic Model JOA provides that if the parties cannot agree on a surrender, the party with the largest interest will take the decision, and this will be binding on all parties:

> *If the Operating Committee cannot decide on the manner of carrying out any Work Obligations or surrender of acreage required under the Licence in sufficient time to fulfil those obligations within the Licence terms and in accordance with the Licence conditions, then such Work Obligations will be carried out or satisfied or surrender of acreage effected in such manner as shall be favoured by the Party or Parties holding individually or in aggregate the greatest Percentage Interests, and all Parties shall be bound by any such decision and such manner of carrying out the Work Obligations or surrender of acreage shall be deemed adopted as part of the Programme and Budget for the year in question.*[1003]

1002 AIPN JOA §11.1.A.
1003 Article 4.7.4 of the Greenlandic Model JOA.

It is also important to understand that the decision to surrender the license as well as the fact that the license has been surrendered might not mean that no further winding-up activities will be required. With this in mind, it is important to identify what kind of activities remain after the decision on surrender has been taken, what the operator is entitled to do and within which period? Would the winding-up activities be charged to the joint account and shall the participants pay for this?

The Norwegian JOA provides with the specific provisions in relation to the costs of winding up after relinquishment, for example Article 1.3.4. Relinquishment of production licenses specifically says that the Operator may charge the Joint Account only for expenses necessary to properly wind up the activities after the Production Licence has been surrendered. Unless otherwise agreed, this shall take place within six months following the month of surrender. Debits/credits stemming from past calculations, corrections or audits shall carry interest in accordance with the joint operating agreement.[1004]

The situation with respect to outstanding costs when all of the licenses are surrendered (which leads to the termination of the joint venture) will be specifically covered in Chapter 3, Section 3 of this book.[1005]

15.3 Discussion

Since withdrawal and relinquishment issues are sensitive for both national and international oil companies, it is important that the model JOAs offer robust provisions in this respect. Importantly, the interest of the host government to ensure that at least the minimum exploration work obligations are met prior to withdrawal is embedded in most of the existing JOAs. At the same time, the current model JOAs provide for the possibility of withdrawals once minimum exploration work obligations are met.

1004 Article 1.3.4. of Norwegian JOA.

1005 The difference between surrender and whole termination situations is that in case of surrender the joint venture continues to operate and thus the abandonment costs will be addressed in the abandonment plan approved by the relevant committee and the costs will be referred to the joint account, whereas with termination the joint venture ceases to exist and the residual liability of the partners will be addressed by special provisions of the joint operating agreement or the law.

2. Funding and accounting

While Chapter 1 deals with the essence of the operations, contemplated by the joint operating agreements, this chapter will deal with the no less important matter of how the operations are financed and how records in relation to spending on operational activities are organised.

The chapter begins by elaborating on the starting point of each funding process – the work programme and budget. It will particularly deal with the preparation process, the participation of non-operators in decision making, the matter of mandatory minimum work obligations and related aspects of petroleum title, the level of detail and its impact on non-operators' rights and other important aspects.

Authorisation for expenditures logically follows the section on work programme and budget and will provide more information on how the spending of money and significant expenditures could be controlled, financial discipline issues, involvement of the participants in the process and the role of the operator.

Insurance, decommissioning and default also form part of funding process. Thus, decommissioning deals with the obligations and plans for expenditures upon termination of hydrocarbon operations. Decommissioning is normally the subject of a dedicated work programme and budget which requires separate approval by the operating committee. Its scope and contact is heavily influenced by the need to meet the requirements of local law and is subject to specific commercial arrangements between the parties.

The insurance section will demonstrate how important it is for operator and non-operators to have a certain level of security against any misfortunes during the conduct of hydrocarbons activities. The existence of a procedure for obtaining insurance might assist in the negotiations with the operator in relation to the operator's indemnity clause in the JOA on the argument that if the operator's liability will be insured to some degree, the operator might consider this a sufficient level of protection against its liability and it may then demonstrate more flexibility in its position on indemnity clauses.

Non-fulfillment of funding obligations will lead to default. Failure to meet cash calls requests will, in all cases, be the basis for default. Among other events, constituting grounds for default could be bankruptcy, material breach and other significant circumstances. It is important to understand what will be the consequences of an event of default and whether the situation could be cured. All these aspects will be touched upon in the default section.

The second part of the chapter will deal with the accounting process, how non-operators can influence the operator's financial performance by exercising the rights they have under the accounting procedure; how the cash calls are organised, who is responsible for the process, and how indirect costs and overheads shall be reflected in the particular line items of the work programme and budget.

The final part of the chapter is dedicated to the important issue of the process by which the participants recover their costs of investment from the cash generated from hydrocarbon production and specific rules on this topic in terms of the granting instrument as well as the general prohibition on the commingling of the operator's own funds with the funds of the joint venture.

As with the first chapter of this book, this second chapter provides the sometimes differing views of international and national oil companies in relation to the funding and accounting processes and analyses the most commonly used joint operating agreement models on these topics.

1. Work programme and budget

1.1 General principles

As mentioned in the previous chapter, commonly the operator acts on the behalf of the joint venture. One of the operator's main duties is to prepare the work programme and budget for approval by the Opcom[1] (if applicable, or by the other parties).[2] This role and obligation are likely to be exercised by an international oil company (at least in the exploration stage) as the main investor in the consortium, but in some cases the national oil company will lead the consortium.

There is no doubt about such an obligation,[3] but the extent to which it occurs in practice is questionable. Is there any limit, or does the operator freely decide the expenditure required during the existence of the enterprise? The nature of this agreement is self-explanatory: as the parties will jointly share the costs involved, it is logical that all parties together will share decisions on running the enterprise.[4] This is the exact aim of the work programme and budget provision as it establishes the overall destination of the consortium expenditure. The operator can only proceed with any form of expenditure if it has been established in the work programme and budget. This is very important for the national oil company and the international oil companies as commonly there will be more than one international oil company in the consortium and each of them will want to control the consortium's expenses.[5]

---

1 References to the OpCom within this section apply to those JOA Models that provide for an OpCom. For those models that do not, the OpCom should be read as the approval or determination of the contracting parties.

2 BG Taverne, *Co-operative Agreements in the Extractive Petroleum Industry*, Kluwer Law International, 1996, pp66–67.

3 H Dundas, *Joint Operating Agreements: An Introduction*, 1994 Summer Programme: UK Oil and Gas Law, CPMLP 09/09, 1994, p5, C Duval, H Le Leuch, A Pertuzio and JL Weaver, *International Petroleum and Exploration Agreements: Legal, Economic & Policy Aspects*, 2nd edn, Barrows, 2009, p290; JS Dzienkowski, EE Smith, OL Anderson, JS Lowe, BM Kramer and JL Weaver, *Materials on International Petroleum Transactions*, 3rd edn, RMMLF, 2010, p543; T Daintith, "Right to Explore For and Exploit Petroleum: The Licence" in T Daintith and G Willoughby (eds), *Adrian Hill, United Kingdom Oil and Gas Law*, 3rd edn, Sweet & Maxwell, 2009, p1140; A Jennings, *Oil and Gas Exploration Contracts*, 2nd edn, Sweet & Maxwell, 2008, p25; BG Taverne, *An Introduction to the Regulation of the Petroleum Industry: Law, Contracts and Conventions*, Graham & Trotman, 1994, p136; C Thorpe, *Fundamentals of Upstream Petroleum Agreements*, CP Thorpe, 2008, p126; J Wilkinson, *Introduction to Oil and Gas Joint Ventures*, OPL, 1997, pp41–42; GMD Bean, *Fiduciary Relationships, Fiduciary Duties and Joint Ventures: The Joint Operating Agreement*, University of Cambridge, 1992, p15.

4 P Roberts and R Fowler, *Joint Operating Agreements: A Practical Guide*, 4th edn, Globe Law and Business, 2020, p168.

5 MPG Taylor and SM Tyne, *Taylor and Winsor on Joint Operating Agreements*, 2nd edn, Longman, 1992, p36.

On the other hand, the operator might seek more flexibility so it can incur expenditure outside that determined by the work programme and budget.[6] As a general rule, such unauthorised action is not allowed. However, it is important to note that it is not possible to predict the precise budget for the entire operation and/or annual work. There are several factors that might require adjustment and which might be outside the control of the parties, such as market fluctuation in the cost of supplies, the geological conditions of the reservoir, technical difficulties and emergencies, among others.[7] As a consequence, the work programme and budget is an estimated[8] prediction, and may be modified if technical or other issues justify such a procedure.[9]

Nevertheless, from a non-operator's perspective, a fairly detailed work programme and budget might facilitate control over the operations such that less discretion is provided to the operator.[10]

The general rule provides that the operator must obey the precise determination of the work programme and budget as approved by the OpCom. However, as an exception, it may be modified. In this case, it is important to note the distinction between modifications imposed by the OpCom and modifications imposed by the operator. The right to make the former kind of modification is a right which is commonly provided within the powers of the OpCom, as it is the highest authority of the JOA; the OpCom may, at any time, change any approved work programme and budget, if it obtains the necessary passmark.[11] The latter kind of modification is a certain amount of flexibility which the JOA provides for the operator to disregard the work programme and budget already approved by the OpCom. If the required modification is no more than a fixed percentage (commonly 10%), the operator does not need to obtain further approvals (as the parties previously accepted such discretion), but if the amount of additional expenditure is anything above the agreed percentage, the operator must obtain the approval of the parties.[12]

This is a very practical and efficient provision. If the modification to expenditure is not significant (ie, it is minor), from a business perspective it should not need any further consents and delays; but if the variation is considerable, then it must be reviewed by the OpCom. This is especially important for an international oil company if there is a national oil company in the consortium, as the national company's level of approval could be fairly complex and take a long time to achieve.

In addition to this tolerance, there is only one specific situation where it is possible for the operator to modify the work programme and budget without the

6 DF Asmus, "The 1995 Model Form International Operating Agreement", *Journal of Energy & Natural Resources Law* 14 (1996) 22.

7 MPG Taylor and SM Tyne, *Taylor and Winsor on Joint Operating Agreements*, 2nd edn, Longman, 1992, p41.

8 T Daintith and G Willoughby (eds), *Adrian Hill, United Kingdom Oil and Gas Law*, 3rd edn, Sweet & Maxwell, 2009, p1145.

9 See also: BG Taverne, *Co-operative Agreements in the Extractive Petroleum Industry*, Kluwer Law International, 1996, pp66–67; P Roberts and R Fowler, *Joint Operating Agreements: A Practical Guide*, 4th edn, Globe Law and Business, 2020, pp176–177; MPG Taylor and SM Tyne, *Taylor and Winsor on Joint Operating Agreements*, 2nd edn, Longman, 1992, p42; S Shaw, "Joint Operating Agreements" in MR David, *Upstream Oil and Gas Agreements*, Sweet & Maxwell, 1996, p20; S Styles, "Joint Operating Agreements" in J Paterson and G Gordon (eds), *Oil and Gas Law: Current Practice and Emerging Trends*, Dundee University Press, 2007, p288.

10 P Roberts and R Fowler, *Joint Operating Agreements: A Practical Guide*, 4th edn, Globe Law and Business, 2020, pp171–172.

11 *Ibid*, pp176–177.

12 C Duval, H Le Leuch, A Pertuzio and JL Weaver, *International Petroleum and Exploration Agreements: Legal, Economic & Policy Aspects*, 2nd edn, Barrows, 2009, p298.

OpCom's consent.[13] In the case of emergencies (such as pollution, explosion and fire, among others[14]), an immediate response is necessary, with no time to obtain the other parties' consent. Nevertheless, the operator must inform the non-operators immediately of such an emergency situation and should act reasonably in accordance with good oil practices.[15]

If the operator exceeds the level of flexibility mentioned above in a situation that is not an emergency procedure, it must follow the exact provisions of the work programme and budget or request a revision in the Opcom. This is a very critical position for all the parties in the consortium (both national and international oil companies) as they should know their exact financial exposure towards the joint operations.

This begs a further question: are the joint-venture parties free to vote their participating interests when asked to approve a work programme budget by the operator? As discussed in Chapter 1, Section 8, generally JOAs under common law expressly exclude any duty of good faith or fiduciary duty owed by joint-venture parties exercising their OpCom vote. Furthermore, English law would certainly recognise and enforce such express exclusion.[16] However, there are foreseeable circumstances where the OpCom may vote down a work programme and budget for expenditure which the operator must expend in order to meet legal obligations already incurred with the full approval of the OpCom. Such situation arose in the facts behind the case of *Spirit Energy Resources v Marathon*,[17] where Marathon as operator sought approval for a programme and budget including £68 million of additional pension charges, to pay for the superannuation benefits of Marathon employees, the cost of whose salaries and superannuation benefits had been previously approved by the OpCom. Given that Marathon was obliged by law to make good the relevant pension shortfall, whether or not the OpCom approve the expenditure, the court had to balance two opposing JOA principles – the principle that an operator should incur no loss by reason of its operator capacity, and the principle that expenditure may only be recovered if it has been approved in accordance with the JOA, for example by reason of its inclusion within an approved programme and budget. The court resolved the conflict by holding that the OpCom must approve expenditure which is necessitated by work undertaken by the operator in the past in compliance with the relevant JOA rules. This is a very significant decision for all JOA parties; it can no longer be assumed that the parties may avoid expenditure by voting down the costs of a particular project in subsequent years. Parties need to pay greater attention to the "regret costs" of the multi-year projects they approve because they will not be able to avoid such regret costs in future by voting down the request for its approval in the OpCom.

13 MPG Taylor and SM Tyne, *Taylor and Winsor on Joint Operating Agreements*, 2nd edn, Longman, 1992, p36.

14 P Roberts and R Fowler, *Joint Operating Agreements: A Practical Guide*, 4th edn, Globe Law and Business, 2020, p177.

15 KCMildwaters, *Joint Operating Agreements, A Consideration of Legal Aspects Relevant to Joint Operating Agreements used in Great Britain and Australia by Participants thereto to Regulate the Joint Undertaking of Exploration for Petroleum in Offshore Areas with Particular Reference to their Rights and Duties*, PhD Thesis presented to the University of Dundee, 1990, p561.

16 *Ross River Ltd v Waverley Commercial Ltd* [2013] EWCA Civ 910.

17 *Spirit Energy Resources Ltd v Marathon Oil UK LLC* (2019] EWCA Civ 11.

A critical problem may arise if the non-operators can exert an effective control on the Opcom by a higher passmark and reject the operator's proposal for the work programme and budget. As a general rule, the operator would then have to revise its proposal and resubmit it. But the critical part goes back to the deadlock situation, which was discussed in Chapter 1, Section 6.[18] For the sake of argument, if the non-operators keep rejecting a proposal made by the operator, what would happen? If it involves the minimum work programme (provided that exclusive operation is forbidden)[19] the answer is quite drastic, as it could lead to the termination of the petroleum title and thus the termination of the joint venture, and also it could affect future applications with that host government.[20]

Deadlocks can be even more complicated if the consortium includes a national oil company. National oil companies may have different views and concerns about the speed of the joint operations as commonly the host government has a higher input on the strategy and decision-making process of most national oil companies. For example, the ministry of petroleum may wish for more investments on the ground and require a more aggressive work programme or vice versa.[21]

It is regularly the case under production sharing agreements and service agreements that the joint venture's activities will be governed by work programmes and budgets which will be subject to approval by the state. In effect, the state acts as another approving party, albeit not as a party to the JOA. Even if the non-operators approve the work programme and budget, it may not be approved by the state, triggering an iterative process in which the operator shuttles between the OpCom and the state, often acting through a management or steering committee under the relevant granting instrument, trying to get approval of the OpCom and the state to one form of programme and budget. Such joint ventures should draft their JOAs to ensure that the programmes and budgets are presented to the OpCom in good time to allow for such iterations, and any deadlock provision in the JOA should be compatible with any deadlock procedures in the relevant granting instrument.[22]

Therefore, it is very important to adopt a resolution process for work programme and budget deadlocks in order to preserve the existence of the petroleum licence and joint venture. There are several procedures available to address this issue, such as mediation, mini-trial, and expert determination, among others. These options could take a long time and may not be the most suitable to reach a quick solution.

A simple solution is to give the decision-making power to the operator if the consortium cannot reach an agreement. This may be the easiest solution to protect the consortium's interests but, on the other hand, it does not prevent

18 P Roberts and R Fowler, *Joint Operating Agreements: A Practical Guide*, 4th edn, Globe Law and Business, 2020, pp153–154.

19 HH Fawzi, *The Evolution of the Legal and Contractual Framework for Exploration and Production of Oil in Sudan and the United Kingdom, A Comparative Approach to Developing and Developed Countries*, PhD Thesis presented to the University of Dundee, 1996.

20 For further information about minimum work obligations see: DAW Maloney, "Australia's Offshore Petroleum Work Programme Bidding System", 21 *Journal of Energy & Natural Resources Law* (2003) 127.

21 P Roberts and R Fowler, *Joint Operating Agreements: A Practical Guide*, 4th edn, Globe Law and Business, 2020, p51.

22 The AIPN JOA is one of the few that addresses this problem; Article 6.1 through to Article 6.5 recognises that programmes and budgets may require state approval for which extra time may be required.

abuse by the operator, which will have the final decision on the minimum work obligations. In other words, it is not a balanced solution but, rather, the most practical alternative.

Another, perhaps more reasonable, solution is to allow the proposal that receives the most support to prevail.[23] This alternative may solve the problem of securing the existence of the petroleum title and ultimately the consortium. However, it also puts the non-operators in a difficult situation if the operator has the largest participating interest in the consortium.

On the other hand, the alternative described by Anthony Jennings may be more balanced if such a right of final decision could alternate between the parties, that is, a rotation process.[24] Thus, if the operator used such a right for a particular work programme and budget proposal, then this right would pass to the non-operators for the next work programme and budget, and so on. This is an interesting provision in the long term but certainly not the best for the short term as initially one party will have more powers.

A radical alternative would be to prohibit the operator from voting on any proposal prepared exclusively by itself. The operator would be forced to gather the non-operators' input or otherwise would have to prepare the work programme and budget, bearing in mind that it would not be permitted to vote on the proposal. This could provide an alternative to balance the participation of the parties regarding the approval of the work programme and budget. However, it is unlikely that any operator would accept such terms, as it would provide far too many powers to the non-operators.

A moderate alternative would be to limit the number of rejections, so that after a specific number the operator would lose its powers to prepare the work programme and budget and the non-operators would take over the role and submit the work programme and budget as an *ad hoc* provision. However, in this approach the operator might also block the proposal and the problem would persist.

The best solution would be balanced provisions imposing a duty on the operator to prepare a reasonable work programme and budget proposal in collaboration with the non-operators, which could not be rejected by any party without reasonable grounds. If there were reasonable grounds to reject the proposal, alternative dispute resolution procedures could be installed to resolve the deadlock by third-party determination or whatever means to reach a quick and fair solution to the conflict.

The approval of any work programme and budget, especially where state approval is also required, can test the mettle of any operator. It can become the forum in which several tensions are worked out, year after year, such as the state's desire to force the joint venture to increase expenditure on local suppliers and services, or its desire to generate cash aggressively, or even to subsidise downstream gas prices. There is a danger that the individual budget items will be "horse traded" with the result that the approving parties are moderately satisfied with the result, but the component budget items are not approved on operationally reasonable terms. The parties need to bear in mind that programmes and budgets should be treated as holistic business

---

23 C Duval, H Le Leuch, A Pertuzio and JL Weaver, *International Petroleum and Exploration Agreements: Legal, Economic & Policy Aspects*, 2nd edn, Barrows, 2009, p291.

24 A Jennings, *Oil and Gas Exploration Contracts*, 2nd edn, Sweet & Maxwell, 2008, p27.

plans, the components of which are consistent with an overall strategy but also reasonable on a stand-alone basis. All too often such objectives are compromised in the interests of a commercial bargain.

It is obvious, but nevertheless important, to comment briefly on the distinction between the work programme and the budget The work programme details the activities that the joint venture will perform and the budget provides an estimate of the cost of those activities.[25] Commonly, the budget is divided between capital budget and operating budget. Capital budget relates to the costs of the main activities, such as seismic acquisition and drilling costs.[26] Operating budget relates to the manpower and overhead costs.[27] The latter is a potential area of conflict between operator and non-operators as the operator may wish to increase its revenues by setting the overheads as high as possible.[28] The non-operators should check carefully whether the accounting procedures control the extension of the application of overheads.[29]

The work programme and budget will cover a certain period of time. In this case, it is based on a specific phase of the enterprise, such as exploration, development or production.[30]

As a general rule, the operator will prepare the work programme and budget programmes on an annual basis.[31] However, this may not be the case for certain phases of the project.[32] The exploration phase deals primarily with the minimum work programme, which must be performed entirely as set out in the petroleum title.[33] Thus, in the exploration phase the parties might provide just one programme and budget to cover the whole minimum work programme, but this can be subject to amendment if further work is necessary to progress towards the development

---

25 S Styles, "Joint Operating Agreements" in J Paterson and G Gordon (eds), *Oil and Gas Law: Current Practice and Emerging Trends*, Dundee University Press, 2007, p288; S Shaw, "Joint Operating Agreements" in MR David, *Upstream Oil and Gas Agreements*, Sweet & Maxwell, 1996, p20.

26 S Styles, "Joint Operating Agreements" in J Paterson and G Gordon (eds), *Oil and Gas Law: Current Practice and Emerging Trends*, Dundee University Press, 2007, p288; S Shaw, "Joint Operating Agreements" in MR David, *Upstream Oil and Gas Agreements*, Sweet & Maxwell, 1996, p20.

27 S Styles, "Joint Operating Agreements" in J Paterson and G Gordon (eds), *Oil and Gas Law: Current Practice and Emerging Trends*, Dundee University Press, 2007, p288; S Shaw, "Joint Operating Agreements" in MR David, *Upstream Oil and Gas Agreements*, Sweet & Maxwell, 1996, p20.

28 MPG Taylor and SM Tyne, *Taylor and Winsor on Joint Operating Agreements*, 2nd edn, Longman, 1992, p44.

29 "Sensitive questions arise with regard to the audit of company overhead ..." T Daintith, "Right to Explore for and Exploit Petroleum: The Licence" in T Daintith and G Willoughby (eds), *Adrian Hill, United Kingdom Oil and Gas Law*, 3rd edn, Sweet & Maxwell, 2009, p1146.

30 Some scholars and JOAs add another phase, "appraisal", between the exploration and development phases. For further information see: MPG Taylor and SM Tyne, *Taylor and Winsor on Joint Operating Agreements*, 2nd edn, Longman, 1992, pp36–41; S Shaw, "Joint Operating Agreements" in MR David, *Upstream Oil and Gas Agreements*, Sweet & Maxwell, 1996, pp19–20; C Golvala, "Upstream joint ventures – bidding and operating agreements" in G Picton-Tubervill (ed.), *Oil and Gas: A Practical Handbook*, Globe Law and Business, 2009, p47.

31 BG Taverne, *An Introduction to the Regulation of the Petroleum Industry: Law, Contracts and Conventions*, Graham & Trotman, 1994, p136; C Thorpe, *Fundamentals of Upstream Petroleum Agreements*, CP Thorpe, 2008, p126; J Wilkinson, *Introduction to Oil and Gas Joint Ventures*, OPL, 1997, pp41–42; GMD Bean, *Fiduciary Relationships, Fiduciary Duties and Joint Ventures: The Joint Operating Agreement*, University of Cambridge, 1992, p14; S Shaw, "Joint Operating Agreements" in MR David, *Upstream Oil and Gas Agreements*, Sweet & Maxwell, 1996, p19; P Roberts and R Fowler, *Joint Operating Agreements: A Practical Guide*, 4th edn, Globe Law and Business, 2020, p168.

32 C Golvala, "Upstream joint ventures – bidding and operating agreements" in G Picton-Tubervill (ed.), *Oil and Gas: A Practical Handbook*, Globe Law and Business, 2009, p47.

33 Model Clause 16 (1) – Petroleum Licensing (Production) (Seaward Areas) Regulations 2008.

phase.[34] A similar situation applies for the development phase[35] as, commonly, before moving to such a phase the host government must approve the work programme and budget plan, and it will be looking to maximise its economic recovery.[36] On the other hand, some parties may use a multi-year work programme and budget in order to deal with such situations.[37] The production phase will be more straightforward on an annual basis and is likely to be accepted without major amendment.[38]

It could be suggested that in practical terms such distinction between an annual basis and a programme of activities will not affect the non-operators provided the Opcom has powers to amend any approved work programme and budget.[39] Nevertheless, an annual work programme and budget will ensure a higher degree of participation by the non-operators, as successful exploration and development phases may take a year or more before reaching the production stage, so they will have more opportunities to give their input on each proposal of the work programme and budget.

From a non-operator's perspective, the establishment of a work programme and budget provision is an excellent opportunity to exert control over the expenditure – they can participate in the decision that will determine the allocation of expenditure.[40] However, the work programme and budget will only represent an effective procedure to control the operator's discretion to conduct the joint operations if the non-operators have effective control in the Opcom.

Additionally, the preparation of the work programme and budget might be difficult for non-operators given their position in the JOA, as the operator will prepare all the programmes and budgets required for the execution of the joint operations.[41] Thus, it is essential to allow the non-operators to participate in the ongoing process of formulation and preparation of the programmes, or at least include a requirement to consult them, so that full control and participation is provided for the non-operators.[42] In fact, such participation may reduce the chance of deadlocks over the work programme and budget proposals as all parties would have taken part in the development of each proposal.

---

34 However, the practice may vary in the exploration phase as some parties may still prefer to approve an annual programme and to address the minimum work programme accordingly. See: MPG Taylor and SM Tyne, *Taylor and Winsor on Joint Operating Agreements*, 2nd edn, Longman, 1992, pp36–37.

35 P Roberts and R Fowler, *Joint Operating Agreements: A Practical Guide*, 4th edn, Globe Law and Business, 2020, p170.

36 Model Clause 17 (1) and (2) – Petroleum Licensing (Production) (Seaward Areas) Regulations 2008.

37 PR Weems and M Bolton, "Highlights of Key Revisions – 2002 AIPN Model Form International Operating Agreement" *OGEL* 1 (2003) 5.

38 P Roberts and R Fowler, *Joint Operating Agreements: A Practical Guide*, 4th edn, Globe Law and Business, 2020, p170.

39 The same principle applies for multi-year programmes since the programme may need revision as the activities evolve. C Golvala, "Upstream joint ventures – bidding and operating agreements" in G Picton-Tubervill (ed.), *Oil and Gas: A Practical Handbook*, Globe Law and Business, 2009, p47.

40 P Roberts and R Fowler, *Joint Operating Agreements: A Practical Guide*, 4th edn, Globe Law and Business, 4th edn, 2020, p173.

41 H Dundas, *Joint Operating Agreements: An Introduction*, 1994 Summer Programme: UK Oil and Gas Law, CPMLP 09/09, 1994, p5; C Thorpe, *Fundamentals of Upstream Petroleum Agreements*, CP Thorpe, 2008, pp125, 126; J Wilkinson, *Introduction to Oil and Gas Joint Ventures*, OPL, 1997, p39; GMD Bean, *Fiduciary Relationships, Fiduciary Duties and Joint Ventures: The Joint Operating Agreement*, University of Cambridge, 1992, p15.

42 KC Mildwaters, *Joint Operating Agreements, A Consideration of Legal Aspects Relevant to Joint Operating Agreements used in Great Britain and Australia by Participants thereto to Regulate the Joint Undertaking of Exploration for Petroleum in Offshore Areas with Particular Reference to their Rights and Duties*, PhD Thesis presented to the University of Dundee, 1990, p561.

Although the work programme and budget provision is a valuable protection for the non-operators, it is important to note that it is not widely established in the JOA forms – some JOAs do not provide for the existence of such a mechanism of control.[43] The following paragraphs will examine how each JOA Model deals with such provisions and, if there is no implementation of a work programme and budget provision, the reason why will also be discussed.

1.2 Analysis of the model JOAs

AAPL Form 810 provides for the existence of the work programme and budget provision, which is referred as the "Annual Operating Plan". However, the work programme and budget mechanism adopts a soft approach. Such a soft approach is clearly stated in Article 6.4.1 of the form.

In effect, this work programme and budget provision is a bureaucratic mechanism, as it secures nothing apart from information for the non-operators. There is no effective participation of the non-operators, except for the right to make suggestions, additions or deletions to the annual operating plan, but these do not bind the operators – the operator is not obliged to incorporate any input from the non-operators.[44] The strong position of the operator is very clear under this model, as it provides that the operator has the exclusive right and duty to conduct the consortium activities.[45]

Thus, AAPL Form 810 provides the non-operators with similar rights to an investor, as they will have access to information but no effective participation in the activities that are performed by the joint venture. However, it is important to stress that the exclusion of an effective work programme and budget provision does not necessarily mean that the non-operators have no right to control the expenditure incurred by the operator, as there are other methods to control this. This model form 810 also provides for the existence of an authorisation for expenditure mechanism, which is an efficient and effective method to control the expenditure.

In conclusion, the AAPL JOA Model Form does not secure the participation of the non-operators in the work programme and budget provisions, as they allow extensive discretion to the operator, allowing it to act freely without control of its expenditure by other parties. Nevertheless, the model secures the non-operators' position as they can exert effective control of the expenditure via the authorisation for expenditure mechanism, as will be discussed in another section.

The long-standing RMMLF Model Form does not provide for the existence of a work programme and budget provision. A simple analysis of paragraph 4.1 leaves no doubt about the total control of the operation, since the "Operator shall direct and have control of all operations conducted hereunder and shall have exclusive custody of all materials, equipment and other property owned by the Parties."[46]

In other words, under this model form the operator is in a very strong position and has extensive discretion to conduct the joint operations. However, the non-operators may have an opportunity to participate in the preparation of the work programmes as the operator must "Consult freely the other Parties concerning

43 P Roberts and R Fowler, *Joint Operating Agreements: A Practical Guide*, 4th edn, Globe Law and Business, 2020, pp168–169.
44 AAPL JOA Form 810 §6.4.3.
45 AAPL JOA Form 810 §5.1.
46 RMMLF JOA §4.1.

operations hereunder and keep them advised of all matters arising in operations hereunder which Operator deems important in the exercise of its best judgement."[47]

The Canadian Operating Procedure Model Form adopts a similar approach to the American JOA Model Forms, as there is no provision on the work programme and budget. The operator has extensive discretion to conduct the operations.

However, this model suggests more participation by the non-operators in comparison with the American Models as it requires the operator to consult the other parties on exploration, development and operation of joint lands.[48, 49]

In this case, the operator must consult the non-operators, which is a valuable provision for them. Nevertheless, it is important to stress that such consultation has no influence on the operator's decision, as the operator is not obliged to accept any input from the non-operators. Consequently, this is not a proper participation as there is no guarantee that the non-operators can effectively contribute to setting each work programme and budget.

Considering the work programme and budget provision, this model puts the non-operators in a weak position as there is no procedure to control the expenditure of the joint operations. However, it is not correct to state that under the CAPL Operating Procedure Model form there is no control whatsoever of the expenditure as the work programme and budget gap is addressed via the authorisation for expenditure mechanism.

Therefore, the Canadian Model Form provides a similar approach to the American JOA Model Form, as it provides a great discretion for the operator's conduct of the joint operations, with no effective control over the work programme and budget for the non-operators. However, it does contain an authorisation for expenditure mechanism, which is another procedure to control the expenditure of the joint venture.

The OGUK JOA Model Form clearly provides for the existence of a work programme and budget provision. The operator is obliged annually to submit the work programme and budget for the following year, which must be approved by the OpCom.[50] Additionally, the OpCom has powers to revise, and also to make adjustments to, any work programme and budget previously approved.[51]

This model follows the general rule that the operator cannot incur any expenditure until it is approved by the OpCom. However, it allows more flexibility for the operator if commitments are required in advance as the Opcom may call special meetings to consider such requests.[52]

In general terms, this may be a positive provision as certain issues will need to be approved more urgently than others, and ultimately this will benefit the consortium as a whole. On the other hand, the operator could use the provision to pressure the OpCom into approving its preferred issues as there is no clear regulation on who will

47 RMMLF JOA §5.1(B).

48 CAPL OP §3.01.

49 The CAPL JOA includes an unusual provision whereby a non-operator may "challenge" the operator to commit to running joint operations in accordance with that non-operator's proposal ("the Challenge"). If the operator does not agree to adopt such Challenge, it will be replaced as operator by another party, including the challenging party as a last resort. If the replacement operator fails to implement joint operations in accordance with the Challenge, any incremental cost is for its sole account. See CAPL JOA article 2.03.

50 OGUK JOA §10.1.1.

51 OGUK JOA §10.1.2, 10.3.

52 OGUK JOA §10.1.2.

determine which commitments require approval before the work programme and budget is set and how such a right could be controlled.

In order to maintain the petroleum title, this model avoids minimum work programme deadlocks by providing a practical solution.[53] It allows extensive discretion to the operator, as the programme proposed by the operator will be deemed to be approved unless an alternative plan is approved by a simple majority of votes. In other words, if the non-operators cannot control the OpCom, the operator is likely to determine the work programme and budget by itself, which might happen in the majority of the cases. Nevertheless, the deadlock cannot be resolved if it concerns anything that is not related to the minimum work programme. This could be problematic as, if no work is approved, the consortium will face critical challenges because the licence rigorously imposes several deadlines, but the model appears to address the situation as an exclusive operation, as will be analysed further.

The minimum work programme is not the only flexibility provided within the British JOA Model Form as the operator may overspend the overall terms defined in the budget. However, the limitation is left blank, so the parties can define the limitation during the negotiation process.[54] The model does not put any obligation on the operator to notify the non-operators about such overspending, but only to obtain the OpCom's approval if the limit is exceeded. On the other hand, such an obligation is clearly imposed whenever the operator is required to take action to deal with emergencies.[55]

No indication whatsoever is given that the operator must obtain the non-operators' input during the process of setting the work programme and budget, and even direct consultation is not required.[56] On the other hand, it is important to stress that the general duties of the operator establish that the "Operator shall freely consult with the Participants and keep them informed of matters concerning the Joint Operations."[57] This provision gives grounds for non-operators to insist on participating in the discussion process but does not force the operator to implement their views, and the mention of 'freely' also indicates that more discretion is provided to the operator.

Therefore, it could be said that this approach is definitely not beneficial to the non-operators, as their participation is restricted to the OpCom's approval. The approach could lead to two different scenarios. The first is when the operator has overall control of the OpCom. In this case, the non-operators are mere observers, as they cannot participate in the discussion process or in the determinations of the OpCom. The second is when the non-operators have negative control of the OpCom, as they can block decisions. In this case, the non-operators can minimise their lack of participation in the ongoing discussions of the work programme and budget proposals by blocking them. However, this will not apply to the minimum work programme as the operator has more discretion to deal with this. Therefore, it could be suggested that the British JOA Model does not provide for effective participation by the non-operators regarding the work programme and budget provision and

53 OGUK JOA §9.9.1.
54 OGUK JOA §§ 0.5, 11.4, 12.4, 13.4.
55 OGUK JOA §6.10.2.
56 OGUK JOA §10, 11, 12, 13, 14.
57 OGUK JOA §6.9.1.

that partial participation will only be effective if the non-operators can control the OpCom; otherwise, they will be mere spectators in the process.

On the other hand, this model secures a higher level of detail that must be provided by the operator in any work programme and budget proposal.[58] Such a provision is very valuable for the non-operators as they will have a better basis to vote on the OpCom. Possibly this provision seeks to minimise the effect of the non-operators being unable to participate in the discussion of the work programme and budget proposals.

In conclusion, it could be suggested that the British JOA Model puts the non-operators in a relatively weak position, as the model allows extensive discretion to the operator in preparing the work programme and budget, as well as in dealing with minimum work programmes and not placing limitations on overspending the budgets. However, the model also has a positive side for the non-operators, as a higher level of information must be provided on each work programme and budget proposal and it is possible for the non-operators to block a proposal if they can effectively block it in the OpCom. The AAPL, CAPL, RMMLF and OGUK JOA are appropriate for petroleum licence regimes where the state does not routinely require to approve exploration or production programmes and budgets; in some cases, the state would expect to approve a development plan and budget. For these reasons, these model form JOAs do not allow for the additional effort and time required to obtain such state approvals and need more robust "anti-deadlock" mechanisms for this purpose.

Under the Norwegian JOA Model, the operator is responsible for preparing the overall proposals for submission to the OpCom.[59] However, this model clearly requires the participation of the non-operators, as follows: "When preparing proposals for work programmes and budgets, the operator shall involve the Parties before the proposal is submitted to the Opcom for final adoption."[60] This is a valuable provision for the non-operators as they will have a chance to participate in the discussion on the work programme and budget.

Any party may propose amendments to the approved work programme and budget to the OpCom.[61] The OpCom has authority to change any limitation or content approved in a work programme and budget programme.[62] This is a positive provision for non-operators, as it clearly provides the right for any non-operator to call for amendments. Nevertheless, such a right is commonly provided in the OpCom regulations, as any party can add topics to the agenda before the relevant meeting within a specific time period.[63]

This model requires detailed provisions about the work programme and budget proposals.[64] After such a general statement, it separates the provisions between the work programme proposal and the budget proposal in order to address the minimum requirements for each category. The work programme should:

---

58 OGUK JOA §10.4.
59 Norwegian JOA §3.3.
60 Norwegian JOA §12.2.
61 *Ibid.*
62 *Ibid.*
63 Norwegian JOA §12.1.
64 *Ibid.*

a) Define clear goals, deliverables and deadlines for significant activities; b) Clarify how the activities in the coming Year will contribute to realizing goals set forth for activities; and c) Identify significant risk factors and relevant actions to manage risk.[65]

There are fairly detailed provisions on the budget proposal, as the operator shall "explain the allocation procedures for charging costs".[66] However, the most important provision concerns the structure and content of the budget items, specifying the items according to the activity that should be performed by the joint venture.[67] This is a valuable approach for the non-operators as it secures a fairly detailed provision to exert control over the overall work programme and budget.

This model also provides a certain flexibility for the operator, as it is allowed to exceed the budget line by up to 10%, although not by more than 5% of the overall budget.[68] In cases of emergency, the operator may incur a liability or expenditure outside the approved work programme and budget in order to protect life, health or property.[69] The model also mentions the power to expend up to a limit of 3 million Norwegian kroner a year, subject to adjustment by the OpCom. However, the operator must provide the OpCom, "with no undue delay", a written notice detailing all unforeseen expenditure and expenditure that may exceed the approved work programme and budget.[70]

However, it is important to note that any event will only be considered an emergency "if there is not sufficient time to present the matter to the committee", which implies that if the operator is going to prepare an emergency plan, it must consult the non-operators, which is a valuable protection for them. In addition, it is not very clear whether the three million Norwegian kroner allowance is included in the aforementioned percentages or if this is a supplementary sum. The grammatical interpretation suggests a supplementary allowance as it uses the terminology "may also", but a logical analysis indicates that they are all connected.

The major flaw in the Norwegian Model is its lack of a resolution process for deadlocks. As mentioned previously, it is very important to perform the minimum work programme as established in the relevant licence so that the consortium is preserved. On the other hand, the model does allow for sole risk operations, which might be a way of resolving a deadlock, but this resolution is forbidden in situations that include a minimum work obligation.[71] Nevertheless, it is important to verify that any alternative adopted does not provide excessive powers to the operator when it deals with the situation. Consequently, flexibility and balance are the key words to describe any alternative chosen by the parties to address deadlocks related to a minimum work programme or even the work programme and budget as a whole.

The Norwegian JOA Model appears to secure a fairly positive position for the non-operators and, most importantly, a higher level of participation from the

65 Norwegian JOA §12.1.
66 Norwegian JOA §12.3.
67 Norwegian JOA §12.4.
68 Norwegian JOA §12.5.
69 Norwegian JOA §12.5.
70 *Ibid.*
71 Norwegian JOA §18.3(d).

non-operators in the preparation of the work programme and budget. However, it fails to provide a resolution process for deadlocks, which might jeopardise the existence of the consortium.

The AIPN form provides for the existence of a work programme and budget provision, which is a valuable procedure for the non-operators as it allows them to exert more control over the key elements of the joint operations – that is, the costs and expenditure.[72]

This form follows the common procedure, under which the operator has the duty to prepare the work programme and budget.[73] However, there is no doubt about the supremacy of the OpCom, as the form clearly establishes the requirement to obtain the decision-making body's approval and also the authority of this committee to make modifications to any work programme and budget that has been already approved.[74]

It is important to note the provision requiring the operator to consult with the OpCom or applicable subcommittees on the contents of the work programme and budget plans.[75] This is a very positive provision for non-operators, as it allows them the opportunity to give their input on such important issues. However, the provision only mentions "consult", which means that the operator may not necessarily use the non-operators' suggestions. In addition, the AIPN Model allows a multi-year work programme and budget, which might cause problems.[76] On the other hand, the model also requires a fairly reasonable amount of detail in the work programme and budget proposal, so it is much easier for a non-operator to exert control when voting on the work programme and budget proposals in the OpCom.[77]

This model also secures certain flexibility for the operator, as it may overspend by 10% on each item approved, but it must not exceed 5% of the total work programme and budget approved for the year.[78] If the operator exceeds these percentages, it must obtain the approval of the OpCom.[79]

However, this restriction does not apply to urgent matters (eg, explosion, sabotage, crude oil release), when the operator is allowed to incur expenditure without obtaining the OpCom's consent.[80] Nevertheless, the operator shall "as soon as reasonably practicable, report to Non-Operators the details of such event and any measures Operator has taken or plans to take in response thereto".[81] It could be suggested that this provision achieves sufficient flexibility to protect both the operator's and the non-operators' interests, but this is not entirely true. First, "as soon as reasonably practicable" is not the best wording for urgent measures. It should provide that "immediately after the event" the operator should report to the non-operators. Secondly, an immediate response from the non-operators may allow their input on alternative plans and decisions to deal with such a catastrophic event. Thirdly, for a plan to address the emergency, the operator must obtain the

72 AIPN JOA §6.
73 AIPN JOA §4.2(B)(6).
74 AIPN JOA §6.1(E).
75 AIPN JOA §6.4(A).
76 DF Asmus, "The 1995 Model Form International Operating Agreement", *Journal of Energy & Natural Resources Law* 14 (1996) 14, 16.
77 AIPN JOA §6.1(F), 6.2(A).
78 AIPN JOA §6.8(A).
79 AIPN JOA §6.8(B).
80 AIPN JOA §§6.8(C), 13.5.
81 AIPN JOA §4.2(B)(13).

non-operators' approval – the consequences of the measures will affect all the contracting parties, so it is reasonable to allow them to participate at such a critical moment.

This model adopts a resolution process for deadlocks regarding the minimum work programme:

> *The Work Program and Budget agreed pursuant to this Article shall include at least that part of the Minimum Work Obligations required to be carried out during the Calendar Year in question under the terms of the Contract. If within the time periods prescribed in this Article 6.1 the Operating Committee is unable to agree on such a Work Program and Budget, then the proposal capable of satisfying the Minimum Work Obligations for the Calendar Year in question that receives the largest Participating Interest vote (even if less than the applicable percentage under Article 5.9) shall be deemed adopted as part of the annual Work Program and Budget. If competing proposals receive equal votes, then Operator shall choose between those competing proposals. Any portion of a Work Program and Budget adopted pursuant to this Article 6.1(D) instead of Article 5.9 shall contain only such operations for the Joint Account as are necessary to maintain the Contract in full force and effect, including such operations as are necessary to fulfil the Minimum Work Obligations required for the given Calendar Year.*[82]

This resolution process is very positive in terms of preserving the integrity of the petroleum title and, as a consequence, the consortium. However, it clearly gives more powers to the operator, as this is the party which is likely to retain the largest percentage interest. It is also important to stress that this procedure does not follow the usual voting processes, as it does not consider the number of parties but only the level of percentage interests.[83] Nevertheless, it is a significant improvement on previous editions of the model, as the operator used to have even more discretion to perform the minimum work obligations if consensus was not reached in the OpCom.[84]

On the level of detail that the operator must provide, this JOA Model Form is very positive for non-operators as it adopts two procedures. First, it imposes an obligation on the operator to provide "detailed" information on the joint operations, which generally must be met.[85] Secondly, it imposes an obligation on the operator to provide certain detailed information during different stages of the operations.[86] Consequently, this system provides the non-operators with two layers of protection similar to the right to information.

Finally, it can be seen that the AIPN JOA Model secures reasonable protection for the non-operators, if they can exert effective control over the OpCom. The non-operators have valuable participation rights during the work programme and budget

82 AIPN JOA §6.1(D).

83 AIPN JOA §5.9.

84 DF Asmus, "The 1995 Model Form International Operating Agreement", *Journal of Energy & Natural Resources Law* 14 (1996) 14.

85 AIPN JOA §6.1(A), (B), (C).

86 AIPN JOA §6.1(F), 6.2(A).

negotiations. However, if the operator has absolute control over the OpCom, from a non-operator's perspective this provision may be useful for information purposes only, rather than effective participation as consultation does not ensure acceptance of the non-operator's suggestions. In addition, this model fails to secure an immediate notification for the non-operators in an emergency situation, where they could provide assistance or, at least, their advice about an issue that clearly will affect their interest. Also, the model fails to provide for project teams, which could provide a higher level of participation in preparing the work programme and budget proposals, but this could be addressed by implementing a subcommittee to deal with the task.

Under the Greenlandic JOA Model Form, the operator prepares and submits each work programme and budget proposal, which must be approved by the OpCom.[87] As usual, the OpCom also has the authority to amend any approved work programme and budget.[88]

It is important to note that there is no requirement to gather the non-operators' input or even to consult them during the discussion and preparation process of the work programme and budget proposals. However, there is a general provision stating that "The Operator shall freely consult with the Parties and keep them informed of matters concerning the Joint Operations."[89] As previously mentioned, such flexible terms indicate that the operator will have extensive discretion to determine the consultation, which includes the activities where consultation may be required.

As a consequence, the operator may choose not to consult with the non-operators, and their lack of participation may increase the chance of the proposal then being rejected by the OpCom. This situation is much more complicated during the exploration phase, as here there is no requirement to provide sufficient detail on any proposal.[90] Thus, the non-operators are likely to examine the work programme and budget proposal for the first time in the OpCom, without any relevant detail – that is, they will be voting on something they are not entirely sure about, which is clearly a dangerous situation. On the other hand, the development phase requires more detail on all proposals, which gives more protection to the non-operators as, even if they cannot participate in the discussion process, at least enough information is provided to allow them to make an informed decision in the OpCom.[91] There are no requirements to provide detail during the production phase, but there is less need for detail in this case because the parameters of production will have been set by the scope and design of the development plan which naturally precedes it.[92]

It is important to stress that the Greenlandic Model recognises the importance of dealing with deadlocks, as follows:

> *If the Operating Committee cannot decide on the manner of carrying out any Work Obligations or surrender of acreage required under the Licence in sufficient time to fulfil those obligations within the Licence terms and in accordance with the Licence conditions, then such Work Obligations will be carried out or satisfied or surrender of*

---

87 Greenlandic JOA §5.1, 5.2, 5.3.1, 5.3.2, 5.4.1, 5.4.2, 5.5, 5.6.
88 Greenlandic JOA §5.11.
89 Greenlandic JOA §3.10.
90 Greenlandic JOA §5.1, 5.2.
91 Greenlandic JOA §5.4.1.
92 *Ibid.*

acreage effected in such manner as shall be favoured by the Party or Parties holding individually or in aggregate the greatest Percentage Interests, and all Parties shall be bound by any such decision and such manner of carrying out the Work Obligations or surrender of acreage shall be deemed adopted as part of the Programme and Budget for the year in question.[93]

This procedure is a practical solution to deal with work obligation deadlocks, but the mechanism provides extensive discretion to the strongest party in the consortium, that is, the operator. Thus, the operator could abuse such powers by creating artificial difficulties to get work obligations approved in the OpCom, where it can decide unilaterally, avoiding OpCom approval. It should be noted that this resolution applies only for work obligations and surrender of acreage, which are imposed by the licence, so it does not deal with any other work programme and budget proposals that may be necessary during the consortium's life-span. Again, this procedure seems to apply the exclusive operation approach to resolving deadlocks in the OpCom.

This model also provides flexibility to the overall conduct of the operations, as the operator is permitted to incur expenditure that is not authorised by the approved work programme and budget in an emergency situation, or over-expenditure of up to 10% or a defined amount.[94] In the case of emergencies, the operator must promptly notify the non-operators about the emergency (including actions taken).[95] However, in the case of over-expenditure, there is no provision in the JOA requiring the operator to notify the non-operators about the situation; instead the model prefers to deal with this issue in the accounting procedures.

The Greenlandic JOA, as with the other model formats, does not expressly state that the operator has no right to recover from the joint-venture expenditure which has not been incurred in accordance with the JOA rules. This would include cases where the relevant expenditure exceeded the approved budget amount, subject to any tolerance allowed for by the JOA. However, the better legal view would be that the operator may not recover such non-compliant expenditure. This outcome would not conflict with the principle that the operator may incur no loss from its role: it simply reflects the fact that the principle of "no gain and no loss" only applies within the scope of joint operations carried out within the rules of the JOA.[96]

In conclusion, the Greenlandic Model provides extensive discretion to the operators since (a) the operator is not obliged to allow the non-operators to participate in the preparation process of any work programme and budget proposal or in the case of emergencies, (b) the model also provides that for work obligations the ultimate decision is likely to be for the operator, and (c) few details are required on each work programme and budget proposal, except for the development phase. The only effective control and participation available to the non-operators is via Opcom

93 Greenlandic JOA §4.7.4.
94 Greenlandic JOA §5.10.
95 Greenlandic JOA §3.11.
96 R Fowler, "The Blank Cheque and the Cliff Edge", *Journal of World Energy Law and Business* 12(6) (2019), pp513–526.

approval, if they have enough control to block a decision, otherwise the operator will have the total control under the work programme and budget provision.

1.3 Discussion

Initially, it is possible to make a distinction between the North American JOA models and all the others. The North American Models do not provide control of operations via a work programme and budget, so the operator has total discretion under those models. On the other hand, the remaining models clearly secure the control of the operations via work programme and budget provisions.

It is worth noting that such a situation is similar to the OpCom provision, as the North American Models do not provide for the existence of an OpCom but all other JOAs do. Thus, it could be suggested that the existence of an OpCom is directly connected to the existence of a work programme and budget.

As usual, the AIPN and British Models provide the non-operators with this essential participation and control.[97] On the other hand, the Canadian Model does not contain any such provision, and the AAPL adopts a soft approach as it provides that the operator shall formulate the work programme, but the non-operators may only suggest modifications to the operator. Thus, the question arises whether it is possible to suggest that the British or international non-operators are in a safer position to determine and control the expenditure of the joint operations, and whether, on the other hand, the North American non-operators are in a dramatically weaker position as they do not have any obligation jointly to approve a work programme and budget. This seems unlikely as work programmes and budgets are not the only means to control costs and expenditure – other procedures are available, which are briefly examined below.

However, the main problem is the non-operators' participation as the majority of the JOAs do not require the non-operators' input during the preparation process of work programme and budget proposals, except the AIPN and Norwegian JOA Models, which strongly indicate the importance of the non-operators' collaboration at such a stage. The lack of participation by the non-operators is very negative for the consortium as a whole, since the non-operators can add valuable input towards best practices and higher efficiency.

On the other hand, the non-operators may protect themselves by ensuring that the accounting procedure effectively regulates the operator's operational and financial performance, enabling the non-operators to challenge expenditure (and their liability to pay for it) after the event, through the process of audit and adjustment of the joint account. This may be an effective compromise – whereby the operator is not required to consult the OpCom during the management of operations, but can be held to account at a later date for failing to comply with the JOA.[98]

The historically dominant position retained by the operator provides it with extensive powers to conduct the joint operations. A balanced scenario would make an important distinction between discussion and implementation. This balance is more

---

97 The British and international models allow a certain flexibility to the operator's procedure as it may overspend on the limit established in the work programme and budget by up to 10% for each specific item, if this does not affect more than 5% of the overall budget. However, if the limit is exceeded, the operator must obtain the OpCom's approval. See: AIPN JOA item 6.8 and OGUK JOA items 10.5, 11.4, 12.4 and 13.4.

98 P Roberts and R Fowler, *Joint Operating Agreements: A Practical Guide*, 4th edn, Globe Law and Business, 2020, p323.

likely to be required when a national oil company participates in the consortium or several IOCs participate in it.

The discussion stage is a very important part of any work programme and budget proposal, as it addresses the main elements of the consortium – that is, the operations and costs involved. Thus, a higher level of participation from all parties not only minimises the chance of rejection in the OpCom, but also allows joint collaboration towards an efficient and effective operation. The best way to obtain input from the non-operators is to create a subcommittee or project team to deal only with work programme and budget proposals, with all parties putting forward a representative. This would give the non-operators the opportunity to participate in any work programme and budget proposal, even if they cannot control the OpCom's decisions. On the other hand, implementing a work programme and budget will have a different procedure. In order to maintain the efficiency of the joint operations, the implementation of the work programme and budget will fall under the operator's powers, and this can be controlled by other means, for example, information provided, right of audits, authorisation for expenditure.

This lack of participation by the non-operators increases the chances of rejection by the OpCom, if the non-operators can block such a proposal. It may lead to deadlock, which is a very important issue to be addressed, even though some JOAs try to resolve this concern. It should also be noted that, whenever JOA Models deal with deadlock, the provision is focused on minimum work obligations, which are imposed by the licence. However, the outcome is very negative for the non-operators as the mechanism adopted to resolve deadlocks shows a clear preference for the easiest solution – that is, a greater discretion to the strongest party of the joint venture.

Another way to minimise the non-operators' lack of participation during the discussion process is the level of detail that is required in any proposal submitted by the operator. A higher level of detail facilitates the non-operators' decision to approve or reject a work programme and budget proposal; less detail may make the non-operators' decision difficult. The JOA Models vary in their approach, from requiring a high level of information to a lower one.

The most effective way to control the work programme and budget proposals in any JOA is the requirement for the OpCom's approval. If the non-operators have at least a negative control of the OpCom (ie, if they can block any decision), effectively this control will exist. On the other hand, if the operator has overall control of the OpCom, the JOA Models will provide only a bureaucratic work programme and budget provision, as the non-operators will be unable to participate at all, but only observe the decisions taken by the operator. Their only available alternative will be the right of non-consent or sole risk (if available).

Finally, it is important to stress that the work programme and budget is one of several mechanisms to control the expenditure of the joint operations. For this reason, it is not correct to say that North American JOA Models do not secure any control of expenditure as they provide other routes to control expenditure.

In cases where the state also approves the relevant programmes and budgets for the purposes of the corresponding granting instrument, the position of the non-operators is significantly different. In such cases it will be the granting instrument that defines the level of detail and supporting information which the operator must provide on behalf the joint venture to the state. Accordingly, irrespective of the level of information that the operator must provide to the non-operators under the JOA, the non-operators will expect to see and approve the programme and budget and supporting information which is presented to the state for the purposes of the granting instrument. After all, the non-operators are themselves party to the granting instrument, are entitled to see the reports and information provided on their behalf to the state by the operator and are likely to have their own rights to be represented, or at least to be present at, meetings between the operator and the state in accordance with the relevant instruments. However, non-operators should be careful not to jeopardise the joint venture's representation before the state; in *Euroil Ltd v Cameroon Offshore Petroleum SARL*, the operator obtained an injunction against one another preventing it from engaging with the state in a manner which conflicted with the operator's strategy.[99]

Therefore, there is no doubt that several mechanisms exist to exert control over the consortium's expenditure. One effective mechanism is the authorisation for expenditure, which is examined in the next section.

2. Authorisation for expenditure

2.1 General principles

An authorisation for expenditure is exactly what it sounds like – a request made by the operator to the non-operators requiring authorisation to proceed with a specific expenditure, described in a document. In other words, the operator must request the non-operators' consent to incur specific expenditure.[100]

From a non-operator's perspective, this provision is a very efficient way to control expenditure as it allows a case-by-case examination.[101] Thus, it is a very relevant provision for both international and national oil companies as financial exposure is one of the key areas of conflict between them.

It is worth noting that an authorisation for expenditure is even more precise than the work programme and budget as it is not just an estimated calculation of the expenditure, but actually sets out the precise expenditure to be incurred.[102] Nevertheless, some scholars consider that the authorisation for expenditure is also an estimate or prediction of the expenditure.[103] Both views are correct to a certain extent. The former is generally true, as an authorisation for expenditure is far more precise than a work programme and budget. However, specific situations may require over-expenditure, a supplementary authorisation for expenditure or even revision of the work programme and budget if events outside the parties' control occur.

Therefore, work programme and budgets are very positive and effective instruments for a non-operator, but only if they are combined with authorisation for expenditures so that control of expenditure can be exerted in an effective way.[104] Consequently, a combination of the work programme and budget and the

---

99 *Euroil Ltd v Cameroon Offshore Petroleum SARL* [2014] EWHC 12 (Comm). P Roberts and R Fowler, *Joint Operating Agreements: A Practical Guide*, 4th edn, Globe Law and Business, 2020, p48.

100 BG Taverne, *Co-operative Agreements in the Extractive Petroleum Industry*, Kluwer Law International, 1996, p67.

101 MPG Taylor and SM Tyne, *Taylor and Winsor on Joint Operating Agreements*, 2nd edn, Longman, 1992, p42.

102 Terence Daintith and Sandy Saw describe a similar concept of authorisation for expenditure. See: T Daintith and G Willoughby (eds), *Adrian Hill, United Kingdom Oil and Gas Law*, 3rd edn, Sweet & Maxwell, 2009, p1145.

103 GMD Bean, *Fiduciary Relationships, Fiduciary Duties and Joint Ventures: The Joint Operating Agreement*, University of Cambridge, 1992, p17.

104 S Shaw, "Joint Operating Agreements" in MR David, *Upstream Oil and Gas Agreements*, Sweet & Maxwell, 1996, p20.

authorisation for expenditure is an effective and efficient mechanism to control the operator's discretion over the expenditure of the joint operations. However, from an operator's point of view, a lower burden of control by the non-operators is likely to be the best for an efficient operation.[105]

If a work programme and budget is in place, the authorisation for expenditure will make reference to the line item approved in that programme and budget, so the non-operators should control the determination of the overall scope of the work programmes and budgets, and the authorisation for expenditure mechanism will provide detailed control of each operation. The more detail that is provided in the work programmes and budgets, the easier it will be to exert control in the authorisation for expenditure mechanism.[106]

On the other hand, if the work programme and budget is the only mechanism of expenditure control, it will provide too much discretion to the operator and too little control to the non-operators, even though some control could be exercised in the award of contracts.[107]

A practical explanation for the necessity of an authorisation for expenditure was clearly described by Professor Ernest E Smith in his comments on the *Haas v Gulf Coast Natural Gas Co* case.[108] In summary, the decision of this case upheld the defendants' (the non-operators') arguments, providing that there was not enough evidence to prove that the claimant (the operator) followed the authorisation for expenditure procedures in order to demonstrate the legality of its operations. However, it is important to note that Smith raised questions about what is to be considered compulsory in the authorisation for expenditure. Is it the operation *per se*? Or is it the details of the expenditure (including costs)? Smith cited the case of *Cleverock Energy Corp v Trepel*,[109] which found that the consent of a non-operator is related to the operation as a whole and not to the amount of expenditure. In other words, from this perspective, an authorisation for expenditure is an estimated cost;[110] but it is possible to argue that this opinion is not unanimous.[111] Moreover, why would an allowance for excess expenditures without prior approval exist if the authorisation for expenditure had to give every detail of the overall operation? There is no straightforward answer, but the authorisation for expenditure certainly

---

105 C Duval, H Le Leuch, A Pertuzio and JL Weaver, *International Petroleum and Exploration Agreements: Legal, Economic & Policy Aspects*, 2nd edn, Barrows, 2009, p298.

106 C Duval, H Le Leuch, A Pertuzio and JL Weaver, *International Petroleum and Exploration Agreements: Legal, Economic & Policy Aspects*, 2nd edn, Barrows, 2009, p298.

107 MPG Taylor and SM Tyne, *Taylor and Winsor on Joint Operating Agreements*, 2nd edn, Longman, 1992, p42.

108 *Haas v Gulf Coast Natural Gas Co* 484 S.W.2d 127 (Tex Civ App – Corpus Christi 1972) in JS Dzienkowski, EE Smith, OL Anderson, JS Lowe, BM Kramer and JL Weaver, *Materials on International Petroleum Transactions*, 3rd edn, RMMLF, 2010, pp583–592.

109 *Cleverock Energy Corp v Trepel* 609 F2d 1358, 1360-61 (10th Cir 1979), cert Denied, 446 US 909) in JS Dzienkowski, EE Smith, OL Anderson, JS Lowe, BM Kramer and JL Weaver, *Materials on International Petroleum Transactions*, 3rd edn, RMMLF, 2010, pp583–592.

110 JS Dzienkowski, EE Smith, OL Anderson, JS Lowe, BM Kramer and JL Weaver, *Materials on International Petroleum Transactions*, 3rd edn, RMMLF, 2010, p589.

111 See: MPG Taylor and SM Tyne, *Taylor and Winsor on Joint Operating Agreements*, 2nd edn, Longman, 1992, p42; TDaintith and G Willoughby (eds), *Adrian Hill, United Kingdom Oil and Gas Law*, 3rd edn, Sweet & Maxwell, 2009, p1145; S Shaw, "Joint Operating Agreements" in MR David, *Upstream Oil and Gas Agreements*, Sweet & Maxwell, 1996, p19; C Duval, H Le Leuch, A Pertuzio and JL Weaver, *International Petroleum and Exploration Agreements: Legal, Economic & Policy Aspects*, 2nd edn, Barrows, 2009, p298; P Roberts and R Fowler, *Joint Operating Agreements: A Practical Guide*, 4th edn, Globe Law and Business, 2020, p180.

provides more control to the non-operators, as it is a much more precise procedure than the work programme and budget.

Therefore, the importance of an authorisation for expenditure mechanism for a non-operator is more than clear; however, what will determine the efficiency of such a mechanism is the purpose of the authorisation for expenditure, which must be defined by the parties.

The authorisation for expenditure can be divided into two main but different categories, namely information and control. Control can be subdivided into two categories: broad and limited. The information category is purely a bureaucratic procedure, as the operator needs only to issue an authorisation for expenditure to inform the non-operators of the operation *per se* and no further approvals are required.[112] The control category goes far beyond this as it allows an effective system to assess whether each operation proposed by the operator is efficient and in the best interests of the consortium. The parties can choose whether the level of control will be broad or limited. Broad control means the operator must obtain the OpCom's approval for the specific operation. Limited control restricts the need for OpCom approval as the authorisation for expenditure may only be rejected on a limited number of grounds.[113]

Thus, it could be said that the informative procedure is very negative from a non-operator's perspective as the work programme and budget gives no precise details about the joint operations, so the operator will end up with too much discretion to execute the joint operations.[114] On the other hand, the approval procedure is very positive from a non-operator's perspective as it creates a second and more precise mechanism to control the expenditure of the joint operations.[115]

As mentioned above, from a non-operator's perspective, an authorisation for expenditure provision is an excellent mechanism to control the expenditure of the joint operations, but JOAs that also contain a work programme and budget provision may create difficulties for implementing an authorisation for expenditure mechanism. The operator will seek to minimise the necessity of further approval by authorisation for expenditures,[116] but, on the other hand, the non-operators will seek to increase their control of expenditure by requiring further approvals via authorisation for expenditures.[117]

The easiest solution would be to adopt a regime of authorisations for expenditure for information purposes only, as the operators would have no objection to this approach, but it will also be the worst solution for the non-operators as the work programme and budget will not contain any detail about the joint operations. So, if the authorisation for expenditure system is not fully implemented, the JOA will provide too much discretion for the operator and the non-operators will have poor control over the expenditure of the joint operations. This is likely to be the preference of an international oil company if it is the operator of the consortium. The non-operators should rely on strong controls of the mechanism to award contracts and auditing to control the consortium's costs.

On the other hand, the implementation of an effective authorisation for expenditure system, which will require the OpCom's approval (total/broad or

112 MPG Taylor and SM Tyne, *Taylor and Winsor on Joint Operating Agreements*, 2nd edn, Longman, 1992, p43.
113 P Roberts and R Fowler, *Joint Operating Agreements: A Practical Guide*, 4th edn, Globe Law and Business, 2020, p179.
114 C Duval, H Le Leuch, A Pertuzio and JL Weaver, *International Petroleum and Exploration Agreements: Legal, Economic & Policy Aspects*, 2nd edn, Barrows, 2009, p298.
115 *Ibid.*
116 MPG Taylor and SM Tyne, *Taylor and Winsor on Joint Operating Agreements*, 2nd edn, Longman, 1992, p42.
117 *Ibid.*

limited), may be much more difficult. The strongest argument against this approach is that the JOA would allow a second chance for the non-operators to approve or reject an operation which had already been approved in the work programme and budget.[118] In this sense, a system of limited approval should be easier to implement as there is a clear and restricted basis with which to examine the proposed authorisation for expenditure.[119] In one sense the work programme and budget is an estimate or prediction of the joint operations and only the authorisation for expenditure allows a precise verification of the proposed work and costs. Consequently, the non-implementation of a full mechanism of authorisation for expenditure would be equivalent to a scenario where both parties determine together the destination of a journey, but the operator would decide the route to get there.

However, if the state approves the programme and budget for the purposes of the granting instrument, it may be that the parties are then required to perform that programme within the limitations of that budget. In such circumstances, the non-approval of a related authorisation for expenditure under the JOA may put the joint venture in breach of the granting instrument. Authorisations for expenditure are rarely a feature of concession agreements and the programme and budget are the key governance documents by which the joint-venture activities are defined and approved by the state.

At times, such a complicated situation may be the factor that causes negotiations to break down. The operator is unlikely to allow the non-operators another chance to consider approving an operation and, on the other hand, the non-operators may not consider another possibility of allowing too much discretion for the operator. The situation may be even more complex if the national oil company has a carried interested. The international oil company will be bearing the exploration costs by itself, so may not accept too much interference from the national company on the detail of a cost which it will not be paying, or at least not initially. On the other hand, the national oil company could argue that the carried interest will be duly compensated with production so it has an interest in how these costs are executed.

However, there are alternatives, which may provide a middle ground between such diverse views, namely:

- a financial cap;
- separation of operational and capital budgets;
- exclusion of certain items;
- a lower passmark in the OpCom;
- a deemed approval in the OpCom;
- special provisions for over-expenditure; and
- special provisions for emergencies.

A financial cap is a simple solution as the authorisation for expenditure would require further approval from the OpCom only if the financial cap were exceeded.[120] However, the difficulty with this approach is the determination of the financial limitation, especially from a non-operator's perspective, as commonly the operator retains the strongest position. Also, this solution may have a critical problem: since

118 *Ibid*, p43.

119 H Dundas, *Joint Operating Agreements: An Introduction*, 1994 Summer Programme: UK Oil and Gas Law, CPMLP 09/09, 1994, p9.

120 MPG Taylor and SM Tyne, *Taylor and Winsor on Joint Operating Agreements*, 2nd edn, Longman, 1992, p42.

the smaller operations will not be subject to control, the operator could break larger operations down into several smaller operations to avoid further control from the non-operators. In addition, if the financial cap is implemented, the financial cap must vary according to the phase of the project.[121]

Another alternative relates to the distinction between operational and capital budgets. The former are ongoing costs of the joint operations, which will require specific approval at the OpCom, but the latter should be contained in an informative authorisation for expenditure.[122] Such an approach is based on the fact that the work programme and budget will have already approved the capital budget so the non-operators must control the ongoing costs which are not directly related to the joint operations, such as overheads.[123]

The positive side of this approach is that costs can be effectively controlled. However, the non-operator would lose a great deal of control over the most expensive operations as the capital budget deals with these operations.

Exclusion of certain items may solve specific problems, but this approach is unlikely to provide the necessary balance in all situations, as it is difficult to predict in advance which items should be excluded. The operator will seek to exclude as many items as possible and the non-operators will seek the opposite. However, the operator's bargaining power is much stronger than the non-operators', so the operator is likely to obtain better terms with such a provision.

Typically, minimum work obligations should be excluded from the scope of activities subject to authorisation for expenditure, to avoid a situation where non-approval puts the granting instrument at risk. Indeed, there is much to be said for going one step further and including a condition that authorisations for expenditure must be approved to the extent that the expenditure is necessary to keep the granting instrument in good standing. Alternatively, some form of "anti-deadlock" provision could be included to ensure that the operator is given the opportunity to resubmit an amended authorisation for expenditure which protects the granting instrument and must then be approved by the OpCom.[124]

The same principle applies for an emergency as the JOA prefers to secure an immediate response without any delay.[125]

However, the system is not very efficient and is a long way from the best practices of the industry, as the non-operators have no power to participate in the decisions regarding the approach to dealing with any emergency. It is true that the parties' liabilities will remain the same regardless of the non-operators' participation in actions to address emergencies. However, if there is an emergency, it is very important to impose a duty on the operator to notify the non-operators immediately when it becomes aware of the situation so that the non-operators can participate in such a highly sensitive issue.

The exclusion of certain items is relatively beneficial for the consortium in practical terms, because the operations can be conducted more efficiently.[126]

---

121 *Ibid*, p43.

122 *Ibid.*

123 For more information see: www.dundee.ac.uk/cepmlp/gateway/?news=28099.

124 MPG Taylor and SM Tyne, *Taylor and Winsor on Joint Operating Agreements*, 2nd edn, Longman, 1992, p42.

125 P Roberts and R Fowler, *Joint Operating Agreements: A Practical Guide*, 4th edn, Globe Law and Business, 2020, p177.

126 Terence Daintith and Sandy Saw describe a similar concept of authorisation for expenditure. See: T Daintith and G Willoughby (eds), *Adrian Hill, United Kingdom Oil and Gas Law*, 3rd edn, Sweet & Maxwell, 2009, p1145.

However, it is a negative approach for the non-operators as they will have little or no control over the joint venture's initial activities, which may determine the success or failure of the consortium (the minimum work obligations), or they may be excluded from very important decisions that will affect the existence of the consortium (eg, emergencies), as occurred with the Deepwater Horizon accident in the Gulf of Mexico. In other words, it is difficult to find the balance between the exclusions sought by the operator and the exclusions accepted by the non-operators. However, if exclusions are accepted, it may also provide some measure of control by the non-operators and excessive discretion to the operator could be avoided.

Another important mechanism to minimise the use of authorisation for expenditures is to allow over-expenditure. This is a valuable provision to secure a certain level of flexibility in the conduct of the joint operations as, up to a certain limit (commonly 10%),[127] the operator can exceed the budget approved without a requirement to obtain the OpCom's consent.[128] However, it is important to note that some JOAs do not permit any over-expenditure without the formal approval of the OpCom.[129] Others provide that a right without consent should apply under certain circumstances.[130]

As mentioned previously, such flexibility in allowing over-expenditure in approved authorisation for expenditures is essential to keep the consortium together. The dynamics of the oil and gas industry may require a certain discretion to the operator in the conduct of operations, but also this discretion must be clearly regulated and controlled by the non-operators in order to avoid any abuse.

Claude Duval raises an interesting scenario where the operator seeks to exceed the over-expenditure limit.[131] It is not straightforward, although he suggested a solution for the problem. In a case like this, it will be important to establish whether the operator acted diligently and in accordance with good practice, otherwise the operator would have unlimited discretion to exceed limits for a day or two or a week and so on. If the operator is conducting the operations carefully and diligently, it is likely to predict any difficulty in complying with the over-expenditure limits and it must revise the specific budget and request the non-operators' approval in time, or at least report the situation and request a further extension to prove it is acting with due diligence and according to best practice.[132]

There seems to be agreement that best practice in the oil and gas industry clearly requires an operator to be diligent and aware of all circumstances that might delay or harm the joint operations and report those circumstances, as soon as possible, to the non-operators so they can plan how to address those issues

127 See: T Daintith and G Willoughby (eds), *Adrian Hill, United Kingdom Oil and Gas Law*, 3rd edn, Sweet & Maxwell, 2009, p1145; P Roberts and R Fowler, *Joint Operating Agreements: A Practical Guide*, 4th edn, Globe Law and Business, 2020, p169; C Duval, H Le Leuch, A Pertuzio and JL Weaver, *International Petroleum and Exploration Agreements: Legal, Economic & Policy Aspects*, 2nd edn, Barrows, 2009, p298; H Dundas, *Joint Operating Agreements: An Introduction*, 1994 Summer Programme: UK Oil and Gas Law, CPMLP 09/09, 1994, p5.

128 BG Taverne, *Co-operative Agreements in the Extractive Petroleum Industry*, Kluwer Law International, 1996, pp68–69.

129 See: T Daintith and G Willoughby (eds), *Adrian Hill, United Kingdom Oil and Gas Law*, 3rd edn, Sweet & Maxwell, 2009, p1145.

130 H Dundas, *Joint Operating Agreements: An Introduction*, 1994 Summer Programme: UK Oil and Gas Law, CPMLP 09/09, 1994, p9. However, the non-consent application will be elsewhere in the book.

131 C Duval, H Le Leuch, A Pertuzio and JL Weaver, *International Petroleum and Exploration Agreements: Legal, Economic & Policy Aspects*, 2nd edn, Barrows, 2009, p298.

132 *Ibid.*

adequately. However, as mentioned previously, emergency cases are excluded from the over-expenditure limitation.[133]

Another alternative to the use of authorisation for expenditures is to lower the passmark required in the OpCom for approval of operations. The justification for this is that authorisation for expenditures deal with operations that, in theory, have been approved by a work programme and budget. This approach would reduce the approval burden, but at the same time it would give some measure of control to the non-operators.[134] In theory, this alternative sounds like a positive balance between the operator's and non-operators' views. However, the practical result of such an approach is highly in favour of the operator as, commonly, the operator is in a dominant position even in the negotiation period, so it is difficult to expect a non-operator to control the OpCom. In other words, if the operator has overall control of the OpCom, the reduction of the passmark may have no practical application as the operator is likely to approve any decision with or without such a lower passmark, as illustrated in Example 1.

Example 1

	Company A	Company B	Company C
Role	Operator	Non-operator	Non-operator
Interest	80%	10%	10%
Ordinary passmark	70%		
Lower passmark	40%		

On the other hand, if the non-operators have strong control in the Opcom, such a reduction may not make any difference, as the result will remain the same as for any other approval in the Opcom (Example 2).

Example 2

	Company A	Company B	Company C
Role	Operator	Non-operator	Non-operator
Interest	40%	30%	30%
Ordinary passmark	60%		
Lower passmark	50%		

Consequently, such an approach may only suit a situation where the consortium has many parties and this lower passmark would reduce the number of non-operators needed for approval (Example 3).

133 *Ibid.*

134 BG Taverne, *Co-operative Agreements in the Extractive Petroleum Industry*, Kluwer Law International, 1996, p67.

Example 3

	Company A	Company B	Company C	Company D	Company E
Role	Operator	Non-operator	Non-operator	Non-operator	Non-operator
Interest	40%	20%	20%	10%	10%
Ordinary passmark	80%				
Lower passmark	60%				

A similar alternative is to assume the OpCom's approval, whereby the authorisation for expenditure is deemed to be approved unless a specific number of negative votes are cast.[135]

Such an approach also faces the same problem that has been mentioned before, which is that a passmark is required. If the number of negative votes required is too high, the non-operators may not succeed. If the negative vote is too low, the non-operators may block everything. This approach will not provide a balanced mechanism between the operator's and non-operators' wishes regarding authorisation for expenditure implementation. Therefore, such a system might only suit the situation where the consortium has several parties involved and the requirement for authorisation for expenditures can be reduced without unduly benefiting any party.

In summary, a requirement for non-operators to approve an authorisation for expenditure in every case is unlikely to happen as it would give too much control to the non-operators,[136] even though this is the best mechanism for any non-operator to control the expenditure of the joint operations.[137]

At the other extreme is the implementation of informative control, which is unlikely to be accepted by the non-operators. Therefore, the balance will usually be a combination of several of the mechanisms mentioned above, such as financial caps, exclusions of items and limited approval.

As previously described, the difficulty in implementing an authorisation for expenditure mechanism only exists in JOAs where the work programme and budget is established. However, this is not the case for the North American JOA Models, where the situation is completely different.

An important issue for smaller non-operators is the point when the operator must issue an authorisation for expenditure. Commonly, the industry provides that the operator must issue "an invoice for approved expenditures in that month".[138] On the other hand, this may be too short a time if the amount of expenditure is

135 P Roberts and R Fowler, *Joint Operating Agreements: A Practical Guide*, 4th edn, Globe Law and Business, 2020, p179.

136 C Duval, H Le Leuch, A Pertuzio and JL Weaver, *International Petroleum and Exploration Agreements: Legal, Economic & Policy Aspects*, 2nd edn, Barrows, 2009, p298.

137 S Styles, "Joint Operating Agreements" in J Paterson and G Gordon (eds), *Oil and Gas Law: Current Practice and Emerging Trends*, Dundee University Press, 2007, p288.

138 C Thorpe, *Fundamentals of Upstream Petroleum Agreements*, CP Thorpe, 2008, p128.

very high, when it would be better for a smaller non-operator if certain expenditure required earlier notice so the party has enough time to prepare itself.[139]

Full implementation of the authorisation for expenditure mechanism is clearly related to the approval of the OpCom (if applicable) or to the non-operators. What will happen if the non-operators can block such approval? There are two possible solutions. The first is revision, by the operator, of the proposed authorisation for expenditure so it can be resubmitted in the OpCom.[140] The second is to propose the work as an exclusive operation.[141] The former has been discussed above and the latter is discussed in Chapter 1, Section 9.

If an authorisation for expenditure is approved, what will happen? As a general rule, each party shall contribute according to their share in the joint venture, that is, they will contribute in the same proportion as their participating interest in the joint venture.[142] However, there are exceptions, such as the implementation of a carried interest, as explained in Chapter 1, Section 2.[143]

Participating interests are carried in two possible scenarios: where the state has the right to participate in the joint venture through the national oil company whose costs are carried by the other joint venture parties during the exploration and appraisal phase, and where a third party enters the joint venture through a transaction with one or more party existing participants, whereby the new entrant carries the costs of the existing participants as the price it pays for acquiring some or all of their participating interest. In both cases, the relevant agreements should specify whether the carried party has the right to vote on programmes and budgets and/or authorisation is expenditures in respect of which it is carried – bearing in mind that some carries are "soft", in the sense that the amount paid under the carry is repayable when it expires.

It is important to remember that the same procedure explained in the work programme and budget applies to the authorisation for expenditure, as it is possible to amend or revise the authorisation for expenditure if determined by the OpCom (if applicable) or the non-operators. However, this will not affect any authorisation for expenditure approved prior to such a decision.[144]

Finally, it is possible to suggest that a non-operator should be looking for an authorisation for expenditure mechanism requiring the approval of all contracting

139 *Ibid.*

140 P Roberts and R Fowler, *Joint Operating Agreements: A Practical Guide*, 4th edn, Globe Law and Business, 2020, p179.

141 C Duval, H Le Leuch, A Pertuzio and JL Weaver, *International Petroleum and Exploration Agreements: Legal, Economic & Policy Aspects*, 2nd edn, Barrows, 2009, p298.

142 S Styles, "Joint Operating Agreements" in J Paterson and G Gordon (eds), *Oil and Gas Law: Current Practice and Emerging Trends*, Dundee University Press, 2007, p288; C Thorpe, *Fundamentals of Upstream Petroleum Agreements*, CP Thorpe, 2008, p126; BG Taverne, *An Introduction to the Regulation of the Petroleum Industry: Law, Contracts and Conventions*, Graham & Trotman, 1994, pp136–137; H Dundas, *Joint Operating Agreements: An Introduction*, 1994 Summer Programme: UK Oil and Gas Law, CPMLP 09/09, 1994, pp4–5; T Daintith, "Right to Explore For and Exploit Petroleum: The Licence" in T Daintith and G Willoughby (eds), *Adrian Hill, United Kingdom Oil and Gas Law*, 3rd edn, Sweet & Maxwell, 2009, p1145; C Duval, H Le Leuch, A Pertuzio and JL Weaver, *International Petroleum and Exploration Agreements: Legal, Economic & Policy Aspects*, 2nd edn, Barrows, 2009, p297.

143 T Daintith, "Right to Explore for and Exploit Petroleum: The Licence" in T Daintith and G Willoughby (eds), *Adrian Hill, United Kingdom Oil and Gas Law*, 3rd edn, Sweet & Maxwell, 2009, pp1145–1146.

144 KC Mildwaters, *Joint Operating Agreements, A Consideration of Legal Aspects Relevant to Joint Operating Agreements used in Great Britain and Australia by Participants thereto to Regulate the Joint Undertaking of Exploration for Petroleum in Offshore Areas with Particular Reference to their Rights and Duties*, PhD Thesis presented to the University of Dundee, 1990, p569.

parties. However, this may not be possible in all JOAs, so the non-operator should implement a mechanism to ensure effective controls over the expenditure, but at the same time allow some flexibility to the operator in the conduct of the joint operations. Any alternative method which minimises the application of the authorisation for expenditure mechanism could achieve this purpose, but the non-operator should analyse carefully any limitation to the authorisation for expenditure implementation so that the operator does not end up with too much discretion. It is also important to provide a connection between authorisation for expenditure approval and the information provided, so over-expenditure (above a certain limit) should require a supplementary authorisation for expenditure to allow the non-operator to control the operation as a whole.

Additionally, the non-operators must secure a reasonable amount of time between the issue of an authorisation for expenditure and the payment of such costs, as smaller non-operators may find it difficult to comply with the payment provision quickly as they are likely to need to obtain external funds to cover major costs.[145]

2.2 Analysis of model JOAs

The following paragraphs examine the application of authorisation for expenditures in each JOA standard model form. It will also be demonstrated that there is sometimes a benefit in not having a work programme and budget provision. Arguably, using only authorisation for expenditures can provide a better system to control expenditure than most combinations of work programme and budgets and authorisation for expenditures. However, using only authorisation for expenditures does not provide as much control to non-operators as a full implementation of work programme and budgets and authorisation for expenditures, which will provide a higher degree of control for any non-operator.

AAPL Model Form 810 clearly imposes an obligation on the operator to issue an authorisation for expenditure before incurring any expenditure.[146] However, there are mechanisms in place to minimise the impact of the authorisation for expenditure system.

The main criterion to determine the use of the authorisation for expenditure mechanism is the value of the expenditure. In other words, there is a financial limitation which will determine what procedures the operator must follow. If the expenditure exceeds the financial cap, the operator must obtain the non-operators' approval; if the expenditure is below the financial cap the operator must inform the parties about such expenditure, with no further requirements.[147] Thus, the value of the expenditure will determine whether the authorisation for expenditure will be for an informative or an approval purpose. This is an interesting provision to balance the interest between the operator and non-operator. However, such a financial cap is left blank so the parties can negotiate and establish the most suitable level for the deal. In practice, the non-operators are unlikely to obtain a positive outcome in current operations, as the operator will overrule the non-operators by its dominant position.

145 Commonly, such mechanism is addressed by the accounting procedure as it involves cash calls, so it will not be discussed further here.
146 AAPL Form 810 §6.2.
147 AAPL Form 810 §6.2.

This model form also recognises the importance of providing a certain amount of flexibility to the operator in the conduct of the joint operations, so it establishes the authority of the operator to overspend an approved authorisation for expenditure up to a certain limit.[148] Nevertheless, the operator must issue an authorisation for expenditure for informative purposes, to make the non-operators aware of any over-expenditure. As previously mentioned, such flexibility is fairly common among JOAs; however, the interesting provision is the express obligation to issue a supplementary authorisation for expenditure if the amount is exceeded.[149] If the operator predicts that the over-expenditure limit will be exceeded, it must issue a supplementary authorisation for expenditure for the additional costs.

Another procedure to minimise a potentially negative impact of an authorisation for expenditure was established for situations such as emergencies and *force majeure* (chance occurrence) cases, which are excluded from such scrutiny.[150] Such flexibility is important to maintain the good standing of the petroleum title. However, there is no obligation to gather the non-operators' input on any action to address emergencies, as the model provides that the operator must make the decision based on "its opinion as a reasonable and prudent operator".[151] The operator's only obligation to the non-operators is to "report to the Participating Parties, as promptly as possible, the nature of the emergency, the action taken, and the Costs incurred".[152] Nevertheless, when the emergency or *force majeure* is over, the operator must then issue a supplementary authorisation for expenditure to continue or to finish any of these operations.[153]

It is important to note that JOA Model Form 810 provides for a special type of authorisation for expenditure for the long lead development system in order to secure approval for critical long lead item expenditure before a formal development AFE is presented.[154]

Such a procedure gives extensive rights and discretion to the operator as it minimises the precision and specification of an authorisation for expenditure. As a consequence, the application of this mechanism could put the non-operators in a difficult position when trying to exert effective control over the expenditure. Nevertheless, it establishes the necessity of unanimous consent to proceed with such a special authorisation for expenditure.[155]

It is also important to note that minimum work obligations are not excluded from the authorisation for expenditure mechanism. This is a positive provision for non-operators as they can participate in the important operations, which usually occur during the early stages of the consortium. On the other hand, if a deadlock occurs on such approval, it may jeopardise the whole existence of the joint venture, as it would not allow the performance of the licence obligations.

Therefore, the authorisation for expenditure mechanism is very important in AAPL Model Form 810, as the work programme and budget has only an informative purpose.[156] In other words, the authorisation for expenditure is the only procedure

148 AAPL Form 810 §6.2.1.
149 AAPL Form 810 §6.2.2.
150 AAPL Form 810 §6.2.3.
151 AAPL Form 810 §6.2.
152 *Ibid.*
153 AAPL Form 810 §6.2.3.
154 AAPL Form 810 §6.2.4.
155 AAPL Form 810 §6.2.4.1.
156 AAPL Form 810 §6.4.1.

available for the non-operators to exert control over the expenditure. In these circumstances, the procedures which minimise the use of the authorisation for expenditure mechanism should be as weak as possible. Indeed, the mechanism implemented to minimise the impact of the authorisation for expenditures is reasonably balanced, as it allows the non-operators to control the majority of operations and also allows a certain discretion for the operator in its operations. However, the critical issue is the determination of the financial cap, as this will determine the purpose of the authorisation for expenditure, that is, for informative or approval purposes.

The RRMLF JOA Model gives a concise provision regarding authorisation for expenditures, but, in theory, this conciseness should not jeopardise the effectiveness of such a mechanism of control of the expenditure of the joint operations. However, the limited restrictions on the use of authorisation for expenditures may reduce the discretion of the operator.

Under the RMMLF JOA Model, the major limitation on the use of authorisation for expenditures is the financial consideration. The parties must define the financial limitation in American dollars. If the operator exceeds this level, the non-operators' approval is required.[157] The only exception to this rule is related to emergencies, as the operator does not need to obtain the non-operators' approval to incur expenditure in an emergency. However, the operator must report such emergencies to the non-operators "as promptly as possible".[158]

It could be suggested that the RMMLF JOA Model secures a higher degree of control of expenditure for the non-operators by implementing a simple mechanism of authorisation for expenditures (provided that the financial cap is not too high). One question is why a dominant operator would accept such strong control by the non-operators.

The major flaw in the control exerted by the non-operators is the specification that the authorisation for expenditure contains only an estimated cost, as can be seen in the following clause: "the operator shall not, without the consent of all Parties chargeable with the Costs thereof, undertake any single project reasonably estimated to require an expenditure in excess of".[159] Consequently, the non-operators shall approve an estimated cost and there is no regulation on further adjustments. The wording of this clause requires the non-operators to approve the operation itself, but not the details provided in the authorisation for expenditure. In other words, the non-operators can exert effective control until the approval of the authorisation for expenditure, but once the operation is approved the discretion goes back to the operator.

In theory, the limiting restriction on the operator's expenditure seems to favour the non-operator. But it is clear that the lack of any provision on over-expenditure is, in fact, negative for the non-operators, as there is no regulation whatsoever on the limitation of over-expenditure and the requirement for supplementary authorisation for expenditures. However, as noted above, the terms of most JOAs and accounting procedures are sufficiently clear that the operator cannot recover costs which exceed approved levels, unless the additional expenditure is covered by a tolerance or is expressly approved by the OpCom.

157 MMLF JOA §5.5.
158 RMMLF JOA §5.5.
159 *Ibid.*

Therefore, the non-operators can exert a high degree of control over the authorisation for expenditure of the overall operation. On the other hand, the estimative basis of the authorisation for expenditure and the lack of clear regulation about over-expenditure are the most critical concerns for the non-operators. In other words, once the operation is approved, it gives extensive powers to the operator to freely conduct the joint operations.

The Canadian Model provides for the existence of an authorisation for expenditure mechanism.[160] However, the mechanism will only apply if a financial cap is reached, namely 50,000 Canadian dollars.[161] Such a limitation is not important for any non-operator, as oil and gas operations usually involve very high costs and it is more important to exert control over major expenditure than minor expenditure. The discretion over minor expenditures will make the joint venture more efficient even though several minor expenditures combined could become a larger sum.

If the expenditure exceeds the financial cap, the operator is obliged to issue an authorisation for expenditure, which must be approved by all non-operators.[162] This is by far the best control provided in this model form, even though there is no control via work programme and budgets.

It is important to note that the financial cap is not the only limitation on the authorisation for expenditure mechanism, as exclusions of items and over-expenditure are also allowed. The former mainly excludes emergency situations and expenditure required by regulations.[163] In both circumstances, the operator must report to the non-operators any anticipated costs, including details about the event, nature, scope and schedule of the expenditure.[164] This is a positive provision allowing the non-operators to participate in the decision in such events; however, there is no obligation to obtain the non-operators' opinions, as this is only an informative provision. The emergency exclusion is fairly common in the oil and gas industry, but the regulations exclusion is far too broad, as it might even include minimum work obligations. Thus, the non-operators could face critical problems with the interpretation and application of such a clause, as the operator may use this extension in expenditure as much as possible. The over-expenditure provision authorises over-expenditure almost without limitation, as the authorisation for expenditure authorises the operation itself, so any over-expenditure will require no further approval, only an informative authorisation for expenditure.[165] In other words, the permission granted by an authorisation for expenditure is not limited by the terms of the authorisation for expenditure itself, but extends to any expenditure required to perform the activity described by it, as outlined by Ernest Smith.[166]

---

160 CAPL OP Form 610 §3.01(B).

161 *Ibid.*

162 CAPL OP Form 610 §7.01(A).

163 CAPL OP Form 610 §3.01(B).

164 *Ibid.*

165 CAPL OP Form 610 §3.01 (C).

166 See: JO Young, "Oil and Gas Operating Agreements: Producers 88 Operating Agreements, Selected Problems and Suggested Solutions" *Rocky Mtn Min L Inst* 20 (1975) 197, 207 in JS Dzienkowski, EE Smith, OL Anderson, JS Lowe, BM Kramer and JL Weaver, *Materials on International Petroleum Transactions*, 3rd edn, RMMLF, 2010, p589. US and Canadian cases which have addressed this question are discussed in the AIPN research paper by T Martin, J Gilbert and M Gusy, "A Global Review of Joint Operating Agreement Disputes" AIPN research paper 2020. The position under English law as discussed by R Fowler, "The Blank Cheque and the Cliff Edge", *Journal of World Energy Law and Business* 6 (2019).

As a consequence, the non-operators face very positive and negative situations at the same time. At first glance, the non-operators' position is fairly strong because they have to approve the operation by an authorisation for expenditure. In fact, the lack of a work programme and budget in this model gives more powers to the non-operators to control the operation via the authorisation for expenditure mechanism.

On the other hand, once the non-operators authorise the operation via the authorisation for expenditure, the model gives extensive rights to the operator to incur any over-expenditure, with only a few limitations, such as the completion of wells. In this case, the position of the non-operators is weak, as the operator may exceed the overall prediction of the authorisation for expenditure and the non-operators will only verify such procedures as mere observers by informative authorisation for expenditures, rather than by supplementary authorisation for expenditures.[167]

Additionally, this model form recognises the importance of the use of the authorisation for expenditure, as the operator must commence an operation within 120 days of the authorisation for expenditure approval.[168] This is an important provision, as the operator must commence the operations within a time limit otherwise the authorisation for expenditure loses effect.

In conclusion, the Canadian OP Model provides an excellent control of expenditure for the non-operators, but only at an early stage in the operations. As a general rule, the operator will have more discretion after the authorisation for expenditure is approved, as this approves the operation as a whole and not the precise costs involved. At this later stage, the non-operators may face more difficulty in controlling the joint operations.

The British Model provides for the existence of an authorisation for expenditure mechanism, but its implementation depends on the phase of the project – this changes depending whether the project is at the exploration or decommissioning stage.

During the exploration stage, the operator must issue an authorisation for expenditure for the OpCom's approval before any commitment of capital or seismic expenditure that exceeds the financial limit of the approved work programme and budget.[169] The financial cap will determine whether the authorisation for expenditure is used. However, the limitation is left blank so the parties can negotiate the best value for the deal. In practice, where there is a power imbalance, such an approach is likely to benefit the operator. Nevertheless, the approved authorisation for expenditure can be revised or amended by the determination of the OpCom.[170]

The financial cap is not the only procedure which minimises the authorisation for expenditure's impact: emergencies are also excluded from this mechanism.[171] The only obligation for the operator is to report such circumstances to the non-operators, as well as the expenditure incurred to date. The model does not require the non-operators to participate in such important decisions, only gives them the right to be informed. Minimum work obligations are not excluded, but are automatically deemed to be approved if the OpCom does not reject a proposal within 28 days from its submission.[172] Another procedure established to minimise the authorisation

167 H Dundas, *Joint Operating Agreements: An Introduction*, 1994 Summer Programme: UK Oil and Gas Law, CPMLP 09/09, 1994, p9.
168 CAPL OP Form 610 §7.01(A).
169 OGUK JOA §10.2.
170 OGUK JOA §10.3.
171 OGUK JOA §6.10.2.
172 OGUK JOA §10.4.

for expenditure's impact is the allowance of over-expenditure of up to 10% of the amount approved in it or a specific amount in pounds sterling, whichever is lower.[173]

The same procedures apply for the development, production and decommissioning phases.[174] However, there are some limitations on the right to reject an authorisation for expenditure in the decommissioning phase as the model provides that the approval of an authorisation for expenditure shall not be "unreasonably withheld or delayed where the authorisation for expenditure is consistent with the approved decommissioning programme and budget".[175]

It is clear that there is concern over minimum work obligations and decommissioning obligations, as more restrictions are put on the non-operators' control of expenditure in relation to these matters. However, as a general rule, the British Model provides strong control of expenditure by a combination of work programme and budget and authorisation for expenditure provisions. Such control is only effective if the non-operators can truly obtain some measure of control over the OpCom, otherwise the control is rather illusory. In addition, it is important to stress that the non-operators cannot participate in decisions regarding emergencies, which could be very disadvantageous for them in a catastrophic situation that affects the whole consortium.

The Norwegian JOA Model contains not only work programme and budget provisions, but also an authorisation for expenditure mechanism.[176] In theory, these are very positive provisions for non-operators, but it is necessary to analyse the extent to which both control mechanisms work together.

Initially, it is important to stress that the body that approves the work programme and budget is the same body that approves authorisation for expenditures, namely the OpCom. As previously mentioned, the existence of the OpCom is an effective way of exerting control over the joint operations. However, the efficacy of such control is directly connected to the voting procedures since if a lower passmark is established, usually the operator will have total control of the OpCom. If this is the case, the OpCom will be an ineffective method of control.

It is interesting to note that the Norwegian JOA Model Form clearly provides flexibility to the authorisation for expenditure mechanism, such as by allowing over-expenditure of up to 10% of an approved authorisation for expenditure and the exclusion of formal procedures regarding emergencies.[177] Both cases must be reported to the OpCom, so the non-operators must be informed of such situations, but the model does not require OpCom participation in emergency situations, which could have a very negative effect on non-operators. On the other hand, the model does not give further details on the use of the authorisation for expenditure mechanism, except for the requirement of OpCom approval.[178]

However, the model does clearly mention the implementation of another mechanism of control of expenditure referred to as the "master control estimate", as follows:

---

173 OGUK JOA §10.5.
174 OGUK JOA §§11.2, 11.3, 11.5, 12.2, 12.3, 12.4, 13.2, 13.3, 13.4.
175 OGUK JOA §13.2.
176 Norwegian JOA §12.5.
177 Norwegian JOA §12.5.
178 Norwegian JOA §12.5.

A master control estimate and master control plan to be created prior to the initiation of the project shall be used for the management and progress control of significant development and modification projects. The master control estimate and master control plan shall be amended in case of significant changes to the scope of the project or the assumptions on which the project are based. When updated, changes to the assumptions shall be clarified and submitted to the management committee for consideration.
The applicable control estimate and control plan shall represent the best estimate at the time of the estimate and reflect the approved budget limits. The Operator shall submit the current control estimate and control plan to the management committee together with an analysis of opportunities for added value/cost reductions and potential risks, which may influence the planned target achievements. The current control estimate and control plan shall be revised and submitted to the management committee for consideration twice a year, unless otherwise decided by the management committee.[179]

Therefore, the Norwegian JOA Model provides a highly effective control of expenditure via a combination of an authorisation for expenditure mechanism a master control estimate and a work programme and budget provision. However, the model does not require the non-operators' participation in decisions concerning emergencies. As these potentially could cause a non-operator to suffer substantial loss, there must be concerns for non-operators, for example if an emergency had major effects such as oil pollution – a risk highlighted by the recent terrible accident in the Gulf of Mexico (the Deepwater Horizon disaster).

The AIPN Model also contains an authorisation for expenditure provision, but it is only optional.[180] Like most JOAs, it contains a financial cap so only expenditure which exceeds a specific limit, defined by the parties, will require an authorisation for expenditure.[181] The financial cap is similar to the British JOA Model, as it separates expenditure according to the phase of the project, namely exploration, development and production. However, this model does not provide a specific authorisation for expenditure for decommissioning.

The model also allows some flexibility to secure the better efficiency of the joint venture. Such flexibility is established by provisions on over-expenditure and excluded items.[182] The former provisions allow over-expenditure of up to 10% of the line item, but no more than 5% of the approved work programme and budget.[183] If the operator is going to exceed this limit, the parties can decide whether the operator must revise the work programme and budget and resubmit it for OpCom approval[184] or if the operator must only submit a supplementary authorisation for expenditure to the OpCom for approval.[185] In addition, the operator is not obliged to issue an

179 Norwegian JOA §12.6.
180 AIPN JOA §6.7.
181 AIPN JOA §6.7(A).
182 AIPN JOA §6.7(A), 6.8(A), (C).
183 AIPN JOA §6.8(A).
184 AIPN JOA §6.8(B) alternative 1.
185 AIPN JOA §6.8(B) alternative 2.

authorisation for expenditure for minimum work obligations and emergencies.[186] It is worth noting that these exclusions were introduced only in the last revision of the AIPN Model Forms and from 1990 to 1995 an authorisation for expenditure was also necessary for minimum work obligations.[187]

This procedure is fairly common among JOAs. However, the model contains a rather unique provision regarding the scope of the authorisation for expenditure. It allows three main scenarios for the operator.[188] The first provides that the authorisation for expenditure procedure will be solely for informative purposes.[189] The second provides that the total approval of the OpCom must be obtained for the authorisation for expenditure.[190] The third option involves limited approval such that the OpCom may only reject an authorisation for expenditure on restricted grounds.[191] However, all these options are available for the parties to decide which one they prefer to bind their JOA.

Thus, the AIPN Model allows the parties to negotiate the procedure of the authorisation for expenditure. From a non-operator's perspective, the second scenario is the most interesting, as it allows for the creation of a robust second layer of protection regarding control of expenditure. In this case, the non-operators will participate with regard to the contents of the work programme and budget and subsequently control each specific item of expenditure on a case-by-case basis via the authorisation for expenditure procedures. On the other hand, if an informative procedure is agreed, it will give the operator more freedom to execute the work programme and budget, which commonly is an estimate of the overall expenditure.[192] However, the most balanced procedure is the third scenario as it is a compromise between the interests of the operator and the non-operators.

As Taylor and Tyne mention,[193] the limited approval mechanism is not the ideal scenario for a non-operator, but it protects the non-operator from abuse and unreasonable expenditure. At the same time it gives some comfort to the operator that it will not face rejections of authorisation for expenditures if its expenditure is based on the approved work programme and budget and reasonable grounds.

Additionally, it is important to stress that there is a highly positive provision for the non-operators in the model, as the AIPN JOA Model requires a fairly detailed authorisation for expenditure:

> *6.7 (C) Each authorisation for expenditure proposed by Operator shall:*
> *(1) identify the operation by specific reference to the applicable line items in the Work Program and Budget;*
> *(2) describe the work in detail;*

186 AIPN JOA §6.7(A) and 6.8(C).

187 DF Asmus, "The 1995 Model Form International Operating Agreement" *Journal of Energy & Natural Resources Law* 14 (1996) 14, 11.

188 AIPN JOA §6.7(B).

189 AIPN JOA §6.7(B) alternative 1.

190 AIPN JOA §6.7(B) alternative 2.

191 AIPN JOA §6.7(B) alternative 3.

192 PR Weems and M Bolton, "Highlights of Key Revisions – 2002 AIPN Model Form International Operating Agreement" *OGEL* 1 (2003) 5.

193 MPG Taylor and SM Tyne, *Taylor and Winsor on Joint Operating Agreements*, 2nd edn, Longman, 1992, pp42–43.

> *(3) contain Operator's best estimate of the total funds required to carry out such work;*
> *(4) outline the proposed work schedule;*
> *(5) provide a timetable of expenditures, if known; and*
> *(6) be accompanied by such other supporting information as is necessary for an informed decision.*

In other words, such a detailed requirement is a very positive provision for any non-operator because it can exert effective control of the expenditure by comparing the line item approved in the work programme and budget provision with the proposed authorisation for expenditure.

Therefore, the AIPN Model provides an excellent authorisation for expenditure mechanism for a non-operator (a total approval mechanism), an excellent authorisation for expenditure mechanism for an operator (an informative mechanism) and a reasonable authorisation for expenditure for both parties (a limited approval mechanism). Even the best-case scenario for the non-operators (the total approval mechanism) will only be effective if their support is needed in the OpCom for the AFE to be approved.

The Greenlandic JOA Model Form also contains an authorisation for expenditure mechanism.[194] The most noteworthy aspect of the mechanism is the absence of a financial cap – that is, any expenditure shall be subject to the OpCom's approval.[195]

On the other hand, there are two procedures available to minimise the impact of an authorisation for expenditure: over-expenditure and exclusion of items.[196] The former allows over-expenditure of up to 10% of an approved authorisation for expenditure or a determined amount of capital, whichever is lower. The latter excludes the necessity of authorisation for expenditure procedures in emergency situations. However, it does not exclude the obligation promptly to notify the non-operators about such emergencies. From a non-operator's perspective, such prompt notice is positive, but it is not highly effective as there is no obligation on the operator to obtain the non-operators' input before making important decisions regarding the emergency, decisions which will affect and bind the consortium as a whole.

It is also important to highlight the existence of a mechanism to avoid deadlock when a party neglects to vote. If the non-operator does not clearly express its rejection (including its reasons), the operation will be considered approved by default. It is not a positive provision for the non-operators, as it imposes a restriction upon their rights, but it is a positive provision for an effective and efficient consortium.[197]

However, from an operator's perspective, the model offers a possible opening flexibility; the model states that "Each authorisation for expenditure shall describe the expenditure, give an estimate of the cost and estimated phasing by Quarter for the current Year and by Year thereafter of such expenditures."[198] An operator could use this wording to argue that each approved authorisation for expenditure grants it some

---

194 Greenlandic JOA §5.10.
195 *Ibid.*
196 *Ibid.*
197 *Ibid.*
198 *Ibid.*

tolerance. On the other hand, a non-operator may contest such an argument by making the point that the reference to an estimate refers to the allowance of over-expenditure, but beyond such limitation the operator must obtain further approval by the OpCom.

Thus, it can be suggested that any non-operator will have strong control of expenditure under the Greenlandic JOA Model Form as there is a highly effective combination of work programme and budget and authorisation for expenditure provisions, which exert a high degree of control over any tendency by the operator to incur additional expenditure. However, such strong control only exists if the non-operators can truly control the OpCom, either positively or negatively, otherwise there will be no control whatsoever available for them.

2.3 Discussion

In general, the non-operators are in a good position regarding the authorisation for expenditure control, as such a mechanism is a common provision in all JOA Model Forms.[199] After analysing all those JOA Models that provide for the use of authorisation for expenditures, it is possible to separate the models into two different categories. One category provides for only an authorisation for expenditure mechanism to control the expenditure and the other establishes a combination of work programme and budget provisions with authorisation for expenditure provisions.

As mentioned previously, the North American JOA Models' weakness for the non-operators' position is that the models do not allow the non-operators to participate in the decisions on operations, as there is no provision for work programme and budgets or OpCom. On the other hand, all the remaining JOA Models, which clearly provide for work programme and budgets and OpComs, put the non-operators in a better position to exert a higher degree of control over the joint operations.

However, the situation is different for the authorisation for expenditure mechanisms, as the North American JOAs provide a higher degree of control of expenditure compared with the other JOA Models.

First, as previously discussed, the work programme and budget is a rough estimate of the work and budget that will be incurred on an annual (or activity) basis, whereas an authorisation for expenditure is rather more precise and detailed.[200] In other words, the use of a work programme and budget by itself is not sufficient to secure enough control over the expenditure, so it is essential to implement an authorisation for expenditure mechanism as well.[201] It is noticeable that there is a tendency with each committee revision of the AIPN Model to provide an increasingly higher degree of information in both mechanisms of control of expenditure, namely work programme and budgets and authorisation for expenditures.[202] However, the AIPN recognises a higher degree of information must be provided in an authorisation for expenditure compared with a work programme and budget.[203]

---

199 H Dundas, *Joint Operating Agreements: An Introduction*, 1994 Summer Programme: UK Oil and Gas Law, CPMLP 09/09, 1994, p9.

200 H Dundas, *Joint Operating Agreements: An Introduction*, 1994 Summer Programme: UK Oil and Gas Law, CPMLP 09/09, 1994, p9. See also R Fowler, "The Blank Cheque and the Cliff Edge", *Journal of World Energy Law and Business* 6 (2019).

201 C Duval, H Le Leuch, A Pertuzio and JL Weaver, *International Petroleum and Exploration Agreements: Legal, Economic & Policy Aspects*, 2nd edn, Barrows, 2009, p293.

202 DF Asmus, "The 1995 Model Form International Operating Agreement" *Journal Energy & Natural Resources Law* 14 (1996) 14, 11.

203 *Ibid.*

Secondly, all JOAs that provide for a work programme and budget face the dilemma that it is unfair (from an operator's perspective) to give non-operators a second chance to reject an operation that has already been approved in the work programme and budget. Therefore, several approaches are used to reduce the significance of authorisations for expenditure, such as requiring operators to issue authorisations for expenditures for information or only for the purpose of reducing expenditure in response to deteriorating economic conditions. On the other hand, a JOA which does not contain work programme and budget provisions (eg, the North American JOA Models) escapes this dilemma and can clearly implement the authorisation for expenditure mechanism with only minor restrictions to allow efficiency and security of the operations.

Thirdly, some JOAs such as the CAPL form which do not provide for the existence of work programme and budgets also do not provide for the existence of OpComs, so the parties vote unanimously instead of by pre-determined passmark. By contrast the AAPL 810 form envisages approval of an authorisation for expenditure by vote or unanimously, as the parties may select.[204] If OpCom approval is required, the non-operators rely on their control in the OpCom to exert control over the expenditure, so if the operator has complete control of the OpCom the non-operators are left with no control whatsoever over the expenditure. However, in JOAs which do not provide for OpCom control the non-operators have a higher degree of control of expenditure if the authorisation for expenditures must be approved by the non-operator unanimously.

Therefore, the major difference between the JOAs is the body responsible for approving the authorisation for expenditures. In the international, British, Norwegian and Greenlandic JOA Models, the OpCom's approval is required and in the North American Models, the non-operators' approval is required.[205] Consequently, for the first time in this discussion, it is possible to suggest that the North American Models put the non-operators in a stronger position compared with the other models, as each non-operator, acting in its own discretion, shall approve the authorisation for expenditures instead by committee, in which the operator is also represented, on a passmark basis. This fact is easy to understand in practical terms: if in a particular case the operator retains the majority of interest in the joint venture, or if a low passmark exists, the operator will be able to overcome this issue without any major difficulty as it would have the final decision in the OpCom. However, some authors disagree with this view, such as Hugh Dundas:

> *... the UKCS norm is for authorisation for expenditure to require Operating Committee approval prior to Operator making any commitment, while the North American approach is generally that authorisation for expenditures are provided to non-operators more by way of information and do not require prior approval.*[206]

The respected author is not entirely correct in this statement, as the joint operation can only occur if the non-operators approve the authorisation for expenditure, but

204 AAPL 810 Form §6.2.

205 C Duval, H Le Leuch, A Pertuzio and JL Weaver, *International Petroleum and Exploration Agreements: Legal, Economic & Policy Aspects*, 2nd edn, Barrows, 2009, p289.

206 H Dundas, *Joint Operating Agreements: An Introduction*, 1994 Summer Programme: UK Oil and Gas Law, CPMLP 09/09, 1994, p9.

it does not mean that the operator cannot continue this operation as an exclusive operation, which is discussed in Chapter 1, Section 9.[207] Thus, it could be suggested that under the North American JOAs, joint operations will only exist and bind the non-operators if they approve the relevant authorisation for expenditures. In other words, in North America there is a higher degree of control by the non-operators.

It is also important to stress that the lack of work programme and budget provisions increases the power of non-operators to control the expenditures of the consortium if the JOA implements a full authorisation for expenditure mechanism with little flexibility in its place. However, a JOA with work programme and budgets and authorisation for expenditures might not result in a higher degree of control of expenditure, but rather a balancing of control from one mechanism to the other. This is a problem that was present even in early editions of the AIPN JOA Model Forms and still exists.[208]

However, it is important to note that these provisions will not commonly apply for the fulfilment of the minimum work programme imposed by the petroleum legal regime and any emergency procedures, as the operator has to execute these operations and any objection to an authorisation for expenditure could jeopardise the existence of the entire joint venture.[209] One could argue that it is reasonable to accept some measure of flexibility under those circumstances, but the non-operators should have more than a right to be informed as these decisions could affect the future and the existence of the consortium. All of the JOAs fail to provide adequate participation in emergency situations.

The question of whether an authorisation for expenditure should be regarded as a flexible estimate or a specific fixed quote is highly controversial. The most reasonable interpretation is that the authorisation for expenditure is strict as to the procedures determined in the JOA, but also flexible to the extent the JOA allows modifications. Consequently, once an authorisation for expenditure is approved, the operator can only modify it up to the level authorised in the JOA otherwise it will be subject to further approval from the remaining parties. In other words, the authorisation for expenditure is precise and flexible at the same time. An authorisation for expenditure is an estimate in the sense that it can be subject to amendments or revisions, but the rules are strict, as any amendment shall be subject to the approval of the non-operators or the OpCom.

In practice, the operator should avoid putting multiple operations in a single authorisation for expenditure as it would be far more difficult to control the expenditure and might lead to complications where an authorisation for expenditure needs to be reconsidered by the OpCom simply because one item within it needs to be updated.

Therefore, the authorisation for expenditure requirement is an extremely important provision, in that it helps to maintain an effective and precise system of control of expenditure. All the models recognise the importance of authorisation for

---

207 DF Asmus, "The 1995 Model Form International Operating Agreement", *Journal of Energy & Natural Resources Law* 14 (1996) 11.

208 *Ibid.*

209 AIPN JOA items 6.1, 6.2, 6.3. OGUK JOA items 10.1, 11.1, 12.1, P Roberts and R Fowler, *Joint Operating Agreements: A Practical Guide*, 4th edn, Globe Law and Business, London, 2020, pp178–181; T Daintith and G Willoughby (eds), *Adrian Hill, United Kingdom Oil and Gas Law*, 3rd edn, Sweet & Maxwell, 2009, pp1143–1150.

expenditures, so a system for their use is clearly implemented in each model studied. However, it is possible to consider two potential pitfalls from a non-operator's perspective. First, the AIPN Model could eventually create a purely bureaucratic authorisation for expenditure which aims to provide information, without any effective control by the non-operator, if such an alternative is chosen by the parties, although it is more likely to be imposed by a strong operator during negotiations. Furthermore, as was described by Taylor and Tyne, an operator might not accept the existence of a second chance to control an expenditure previously approved by the work programme and budget.[210] Secondly, it is possible to argue that the existence of the OpCom, which commonly is intended to assure and protect the interest of non-operators, is, for the purposes of an authorisation for expenditure, not the best instrument to secure the interest of the non-operators. In this case, the North American Models, which do not provide for the existence of an OpCom to control the joint operations, allow the non-operators to exercise a more important role, as each one has to approve each authorisation for expenditure. Thirdly, the implementation of the work programme and budget provision could reduce the non-operators' overall control of expenditure, as the non-operators are unlikely to achieve full implementation of both mechanisms but are more likely to accept some degree of control using each provision. Therefore, the necessity for authorisation for expenditures is more than clear, but balance should be the main principle in determining the conduct and control of the joint operations.

From a non-operator's perspective, the importance of the authorisation for expenditure is more than clear, but it is important to remember that the JOA is not the only document which will regulate the expenditure of the joint venture. Detailed information on the authorisation for expenditure mechanism should be provided in the accounting procedure, which commonly is an attachment to the JOA.[211] This document will determine the practical operations regarding the chargeability for the joint operations. Consequently, the non-operators must verify that all terms established in the accounting procedure follow the provisions in the JOA.

Another key issue related to expenditure is the records of the expenditure, which are clearly regulated by the accounting procedure. The operator must keep records of the joint operations, including the expenditure incurred on behalf of the consortium. Consequently, the non-operators may also verify the correctness of the charges incurred by the operator via audits, and these may result in correction of the charges.[212]

The argument raised by Chris Thorpe stating that non-operators must pay an invoice even if it is incorrect, imprecise or void, otherwise they will be considered a defaulting party, is very controversial. It could be argued that such a procedure legalises abusive actions by operators towards non-operators that are in a weaker financial condition. This issue will be discussed in the section on default.[213]

A non-operator is in a difficult situation, because if a high degree of control is exercised by the work programme and budget, it may at the same time reduce

210 MPG Taylor and SM Tyne, *Taylor and Winsor on Joint Operating Agreements*, 2nd edn, Longman, 1992, p42.

211 BG Taverne, *Co-operative Agreements in the Extractive Petroleum Industry*, Kluwer Law International, 1996, p67.

212 C Thorpe, *Fundamentals of Upstream Petroleum Agreements*, CP Thorpe, 2008, p138.

213 *Ibid.*

the chances of obtaining a full implementation of a robust authorisation for expenditure mechanism. The reason for this is that the operator may consider the authorisation for expenditure as a second chance to reject an operation which was previously authorised by the work programme and budget. In this case, the non-operators would face a dilemma. On the one hand, they could gain an advantage by participating in important decisions on the joint operations through the work programme and budget, but lose control of the details. On the other hand, they could exert far more control on individual operations by the authorisation for expenditure mechanism, but lose the power to participate in deciding the content of the activities. Consequently, the non-operators must consider carefully what kind of control they are looking for, so that the most suitable terms are in place.

Therefore, in practical terms, the operator may seek to avoid the implementation of an authorisation for expenditure procedure, or at least minimise the use of authorisation for expenditures by increasing the amount of work contained in a single authorisation for expenditure,[214] and the non-operators may seek the opposite so that they can exercise better control over the expenditure.[215]

However, the goal of all parties should be balance, so that efficiency can be improved. Operators should also consider the advantages of authorisations for expenditure. As stated above, work programmes and budgets provide at best a business plan and cash flow forecast for the activity envisaged; they are estimates derived from the operator's best guess of the scope and cost of those activities many months in advance. If the JOA requires an authorisation for expenditure to be issued, that authorisation will be issued at a point in time when the expenditure can be more easily quantified and the relevant information is more precise and reliable. As long as the OpCom approves that authorisation for expenditure, the operator is in a better position because it has then obtained more specific and up-to-date approval of the activity. Accordingly, it will be much harder for the non-operators to contest their liability to pay the corresponding cash calls or invoices by arguing that the relevant activity had not been approved and/or fell outside the approved work programme and budget. In this way, the authorisation for expenditure updates the work programme and budget, even if the work programme and budget is not formally amended.[216]

In conclusion, the outcome of the authorisation for expenditure negotiations will vary on each position that the national oil company and the international oil company takes in the consortium (ie, operator or non-operator), which will encourage them to take a more flexible approach (eg, authorisation for expenditure for information) or a more conservative approach (eg, authorisation for expenditure for approval). Those granting instruments which require the joint venture to submit its programmes and budgets for approval by the state do not normally include in their terms a concept of authorisations for expenditure. This could mean that the national oil company in the joint venture may wish to represent the state's interests when approving for the purposes of the JOA any authorisation for expenditure implementing a programme and budget approved by the state. On the other hand, it may be in the interests of the joint venture to include

214 MPG Taylor and SM Tyne, *Taylor and Winsor on Joint Operating Agreements*, 2nd edn, Longman, 1992, pp42–43.

215 H Dundas, *Joint Operating Agreements: An Introduction*, 1994 Summer Programme: UK Oil and Gas Law, CPMLP 09/09, 1994, p9.

216 R Fowler, "The Blank Cheque and the Cliff Edge", *Journal of World Energy Law and Business* 6 (2019).

the concept of authorisations for expenditure within the scope of the granting instrument – precisely so that the relevant programme and budget is kept up-to-date and accurately reflects the authorised activities. This may be cumbersome to implement, but will enhance the joint venture's prospects of obtaining cost recovery for those expenditures from the state, avoiding "post-hoc" arguments that the relevant expenditure fell outside the scope of activities authorised for the purposes of the granting instrument. After all, it does not help the joint venture at all if the expenditure was authorised for the purposes of the JOA, but not by the state for the purposes of the granting instrument.

3. Insurance

3.1 General principles

In essence, oil and gas operations are risky. That is why most host government contracts and hydrocarbon laws are likely to request insurances from the concessionaires/licensees/contractors to ensure that operations can be reinstated and facilities rebuilt after a catastrophic loss. After all, under certain granting instruments, the contractor may have been compensated by the state for the cost of installing those facilities, and the state is likely to be the ultimate payer of the costs of restoring of such facilities following such accident, unless they are insured. The state therefore has the lion's share of the insurable interest in the facilities.

JOAs must follow what is provided in the relevant laws and the granting instrument. Any JOA is likely to provide a high-level statement of the basic obligations concerning insurance than the detail behind this provision.[217] The key issue is to provide assurance for the host government (if applicable) that the conduct of the operations is secured by adequate insurance, as described below.

3.2 Analysis of model JOAs

Since the operator is the party elected to conduct operations on the behalf of the consortium, it is likely to be the party responsible for the insurance provision. This is clearly provided in the Australian JOA Model:

> *In the course of managing, supervising and conducting Joint Operations, the Operator is entitled to have possession and control of all Joint Venture Property and must, either itself or through such third parties as it may engage:*
>
> ...
>
> *– (insurances) effect and maintain all insurances appropriate in relation to Joint Venture Property and Joint Operations, or as required by Law, and any additional insurances which the Operating Committee requires to be effected, provided that the Operator must wherever possible procure that all such insurances include a provision that the insurer has no right of subrogation against any Participant or the Operator and that the Participants and Operator are to be named, to the extent of their interests, on each policy of insurance;*

217 AIPN JOA §4.7(A).

– (insurance certificates) if requested, provide full details to a Participant of all insurances effected by the Operator under this agreement, including certificates of currency; ...[218]

The operator must take out insurance on behalf of the consortium. However, the non-operators may prefer to take out their own insurance to cover their individual working interests. The Norwegian Model says:

A Party is entitled to take out his own insurance or in other equivalent ways ensure coverage. In such case he shall notify the Operator well in advance before the Operator takes out insurance on behalf of the joint venture, and give the Operator and the other Parties the necessary information on his insurance coverage, and ensure that recourse against the other Parties has been waived.
The Operator shall in such cases give the Party requiring it, the information necessary to establish the insurances and duly assist a Party promoting claims under such insurances. Extra cost arising in this respect shall be covered by the Party concerned.[219]

Another important duty of the operator is to ensure that any service provider contracted to the consortium's operations also maintains its own insurances. The Norwegian Model says that:

The Operator shall ensure that suppliers of goods and services to the joint venture activities take out and maintain such insurances as are required by laws and regulations and other requirements by the authorities, or which are decided by the management committee. The Operator shall endeavour to secure waivers of recourse actions against the Parties.[220]

The above provisions are unlikely to need much discussion during negotiations between an international and a national oil company. In general, they follow the obligations derived from the host government contract and applicable laws.

But the key concerns should be: (a) what happens if one party wishes to self-insure and (b) what happens if the operator fails to provide the required insurance?

Although it may not be relevant in all jurisdictions, the AIPN Model Form provides an alternative provision, covering the situation where the operator self-insures:

---

218 AMPLA JOA §7.2(m), (n).
219 Norwegian JOA §14.2.
220 Norwegian JOA §14.4.

OPTIONAL PROVISION, CHOOSE ARTICLE 4.7.E, IF DESIRED. RENUMBER FOLLOWING PARAGRAPHS AND CHECK CROSS-REFERENCES, IF ARTICLE 4.7.E IS NOT CHOSEN.
If Operator elects, to the extent permitted by the Contract and Laws, to self-insure all or part of the coverage to be procured under Articles 4.7.A and/or 4.7.B, Operator shall so notify the Operating Committee and provide a qualified self-insurance letter stating what coverages Operator is self-insuring. Any risk to be covered by insurance to be procured under Articles 4.7.A and 4.7.B, that is not identified in the self-insurance letter shall be covered by insurance and supported by a current certificate of adequate coverage. If requested by the Operating Committee from time to time, Operator shall provide evidence of financial responsibility, acceptable to the Operating Committee that fully covers the risks that would be covered by the insurance to be procured under Articles 4.7.A and 4.7.B.[221]

Some JOAs treat any breach of the operator's duty to comply with its insurance obligation as a very serious issue, since this could lead to termination of the granting instrument and high exposure for the consortium. The industry's main solution has been to treat a breach of the obligation by the operator to secure the required insurances as a particularly serious breach of the operator's duties. However, this solution is not widely adopted by the model forms. The CAPL form Article 4.02 (C) provides that an operator remains liable for losses which should have been insured and were not by reason of its failure to comply with the JOA's insurance provisions. The OGUK JOA takes the same approach, only excusing the operator from the failure to insure if it used reasonable endeavours to obtain the relevant insurance policy, and notified the non-operators of its failure to do so.[222] The AIPN JOA expects the operator to procure and maintain the insurances required to meet applicable law and any additional insurance as required by the JOA, but does not expressly provide that a failure to insure in breach of the JOA terms would automatically disqualify the operator from indemnification.

The Greenlandic Model also adopts this option:

Except as set out in Article 3.3.3.C the Operator shall not bear (except as a Party to the extent of its Percentage Interest share) any damage, loss, cost or liability resulting from performing (or failing to perform) its duties and functions as Operator.
Except as set out in Article 3.3.3.C the Parties shall (in proportion to their Percentage Interest share) defend and indemnify the Operator and its Affiliates from any damage, loss, cost or liabilities incident to claims, demands or causes of action brought by any or on behalf of any person or entity, which claims, demands or causes of action arise out of, are incident to or result from Joint Operations.
Notwithstanding Articles 3.3.3.A or 3.3.3.B:

221 AIPN JOA §4.7(E).
222 OGUK JOA §6.2.4 (a) (ii); AIPN JOA §4.7.A.

> (a) *if any Managerial or Supervisory Personnel of Operator or its Affiliates engage in gross negligence, wilful misconduct or wilful failure to act and this causes the Parties to incur damage, loss, cost, expense or liability for claims, demands or causes of action referred to in Articles 3.3.3.A or 3.3.3.B, or*
> (b) *if Operator fails to obtain or maintain any insurance which it is required to obtain or maintain under Article 3.12, except where it has used all reasonable endeavours to obtain or maintain such insurance but has been unable to do so and has promptly notified the Parties of such fact, and such failure causes the Parties to incur damage, loss, cost, expense or liability for claims, demands or causes of action referred to in Articles 3.3.3.A or 3.3.3.B then in addition to its Percentage Interest share, the Operator shall bear all such damages, losses, costs, expenses and liabilities. Notwithstanding the foregoing, the Operator shall in neither case be liable for any consequential loss or damage. For the purposes of this Article 3.3.3 consequential loss or damage shall include, but not be limited to, inability to produce Hydrocarbons, environmental damage caused by a discharge of Hydrocarbons, lost production or loss of profits.*[223]

3.3 Discussion

Although the insurance provision is unlikely to be a main focus in negotiations between an international and a national oil company, both parties should ensure that the petroleum title is secured by the required insurances, which cover both the operations and the property related to the consortium. One key issue which is sometimes missed is whether the granting instrument also requires the contractor to insure joint property, precisely because the state is particularly exposed to loss or damage to the production facilities. If so, the prudent course would be to arrange insurances on terms that satisfy both the granting instrument and the JOA, including the state as a named insured on those policies. This would avoid paying two sets of premia for effectively the same insurance cover.[224]

4. Decommissioning

4.1 General principles

Oil and gas are non-renewable commodities. Every oil and/or gas field has a life cycle. This starts with a commercial discovery and a large amount of infrastructure is required to develop the field. Commonly, the production facilities involve platforms, offshore pipelines and storage facilities. Once oil and/or gas is extracted, it needs to be lifted to a pipeline or terminal for transporting to its final destination. When the oil and/or gas production ends, all installations and structures must be decommissioned as they cannot not be left *in situ*. The reasons are, first, for navigational and sea users' safety and, secondly, for environmental safety (ie, to prevent pollution). Therefore, decommissioning refers to the decision-making process relating to, or the act of, disposal of any infrastructure installed to explore, produce or to lift oil and gas to a final destination. Originally, decommissioning was referred to as 'abandonment'.

---

223 Greenlandic JOA §3.3.3.

224 P Roberts and R Fowler, *Joint Operating Agreements: A Practical Guide*, 4th edn, Globe Law and Business, 2020, p56.

However, for environmental and public opinion reasons the term 'decommissioning' is more suitable than abandonment, even though some countries still maintain the traditional references to abandonment.[225]

There are several international, regional and local laws covering decommissioning.[226] All oil and gas companies must obey all of the regulations that apply to their operations. However, the number of applicable regulations may vary depending on the number of treaties to which the relevant host government is a signatory.

Commonly, the proprietary rights of oil and gas *in situ* (or the exploitation rights) belong to the host government, except in a few cases (eg, private property in the United States). Host governments have several options for exploiting these natural resources,[227] but in general use three different types of arrangement:

- exclusive licence,[228] under which all rights to exploration and production are assigned to the licensee and the government benefits from the revenue through its petroleum tax regime;
- production sharing agreement,[229] under which part of the production is assigned to the contractor (subject to tax or not), but commonly the majority of the production will remain government property; and
- service contract, which assigns no right of oil and gas (to the extent it is a purely service agreement), but only remuneration on a service fee basis.

The distinction between such arrangements is relevant from a decommissioning perspective because they have different approaches to the ownership of the infrastructure. In a licence regime, the infrastructure is likely to belong to the licensee as this body will bear all the costs and risks involved in implementing the infrastructure. In a production sharing agreement regime, the infrastructure should revert to the government in accordance with the agreement usually after the joint venture has been compensated for the costs of its investment in the infrastructure through the allocation to it of cost petroleum. In a service agreement regime, likewise, the joint venture will have been compensated for the cost of the infrastructure it has installed through the appropriate service fee.

The Brazilian approach is a good example of how decommissioning is regulated from a host government's perspective. The concession agreement agreed at the 10th licence round provides contractual obligations for decommissioning in the following terms:[230]

---

225 For the purposes of this book decommissioning and abandonment are used interchangeably.

226 For example, UN Convention on the Law of the Sea (UNCLOS) 1982, Convention on the Prevention of Marine Pollution by Dumping of Wastes and Other Matter (London Convention) 1972, Convention for the Protection of the Marine Environment of the North-East Atlantic (OSPAR Convention) 1992.

227 For further information see: BG Taverne, *Petroleum, Industry and Governments: A Study of the Involvement of Industry and Government with the Production and Use of Petroleum*, 2nd edn, Kluwer Law International, 2008; BG Taverne, *An Introduction to the Regulation of the Petroleum Industry: Law, Contracts and Conventions*, Graham & Trotman, 1994; EV Rostow, *A National Policy for the Oil Industry*, Yale University Press, 1948, pp3–26; D Barberis, *Negotiating Mining Agreements: Past, Present and Future Trends*, Kluwer Law International, 1998, pp4–60.

228 Licence is also referred to as concession agreement or lease. These terms are used interchangeably in the petroleum industry – they have the same meaning.

229 Production sharing agreements are also referred to as petroleum sharing contracts.

230 www.anp.gov.br/brasil-rounds/round10/index_e.asp.

- Compliance with applicable regulations and industry best practices:

13.19 The Concessionaire may interrupt the drilling of a well and abandon it before reaching the expected geological goal, in accordance with the applicable Brazilian laws and the Best Practices of the Oil Industry. If the well represents part of the Minimum Exploration Program and it does not reach the expected goal, the well shall not take into account in the compliance with the Minimum Exploration Program unless the ANP, at its sole discretion, determines otherwise.
18.8 When performing all and any relinquishment of the Blocks within the Concession Area, the Concessionaire shall rigorously comply, not only with the provisions of paragraphs 3.5, 18.11 to 18.19 and Clause Twenty-One, but also with all other legal provisions and instructions of the ANP, in accordance with the Best Practices of the Oil Industry, regarding the relinquishment and abandonment of areas and removal and reversion of assets.
18.11 The Planning and performance of any Inactivation and Abandonment Operations, including areas, wells, structures, fields, transfer lines, parts or units of surface or sub-surface facilities, offshore or onshore, shall be made in accordance with the applicable Brazilian legislation and the Best Practices of the Oil Industry and also according to Clause Twenty-One.

- Allocation of responsibilities and liabilities for decommissioning obligations:

18.9 In accordance with the applicable Brazilian legislation, the relinquishment mentioned herein shall not exempt the Concessionaire from the fulfilment of all outstanding obligations, nor for any liabilities, irregularities or infractions occurring at a later date.
18.10 In the event of a pre-existing well or production infrastructure in the Concession Area that the Concessionaire may, at any time during the life of this Agreement, use or dispose of for any purpose, the Concessionaire shall assume the responsibilities of the obligations and has no right to waiver or any kind of indemnification in relation to the ANP or Union, pursuant to Clause Eighteen and Twenty-One.

- Allocation of costs and guarantees:

18.12 When it refers to a field, the inactivation planning and abandonment and the organization to provide the necessary funds shall be contemplated in the respective Development Plan, pursuant to paragraph 9.1 and periodically reviewed, during the Production Phase. Such revisions will be subject to paragraph 9.8.
18.13 The costs of the Inactivation and abandonment Operations in a field shall be established, in order to cover the activities of definitive well abandonment, the inactivation and removal of lines and facilities and the recovery of areas, pursuant to the applicable Brazilian legislation.

18.14 Upon request by the ANP, the Concessionaire shall deliver an inactivation and abandonment guarantee, by means of insurance, letter of credit, provisional guarantee fund, or other form of acceptable guarantee to the ANP, in conformance with the applicable Brazilian legislation.
18.15 The value of the inactivation and abandonment guarantee for a Field will be revised if there are approved revisions to the Development Plan of this Field that will alter the cost of inactivation and abandonment operations.
18.16 If the inactivation and abandonment guarantee is constituted by a provisional guarantee fund, the calculated balance after the completion of all the necessary operations to inactivate and abandon the Field will revert exclusively to the Concessionaire.
18.17 The presentation of the inactivation and abandonment guarantee does not discharge the Concessionaire's obligation to complete, at its own cost and risk, all of the Operations necessary to inactivate and abandon the Field.

These provisions do not differ from the majority of licence regimes. First, they require compliance with the applicable law (including environmental law) and international best practice. Secondly, they allocate responsibility for all and any liability and costs related to decommissioning to the licensee. Thirdly, they require certain guarantees at the development plan stage to secure the performance of the decommissioning obligations.

In Brazil, in addition to the petroleum title the National Petroleum Agency also provides a specific regulation, Ordinance 25/2002, which regulates "abandonment". The main substance of this ordinance is its technical requirements for the abandonment process.[231] Its overall aim is to prevent the migration of fluids (in particular to the surface or seabed).[232] The general obligations can be described in the following terms:

- the National Petroleum Agency must be notified before any abandonment;[233]
- the National Petroleum Agency's approval must be obtained before any production well is abandoned;[234]
- no well may be abandoned while it can still jeopardise neighbouring wells, except for safety or environmental reasons;[235]
- references to American Petroleum Institute specifications;[236]
- testing equipment;[237]
- structure clearance;[238]
- navigation charts adjusted;[239] and
- emergency plan.[240]

---

231 Ordinance 25/2002 refers to "abandonment" rather than "decommissioning", which indicates the absence or lack of public sensitivity about this issue in comparison with mature provinces such as the United Kingdom and Norway.
232 Article 1.
233 Article 4.
234 Article 5.
235 Article 6.
236 Article 7.
237 Article 8.
238 Article 6.
239 Article 27.
240 Articles 19, 20 and 21.

Host governments should be aware of the different contractual arrangements and their distinctions before deciding on the structure of their legal regime. Oil and gas companies should be aware of the full regulatory and contractual obligations regarding decommissioning before investing in any province, since decommissioning is a critical factor in determining the economics of their projects.

As previously mentioned, the JOA is derived from the rights and obligations given to the consortium in a granting instrument (except in the United States where private parties might own the subsurface). Therefore, the JOA must be consistent with the granting instrument.

In general, the JOAs are unlikely to provide extensive detail on decommissioning as this should be regulated in the granting instrument and applicable laws. In this sense, there is little room for negotiation and discussion between the national and international oil companies regarding decommissioning provisions: regulations and laws must be applied and the JOA should make reference to the key obligations.

One possible cause of tension could be a request from any party to increase the decommissioning procedures and requirements above those required by the granting instrument and local laws. The operator is likely to wish to avoid any proposal that will increase its administrative burden, and most parties are likely to be concerned about the need for further reserve funds to cover the costs of any decommissioning procedures beyond those required by law. In theory, the international and national oil companies should agree on this matter, as they will not wish to increase their costs beyond any legal obligation. However, the national oil company may wish to increase these obligations for the benefit of a wider public interest.

4.2 Analysis of model JOAs

Most JOAs follow a similar approach to decommissioning. First, they ensure that the JOA is valid and enforceable up to the end of the decommissioning process.[241] Secondly, they require that an estimated decommissioning work programme and budget is included in the development plan.[242] Thirdly, they may require special approval for some decommissioning costs, for example in the award of contracts and authorisation for expenditure mechanisms.[243] Some JOAs may include a requirement for the parties to put up financial security for their decommissioning obligations, particularly if the host government agreement requires it or to ensure that withdrawing parties do not escape paying their share of such obligations by means of such withdrawal.[244]

4.3 Discussion

A national oil company participating in a joint venture may have a different perspective on decommissioning facilities at the end of field life. It is more likely than the participating international oil companies to have other interests in the relevant basin or region and may have other prospects into which the existing facilities may tie in, avoiding having to make significant investment in duplicative transportation and processing infrastructure.[245] This may mean that the national

241 AIPN JOA §2.1(B).
242 AIPN JOA §6.3(A).
243 AMPLA JOA §9.1.
244 Greenlandic JOA §3.18.3 and AIPN JOA §13.8.
245 P Roberts and R Fowler, *Joint Operating Agreements: A Practical Guide*, 4th edn, Globe Law and Business, 2020, p230.

oil company will take particular interest in the sole risk provisions which apply to the decommissioning phase, with a view to continuing using the facilities after the point at which continued production is not economic. On the other hand, it may not need to do so if, at the end of the granting instrument, the state takes over the facilities which it has paid for by compensating the joint venture for its costs. This would enable the state to make the facilities available for use by a fresh consortium, which may continue exploiting the original reservoir or indeed using the facilities for hydrocarbons produced from adjacent fields.

The main risk most JOAs fail to address is the consequence of any breach of the decommissioning obligations. If the breach occurs towards the end of the consortium's life, the consortium is unlikely to have any assets (production, facilities) to guarantee any failures in performance, and a default would not resolve the problem (ie, the liability will remain). The party should bear in mind that their decommissioning obligations overlap – they owe an obligation to the state to decommission, or at least finance the decommissioning of, production facilities at the end of field life, and they effectively owe the same obligation to each other under the terms of the JOA. Prudently, the parties should adapt any regime for financial security under the JOA so that it meets the purposes of any financial security requirement under the granting instruments as well if the granting instrument allows partial termination to the relevant defaulting party.

5. Default

5.1 General principles

The JOA provisions on default[246] aim to secure the financial resources required to execute the joint operations, which should be funded by the parties in proportion to their respective interests.[247] If any party cannot contribute its share of the costs, the default[248] provision will be activated. Default is a critical matter – no operation can be executed without the financial means to cover its costs.[249]

Traditionally, the JOA default provision was not intended to be used (as with the sole risk provision). Its purpose was to act as a deterrent to the parties against failing to meet their financial commitments to the joint operations. However, in the early days of oil and gas operations, their reputation was very valuable to the parties and protecting this was sufficient deterrent against default.[250]

246 For further information see: RW Bentham, "Joint Operating Agreements – Default" *JERL* 8(1) (1990) 63; P Roberts, "Fault Lines in the Joint Operating Agreement: Forfeiture" *IELR* 7 (2008) 274–278 D Dawborn and J Waite, "Contractual Forfeiture of Joint Venture Interests: Are Such Clauses Enforceable" *OGLTR* 8 (1990) 389–392; C Parr, "Relief against Forfeiture under Joint Operating Agreements" *OGLTR* 5(10) (1986/87) 253–255; T Daintith and G Willoughby (eds), *Adrian Hill, United Kingdom Oil and Gas Law*, 3rd edn, Sweet & Maxwell, 2009, pp1143–1150; MPG Taylor and SM Tyne, *Taylor and Winsor on Joint Operating Agreements*, 2nd edn, Longman, 1992, pp77–96; P Roberts and R Fowler, *Joint Operating Agreements: A Practical Guide*, 4th edn, Globe Law and Business, 2020, pp321–351.

247 BG Taverne, *An Introduction to the Regulation of the Petroleum Industry: Law, Contracts and Conventions*, Graham & Trotman, 1994, p138.

248 GMD Bean, *Fiduciary Relationships, Fiduciary Duties and Joint Ventures: The Joint Operating Agreement*, University of Cambridge, 1992, p17.

249 S Styles, "Joint Operating Agreements" in J Paterson and G Gordon (eds), *Oil and Gas Law: Current Practice and Emerging Trends*, Dundee University Press, 2007, p289.

250 P Roberts and R Fowler, *Joint Operating Agreements: A Practical Guide*, 4th edn, Globe Law and Business, 2020, p322.

As a consequence, the JOA default provision has not been properly explored or tested in the courts until recently, not least because in some mature oil provinces, the major companies are being replaced by smaller, independent companies, and repeated oil price shocks are testing the financial strength of international oil companies and national oil companies.[251, 252]

Therefore, it is important to examine the implications of the default provision, as defaults are likely to occur more often now than they used to. Although a default will affect all the JOA parties, the non-operators are less likely to enforce the application of a default provision than the operator because it is the operator that is immediately exposed to any failure by non-operators to fund cash calls. All the JOA parties are nevertheless affected by any hiatus in cash flow for joint operations, not least because it may cause a breach of the relevant granting instrument.

Richard H Bartlett provides an extensive analysis of the parties' positions in a default situation in an article in the Alberta Law Review.[253] It is unlikely that the default provision will provide a remedy for a non-operator against the operator, but not impossible.[254] However, it is more likely to offer a remedy for the operator against a non-operator or even for one non-operator against another as any default will affect all the JOA parties.

Once a party fails to contribute to its participating interest share of the financial commitments of the consortium, it will, depending on the precise JOA definition of default, and the applicable law, be treated as in default.[255] This is a common approach in the petroleum industry,[256] but implementation of such a provision and the range of default remedies may vary between different JOAs.[257]

As a starting point, any national oil company will equally be affected by the default of another party because of its impact on joint operations cash flow and its threat to the good standing of the granting instrument. More than that, like the other non-defaulting parties, the national oil company will be required to contribute its participating interest share of the default, pending any recovery that can be made against the defaulting party's interest. The default may most likely arise in the exploration and appraisal phase of the joint venture when the national oil company's costs are being carried by the other parties – when the national oil company itself

---

251 S Styles, "Joint Operating Agreements" in J Paterson and G Gordon (eds), *Oil and Gas Law: Current Practice and Emerging Trends*, Dundee University Press, 2007, p289.

252 Two recent examples are discussed in ICC Dispute Resolution Bulletin 3 "Joint Operating Agreements in the International Oil & Gas Industry: ICC Arbitral Awards".

253 RH Bartlett, "Rights and Remedies of an Operator vis-à-vis a Defaulting Non-operator under Joint and Unit Operating Agreements", *Alberta Law Review* 10 (1972) 288, 291.

254 The AIPN JOA and OGUK JOA allow for default remedies to be triggered by any party serving the appropriate notice; AIPN JOA §8.1.A and OGUK JOA §17.9. See also P Roberts and R Fowler, *Joint Operating Agreements: A Practical Guide*, 4th edn, Globe Law and Business, 2020, p326.

255 See: S Shaw, "Joint Operating Agreements" in MR David, *Upstream Oil and Gas Agreements*, Sweet & Maxwell, 1996, p25; BG Taverne, *An Introduction to the Regulation of the Petroleum Industry: Law, Contracts and Conventions*, Graham & Trotman, 1994, p141; C Thorpe, *Fundamentals of Upstream Petroleum Agreements*, CP Thorpe, 2008, pp138–140; C Golvala, "Upstream joint ventures – bidding and operating agreements" in G Picton-Tubervill (ed.), *Oil and Gas: A Practical Handbook*, Globe Law and Business, 2009, pp49–51; C Duval, H Le Leuch, A Pertuzio and JL Weaver, *International Petroleum and Exploration Agreements: Legal, Economic & Policy Aspects*, 2nd edn, Barrows, 2009, p299; A Jennings, *Oil and Gas Exploration Contracts*, 2nd edn, Sweet & Maxwell, 2008, p25; J Wilkinson, *Introduction to Oil and Gas Joint Ventures*, OPL, 1997, p44; H Dundas, *Joint Operating Agreements: An Introduction*, 1994 Summer Programme: UK Oil and Gas Law, CPMLP 09/09, 1994, p10.

256 MPG Taylor and SM Tyne, *Taylor and Winsor on Joint Operating Agreements*, 2nd edn, Longman, 1992, p77.

257 C Thorpe, *Fundamentals of Upstream Petroleum Agreements*, CP Thorpe, 2008, pp139–140.

has no liability for costs and cannot be in default. Usually, the carry arrangement is drafted in such a way that the carrying parties have joint and several liability for the carry, with the result that the national oil company may be unaffected, as long as the remaining non-defaulting international oil companies have the wherewithal to continue paying the carry, albeit in increased shares. Finally, another way to minimise the effects of forfeiture is the power given to the defaulting party to reacquire its forfeited interest at a later date.[258]

The JOA should provide a very detailed procedure for the default application process.[259] Initially, the JOA will provide the requirement for a notice and a specific time (commonly between 6 and 12 days)[260] for the defaulting party to remedy its failure by paying the relevant cash call. During this time, some restrictions will be placed on its rights under the JOA, such as the right to obtain information, the right to vote in the OpCom, the right to take its share of the production,[261] the right to transfer its interest, among others.[262] If the defaulting party does not remedy the default within a specified time (commonly 60 days), the non-defaulting parties are entitled to claim its interest.

However, if the non-defaulting parties do not wish to invoke forfeiture and carry the defaulting interest, the consortium will terminate.[263]

It is important to note that the non-defaulting parties have an obligation to cover the defaulting party's share, otherwise they will also be in default.[264] Although it may seem unfair to enforce the obligation to cover someone else's expense, this is necessary to continue to perform operations and to avoid liability to the state for non-performance of concession agreement obligations. Another major problem that may arise from the default provision is the liability related to decommissioning obligations. If a default occurs at the beginning of the life of the consortium, the decommissioning obligations are unlikely to be a problem since the production will secure such costs. However, default could create a major problem at the final stage of the development, when the petroleum title is no longer an asset but rather a burden as the decommissioning costs are greater than the monetary value of the remaining production.[265]

In this situation, a defaulting party will be "happy" to lose all of its interest as it will be losing liabilities rather than an asset. If there is no decommissioning

---

258 P Roberts and R Fowler, *Joint Operating Agreements: A Practical Guide*, 4th edn, Globe Law and Business, 2020, p339.

259 S Styles, "Joint Operating Agreements" in J Paterson and G Gordon (eds), *Oil and Gas Law: Current Practice and Emerging Trends*, Dundee University Press, 2007, p289.

260 MPG Taylor and SM Tyne, *Taylor and Winsor on Joint Operating Agreements*, 2nd edn, Longman, 1992, p77.

261 As previously mentioned, the non-defaulting parties may be able to market the production to cover the default. The risk of this approach is the connection with partnership requirements under the UK Partnership Act 1890.

262 P Roberts and R Fowler, *Joint Operating Agreements: A Practical Guide*, 4th edn, Globe Law and Business, 2020, pp328–330.

263 See: H Dundas, *Joint Operating Agreements: An Introduction*, 1994 Summer Programme: UK Oil and Gas Law, CPMLP 09/09, 1994, p10; C Duval, H Le Leuch, A Pertuzio and JL Weaver, *International Petroleum and Exploration Agreements: Legal, Economic & Policy Aspects*, 2nd edn, Barrows, 2009, p299; S Shaw, "Joint Operating Agreements" in MR David, *Upstream Oil and Gas Agreements*, Sweet & Maxwell, 1996, p25; C Thorpe, *Fundamentals of Upstream Petroleum Agreements*, CP Thorpe, 2008, pp138–140; C Golvala, "Upstream joint ventures – bidding and operating agreements" in G Picton-Tubervill (ed.), *Oil and Gas: A Practical Handbook*, Globe Law and Business, 2009, pp49–51.

264 T Daintith and G Willoughby (eds), *Adrian Hill, United Kingdom Oil and Gas Law*, 3rd edn, Sweet & Maxwell, 2009, p1147; P Roberts and R Fowler, *Joint Operating Agreements: A Practical Guide*, 4th edn, Globe Law and Business, 2020, p328.

265 S Shaw, "Joint Operating Agreements" in MR David, *Upstream Oil and Gas Agreements*, Sweet & Maxwell, 1996, p25.

arrangement in place,[266] the parties should take extra care before drafting the default provision. A similar case occurs with default during an unsuccessful operation where there is no production[267] to compensate for the "failure of cash performance".[268]

In both cases the establishment of liens and securities outside the provisions of the JOA may ensure payment of the ongoing costs.[269] However, in the case of decommissioning, a lien over the defaulting share of the joint property or production may not be a reliable protection at such a late stage of the field.[270]

Consequently, it can be said that the default provision serves as a real threat to all parties, just like the sole risk provision, because the consequences of its implementation are quite severe for the defaulting party.[271]

JOA default clauses are controversial for commercial and legal reasons. The commercial objection arises from the fact that the non-payment by a party of amounts due under the JOA can lead to it being deprived of its participating interest, wholly or partly, regardless of the fact that the commercial value of that participating interest may vastly exceed the debt which gave rise to the default. That in turn explains the legal controversy; the clause may be challenged by civil law principles which allow the courts to review and revise a clause which has an extravagant or exorbitant effect or is unconscionable.[272] Applying common law principles, the same clause may be impugned by the rule against penalties and/or may be subject to review under the equitable principle of relief against forfeiture. The highest courts in Australia[273], England[274] and Singapore[275] have each reconsidered these rules in the last eight years and in particular the rule against penalties has been significantly revised. However, there are few reported cases applying the rule against penalties or the relief against forfeiture to JOA default clauses.[276] This section does its best

266 C Golvala, "Upstream joint ventures – bidding and operating agreements" in G Picton-Tubervill (ed.), *Oil and Gas: A Practical Handbook*, Globe Law and Business, 2009, p50.

267 S Shaw, "Joint Operating Agreements" in MR David, *Upstream Oil and Gas Agreements*, Sweet & Maxwell, 1996, p26.

268 S Styles, "Joint Operating Agreements" in J Paterson and G Gordon (eds), *Oil and Gas Law: Current Practice and Emerging Trends*, Dundee University Press, 2007, p289.

269 For further information on insurance and liens see: DO Sabey and JL Fingarson, "Indemnity and Insurance Clauses in Joint Venture, Farmout and Joint Operating Agreements", *Alberta Law Review* 8 (1970) 210; JD Weidman, "Oil and Gas, Operator's Liens in Bankruptcy, The Model Form Operating Agreement Versus the Trustee in bankruptcy's Avoiding Powers", *Oklahoma Law Review* 37 (1984) 141 and DD Peng, *Insurance and Legal Issues in the Oil Industry*, Graham & Trotman, 1993.

270 H Dundas, *Joint Operating Agreements: An Introduction*, 1994 Summer Programme: UK Oil and Gas Law, CPMLP 09/09, 1994, pp12–15.

271 C Thorpe, *Fundamentals of Upstream Petroleum Agreements*, CP Thorpe, 2008, p140.

272 In *Cavendish*, the English Supreme Court took into account comparable legislation under French, German, Swiss and Belgian law as well as New York and Hong Kong laws (*Cavendish Square B.V. v Makdessi, Parking Eye Limited v Beavis* [2015] UKSC 67, paragraph 1 6 4–16 6). In Denka, the Singaporean Supreme Court also looked at legislation and case law on penalties in Canada, New Zealand, Hong Kong, Malaysia and Australia (*Denka Advantech Private Limited and another v Seraya Energy PTE Ltd and another*, [2020] SGCA 119, paragraphs 101–149.

273 *Andrews and others v Australia and New Zealand Banking Group Limited* (2012) 247 CLR 205.

274 *Cavendish Square B.V. v Makdessi, Parking Eye Limited v Beavis* [2015] UKSC 67, paragraph 1 6 4–16 6.

275 *Denka Advantech Private Limited and another v Seraya Energy PTE Ltd and another*, [2020] SGCA 119, paragraphs 101–149.

276 Three arbitration awards considering the effectiveness of JOA default clauses are discussed in ICC Dispute Resolution Bulletin 3 "Joint Operating Agreements in the International Oil & Gas Industry: ICC Arbitral Awards". *Mosaic Oil N.L. v Angari Pty. Ltd*, Supreme Court of New South Wales, (1990) 8 ACLC 780 (NSW) considered the validity of a JOA default clause triggered by insolvency of a JOA party, and decided it was unenforceable because it both infringed insolvency laws and the rule against penalties, particularly as it deprived the defaulting party of its participating interest without compensation.

to predict what may now happen if a JOA default clause is challenged by courts applying English-based legislation.

Chapter 1, Sections 7 and 8 looked at the principle "pay first, argue later", according to which the operator may call upon the parties to pay their participating interest shares of a cash call or invoice in full and on time, regardless of any concern that the payers may have with the legality or accuracy of the demand to the extent it follows the procedures established in the JOA and applicable law. The purpose of this provision is to prevent the operator from being faced with a cash flow crisis in the event that one or more of the parties decide to dispute the relevant demand for payment. This would force the operator either to finance the shortfall pending resolution of the dispute, or to incur liability to third parties supplying goods and services for joint operations for failure to pay them in accordance with the relevant procurement contract.[277] More significantly, it avoids the parties defaulting in respect of any payment due to the state with respect to the petroleum production licence or concession agreement, putting their petroleum title at risk. It is also in keeping with the principle that the operator should suffer no loss by reason of its role, save in the event of its wilful misconduct or gross negligence. Nor is it out of proportion because the non-operators will retain their rights to conduct an audit of the joint account and to raise, albeit retrospectively, any challenge to the correctness of payments they have previously made.[278]

To understand the relevance of the rule against penalties, it is first essential to describe the purpose and process of the standard JOA default clause. The clause provides remedies both to the operator and the non-defaulting parties for a non-payment by one party of amounts due under the JOA. Typically, this would involve a failure to pay that party's participating interest share of an invoice or cash call for funds required by the joint account. However, the JOA may define "default" in wider terms, including a failure to provide or maintain financial security when required to do so under the JOA, or a failure to make payment under an express indemnity set out in the JOA.[279] It is important to note that the default clause rarely applies to the breach of a non-pecuniary obligation, such as the obligation to lift a party's participating interest share of joint petroleum or to respect the confidentiality provisions of the JOA, where the appropriate remedy is not an action in debt, but ordinary damages instead, if not possibly specific performance. The significance of this point stems from the fact that the modern law with respect to penalties distinguishes between cases where the harm caused by breach of the relevant contract can be made good by the payment of damages or settlement of the debt, and cases where the harm cannot be adequately assessed in terms of any financial figure because of the nature of the interests put at risk by non-performance of the contract.

The Accounting Procedure will normally define the requirements for a valid cash call or invoice, as well as the required timing for its payment.[280] If these payment provisions are breached, the payer will be treated as a defaulting party for so long as the default persists. Typically, the operator will immediately issue the defaulting

277 P Roberts, R Fowler and E Pereira (eds), *The AIPN Joint Operating Agreement: A Practical Guide*, Globe Law and Business, 2019, 184.

278 See Section 6 of this chapter, "Accounting".

279 AIPN JOA §8.1.A; OGUK JOA §17.2; AMPLA JOA §& 15.2; Unusually, the AMPLA JOA provides two definitions of default; the "Breach Default Event" and the "Unpaid Monies Default Event", the former being connected with insolvency.

280 See Section 6 of this chapter, "Accounting".

party with a notice identifying the non-payment and giving the defaulting party a short grace period within which to make good the default.[281] A defaulting party could abuse such a provision by being guilty of defaults repeatedly, providing each breach is remedied before the establishment of forfeiture. In other words, a party may wrongfully use the other parties as temporary lenders. For this reason, some JOAs extend the definition of default to cover repeated late payments.[282]

If that grace period expires without payment, three consequences will likely follow according to the default clause; first, the relevant debt will accrue interest usually at a default rate, starting immediately on default or after a short grace period, until the default is paid.[283] Secondly, the defaulting party will be deprived of certain rights under the JOA for so long as the default persists; these routinely include:

- the right to attend and vote at OpCom;
- the right to receive information and reports with respect to joint operations;
- the right to approve transfers and/or pre-empt them;
- the right to receive its participating interest of joint petroleum; and
- the right to receive its participating interest share of the participating interest of any withdrawing or defaulting party.[284]

For the duration of the default, the defaulting party will be treated as having voted against any proposal for joint operations or exclusive operations.[285] If the default is subsequently made good, it is likely that the defaulting party will receive the information and reports held back during its default, but it will not be compensated for the missed opportunities to exercise its other rights during the default period.

The third consequence is particularly important for considering the legal implications of a default. Once the grace period has expired, the operator has the right to issue a notice to the non-defaulting parties, requiring them to pay their respective participating interest shares of the default to the joint account. If any non-defaulting party fails to make this payment, they are also treated as in default.[286] In this way, the impact of the default is "socialised", the shortfall in the joint account is made good and the operator is no longer exposed to direct liability from third parties or the state for failing to make payments due with respect to joint operations. However, if a non-defaulting party fails to pay its share of the default, then the risk arises that the default's impact will 'snowball' as each new default increases the amount payable by the remaining defaulters obliged to contribute – to the point where the overall default is not made good.[287] The AIPN JOA provides that in such circumstances the JOA and joint venture will be treated as terminated.[288]

If the default persists for a significant length of time, typically 30–60 days, the non-defaulting parties accrue the right to exercise certain further remedies

281 AIPN JOA §8.1.A; OGUK JOA §17.1; AMPLA JOA §15.1(a), 15.2(a).

282 P Roberts and R Fowler, *Joint Operating Agreements: A Practical Guide*, 4th edn, Globe Law and Business, 4th ed, 2020, p324.

283 AIPN JOA §8.1.B; OGUK JOA §17.3.1; AMPLA JOA §15.1(a), 15.3(a).

284 AIPN JOA §8.2.A; OGUK JOA §17.4, 5.

285 AIPN JOA §8.2.C.4; OGUK JOA §17.5.1.

286 AIPN JOA §8.3.A; OGUK JOA §17.2(b); AMPLA JOA §15.2(c). The AMPLA JOA is unusual in providing that the non-defaulting parties have the option to make good a default, at least until the default is lasted for 14 days, at which point the operator is obliged to serve them with a notice requiring them to make good the default.

287 AIPN JOA §8.3.B; OGUK JOA §17.2(c); AMPLA JOA §15.5(c).

288 AIPN JOA §8.3.E.

exercisable against the defaulter's participating interest.[289] The AIPN JOA offers the non-defaulting parties a range of options which they can choose to exercise depending on the circumstances; some model JOAs will provide only one option, or perhaps several options, expecting the drafters to choose a preferred single option for implementing in the final form of the agreement. In principle, the parties could choose between any of the following.

5.2 **Forfeiture**

The non-defaulting parties have the right to terminate the defaulting party's participation in the JOA, and to take its participating interest, each acquiring its respective participating interest share for no consideration whatsoever. Legally this may be expressed as an option to call upon the defaulter to withdraw from the JOA or by requiring the defaulter to transfer its participating interest to each non-defaulting party, possibly making use of a standing power of attorney.[290]

5.3 **Buy-out**

As a variant of the forfeiture mechanism, the non-defaulting parties may have the right to call upon the defaulter to sell its participating interest to them in proportion to their participating interests for a price normally expressed to be consistent with arm's-length market terms. Given the likelihood of a dispute on the valuation of the defaulter's participating interest, this variant usually provides for the sale price to be assessed by an expert. The default amount (including accrued interest), the cost of sale and possibly an additional allowance will then be deducted from the assessed value of the defaulter's participating interest and the balance paid to the defaulter, who then ceases to be a party to the JOA.[291]

5.4 **Forced sale**

This is another variant of the forfeiture mechanism, under which the non-defaulting parties may have the right to call upon the defaulter to put its participating interest on the market, and to sell it, applying the proceeds first to compensating the non-defaulting parties for the default amount. Again, the operator will conduct such sale, if there is a power of attorney in place enabling it to act instead of the defaulter.

5.5 **Withering interest**

Under this mechanism, the defaulting party is required to transfer to the non-defaulting parties a proportion of its participating interest which is valued to be equivalent to the amount in default (usually with an allowance for transaction costs). In the AIPN JOA version of this mechanism, allowance is also made for the defaulting party's previous payments of cash calls, allowing the defaulter to keep more of its participating interest if it has properly paid a significant proportion of its cash calls in the past and has in that sense 'earned' the right to keep its rights to a greater proportion of the joint property in which it has invested.[292]

---

289 AIPN JOA §8.4.D; OGUK JOA §17.6.1; AMPLA JOA §15.6.
290 AIPN JOA §8.4.E; OGUK JOA §17.6.
291 AIPN JOA §8.4.F; OGUK JOA §17.7; AMPLA JOA §15.6(a)(ii).
292 AIPN JOA §8.4.G.

5.6 Mortgage foreclosure

The JOA may provide that the parties grant each other a charge or mortgage over their respective participating interests, on terms that allow that charge to be foreclosed in the event of default, entitling the non-defaulting parties to exercise their right of sale as mortgagees. As such, the non-defaulting parties will hold the proceeds of such sale for the account of the defaulting party, with the right to deduct the default amount in satisfaction of the debt owed to them.[293]

These default remedies share two weaknesses in common; their implementation relies upon some level of cooperation by the defaulting party, in default of which the parties may need to resort to legal action in the appropriate court to force the defaulting party's hand, and secondly, the non-defaulting parties will need the approval and consent of the state and/or local regulator to the change in participating interests and (where applicable) the elimination of the defaulting party from the joint venture.

As explained at the beginning of this section, a default has three potential outcomes: (i) the defaulting party loses certain rights under the JOA for so long as the default lasts; (ii) the non-defaulting parties are obliged to pay their participating interest shares of the default; and (iii) ultimately the defaulting party is at risk of being deprived of some or all of its participating interest, through the application of one of the enforcement mechanisms described above. Only (ii) is a consequence of the default which requires the payment of money, in this case by non-defaulting parties and in this case without any increase or incremental compensation to the operator which could be argued as penal. Step (iii) involves the payment of money to the defaulting party in consideration of the interest it is forced to give up only in the cases of buy-out, forced sale, withering interest and mortgage interest options discussed above.

However, in *Cavendish v Makdessi*, the English Supreme Court concluded that the rule against penalties could be applied to any remedy, not only a remedy requiring the payment of money (with the possible exception of deprivation of proprietary or possessory rights in land, for which relief against forfeiture may be the exclusive remedy).[294] The cases of non-payment remedies considered by the court as potentially penal included, typically, the non-refund of deposits or instalments of the contract price paid in advance.[295, 296] Generally, there are few reported English cases where the defaulting party is deprived of contractual rights and effectively expelled from the joint venture as an alternative to the recovery of a debt or claim for money damages.[297] In *Cavendish*, Makdessi was held in breach of certain restrictive covenants in connection with the sale of his company before certain instalments of the purchase price were due, entitling the purchasers to require Makdessi to sell his remaining shareholding at a reduced price, compared to the price applicable had

---

293 AIPN JOA §8.4.H.

294 *Cavendish Square B.V. v Makdessi, Parking Eye Limited v Beavis* [2015] UKSC 67 Para 17.

295 *Ibid*, Para 35.

296 *Cavendish* also considered the case of *Jobson v Johnson* ([1989] 1 WLR 1026) where a purchaser of shares in a football club was required to re-transfer the shares back to the sellers at an undervalue for failure to pay an instalment of the purchase price, which the Court of Appeal recognised as penal.

297 There have been two Australian cases of note: *Mosaic Oil N.L. v Angari Pty. Ltd*, and *CRA Ltd v New Zealand Goldfields Investments* [1989] V.R. 873, analysed in M Lishman, "Penalties and Relief against Forfeiture of Joint Venture Interests" *AMPLA Yearbook* available at http://classic.austlii.edu.au/au/journals/AURELawJl/2008/26.pdf.

Makdessi performed his restrictive covenants; it was not a case where the breach gave the innocent parties the right to expel Makdessi from his shareholding against his will. In *BICC v Burndy*,[298] the English Court of Appeal considered the contractual provisions in place to handle the dissolution of the joint venture between two parties triggered by Burndy's breach of the joint-venture agreement but considered the applicability of the relief against forfeiture and not the rule against penalties. Lastly, *Richards and another v IP Solutions* considered the validity of a provision which required director employees summarily dismissed from the company to sell their shares for a nominal consideration and decided that the provision would be enforceable as a secondary obligation.[299]

The Australian, English and Singaporean courts have gone three different ways in deciding whether the rule against penalties is only applicable to remedies defined by contract and triggered by the breach of another obligation in that contract – otherwise defined as "secondary obligations". *Prima facie*, this distinction is not important for JOA default clauses because the definition of default in each of the industry model JOAs links the remedy squarely to breach of a JOA provision. In *Cavendish*, the Supreme Court commented that the law should follow substance and not form in distinguishing between such secondary obligations and "conditional primary obligations" where the relevant clause offered a party an alternative means of performance, rather than a mechanism for compensating a failure to perform.[300]

However, this is an oversimplification. The judges in *Cavendish* refused to classify a clause expelling a joint-venture party as a primary or secondary obligation, leaving it open for later cases to take either approach depending on the facts the individual case. However difficult and artificial it may seem, a distinction needs to be drawn between a financial provision which sets the price which the defaulting party must accept for its participating interest shares as part of the mechanics for expelling that party (a primary obligation) and a provision which sets out to compensate the non-defaulting parties by allowing them to take the defaulting party's participating interest at an undervalue (a secondary obligation).[301] In the confusion, English courts and Australian courts have parted company; the English court in *Richards* was not concerned that the directors having employment contracts with the company would have been compensated for £1 for their shares, whereas the Australian court in *Ringrow*[302] considered that any discount to the market price must be extravagant and unconscionable, and out of all proportion, making reference to Lord Dunedin's tests in *Dunlop*, if it was to be considered penal.

In other respects, the *Cavendish* decision simplified the rule against penalties as it might apply to JOA default clauses. First, it dismissed the argument that clauses were potentially penal if they had the purpose of deterring a party from breaching a contractual provision.[303] Secondly, the court clarified the manner in which the tests

298 *BICC plc v Burndy Corpn* [1985] Ch 232; discussed in Cavendish at Para 17.

299 [2016] EWHC 1835 (QB). The court also held that the pricing provision could be considered a primary obligation in so far as it simply defined the price payable for shares transferred on departure of the director employee, the same clause providing that a market price will be payable to direct employees departing as "good leavers".

300 *Cavendish*, paras 15, 23, 28, 152.

301 In *Richards*, the court placed much store by the fact that the relevant pricing provision was in a separate document to the Company's Articles of Association which provided for expulsion of a "bad leaver".

302 *Ringrow Pty Ltd v BP Australia Pty Ltd* (2005) 222 ALR 306.

303 *Cavendish*, Paras 31, 248.

set out in Lord Dunedin's judgment in *Dunlop*[304] should be applied – not as hard and fast defining criteria, but as guidance,[305] expressing the general scope of the rule against penalties in these words:

> *The true test is whether the impugned provision is a secondary obligation which imposes a detriment on the contract breaker out of all proportion to any legitimate interest of the innocent party in the enforcement of the primary obligation. The innocent party can have no proper interest in simply punishing the defaulter. His interest is in performance or in some appropriate alternative to performance. In the case of a straightforward damages clause, that interest will rarely extend beyond compensation for the breach, and we therefore expect that Lord Dunedin's four tests would usually be perfectly adequate to determine its validity. But compensation is not necessarily the only legitimate interest that the innocent party may have in the performance of the defaulter's primary obligations.*[306]

It is significant that Lord Dunedin's tests for penalties set out in his judgment in *Dunlop* were approved by the court in *Cavendish*, albeit as guidance and not exhaustive rules, because Lord Dunedin's second test states:

> *It will be held to be a penalty if the breach consists only in not paying a sum of money, and the sum stipulated is a sum greater than the sum which ought to have been paid.*[307]

The case for JOA default clauses to answer is simply stated – if the trigger for a default is failure to make a payment, why is the remedy which deprives the defaulting party of its participating interest, not penal, given that the value of the participating interest may vastly exceed the default amount and may significantly overcompensate the non-defaulting parties? Furthermore, why is it not penal to deprive the defaulting party of certain rights (to receive information, to vote and attend OpCom) before it has been expelled from the joint venture as a result of the forfeiture mechanisms which only apply if the default persists? Put positively, can a "legitimate interest" be identified which justifies these provisions, despite the fact that the loss to the defaulting party, and the gain to the non-defaulting parties, may be out of all proportion with the default which triggered the remedy?

Dunlop and *Cavendish* give examples as to the kind of legitimate interest that might be engaged; in *Dunlop*, Lord Atkinson considered that it was legitimate for Dunlop to recover the sum of £5 for every occasion when a garage resold Dunlop products in breach of recommended resale prices, because Dunlop had an interest in maintaining an overall marketing business system which required there to be no exception to its pricing strategy.[308] In *Cavendish*, goodwill formed a considerable proportion of the value of the marketing company the claimants purchased, the value of such goodwill being effectively eliminated in the event that Makdessi not only failed to support the company after he sold it, but set up in competition with it.

---

304 *Dunlop Pneumatic Tyre Co Ltd v New Garage and Motor Co Ltd* [1915]AC 79.

305 *Cavendish*, Para 142.

306 *Cavendish*, Para 32.

307 Quoted in *Cavendish*, Para 142.

308 Considered in *Cavendish*, Para 23.

In the leading judgment in *Cavendish*, the judges placed some emphasis on contractual provisions triggered by a breach of loyalty upon which the contract relied. Makdessi had in a sense overturned the rationale behind the deal for the purchase of his shares by showing disloyalty to the business as a going concern. The judges said:

> *Loyalty is indivisible. Its absence in a business like this introduces a very significant business risk whose impact cannot be measured simply by reference to the known and provable consequences of particular breaches.*[309]

Can it be argued that a defaulting party that has caused the non-defaulting parties to have to make good its default on short notice and has persisted in failing to pay no longer represents a reliable counterparty? Given that the non-defaulting parties must pay and argue later, is it not legitimate for them to have the right to expel a defaulting party to avoid repetition of such defaults? Unless the default is redeemed, the non-defaulting parties can reasonably expect to have to carry on making good default after default, and, until the defaulting party's participating interest is forfeited, their claim against the defaulting party is unsecured. Before an English court, the non-defaulting parties can say that there was a legitimate interest in eliminating an unreliable party from the joint venture after its default; and before an Australian court, and the court in *Richards*, they could also argue that the sale of the participating interest, even at an undervalue, was a primary obligation triggered by certain events, including a defaulted cash call or invoice.

There are several problems with these lines of argument; first, the JOA terms are not entirely consistent with them. As discussed in Chapter 1, Section 8, JOAs routinely exclude any fiduciary duty or duty of good faith as between the JOA parties,[310] and English law respects that choice.[311] The relationship between the parties is in that sense at arm's length and is intended to be fully described by the express terms of the JOA. Apparently, loyalty does not come into it.

Secondly, the parties run the risk that one of their number will leave the joint venture and cause their exposure to cost and liability to increase proportionately, if a party elects to withdraw, a matter which is entirely beyond their control.[312] The withdrawing party is not in breach of any obligation of loyalty by doing so. For the non-defaulting parties, there is no difference in the outcome between the case where a defaulting party which remedies its default and then serves notice to withdraw, and a party which simply exercises its right to withdraw.[313] The position might be different if the JOA required a withdrawing party to provide financial security for its ongoing liabilities, especially for decommissioning costs[314] – which a party may avoid if it is expelled from the JOA through the default mechanism. If that were the case, it would be more convincing to argue that the taking of a defaulting party's interest regardless of the amount in default is legitimate, because it would go some

309 *Cavendish*, Para 75.
310 AIPN JOA§14.1.
311 *Ross River Ltd and another v Waverley Commercial Ltd and others* [2013] EWCA Civ 910.
312 AIPN JOA§13.1; OGUK JOA§24.2; AMPLA JOA§12.2(b).
313 See Chapter 1, Section 15, "Relinquishment, surrender and withdrawal".
314 AMPLA JOA 12.2(c).

way to compensate the non-defaulting parties for the lack of financial security that they would have obtained from the defaulting party had it withdrawn from the JOA, and provided financial security in accordance with that provision. The loss that may be caused to the non-defaulting parties by reason of a defaulting party leaving the joint venture without leaving any security for its ongoing liabilities would be unascertainable, but tangible, potentially justifying liquidated damages, if not forfeiture of the defaulting party's interest.

As previously mentioned, the AIPN JOA provides the non-defaulting parties with a range of remedies to choose from, and in principle allows each non-defaulting party to make their own choice of remedy. This optionality would make it harder to argue that the parties have a common legitimate interest in the elimination of unreliable parties – because there would then be a choice to expel the defaulter (by choosing a forced sale or forfeiture option) or to allow the defaulter to remain (by choosing the withering interest option).[315]

Another example of how JOAs respond to behaviour by a party that may jeopardise the relationship of reliability fundamental to a joint venture relates to the breach of anti-bribery and corruption covenants. The AIPN 2012 Model introduces a new optional provision permitting a party to withdraw from the JOA if its withdrawal is motivated by another party's breach of anti-bribery and corruption undertakings, without prejudice to the withdrawing party's right to an indemnity for losses arising from that breach of covenant.[316, 317] While this provision is consistent with the notion that joint ventures require the participants to follow minimum standards of reliability and compliance, the remedy for breach in this case is the complete opposite of the default clause, anticipating the innocent party having to leave the joint venture, albeit potentially with financial compensation, and leaving the defaulting party on seat. Would it not be more consistent with the concept of joint-venture loyalty if the breach of anti-bribery and corruption covenants would entitle the other parties to expel the perpetrator, by forcing a sale of its participating interests, out of the proceeds of which the other parties might legitimately be compensated for any pecuniary loss arising from such breach? Indeed, the reputational damage which the right to withdraw seeks to protect or mitigate is exactly the form of unascertainable loss which the courts recognise may justify liquidated damages, even in very significant amounts.[318]

It is wrong to suggest that the preservation of contractual relations based on loyalty is the only form of legitimate interest that might justify a penalty. The garage dealing with Dunlop operated at arm's length. But the point remains that the JOA

315 AIPN JOA 8.4.K provides that the non-defaulting parties can exercise whichever remedy whenever and how so often as they may jointly desire.

316 A similar point can be made with respect to sanctions legislation. In 2014, the United States introduced Ukraine-Related Sanctions Regulations, 31 C.F.R. part 589, prohibiting relevant persons from transacting with individuals connected with Ukraine crisis and listed on the list of specially designated individuals maintained by the Office of Foreign Assets Control of the US State Department. These regulations make it unlawful for relevant persons to deal with the property and interests of specially designated individuals, which include significant leaders in the Russian oil and gas industry. None of the model JOAs adequately address the position of the operator and other non-operators in the event that a joint-venture party is managed and/or owned by such an individual.

317 AIPN JOA §13.3.

318 *Cavendish*, Para 23.

terms themselves do not protect the non-defaulting parties' interests in a consistent way, making it less easy to argue that a default threatens the parties' 'legitimate interest' in the commercial order and relationships upon which the joint venture is founded.

Alternatively, can it be argued that the parties have a legitimate interest in preserving the financial integrity of the joint venture, particularly when that is linked to compliance with payment obligations under the relevant licence or concession agreement? *Prima facie*, the JOA terms are consistent with that line of argumentation – cash calls and invoices must be paid on time and disputes deferred till later, and the non-defaulting parties are required to make good a default in order to preserve joint-venture cash flow. JOAs routinely control the creditworthiness of any third party to whom an existing party may transfer their interests, either by enabling the non-transferring parties to veto a transfer, or to defeat the transfer by pre-empting it.[319]

However, the AIPN JOA default clause provides that any failure to make good the default ultimately results in the termination of the JOA and joint venture, and not the enforcement of the default against the participating interest of the defaulter.[320] In other words, the default enforcement mechanisms may act as a deterrent against default, may underpin the expectation of financial reliability each party has of each other, may compensate the non-defaulting parties for paying their contribution to the default and may avoid the non-defaulting parties having to make such contribution in future, but it does not ultimately play a role in securing the financial integrity of joint-venture cash flows. Perhaps to protect the operator from having to finance any shortfall, the JOA is terminated forthwith, rather than waiting for the outcome of any enforcement of the default against participating interests.

One final point emerging from *Cavendish*: if there is a legitimate interest justifying a provision that would otherwise be penal, it is not material that the provision might be triggered in cases where the pecuniary loss caused by the relevant breach may be ascertainable and insignificant. The court in *Cavendish* affirmed the decision in *Dunlop* that the mischief which was intended to be addressed by the penalty of £5 for every sale of Dunlop products in breach of the distribution agreement was not any loss of revenue to Dunlop as such arising from each such sale, but rather the potential unravelling of its distribution strategy, the harm to which could not be ascertained.[321] This answers the challenge that the failure to make payment under a JOA may trigger a default and the deprivation of a participating interest which is significantly more valuable, either at the time of default, or later, than the missed payment. But at the same time, it does not detract from the point that such an outcome must still be justified by a legitimate interest of the nature described in *Cavendish*.

This in particular meets the point that the scale of default and its significance may depend on the phase in joint operations when it occurs; if the default occurs when the parties are engaged in performing minimum work obligations, the default may

---

319 AIPN JOA §12.2.D; OGUK JOA §23.2; AMPLA JOA §14.5.

320 AIPN JOA §8.3.E.

321 *Cavendish*, Para 23.

seriously threaten the integrity of the licence at a time when there is no production which the non-defaulting parties can use to recoup their contribution to the default amount. Conversely, if the asset is in production, it could be argued that the non-defaulting parties should simply wait until their contribution to the default has been offset by the proceeds of sale of the defaulting party's share of production. Again, that is not inconsistent with the point that they may have a legitimate interest in expelling a party whose reliability can no longer be taken for granted.

By way of conclusion on the impact of *Cavendish* on JOA default clauses, it can be said that the case opens a door for the justification of default clauses by reference to the parties' legitimate interests in having financially reliable and/or loyal partners and/or by arguing that the default clause merely provides the mechanics by which an unreliable partner is expelled. However, the standard terms of JOAs have evolved over time in such a way that makes it harder to argue that case. The dilemmas which JOAs routinely address (in what circumstances should the partners provide credit support for their obligations? Should partners be permitted to withdraw from the JOA, with or without giving security for accrued obligations? Should partners owe each other a duty of good faith loyalty or fiduciary duties?) have been resolved in a somewhat piecemeal fashion, usually with a preference for a *laissez faire* approach. Accordingly, a JOA default clause may be defensible in isolation in terms of legitimate interests it protects, but any such clause must be interpreted and applied, taking into account all the relevant terms of the JOA, making it potentially more difficult in some cases to persuade a court that the JOA as a whole is consistent with such "legitimate interest". After all, it is no good drafting some self-serving statement into the JOA, claiming that the JOA is consistent with such legitimate interest, if other express provisions of the JOA contradict that statement; after *Cavendish*, if not before, the courts will prefer substance over form.

Some of this uncertainty can be avoided. After all, a clause is not penal unless the disbenefit to the defaulting party is out of all proportion to the harm its breach is likely to cause.[322] If that is not the case, there is no need to justify it by reference to any form of "legitimate interest". Accordingly, JOA drafters should look carefully at the default options, preferring those options such as the withering interest option, and forced sale options, which require the non-defaulting parties to repay the defaulting party the balance (if any) of the proceeds of sale, having deducted the relevant default amount. The disadvantage with the withering interest option to the non-defaulting parties is that the defaulting party remains a participant, albeit with a reduced participating interest. It is submitted that the fairest and most balanced choice of remedy therefore is the forced sale, whereby the defaulting party is expelled, but the compensation it is forced to pay is proportionate. Concerns about the valuation of the participating interest are exaggerated; such issues arise in the valuation of a participating interest for the purposes of pre-emption on transfer, or indeed the enforcement of the right of sale by a mortgagee in possession, and can be mitigated by appointing an expert to resolve any valuation dispute.[323]

The question was asked above whether it was defensible to prevent a defaulting party from exercising certain JOA rights for the duration of its default, even if it subsequently redeemed that default. In one sense, this provision is consistent with the argument that JOA parties expect a minimum level of reliability from each other,

322 *Cavendish*, Para 32, as quoted above.
323 For example OGUK JOA §17.7.

and that the privileges of participation should be withdrawn for so long as such reliability is in doubt. The issue is that these rights are not restored retrospectively when the default is redeemed; the opportunity to vote and participate in joint operations is lost forever even if the default is later redeemed (although some JOAs might be construed to suggest that a defaulting party may buy-back into a sole risk operation which it was deemed to non-consent during its period in default[324]). Arguably, this outcome is not out of proportion with the harm caused to the non-defaulting parties arising from the uncertainty about the reliability and financial creditworthiness of the defaulting party for so long as the default continues. The defaulting party will be aware of the OpCom votes it risks missing, and in principle has the opportunity to make good the default and reinstate its rights to attend and vote before they are lost.

However, the circumstances might provide the defaulting party with the right to invoke equity and the relief against forfeiture. *Cavendish* confirmed that this remedy can apply to the deprivation of rights under a joint venture (commenting on *BICC v Burndy*).[325] As long as the defaulting party can convince the court that it is just and equitable on the balance of conveniences to intervene, the court may allow the defaulting party more time in which to redeem its default, potentially reinstating the defaulting party's privileges on condition that the default is redeemed on terms set by the court. One can foresee the non-defaulting parties objecting strongly, however, to such an outcome because it would be difficult to unravel the outcome of an OpCom vote in which the defaulting party participated, only for it then to fail to redeem its default and for its interests subsequently to be taken.

The rule against penalties tries to define the borderline between parties' freedom to contract on mutually agreed terms, and the jurisdiction of the courts to define the limits of appropriate compensation for breach of those terms. The JOA default clause may also conflict with the rights of a trustee in bankruptcy or liquidator to obtain control of a bankrupt party's assets and to monetise them for the benefit of all that party's creditors in accordance with the principles of insolvency law. Here again, there is a conflict between the freedom of contract and the rights of third parties as creditors of the defaulter. If a party defaults under a JOA and subsequently is the subject of bankruptcy proceedings, the remedies which the non-defaulting parties may have exercised (or be in the process of exercising when the bankruptcy order is made) may be reversed by the courts, forcing the non-defaulting parties to repay compensation recovered from the defaulting party so that it can be allocated to all the creditors in proportion to the debts owed to them (the *pari passu* principle). Alternatively, a party may be subject to bankruptcy proceedings before any default arises, with the result that the non-defaulting parties find that they are unable to exercise their JOA remedies against the defaulter when, in due course, a default arises, because the bankruptcy proceedings initiated a moratorium with respect to dealings in the defaulter's assets. Simply put, it is no good trying to devise a JOA default clause which survives the rule against penalties if it is likely to be defeated by insolvency legislation; if a defaulter has failed to make good the default after 60 days of waiting, the chances that bankruptcy and liquidation will follow are high.

Using the example of English law, insolvency law is likely to be relevant for two different reasons – first, any contractual provision which has the effect of putting

---

324 AIPN JOA §8.2.C.

325 *Cavendish*, Para 17; *BICC plc v Burndy Corpn* [1985] Ch 232.

assets of the defaulting party beyond the reach of bankruptcy proceedings may infringe the anti-deprivation rule in common law; secondly, the provision may also call into play specific statutory rules preventing the defaulter from granting preferences to third parties which unfairly prejudice other creditors. The *pari passu* principle, also a common law rule, is applied almost without exception and the rules applicable to the order of priorities between different classes of creditors are fixed by statute.

As discussed above, default is normally defined in terms of a failure to pay a cash call or invoice, failure to honour an indemnity or put up financial security. The event of insolvency is not normally a separate event of default. As long as insolvency is not included in the JOA definition of an event of default, it is therefore possible to argue that the intention and objective of a JOA default clause is not to defeat the rights of the trustee in bankruptcy and to put the defaulting party's participating interest out of reach of its other creditors. As with the rule against penalties, the non-defaulting parties can claim that the primary objective of the JOA default clause is to expel an unreliable party, and that the treatment of its participating interest as a financial asset is an ancillary matter.

Can the courts be expected to accept such an argument? The trend of English case law is in favour of upholding the commercial transactions which allow for their termination in the event of one party's insolvency, particularly if the transaction is reciprocal and there is no evidence of any blatant intention to put assets beyond the reach of other creditors. Lord Mance in *Belmont Park Investments Pty Ltd v BNY Corporate Trustee Services Ltd* said:

> *Where a contract provides for the performance in the future of reciprocal obligations, the performance of each of which is the quid pro quo of the other, I see nothing objectionable or evasive about a provision entitling one party to terminate if the other becomes bankrupt.*[326]

Whilst the decision in *Belmont* has been heavily criticised by commentators,[327] it has largely been followed by English courts since.[328] However, in another decision relating to the same issue triggered by collapse of the Lehman Brothers bank in 2008, the US Bankruptcy Court of the southern district of New York held that such provisions infringe the US Bankruptcy Code.[329] As discussed in *Fibria Cellulose*, the Canadian and Korean courts would also likely challenge the effectiveness of the clause permitting termination of the contract upon a party's insolvency (*ipso facto* clauses).

Under English law at least, given that a JOA default is triggered by non-payment and not insolvency, it seems only a remote risk that a liquidator will successfully make the case that the exercise of a JOA default clause depriving the defaulter of its participating interest blatantly intended to remove that interest from the defaulter's bankruptcy assets.

However, the English courts may take a more lenient approach to the anti-deprivation rule precisely because English statute law provides the bankruptcy trustee with statutory remedies which can override such contractual provisions.

---

326 [2012] AC 383 para 177.

327 Sarah Worthington, "Good Faith, Flawed Assets and the Emasculation of the UK Anti-Deprivation Rule", *The Modern Law Review* 75(1) (2012) 112–121.

328 *Fibria Cellulose S/A v (1) Pan Ocean Co. Ltd; (2) Mr. You Sik Kim* [2014] EWHC 2124 (Ch).

329 Re Lehman Bros Holdings Inc 422 BR 407.

In a bankruptcy governed by English law, the liquidator can apply to court for an order setting aside a transaction by which the bankrupt party disposed of assets at an undervalue within two years before the onset of insolvency;[330] the liquidator can also ask the court to set aside a transaction by which the bankrupt party puts one of its creditors in a preferential position compared to other creditors, if that transaction took place six months before the onset of insolvency;[331] it can also ask for extortionate credit bargains[332] or floating charges[333] to be set aside by the court if they are entered into shortly before insolvency. Lastly and most significantly, there is a general power for the court to set aside transactions at an undervalue which have the intention of putting assets beyond the reach of the creditor making a claim upon the asset holder – a power which may be exercised inside and outside the context of insolvency and has no special time limitation, save for the ordinary six-year limitation period.[334]

It is irrelevant to the application of these rules whether or not the JOA default clause is a penalty. As noted above, a payment default may presage insolvency and there is every prospect that a JOA default clause will be triggered by a failure to make payment and the appropriate default remedies initiated within the "suspect period" before insolvency when a transaction may in principle be challenged under these powers.

However, there is a case to be made that the relevant transaction from the perspective of the defaulter is not made when it transfers its participating interest pursuant to the default clause under compulsion (which may in any event be performed by the operator or the non-defaulting parties acting under a power of attorney), but when it agreed to the default clause by its signature of the JOA. In that case it will be easier for the defaulting party to argue that it entered into the JOA in good faith, in the conduct of its ordinary business and it had good reasons for believing that the JOA would advance its business, giving it a defence to several of these possible actions. With respect to Section 423, the English Court of Appeal has recently confirmed that the defaulting party must intend to put the relevant assets beyond the reach of a claimant, albeit that may not be the only intention of his actions; that would hardly apply at the time the JOA was signed by its parties.[335]

Is it possible to identify a pathway through the rule against penalties and insolvency legislation that would, as far as possible, guarantee the enforceability of the JOA default clause? One Australian case has recognised the logic and legitimacy behind the non-defaulting parties' right to expel a defaulter because of the costs of offshore drilling, the low prospect of success, and the need to spread risk and the scarcity of high-risk capital.[336] However, if the defaulter is not compensated for the participating interest, it then forfeits. Further, if the other terms of the JOA are not consistent with that logic, and perhaps if the JOA default clause is not automatic but leaves the non-defaulting parties with options whether or not to take the defaulter's participating interest, and if so how much of it, then this "legitimate interest" may

---

330 Insolvency Act 1986 s. 238.
331 *Ibid*, s. 239.
332 *Ibid*, s. 244.
333 *Ibid*, s. 245.
334 *Ibid*, s. 423.
335 *JSC BTA Bank v Mukhtar Ablyazov, Madiyar Ablyazov* [2018] EWCA Civ 1176.
336 *Monarch Petroleum NL v Citco Australia Petroleum Ltd* [1986] WAR 310 at 352.

not look so legitimate when scrutinised by a court. It would assist if JOA parties did not mix up the legitimate objective of expelling an unreliable party and the financial consequences of doing so. When a withdrawing party exercises its right to withdraw, it does so voluntarily, knowing that it will not be rewarded for the participating interest it gives up; by contrast, the defaulting party loses its participating interest against its will, and should be compensated for the residual value in its participating interest, its outstanding debt having been paid from the proceeds. If the priority of the JOA default clause is to achieve the expulsion of a defaulter at a minimum risk of a legal challenge, then any financial windfall to the non-defaulters arising from the defaulter's participating interest should be surrendered. Such an approach would put the non-defaulters in a strong position to resist the rule against penalties, the anti-deprivation principle and the provisions of the Insolvency Act discussed above.

Another major difficulty in implementing the default provision in a JOA arises when a national oil company is a member of the consortium. This is a clear example of a situation where a right may exist, but its implementation could be very complex and risky.[337] The national oil company is unlikely to accept a default process, and the government may intervene to protect the national company's interest, or even terminate the host government contract and award a new contract to the national oil company.

This issue of governmental approval is a reminder of the need to harmonise the procedures established in the JOA and the granting instrument. The parties will face an awkward situation if the provisions in the two instruments do not correspond.[338]

Therefore, the JOA parties must be aware of all the implications of the default provision and its potential alternatives. Even if the courts recognise the enforceability of a total forfeiture provision, the non-defaulting parties may face a series of additional problems, such as the defaulting party being unwilling to assign its interest (ie, if a power of attorney is not provided), ongoing liabilities and governmental approval.[339]

In summary, the necessity of balanced and fair terms in the default provision is clear, because, first, the provision affects all the parties involved. Secondly, the outcome of the default provision may rely on third parties (ie, court ratification or governmental approval). On the other hand, it is also important to stress the seriousness of this provision, as a failure to contribute financially could jeopardise the whole consortium. Thus, this provision must be carefully drafted in order to protect the non-defaulting parties' interests, but also in a way that secures an enforceable and reasonable resolution in accordance with the applicable law. So, the applicable law and the options available might be critical to determine the validity of such remedy and its proportionality. In addition, the stage of the project may be a relevant consideration in certain legal systems.

---

337 P Roberts and R Fowler, *Joint Operating Agreements: A Practical Guide*, 4th edn, Globe Law and Business, 2020, p80.

338 *Ibid*, p113.

339 See: H Dundas, *Joint Operating Agreements: An Introduction*, 1994 Summer Programme: UK Oil and Gas Law, CPMLP 09/09, 1994, p10; C Duval, H Le Leuch, A Pertuzio and JL Weaver, *International Petroleum and Exploration Agreements: Legal, Economic & Policy Aspects*, 2nd edn, Barrows, 2009, p299; S Shaw, "Joint Operating Agreements" in MR David, *Upstream Oil and Gas Agreements*, Sweet & Maxwell, 1996, p25; C Thorpe, *Fundamentals of Upstream Petroleum Agreements*, CP Thorpe, 2008, pp138–140; C Golvala, "Upstream joint ventures – bidding and operating agreements" in G Picton-Tubervill (ed.), *Oil and Gas: A Practical Handbook*, Globe Law and Business, 2009, pp49–51; MPG Taylor and SM Tyne, *Taylor and Winsor on Joint Operating Agreements*, 2nd edn, Longman, 1992, pp77–81.

Assuming that a non-operator has a larger financial interest than the operator, it is important to ensure that the JOA provides fair and balanced provisions to remedy any default within a reasonable time, as well the consequences of the default, and the risk that the operation of the clause will be challenged by the defaulting party or its insolvency trustee.

5.7 Analysis of model JOAs

The following paragraphs examine the approach taken by each JOA in order to understand the consequences of a default and the possible outcomes for the non-operators.

AAPL Form 810 provides a default provision in an attachment to the JOA, rather that within the JOA itself. This approach is not common among JOAs.

Attachment F to AAPL Form 810 contains a default provision. If a party fails to pay its cash call contributions, the operator will issue it with a default notice. The party must remedy the situation within 30 days otherwise it will be in default. It is relevant to note that the AAPL form assumes that the defaulting party is a non-operator, otherwise the operator would have to issue a notice to itself.

Once the default is established, the consequences for the defaulting party are that, first, it will lose most of its rights until a remedy is fully provided, such as losing the right to vote and the right to obtain information, among others. If a proposal for work is made during the default period, the defaulting party will be considered a non-consenting party unless unanimity within the consortium is required.[340] If no payment is made within 60 days, the non-defaulting parties can take more severe action.

AAPL Form 810 does not provide for a forfeiture of interest but rather a security interest and mortgage to secure payment of the consortium's applicable costs and expenditure.[341] The non-operators grant a mortgage and security interest over their participating interest and any production and property participation related to the consortium in favour of the operator. In turn, the operator grants a mortgage and security interest over the same things in favour of the non-operators. However, there is a reciprocal limitation on the applicable mortgage of US$25 million dollars, as this is required by law, otherwise there will be no limitation. In addition, it is important to stress that a reciprocal power of attorney is also provided for all participants in order to execute the applicable security interest.[342]

Therefore, it could be suggested that AAPL Form 810 avoids the risks inherent with the forfeiture option by adopting the mortgage option. However, such a solution must be in full compliance with local legislation and also with the granting instrument, otherwise it will not be an effective solution. Nevertheless, such a solution may work only in the development or production phase; the participating interest during the decommissioning stage may not be worth anything or no production or property will be available to secure such costs. Finally, it is important to note that the form does not address the issue of ongoing liabilities related to the defaulting interest.

In conclusion, the AAPL JOA Model Form avoids the forfeiture option for enforcement of a default by adopting the mortgage security option over the

340 AAPL JOA Model Form 810 Attachment F §6.3(b).
341 AAPL JOA Model Form 810 Attachment F §6.3(a).
342 AAPL JOA Model Form 810 Attachment F §6.3(c).

participating interest or any available production or joint property. The forms' major shortcomings are their failure to address ongoing liabilities related to the default interest and their reliance on the market value of the participating interest or any availability of production or joint property, which may result in the secured interest not having sufficient value to secure the applicable default.

The RMMLF JOA Model provides the shortest default provision of all the JOAs. There is no provision for any procedure involving default, except for the creation of reciprocal liens among the JOA parties and the right to acquire the defaulting share of production.[343] Conversely, such a liberal approach could put a defaulting party in a critical situation, as the time to remedy the default may not be sufficient.

However, this simple provision contains several flaws. First, this approach might work during the development stage when production is available, but it will not be effective during the exploration stage. Secondly, there is no power of attorney so the non-defaulting parties may have problems enforcing the lien. Thirdly, there is no provision regarding decommissioning obligations. Fourthly, there is no suspension of the defaulting party's rights under the JOA. In this sense, the defaulting party maintains its right to receive information and to elect to participate in a proposal of work.

The Canadian Operating Procedure takes a different approach from the other JOAs. It gives authority to the operator to request from each other party proof, in a manner which is satisfactory to the operator, that it has the financial resources to secure the approved work and programme.[344] However, the non-operators may refuse to provide such security if they believe it is unreasonable. In this case, the parties must use a dispute resolution process to resolve the issue. It is important to stress that this provision does not work in reverse, as there is no obligation on the operator to demonstrate its financial resources to the non-operators.

The operator will issue a default notice to the defaulting party and provide the other parties with a copy, but only for their information.[345] If the defaulting party does not remedy its default within five days, it will face several consequences.[346] First, it will have to pay interest on top of the default. Secondly, it will lose its right to receive information. Thirdly, it will not be able to participate in any of the consortium's activities. If the default persists for more than 30 days, the defaulting party will also lose its production share to the other parties and its rights over the joint property. Finally, if the default persists for more than 60 days, the non-defaulting parties may enforce the lien of interest that is established on every party's participating interest.[347] It is important to note that all remedies provided in the agreement are cumulative rather than restrictive.[348]

It is relevant to note that this provision was drafted for the situation where the defaulting party is a non-operator, even though there is a special provision referring to the operator as the defaulting party.[349]

It could be suggested that the Canadian Operating Procedure adopts a fairly similar approach to the American Models as they avoid forfeiture, withering and buy-out options but focus on securities and liens. In this sense, the Canadian Model form

343 RMMLF JOA §4.7.
344 CAPL OP §5.03(C).
345 CAPL OP §5.05(B) (g).
346 CAPL OP §5.05(B).
347 CAPL OP §5.05(A), (B).
348 CAPL OP §5.05(D).
349 CAPL OP § 5.05 (G), 5.06.

also fails to provide clear regulation of the ongoing liabilities of the defaulting party (especially related to decommissioning issues) and also relies on the effectiveness of the lien, which may be something valuable during the exploration phase.

The British JOA Model Form provides a wide definition of default, which includes not only any failure to contribute to the relevant cash call (ie, advances or invoices), but the failure to perform the decommissioning security agreement.[350] There are strict obligations on duty of care for decommissioning in the United Kingdom as it is considered to be a mature province.[351] In other words, most of the operations will soon be moving towards the end of production and will face decommissioning.

The approach taken by the British Model assumes that a non-operator is more likely to breach as the default notice is issued exclusively by the operator.[352] However, it does provide a special paragraph at the end of the clause to address default by the operator.[353] In this situation, the operator's duties will vest in the non-operator that has the largest participating interest for as long as the default persists.

As with any standard JOA, within three days from the default notice, the operator must notify the non-defaulting parties of their obligation to cover the default within six days or else they too will be in default.[354] It is important to note that any money that has been borrowed must incur interest at LIBOR plus 2%, which, in the financial market, is not very high.[355] In other words, although the intention is to create sufficient burden on the defaulting party to force it to remedy, the approach may not be effective.

If the defaulting party does not remedy the breach within six days, there will be a number of consequences. First, the defaulting party will lose its right to take its production share, and the non-defaulting parties may market this production in order to secure payment of outstanding expenditures and costs.[356] Secondly, the defaulting party will lose its right to vote in the OpCom. If any work proposal is submitted, the defaulting party will be considered a non-participant. If unanimous consent is required, the defaulting party will be excluded. Thirdly, the defaulting party will be bound by any decision of the OpCom.[357] Fourthly, the defaulting party will lose its right of access to information.[358] Finally, the defaulting party will lose its right to withdraw from the agreement and to transfer its participating interest (except to the extent allowed in the provision).[359]

If the default persists for more than 60 or 30 days (according to the stage of the project), the forfeiture provision will become available to the non-defaulting parties. It is also relevant to note that this model form addresses the case of repetitive defaults (ie, for more than 60 days within 12 successive calendar months).[360] However, until the default is resolved, by either the default amount being paid, or the execution of the forfeiture provision or a decision to abandon the joint operations, all the operations remain in full force.[361]

350 OGUK JOA § 17.1.
351 See Section 4 of this chapter, "Decommissioning".
352 OGUK JOA §17.1.
353 OGUK JOA §17.9.
354 OGUK JOA §17.2(b), (c).
355 OGUK JOA §17.2(a).
356 OGUK JOA §17.4.
357 OGUK JOA §17.5.1.
358 OGUK JOA §17.5.2.
359 OGUK JOA §17.5.3.
360 OGUK JOA §17.6.1.
361 OGUK JOA §17.6.2.

Execution of the forfeiture provision is subject to several procedures,[362] but the most important relates to the governmental authorities' consent. If the host government does not approve the forfeiture, the non-defaulting parties will face an awkward situation as the defaulting party will maintain its interest in the petroleum title but not in the JOA. The most interesting element of this forfeiture provision is that it allows an option for the defaulter to receive compensation for its interest (though there is also the possibility to provide for the defaulter to be compensated in the case of a default occurring after the development plan).[363] This is in effect a "buy-out" option. This is a reasonable approach as it avoids the threat of full forfeiture. If the parties cannot reach an agreement within 30 days of such election, any party may refer the matter for expert determination, which is a strictly regulated procedure and will bind the parties.[364] However, the non-defaulting parties have the option to refuse an expert determination and withdraw from the agreement. If agreement is reached, the compensation will be deducted from all costs related to the default. Also, a discount of the valuation is provided in the final section of the provision, but this must be determined by the parties during the negotiation stage of the JOA.

Finally, the defaulting parties give a power of attorney to the operator to perform all the necessary actions set out in the default provision.[365] Although the power of attorney is expressly given to the operator, another provision gives the same power to the non-operators if the operator is the defaulting party.[366]

In conclusion, the British JOA Model Form offers a number of balanced options offering some fairness to the non-defaulting parties by not allowing compensation before a development plan has been approved and a neutral determination of compensation after the development is approved even though late exploration and appraisal phases might involve significant expense. This model also addresses decommissioning issues, powers of attorney and governmental consent. On the other hand, its main weakness is the lack of security before the development stage, as no production and no proper asset is available to cover such costs, and the uncertainty that most JOAs suffer from – the requirement for governmental approval.

The Norwegian provision on default adopts most of the key elements that commonly are required. Initially, it defines default as the breach of the financial commitment, but also extends this definition by imposing a duty on the non-defaulting parties to cover the breach.[367]

The defaulting party has five days to remedy its default, otherwise restrictions on its rights to receive information and to vote in the OpCom will be imposed. This model adopts a different approach to the work proposal, as the defaulting party will be bound by the decision of the remaining parties rather than be treated automatically as non-consenting.[368]

One unusual requirement is that the operator must inform the governmental authorities (ie, the ministry) of any default.[369] Commonly, this is a private issue between the JOA parties, but the Norwegian Model may have a national oil company

362 OGUK JOA §17.6.3.
363 OGUK JOA §17.7.
364 OGUK JOA §17.7.1 to 17.7.11.
365 OGUK JOA §17.8.
366 OGUK JOA §17.9.
367 Norwegian JOA §9.1.
368 Norwegian JOA §9.2.
369 *Ibid.*

as a party to the JOA, and so will be keen to impose a higher level of control over the joint operations.

After five days from the default notice, the non-defaulting parties may lift the defaulting party's production to cover the applicable costs. However, if the default persists for more than three months, the non-defaulting parties may demand that the defaulting party transfers its interest to them. The defaulting party will be compensated for its investments, which are deducted from the applicable contributions and costs, but this value must not exceed the book value of its investments.[370]

Most of the ongoing liabilities are transferred to the non-defaulting parties, but the terms agreed for this assignment will vary.[371] In this situation, the parties must draft the assignment's terms very carefully as the defaulting party will remain liable only for the unsettled issues at the time of the assignment. It is important to note that, like the United Kingdom, Norway is also a mature province, but it does not follow the UK's concern and realism over decommissioning issues.

The JOA includes a stipulation for "penal interest", in clause 9.1:

> *If a Party is in default of his obligation to make payments pursuant to Articles 7, 8 or the preceding paragraph, he shall be charged a penal interest pursuant to Article 1.2.2 of Attachment B – Accounting Agreement.*[372]

It could be suggested that the Norwegian JOA provides a balanced provision with regard to the buy-out option, as the defaulting party will not suffer draconian punishment. However, it has several flaws related to the clear determination of unsettled liabilities, penalty characterisation and lack of clarity on operator breach and the implications for suspension of the operator's rights under the JOA.

The AIPN JOA Model Form provides a wider definition of default as it considers not only failure to contribute to a cash call, but also a failure to obtain or maintain security related to the joint operations.[373] However, both alternatives are directly related to the financial resources of the joint operations.

The default notice is strictly regulated and must include certain elements, but overall, the provision aims to clarify the precise reason why the party is receiving the notice. A favourable point is that it was drafted in a way that can apply to any party of the JOA rather than exclusively to the non-operators,[374] and it provides a special paragraph addressing the particularities of an operator breach. In this situation, all payments related to the joint operations will be made to the non-defaulting party that issued the default notice to the operator, and that party also will have the power to request a cash call if applicable.[375]

The default period will start five days after the notice has been issued and will end when the default has been remedied in full.[376] If the defaulting party does not

370 Norwegian JOA §9.3.
371 Norwegian JOA §9.4.
372 Norwegian JOA §9.2.
373 AIPN JOA §8.1(A).
374 AIPN JOA §8.3.
375 AIPN JOA §8.3(C).
376 AIPN JOA §8.1(B).

remedy the breach within five days, it will be in default. However, the non-defaulting parties must cover the breach otherwise they also will be in default.[377]

The consequences of default are fairly severe as the defaulting party will lose almost all of its rights, such as the rights to vote in the OpCom, to transfer its interest, to withdraw from the agreement, to receive information and to lift its production share, among others.[378] If any proposal of work is submitted during the default period, the defaulting party will automatically be excluded from that operation.

During the default period, the non-defaulting parties may use the defaulting entitlement to production to cover the expenditures and costs incurred. Also, they may create a reserve fund to cover the defaulting party's share of future expenditure related to the abandonment and cessation of operations.[379] The former approach is reasonable as it is not fair to allow a party to take and monetise its entitlement without redeeming its default, but the latter could be considered somewhat draconian, although it serves to protect the non-defaulting parties from the consequences of a repeat default at the terminal phase of operations.

In addition to the right to lift the defaulting party's production share, the AIPN JOA Model provides broadly three alternatives for the parties: forfeiture, buy-out and security interest.[380] If the defaulting party does not remedy its breach within 30 days, one or more of these alternatives may apply. The forfeiture alternative is the harshest since the defaulting party will not be compensated for the loss of its interest. However, it will only be applicable if the default persists for more than 30 days, so if the party remedies its default within 30 days it will not face any major consequences. In order to avoid such behaviour, the AIPN Model has an optional provision to adjust the approach to repetitive defaults, giving a repeat defaulter only five days to remedy a default occurring within 12 months of a previous default.[381] This is a harsh provision to discourage a party from using the non-defaulting parties as a form of short-term, low-cost financing. Additionally, the parties may implement security over each participant's interest in order to secure the payment of cash calls. Each non-defaulting party can make its own choice of default remedy to apply as the need arises.

In addition, the accrued but unfulfilled liabilities of the defaulter related to surrender and decommissioning will persist as a continuing obligation regardless of the termination of the granting instrument or JOA.[382]

It could be suggested that the buy-out option is far more balanced than any other alternative (especially in the later stages of the project).[383] The buy-out mechanism is the only alternative that provides for an expert determination to resolve the value of the defaulter's interest (if the parties cannot reach a consensus about the fair market value minus the total amount of default). Also, it allows the payment to be made in four instalments starting 15 days after and finishing 545 days after the transfer date.[384] However, the JOA parties have the flexibility to decide which alternative they will implement during the negotiations.[385]

---

377 AIPN JOA §8.3(B).
378 AIPN JOA §8.2.
379 AIPN JOA §8.4.
380 *Ibid.*
381 AIPN JOA §8.4D.
382 AIPN JOA §8.4 and 8.5.
383 *Ibid.*
384 AIPN JOA §8.4.
385 AIPN JOA § 8.5.

The Greenlandic Model JOA adopts a fairly detailed procedure for establishing a default.[386] However, it is important to stress that a national oil company will be a member of the JOA so it is unsurprising that there is not a single procedure for all parties involved, but instead a procedure applicable only to the private parties.

First, the operator must notify the defaulting party of its default as soon as possible.[387] However, the form does not address the situation where the operator is the defaulting party. Secondly, all the non-defaulting parties must cover the defaulting party's breach in order to secure execution of the ongoing activities.[388] It is interesting to note that the operator must issue another notice to the non-defaulting parties on their additional obligation, which must be performed within six days otherwise they will too be in default.[389] However, there are two interesting provisions regarding such additional funds: (i) the operator has the burden to find the additional resources necessary to cover the breach until the non-defaulting parties' contributions are received, although again the situation where the operator is the defaulting party is not addressed, and (ii) the national oil company's share of the default is carried by the other non-defaulting parties.[390]

The defaulting party can only remedy its breach if the total outstanding amount is paid to the non-defaulting parties.[391] If the defaulting party does not remedy its breach within six days of the default notice, there are several consequences. First, the defaulting party loses its right to lift its production and the non-defaulting parties will take this share to cover the applicable costs.[392] Secondly, the defaulting party will lose its right to participate in the OpCom and any decision taken by the OpCom will bind it. Thirdly, the defaulting party will lose its right of access to information.[393] Finally, if the defaulting party does not remedy its breach within 60 days from the default notice, the non-defaulting parties may forfeit that party's interest.[394] This provision does not apply to the national oil company during the relevant carry, and if none of the non-defaulting parties take the defaulting interest in forfeiture, the consortium will terminate. However, no surrender is allowed before completion of the minimum work obligation.

It is expressly established that the forfeiture will only be valid if governmental approval is obtained and default will not release the defaulting party from its decommissioning obligations.[395] In this sense, the Greenlandic Model secures the interest from the government's perspective as it is unlikely to accept forfeiture of the national oil company's interest and also will wish to keep as many parties as possible liable for the decommissioning obligations.

The Greenlandic JOA Model takes a fairly unique approach as it includes further protections for the national oil company and also imposes strict obligations on the non-defaulting parties. Although it adopts several standard procedures (in relation to the notice, time to remedy the breach and the consequences of default), the model

386 Greenlandic JOA §11.1.
387 Greenlandic JOA §11.1(a).
388 Greenlandic JOA §11.1 (b).
389 Greenlandic JOA §11.1(c), (d).
390 Greenlandic JOA §11.1(b), (c) and (d).
391 Greenlandic JOA §11.2.
392 Greenlandic JOA §11.3.1.
393 Greenlandic JOA §11.3.2.
394 Greenlandic JOA §11.3.3.
395 Greenlandic JOA §11.3.4.

does not properly address operator default, although this is not likely to happen under current operations.

5.8 Discussion

It is important to remember the JOA's basic scope, which is the sharing of risks and costs involved in the execution of the joint operation. Consequently, the financial contribution to cover the expenditure of the consortium is absolutely critical to maintain the good standing of the petroleum title, as the consortium will not be able to perform the obligations without financial means. Thus, default deals with a serious risk for the consortium and for all parties involved as the failure of any party will increase the burden on the other parties to secure the performance of the joint operations.[396]

Furthermore, even though it seems unfair, it is not advisable to refuse to pay an invoice because it is controversial. It is safer to pay first then contest later in order to avoid any chance of default.[397] Nevertheless, although rare, some JOAs will allow the non-operators to pay only the undisputed share of the costs or the JOA may simply not address the point.

In contrast with the JOA provisions governing the removal of the operator, default provisions should apply to all JOA parties including the operator (in its capacity as a JOA party). The operator is obliged to pay its percentage interest share of operating costs as a party to the JOA on the same terms as the non-operators. The same would apply to a national oil company unless its participation is subject to a carry or that carry has expired. The national oil company's interest is not at risk in the event that the other parties carrying its costs are themselves in default.

Default by the operator party is perhaps unlikely because it has been chosen by the venture for its financial and technical robustness. Also, the operator may believe that it is unlikely to be the party that will trigger the provision and may exploit its leverage in the joint venture to insert a harsh form of default provision. For these reasons, the default clauses of most JOAs are drafted with the underlying assumption that they will apply only to non-operators; this is unwise. If the operator is the defaulting party, since by the time they discover the operator's financial position it may already be too late.[398]

Additionally, default is a very important provision for future operations in a mature province as financial strength may be a serious concern for work to be fully executed over a longer timescale. This situation is easy to understand as a mature province is unlikely to attract major companies that have or can easily arrange financial resources to cover their expenditure. The reality is that a mature province will be under licence to small or medium-sized companies that will find it more difficult to raise the required funds and are likely to trade part of their share in the joint venture to raise them.

Therefore, balance and fairness are the key elements of the application of this provision for the present, and especially in the future as it will apply to all the parties involved.[399]

---

396 BG Taverne, *An Introduction to the Regulation of the Petroleum Industry: Law, Contracts and Conventions*, Graham & Trotman, 1994, p141.

397 C Thorpe, *Fundamentals of Upstream Petroleum Agreements*, CP Thorpe, 2008, p141.

398 P Roberts and R Fowler, *Joint Operating Agreements: A Practical Guide*, 4th edn, Globe Law and Business, 2020, p326.

399 *Ibid*, p342.

It is important to protect the joint venture's interest, and as Peter Roberts states: "The business of exploring for and producing petroleum cannot simply stop because a party has decided not to pay for its share of the costs activities".[400] But, on the other hand, the parties should not adopt unreasonable and possibly unenforceable provisions to deal with such a sensitive area for the consortium. Therefore, the goal of the default provision is protection against a lack of financial resources to cover the joint expenditures. However, the JOA must be drafted carefully in order to avoid abuse of the procedures before the full consequences of a default (ie, repetitive defaults) and to be consistent with the applicable law.[401] As discussed, the reasonableness of a default provision for the purposes of the rule against penalties and insolvency law is likely to be decided based on the wording of the clause and not the manner in which it is implemented by the non-defaulting parties. Therefore, a clause which is draconian, unreasonable and imposes an exorbitant penalty upon the defaulting party may be challenged even if the same clause gives the non-defaulting parties some more reasonable and modest options – the non-defaulting parties may not avoid a challenge to the default clause simply by choosing to implement the more reasonable options it provides.

However, the most critical concern and the difficulty that the majority of JOAs will face is the requirement to obtain governmental approval. The right to force a party to forfeit provided in the JOA may not be repeated in the petroleum title, and this can create a critical problem for the non-defaulting parties.

Finally, it is important to note that the default clause may be of no use if no production is available or if the licence interests have no commercial value. In this case, a forfeiture, withering or buy-out to protect the interest of the non-defaulting parties makes no commercial sense. This could be a critical issue for both the national and the international oil companies to consider during the drafting of their JOA. In this case, the only solution available for the non-defaulting parties would be to have financial collateral in place before the event.[402]

6. Accounting

6.1 General principles

As can be seen from many model JOAs, commonly the accounting procedure is the integral part of the JOA and usually it is either embedded in the body of the JOA itself or exhibited as an attachment. Another way in which accounting issues could be addressed in the joint ventures will be the accounting agreement existent together with the accounting procedure. The accounting agreement could also form a part of JOA in case it is concluded with the operator and/or its affiliates and will establish the process where the operator or third party will provide the accounting and possibly other financial services to the joint venture. If it is a third party engaged in such agreement, such service provider might be a professional accountant. The mere existence of accounting agreement, however, does not remove the necessity of existence of joint venture's internal corporate rules, which establish the accounting principles and does not remove the operator's liability to fulfil financial obligations imposed on it by the JOA and accounting procedure.

---

400 *Ibid*, p187.
401 *Ibid*, p189.
402 For further information see: www.oxfordenergy.org/wpcms/wp-content/uploads/2012/05/WPM_47.pdf.

The accounting procedure is an integral part of any JOA. The accounting procedure specifically addresses the issues related to the maintenance of the joint account; specifically determination of appropriate charges and credits applicable to the joint account.[403]

As one of the operator's primary obligations under the JOA is to keep and maintain the financial books and accounts, the accounting procedure provides the rules for the operator in keeping and maintaining the financial books and accounts for the operations. For the non-operator (which may be either the international or the national oil company), it is very important to ensure that the accounting is conducted on the principles of fairness and transparency. As it has been noted above, the operator may also engage an accounting firm to help it in performing its obligations under the JOA; however, the operator will remain at all times primarily responsible for financial issues, such as issuing cash calls, reporting to OpCom as well as other matters which by their nature cannot be delegated to the third-party service provider. A key principle of any JOA will be that liability for performing the role of operator will at all times remain with the entity designated as such.

If an accounting agreement is concluded, its terms and conditions will also address how the financial books and accounts of the operations will be maintained. The more explicit the terms are, the more clarity the operator and non-operators will have about accounting practices. Commonly the accounting agreement will be prepared by the operator with the objective of ensuring that it addresses the requirements of local financial accounting rules and deals with any specific accounting matter which is unique to the joint venture. Controversial issues might be left to a list of reserved matters for the OpCom to decide upon or for the operator to resolve in its discretion. Once agreed with the third-party provider, the agreement will be concluded by the operator.

Another important principle of each model JOA is the "no gain no loss" principle[404] which is important for the operator as it identifies the level of liability of the operator as well as important for non-operators as it provides clarity in relation to operator's responsibility. Despite the fact that some Accounting Procedures Models such as Greenlandic JOA, OGUK JOA, AMPLA JOA apply this principle solely to the operator, other JOA Models such as 2012 AIPN Model form accounting procedure recognises the importance of this principle for all of the partners to the joint venture. The latter approach, however, raises some doubts from a practical point of view as nobody promised that the joint venture will be commercially successful or the parties will enjoy the same level of tax treatment in the jurisdiction of their incorporation.[405]

As it has been discussed in details in this book, the "no gain no loss" principle means that the operator shall not gain any profit during the conduct of operations

403 R Gallun, JW Stevenson, LM Nichols and CJ Wright, *Fundamentals of Oil and Gas Accounting*, 4th edn, Dennwell Books, 2001.

404 See S Shaw, "Joint Operating Agreements" in MR. David (ed.), *Upstream Oil and Gas Agreements*, Sweet and Maxwell, 1996, p16; C Thorpe, *Fundamentals of Upstream Petroleum Agreements*, CP Thorpe, 2008, p126; H Dundas, *Joint Operating Agreements: An Introduction*, 1994 Summer Programme: UK Oil and Gas Law, CPMLP 09/09, 1994, p12.

405 R Fowler, P Roberts and EG Pereira, *The AIPN Joint Operating Agreement: A Practical Guide*, Globe Law and Business, 2019.

as well as to demonstrate sufficient due diligence not to incur any damage of loss during the operations. This important principle finds its practical implementation in the accounting procedure. The accounting procedure, in particular, addresses the objective principles of goods and services supply, specific procedures of attracting the services from the affiliated parties, dealing with levies and damages. Goods and services shall be purchased by the joint venture on market-based economic terms, while contracts with affiliates shall be concluded on arm's length basis and should employ market-based profit margin, which in its turn shall be justifiable for tax purposes. The operator, among other things, will also be responsible for the tax effect of the operational transactions to which the operator (on behalf of joint venture) becomes a party. In this sense the operator shall demonstrate caution not to incur any damages related to possible tax fines and levies for the joint venture.

The main points of disagreement between a national and an international oil company in accounting matters (depending on which party is the operator) are the overheads (which are costs and expenses, and under which circumstances they should be allocated to the joint account as discussed in the previous section) and the frequency and the scope of the audit – in this case the operator's interest would be to limit the number of audits per year and their scope as well, while the non-operator is likely to insist on a broader scope and more frequent audits, including by independent auditors and by the partners themselves.

The same rules that are applied to the joint operations should apply to any sole risk options; it is logical that all operations within the scope of one project, whether they are joint or exclusive, should be subject to the same accounting rules and procedures. It is also important from the point of view of re-joining the sole risk operations, since the non-consenting party will be able to verify the actual costs to be compensated and calculate the payment for re-entering the operations on the basis of the costs (incurred by and recorded under clear and transparent principles for each participant) accounting procedure. Even if the operator is not a consenting party, as a general rule, it still has to manage the operations and maintain the accounts according to the JOA and the accounting procedure.

Commonly, the accounting procedures should contain the cash call procedures and designation of costs (direct charges, such as procurement of goods and services, personnel, pension and common pension increment, material and services from operator and non-operators, damage to or loss of joint property, taxes, duties, levies, insurance etc or indirect charges, eg, general research and development, corporate staff and corporate management etc). They should also contain methods of accounting, inventory, audit timing and procedures, specifics of contract awards for affiliates, including the applicable level of mark-up, currency of operations (in certain circumstances a choice of the currency in which to conduct the operations may be possible, depending on the counterparty), and other aspects, including those which the participants themselves deem necessary.

Usually, the accounting methods used within the operator's group are adopted in the accounting procedure, since the operator is responsible for keeping the financial accounts and will prefer to follow the rules with which is it familiar. The operator may wish to maintain accounting records consistent with this agreement and generally accepted accounting practices (eg, in the United States: Generally Accepted Accounting Principles – GAAP; International Financial Reporting Standards – IFRS; and International Accounting Standards – IAS).

Any JOA party which issues securities under US security exchange or is incorporated in the US will also be concerned to make sure that the joint account is maintained and whole financial and other types of operations are conducted in a manner which complies with the Foreign and Corrupt Practices Act 1977 ("FCPA"). Although that Act does not extend its jurisdiction to include non-US entities and/or entities which do not issue securities on US security exchanges, any party within the scope of the Act faces two concerns. First, it must rely on the accounting information provided by the operator with respect to the joint account in filing its own US statutory reports; any failure to disclose a suspicious payment may incur it significant penalties under US law, unless it can show that it took reasonable steps to verify the information it relied upon. Secondly, any allegation of breach of the FCPA will damage the reputation of all of the JOA parties, even if the relevant US legislation is not applicable to them.

The same considerations might apply in relation to the compliance with the UK Anti Bribery Act as well as any sanctions restrictions in relation to financial aspects of the joint venture.

The problems arise when the operator is a national oil company – it is very possible that it will not be using the best industry methods of accounting and will be satisfied with minimum possible requirements of the local law. If the non-operator is an international oil company, it will insist on using the more developed methods in the accounting procedure, and usually will be willing to support the operator (the national oil company), in adopting and getting accustomed to the more developed practices and procedures. Country-specific requirements may also impose certain additional obligations on the operator and could form a compromise between the international and the national oil companies' approach. The requirements of the country of operations may mean that the operator has to maintain accounting records under more than one accounting standard.

6.2 Analysis of model JOAs

Whilst there are accounting procedure precedents available to accompany the AIPN, OGUK, AMPLA, Norwegian and Greenlandic JOAs, they are less likely to be adopted unchanged by joint ventures as a part of their corresponding JOAs. This is because each IOC operator will seek to use its own in-house form accounting procedure to make sure that all of the joint ventures for which it acts use a common set of accounting principles. Otherwise, it will not be able to show that it met those principles in a consistent manner when audited by the non-operators of each joint venture paying or contributing to its costs. However, the non-operators will also have a "say" while discussing and adopting accounting procedure as they also have their in-house rules and procedures which shall be also reflected in the joint venture's accounting procedure.

Following the general rule, in the AMPLA JOA the accounting procedure is attached to its Exhibit 3. However, the JOA itself also contains general principles for accounting and financial reporting by the operator. If there is a conflict between the rules and provisions of the accounting procedure and the JOA, the JOA provisions will prevail.

Under the AMPLA JOA it is the operator's general obligation to establish, maintain and conduct the joint accounts and accounting, as well as to obtain and keep all primarily supporting documentation. The operator must ensure that these accounts and books are kept separately to prevent them becoming mixed up with the operator's own ones. The joint-venture accounting is the basis for financial reporting to OpCom and the participants. It is also the operator's responsibility to prepare the accounting procedures and to report to the participants in the format established by the accounting procedure.

The Operator must maintain separate books, accounts and records for the Joint Venture of Joint Expenditure in accordance with the Accounting Procedure and generally accepted accounting principles adopted from time to time by the Institute of Chartered Accountants in Australia, consistently applied.
The Operator must develop and provide to the Participants standard accounting procedures, expenditure classifications and reporting formats in accordance with the Accounting Procedure as appropriate to the Joint Venture to satisfy the requirements of the Operating Committee and the Auditor.[406]

The AMPLA accounting procedure contains the no gain, no loss principle which is fundamental for each JOA, stating that:

It is the intent of this Accounting Procedure that, except as otherwise expressly provided by this agreement, no party (including the Operator) will gain or lose by reason of carrying out its duties and responsibilities pursuant to this agreement.[407]

Further, the AMPLA accounting procedure contains the standard obligations of the operator to maintain the records and the accounting:

The Operator must maintain the Joint Account and the Joint Venture Asset Register in accordance with the Accounting Procedures on behalf of the Participants in their Participating Interests.
The Operator must make available to any Participant on request copies of the accounting procedures, expenditure classifications and reporting formats underlying the Joint Account.
The Operator must retain all receipts, vouchers and other documents relating to Joint Expenditure until directed otherwise by the Operating Committee.[408]

The AMPLA accounting procedure also contains some other standards for each JOA provision, such as designation of costs, labour, acquisition of materials, operator's rights of purchase and disposal and inventory.

---

406 Article 10.1 of the AMPLA JOA.
407 Article 1(b) of the AMPLA JOA accounting procedure.
408 Article 1(b) of the AMPLA JOA accounting procedure.

However, there is also a specific provision in the AMPLA JOA accounting procedure that distinguishes it from many other accounting procedures: it sets out the rules of accounting for the sole risk operations.

> *If under the Operator is conducting a Sole Risk Operation under this agreement, the computation of sole risk costs and expenses as incurred by the Sole Risk Participants must be made in accordance with this Accounting Procedure. If it is necessary to allocate any kind of cost or expense, including, but not limited to, direct drilling, rig mobilisation and demobilisation, general and administrative, overhead and depreciation of material and equipment to the Sole Risk Operation and to the Joint Account an equitable procedure previously approved by the parties will be used.*
> *The costs and expenses of a Sole Risk Operation must not be reflected in the statement and invoices rendered by the Operator for the Joint Account.*
> *The Operator is entitled to request and obtain timely cash advances from the Sole Risk Participants in accordance with the provisions of the Accounting Procedure against costs and expenses such as will reasonably protect the Operator for the necessity of using its own or Joint Account funds for such purposes and the Operator is not obliged to commence the Sole Risk Operation until all such cash advances have been received from the Sole Risk Participants.*[409]

In accordance with the sole risk accounting principles under the AMPLA JOA, the main principle is that the funds to pay for conducting the joint operations must not be commingled with the funds being cash-called and designated for conducting the sole risk operations. There may also be a requirement to keep a separate bank account for the purpose of funding the exclusive operations. Also, the operator must separately cash call a consenting participant for the amounts necessary for the exclusive operations. The operator is not obliged to commence the joint operations until it receives the funds necessary for the exclusive operations from the party consenting to the exclusive operations. Usually, the exclusive operations are the operations that go beyond the minimum obligations under the relevant licence and thus any delay in their conduct or any non-fulfilment will not lead to negative consequences for the licence.[410] Therefore, the operator can be flexible and can afford to wait until the funds for the exclusive operations are received from the consenting participant.

Under Article 3.8 of the Greenlandic JOA, the operator must prepare and maintain the joint records and conduct the accounting for the joint purposes. The Greenlandic JOA also provides the timing within which such records and the accounting documents must be kept.

---

409 Article 9 of the AMPLA JOA accounting procedure.

410 An exception may arise if the sole risk operation is treated as part of a work programme and budget approved by the state under the relevant granting instrument; performance of that work may then be obligatory for all the granting instrument parties so that each JOA party will be liable for the performance of that sole risk operation under the terms of the granting instrument as if it was part of joint operations.

The Operator shall prepare and maintain proper books, records and inventories in respect of the Joint Operations which shall be kept in compliance with the Accounting Procedure and with due regard to the requirements of the Licence and any applicable laws or regulations. The books, records, and inventories shall, however, be preserved at least until two (2) Years after the total deficit carried forward has been recovered and the depreciation of investments has been completed or if arbitration proceedings have been instituted, until such date as such proceedings have been terminated, whichever date is the later.

Under Article 4.6 of the Greenlandic JOA, an accounting committee should be established to deal with accounting issues. This is quite a unique provision for the Greenlandic JOA, since other model JOAs do not establish a specific committee to deal with accounting matters.

Article 6 of the Greenlandic JOA provides that the accounting procedure is part of the agreement and that, as a general rule, the participants must pay their share of the joint operation's costs and expenses in proportion to their participating interests in the project:

The Accounting Procedure attached hereto as Appendix A is hereby made a part of this Agreement. In the event of any conflict between any provision in the main body of this Agreement and any provision in the Accounting Procedure, the provision in the main body shall prevail.
Subject to Article 2.4, each Party agrees to pay to the Operator its respective share of costs and expenses and in accordance with the Accounting Procedure.[411]

Under the Article 7 of the Greenlandic JOA, the accounting procedure is also applicable to exclusive operations.

The Norwegian Model JOA regulates the accounting issues via a specific accounting agreement (which is exhibited to the JOA as an integral part).

As with other model JOAs, Article 10 of the Norwegian JOA provides the operator's obligations to keep the accounting records and books:

The Operator shall keep accounts in Norway for all activities pursuant to this Agreement, in accordance with laws and regulations and accounting practices in Norway, and the provisions of Attachment B – Accounting Agreement. The accounts shall be so kept that the other Parties may supervise the activities of the Operator. Thus, the accounts shall reflect the joint operations and activities in each Deposit in the licence area.

411 Article 6 of the Greenlandic Model JOA.

The OGUK JOA also provides for the operator' obligation to keep and maintain the accounting records for the operations of the project:

The Operator shall prepare and maintain separate books, records and inventories of the Joint Operations which shall be kept in compliance with the Accounting Procedure and with due regard to the requirements of the Acts, the Licence, and all applicable Legislation.[412]

The OGUK Model JOA contains two types of accounting procedures: short form and long form. The short form procedure contains the following details:

- purpose and intent;
- responsibilities;
- accounting basis and currency (the applicable currency is pounds sterling);
- funding and finance fee;
- billing statements;
- materials;
- audit and audit principles.

The long form accounting procedure provides a much more detailed description of, for example, expenses and costs, the procedure for contract awards to affiliates and inventory.

The 2012 AIPN JOA Model accounting procedure is probably the most comprehensive and user-friendly. It has been revised together with the AIPN JOA Model and is currently one of the most updated and developed models. As with other model JOAs, the 2012 AIPN Model JOA contains the no gain, no loss principle for the operator:

Subject to Article 4.6 and the Accounting Procedure, neither gain a profit nor suffer a loss as a result of being the Operator, provided that Operator may rely upon Operating Committee approval of specific accounting practices not in conflict with the Accounting Procedure.[413]

As with many other model JOAs, the operator must use the general accounting procedure while conducting the exclusive operations. Article 7.12(C) of the 2012 AIPN Model JOA contains this principle:

Operator shall maintain separate books, financial records and accounts for Exclusive Operations which shall be subject to the same rights of audit and examination as the Joint Account and related records, all as provided in the Accounting Procedure.

412 Article 6.7 of the OGUK JOA.
413 Article 4.2(B) 5 of the 2012 AIPN Model JOA.

> *Said rights of audit and examination shall extend to each of the Consenting Parties and each of the Non-Consenting Parties so long as the latter are, or may be, entitled to elect to participate in such Exclusive Operations.*

The accounting procedure itself is exhibited to the 2012 AIPN Model JOA and contains the following sections, which deal most comprehensively with many accounting issues:

- Section 1 – General provisions deals with purpose, interpretation, definitions, joint account records and currency issues, cash calls, adjustments, allocation, and audit provisions;
- Section 2 deals with direct charges and costs that can be allocated to the direct charges, such as salaries, other labour costs, equipment, facilities, and other costs;
- Section 3 deals with indirect changes, the cap on them, costs and expenses which can be allocated to indirect charges;
- Sections 4 and 5 deal with the principles and the procedures of acquisition and disposal of materials; and
- Section 6 deals with inventories, their frequency and special purpose inventories.

As it can be seen, the 2012 AIPN JOA Model and its accounting procedure provide the most developed and comprehensive accounting documents among the current JOAs and accounting procedures.

6.3 Discussion

Both the national and the international oil companies will wish to have a clear and transparent basis for the accounting. However, unlike the international oil company, the national oil company may insist on using the less developed local accounting standards if this is a requirement of the local law.

7. Cash calls

7.1 General principles

Cash calls are requests for payment for anticipated future capital and operating expenditures, usually sent by joint-venture operators to their non-operating parties [414]

Most JOAs include a provision that allows the operator to issue cash calls to non-operating partners. The basic obligations of each operator include keeping the financial statements of the joint operations and issuing the cash calls. Both national oil companies and international oil companies, if acting as non-operators, will want this basic obligation to be performed in the most diligent manner, since the future expenditures, calculated under the approved work programme and budget, and proper forecasts for the anticipated expenditures are important for the successful conduct of operations and meeting granting instrument obligations.

---

414 However, under certain circumstances it is possible for the non-operators to issue the cash calls to operator, for example, when the operator fails to do so.

If either the international or the national oil company is the operator, it will be under the strict requirements of almost every model JOA to properly issue cash calls and ensure that all parties to the JOA make payments as required to meet operational cash flow demands. Usually, the operator also issues cash calls to itself, but the actual payments for such cash calls may not be made by the operator to its own account; instead, the operator will make a book entry and will pay on behalf of the joint operations the whole amount of the cash-called expenditures designated for that month. However, if the relevant JOA provides that the operator cannot commingle its own money with the project money, the cash call procedures will be fully applicable to the operator, namely they must be issued and actually paid by the party acting as operator.

The OGUK Model JOA provides the following definition of cash calls:

> *"Cash Call" means any request for payment of cash in advance made by the Operator to the Participants in connection with the Joint Operations or, where the context so requires, to the Sole Risk Participant in connection with any Sole Risk Project.*[415]

Clearly, under this definition cash calls may be issued not only for standard joint operations, but also when a participant undertakes sole risk operations. Thus the operator, which may not be the sole risk participant, can still issue such calls and conduct the sole risk operations. However, a separate operator may be appointed to conduct the sole risk operations and then that operator will be issuing the cash calls.

The Greenlandic Model JOA also specifically deals with the situation where the sole risk operations are conducted by the operator on behalf of the sole risk participant, emphasising that the operator must never use its own funds, designated for the joint operations, to fund the sole risk activity. However, the operator is not prohibited from conducting such operations for the benefit of the sole risk participant.[416]

> *If the Operator is carrying out a Sole Risk Project on behalf of a Sole Risk Party, the Operator shall be entitled to request Cash Calls and raise Invoices against the Sole Risk Party and to require such security as it may reasonably request for costs which it may incur in connection with the Sole Risk Project and shall not use its own or Joint Account funds for the purpose of paying the costs and expenses of the Sole Risk Project.*[417]

A typical cash call transaction follows the following steps:

- a cash call is issued;
- a cash call payment is posted;
- an expense for which the cash call was issued is posted in the joint account;
- the cash call is reclassified for clearing.

415 Preamble of the OGUK Model JOA.

416 Sole risk operations and operator's rights and duties in these circumstances are discussed in Chapter 1, Section 9.

417 Article 7.2(e) of the Greenlandic Model JOA.

Commonly, the cash calls are used when the project is funded by the participants themselves. The funding sources could be mixed, meaning that both corporate and external financing are used. In the case of external financing, the operator issues draw down notices to the external financing institutions. External financing is a separate and big topic for consideration and discussion. Usually, the cost of external financing is more expensive in comparison with the situation when the participants provide financing from their group source, so-called corporate financing. It might take longer time to negotiate and organise external financing.[418] Financial institutions providing financing prefer to monitor the implementation of the project and how the funds are utilised. However, external financing has its significant advantages. Among them is that the lender has a limited recourse against the borrower.[419] Others could be that depending on types of accounting model, the participants might not be obliged to consolidate this debt in their group financial accounts. Such a vehicle allows the participants to share some risks with the third party, which is not a direct participant of the project; depending on jurisdiction, such financing structure might have its tax advantages, including tax holidays.

The structure for external financing might be different, it might be the operator itself who enters into the loan agreement, or a special purpose vehicle might be established to be the borrower under such agreement.[420] Different financial institutions, such as commercial banks, funds and multilateral agencies might serve as the lenders in the loan agreements. The funding could be structured as the loan agreements or through third-party equity sponsorship whereby special development or equity funds are set up for the purposes of investing into a different project. Usually, such funds require some involvement at the board level of the special vehicle to monitor the investment.

Terms and conditions upon which the loans are provided are thoroughly negotiated and are usually subject to operating committee or board approval. Typically, such conditions contain a list of project expenditures the loans can be used for. All drawdowns will be credited to special disbursement account, which might have payment waterfall rules for applicability of the remaining money. The reimbursement of the loan will be paid from the proceeds account which is typically funded from actual proceeds from the operations. The interest rate will be either accumulated and paid back together with the body of the loan or alternatively will be invoiced to the participants based on cash calls. In this case the operator working under the no gain, no loss principle, will only include the interest payments in the cash calls and will not be entitled to add any other margin.

7.2 Analysis of model JOAs

Where the operator is funded by cash calls, as is the standard practice, the operator is not always entitled to add interest to the pool of the joint expenses. Article 4.6 of the OGUK Model Short Form Accounting Procedure specifically deals with this matter, and excludes corporate finance fees for cash calls; however, it does not prohibit the operator to charge the external finance fees to the joint account:

---

418 H Thomas and A Skinner (eds), *Energy and Resources Financing*, Globe Law and Business, 2015.

419 This principle was recognised by English courts long ago as 1877 well-known case *Williams v Hathaway* (1877) GCH D544 "to bind the fund and not the trustee in their personal capacities".

420 Typically, if special purpose vehicle is used for external financing, then it will be owned by all participants to the project, including the operator.

During periods of major expenditure, for example during a development, the implementation of any alternative funding mechanism to the foregoing, such as a cash call procedure, shall be the decision of the Joint Operating Committee. No finance fee shall apply to payments funded by Cash Call.

It might be assumed that under the OGUK Model JOA, the operator is carrying the other participants' expenses in relation to external financing fees. The OGUK Accounting Procedure provides that the operator will invoice the participants for operating costs it has already financed, justifying its recovery of a modest financing fee. When the level of capital and operating expenditure increases significantly in the development phase, it may be unreasonable to expect the operator to finance the expenditure from its own resources, at which point a cash call mechanism may be introduced. If so, the operator would not be entitled to a financing fee.

In comparison with the other current AMPLA Model and the OGUK JOA, the JOA 2012 AIPN Model Form accounting procedure contains very detailed principles and mechanisms for the cash calls. It provides the following principles:

- each cash call shall be based on the approved work programme and budget and contain the same categories of expenditures;
- in the normal conduct of operations, it is not assumed that the operator will incur the project expenditures out of its own funds and thus the principle of each cash call is that it requires a pre-payment for the expenditures to be incurred in the forthcoming month.

As with the other model JOAs, the AIPN accounting procedure also provides the timing for the issue of cash calls and payments and makes clear the non-operator's obligations to pay cash calls on a timely and due basis.

The other important principle of the accounting procedure is that the non-operators must pay the cash calls regardless of whether they are disputable or not. Even if the non-operator has any concerns about the correctness of the requested amount in a particular cash call, it must still pay. However, this does not mean that the disputing party cannot raise its concerns. It may bring its arguments to the operator, including on the basis of the audit, and if successful the future cash calls will be adjusted to the extent of the disputed amount.[421]

Upon approval of any Work Program and Budget, Operator may submit to the Non-Operators a Cash Call for the next Calendar Month's operations. The Cash Call shall equal the Operator's estimate of the money to be spent in the currencies required to perform its duties under the approved Work Program and Budget during the next Calendar Month. For informational purposes Operator shall submit with

421 Article 1.7 of the 2012 AIPN Model Accounting Procedure specifically deals with this matter: "*Payment by a Non-Operator of any Cash Calls or amounts billed in a statement shall not prejudice the right of that Non-Operator to protest or question the correctness of the Cash Calls or amounts billed; however, all statements rendered to Non-Operators by Operator during any Calendar Year shall conclusively be presumed to be true and correct after 24 Calendar Months following the end of the Calendar Year unless within that 24-Calendar Month period a Non-Operator takes written exception to a charge and makes claim on Operator for adjustment. Operator shall provide a response to all written exceptions whether or not contained in an audit report within the time period prescribed in Section 1.8.5.*"

the Cash Call an estimate of the funds required for each of the two Calendar Months following the Calendar Month for which the Cash Call is made. The Cash Call and the two-Calendar Month estimate shall be detailed by the categories designated in the approved Work Program and Budget.

Operator shall submit each Cash Call in writing and deliver it to all Non-Operators not less than 15 Days before the due date for payment of the Cash Call. Operator shall set the due date, but the due date shall be no sooner than the first Business Day of the Calendar Month for which the funds subject of the Cash Call are required.

Each Non-Operator shall pay any Cash Call free of bank charges. Any bank charges deducted from the payment of a Cash Call shall be borne by the Non-Operator that made the payment.

Each Non-Operator shall wire transfer to Operator at a bank designated by Operator the share corresponding to the Non-Operator of the full amount of each Cash Call in the currencies requested or any other currencies acceptable to Operator. Operator may charge the Non-Operator the entire cost of converting the currency furnished to the currency requested in the Cash Call.

Each Party shall pay the amount requested of that Party by a Cash Call on or before the due date specified in the Cash Call. The due date for any amount billed to a Party in a statement from Operator shall be 15 Days following receipt of the statement from Operator. Any late payment of a Cash Call or an amount billed in a statement by a Party prior to a Default Period applicable to that Party, should it become a Defaulting Party, shall accrue interest in favour of Operator at the Agreed Interest Rate from its due date until the earlier of the date payment is received by Operator or the beginning of a Default Period as to that Party as a Defaulting Party.[422]

Cash calls may result in deficit and overpayment situations. In case of a deficit and in the event the cash-called participant does not pay the requested amount of money, the future cash call will include not only the amount of the expenditures to be incurred in the forthcoming month, but also the amounts underpaid in the previous month. In the case of overpayment, the future cash calls will be reduced by the overpaid amount or, alternatively, the overpaid amounts will be returned by the operator.

- *If Operator issues a Cash Call for a Calendar Month but becomes aware of additional sums of money needed for that Calendar Month, then Operator may revise the outstanding Cash Call if the revision is made before the 15-day period prior to the due date of the outstanding Cash Call. Otherwise, Operator may make an additional Cash Call for the Calendar Month in question. The due date for payment of the additional Cash Call shall be 10 Days after receipt of the Cash Call by each Non-Operator, but no sooner than the first Business Day of the Calendar Month for which the additional Cash Call is made.*
- *If payment of a Cash Call by a Non-Operator exceeds its share of cash expenditures for a Calendar Month, then the next Cash Call for that Non-Operator shall be reduced by the excess. However, if the excess is greater than the estimated Cash*

422 AIPN Accounting Procedure, §§1.6.1–1.6.3, 1.6.10.

Call for that Non-Operator for the next Calendar Month, then the Non-Operator may request a refund from Operator of the difference between the excess and the estimated Cash Call for that Non-Operator for the next Calendar Month if the difference is more than U.S.$. Operator shall refund the difference within 15 Days after receipt of a request from the Non-Operator. Optional

- *If Operator does not refund the money within the time required, then Operator shall, at the sole cost and expense of Operator, pay the Non-Operator that requested the refund interest on the unpaid balance at the Agreed Interest Rate from the due date until the payment is received by the Non-Operator that requested the refund.*
- *If the amounts paid by a Non-Operator pursuant to a Cash Call are less than its share of cash expenditures for the Month covered by the Cash Call, then Operator may add the deficiency to subsequent Cash Calls or bill the Non-Operator for the deficiency in the statement rendered by Operator to Non-Operators under Section 1.5.1.*[423]

If permitted by the relevant JOA, the operator may place the funds received under the cash calls, excluding the used amounts, in bank deposit accounts. The interest received as a result of the deposited funds will be counted against the next cash calls amounts. If allowed, the operator may also change the received amounts into another currency. This may be appropriate for hedging the FX risks, or may be required when foreign contractors are paid in their own currency.

- *Interest paid into a bank account into which funds received by Operator from the Parties are deposited shall be applied against the next Cash Call or, if directed by the Operating Committee, paid to the Parties. The interest thus received shall be allocated to the Parties on a proportionate basis taking into consideration the date of funding by each Party of the account in proportion to the total funding of the account. Operator shall provide the Parties a monthly statement summarizing receipts, disbursements, and transfers and beginning and ending balances for each bank account.*
- *Subject to the Laws, Operator shall have the right, at any time and from time to time, to convert the funds received pursuant to a Cash Call or any part of those funds to other currencies to the extent that the currencies are then required for operations. The cost of any conversion of funds shall be charged to the Joint Account.*
- *Operator shall try to maintain funds held for the Joint Account in bank accounts at a level consistent with that required for the prudent conduct of Joint Operations.*[424]

Like the 2012 AIPN Model JOA, the Norwegian JOA Model Form contains provisions dealing with cash calls, although in a specific, less robust manner. The Norwegian Model provides for the timing for payments, overpayment and deficit issues. It also provides that when the total request for payment is less than 5 million Norwegian kroner, cash calls are not required. The management committee may resolve to change the 5 million Norwegian kroner limit:

---

423 AIPN Accounting Procedure, §§1.6.4–1.6.6.

424 AIPN Accounting Procedure, §§1.6.8, 1.6.11–1.6.12.

At least 10 days prior to the beginning of each month, the Operator shall submit to the Non-operators a 3 month forecast, specified by month, of estimated cash requirements.
Upon request, the Non-operators shall advance their share of estimated cash requirements for the following month. The Operator shall submit a written request for advances at least 15 days prior to the due date. The due date shall be set by the Operator, but shall be no earlier than the first working day of the month for which the advances are requested.
Notwithstanding the terms of Article 1.2.3, the Operator shall avoid accumulating unnecessary cash balances from cash advances.
To avoid build-up of such cash balances, substantial cash advances may be divided into two payments to coincide with disbursements.
The prognosis for cash requirements and the request for cash advances shall specify the currencies in which the advances are to be made. Cash advances shall be called in currency when the Operator is obliged to make a payment in that currency exceeding more than the equivalent of NOK 50 million annually. The amount may be altered by the management committee.
If the advance payments prove insufficient, the Operator may make a written request for additional advances. Such request shall state which expenditures the unpredicted payments refer to. The due date shall be set by the Operator, but shall at the earliest be set at 5 working days after the receipt of the request.
If the actual monthly need for cash proves to be significantly less than the advances called for, the Operator shall refund the excess amounts as soon as possible, unless the Parties agree to transfer the amount to the following period. If the Operator sees that the cash requirement will be reduced before due date, the Parties shall be so informed through a revised cash call to the extent this is feasible.
The difference between the monthly cash advances and the actual payments in each currency shall be stated, and the next request for advances shall be adjusted accordingly.
Where the total cash requirement is less than NOK 5 million a month, the Operator is not required to make cash calls. The amount may be altered by the management committee.
If the Operator has made no request for advance payments, the Non-operators shall pay their proportionate share of the actual monthly payments within 15 days after receipt of the Operator's billing with request for payment.[425]

Unlike the 2012 AIPN Model Form, in which the detailed procedures for cash calls are contained in the accounting procedures rather than the JOA agreement, the AMPLA Model JOA contains the provisions on cash calls in the agreement itself.

The AMPLA Model JOA places issuance of the cash calls under the approval of the relevant authorisation for expenditure, which is a different approach from other JOAs, which place issuance of the cash calls under the approved work programme and budget. Like other model JOAs, the AMPLA JOA has provisions for the timing of payments, overpayments and deficit issues.

425 Article 1.2 of the Accounting Procedure, Attachment B of the Norwegian Model JOA.

> *(a) Approval of an AFE constitutes authority for the Operator to issue Cash Calls to the Participants in respect of that expenditure. A Cash Call must include an estimate of the cash requirement for each of the next ensuing 3 months and include a cost break-up of the main expenditure components.*
> *(b) A Participant must pay each Cash Call to the Operator within 7 days of approval of an AFE. If a Participant is late in paying a Cash Call, the Participant must pay with interest on the late payment calculated from the due date to date of payment at the Agreed Interest Rate in the next Cash Call payable by it.*
> *(c) The payment of any Cash Call or other monies under this agreement is without prejudice to the right of a Participant to later contest the payment.*
> *(d) All payments must be in the currency determined by the Operator and made to a bank account in Australia nominated by the Operator.*[426]

The AMPLA Model JOA specifically prohibits the commingling of joint funds with the operator's own funds and requires the establishment of a separate bank account for the purposes of the project's funding. The money from this account can be withdrawn by the operator only for the specific purpose of funding the joint operations.

> *(a) All funds received by the Operator under this agreement (other than funds received for the purpose of a Sole Risk Operation) must be lodged by the Operator in a Joint Venture bank account in Australia maintained by the Operator for the purposes of the Joint Operations. Pending expenditure in accordance with this agreement, funds advanced by any Participant must be held by the Operator in trust for the respective Participant.*
> *(b) Each Participant is entitled to receive or be credited with any interest earned on its funds while they are held on trust by the Operator.*
> *(c) The Operator is authorised to withdraw funds from the Joint Venture bank account as required to pay Joint Expenditure.*[427]

7.3 Discussion

It is clear that the interests of both a national and an international oil company in relation to the cash calls procedure mainly coincide. Both will require a procedure that is transparent and efficient to ensure the smooth conduct of the joint operations.

Most of the model JOAs have fairly robust provisions on cash calls and the relevant procedures. However, it could be concluded that the 2012 AIPN Model Accounting Procedure has the most developed and expanded procedures in this area.

8. Indirect costs and affiliate overheads

8.1 General principles

In hydrocarbons operations, indirect costs or overhead can be defined as a cost necessary for such operations but which is difficult to attribute to any specific

---

426 Article 8.5 of the AMPLA Model JOA.
427 Article 8.6 of the AMPLA Model JOA.

line item in the work programme and budget. Somewhat confusingly, accounting procedures will also address the issue of "general and administrative overheads", being a further allocation of costs, which may be recovered by the operator from the joint account on account of expenditure incurred by it and its affiliates in supplying corporate support to the operator and indirectly to the joint venture. However, such costs might be incurred not only by the operator, but by the other participants' non-operators and their affiliates. 'Overheads' should not be confused with over-expenditure, which is best defined as expenditure incurred by the operator which exceeds the permitted allocation of budgeted funds (subject to any tolerance, if established in the particular JOA) under the applicable programme and budget.[428] In order to bring some clarity to this analysis, the table below summarises the different terms for overheads used by different accounting procedures.

Terminology used by model agreements for overheads and related charges

	Direct costs	**Indirect costs**	**General and administrative overhead**
Alternative terms	Direct charges	Indirect charges, overheads	Parent Company Overhead, G&A.
Term as used in this section	Costs attributable to only one budget line item; eg, drilling costs, capital project costs	Costs attributable to several budget line items and allocated between them; eg, office & accommodation costs, support functions, utilities	An allowance chargeable by the Operator on account of head office support costs, usually incurred outside the country of operations. Often capped or fixed as a % of other costs
AIPN JOA Accounting Procedure	Included in defined term "Direct Charges" without distinguishing indirect costs	Included in defined term "Direct Charges" without distinguishing indirect costs	Indirect Charges
Greenlandic Accounting Procedure	Included in costs generally without distinguishing indirect costs	Included in costs generally without distinguishing direct costs	Not permitted
Norwegian Accounting Procedure	Direct charges	Indirect charges	General Research and Development, Corporate Staff and Corporate Management
Australian Accounting Procedure	Direct Costs	Direct Costs	Indirect costs – administrative overhead

428 See discussion in Section 1 "Work programme and budget" and Section 2 "Authorisation for expenditure" in this chapter.

Each indirect cost may be fairly low, but their cumulative total could be significant. Indirect costs are all costs not including or related to direct labour (excluding geological and geophysical costs), materials and administration costs.

For example, the payment of actual employees' wages (which are operating expenditures, 'OPEX') and an investment that improves the useful life of an existing capital asset (eg, capitalisation of costs, research and development, central engineering, process engineering – capital expenditures 'CAPEX') beyond the level designated in the work programme and budget under certain circumstances might still be considered as indirect costs.

Although the overheads (indirect costs, indirect charges, administrative charges) will not be directly related to a particular well or project, they contribute to bringing that well into production and thus are essential for successful operations.

The general or administrative expenses are the expenses associated with the functioning of the JOA participant in the country of operations as well as abroad. They may also be related to the general assistance and the headquarters services necessary for the study, planning and execution of hydrocarbons operations. General and Administrative overhead costs are deemed to cover the actual costs incurred by the operator and/or participants or their affiliates and related to general and administrative services. In practice, the basis for them could be separate services agreements, including financial, technical, staffing and other services and they may be higher than estimated when the relevant work programme and budget was prepared. Such costs might sometimes be attributed to a specific line item in the work programme and budget.

An international oil company as a JOA participant is likely to be undertaking several projects in different areas and countries, and thus incurring not only costs related to the particular operations under the JOA, but also costs attributable to its head office, parent company and shareholders. This is inherent to the continuing operations under the JOA and not designated as specific line items in the project work programme and budget. Conversely, a national oil company is unlikely to incur separate additional costs, although it will be more likely to incur additional costs related to the specific line items.

The distinction between (i) indirect costs and overheads and (ii) general and administrative costs is straightforward, if only the terminology was used consistently. Indirect costs are costs which are incurred uniquely for the purpose of joint operations or exclusive operations under one JOA, but are properly attributable to several budget line items approved by OpCom. While general and administrative costs are attributable to the activities of the operator, or its affiliates, in several different projects governed by different JOAs, but because such activities contribute to joint operations or exclusive operations, an agreed proportion of such costs is chargeable to the joint account.

These general and administrative overheads may include all main offices, field offices and associated general and administrative costs, including, but not limited to, supervisory, accounting and employee relations services. A common point of contention is whether the operator can include the cost of maintaining its brand and intellectual property through the mechanism of general and administrative overheads.

Whether the general and administrative overhead costs can be included in the pool of costs to be recovered is a disputed issue. The host government's position, and thus the position of the national oil company (unless of course the national oil company is also the operator) will be that such costs should not be included in the costs to be recovered under the production sharing agreement, since the overhead costs' recovery concept will delay the appearance of the profit oil for the national oil company. Some production sharing agreements have explicitly excluded overheads from the pool of costs to be recovered under the relevant production sharing agreement (or only permit recovery at a lower amount).[429] Other agreements recognise the inclusion of overheads in the recoverable costs pool.[430]

If the host government recognises that the overhead costs may be compensated or if the granting instrument does not but the concession or other agreement does, and the concept of overheads exists within the JOA, the calculation of overheads may be based on three general approaches:

- time sheets;
- generalised approach; and
- sliding scale percentage.

In the time sheets approach, the personnel costs are charged to the joint account and must be determined according to the actual time spent by the personnel on the project, as evidenced by the summary of the time sheets adopted by the operator's organisation. This approach has been considered to be complicated, unmanageable and inefficient for a long time. In practice, it has been shown that this approach is not sufficiently transparent; on the contrary, it is very easy to abuse by adding extra, fictitious time. It is very difficult for operators to provide effective monitoring of the overheads with this system, and it increases the administrative burden.

Where the operator's affiliate dedicates additional human resources or consultancy to the joint venture, the preferred approach is for such services to be provided under a technical services agreement between the affiliate and the operator, the charges being supported by time-writing documentation, such as time sheets. To satisfy the concerns of the non-operators and the state that the services may not be charged at market rates and/or the relevant affiliate may make a profit from providing the service, the relevant accounting procedure may require that the relevant agreement is approved by OpCom as the related parties' agreement.[431] The difficulty with this is that the operator may seek to charge the services across all the joint ventures and JOAs that benefit from it, an objective that may be defeated if it has to obtain the approval of every affected OpCom. As an alternative, the accounting procedure may require each service provider to issue a certificate by its statutory auditors confirming that the service charge includes no element of profit or mark-up.[432] The same approach will be valid for the costs incurred by the non-operators and their affiliates; such agreements shall also be approved by OpCom which is the common approval process for agreements with interest parties such as partner affiliates. The costs of such services would normally be treated as direct costs if attributed to one line item, or indirect costs if they were attributable to several budget line items.

---

429 For example, Equatorial Guinea production sharing agreement (1998 Model Petroleum Production Sharing Contract of Republic of Equatorial Guinea). The same applies to the Greenlandic JOIA Accounting Procedure §3.18.

430 For example, Indian and Yemen production sharing agreements.

431 AIPN Accounting Procedure §2.8.1.

432 OGUK Accounting Procedure §7.6.

Due to the time sheet system's potential to increase administration time, the industry practice has evolved a so-called generalised approach, under which the operator and the non-operator in the JOA may incur necessary, appropriate and economically justifiable overheads and will be regularly allocating such overheads to the joint account.

8.2 Analysis of model agreements

The AIPN recommendation is to use a system of percentage-based overhead charges.

Some countries, such as Sudan and Yemen, use a sliding scale allowance for general and administrative overheads, based on total petroleum costs each year.

Sudan's production sharing agreement[433] stipulates that any general and administrative overhead incurred by a contractor's affiliates will be deemed compensated by an annual charge based on a sliding scale percentage and charged monthly. The basis for applying this percentage will be the total expenditure incurred during each calendar year or fractions thereof:

- first 1 million US dollars: 4%
- next 3 million US dollars: 3%
- next 4 million US dollars: 2%
- over 8 million US dollars: 1%

The limitation of the corresponding annual charges is widely spread during the first exploration period. For example, Sudan's production sharing agreement provides limitation to 300,000 US dollars.[434]

In Myanmar, the basis for applying general and administrative overhead charges is the total petroleum costs incurred during each financial year or fractions thereof. The sliding scale percentage is as follows:

- first 5 million US dollars: 4%
- first 3 million US dollars: 2%
- first 4 million US dollars: 1%
- over 8 million US dollars: 0.5%[435]

The contractor or operating company's general and administrative overheads outside Yemen applicable to the participating interest under this agreement are charged quarterly as percentages of the total exploration expenditures, development expenditures and operating expenses for the year, as specified below:

- first > 1 million US dollars: 3%
- first 1 million to 5 million US dollars: 1.5%
- first < 5 million US dollars: 1%

General costs incurred by the operator during the exploration phase are charged to petroleum costs in proportion to the annual amount of direct petroleum costs incurred and subdivided into tranches.[436]

---

433 Production sharing contract concluded between Sudan and SUN Oil in 1982.

434 Production sharing contract concluded between Sudan and SUN Oil in 1982.

435 Production Sharing Contract for Offshore Petroleum Operations between Myanmar Oil and Gas Enterprise and Premier Petroleum Myanmar Limited, dated 3 May 1990.

436 Yemen model production sharing contract.

The AIPN Model Accounting Procedure uses the term "indirect charges", and has a detailed Section 3 on indirect charges. The model employs the generalised approach, and has an important principle of no double charging. It specifically states that no costs charged under the indirect section costs may be also charged under the direct section.

Operator may charge the Joint Account monthly for the cost of indirect services and related office costs of Operator and its Affiliates not otherwise provided in this Accounting Procedure. Indirect costs chargeable under this Section 3 represent the cost of general assistance and support services provided by the organizational units of Operator and its Affiliates not directly involved in Joint Operations and are costs that are not practical to identify or associate with Joint Operations but are for services that provide Joint Operations with needed and necessary resources. No cost or expenditure included under Section 2 shall be included or duplicated under Section 3. The charges under Section 3 are not subject to audit under Sections 1.8.1 and 1.8.2 other than to verify that the overhead percentages are applied correctly to the expenditure basis.

3.2 Amount

3.2.1 Operator's indirect charge under Section 3.1 for any month shall equal the greater of (1) the total amount of indirect charges for the period beginning at the start of the Calendar Year through the end of the period covered by Operator's invoice ("Year-to-Date") determined under Section 3.2.2, less indirect charges previously made under Section 3.1 for the Calendar Year in question, or (2) the amount of the minimum assessment determined under Section 3.2.3, calculated on an annualized basis (but reduced pro rata for periods of less than one year), less indirect charges previously made under Section 3.1 for the Calendar Year in question.

3.2.2 Unless exceeded by the minimum assessment under Section 3.2.3, Operator's aggregate Year-to-Date indirect charges shall be a percentage of the Year-to-Date expenditures, calculated on the following scale (US dollars):

Annual Expenditures

$0 to $ of expenditures = __%

Next $ of expenditures = __%

Excess above $ of expenditures = __%

3.2.3 Operator may charge a minimum amount of US $ _______ assessed each Calendar Year calculated from the Effective Date and shall be reduced pro rata for periods of less than a year.

3.2.4 Indirect Charge for Projects

Regarding major projects (including pipelines, gas reprocessing and processing plants, final loading and terminalling facilities, and dismantling for decommissioning of platforms and related facilities), when the estimated cost of each project amounts to more than US $ _____________, Operator may make a separate indirect charge for the project if approved by the _______________ (here insert either "Operating Committee" or "Parties") at the time of approval of the project.

Optional

> *During its process of winding-up Joint Operations, Operator shall charge the greater of the sliding scale percentage rate or the minimum indirect charge for a period of ___ months. If the winding-up process continues beyond the end of the period, then the charge shall be confined to and based upon the sliding scale percentage rate.*
> *Optional*
> *Notwithstanding the foregoing, the _________ (here insert either "Operating Committee" or "Parties") must approve of the Operator's indirect rates and related calculation method for development operations, production operations, and dismantling for decommissioning of platforms and related facilities before the submission of the first annual budget for those phases of operations.*
> *Optional*
> *At the beginning of each year, the dollar amounts noted in Section 3.2 shall be adjusted based on the previous year's annual change in the ________________ Index as published by ______________________. For this purpose, the starting index base shall be ______________ as published on ______________, 20___.*[437]

The AIPN Model directly excludes from the indirect costs section those costs which are explicitly attributable to particular line items of the WP&B and thus need not be split among several line items, thus avoiding the ambiguity the cost allocation process may cause.

> *3.3 Exclusions*
> *When calculating the monthly indirect charge, the Operator shall not include in the expenditures the indirect charge (calculated either as a percentage of expenditures or as a minimum monthly charge), rentals on surface rights acquired and maintained for the Joint Account, guarantee deposits, pipeline tariffs, concession acquisition costs, bonuses paid in accordance with the Contract, royalties and taxes on production or revenue to the Joint Account paid by Operator, expenditures associated with major construction projects for which a separate indirect charge is established hereunder, payments to third parties in settlement of claims, and other similar items.*
> *Credits arising from any government subsidy payments, disposition of Material, and receipts from third parties for settlement of claims shall not be deducted by Operator from total expenditures in determining the indirect charge.*[438]

The Norwegian Agreement concerning petroleum activity contains very detailed provisions on indirect costs or, in other words, the overheads. It deals with the nature of overheads, thresholds, procedures and so on.

---

437 AIPN Accounting Procedure §3.
438 Section 3 of the AIPN Model Accounting Procedure.

Indirect cost is cost related to organizational units/functions[439] which are by nature indirect, eg:

- *Corporate management;*
- *Support and staff functions such as economy and finance, personnel, organisational;*
- *Legal and joint service functions;*
- *Indirect functions in operational departments;*
- *Indirect cost of Affiliated companies.*

Moreover, cost can be indirect according to their nature, and may include financing cost and depreciation, office leasing and communications cost.
Finally, certain activities may entail Indirect cost, such as General Research and Development.
Services rendered by the aforementioned or similar departments and which are directly chargeable to the Joint operation shall, to the extent practicable, be charged as direct cost in accordance with Article 2.1.4 a) Material above.
According to different systems for intermediate distribution, Indirect cost shall ultimately be charged to the individual Joint operation or to activities for which the Operator himself bears the cost. The charges shall be made pursuant to fair distribution methods. Examples of such methods are:

- *According to direct time, applied to direct personnel cost;*
- *According to direct Material consumption, applied to direct material cost;*
- *According to turnover ratios, including sliding scale systems;*
- *Other capacity and/or consumption-based distribution methods.*

Charges related to such distribution methods shall be calculated on the basis of time and cost studies and be reviewed annually to verify that they compensate the Operator fairly for the charges they are intended to cover. If the Operator uses provisionally budgeted hourly fees etc. for the charges throughout the Year, and does a recalculation the following Year, see Article 1.3.3, the recalculation shall be terminated and charged/credited to the Joint operation including interest, preferably within the first Quarter of the following Year, but at the latest 1 June of the following Year.
In order to provide the basis for such annual review, the Operator shall provide the Nonoperators with a current organization chart together with the basis for charging cost to the Joint Account and an identification of those sections of the organization for which cost will be charged directly to the Joint account under Articles 2.1.2, 2.1.3 a) and 2.1.8, and those parts of the organisation that are covered by charges under this Article.
General Research and Development
The Operator's cost for General Research and Development may be charged to the Joint Account in proportion to the exploration, development and operating cost of the year in accordance with the following provisions:

439 Norwegian Agreement concerning petroleum activity.

Projects which are not subjected to unlimited audit may be charged to the Joint Account according to the following per cent rates and limits based on annual costs except for area fees, CO^2 duty, NO^X duty when directly imposed on the Joint operation, purchase of gas for injection and tariffs paid in connection with the processing of petroleum on a third party's field installation:

Exploration cost: 0–300 million NOK 2.5%

Operating cost: 0–1000 million NOK 2.7%

1000–2500 million NOK 1.0%

Development cost: 0–1000 million NOK 2.5%

1000–2000 million NOK 1.0%

2000–3500 million NOK 0.5%

Tariffs received for the processing of other companies' petroleum and other revenues that are credited to the Joint Account shall not be deducted at the calculation of the above-mentioned cost.

Exploration cost means all cost charged to the Joint Account as exploration cost by decision of the management committee, ie, normally cost until an approved development plan is established, and in addition all cost outside the area comprised by the development plan.

Operating cost means all cost charged to the Joint Account as operating cost by decision of the management committee, ie, normally direct cost of production and direct and indirect expenses of the operating organisation before and after commencement of production, excluding exploration cost.

Development cost means all cost charged to the Joint Account as investments by decision of the management committee, ie, normally all cost excluding operating cost (including cost related to preparation for operation) for activities in the area comprised by the development plan.

Removal cost shall be dealt with as development cost.

The Operator shall each Year document that General Research and Development cost has a useful effect for the Norwegian Continental Shelf and has been charged to an extent at least corresponding to the chargeable amounts against the relevant Joint Accounts. The Operator shall charge the Joint Account with the percentage additions at the time of periodic settlement of accounts. Cost charged to the Joint Account in accordance with this Article is not to be included in the basis of calculation.

To the extent the Operator is unable to document a cost level sufficient to fully charge the percentage additions to the relevant Joint Accounts, the charges made by the Operator to the relevant Joint Accounts shall be reduced correspondingly on a pro rata basis.

The intervals above will be adjusted at the beginning of each Year on the basis of the consumer price index as published by Statistics Norway per 15 July of the current year. The starting basis is 15 July 2004.

2.2.3 Corporate Staff and Corporate Management

The Operator's cost for Corporate Management and Corporate Staff may be charged to the Joint Account with 0.65% of the annual costs for exploration, operation and development of the Joint operation, with the exception of charges for General Research and Development which may be charged to the Joint Account according to

Article 2.2.2. Costs for exploration, operation and development shall have the same meaning as in Article 2.2.2.
The percentage shall cover the Operator's Corporate Management and Corporate Staff cost to the extent that Corporate Management and Corporate Staffs perform work of a general nature for the Operator that does not refer directly to the operation of one or several fields on the Norwegian Continental Shelf. The activities covered by the percentage shall comprise the Corporate Management and Corporate Staff's cost related to the preparation and maintenance of management documentation and procedures covering the group as well as services that are not covered by Article 2.2.3 fourth paragraph. The percentage shall cover internal services as well as services bought externally.
The expenses covered by the percentage shall not be subject to any audit.
Services of an extraordinary nature which are beneficial to one or several joint ventures on the Norwegian Continental Shelf shall be chargeable directly to the relevant joint ventures in addition to the percentage. If the expenses for services of an extraordinary nature are known at the time when the Operator submits the budget proposal for the coming year, these expenses are to be included in the budget proposal. In all cases, the management committee shall be informed of any such expense in the monthly report. Extraordinary nature means work performed by the Group Staffs of a particularly large or unusual scope and not comprising work which forms part of the ordinary operation of one or several joint ventures (major investigations, reports and crisis management related to accidents and the like, the establishment of new group systems and other extraordinary activities). Expenses related to services of an extraordinary nature shall be documented by way of work description and may be subject to an audit.
Expenses covered by this Article 2.2.3 shall not be charged to the joint ventures in any other way.
2.2.4 Additional Indirect cost
The Indirect cost not covered by Articles 2.2.2 and 2.2.3 and which accrue to the Operator or the Operators' Affiliated companies for the Joint operation in Norway, shall be calculated on the basis of cost studies and shall be charged to the Joint Account each month pursuant to the distribution key described in Article 2.2.1.[440]

8.3 Discussion

There is potential misalignment between the participants not incurring and charging the costs as overheads and those who are charging. It will most likely be the operator who will largely charge the overheads to the joint account. In this case the non-operators and the state will seek to ensure that the operator keeps adequate accounting records, enabling them to identify any double recovery or overcharging. This is particularly relevant where the operator may have a choice as to how the costs are charged to the joint venture – either by agreeing a specific services agreement between the service provider and the operator or joint venture,

440 Article 2.2 of the Norwegian Agreement concerning petroleum activity.

or by including them in the scope of the general and administrative overhead; the state and non-operators will wish to ensure that one or other option has been chosen, not both. The same approach will be valid for those non-operators who will seek to charge the overheads to the joint account.

9. Cost recovery

9.1 General principles

Usually, the issue of cost recovery is not covered in a JOA. The most appropriate place for it is in the production sharing agreements or service agreements, since these are the instruments that establish the relationship between the host government and the private parties and thus are designated to deal with cost recovery, the national oil company's share, costs recovery procedures and other issues.

Cost recovery is the allocation to the contractor of a certain portion of oil and gas as reimbursement for its sunk costs, often incurred at the project's exploration stage.[441] This portion of project production relates to costs recovery in oil and gas. The following costs and expenditures may be referred to as the sunk costs to be recovered from the production share:

- direct costs relating to exploration, appraisal, development, production, marketing and abandonment; and
- indirect costs, relating to the payment of interest and overheads, administrative costs, and any other costs that may be designated in the accounting procedure or alternatively in the accounting agreement[442] as the indirect costs.

Not all costs incurred qualify for recovery out of production. There are recoverable and non-recoverable costs. Non-recoverable costs are costs incurred by the contractor when it deviates from the rules of the contract.

It is likely that the following costs will be excluded from the scope of the recoverable costs: unauthorised work, the costs incurred as a result of gross negligence and wilful misconduct, contract awarded contrary to the tender procedures, costs that are not specified in the work programme and budget.

Many contracts provide a list of the recoverable and non-recoverable costs, with the criteria to which category the particular contract will be referred.

Recoverable costs include most of exploration costs, capital expenditures, operating costs and abandonment costs. Each cost category, except for abandonment costs, may be recovered in accordance with the rules of amortisation and depreciations applicable to the category. Abandonment costs arise at the end of the contract and thus it is not possible for them to be recovered after production ends.

---

441 In certain circumstances, if specifically envisaged in the production sharing agreement, the investor (international oil company) may be entitled to recover the costs in the later stages of the project (eg, costs incurred during the development and production stages).

442 The difference between accounting procedure and accounting agreement is described in Section 6 of this chapter, "Accounting".

Regarding the recovery of costs and expenses incurred by the parties to production sharing or services agreements during the exploration, development and production phases, both the international and the national oil companies are entitled to an equivalent amount of the oil produced (in other words, 'cost oil'). Commonly, the amount of oil to be used for the cost recovery will be capped in the production sharing agreement to provide a cost oil ceiling and ensure that the host government receives a share of revenue in the early part of the field's production life cycle. The host government is entitled to receive its portion of revenues in the form of royalties and other mandatory payments. Usually, the host government receives its portion before the entitlement in the form of costs recovery is available for the production sharing agreement participants, and is received by government revenue in the form of taxes under the service agreements.

The oil remaining after the cost oil ceiling revenue, the so-called 'excess cost oil' or 'profit oil', is available for sharing between the international and national oil companies in a proportion predetermined under the relevant production sharing agreement, equal to each of the parties' percentage of participating interest. Typically, the international oil company's share of these revenues declines as production and project profitability increase.[443]

Unless otherwise provided by the production sharing agreement, typically after costs recovery and payment of royalties, the parties to the production sharing agreement split the remaining portion of the produced hydrocarbons. This is known as profit oil/profit gas.

In traditional production sharing agreements, the process of production allocation will be as follows:

- the contractor extracts cost petroleum from the reserved gross production;
- royalties are paid from the remaining amount;[444]
- profit petroleum (ie, the part remaining after the recovery of the sunk costs and royalties payments) is split between the state and the contractor. If the contractor's side includes several entities, the contractor's profit petroleum is split between all contractors. If a national oil company participates in the JOA, it will be allocated a share of profit petroleum on account of its participating interest. This is distinct from the state's allocation of profit petroleum;
- contractors pay taxes to the host government;[445]
- after all payments are duly made, the contractors become the owners of the profit petroleum, net after all payments and taxes.

The scheme under the production sharing agreement is shown in Figure 1 and the cost recovery process under the services agreements is shown in Figure 2 (both overleaf).

443 Dr R Kombargi, D Tideman, D Branson and A Sastry, *Maximising the Value of Oil Resources in the MENA Region the Critical Role of Petroleum Fiscal Systems*, ebook, Booz and Company, 2011, pp6–8.

444 Royalties may be the first priority in some production sharing agreements.

445 Historically, tax payments were not included in payments under production sharing agreements; however, more recently they have been included.

Figure 1: The scheme under the production sharing agreement

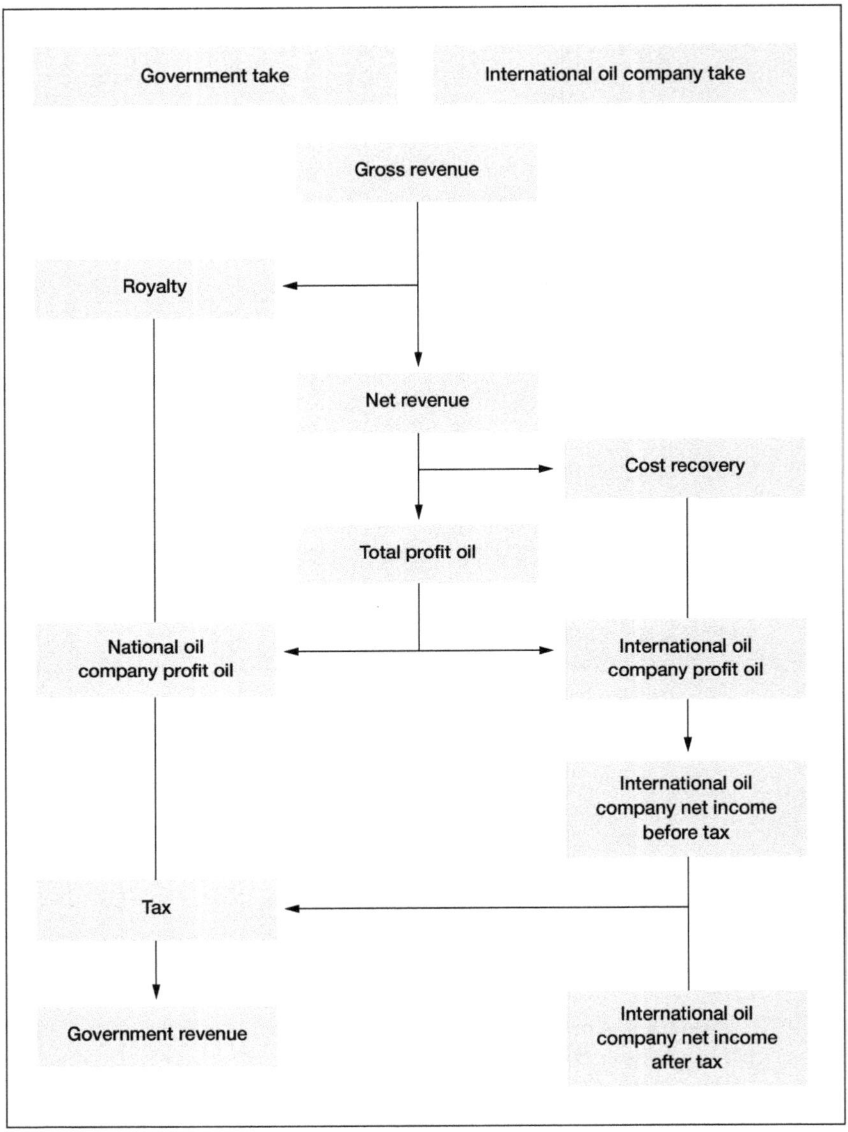

Figure 2: The cost recovery process under the services agreements

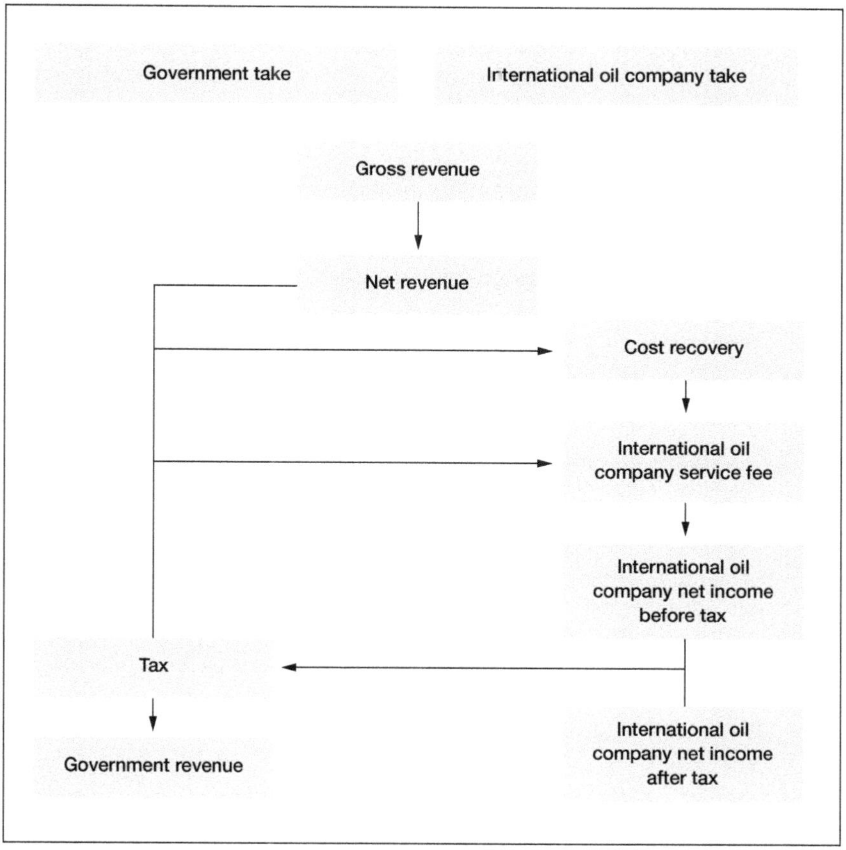

Under the services agreements the cost recovery amounts are paid to the contractor (including any participating national oil company) out of net revenue received as a result of the hydrocarbons operations.

Often, allocation of the oil production starts with separating a portion of oil, designated for the state as payment in kind of the royalties under the granting instrument. The percentage may vary and may also depend on the amount of daily and yearly production. The remaining portion of oil (within or without limits under the relevant contract) may be put at the disposal of the contractors for recovery of the costs and expenses they have incurred while carrying out the petroleum operations. This portion is referred to as the cost recovery oil.

The production remaining after deduction of royalty oil and cost recovery oil is referred to as profit oil. This portion is shared in complex proportions between the national and the international oil companies.

The cost recovery rules for any project will be set out in the relevant granting instrument. The JOA still has a vital role to play, especially where exclusive operations take place. Generally, the granting instrument will ignore exclusive operations, in the sense that it will treat such operations as conducted by the license holder (as being all the JOA parties) as if it were joint operations. In the case of production sharing agreements, the costs of joint operations and exclusive operations will not be treated separately, and cost petroleum will be allocated to the contractor on account of all such costs without discrimination. It is therefore for the JOA parties to decide if cost petroleum should be further subdivided between them to distinguish between cost petroleum earned through investment in joint operations and cost petroleum earned through investment in exclusive operations. There are strong commercial justifications for making this further reallocation. Typically, joint project and exclusive operations will be at a different phase of investment. A mature producing asset, developed as joint operations, may incur modest operating costs, and therefore earn comparatively low allocation of cost petroleum; simultaneously, an exclusive operations project may be under development, and earn substantially more cost petroleum because of higher capital and operating costs. The host government agreement will "socialise" cost petroleum, in effect awarding cost petroleum earned by the exclusive project to joint operations. This is unfair for the exclusive operations project because it defers cost recovery. It is also potentially unfair for joint operations, because the share of profit petroleum earned by it may be diluted by the additional allocation of cost petroleum earned by the exclusive operations project. Only the AIPN JOA addresses this issue in Article 19, which requires the JOA parties to enter into a specific allocation agreement for cost petroleum; broadly it offers two solutions, either different exploitation areas are "ring fenced" as if they were separate projects with their own allocation of cost petroleum and profit petroleum, or more simply, cost petroleum and profit petroleum are split between joint operations and exclusive operations.[446]

9.2 Analysis of model JOAs

Some model agreements, such as 2012 AIPN Model JOA, correlate the granting instrument (eg, production sharing agreement, service agreement etc) and the JOA, specifically providing the definition of the costs to be recovered under the production sharing agreement, service agreement and so on:

> *Cost Hydrocarbons means the portion of the Total Available Production of Hydrocarbons that is allocated to the Parties under the Contract and this Agreement for the recovery of the costs incurred by the Parties and recoverable under the Contract.*[447]

The 2012 AIPN JOA Model further provides with a general rule on costs recovery for oil and profit oil allocation:

> *The total quantity of Hydrocarbons produced and measured at the Delivery Point (as determined under Article 9) from each Exploitation Area and to which the Parties*

446 R Fowler, P Roberts and EG Pereira, *The AIPN Joint Operating Agreement: A Practical Guide*, Globe Law and Business, 2019, pp467–473, 580–584.

447 See the terms and definitions section of the 2012 AIPN Model JOA.

are collectively entitled under the Contract shall be composed of Cost Hydrocarbons and Profit Hydrocarbons under the Contract.
Operator shall develop and the Operating Committee shall approve procedures for allocating such Cost Hydrocarbons and Profit Hydrocarbons during each Calendar Quarter among the individual Exploitation Areas.[448]

9.3 Discussion

As mentioned above, the cost recovery issue is a crucial area for both national and international oil companies. The state will be motivated to reduce cost, reduce the allocation of cost petroleum and therefore increase its allocation of profit petroleum. In a properly balanced production sharing regime, the contractor will also wish to reduce cost to maximise its share of profit petroleum for the same reason, but it will also seek to have all its costs reimbursed. It is in a privileged position unlike other risk-taking businesses, because it has some assurance that it will recover its costs ahead of the state which is the ultimate investor in the upstream projects conducted under the agreement. A national oil company participating in the JOA is therefore potentially conflicted because contractually it has the same entitlement to cost recovery as any other JOA participant, but may be influenced by its stakeholders in the state to argue more aggressively for cost reductions. This should not be seen by the international oil companies as an entirely bad thing because the national oil company will share their interests in ensuring that all costs are recovered through cost petroleum and that non-recoverable costs are minimised; in that sense at least, there is alignment on this point.

10. Commingling of funds

10.1 General principles

Basically, the crux of commingling of funds lies in the concept of trust. The operator is entrusted by virtue of the JOA to handle the money received from the non-operators and spend that money solely for the specific purposes of supporting the joint operations. Since the money received from the non-operators on the basis of the cash calls (or from external financing for the purposes of conducting joint operations) is not money owned by the operator, in most cases the JOAs and the applicable law impose strict duties on the operator. The situation might be different if the external financing is provided for the project. In this case the security arrangements for such financing will likely require there to be a separate disbursement account over which the lender has certain controls. The money available at this account is prohibited to be commingled with any other money involved in the project.

Certainly, it is prudent practice for the operator to separate the joint funds from its own funds, but in some situations the operator may be expressly or impliedly authorised to commingle the funds with its own funds. However, the express or implied right to commingle does not give the operator the right to breach fiduciary

448 Article 19 of the 2012 AIPN Model JOA.

obligations it will have under any JOA.[449] Usually, the JOAs provide that the funds may be applied "only to their intended use". The operator does not have a right to borrow the commingled funds and use them for its own separate purposes. Whether commingled or not, the operator may only expend joint funds on purposes authorised by the JOA.

The issue of the funds commingling is probably more sensitive for the non-operators, since they will be concerned that the funds invested in the project are utilised in due manner and specifically for the purposes of the project. The non-operators will also require that the operator is prohibited from using the funds for its own purposes. Whether the operator is a national or an international company, the non-operators (international or national company, as applicable) will be raising their concerns in relation to the commingling of funds. The best-case scenario for the non-operators would be to have a complete prohibition on the operator commingling the funds. However, this will not always be beneficial for the project, since placing the funds (even commingling them with the operator's own funds) in an interest-bearing account may be more beneficial than keeping them in a separate account that does not provide such a good interest rate.

10.2 Analysis of model JOAs

There are several options under the 2012 AIPN Model Accounting Procedure. The first alternative is that the:

> *Operator may not commingle with Operator's own funds the monies that Operator receives from or for the Joint Account under this Agreement. However, Operator reserves the right to make future proposals to the Operating Committee concerning the commingling of funds to achieve financial efficiency.*[450]

If that alternative is adopted, the operator must open a bank account specifically and only for use by the joint operations. The operator and non-operators will pay cash calls directly into that account and all expenditures will be paid from that account.

The first sentence of the alternative provision could be interpreted as requiring the operator to pay bills by issuing two checks: one drawn on its own account for its share and another drawn on another account containing the non-operators' funds. Since this is not industry practice and the main intent of the JOA provision is to avoid commingling the non-operators' funds with operator funds that are unrelated to operations under the JOA (which is how Section 1.6.7 of the AIPN accounting procedure construes the particular JOA provision), the parties may consider

449 It is a matter for debate whether the operator owes such fiduciary duties, and much will depend on the express wording the JOA and its applicable law. The model JOAs routinely governed by US or English law (AIPN and OGUK JOAs) include clauses which exclude any fiduciary duty on the part of the operator with respect to joint property, monies in the joint account or generally. See for example AIPN JOA §14.1; OGUK JOA §6.2.4 and for the definition of "Consequential Loss". The present state of English law on this issue is summarised in P Roberts and R Fowler, *Joint Operating Agreements – A Practical Guide*, Globe Law and Business, 2020, pp131–141.

450 Article 4.8(A) of the 2012 AIPN Model Accounting Procedure.

modifying the first sentence of the alternative JOA provision to specify operator funds not related to operations under the JOA rather than just the operator's own funds, and provide that the operator must deposit its funds to be used for joint operations with those of the non-operators in a separate bank account.

The 2012 AIPN Model JOA contains a separate section dedicated to commingling of funds by the operator. Several options are provided for the participants. The first is the strictest one. It prohibits the operator from commingling the joint-venture funds with its own funds and only provides the option to request the possibility for commingling the funds in an interest-bearing account in the future.

Under the second option, the operator may commingle the funds, but it will still be liable before the non-operators for the funds received from the non-operators and it must spend such funds solely for the purposes of the joint operations. It is also interesting to note that the operator might be entitled to place the money in an interest-bearing deposit account only once the development plan is approved. This might be explained by the fact that at the development stage much more money is being invested in construction and other capital works and not all of them might be spent immediately upon receipt. That said, it is important that the remaining amounts earn some return and accrue some interest rather than staying on the account without earning some interest.

ALTERNATIVE PROVISION, CHOOSE ONE
ALTERNATIVE #1
Operator may not commingle with Operator's own funds the monies that Operator receives from or for the Joint Account under this Agreement. However, Operator reserves the right to make future proposals to the Operating Committee concerning the commingling of funds to achieve financial efficiency.
ALTERNATIVE #2
4.8.A Operator may commingle with Operator's own funds the monies that it receives from or for the Joint Account under this Agreement. Despite that monies of a Non-Operator have been commingled with Operator's funds, Operator shall account to the Non-Operators for the monies of the Non-Operators advanced or paid to Operator, whether for the conduct of Joint Operations or as proceeds from the sale of Hydrocarbons or Joint Property under this Agreement. Such monies of the Non-Operators shall be applied only to their intended use and shall in no way be deemed to be funds belonging to Operator.
OPTIONAL PROVISION, CHOOSE IF DESIRED, IN RELATION TO ALTERNATIVE #2
Despite the foregoing, the Operating Committee shall have the right to require Operator to segregate from Operator's own funds the monies that Operator receives:
ALTERNATIVE PROVISION, CHOOSE ONE
ALTERNATIVE #2-1
from or for the Joint Account under this Agreement.
ALTERNATIVE #2-2
from the Parties in connection with operations on each Exploitation Area.
OPTIONAL PROVISION, CHOOSE IF DESIRED – INTEREST BEARING ACCOUNT. IF NOT CHOSEN CHECK CROSS-REFERENCES.

The Operating Committee may require Operator to deposit monies received for the Joint Account in an interest-bearing account
ALTERNATIVE PROVISION, CHOOSE ONE
ALTERNATIVE #1
at any time.
ALTERNATIVE #2
after the approval of the Development Plan.
Operator shall allocate interest earned among the Parties on an equitable basis taking into account the amounts received from each Party and the date of receipt. Operator shall apply each Party's allocation of earned interest to such Party's next succeeding Cash Call or, if directed by the Operating Committee, pay it to each such Party.[451]

The concept of keeping the money in trust is contemplated by the AMPLA JOA. Also, the JOA specifically designates that the non-operators will be entitled to receive the interest in proportion to their share if the money is deposited in an interest-bearing account:

Banking of funds
(a) All funds received by the Operator under this agreement (other than funds received for the purpose of a Sole Risk Operation) must be lodged by the Operator in a Joint Venture bank account in Australia maintained by the Operator for the purposes of the Joint Operations. Pending expenditure in accordance with this agreement, funds advanced by any Participant must be held by the Operator in trust for the respective Participant.
(b) Each Participant is entitled to receive or be credited with any interest earned on its funds while they are held on trust by the Operator.
(c) The Operator is authorised to withdraw funds from the Joint Venture bank account as required to pay Joint Expenditure.[452]

10.3 Discussion

As noted already, if commingling is allowed under the JOA, the funds received from the participants are mixed with the funds belonging to the operator and thus with the funds to which the operator's creditors can make recourse. This makes banking and accounting easier for the operator, but also creates problems for the participants in identifying or tracing funds, especially in the case of bankruptcy.

In the event of bankruptcy, the participants' funds should not become part of the bankruptcy estate. These funds always belong to the participants in proportion to their participating interest.

451 Article 4.8 of the 2012 AIPN Model JOA.
452 Article 8.6 of the AMPLA Model JOA.

The operator is merely holding the participants' money. In the event of the operator's bankruptcy, its creditors, even with appropriate bankruptcy orders, may be entitled only to payments out of the operator's bankruptcy estate. This concept can be a very important defence to a preference claim in bankruptcy, since the participants will have preference claims over the money held for them in trust. However, there are two problems here: (i) the first is how to identify which funds belong to the participant and which funds are held for the participants in trust; (ii) and the second is that some courts have stated that they are "not inclined to allow creditors to utilize a trust theory as a means of obtaining preferential treatment in a bankruptcy", since "equality of distribution among creditors is a central policy".[453]

There is specific case law in relation to the general concept of commingling funds. The court of Appeal of Alberta has considered and rendered a decision with regards to this issue.[454]

In the case considered by the court of Appeal of Alberta, Vanquish Oil & Gas was the operator of a certain oil well.

It was required to remit 45% of the net production revenues to the owner of that proportional interest in the well – Karl Oil and Gas Ltd and Choice Resources.

Under Section 5.07 of the 1990 Canadian Association of Petroleum Landmen operating procedure, the operator may commingle with its own funds the moneys that it receives from or for the account of the non-operators under the operating procedure. Notwithstanding that moneys of a joint operator have been commingled with the operator's funds, the moneys of a joint operator advanced or paid to the operator, whether for the conduct of operations or as proceeds from the sale of production under the operating procedure, will be deemed to be trust moneys, and will be applied only to their intended use and shall in no way be deemed to be funds belonging to the operator, other than in its capacity as the joint operators' trustee.

As the court of Appeal of Alberta ruled:

This appeal demonstrates the shortcomings of a practice, which is apparently an industry-wide practice, of letting oil well operators commingle trust funds with non-trust funds, while purporting to limit the ability of the operator to use those funds only for operation of the specific well. It must be remembered that it is the respondents who created the risk of these circumstances arising by agreeing that trust and non-trust money could be commingled. Where the conduct of one party creates the problem, that is a relevant consideration in deciding whether a constructive trust should be imposed: D.M. Paciocco, The Remedial Constructive Trust: A Principled Basis for Priorities Over Creditors (1989), 68 Can. Bar Rev. 315 at pp. 348-9. It was a reviewable error to impose a constructive trust in this situation.

453 In re Kulzer Roofing, Inc, 139 BR 132, 138 (Bankr E D Pa 1992); see also In re Morales Travel Agency, 667 F.2d 1069, 1071 (1st Cir PR 1981). If a ritualistic incantation of trust language were deemed conclusive, it would be a simple matter for one creditor, at the expense of the others, to circumvent the rules pertaining to the creation of *bona fide* security interests. See: www.fullertonlaw.com/construction-law-survival-manual/trust-fund-laws-and-agreements.html. See also discussion of undervalue preferences in Section 5 of this chapter, "Default".

454 See: http://caselaw.canada.globe24h.com/0/0/alberta/court-of-appeal/2009/05/14/brookfield-bridge-lending-fund-inc-v-karl-oil-and-gas-ltd-2009-abca-99.shtml.

In conclusion, it was an error of principle to impose a constructive trust in the circumstances of this case. The express trust agreed to by the parties only attached to the lowest balance of the account on 14 March 2007, plus the respondents' proportion of the additional trust funds deposited on 16 March 2007. The appeal is allowed.

The prudent course under English law may be to establish an express trust of the joint account funds under the terms of the JOA. Such an arrangement would be sufficiently specific to meet the technical legal requirements for an express trust. If the trust was established by the terms of the JOA, it is likely to defeat any challenge that constitutes an unfair preference, putting the joint account monies out of reach of the operator's other creditors, simply because that trust would be established well before the 'suspect period' when the operator's insolvency was in prospect.

As can be seen from the court's decision, the JOA participants, in allowing the operator to commingle the funds, have themselves created risks and difficulties in claiming damages from the operator in the event that it disposed of the funds in trust. As a result, non-operators may be unwilling to accept provisions in the JOA that allow the operator to commingle the funds or may be willing to establish a proper express trust to ensure their interests are protected better.

11. Tax

11.1 General principles

The taxation clause tends to be straightforward during JOA negotiations. Usually, both international and national oil companies agree with the general concept behind this clause. It should be a matter of compliance with the applicable law.

11.2 Analysis of model JOAs

The key concept is that each party will be responsible to pay its own taxation in relation to its participating interest in the consortium. This is exactly the approach taken by the AIPN JOA Model Form:

> *Each Party shall be responsible for reporting and discharging its own tax measured by the profit or income of the Party and the satisfaction of such Party's share of all contract obligations under the Contract and under this Agreement. Each Party shall protect, defend, and indemnify each other Party from any damage, loss, cost or liability arising from the indemnifying Party's failure to report and discharge such taxes or satisfy such obligations. The Parties intend that all income and all tax benefits (including deductions, depreciation, credits and capitalization) regarding the expenditures made by the Parties under this Agreement will be allocated by the Government tax authorities to the Parties based on the share of each tax item actually received or borne by each Party. If such allocation is not accomplished due to the application of the Laws or other Government action, the Parties shall attempt to adopt mutually agreeable arrangements that will allow the Parties to achieve the*

financial results intended. Operator shall provide each Party, in a timely manner and at such Party's sole expense, with such information concerning Joint Operations as such Party may reasonably request for preparation of its tax returns or responding to any audit or other tax proceeding.[455]

A similar approach is provided by the Norwegian JOA Model Form:

7.1 Unless otherwise specified in this Agreement, the Parties shall be primarily liable to each other on a pro rata basis, secondarily jointly and severally liable for all obligations arising by virtue of the joint venture's activities. This applies irrespective of a liability towards third parties.
7.2 Each Party is responsible for his share of the area fee. If a Party does not pay his share, the Operator shall make the payment on his behalf and apportion the amount between the other Parties in accordance with their Participating interest.
7.3 None of the other Parties may be held liable pursuant to Article 7.1 for direct taxes which a Party is obliged to pay. Each Party is obliged to pay the direct taxes charged to him.[456]

However, the general taxation on the joint operations will be paid by the operator and charged to the joint account. The Greenlandic and Canadian JOA Model Forms provide, respectively, a good example of this approach:

The Operator shall pay for the Joint Account all rentals, taxes (except taxes based on income and profits), fees and charges which may be levied or assessed by, or due or payable to the Government of Greenland, any sub-division thereof or any Greenland municipality on or with respect to the respective Percentage Interests of the Parties, except that each of the Parties shall pay all surplus royalties which become due and payable on and with respect to such Party's share of the Joint Hydrocarbons including on any proportionate share of Hydrocarbons which may be purchased from NUNAOIL in accordance with Section 13.01 of the Licence.[457]
The Operator will initially pay, for the Joint Account, all taxes levied against the Joint Property (including, subject to the Regulations, the Working Interest share of any freehold mineral taxes), except income taxes and other levies assessed against the Parties individually. However, the Operator may decline to pay freehold mineral taxes if it is not the lessee under the particular Title Document under which they accrue. The Operator will promptly forward to each Party a copy of any tax notice or assessment it receives for any tax or assessment against the Joint Property that is not borne for the Joint Account.[458]

455 AIPN JOA §14.2.
456 Norwegian JOA §7.1, 7.2, 7.3.
457 Greenlandic JOA §3.14.
458 CAPL JOA §3.13.

This refers to the standard process in the petroleum industry. However, it is possible that the national oil company will be responsible for paying the taxes on behalf of the international oil company, or that eventually a specific tax exemption will be given in the hydrocarbon laws or the host government contract. In any case, the JOA parties should comply with the applicable laws and host government contract.

Some JOA Model Forms may clearly express their intention to avoid any consideration of partnership as this may have tax implications, especially in common law jurisdictions.[459]

In addition, corporate planning should be considered well ahead of the conclusion of drafting the JOA. All international investors should establish whether their home country has a bilateral investment treaty with the host government where they intend to invest and sign their JOA. Furthermore, without a double tax treaty, an international investor could end up paying twice for the same taxation (ie, at the place of the business and in its home country). In turn, the national oil company is likely to ensure that the consortium will comply with local laws and make use of any mechanism to avoid local taxation.

11.3 Discussion

Therefore, from an international oil company's perspective, the JOA parties should check beforehand which company should sign the relevant JOA, but always in compliance with the applicable laws (especially the law of the country where they intend to do business as in some countries, eg, Brazil, as only a company incorporated in the country may be the owner of the oil and gas licence interests) to secure adequate tax planning for the business.

Finally, taxation is unlikely to be included in the negotiation process of the JOA, but instead will be treated as a compliance issue. Corporate planning should be considered well in advance, as this may affect the taxation of the project as a whole and the entities involved. In addition, investors may wish to negotiate taxation issues at the governmental level (if applicable), as the government and/or the legislature has discretion to provide further incentives for both international and local companies.

---

459 *Ibid.*

3. Boiler plate

1. Governing law

1.1 General principles

Governing law is a very short but important provision in any JOA. It dictates which laws and rules will apply to the performance and validity of the agreement. Most international oil companies are likely to prefer the JOA to be governed by a foreign regime of law, such as English, New York, Swiss, French or Swedish law, among others, depending on the region of the transaction and the parties involved. On the other hand, most national oil companies are likely to prefer to be governed by local laws.

The international oil companies may argue that the JOA is a separate agreement from the host government agreement and therefore different governing laws can be negotiated. The national oil company may argue that this contract governs its parties' performance of the host government contract and operations should respect the local laws. If the JOA has to be approved by the host government, it will be more difficult to negotiate a foreign law in the JOA (eg, Norway, Morocco and Mozambique);[1] otherwise, the parties may be free to negotiate which law shall govern their JOA to the extent the local laws and regulations are observed.

1.2 Analysis of model JOAs

The AIPN JOA Model Form is the only model that leaves the choice of governing law open for the parties to negotiate, as follows:

> *18.1 Applicable Law*
> *In other words, there is no doubt about the expectation that the operations will be performed jointly.*
> *ALTERNATIVE PROVISION, CHOOSE ONE*
> *ALTERNATIVE #1*
> *The substantive laws of ______________, exclusive of any conflicts of laws principles that could require the application of any other law, shall govern this Agreement for all purposes.*
> *ALTERNATIVE #2*

1 A Ovcharova, TP Gormley and EG Pereira, "To What Extent Should a Host Government Interfere in the Drafting and Conclusion of a Joint Operating Agreement?" *LEF Energy Law Review* (2016) 1.

The laws of _____________, to the extent consistent with international law, shall govern this Agreement for all purposes. To the extent the laws of _____________ are not consistent with international law, then international law shall prevail.[2]

The majority of the JOA Model Forms define the governing law and this tends to be the same as the location of the asset/operation. Some examples are given below.

- Australian Model
  This agreement is governed by and must be construed in accordance with the laws of the Nominated State. The parties submit irrevocably to the non-exclusive jurisdiction of the Courts of the Nominated State and all Courts competent to hear appeals from those Courts.[3]
- Norwegian Model
  Unless the Parties agree to bring a dispute before the courts of law, any dispute arising in connection with this Agreement shall be settled by arbitration in Norway pursuant to Norwegian law. The provisions of the Act No 25 of 14 May 2004 relating to arbitration shall apply unless otherwise agreed.[4]
- British Model
  This Agreement shall be governed by and shall be construed according to the laws of England and in respect of any dispute regarding the validity, enforceability or interpretation of this Agreement; each of the Participants (including the Participant acting in the capacity of Operator) hereby irrevocably submits to the [exclusive] jurisdiction of the English courts.[5]
- Greenlandic Model
  This Agreement shall be governed by and construed in accordance with Danish law and subject to Article 12.6; each of the Parties hereby submits to the jurisdiction of the courts of Denmark.[6]
- Moroccan Model
  This Contract shall be governed and interpreted in conformity with Moroccan Law, in conformity with the terms of Article 7 of the Petroleum Agreement.[7]

1.3 Discussion

In general, it is quite difficult for an international oil company to negotiate with a national oil company to secure a foreign law to govern the JOA. However, in certain cases this may be possible if the government does not participate in the JOA approval process and if the international company has a strong bargaining power in the jurisdiction.

It is important to distinguish between the laws that will be applicable to the JOA by reason of the choice of its governing law, the laws that will apply mandatorily by reason of the location where operations take place, the laws that apply to the parties by reason of their country of incorporation and/or citizenship of the individuals

2 AIPN JOA §18.1.
3 AMPLA JOA §25.7.
4 Norwegian JOA §29.1.
5 OGUK JOA §29.1.
6 Greenlandic JOA §12.7.
7 ONHYM JOA §16.

participating in operations, and the laws applicable to disputes in the forum for dispute resolution chosen by the JOA. Using the example of English law, the legislation and common law applicable to the interpretation of contracts[8] will apply to any contract which is expressly governed by English law, but certain provisions of the UK Bribery Act are applicable to any person connected with the UK carrying out operations in any part of the world.[9] The reality is that the governing law of the JOA is only one body of law that will be applicable to operations and it will only apply to the interpretation of the JOA and the relations between parties to it. Operations themselves will be governed by local laws and regulations including petroleum laws, the terms of the host government agreement as interpreted by its governing law and potentially the laws of other countries which have extraterritorial effect. The JOA is unlikely to detail all of the laws and regulations applicable to operations conducted under it (eg, environmental regulations, labour regulations, compliance regulations). It is more likely to contain a general statement requiring compliance with the applicable law and the host government contract. Local laws and regulations including petroleum laws will apply automatically and compulsorily to operations conducted within their territorial scope, regardless of the JOA's terms. This is why the JOAs tend to be silent on the matter. This is also why JOAs commonly include a provision which excuses the operator from failing to comply with any JOA provisions, if and to the extent that such local laws require the operator to act in breach of such JOA provision; local laws governing operations will necessarily prevail over any conflicting JOA requirement.

However, if the parties decide to adopt a foreign law to govern their JOA, they should include a provision on performing the operations and activities in compliance with the local laws and regulations.[10] AAPL Model Form 810 gives a good example of this.[11] It is important for the operator to ensure that all parties understand and acknowledge that the liabilities they may incur for which they expect indemnification from the JOA parties may arise under local laws, in circumstances which would not be a breach of the JOA governing law or the terms of the JOA itself.

Generally, the regulatory regime will not be a negotiable item between the JOA parties as they must comply with the local laws of the country in which they intend to do business. However, an international oil company may be able to negotiate with the host government the implementation of certain law reforms or protections before it decides to realise any investment in that country. However, this is a matter for vertical negotiation with the host government, not a direct joint-venture discussion. Nevertheless, the question of the law governing the JOA could lead to a heated discussion between the international and national oil companies. The importance of this discussion can be exaggerated because, as discussed, the governing law of the JOA simply establishes the legal rules applicable to its interpretation. However, the parties may prefer to choose a common law regime such as English or New York law because such laws have a strong respect for the freedom of the parties to contract on their own terms, and are less disposed to interfering with, and rewriting, the terms of the contract, when compared to civil law regimes. What is more significant and more controversial is the choice of dispute resolution forum.

---

8 For example, Law Reform (Frustrated Contracts) Act 1943.
9 Bribery Act 2010 Section 12.
10 ONHYM JOA §16.
11 AAPL JOA Form 810 §26.4.

2. Dispute resolution

2.1 General principles

The traditional approach to resolving a dispute is through the courts of justice via litigation. As the main and general dispute resolution process, litigation offers some well-known characteristics, such as:

- high cost;
- long duration;
- no privacy for the outcome;
- non-specialised knowledge of the judges involved; and
- state control of the due process.

Nowadays, litigation is still the main procedure used to resolve disputes between parties. However, the oil and gas industry has a different perspective and a number of specific needs, which are discussed here.

The oil and gas industry usually involves a large amount of investment and risk. Therefore, disputes should be resolved in the most efficient way in order to maximise the return on the investments.

In addition, the number of participants in the oil and gas industry that may work together on a global scale is relatively low. Litigation may harm their relationships, and future negotiations or businesses may be at risk. Therefore, it is important to maintain strategic and positive relationships between all parties.

Participants in the oil and gas sector will wish to avoid public exposure of their problems, so privacy is a key element of dispute resolution. Furthermore, the oil and gas industry relies on specialised technical knowledge, which will be required in any conflict determination. If the person hearing and deciding the dispute does not have industry knowledge, a lot of time will be lost while he or she learns about the specialised issues.

Therefore, oil and gas companies are likely to seek the following characteristics in a dispute resolution process:

- quick;
- low cost;
- specialist knowledge of the decision maker;
- privacy; and
- control of the process.

In this context, Margaret Ross comments on the peculiarity of the oil and gas industry, as follows:

> *There is a need for processes that are fast, effective and cause minimum disruption to working processes and relationships. The preference is for processes which are both private and flexible. They require to be capable of crossing both international boundaries and business culture. There is a limited pool of industry players, but they operate within a global marketplace. These factors combine to create an incentive to avoid making future enemies out of the present dispute, and draw into the range of choices the dispute resolution experiences and preferences of many nationalities and professions.*[12]

---

12 M Ross, "Dispute Management and Resolution" in G Gordon and J Paterson (eds), *Oil and Gas Law: Current Practice and Emerging Trends*, Dundee University Press, 2007, p431.

In other words, for most oil and gas companies, efficiency is the essential element of any dispute resolution process. This is likely to be implemented in the JOA whenever only private parties are involved. However, if the joint venture involves a national oil company it may be more difficult to negotiate a dispute resolution provision in a similar manner, as the national oil company may wish to negotiate a dispute resolution in line with the host government contract and/or state policy.

Most national oil companies are unlikely to want their disputes to be governed by international rules or resolved at international venues. They may view these as procedures to limit their control of a dispute. In some cases, a national oil company may prefer to resolve a dispute through a local court, as it may be familiar with its procedures. However, in some cases the national oil company may be as large as any international oil company and have a range of international operations and may prefer the same dispute resolution procedure as an international oil company. On the other hand, an international oil company or eventually a national oil company with international operations may not view local courts as an impartial process to resolve the dispute because of eventual governmental interference in the outcome.

In summary, the negotiation of a dispute resolution clause may lead to some tension between international and national oil companies. It is important to analyse whether the existing JOA Models provide flexibility for the companies to negotiate this clause to the extent that government approval is not required or interferes with the JOA negotiation, for example, in Norway, Mozambique and Morocco.

2.2 Analysis of model JOAs

The AIPN JOA Model Form is extremely flexible since it foresees different routes for the parties to elect the options they wish to adopt. The first optional provision is called "notification". This provision aims to inform the other party or parties about the existence of a claim within a summary of the case, as follows:

> *OPTIONAL PROVISION – NOTIFICATION, CHOOSE ARTICLE 18.2.A IF ARTICLE 18.2.B OR 18.2.C IS CHOSEN. RENUMBER FOLLOWING PARAGRAPHS AND CHECK CROSS-REFERENCES, IF NEITHER ARTICLE 18.2.B NOR 18.2.C IS CHOSEN.*
> *Notification. A Party who desires to submit a Dispute for resolution shall commence the Dispute resolution process by providing the other parties to the Dispute written notice of the Dispute ("Notice of Dispute"). The Notice of Dispute shall identify the parties to the Dispute and contain a brief statement of the nature of the Dispute and the relief requested. The submission of a Notice of Dispute shall toll any applicable statutes of limitation related to the Dispute, pending the conclusion or abandonment of Dispute resolution proceedings under this Article 18.*[13]

This provision is commonly found in JOAs since it helps the parties to negotiate or to take the necessary measures before an adjudicatory process takes place. The second optional provision is called "senior executive negotiation". Its purpose is to enable the parties to resolve the dispute before their position becomes entrenched,

13 AIPN JOA §18.2.

when there is still an opportunity to prioritise the relationship over the specific matters at stake. Some JOAs provide that the relevant negotiators should not be senior managers involved in operations under the JOA; this may seem surprising, but it has the advantage of placing the decision making and dispute resolution in the hands of individuals whose responsibilities are wider than the financial performance of the particular asset and have greater authority to make the compromises necessary to reach a solution. It can be described in the following terms:

OPTIONAL PROVISION – SENIOR EXECUTIVE NEGOTIATIONS, CHOOSE ARTICLE 18.2.B, IF DESIRED. RENUMBER FOLLOWING PARAGRAPHS AND CHECK CROSS-REFERENCES, IF ARTICLE 18.2.B IS NOT CHOSEN.
Negotiations. The parties to the Dispute shall seek to resolve any Dispute by negotiation between Senior Executives. A "Senior Executive" means any individual who has authority to negotiate the settlement of the Dispute for a Party. Within thirty (30) Days after the date of the receipt by each party to the Dispute of the Notice of Dispute (which notice shall request negotiations among Senior Executives), the Senior Executives representing the parties to the Dispute shall meet at a mutually acceptable time and place to exchange relevant information in an attempt to resolve the Dispute. If a Senior Executive intends to be accompanied at the meeting by an attorney, each other party's Senior Executive shall be given written notice of such intention at least three (3) Days in advance and may also be accompanied at the meeting by an attorney. Despite the above, any Party may initiate arbitration proceedings under Article 18.2.D or mediation proceedings under Article 18.2.C concerning such Dispute within thirty (30) Days after the date of receipt of the Notice of Dispute.[14]

It is clear that the parties involved should have the authority to settle an agreement and retain significant knowledge about the case. However, this option does not have a third party to conduct and evaluate the case, as is provided in a mini-trial and other forms of dispute resolution. Nevertheless, it is important to stress that this option will not bind the parties, unless it is their intention to do so.

The third optional provision is the mediation route, which can be requested by senior executives (if the previous option is chosen) or by the parties:

OPTIONAL PROVISION – MEDIATION, CHOOSE ARTICLE 18.2.C, IF DESIRED. RENUMBER FOLLOWING PARAGRAPHS AND CHECK CROSS-REFERENCES, IF ARTICLE 18.2.C IS NOT CHOSEN.
Mediation. [Subject to the requirements of negotiation between Senior Executives under Article 18.2.B], [t]he parties to the Dispute shall seek to resolve the Dispute by mediation. Within thirty (30) Days after the date of the receipt by each party to the Dispute of the Notice of Dispute, thirty (30) Days after the date of the first negotiation meeting among Senior Executives under Article 18.2.B, any party to the Dispute may

14 AIPN JOA §18.2.

initiate such mediation pursuant to the [________ mediation rules then in effect, as modified herein] by sending all other parties to the Dispute a written request that the Dispute be mediated. The Parties receiving such written request will promptly respond to the requesting Party so that all parties to the Dispute may jointly select a neutral mediator and schedule the mediation session. The mediator shall meet with the parties to the Dispute to mediate the Dispute within thirty (30) Days after the date of receipt of the written request for mediation. Despite the above, any Party may initiate arbitration proceedings under Article [18.2.D] concerning such Dispute within thirty (30) Days after the date of receipt of the Notice of Dispute within sixty (60) Days after the date of receipt of the Notice of Dispute.[15]

The consensual process involved within this option is very clear, as the parties may still go forward within arbitration proceedings. Another provision that is very common within the oil and gas industry is expert determination. The AIPN Model also provides, as an option, an expert determination clause, in the following terms:

OPTIONAL PROVISION (ARTICLE 18.3), CHOOSE ARTICLE 18.3, IF ANY OF ARTICLE 8.4 – ALTERNATIVE #2, ARTICLE 12.2.F – ALTERNATIVE #2, OR ARTICLE 12.3.C – ALTERNATIVE #2 IS CHOSEN. RENUMBER FOLLOWING ARTICLE AND CHECK CROSS-REFERENCES, IF ARTICLE 18.3 IS NOT CHOSEN.
Expert Determination
For any decision referred to an expert under Article [8.4, 12.2 or 12.3], the Parties hereby agree that such decision shall be conducted expeditiously by an expert selected unanimously by the parties to the Dispute. The expert is not an arbitrator of the Dispute and shall not be deemed to be acting in an arbitral capacity. The Party desiring an expert determination shall give the other parties to the Dispute written notice of the request for such determination. If the parties to the Dispute are unable to agree upon an expert within ten (10) Days after receipt of the notice of request for an expert determination, then, upon the request of any of the parties to the Dispute, the International Centre for Expertise of the International Chamber of Commerce (ICC) shall appoint such expert and shall administer such expert determination through the ICC's Rules for Expertise. The expert, once appointed, must not have any ex parte communications with any of the parties to the Dispute concerning the expert determination or the underlying Dispute. All Parties agree to cooperate fully in the expeditious conduct of such expert determination and to provide the expert with access to all facilities, books, records, documents, information, and personnel necessary to make a fully informed decision in an expeditious manner. Before issuing his final decision, the expert shall issue a draft report and allow the parties to the Dispute to comment on it. The expert shall endeavour to resolve the Dispute within thirty (30) Days (but no later than sixty (60) Days) after his appointment, taking into account the circumstances requiring an expeditious resolution of the matter in Dispute. The expert's decision shall be final and binding on the parties to the

15 AIPN JOA §18.2.

Dispute unless challenged in an arbitration under Article 18.2.D within sixty (60) Days of the date the expert's final decision is received by the parties to the Dispute. In such arbitration (i) the expert determination on the specific matter under Article [8.4, 12.2 or 12.3] shall be entitled to a rebuttable presumption of correctness; and (ii) the expert shall not (without the written consent of the parties to the Dispute) be appointed to act as an arbitrator or as adviser to the parties to the Dispute.[16]

The expert determination process has several characteristics which make it most suitable for the resolution of technical disputes, where the key matters at stake require an expert decision, deploying specific industry knowledge. For example, that might include a decision on the prevailing market price of a participating interest, the scope of "industry good oil field practice" in relation to an alleged breach of the JOA or the correct classification of costs for the purposes of the accounting procedure. In these cases, the parties may wish to prioritise obtaining a resolution swiftly and confidentially, according to a process they control and have confidence in, over the specific financial impact of the outcome. However, the parties should be encouraged to identify which types of dispute should be subject to expert determination expressly in the terms of the JOA, because it will be difficult for the parties to agree to apply the expert process by agreement between them when a dispute actually arises.

A disadvantage with the expert determination process is that its judicial status is ambiguous. Most legal regimes will not provide for any form of judicial intervention in the expert process, unless a party is in breach of the express terms of the JOA governing the expert determination process. The expert determination clause should be carefully and exhaustively drafted to minimise the risk that these ambiguities are exploited by a party to derail the process. As a general rule, the decision taken by the expert is final and will bind all the parties involved. The inclusion of this option in JOA Models is very common because the decision is taken by an impartial expert within a short time. However, it is not suitable for all claims, as was mentioned above.

Finally, the main dispute resolution process in the AIPN Model is arbitration, which is not an optional inclusion. The clause clearly mentions previous failures of the other alternatives to dispute resolution (when they have been selected), described as follows:

Arbitration. Any Dispute [not finally resolved by alternative Dispute resolution procedures set forth in Articles 18.2.B and 18.2.C] shall be resolved through final and binding arbitration, it being the intention of the Parties that this is a broad form arbitration agreement designed to encompass all possible Disputes, including Disputes about the arbitrability of a Dispute.

Rules. The arbitration shall be conducted under the arbitration rules (as then in effect) of ________________ (the "Rules").

Number of Arbitrators. The arbitration shall be conducted by three arbitrators, unless all parties to the Dispute agree to a sole arbitrator within thirty (30) Days

16 AIPN JOA §18.3.

after the commencement of the arbitration. For greater certainty, for purposes of this Article 18.2.D, the commencement of the arbitration means the date on which the claimant's request or demand for, or notice of, arbitration is received by the other parties to the Dispute.

Method of Appointment of the Arbitrators. If the arbitration is to be conducted by a sole arbitrator, then the arbitrator will be jointly selected by the parties to the Dispute within thirty (30) Days after the commencement of the arbitration. If the arbitration is to be conducted by three arbitrators and there are only two parties to the Dispute, then each party to the Dispute shall appoint one arbitrator within thirty (30) Days of the commencement of the arbitration, and the two arbitrators so appointed shall select the presiding arbitrator within thirty (30) Days after the latter of the two arbitrators has been appointed by the parties to the Dispute.

Place of Arbitration. Unless otherwise agreed by all parties to the Dispute, the place of arbitration shall be __________________.

Language. The arbitration proceedings shall be conducted in the [English] language and the arbitrator(s) shall be fluent in the [English] language.

Entry of Judgment. The award of the arbitral tribunal shall be final and binding. Judgment on the award of the arbitral tribunal may be entered and enforced by any court of competent jurisdiction.

Notice. All notices required for any arbitration proceeding shall be deemed properly given if sent under Article 17.

OPTIONAL PROVISION, CHOOSE IF DESIRED.

Without limiting the generality of the foregoing, any party to the Dispute may have recourse to and shall be bound by the Pre-arbitral Referee Procedure of the International Chamber of Commerce under its rules then in effect.

Interest. The award shall include interest, as determined by the arbitral tribunal, from the date of any default or other breach of this Agreement until the arbitral award is paid in full. Interest shall be awarded at the Agreed Interest Rate.

Currency of Award. The arbitral award shall be made and payable in United States dollars, free of any tax or other deduction.

Exemplary Damages. The Parties waive their rights to claim or recover from each other, and the arbitral tribunal shall not award, any punitive, multiple, or other exemplary damages (whether statutory or common law) except to the extent such damages have been awarded to a third party and are subject to allocation between or among the parties to the Dispute.

OPTIONAL PROVISION, CHOOSE ARTICLE 18.2.D.11, IF DESIRED.

Consolidation. If the Parties initiate multiple arbitration proceedings, the subject matters of which are related by common questions of law or fact and that could result in conflicting awards or obligations, then all such proceedings may be consolidated into a single arbitral proceeding.

OPTIONAL PROVISION, CHOOSE ARTICLE 18.2.E, IF DESIRED.

Confidentiality. All negotiations, mediation, arbitration, and expert determinations relating to a Dispute (including a settlement resulting from negotiation or mediation, an arbitral award, documents exchanged or produced during a mediation or arbitration proceeding, and memorials, briefs or other documents prepared for the arbitration) are confidential and may not be disclosed by the Parties, their employees, officers, directors, counsel, consultants, and

> *expert witnesses, except (under Article 15.2) to the extent necessary to enforce this Article 18 or any arbitration award, to enforce other rights of a Party, or as required by law; provided, however, that breach of this confidentiality provision shall not void any settlement, expert determination or award.*[17]

This model gives the parties the option to choose the arbitration rules and the method of appointing the arbitrators. In addition, other arbitration provisions are addressed, such as the number of arbitrators, place of arbitration, language, entry of judgment, notice, qualification/conduct of the arbitrators and interim measures, among others.

Therefore, the AIPN Model provides for an increased number of optional mechanisms for the parties in order to resolve their disputes. In addition, it adopts arbitration as the main dispute resolution process, allowing for the use of a court process for the purpose of registration and enforcement of arbitration awards. The option of international arbitration has much to recommend it, because it is a private and confidential mechanism, but especially because it enables the parties to choose the members of the arbitration tribunal. Through that choice, the parties can ensure that the tribunal has adequate expertise to understand the industry issues at stake and that the tribunal is properly objective and not aligned with a particular party. This enhances the confidence of the parties in the process, and therefore the acceptability of the outcome. States themselves may accept an international arbitration mechanism in the host government agreement because it offers a reasonable guarantee of fair treatment for foreign investors. If the state accepts arbitration for the purposes of the host government agreement, it will be easier for the IOCs to persuade any NOC to accept the same arbitration solution in the JOA. The main dispute resolution provision in the British JOA Model Form is traditional court litigation, as provided in clause 2.9:

> *2.9 Applicable Law*
> *2.9.1 This Agreement shall be governed by and shall be construed according to the laws of England and in respect of any dispute regarding the validity, enforceability or interpretation of this Agreement each of the Participants (including the Participant acting in the capacity of Operator) hereby irrevocably submits to the [exclusive] jurisdiction of the English courts.*[18]

As a general rule, this provision is not very common in the oil and gas industry (especially among oil and gas companies). The parties will wish to avoid litigation through the courts because it is costly and time-consuming. Certainly, on some occasions it will be necessary to proceed with litigation, but not as the main solution for any dispute resolution. National oil companies may prefer the system adopted in the British JOA Model Form for UK operations, but they are unlikely to accept English courts resolving those disputes that arise outside the United Kingdom.

17 AIPN JOA §18.2.
18 OGUK JOA §29.

The UK Model is much simpler than the AIPN Model. There are no options available for the parties. There is only one alternative available, which is expert determination.[19]

Therefore, it is clear that the UK Model does provide for consensual methods of alternative dispute resolution, but prefers to focus on adjudicatory methods such as expert determination and litigation.

AAPL Form 610 is the simplest of all the models available.[20] Its provision is very short, and states that any conflict shall be resolved in accordance with the rules and laws of the state (province) in which the licence/lease is in force – that is, unless the state has an alternative dispute resolution provided in its legislation (which is not common), any conflict must be resolved via litigation.

The Greenlandic JOA Model Form uses a similar approach to AAPL JOA Model Form 610 and the British JOA Model Form, as no consensual alternative dispute resolution process is provided. However, in this case the dispute resolution will be conducted by arbitration, as provided by clause 12.6:

> *12.6. Arbitration*
> *Any dispute between the Parties arising out of or in connection with this Agreement shall be finally settled by a board of arbitration consisting of an umpire and two other arbitrators. The board of arbitration shall be appointed at the request of any one of the Parties to the Dispute. When such request has been made, the Party or Parties, which are complainants to the case, shall nominate a single arbitrator, and the Party or Parties, which are defendants to the case, shall nominate a single arbitrator, such nominations to be made within thirty (30) days of receipt of the referring of the dispute to arbitration. ... Any awards made by the board of arbitration shall be final and binding upon the Parties to the case and shall be enforceable without the necessity of any judgement being rendered thereupon. Subject to the provision hereof, the arbitration shall be conducted according to the rules of Danish law, including the Danish Act on Arbitration, and to the extent specified in said rules, the Danish courts shall have jurisdiction to Section 12.7.*[21]

In addition, this arbitration clause foresees the intervention of court proceedings in specific situations, under the Danish Act on Arbitration. However, the model does not provide any form of consensual alternative resolution or expert determination, which would be very useful to resolve a dispute in an efficient and practical manner.

A much-debated topic is the waiver of sovereign immunity. A national oil company could argue that it does not represent its government and therefore cannot waive immunity. Some international oil companies may prefer to implement a waiver of sovereign immunity as a precaution, to ensure that they can enforce their international dispute resolution process (if applicable). The AIPN Model is the only JOA Model Form to include a provision on this issue:

19 OGUK JOA §17.
20 APPL JOA Model Form 610 §XIV.
21 Greenlandic JOA §12.

18.4 Waiver of Sovereign Immunity
Any Party that now or later has a right to claim sovereign immunity for itself or any of its assets hereby waives any such immunity to the fullest extent permitted by the laws of any applicable jurisdiction. This waiver includes immunity from:
any expert determination, mediation, or arbitration proceeding commenced under this Agreement;

any judicial, administrative or other proceedings to aid the expert determination, mediation, or arbitration commenced under this Agreement; and

any effort to confirm, enforce, or execute any decision, settlement, award, judgment, service of process, execution order or attachment (including pre-judgment attachment) that results from an expert determination, mediation, arbitration or any judicial or administrative proceedings commenced under this Agreement.

For the purposes of this waiver only, each Party acknowledges that its rights and obligations under this Agreement are of a commercial and not a governmental nature.[22]

2.3 Discussion

In conclusion, several alternatives for dispute resolution are available for oil and gas companies to adopt in their JOA standard models. As a general rule, the best solution would be an escalation process, which should include consensual alternatives, such as negotiation and mediation, and adjudicatory methods, such as arbitration (the main dispute resolution process), expert determination (for technical issues), and litigation (for specific procedures and matters), in order to achieve an efficient result.[23] It is also important for the dispute resolution clause to help address any conflict of interest affecting the NOC, as a party to the JOA and as a state-controlled entity. The IOCs would reasonably expect the NOC not to participate in decision making and information sharing with respect to the joint venture's management of any dispute with the state, and indeed NOCs may welcome having a clear contractual mechanism enabling them to step out of such a process for reasons of reputation and transparency. Finally, the main issue between an international and a national oil company is to find a common ground to negotiate this clause as they are likely to have different views on how to implement a fair dispute resolution process.

3. Termination

3.1 General principles

When discussing termination provisions in JOAs, it is important to remember the relationship between the JOA and a granting instrument. In many situations, there will be one granting instrument, which might take different forms: a concession agreement, licence, production sharing agreement or service contract, applying to each JOA. However, there are situations where one JOA may be applicable to several

---

22 AIPN JOA §18.4.

23 The oil and gas parties will seek the following characteristics in a dispute resolution process: (i) quick; (ii) low cost; (iii) specialist knowledge of the decision maker; (iv) privacy; and (v) control of the process.

granting instruments, in which case the JOA will survive the termination of any one of those licences or agreements, and will continue to apply in relation to the licences or the granting instruments which are still valid.

Typically, the JOA has the potential to be valid for the whole term of the granting instrument, if not terminated earlier in accordance with its terms. However, the opposite situation is perfectly possible: for the granting instrument to exist without a JOA and this could be particularly the case where only one entity is party to the granting instrument as sole investor or when only one investor remains after all the rest have left the project for some reasons. It may need to introduce a JOA if it subsequently farms out its interest to new third parties. The purpose of the JOA is facilitative, not mandatory – privately as a form of constitution for the joint venture regulating the horizontal relationship between the parties and establishing the rules which the parties to it voluntarily agree to obey.

Usually, JOAs terminate in accordance with their rules, which may be classified into two groups:

- voluntary, or by agreement of the parties;
- on the occurrence of a trigger event, such as the failure to make a commercial discovery or lack of agreement on the development plan.

It is important to note that like many multiparty agreements, JOAs typically do not include provisions which allow unilateral termination of the agreement by one of the parties. The logic for this is clear, and first of all relates to the fact that the granting instrument itself provides limited grounds for termination and JOAs tend to be valid during the lifetime of the granting instruments. The other reason is that it would not be acceptable for the other parties for one party to have the right to terminate the JOA unilaterally for its own reasons, depriving those other parties of their rights and obligations in circumstances beyond their control. JOAs are voluntary arrangements between the parties; the parties' obligations are widely acknowledged under JOAs and thus should have strong reasons to stop complying with the obligations. Commonly, multiparty contracts tend to have very limited grounds for unilateral termination and aim to support contractual and commercial stability, which is vital to business stability.

3.2 Analysis of model JOAs

The AIPN Model JOA contains only optional termination provisions, which means that if those are not chosen to be used in the particular JOA, the cross-references to the particular grounds of termination, reflected in different parts of the agreement, will be used:

OPTIONAL PROVISION, CHOOSE IF DESIRED. IF NOT CHOSEN CHECK CROSS-REFERENCES.

Termination

The Parties shall proceed to terminate the Contract in accordance with the Contract and applicable Law, if any of the following events occur:

- *The Parties unanimously determine under this Agreement to terminate the Contract;*

> - *All of the Parties are Defaulting Parties and are deemed to have elected to withdraw under Article 8;*
> - *The Parties unanimously determine under Article 11 to surrender the Contract Area, including any Exploitation Areas; and/or*
> - *All of the Parties elect to withdraw under Article 13.*[24]

It is interesting to analyse the second bullet of this list: "All of the Parties are Defaulting Parties and are deemed to have elected to withdraw". The expression "deemed to have elected" is a particular cross-reference to AIPN JOA Article 8.3.E which provides that the parties are deemed to have each decided to withdraw from the joint venture with the effect of triggering termination of it and the JOA on the terms set out in AIPN JOA Article 2. This would be triggered only in circumstances where one JOA party was in default and the other non-defaulting parties had failed to pay their respective shares of the amount in default when called upon to do so by the operator in accordance with AIPN JOA Article 8. The implications of this article are discussed further in Chapter 2, Section 5, "Default".

The AMPLA Model JOA offers the following provisions on termination:

> *Term of agreement*
> *This agreement commences on the date of this agreement and continues until the earliest to occur of any of the following Termination Events:*
> *(a) all of the Non-Defaulting Participants (for themselves and as attorney for each Defaulting Participant) agree in writing to terminate the Joint Venture;*
> *(b) the Operating Committee determines by Unanimous Vote that all economically recoverable reserves of Petroleum in the Title Area have been recovered;*
> *(c) the Operating Committee determines by Unanimous Vote that Joint Operations should cease due to a failure to obtain approval under the Act for any required proposals for the production of any recoverable reserves of Petroleum within the Title Area upon terms and conditions acceptable to all the Participants; or*
> *(d) the Participants cease to hold any interest in any Petroleum Title, and further until completion of the winding up of all Joint Operations.*[25]

3.3 Discussion

Recent political developments have given the termination provisions of the JOA increased importance. IOCs are concerned that either the NOC itself or the entity through which the NOC participates in the joint venture will be caught by the scope of economic sanctions introduced by the UN, US and EU authorities (by reason of being included on the US sanctioned persons list or the EU equivalent).[26] For many

24 AIPN Model JOA Article 2.2.

25 AMPLA Model JOA Article 17.

26 The latest status of economic sanctions can be checked at www.un.org/securitycouncil/sanctions/ information for UN sanctions, https://home.treasury.gov/policy-issues/office-of-foreign-assets-control-sanctions-programs-and-information for US sanctions and https://sanctionsmap.eu/#/main for EU sanctions.

IOCs it will be impossible to continue in a contractual association with NOCs if the latter become sanctioned and/or a blocked person. The IOCs will use every relevant provision of the JOA to ensure compliance with the economic sanctions applicable to them in this situation. The following JOA provisions are especially relevant for a non-sanctioned party under the JOA: (i) compliance with laws/restrictive regulations (though this may not assist if the relevant economic sanctions legislation applies to a party by reason of its country of incorporation, which will likely not bind the other parties); (ii) transfer provisions (possibly structured through put and call options); (iii) withdrawal (commonly the withdrawing party remains liable for all expenditures approved before withdrawal); (iv) inclusion of government's restrictive measures in the events of *force majeure*, which would exclude the liability for non-performing party; (v) removal and replacement of the operator.[27] These provisions are the most typically used. Subject to the comments made above about unilateral termination generally, there could be circumstances in which a party might reasonably insist upon an option to terminate the joint venture and JOA if it becomes subject to economic sanctions preventing it from maintaining an association with an NOC. This might be the case where the joint venture comprises that IOC and NOC only, or where the joint venture takes the form of an incorporated vehicle which can be liquidated or left in the ownership of the NOC upon termination of the joint venture.

In fact, all the model JOAs follow a consistent pattern with respect to the termination process; they provide that the JOA will remain in force after the termination of the granting instrument, while the parties settle outstanding matters with the state, complete any abandonment or decommissioning obligations and dispose of joint property.[28] It is essential for the JOA to remain in force during this critical period because it will involve potentially complex negotiations with the state, particularly with respect to decommissioning and the legal status of facilities, plants and pipelines which are not removed and are left for further use by third parties. In this respect, NOCs and/or the joint venture may wish to carry on using such facilities in support of their other projects in the region. Whether this is carried out by an exclusive operation under the current JOA or is the subject of a separate granting instrument and JOA will need to be agreed by the parties and the government.

In short, the negotiations in between NOCs and IOCs shall not be controversial if the termination of the JOA is linked to the duration of the granting instrument. However, it will be more objectionable if the relevant termination provisions are more likely to terminate the JOA in circumstances where foreseeably some of the parties may wish it to continue.

4. *Force majeure* (chance occurrence)

4.1 General principles

In general, *force majeure* provisions allow the parties to a JOA to suspend fulfilling their obligations under the relevant agreements in circumstances when a supervening force beyond their control prevents the party from performing. Such suspension will not be considered a failure or breach under JOA, while under non-*force majeure*

27 AB Derman, A Melsheimer, TJ Auner and SK Sikes, "The Compliance Dilemma: Economic Sanctions and the APN Model Form International Joint Operating Agreement, Final Draft", *The Journal of World Energy Law & Business*, 12(5) (August 2019) 331–347.

28 OGUK JOA §2; Norwegian JOA §25; Greenlandic JOA §1.2; CAPL JOA §1.14.

circumstances such a delay and/or non-performance would be likely to constitute a breach of the relevant contractual provisions. *Force majeure* has the effect of socialising within the joint venture to some extent the loss incurred by one party by reason of the inability of its failure to perform its JOA obligations, but that should not extend to a party's lack of funds, which is a risk best allocated to that party alone because it alone controls its finances and the financial risks it takes. However, it may be that sanctions legislation makes it unlawful for a party to pay or receive funds which it is required to pay or receive under the JOA, even though such funds are available. In such a case, it may be legitimate for a *force majeure* clause to allow the relevant party more time within which to obtain approval to make or receive the payment, or to find an alternative mechanism for complying with its JOA obligations, but it cannot release the party from its financial obligation permanently.

An important aspect of *force majeure* provisions is that they may only be applied to that portion of the obligation which genuinely could not be fulfilled due to the *force majeure*, while the rest of the obligations must be fulfilled on a timely basis. Practically speaking, a party can only invoke *force majeure* in respect of those obligations which are affected by the relevant *force majeure* event. For example, a party which cannot lift its share of hydrocarbons because of inclement weather at the relevant loading port (which qualifies as *force majeure*) could not invoke such a *force majeure* event as a reason not to pay cash calls or attend OpCom meetings, unless extraordinarily such inclement weather also prevented it from paying cash calls or attending OpCom meetings.

The *force majeure* provisions are unlikely to cause disputes between an international and a national oil company during the course of negotiations. However, the company that acts as the operator and is thus responsible for day-to-day conduct of operations will be more interested in having well-developed force majeure provisions that will allow the operator to suspend the performance of its obligations with a minimum of negative consequences. The JOA may provide that if the operator experiences the *force majeure* circumstances over an extended time, it should resign from its operatorship and transfer that capacity to a party (or person) which is not affected by the *force majeure* circumstances. This provision serves to ensure the uninterrupted and ongoing character of hydrocarbon operations and helps the non-operators to protect their interest in maintaining the pace of joint-venture operations.

If the non-operator's most important obligation is to finance the project activity and if payment obligations generally cannot be suspended due to the *force majeure* provisions, it may appear less likely that the non-operator will be able to use the *force majeure* provisions.[29] The parties may now pay greater attention to the *force majeure* clause, because it may provide them with some relief from their payment obligations if and to the extent that economic sanctions legislation prevents or hinders them from performing such obligations. NOCs and other IOCs not affected by the sanctions legislation may object to the cash flow issues that such sanctions legislation may cause, though the alternative of holding a party in default for delayed payment is

29 International sanctions legislation may, however, prevent a party from meeting its obligations to finance, depending on the laws applicable to it and the banks it uses by virtue of its (and their) country of incorporation. The issue of non-fulfillment of the affected parties obligations due to sanctions restrictions is considered in A Derman, A Melsheimer, TJ Auner and SK Sikes, "The Compliance Dilemma: Economic Sanctions and the AIPN Model Form International Joint Operating Agreement" *The Journal of World Energy Law & Business*, 12(4) (August 2019) 331–347.

also unattractive. Allowing for a delay in payment may be sensible if the affected parties wish to challenge the legality of the sanctions legislation or obtain a licence under that legislation to make the relevant payment. However, the joint venture will need to find a permanent solution, to avoid repeated delays. After all, once the sanctions legislation is in place, its impact is foreseeable and the affected parties must take all reasonable steps to mitigate or avoid its impact on further payments. The parties may consider that economic sanctions should not be included within the scope of JOA "*force majeure* events" because such sanctions constitute a risk which is better managed by each party and their respective parent corporations in their own jurisdictions, and should not therefore be "socialised" across all joint-venture participants. A solution may be for the JOA to provide that a party unable to make payment due under the JOA for a continuous period may be obliged to withdraw from the JOA (with compensation as applicable), after a suitable period of notice, giving it the opportunity to explore other options.

The application of *force majeure* clauses in JOAs is something of a conundrum. First, the operator arguably has less need for *force majeure* protection than an independent contractor because the parties will be obliged to indemnify it for all the consequences of any failure to perform, even by reason of its negligence, let alone an event of *force majeure*. Indeed, the parties should focus on the *force majeure* provisions of their granting instruments to ensure that they can avoid liability or suspend performance of their obligations under the granting instrument when they become impossible to perform. Secondly, it is wrong for the non-operators to consider the *force majeure* clause solely in its application to the operator's performance of its duties. In addition to the obligation to make prompt payment against cash calls or invoices, the non-operators also have the obligation to lift their respective shares of petroleum on a timely basis and may be liable to the joint venture for failure to do so; they should consider the *force majeure* clause carefully from this perspective as well. Indeed, it might be prudent to amend the *force majeure* clause to make it clear that it shall not apply to the lifting of hydrocarbons and that the parties will agree a separate *force majeure* provision for that purpose in the relevant hydrocarbon lifting agreements.

Since there is no doctrine or legal definition of *force majeure* in the common law countries, the definition depends on the particular agreement of the parties and how it is formalised in the wording of the JOA.[30] Some civil law countries define the term *force majeure* in their civil codes. However, irrespective of whether it is defined in the legislation, it may be advisable to repeat the granting instrument definition in the JOA – fewer discrepancies between the two agreements will increase their applicability.[31] However, caution should be exercised here; the *force majeure* clause as formulated in the granting instrument may be the output of a compromise between the state's and the JOA parties' preferred commercial positions, and there is no reason why the JOA parties should adopt that compromise in the JOA against their own interests. Particularly, the state may have insisted that the parties can only invoke *force majeure* if none of the parties of the joint venture is capable of performing

30 "Force majeure is not the term of art under the English law": P Roberts and R Fowler, *Joint Operating Agreements: A Practical Guide*, 4th edn, Globe Law and Business, 2020, p367.

31 "preferably *force majeure* shall be defined in the same terms as are used in the underlying authorization": BG Taverne, *Petroleum, Industry and Governments: A Study of the Involvement of Industry and Government with the Production and Use of Petroleum*, 3rd edn, Kluwer Law International, 2008, p376.

granting instrument obligations – that would be consistent with the principle that the parties are jointly and severally liable for the joint venture's performance of the granting instrument.

Despite there being no fixed definition of the term, there are constantly certain characteristics which must be present for the event to be considered a genuine *force majeure* event. It must be unforeseeable and beyond the control of the party that is claiming the relief on the grounds of *force majeure*. A party that is affected by a *force majeure* event must notify the non-affected party about it immediately, or within a reasonable time after its occurrence. Failure to do so is likely to deprive the affected party of the ability to refer to the *force majeure* provisions once it is no longer able to conduct the performance of the operations. Examples of *force majeure* events include labour disputes, natural disasters and governmental actions.

4.2 Analysis of model JOAs

The JOA Models provide different approaches to the *force majeure* provisions. For example, the AIPN Model JOA proposes the following definition of *force majeure*:

> *Force Majeure*
> *ALTERNATIVE PROVISION, CHOOSE ONE*
> *ALTERNATIVE # 1*
> *shall have the same meaning as is set out in the Contract.*
> *ALTERNATIVE # 2*
> *means for the purposes of this Agreement those circumstances beyond the reasonable control of the Party concerned,*
> *OPTIONAL PROVISION, CHOOSE, IF DESIRED.*
> *that could not have been avoided or mitigated by foresight, planning, and implementation consistent with generally accepted practices of the international petroleum industry,*
> *including strikes, lockouts, and other industrial disturbances even if they were not beyond the reasonable control of the Party.*

As can be seen from this definition, the AIPN Model JOA provides a choice of options, either to reiterate the granting instrument definition or to define the event of *force majeure* as an enforceable event that is beyond the party's control. The AIPN Model specifically emphasises that the parties to a JOA will not be obliged to settle labour disputes:

> *If as a result of force majeure any Party is rendered unable, wholly or in part, to carry out its obligations under this Agreement, other than the obligation to pay any amounts due or to furnish Security, then the obligations of the Party giving such notice, so far as and to the extent that the obligations are affected by such force*

majeure, shall be suspended during the continuance of any inability so caused and for such reasonable period afterwards as may be necessary for the Party to put itself in the same position that it occupied before the force majeure, but for no longer period. The Party claiming force majeure shall notify the other Parties of the force majeure within a reasonable time after the occurrence of the facts relied on and shall keep all Parties informed of all significant developments. Such notice shall give reasonably full particulars of the force majeure and also estimate the period of time that the Party will probably require to remedy the force majeure. The affected Party shall use all reasonable diligence to remove or overcome the force majeure situation as quickly as possible in an economic manner but shall not be obligated to settle any labour dispute except on terms acceptable to it, and all such disputes shall be handled within the sole discretion of the affected Party.[32]

The definition of a *force majeure* event in AMPLA Model JOA also provides that the affected party cannot rely upon *force majeure* relief if the matter concerns payment obligations. In addition, and in comparison, with the AIPN JOA Model, the AMPLA Model states that an event that could have been prevented will not constitute *force majeure*:

MEANING OF FORCE MAJEURE
In this agreement, "force majeure" means any cause which is not reasonably within the control of the Participant or the Operator claiming relief by reason of force majeure, which cause may include:
In other words, there is no doubt about the expectation that the operations will be performed jointly.
(a) an act of God, earthquake, lightning, fire, flood, storm, cyclone, explosion or epidemic;
(b) strike, lockout, stoppage, ban or other types of labour difficulty whether at the Title Area, railway or port or otherwise;
(c) war (whether declared or undeclared), blockade, act of a public enemy, act of terrorism, revolution, insurrection, riot, civil commotion, sabotage, malicious damage, radioactive contamination, toxic or dangerous chemical contamination;
(d) action or inaction by a competent Authority (including heritage related restraints and, refusal or failure to grant any Authorisation despite timely reasonable endeavours to obtain the same);
(e) inability to access all or any part of a Title Area because of Native Title Claims or Native Title Rights or otherwise;
(f) unavailability or mechanical and electrical breakdown and failure of equipment, plant, pipelines, transmission lines or transport; or
(g) any other cause whether specifically listed above or otherwise which is not reasonably within the control of the party claiming force majeure except where:

32 AIPN JOA Article 16.

> *(h) the cause is the inability to obtain, use or pay, moneys for any reason; or*
> *(i) the consequences of the cause could have been prevented, overcome or remedied by the exercise by the party affected of care and diligence consistent with Good Australian Oilfield Practice.*[33]

The Greenlandic JOA contains a fairly classical section on *force majeure*. Similarly, to the AIPN Model JOA, it does not require the parties to settle labour disputes:

> *The obligations of each of the Parties hereunder, other than the obligations to make payments of money, shall be suspended during the period and to the extent that such Party is prevented or hindered in whole or in part from complying therewith by "force majeure" (as hereinafter defined). In such event, such Party shall give notice of suspension as soon as reasonably possible to the other Parties stating the date and extent of such suspension and full particulars of the cause thereof. Any of the Parties whose obligations have been suspended as aforesaid shall resume the performance of such obligations as soon as reasonably possible after the removal of the cause and shall so notify all the other Parties.*
> *In this Article 12.5, "force majeure" means any circumstance which could not reasonably be foreseen and/or reasonably overcome and is beyond the reasonable control of such Party including (in so far as beyond such control but without prejudice to the generality of the foregoing expression) strikes, lock-outs and labour disputes, but such Party shall not be obliged to settle any labour dispute except in such manner as it shall in its sole judgement consider fit, and in compliance with any law or governmental order, rule, regulation or direction, if (and only if) the same is issued by governmental agencies or bodies in Greenland or Denmark or by any other organization with authority within Greenland or Denmark. A lack of funds shall not constitute "force majeure".*[34]

4.3 Discussion

In the last five years, new risks threatening the continuity of hydrocarbon operations have emerged or intensified; threats to the integrity of computer systems through hacking and other forms of cybersecurity interference have occurred, climate change is manifesting itself in extreme storm and flooding events around the globe, and the COVID-19 epidemic has wreaked havoc on supply chains, employment and hydrocarbon prices. Some model JOAs clarify the scope of *force majeure* by listing specific circumstances which would qualify as a *force majeure* event, such as an act of God; of these model JOAs, only the AMPLA JOA expressly includes epidemics, and none of them specifically refer to cybersecurity risks. But would the stakeholders of the joint project accept the cybersecurity risks as the event of *force majeure* after hackers have exploited the vulnerability of the joint-venture IT systems because

33 AMPLA JOA Article 21.1.
34 Greenland JOA Article 12.5.

of lack of due diligence on the part of joint-venture IT manager? Would it be a reasonable excuse for suspension of contractual obligations if such risks could have been prevented and controlled by the installation of appropriate IT systems and controls? Cybersecurity risks are well known and countermeasures widely available; accordingly, avoidable cybersecurity interference will likely not qualify for *force majeure* relief.

However, cybersecurity breaches, climate change events and epidemics will generically be caught within the scope of *force majeure* definition, either as an act of God, or other event beyond the reasonable control of the affected party.

In each case the parties to the particular JOA, while considering the *force majeure* clause, should consider the nature of operations, their location, the availability of insurance and a balanced allocation of risks between them, as well as the existing obligations of the consortium to the host government under the granting instrument.

For the reasons explained above, a JOA *force majeure* clause has limited practical application because the costs and risks of hydrocarbon operations are naturally socialised within the joint venture through the operator indemnity discussed in Chapter 1, Section 3. Any event of gross negligence or wilful misconduct by the operator which disapplies that indemnity is also not going to qualify as an event of *force majeure*.

That said, events such as the COVID-19 pandemic have tested the robustness of JOAs and the relationships between IOCs and NOCs within the joint venture. On 20 April 2020, world oil prices fell below zero for the first time in their history; WTO prices reached negative US dollars 37.63 per barrel. That event and the lingering depression in prices gave rise to a sharp contraction in activity as discretionary investments were deferred and contracts cancelled in an attempt to save cash by IOCs and NOCs facing significant economic loss. On the one hand, the sharp destruction in hydrocarbon demand aligned IOCs and NOCs in taking such rapid and drastic measures. However, different perspectives arose with respect to the impact of these measures on local employment and supply chain issues; the state, influencing the joint venture through any NOC representation, would wish to avoid large-scale contract cancellation, triggering redundancy and loss of income in the local community at a critical moment. Furthermore, the closure of international borders to the movement of foreign labour and foreign goods supported the argument from the host state for local content and increased technological autonomy. The pandemic particularly stressed supply chains as manufacturing in different countries closed down intermittently at different times. Given the operator's obligation to demonstrate that it has used all measures within its control to avoid or mitigate the impact of any *force majeure* events such as the pandemic, *force majeure* will only have relieved the joint venture's obligations from performing its obligations under the granting instrument for so long as it was impossible to find an alternative means for continuing operations. This dynamic played out in the OpCom discussions relating to the amendment of the work programmes and budgets affected by the pandemic, and in turn in similar discussions between the joint venture and the state regarding the deferral the joint venture's obligations under the granting instrument.

Lastly, the extremely low if not negative oil prices begged the question in what circumstances should the joint venture elect to suspend hydrocarbon operations, pending a price recovery, or should it opt to continue producing hydrocarbons for good technological reasons, at the risk of having to pay the buyer a negative price? Bearing in mind the terms of the granting instrument, does the joint venture have the right to elect to suspend hydrocarbon operations or, if it does, would it constitute a breach of contractual obligations under the granting instrument? Again, the interests of the state in maintaining local hydrocarbon supply may have influenced the decision to continue, whereas the joint venture should be extremely cautious of accepting negative prices for hydrocarbons which it markets and sells on behalf of the relevant host state without the state's full concurrence and cooperation.

5. Assignment

5.1 General principles

In practical terms, the rules on assignment in JOAs establish whether the assignment is possible at all and, if possible, what are the procedures for assignment under different scenarios: for example (i) assignment to affiliates; (ii) assignment to third parties.

Typically assignment may occur as follows:

- mandatory transfers under the applicable law;
- transfer due to the occurrence of the triggering events envisaged by a JOA; and
- voluntary transfers to third parties.

The JOAs are rarely silent on the assignment provisions. Usually, they offer explicit and detailed provisions on all the possible assignment events, imposing certain requirements in relation to them.

Usually, the JOA provisions allow the participant to freely assign its participation interest to an affiliate. However, in particular circumstances such assignment might be restricted as well, if the other parties to the JOA will not be willing to have another group company as their partner. In case of assignment to the affiliate, a common requirement is that the assigning party should give the other parties notice of the planned assignment, which also usually (under English law) serves as a legal assignment.[35] The JOA can also contain the requirements that the assignees shall become party to all existing contractual documentation in relation to the transaction and thus shall exactly "step into the shoes" of the assignor. Among other requirements, the parties could agree on certain requirements to the financial status of assignee, its experience as well as the level of the group control over such assignee. It is increasingly the case that the JOA expressly requires that the assignee is not subject to economic sanctions legislation.

It is very common that in case of the assignment to a third party (ie, an entity that is not party to the agreement and not the affiliate to the existing party), the non-assigning parties will have preferential rights to acquire the assigned interest on similar terms and conditions to those being offered to the third party. JOAs usually provide a detailed procedure, including notification rules about negotiations, conditions of the agreement with the third party, rules and timing for the response from the non-assigning parties. The details of pre-emption procedure contemplating by the relevant JOA can give rise to tension in the JOA negotiations as between IOCs and NOCs, as they may have different perspectives on the conditions a prospective assignee must meet and the procedure for its evaluation. Even so, it is difficult to draft pre-emption language which addresses each and every possible assignment

35 P Roberts and R Fowler, *Joint Operating Agreements: A Practical Guide*, 4th edn, Globe Law and Business, 2020, p238.

scenario, leaving it open to dispute by non-assigning parties which wish to block a particular assignment transaction.

Under English law (which frequently is the applicable law for international projects' JOAs), there is a critical difference between assignment and novation. Thus, in order to ensure that not only the rights but also the obligations are transferred under the JOA, the transferring party must make a novation rather than a simple assignment: "Under the novation the transferor will be replaced completely in favour of the transferee and effectively a new agreement will be created with the consent of all relevant parties."[36] Therefore, a party wishing to transfer all its interests (ie, rights and obligations) in a JOA to another person will require a novation agreement rather than an assignment, and for this the consent of the non-transferring parties (to be realised through the requirement that such parties will execute the novation agreement) will be an inevitable necessity.[37] Under English law for simple assignment rather than novation and given that only rights could be the object of assignment, the consent of the non-transferring parties might not be required.

5.2 Analysis of model JOAs

In the civil law countries, the concept of assignment is straightforward and means the assignment of all rights and obligations. Since the general approach is that the obligations are assigned at all times together with the rights, it is at all times important that the remaining parties give their consent to the assignment. However, it is also possible that the JOA parties could decide differently for the particular circumstances. The OGUK JOA Model contains assignment provisions and certain restrictions on assignment of the participating interest, the main restriction being that assignment is not possible without the consent of the remaining parties:

> *Assignment and Encumbrance*
> *Restriction*
> *No transfer of any interest under the Licence (in so far as it relates to the Licence Area) or this Agreement shall be made by any Participant:*
> - *otherwise than in respect of an undivided interest in all or part of its interest in the Licence (in so far as it relates to the Licence Area) and in and under this Agreement (so that any such transfer shall include all or a corresponding part of any interest of such Participant in a Sole Risk Project) in accordance with the following provisions of this clause or the provisions of clause 24; or*
> - *[if such transfer would result in a continuing Participant and its Affiliates holding in aggregate a Percentage Interest of less than [ ] percent (%).].*[38]
>
> *Conditions*
> *No transfer shall be effective or binding upon the Participants unless the remaining, non-transferring Participants shall each have consented to such transfer in writing (which consent may only be withheld on grounds that the financial responsibility*

36 *Rasbora Ltd v JCL Marine Ltd* [1977] 1 Lloyd's Rep 645.

37 P Roberts and R Fowler, *Joint Operating Agreements: A Practical Guide*, 4th edn, Globe Law and Business, 2020, p238.

38 This optional clause is designed to avoid the administrative and operational inconvenience that may result from having interests divided into very small shares and the resulting increase in the number of partners to be consulted.

and technical capability of the proposed transferee to discharge the obligations under this Agreement as they relate to the interest to be transferred has not been adequately demonstrated).[39]

The Norwegian Model JOA stipulates the need to obtain the approval and consent of the other parties, and the approval of the governmental authorities:

ARTICLE 23 ASSIGNMENT OF PARTICIPATING INTEREST
A Party may assign its Participating interest or a part thereof. The assignment agreement shall contain provisions stipulating that the assignee shall be bound by this Agreement and the conditions of the Production License with subsequent amendments and supplements.
Before the obligatory work commitment pursuant to the Production Licence has been carried out a Party cannot, without the consent of the management committee, assign its Participating interest or part thereof to others than an Affiliated company.
A Party which has entered into an assignment agreement concerning its Participating interest or part thereof, shall notify [the Manager]/[the State, care of the Ministry,] of the price and other terms agreed between the Party and another Party or third Party.
23.3 [The Manager]/[The State, care of the Ministry,] may take over the whole Participating interest at the price and on the conditions agreed. Notice of exercise of this pre-emptive right shall be given to the Party no later than 40 days following the receipt of a notification according to Article 23.2.
This pre-emptive right does not apply when a Party assigns its Participating interest, or part thereof, to an Affiliated company.
A Party may include a clause in the assignment agreement to the effect that the agreement shall be terminated if a preemptive right is exercised.
After the exercise of a preemptive right or the completion of another assignment, the Party shall notify the management committee with no undue delay of the assignment. If the assignment agreement contains other terms than those notified to [the Manager]/[the State, care of the Ministry,] by the assignor, the provisions in Article 23.2 shall apply accordingly.[40]

Since the assignment procedures for participating interests are strictly regulated by the host government, the governmental authority's approval is required in order to complete the assignment. Most of the model JOAs recognise this practical issue and specifically state that an assignment may be completed only on receipt of the relevant authorised body's consent. The same applies to the assignments to affiliates. However, some jurisdictions recognise that certain intragroup assignments will not require the same level of scrutiny as assignment to the third parties and thus simple notification of the governmental body about the transaction might suffice.

39 OGUL Model JOA Article 23.1 and 23.2.
40 Norwegian Model JOA Article 23.

AIPN Model Form
12.2.D A transferee has no rights in the Contract or this Agreement (except any notice and cure rights or similar rights that may be provided to a Lien Holder (as defined in Article 12.2.E) by separate instrument signed by all Parties) unless and until:
12.2.D.1 such transferee expressly undertakes in an instrument reasonably satisfactory to the other Parties to perform the obligations of the transferor under the Contract and this Agreement to the extent of the Participating Interest being transferred and obtains any necessary Government approval for the Transfer and furnishes any guarantees required by the Government or the Contract on or before the applicable deadlines; and
12.2.D.2 in the case of a Transfer to a transferee other than an Affiliate, each Party has consented in writing to such Transfer, which consent shall be denied only if the transferee fails to establish to the reasonable satisfaction of each Party.[41]

5.3 Discussion

It is likely that the national oil company, which might represent the host government in relations with the investors, will insist on having a pre-emption right over the interest intended to be assigned, and may block the assignment. The national oil company will want a stable and legitimate investor and may prefer to take back the participating interest into the government's ownership and control rather than allowing it to be transferred to a less financially capable partner. Here the tricky issue is the price or consideration for the participating interest and other commercial conditions which the assigning party has agreed with the third party and whether NOC will agree to pay such consideration. There may exist other mechanisms under the applicable petroleum legislation, which allow NOC to take the interest on the conditions different to those agreed with the third party. This can be a matter of significant concern and dispute between the parties and the state whether such a new party must be accepted by the existing parties or whether the new party must meet the financial and technical standards required by the terms of the JOA. That said, local and international investment law is likely to require the state to pay full and fair compensation for such participating interest on the basis of bilateral investment treaties or similar instruments even in the absence of agreement between the JOA parties and the state.

But not only is a national oil company interested in having the stable partner; all JOA parties have the same interest. The parties should endeavour to agree a common list of requirements which a prospective assignee must meet as designated above and, in some cases, may set out a list of unacceptable partners in the JOA.

6. Intellectual property rights

6.1 General principles

In general, the model JOAs do not address joint-venture intellectual property ('IP') rights in sufficient detail. Many of them (eg, the AMPLA and OGUK Model JOAs) provide a general definition of the term 'intellectual property rights', but offer no

41 AIPN JOA §12.2.D.

further guidance. The positive exception is the AIPN JOA Model, which devotes a fairly extensive clause to IP rights and, traditionally, provides options for different scenarios. The most common are cases when the proprietary rights are vested solely in the operator and when each of the parties, either contributing to the joint property or producing an invention that attracts IP rights during the course of the operations, will retain the exclusive proprietary rights over such inventions. Another common case arises with the involvement of a national oil company, which, with its local presence, may possess certain valuable proprietary rights and so be reluctant to transfer them, either to the operator or a third party.

An international oil company may also be concerned about the status of the IP rights within the scope of the project's implementation. In most cases international oil companies own some important IP rights, such as various patents, know-how, secret industrial processes and so on, and international oil companies will be interested in ensuring that such rights remain their property, even in the case they are used in the joint operations.

Commonly, the definition of IP rights provided in the JOAs includes a list of the items which may be included in the joint-venture IP rights pool.

6.2 Analysis of model JOAs

The AMPLA Model JOA provides the following definition:

> *JV Intellectual Property means Information, and all business names, trademarks, copyright, patents, patent applications, discoveries, inventions, and similar rights developed by the Operator and paid for from the Joint Account pursuant to an Approved Programme and Budget in the course of Joint Operations.*[42]

The OGUK Model JOA provides a similar definition to the AMPLA one, but extends this to objects that may be unregistered or have another form of protection under the applicable law:

> *"Intellectual Property Rights" means patents, design rights, copyright, database rights, utility models, semiconductor topography rights, rights in know-how and confidential information whether registered or unregistered anywhere in the world, and applications for any of the foregoing, and any other form of protection afforded by law to a person to allow such person to prevent the use of Intellectual Property owned by such person without consent.*[43]

Usually, each party to the joint venture may use the joint venture's intellectual property for its own purposes, but it must give prior notice of its intention to the other parties. Such usage should be subject to the confidentiality provisions of the relevant JOA. The AMPLA Model JOA makes general provision in this regard.

---

42 AMPLA Model JOA Terms and Definitions section.
43 OGUK Model JOA Section "terms and definitions".

JV Intellectual Property
Each Participant and its Affiliates may use, on a non-exclusive world-wide royalty-free basis, JV Intellectual Property, including any modifications and enhancements, outside the Title Area in activities other than Joint Operations provided that the intended use of such JV Intellectual Property is first disclosed to each of the other Participants and is subject to the obligations of confidentiality contained in this agreement.[44]

However, this is the ideal scenario, when usage of the IP rights is free. In most cases, the parties will insist on the prior written consent of all other parties before a party uses the IP rights for its own purposes. For many reasons, the JOA should make a careful distinction between IP contributed by a party for the use of the joint venture and IP which is created or obtained at the cost of the joint account and during joint operations. This distinction helps preserve the uniqueness of any IP contributed by a party and also helps define which party is entitled to any income derived from the licensing of that IP. This issue becomes one step more complex in cases where the parties are entitled to recover the cost of operations under a production sharing agreement from cost petroleum; rights and property paid for by the state through that mechanism are ultimately transferred into the ownership of the state before or at termination of the production sharing agreement. Accordingly, if jointly held IP has been paid for by this mechanism, any income derived from its licensing to third parties should be accounted for to the state. JOAs and production sharing agreements rarely address this point.[45]

As mentioned above, the AIPN Model JOA provides the most robust IP rights section. It deals with some general cases: first, where the IP is held as joint property by all the participants, and, secondly, when all IP rights are vested in the operator and thus the model provides some alternatives:

ALTERNATIVE #1
... all intellectual property rights in the Venture Information shall be Joint Property. Each Party and its Affiliates have the right to use all such intellectual property rights in their own operations (including joint operations or a production sharing arrangement in which the Party or its Affiliates has an ownership or equity interest) without the approval of any other Party. Decisions regarding obtaining, maintaining and licensing such intellectual property rights shall be made by the Operating Committee, and the associated costs shall be charged to the Joint Account. With the unanimous agreement of the Operating Committee concerning ownership, licensing rights, and income distribution, the ownership of intellectual property rights in the Venture Information may be assigned to the Operator or to a Party.

44 AMPLA Model JOA Article 4.6.
45 P Roberts and R Fowler, *Joint Operating Agreements: A Practical Guide*, 4th edn, Globe Law and Business, 2020, pp265–282.

The parties might opt for the first alternative if they think that as a result of joint operations valuable IP rights might be created and it will be important to scrutinise the usage of such IP rights. The decision-making procedure for obtaining, maintaining and licensing such IP rights requires involvement of the Operating Committee, which might not be always convenient. However, the parties could be assured that they will be informed about every decision about IP rights as well as they will have the opportunity to take part in such decision.

ALTERNATIVE #2
15.3.A Subject to Articles 15.3.C and 15.5, all intellectual property rights in the Venture Information shall be owned by Operator unless provided otherwise in the Contract. Each Party and its Affiliates shall have a perpetual, royalty-free, irrevocable license to use, assign, and sublicense all such intellectual property rights in their own operations (including joint venture operations or a production sharing arrangement in which such Party has an ownership or equity interest) without the approval of any other Party. If any Venture Information amounts to a patentable invention, Operator shall be entitled to seek patent protection for such invention. If Operator does not intend to seek patent protection, Operator shall offer to assign to the other Parties Operator's rights to such invention, and shall assign such rights to any requesting Party or Parties. If a license of such rights is granted to a third party other than Affiliates of a Party, the license income shall be shared among the Parties in proportion to their respective Participating Interests. The Party granting any such license shall:

15.3.A.1 Be entitled to deduct from such license income before sharing among the Parties, the granting Party's reasonable costs incurred in registering and maintaining such rights licensed;
15.3.A.2 Keep records of any license income received for any such license; and
15.3.A.3 If requested, provide each Party with a statement, certified by its statutory auditor to be correct and in accordance with this Article 15.3, regarding such income received.

The second AIPN JOA option provides more flexibility and freedom for the Operator. It will be the Operator who will have general proprietary rights over the intellectual property, created in the conduct of the joint operations. The Operator will be responsible for formalising such rights and obtaining patents. The decisions over the IP rights will be taken solely by the Operator during day-to-day operational activity and it will be responsible for reporting and royalty paying to the non-operators in case of sub-licensing.

The following paragraph of the AIPN JOA is important because it secures the rights of each of the parties to the JOA in relation to its own IP results.

Nothing in this Agreement shall be deemed to require a Party to

- *Divulge proprietary technology to any of the other Parties; or*
- *Grant a license or other rights under any intellectual property rights owned or controlled by such Party or its Affiliates to any of the other Parties.*

It is important for the parties to agree in the JOA or in a separate agreement how their respective existing IP rights may be deployed in joint operations; otherwise, parties may be deterred from deploying their IP in the interests of joint operations. The AIPN JOA suggests two different approaches – either that party's IP will be usable by the joint venture under the terms of a specific, non-transferable license or a licence will automatically arise upon the creation of any fresh IP at the cost of the joint account, if such IP uses or incorporates a party's existing IP.

ALTERNATIVE PROVISION, CHOOSE ONE
ALTERNATIVE #1
If a Party or an Affiliate of a Party has proprietary technology applicable to activities carried out under this Agreement that the Party or its Affiliate desires to make available on terms and conditions other than as specified in Article 15.3.A, the Party or Affiliate may, with the prior approval of the Operating Committee, make the proprietary technology available on terms to be agreed. If the proprietary technology is so made available, then any inventions, discoveries, or improvements that relate to such proprietary technology and that result from Joint Account expenditures shall belong to such Party or Affiliate. In such case, each other Party shall have a perpetual, royalty-free, irrevocable license to practice such inventions, discoveries, or improvements, but only in connection with Joint Operations.
ALTERNATIVE #2
15.3.C If while carrying out activities charged to the Joint Account, a Party or an Affiliate of a Party makes or conceives any inventions, discoveries, or improvements that primarily relate to or are primarily based on the proprietary technology of such Party or its Affiliates, then all intellectual property rights to such inventions, discoveries, or improvements shall vest exclusively in such Party and each other Party shall have a perpetual, royalty-free, irrevocable license to use such inventions, discoveries, or improvements, but only in connection with Joint Operations.
Subject to Article 4.6.B, all costs (including reasonable legal costs and attorneys' fees) of defending, settling, or otherwise handling any claim that is based on the actual or alleged infringement of any intellectual property right shall be for the account of the operation from which the claim arose, whether Joint Operations or Exclusive Operations.[46]

6.3 Discussion

There are other aspects relating to the IP rights issue which the parties to the JOA must consider: how to deal with the IP rights (i) when one of the parties withdraws from the JOA and (ii) when the JOA terminates (for any reason). The most important issues here are how to split the IP rights, who will be entitled to own the IP rights, who should be the title holder over any enhancement and improvement of the IP rights. These are only some of the issues – in practice there may be many more. The

46 AIPN Model JOA Article 15. Interestingly, the AIPN JOA sets out the two alternatives as just that – alternatives. In fact they could both be included in a JOA, because the first alternative addresses the deployment of the parties existing IP, and the second alternative addresses the status of IP created or derived from that party's IP, at the cost of the joint account.

model JOAs do not address any of these issues, apart from the AIPN Model JOA, which has a paragraph devoted to the situation when one of the partners ceases to be the party to the agreement. AIPN JOA Article 15.3 sets out a general provision that the obligations of confidentiality over the IP rights remain binding on an exiting party; however, it does not set out the IP property rights of the exiting party nor does it describe the level of control and access it will have over the joint-venture IP rights after its departure (if any):

> *Continuing Obligations*
> *Any Party ceasing to own a Participating Interest during the term of this Agreement shall nonetheless remain bound by the obligations of confidentiality in Article 15.2, and any Disputes in relation thereto shall be resolved under Article 18.2.*[47]

As oil companies deploy increasingly sophisticated technology in their operations and look to protect intellectual property rights in that technology, there is an increasing need to include detailed provisions on intellectual property in model JOAs, to cover issues such as pre-existing intellectual property rights, those rights developed during the conduct of joint operations, the rules applicable to exiting parties, the deployment of JOA parties' existing intellectual property in joint operations and the use of jointly developed intellectual property by the JOA parties in their other ventures. The model JOAs will need to strike a logical balance in drafting around these issues, but they will also need to be carefully negotiated to ensure that the parties are incentivised to deploy intellectual property efficiently.

47 AIPN Model JOA Article 15.3.

About the authors

Reg Fowler
Independent consultant and senior lawyer
fowler1603@gmail.com

Reg Fowler is an independent consultant and senior lawyer. He has worked as in-house counsel in Atlantic Richfield, eni and Shell for a total of 24 years, and in every aspect of the oil and gas business, including trading and shipping, mergers and acquisitions, production sharing agreements, environmental law and joint ventures. He is particularly familiar with operations in Russia and Central Asia, and speaks Russian. He has published books and papers on topics such as Arctic exploration and shipping, the effect of state succession on long-term agreements, corporate social responsibility, the AIPN JOA (with Peter Roberts and Eduardo Pereira) and the ownership of property by joint ventures.

Anna Ovcharova
Vice president legal and compliance, Wintershall Dea Russia
asovcharova@gmail.com

Anna Ovcharova is vice president legal and compliance, Wintershall Dea Russia. Before joining Wintershall Dea Russia, Anna worked as head of legal Russia in Repsol Exploracion, SA. She has also served as head of offshore projects legal support in the major Russian oil and gas company, Rosneft. She received a master's degree in law from Lomonosovs Moscow State University Russia in 2004, a master's degree in international and comparative law from Rijks Universtiteit Groningen in the Netherlands in 2008 and a PhD from the Russian Academy of Science in 2013. She deals with mergers and acquisitions, new ventures, integration in diversified oil and gas projects, including large-scale international projects.

She is a member of AIPN and several professional societies in Russia.

Eduardo G Pereira
Professor of natural resources and energy law
egp.portugal@gmail.com

Professor Dr Eduardo G Pereira is professor of natural resources and energy law and a full-time, part-time, honorary, associate, adjunct, researcher and/or visiting scholar in a number of leading academic institutions around the world (including the Siberian Federal University, the University of the West Indies, University of São Paulo, Strathmore University, Agostinho Neto University, University of Aberdeen and Externado University of Colombia, among others). He has been active in the oil and gas industry for more than 15 years and is an international expert on joint operating agreements. His experience in this area – both academic and practical – is extensive. He has practical experience in over 50 jurisdictions covering America, Europe, Africa and Asia. He concluded his doctoral thesis on oil and gas joint ventures at the University of Aberdeen. He conducted postdoctoral research at Oxford

Institute for Energy Studies (University of Oxford, UK), the Scandinavian Institute of Maritime Law (University of Oslo, Norway) and the Institute of Energy and Environment (University of São Paulo, Brazil). He is also a managing editor for the *GSENRLJ* and an associate editor of *OGEL*. He is also the author and editor of several leading oil and gas textbooks. Further information about his profile and publications can be found at: www.eduardogpereira.com.

About Globe Law and Business

Globe Law and Business was established in 2005. From the very beginning, we set out to create law books which are sufficiently high level to be of real use to the experienced professional, yet still accessible and easy to navigate. Most of our authors are drawn from Magic Circle and other top commercial firms, both in the UK and internationally.

Our titles are carefully produced, with the utmost attention paid to editorial, design and production processes. We hope this results in high-quality publications that are easy to read, and a pleasure to own. Our titles are also available as ebooks, which are compatible with most desktop, laptop and tablet devices. In 2018 we expanded our portfolio to include journals and Special Reports, available both digitally and in hard copy format, and produced to the same high standards as our books.

In the Spring of 2021, we were very pleased to announce the start of a new chapter for Globe Law and Business following the acquisition of law books under the imprint Ark Publishing. We are very much looking forward to working with our new Ark authors, many of whom are well-known to us, and to further developing the law firm management list, among other areas.

We'd very much like to hear from you with your thoughts and ideas for improving what we offer. Please do feel free to email me at sian@globelawandbusiness.com with your views.

Sian O'Neill
Managing director
Globe Law and Business
www.globelawandbusiness.com

www.ingramcontent.com/pod-product-compliance
Ingram Content Group UK Ltd.
Pitfield, Milton Keynes, MK11 3LW, UK
UKHW062251150926
8656IPUK00007B/45

9 781787 424388